GOVERNMENT ACCOUNTABILITY SOURCES AND MATERIALS

AUSTRALIAN ADMINISTRATIVE LAW

SECOND EDITION

Government Accountability Sources and Materials: Australian Administrative Law is designed to accompany the third edition of the textbook *Government Accountability: Australian Administrative Law.*

Following the accessible structure of *Government Accountability*, this book guides students through the real-world operation of administrative law and demonstrates how multiple doctrines and mechanisms can interact in a single situation. Extracts from primary materials – including cases and legislation – provide a clear account of the facts, issues and statutory provisions considered by the courts, and are accompanied by relevant commentary.

This edition has been thoroughly updated to include recent significant cases such as *Minister for Immigration, Citizenship, Migrant Services and Multicultural Affairs v Viane* (2021), *Hocking v Director-General of the National Archives of Australia* (2020) and *MZAPC v Minister for Immigration and Border Protection* (2021).

Written by a team of experts in the field, *Government Accountability Sources and Materials: Australian Administrative Law* is a fundamental and student-friendly introduction to administrative law in practice.

Judith Bannister is Professor of Law at Flinders University.

Anna Olijnyk is a Senior Lecturer at the Adelaide Law School, University of Adelaide.

Stephen McDonald SC is a Senior Counsel at Hanson Chambers and an Adjunct Associate Professor at the Adelaide Law School, University of Adelaide.

GOVERNMENT ACCOUNTABILITY SOURCES AND MATERIALS

AUSTRALIAN ADMINISTRATIVE LAW

SECOND EDITION

Judith Bannister

Anna Olijnyk

Stephen McDonald

CAMBRIDGE UNIVERSITY PRESS

CAMBRIDGE
UNIVERSITY PRESS

Shaftesbury Road, Cambridge CB2 8EA, United Kingdom

One Liberty Plaza, 20th Floor, New York, NY 10006, USA

477 Williamstown Road, Port Melbourne, VIC 3207, Australia

314–321, 3rd Floor, Plot 3, Splendor Forum, Jasola District Centre, New Delhi - 110025, India

103 Penang Road, #05–06/07, Visioncrest Commercial, Singapore 238467

Cambridge University Press is part of Cambridge University Press & Assessment, a department of the University of Cambridge.

We share the University's mission to contribute to society through the pursuit of education, learning and research at the highest international levels of excellence.

www.cambridge.org
Information on this title: www.cambridge.org/highereducation/isbn/9781009101943

First published 2018
Second edition 2023

Cover designed by Anne-Marie Reeves
Typeset by Lumina Datamatics Ltd
Printed in China by C&C Offset Printing Co., Ltd, April 2023

MIX
Paper | Supporting responsible forestry
FSC® C008047

A catalogue record for this publication is available from the British Library.

A catalogue record for this book is available from the National Library of Australia

ISBN 978-1-009-10194-3 Paperback

Please be aware that this publication may contain several variations of Aboriginal and Torres Strait Islander terms and spellings; no disrespect is intended. Please note that the terms 'Indigenous Australians', 'Aboriginal and Torres Strait Islander peoples' and 'First Nations peoples' may be used interchangeably in this publication.

CONTENTS

Preface page xiii
Table of cases xiv
Table of statutes xviii
Acknowledgements xxiii

1 **Introduction** **1**
An introduction to this book 2
Why accountability? 3
AV Dicey, *Introduction to the Study of the Law of the Constitution* (Macmillan, 1915) (first published 1885) 3
Charles de Secondat, Baron de Montesquieu, *The Spirit of Laws* (Thomas Nugent trans, G Bell and Sons, 1914) (first published 1748) 4
Church of Scientology Inc v Woodward (1982) 154 CLR 25 5
A v Hayden (No 2) (1984) 156 CLR 532 6
Accountability for what? Administrative law values 7
Dawn Oliver, 'Accountability and the Foundations of British Democracy – the Public Interest and Public Service Principles' in Nicholas Bamforth and Peter Leyland (eds), *Accountability in the Contemporary Constitution* (Oxford University Press, 2013) 289 7
Chief Justice James Allsop, 'Values in Public Law' (2017) 91 *Australian Law Journal* 118 9
Administrative law and statutory interpretation 11
SZTAL v Minister for Immigration and Border Protection (2017) 262 CLR 362 11
Modern accountability: some challenges 12
Janina Boughey, 'Executive Power in Emergencies: Where is the Accountability?' (2020) 45(3) *Alternative Law Journal* 168 12

PART I ADMINISTRATIVE DECISION-MAKING **17**

2 **Organisation and structure of government** **19**
Introduction 20
The Crown and the executive: terminology and constitutional framework 20
Constitution 20
Sue v Hill (1999) 199 CLR 462 21
Executive entities 22
Public Service Act 1999 (Cth) 22
Private bodies in the public sphere 24
Plaintiff M68/2015 v Minister for Immigration and Border Protection (2016) 257 CLR 42 24

NEAT Domestic Trading Pty Ltd v AWB Ltd (2003) 216 CLR 277 29
Administrative Review Council, *The Contracting Out of Government Services* (Report No 42, 1998) 34
Crown immunity 35
Bropho v Western Australia (1990) 171 CLR 1 35

3 Administrative powers 40
Introduction 41
Administrative powers and discretions 41
Administrative Review Council 41
Administrative Review Council, *Decision Making: Lawfulness* (Best Practice Guide 1, 2007) 41
Commonwealth Ombudsman, *Automated Decision-Making: Better Practice Guide* (2019) 43
Statutory powers 47
Coco v The Queen (1994) 179 CLR 427 47
Minister for Immigration and Citizenship v Li (2013) 249 CLR 332 50
The Pilbara Infrastructure Pty Ltd v Australian Competition Tribunal (2012) 246 CLR 379 51
Non-statutory powers 53
Osland v Secretary, Department of Justice (No 1) (2008) 234 CLR 275 53
Minister for Arts, Heritage and Environment v Peko-Wallsend Ltd (1987) 15 FCR 274 54

4 Delegated legislation 57
Introduction 58
Executive exercise of legislative power 58
Australian Law Reform Commission, *Traditional Rights and Freedoms – Encroachments by Commonwealth Laws* (Report No 129, 2015) 58
Distinguishing acts of legislative and administrative character 62
R G Capital Radio Ltd v Australian Broadcasting Authority (2001) 113 FCR 185 62
Types of delegated legislation 68
Legislation Act 2003 (Cth) 68
Legislative regulation and parliamentary review of delegated legislation 70
Case study: Disallowance of *Aboriginal Land Rights (Northern Territory) Amendment (Delegation) Regulation 2013* (Cth) 70
Judicial review of delegated legislation 76
Minister for Primary Industries and Energy v Austral Fisheries Pty Ltd (1993) 40 FCR 381 76
Plaintiff M47/2012 v Director-General of Security (2012) 251 CLR 1 78
Attorney-General v Corporation of the City of Adelaide (2013) 249 CLR 1 81

PART II PUBLIC ACCOUNTABILITY MECHANISMS 87

5 Public investigatory bodies 89

Introduction 90

Investigation and scrutiny through parliament 90

Williams v Commonwealth (No 1) (2012) 248 CLR 156 90

Egan v Willis (1998) 195 CLR 424 92

New South Wales Legislative Council, *Order for the Production of Documents* (Standing Order 52, May 2004) 95

Auditors-General 96

Auditor-General Act 1997 (Cth) 96

Public Governance, Performance and Accountability Act 2013 (Cth) 98

Auditor-General Performance Audit, *Offshore Processing Centres in Nauru and Papua New Guinea: Contract Management of Garrison Support and Welfare Services* (ANAO Report No 32 2016–17, 17 January 2017) 102

Ombudsmen 106

Ombudsman Act 1976 (Cth) 106

Chairperson, Aboriginal and Torres Strait Islander Commission v Commonwealth Ombudsman (1995) 63 FCR 163 111

King v Ombudsman (2020) 137 SASR 18 115

Royal commissions 119

Royal Commissions Act 1902 (Cth) 119

Royal Commission into the Home Insulation Program (Report, 2014) 119

6 Information disclosure 126

Introduction 127

The duties of public servants 127

Archives Act 1983 (Cth) 127

Hocking v Director-General of the National Archives of Australia (2020) 271 CLR 1 131

Public Service Act 1999 (Cth) 133

Public Service Regulations 1999 (Cth) 133

Confidential information 134

Commonwealth v John Fairfax & Sons Ltd (1980) 147 CLR 39 134

Information security – personal information 137

Office of the Australian Information Commissioner ('OAIC'), *Department of Immigration and Border Protection: Own Motion Investigation Report* (November 2014) 137

Minister for Immigration and Border Protection v SZSSJ (2016) 259 CLR 180 141

Public interest disclosure (whistleblowers) 143

Public Interest Disclosure Act 2013 (Cth) 143

Freedom of information 148
Freedom of Information Act 1982 (Cth) 148
Office of the Australian Information Commissioner ('OAIC'), *FOI Agency Resource 5: Exemptions and Conditional Exemptions Under the Freedom of Information Act 1982* (September 2011) 156
Case study: *Osland v Secretary, Department of Justice (No 1) & (No 2)* 159
Freedom of Information Act 1982 (Vic) 159
Introduction 160
Osland v Secretary, Department of Justice (No 1) (2008) 234 CLR 275 160
Osland v Secretary, Department of Justice (No 2) (2010) 241 CLR 320 164
Reasons for decisions 165
Public Service Board of New South Wales v Osmond (1986) 159 CLR 656 165
Administrative Review Council, *Best Practice Guide 4 – Decision Making: Reasons* (2007) 168
Administrative Review Council, *Federal Judicial Review in Australia* (Report No 50, 2012) 170
Ombudsman Act 1976 (Cth) 172
Administrative Appeals Tribunal Act 1975 (Cth) 172
Administrative Decisions (Judicial Review) Act 1977 (Cth) 173

PART III MERITS REVIEW 175

7 Review on the merits **177**
Introduction 178
Why merits review? 178
Commonwealth, *Commonwealth Administrative Review Committee Report* (Parl Paper No 144, 1971) 178
Internal review 180
Administrative Review Council, *Internal Review of Agency Decision Making* (Report No 44, 2000) 180
A New Tax System (Family Assistance) (Administration) Act 1999 (Cth) 183
Examples of merits review decisions 187
Farrugia v Secretary, Department of Social Services [2022] AATA 11 187
Tipungwuti v Director – Crime Victims Services Unit (No 2) [2016] NTCAT 191 190

8 Administrative review tribunals **196**
Introduction 197
Issues of tribunal design 197
Council of Australasian Tribunals, *Tribunal Independence in Appointments: A Best Practice Guide* (2016) 197
Council of Australasian Tribunals, *Practice Manual for Tribunals* (5th ed, 2020) 199
Re Drake and Minister for Immigration and Ethnic Affairs (No 2) (1979) 2 ALD 634 200

The Australian administrative tribunal framework 206
Commonwealth, *Commonwealth Administrative Review Committee Report* (Parl Paper No 144, 1971) 206
Administrative Appeals Tribunal Act 1975 (Cth) 207
IDF Callinan, *Review: Section 4 of the Tribunals Amalgamation Act 2015* (Cth) (Report, 19 December 2018) 212
Robin Creyke, 'Australian Tribunals: Impact of Amalgamation' (2020) 26(4) *Australian Journal of Administrative Law* 206 213
Drake v Minister for Immigration and Ethnic Affairs (1979) 46 FLR 409 215
Shi v Migration Agents Registration Authority (2008) 235 CLR 286 218
Frugtniet v Australian Securities and Investments Commission (2019) 266 CLR 250 223

PART IV JUDICIAL REVIEW 227

9 Introduction to judicial review 229
Introduction 230
Stephen Gageler, 'The Legitimate Scope of Judicial Review' (2001) 21(3) *Australian Bar Review* 279 231
Statutory review on a question of law 231
Osland v Secretary, Department of Justice (No 2) (2010) 241 CLR 320 232
Administrative Appeals Tribunal Act 1975 (Cth) 234
Judicial review – review of legality 235
Attorney-General (NSW) v Quin (1990) 170 CLR 1 236
Statutory construction 238
Project Blue Sky Inc v Australian Broadcasting Authority (1998) 194 CLR 355 238
Sources of judicial review jurisdiction 241
Constitution 241
Judiciary Act 1903 (Cth) 241
State Supreme Courts 242
Supreme Court Act 1970 (NSW) 242
Supreme Court Act 1935 (SA) 243
Administrative Law Act 1978 (Vic) 244
Origins of common law and constitutional judicial review 246
Re Refugee Review Tribunal; Ex parte Aala (2000) 204 CLR 82 246
Kirk v Industrial Court of New South Wales (2010) 239 CLR 531 247
Statutory judicial review 249
Administrative Decisions (Judicial Review) Act 1977 (Cth) 249
Kioa v West (1985) 159 CLR 550 253
Australian Broadcasting Tribunal v Bond (1990) 170 CLR 321 254
Griffith University v Tang (2005) 221 CLR 99 256
The concepts of jurisdictional error and error of law on the face of the record 258
Craig v South Australia (1995) 184 CLR 163 258

Minister for Immigration and Multicultural Affairs v Yusuf (2001) 206 CLR 323 261
Kirk v Industrial Court of New South Wales (2010) 239 CLR 531 263
Probuild Constructions (Aust) Pty Ltd v Shade Systems Pty Ltd (2018) 264 CLR 1 268
Hossain v Minister for Immigration and Border Protection (2018) 264 CLR 123 272
MZAPC v Minister for Immigration and Border Protection (2021) 95 ALJR 441 275
Nathanson v Minister for Home Affairs (2022) 96 ALJR 737 276
What is the face of the record? 278
Craig v South Australia (1995) 184 CLR 163 278
Supreme Court Act 1970 (NSW) 280
Administrative Law Act 1978 (Vic) 280

10 Limits on judicial review **281**
Introduction 282
Justiciability 282
R v Toohey; Ex parte Northern Land Council (1981) 151 CLR 170 282
Minister for Arts, Heritage and Environment v Peko-Wallsend Ltd (1987) 15 FCR 274 285
Standing to commence judicial review proceedings 288
Australian Conservation Foundation v Commonwealth (1980) 146 CLR 493 288
Onus v Alcoa of Australia Ltd (1981) 149 CLR 27 291
Administrative Decisions (Judicial Review) Act 1977 (Cth) 293
Argos Pty Ltd v Corbell (2014) 254 CLR 394 294
Privative clauses 298
Plaintiff S157/2002 v Commonwealth (2003) 211 CLR 476 298
Kirk v Industrial Court of New South Wales (2010) 239 CLR 531 304
No-invalidity clauses 308
Commissioner of Taxation (Cth) v Futuris Corporation Ltd (2008) 237 CLR 146 308
Restricting access to information before the courts 311
Graham v Minister for Immigration and Border Protection (2017) 263 CLR 1 311

11 Introduction to the grounds of review **316**
Introduction 317
What are the grounds of review? 317
Will Bateman and Leighton McDonald, 'The Normative Structure of Australian Administrative Law' (2017) 45 *Federal Law Review* 153 317
Statutory grounds 319
Administrative Decisions (Judicial Review) Act 1977 (Cth) 319
Administrative Review Council, *Federal Judicial Review in Australia* (Report No 50, 2012) 320

12 Procedural fairness **323**
Introduction 324
The threshold test: when do the rules of procedural fairness apply? 324
Kioa v West (1985) 159 CLR 550 324
Plaintiff S10/2011 v Minister for Immigration and Citizenship (2012) 246 CLR 636 333
Statutory exclusion 336
Re Minister for Immigration and Multicultural Affairs; Ex parte Miah (2001) 206 CLR 57 336
Minister for Immigration and Border Protection v SZMTA (2019) 264 CLR 421 342
BVD17 v Minister for Immigration and Border Protection (2019) 268 CLR 29 344
Plaintiff S10/2011 v Minister for Immigration and Citizenship (2012) 246 CLR 636 347
The hearing rule 349
Re Minister for Immigration and Multicultural and Indigenous Affairs; Ex parte Lam (2003) 214 CLR 1 349
The bias rule 352
Ebner v Official Trustee in Bankruptcy (2000) 205 CLR 337 352
Isbester v Knox City Council (2015) 255 CLR 135 356
Minister for Immigration and Multicultural Affairs v Jia Legeng (2001) 205 CLR 507 359

13 Grounds arising from the statute conferring a power **363**
Introduction 364
Misconceiving the scope of a power 364
New South Wales Registrar of Births, Deaths and Marriages v Norrie (2014) 250 CLR 490 364
Jurisdictional facts 367
Corporation of the City of Enfield v Development Assessment Commission (2000) 199 CLR 135 367
Liversidge v Anderson [1942] AC 206 370
Plaintiff M70/2011 v Minister for Immigration and Citizenship (2011) 244 CLR 144 ('*Malaysia Declaration Case*') 373
Procedural error 378
Forrest & Forrest Pty Ltd v Wilson (2017) 262 CLR 510 378
Improper delegation 387
O'Reilly v Commissioners of the State Bank of Victoria (1983) 153 CLR 1 387
Mandatory and prohibited considerations 390
Minister for Aboriginal Affairs v Peko-Wallsend Ltd (1986) 162 CLR 24 390
Tickner v Chapman (1995) 57 FCR 451 396
Murphyores Inc Pty Ltd v Commonwealth (1976) 136 CLR 1 400

14 Grounds arising from the general law **403**
Introduction 404
Improper purpose 404
R v Toohey; Ex parte Northern Land Council (1981) 151 CLR 170 404
Shop Distributive and Allied Employees Association v Minister for Industrial Affairs (SA) (1995) 183 CLR 552 407
Fettering discretion 411
Green v Daniels (1977) 13 ALR 1 411
Bread Manufacturers of New South Wales v Evans (1981) 180 CLR 404 415
Unreasonableness 417
Minister for Immigration and Citizenship v Li (2013) 249 CLR 332 417
Minister for Immigration and Border Protection v SZVFW (2018) 264 CLR 541 421
Irrationality and illogicality 427
Minister for Immigration and Citizenship v SZMDS (2010) 240 CLR 611 427
CRL18 v Minister for Immigration, Citizenship, Migrant Services and Multicultural Affairs (2020) 171 ALD 50 432
No evidence 437
Australian Broadcasting Tribunal v Bond (1990) 170 CLR 321 437
Minister for Immigration, Citizenship, Migrant Services and Multicultural Affairs v Viane (2021) 96 ALJR 13 439

15 Consequences of unlawful action **445**
Introduction 446
Consequences of breaching a statutory provision 446
Project Blue Sky Inc v Australian Broadcasting Authority (1998) 194 CLR 355 446
Cavo Pty Ltd v Minister for the Environment and Sustainable Development (2016) 313 FLR 241 449
Consequences of jurisdictional error 454
Minister for Immigration and Multicultural Affairs v Bhardwaj (2002) 209 CLR 597 454
Remedies 456
Ainsworth v Criminal Justice Commission (1992) 175 CLR 564 456
Wingfoot Australia Partners Pty Ltd v Kocak (2013) 252 CLR 480 457
Plaintiff M61/2010E v Commonwealth (2010) 243 CLR 319 461
Corporation of the City of Enfield v Development Assessment Commission (2000) 199 CLR 135 463
Statutory remedies 467
Administrative Decisions (Judicial Review) Act 1977 (Cth) 467
Chapman v Tickner (1995) 55 FCR 316 468

Index 470

PREFACE

The cases and materials in this book complement the introduction to administrative law provided in *Government Accountability: Australian Administrative Law* ('the textbook'). It is assumed that readers of this book will also have access to the textbook. The chapters in this book mirror those in the textbook. We envisage that readers will begin their study of a topic by reading the relevant section of the textbook and will turn to this book to study key cases and concepts in greater depth.

TABLE OF CASES

A v Hayden (No 2) (1984) 156 CLR 532, 6–7
Ainsworth v Criminal Justice Commission (1992) 175 CLR 564, 456–7
Argos Pty Ltd v Corbell (2014) 254 CLR 394, 294–7, 451
Attorney-General (NSW) v Quin (1990) 170 CLR 1, 236–7
Attorney-General (SA) v Corporation of the City of Adelaide (2013) 249 CLR 1, 81–5
Austral Fisheries Pty Ltd v Minister for Primary Industries and Energy (1992) 37 FCR 463, 76
Australian Broadcasting Tribunal v Bond (1990) 170 CLR 321, 254–6, 437–8
Australian Conservation Foundation v Commonwealth (1989) 146 CLR 493, 288–91

Bread Manufacturers of New South Wales v Evans (1981) 180 CLR 404, 415–16
Bropho v Western Australia (1990) 171 CLR 1, 35–9
BVD17 v Minister for Immigration and Border Protection (2019) 268 CLR 29, 344–7

Cavo Pty Ltd v Minister for the Environment and Sustainable Development (2016) 313 FLR 241, 295, 449–54
Chairperson, Aboriginal and Torres Strait Islander Commission v Commonwealth Ombudsman (1995) 63 FCR 163, 111–15
Chapman v Tickner (1995) 55 FCR 316, 468–9
Chu Kheng Lim v Minister for Immigration (1992) 176 CLR 1, 25
Church of Scientology Inc v Woodward (1982) 154 CLR 25, 5–6
Coco v The Queen (1994) 179 CLR 427, 47–50
Collector of Customs (New South Wales) v Brian Lawlor Automotive Pty Ltd (1979) 41 FLR 338, 221
Commonwealth v John Fairfax & Sons Ltd (1980) 147 CLR 39, 134–7
Corporation of the City of Enfield v Development Assessment Commission (2000) 199 CLR 135, 367–70, 463–6
Craig v South Australia (1995) 184 CLR 163, 258–61, 278–80
CRL18 v Minister for Immigration, Citizenship, Migrant Services and Multicultural Affairs (2020) 171 ALD 50, 431–7

Department of Justice v Osland (2007) 26 VAR 425, 161
Dickason v Edwards (1910) 10 CLR 243, 357
Dietrich v The Queen (1992) 177 CLR 292, 258
Drake v Minister for Immigration and Ethnic Affairs (1979) 46 FLR 409, 201, 215–18, 221

Ebner v Official Trustee in Bankruptcy (2000) 205 CLR 337, 352–6
Egan v Chadwick (1999) 46 NSWLR 563, 95
Egan v Willis (1996) 40 NSWLR 650, 93
Egan v Willis (1998) 195 CLR 424, 92–5

Farrugia v Department of Social Services (2022) AATA 11, 187–90
Forrest & Forrest Pty Ltd v Wilson (2017) 262 CLR 510, 378–87

Graham v Minister for Immigration and Border Protection (2017) 263 CLR 1, 311–15
Green v Daniels (1977) 13 ALR 1, 411–15
Griffith University v Tang (2005) 221 CLR 99, 256–8

Hocking v Director-General of the National Archives of Australia (2018) 255 FCR 1, 131
Hocking v Director-General of the National Archives of Australia (2019) 264 FCR 1, 131
Hocking v Director-General of the National Archives of Australia (2020) 271 CLR 1, 131–3
Hossain v Minister for Immigration and Border Protection (2018) 264 CLR 123, 272–4

Isbester v Knox City Council (2015) 255 CLR 135, 356–9

King v Ombudsman (2019) SASC 107, 117
King v Ombudsman (2020) 137 SASR 18, 115–19
Kioa v West (1985) 159 CLR 550, 253–4, 347
Kirk v Industrial Court of New South Wales (2010) 239 CLR 531, 247–9, 262–8, 304–8

Liversidge v Anderson (1942) AC 206, 364, 370–3

Metropolitan Borough and Town Clerk of Lewisham v Roberts (1949) 2 KB 608, 389
Minister for Aboriginal Affairs v Peko-Wallsend Ltd (1986) 162 CLR 24, 390–5, 404
Minister for Arts, Heritage and Environment v Peko-Wallsend Ltd (1987) 15 FCR 274, 54–6, 285–8
Minister for Immigration and Border Protection v SZMTA (2019) 264 CLR 421, 341–5
Minister for Immigration and Border Protection v SZSSJ (2016) 259 CLR 180, 141–3
Minister for Immigration and Citizenship v Li (2013) 249 CLR 332, 50–1, 417–21
Minister for Immigration and Citizenship v SZMDS (2010) 240 CLR 611, 427–31
Minister for Immigration and Multicultural Affairs v Bhardwaj (2002) 209 CLR 597, 454–5
Minister for Immigration and Multicultural Affairs v Jia Legeng (2001) 205 CLR 507, 359–62
Minister for Immigration and Multicultural Affairs v Yusuf (2001) 2006 CLR 323, 261–2
Minister for Primary Industries and Energy v Austral Fisheries Pty Ltd (1993) 40 FCR 381, 76–8
MZAPC v Minister for Immigration and Border Protection (2021) 95 ALJR 441, 275–6

Nathanson v Minister for Home Affairs (2022) 96 ALJR 737, 276–7
NEAT Domestic Trading Pty Ltd v AWB Ltd (2003) 216 CLR 277, 29–34
New South Wales Registrar of Births, Deaths and Marriages v Norrie (2014) 250 CLR 490, 364–7

Onus v Alcoa of Australia Ltd (1981) 149 CLR 27, 291–3
O'Reilly v Commissioners of the State Bank of Victoria (1983) 153 CLR 1, 364, 387–90
Osland v Department of Justice (2005) 23 VAR 378, 160
Osland v Secretary, Department of Justice (No 1) (2008) 234 CLR 275, 53–4, 160–4, 232
Osland v Secretary, Department of Justice (No 2) (2010) 241 CLR 320, 164–5, 231–3

Osland v The Queen (1998) 197 CLR 316, 53, 160
Osmond v Public Service Board of New South Wales (1984) 3 NSWLR 447, 165

Pilbara Infrastructure Pty Ltd v Australian Competition Tribunal (2012) 246 CLR 379, 51–3
Plaintiff M47/2012 v Director-General of Security (2012) 251 CLR 1, 78–81
Plaintiff M61/2010E v Commonwealth (2010) 243 CLR 319, 461–3
Plaintiff M68/2015 v Minister for Immigration and Border Protection (2016) 257 CLR 42, 24–9
Plaintiff M70/2011 v Minister for Immigration and Citizenship (2011) 244 CLR 144, 373–8
Plaintiff S10/2011 v Minister for Immigration and Citizenship (2012) 246 CLR 636, 332–6, 347–9
Plaintiff S157/2002 v Commonwealth (2003) 211 CLR 476, 298–304
Probuild Constructions (Aust) Pty Ltd v Shade Systems Pty Ltd (2016) NSWSC 770, 269
Probuild Constructions (Aust) Pty Ltd v Shade Systems Pty Ltd (2018) 264 CLR 1, 268–72
Project Blue Sky Inc v Australian Broadcasting Authority (1998) 194 CLR 355, 238–41, 446–9, 451, 452
Public Service Board of New South Wales v Osmond (1986) 159 CLR 656, 165–7

R v MacKellar; Ex parte Ratu (1977) 137 CLR 461, 325, 326, 331
R v Toohey; Ex parte Northern Land Council (1981) 151 CLR 170, 282–4, 287, 404–6
R G Capital Radio Ltd v Australian Broadcasting Authority (2001) 113 FCR 185, 62–7
Re Drake and Minister for Immigration and Ethnic Affairs (1978) AAT 111, 201, 215
Re Drake and Minister for Immigration and Ethnic Affairs (No 2) (1979) 2 ALD 634, 200–6, 215, 216
Re Minister for Immigration and Multicultural Affairs; Ex parte Miah (2001) 206 CLR 57, 336–41
Re Minister for Immigration and Multicultural and Indigenous Affairs v Lam (2003) 214 CLR 1, 349–52
Re Refugee Review Tribunal; Ex parte Aala (2000) 204 CLR 82, 246–7
Re Shi and Migration Agents Registration Authority (2005) AAT 851, 219

Salemi v MacKellar (No 2) (1977) 137 CLR 396, 326, 331
Secretary, Department of Justice v Osland (No 2) (2009) 25 VR 490, 164
Shi v Migration Agents Registration Authority (2008) 235 CLR 286, 218–23
Shop Distributive and Allied Employees Association v Minister for Industrial Affairs (SA) (1995) 183 CLR 552, 406–11
Stollery v Greyhound Racing Control Board (1972) 128 CLR 509, 357
Sue v Hill (1999) CLR 462, 21–2
SZSSJ v Minister for Immigration and Border Protection (2015) 234 FCR 1, 142
SZTAL v Minister for Immigration and Border Protection (2017) 262 CLR 362, 47–53

Tickner v Chapman (1995) 57 FCR 451, 395–9, 468
Tipungwuti v Director, Crime Victims Services Unit (No 2) (2016) NTCAT 191, 190–5

Viane v Minister for Immigration, Citizenship, Migrant Services and Multicultural Affairs (2020) 278 FCR 386, 441

Williams v Commonwealth (No 1) (2012) 248 CLR 156, 90–2
Williams v Commonwealth (No 2) (2014) 252 CLR 416, 91
Wingfoot Australia Partners Pty Ltd v Kocak (2013) 252 CLR 480, 457–61

TABLE OF STATUTES

AUSTRALIA

A New Tax System (Family Assistance) Act 1999, 183
s 35B(1), 187–8
s 35B(3), 188
A New Tax System (Family Assistance) (Administration) Act 1999, 183–4, 186–8
pt 2 div 5, 186
pt 5 div 1, 183
pt 5 div 1 subdiv A, 183
pt 5 div 1 subdiv B, 184
pt 5 div 2, 183
pt 5 div 2 subdiv D, 186
s 3, 183
s 105, 184, 186
s 105(1)(b), 184
s 105(2), 184
s 105(3), 184
s 105(4), 184
s 108, 184–5
s 108(1), 186
s 108(2A)–108(5), 185
s 108(c)–108(h), 185
s 109A, 184–6
s 109A(2), 186
s 111(1), 186
s 111(1A), 186
s 128(1), 186
Aboriginal and Torres Strait Islander Heritage Protection Act 1984
s 10, 396–7, 468
Aboriginal Heritage Act 1972
s 6(1), 35
Aboriginal Land Rights (Northern Territory) Act 1976, 392, 405
s 3, 293
s 11, 404
s 11(1), 390–1
s 28(3), 70, 71
s 28A(5), 76
s 28A(6), 76
ss 28A–28B, 71–2
s 28B(6), 76
s 28B(7), 76
s 50, 159, 404
s 78, 70, 72
Aboriginal Land Rights (Northern Territory) Amendment Act 2015, 76
Aboriginal Land Rights (Northern Territory) Amendment (Delegation) Regulation 2013, 70
sch 1, 72
Aboriginal Land Rights (Northern Territory) Regulations 2007, 70
Administrative Appeals Tribunal Act 1975
ss 2A–3, 207–8
s 25, 208
ss 27–28, 208–9
s 28, 172–3
s 28(1AA)–28(4), 173
s 30(1)–30(1A), 209–10
s 33(1)–33(1AB), 210
s 43(1), 47–8
ss 43–44, 210–12
s 44, 215, 219, 225, 234–5
Administrative Decisions (Judicial Review) Act 1977, 30, 174, 253, 254, 256, 325, 326, 331, 392, 397, 437, 468
s 3, 127–8
s 3(4), 293
s 3B(1), 294
s 5, 30, 293–4, 319–20, 325
s 5(1), 63, 98–9, 294
s 6(1), 251
ss 7–8(2), 251
s 12, 294
ss 12–13(1), 251–2
s 13, 173–4, 325
ss 13(3)–13(6), 174
ss 13(8)–13(10), 174
s 13A, 174

s 16, 252–3, 467–8
s 16(1)(a), 468
sch 1, 309
Archives Act 1983, 131
s 3(1)–3(2), 127–8
s 24, 128–9
s 31, 129, 131
s 33, 129–30
Auditor-General Act 1997
ss 7–8, 96–7
s 11, 97
s 17, 97–8
Broadcasting Act 1942, 254, 437
s 88(2), 254
Broadcasting Services Act 1992
s 23, 62
s 24(1), 62
s 25(1), 62
s 26(1), 62–3
s 27, 63
s 122, 238
s 158, 238
s 158(h)–158(j), 446
s 160, 238–9, 446, 447
s 160(d), 447
Constitution
s 44, 21
ss 53–54, 90
ss 61–64, 20
s 71, 247
s 73, 247–8
s 75, 241, 262
s 75(iii), 25, 262
s 75(v), 25, 246, 262, 299, 338, 350, 360, 400, 412, 418, 429
s 83, 90
Crimes Act 1914, 135
s 85ZM, 225
s 85ZV(2)(b), 224
s 85ZW, 224, 225
s 85ZZH, 225
s 85ZZH(c), 224
Customs (Prohibited Exports) Regulations 1958
reg 9(3), 400
Environment Protection (Impact of Proposals) Act 1974, 400
Financial Framework Legislation Amendment Bill (No 3) 2012, 91
Fisheries Act 1952
s 7B(1), 76
s 7B(5)(b), 76
Freedom of Information Act 1982, 156
ss 3–4, 148–50
ss 11–11B, 97
s 15, 152
s 15A, 152
s 20, 152–3
ss 22(1)–22(2), 153
s 23(1), 62
s 23(2), 154
ss 24–24AA, 154–5
s 26(1)–26(2), 155
s 31B, 155
Income Tax Assessment Act 1936
s 175, 309
ss 175–175A, 308
s 177(1), 308
s 264, 387, 388
Judiciary Act 1903
s 39(1B), 242
s 39(1C), 242
s 39(1EA), 242
s 39B, 76, 131, 309
ss 39B(1)–39B(1A), 241–2
Legislation Act 2003
s 8, 68–9
s 38, 69
s 42, 69–70
Migration Act 1958, 79, 200, 261, 262, 325, 326
pt 2 div 3 subdiv AB, 338
pt 7, 346
pt 7AA, 346
s 12, 200
s 18, 324, 331
s 31, 78
s 36(1)–36(2), 427
s 46A, 461
s 48A, 333

Migration Act 1958 (cont.)
s 48B, 333, 334
s 54(1), 336
s 54(3), 336–7
ss 56–57, 337
s 57(1)(b), 338
s 65(1), 242
s 69, 337
s 198A(1), 373
s 198A(3), 373
s 198A(3)(a), 374
s 198A(3)(a)(i)–198A(3)(a)(iv), 374
s 198AB(1), 25
s 198AHA, 24–5
s 303(1), 218–19
s 303(1)(f), 219
s 303(1)(h), 219
s 306, 219
s 351, 333–4
s 353, 417
s 357A, 417
s 360(1), 417
s 363(1), 417
s 408, 342
s 415(1)–415(2), 421–2
s 420, 422
s 422, 343
s 422B, 342
s 422B(1), 422
s 425, 426
s 425(1), 422
s 425A, 422, 426
s 426A, 422–3
s 430(1), 428
s 437DA, 346
s 438, 342–3
s 441A, 423, 426
s 441C, 426
s 441C(1), 423
s 441C(4), 423
s 473BA, 344
s 473DA, 344
s 473GB, 344–5
s 473GB(2)(a), 345
s 474, 298–9
s 476, 418, 429
s 476(2)(b), 429
s 476A, 312
s 498, 78
s 501, 360, 440
s 501(2), 349, 350
s 501(3A), 276, 439, 440
s 501(g)(a), 349–50
ss 501–502, 359–60
s 501CA(1), 439–40
s 501CA(3)(b), 440
s 501CA(4)(b)(ii), 440
s 502, 360
s 503A, 311–12
s 504, 78
s 505, 78–9
Migration Regulations 1958
sch 4 cl 4002, 79
Migration Regulations 1994
reg 880.22, 417–18
National Consumer Credit Protection Act 2009
s 80, 225
s 80(1)(f), 223–4
Ombudsman Act 1976
ss 4–5, 106–8
s 8, 108–9
s 15, 172
ss 15–17, 109–11
Paid Parental Leave Act 2010, 183
Privacy Act 1988, 137
Public Disclosure Act 2013
ss 9–11(1), 143–4
Public Governance, Performance and Accountability Act 2013
s 5, 98–9
s 8, 99
ss 12–13, 99–100
ss 15–19, 100–101
s 21, 101
ss 25–29, 101–2
s 40, 102
Public Interest Disclosure Act 2013
pt 3, 148
s 13, 144

ss 14–16, 144
ss 19–20, 144–5
s 20(1), 145
s 20(2), 145
s 20(3), 145
ss 25–26, 145–6
s 29, 148
Public Service Act 1999, 22, 143–4
s 13, 23–4
s 13(13), 133
Public Service Regulations 1999
reg 2.1, 133–4
Royal Commissions Act 1902
s 1A, 119
Social Services Act 1947
s 107, 411–12
Taxation Administration Act 1953
s 8, 388
s 8(1), 388
Trade Practices Act 1974
pt IIIA, 51
s 44H, 51–2
s 44H(4)(f), 52
Tribunals Amalgamation Act 2015, 212
s 4, 212
Wheat Marketing Act 1989, 30
s 57, 29–30
World Heritage Properties Conservation Act 1983
s 6, 285

Australian Capital Territory

Administrative Decisions (Judicial Review) Act 1989, 295
s 5, 451
Planning and Development Act 2007
s 27(1)–27(2), 449
s 29, 449
s 29(1), 451
s 30(1), 449–51

New South Wales

Administrative Decisions Tribunal Act 1997
s 113, 365
Births, Deaths and Marriages Registration Act 1995
s 32A, 364
s 32DA(1), 364
s 32DC, 364–5
Building and Construction Industry Security of Payment Act 1999, 269
s 8(1), 268
s 22, 268–9
Industrial Relations Act 1996, 248, 264
s 179, 304–5
Occupational Health and Safety Act 1983, 248, 264, 305
s 15, 263, 264
s 53, 263–4
Prices Regulation Act 1948
s 20(1), 152–3
s 20(1A), 415
Supreme Court Act 1970
ss 22–23, 242
s 65(1)–65(3), 242
s 69, 242–3, 269
s 69(3)–69(5), 280

Northern Territory

Northern Territory Civil and Administrative Tribunal Act 2014
ss 45–46, 191
s 46(2)(b), 192
Planning Act 1979
s 4, 405
s 165, 405
s 165(1), 405
Victims of Crime Assistance Act 2006
ss 30–31(3), 190–1
s 48(1), 191

Queensland

Development Regulations 1993
reg 16(1), 368
sch 1, 368
Invasion of Privacy Act 1971
s 43, 47–8
Judicial Review Act 1991, 256

South Australia

Development Act 1993
s 35(3)(a), 367–8
Local Government Act 1934
s 667, 82
Ombudsman Act 1972
s 18, 115–16
s 25, 116–17
s 28, 117
Shop Trading Hours Act 1977
s 4, 407–8
s 5, 410
s 5(1), 408
s 13, 408–9
s 14, 409
Supreme Court Act 1935
s 17, 243–4

Victoria

Accident Compensation Act 1985
s 68, 457–8
s 68(2), 458
Administrative Law Act 1978
ss 2–3, 244–5
ss 7–8, 245
s 10, 35–6
s 11, 97
Archaeological and Aboriginal Relics Preservation Act 1972, 291
Domestic Animals Act 1994
s 29(4), 357
s 29(d), 356
s 84P, 357
s 84P(e), 356
Freedom of Information Act 1982, 160
s 13, 159
s 32, 160
s 32(1), 159
s 50(2)–50(3), 159
s 50(4), 160
Victorian Civil and Administrative Tribunal Act 1998
s 148, 231, 232

Western Australia

Aboriginal Heritage Act 1972, 36
s 5, 35
s 10(1), 35–6
s 17, 36
Mining Act 1978
s 71, 378
s 74(1)(ca)(ii), 381
ss 74–74A, 378–81
s 74A, 381
Western Australian Development Corporation Act 1983
s 4(3), 36

NAURU

Asylum Seekers (Regional Processing Centre) Act 2012
s 18C, 25

UNITED KINGDOM

Defence (General) Regulations 1939
reg 18B, 371
reg 18B(1), 370
Tribunals and Inquiries Act 1958, 178

INTERNATIONAL INSTRUMENTS

Convention for the Protection of the World Cultural and National Heritage, 285
Convention Relating to the Status of Refugees, 374, 428
art 1A(2), 428
art 33, 141
Protocol Relating to the Status of Refugees, 374, 428

ACKNOWLEDGEMENTS

The authors and Cambridge University Press would like to thank the following for permission to reproduce material in this book.

Extracts from Commonwealth legislation: Sourced from the Federal Register of Legislation at 1 December 2022. For the latest information on Australian Government law please go to https://www.legislation.gov.au. Reproduced under Creative Commons Attribution 4.0 International (CC BY 4.0) licence: https://creativecommons.org/licenses/by/4.0/.

Extracts from Australian Capital Territory legislation: © Australian Capital Territory 2001.

Extracts from New South Wales legislation: Sourced from the New South Wales Legislation website at 1 December 2022. For the latest information on New South Wales Government legislation please go to https://www.legislation.nsw.gov.au. Reproduced under a CC BY 4.0 licence: https://creativecommons.org/licenses/by/4.0/.

Extracts from Northern Territory legislation and Northern Territory Civil and Administrative Tribunal ('NTCAT') cases: © Northern Territory. Reproduced with permission.

Extracts from Queensland legislation: Sourced from the Queensland Legislation website at 1 December 2022. For the latest information on Queensland Government legislation please go to https://www.legislation.qld.gov.au. Reproduced under a CC BY 4.0 licence: https://creativecommons.org/licenses/by/4.0/.

Extracts from South Australian legislation: Sourced from the South Australian Legislation website at 1 December 2022. For the latest information on South Australian Government legislation please go to https://www.legislation.sa.gov.au/. Reproduced under Creative Commons Attribution 4.0 International (CC BY 4.0) licence: https://creativecommons.org/licenses/by/4.0/.

Extracts from Victorian legislation: © State of Victoria. Copyright in all legislation of the Parliament of the State of Victoria is owned by the Crown in right of the State of Victoria. This product or service contains an unofficial version of the legislation of the Parliament of State of Victoria. The State of Victoria accepts no responsibility for the accuracy and completeness of any legislation contained in this product or provided through this service.

Extracts from Western Australian legislation: Sourced from the Western Australian Legislation website at 1 December 2022. For the latest information on Western Australian legislation please go to https://www.legislation.wa.gov.au. Reproduced under Creative Commons Attribution 4.0 International (CC BY 4.0) licence: https://creativecommons.org/licenses/by/4.0/.

Extracts from Administrative Review Council, *Rule Making by Commonwealth Agencies* (Report No 35, 1992): © Commonwealth of Australia 1992; Administrative Review Council, *The Contracting Out of Government Services* (Report No 42, 1998): © Commonwealth of Australia 1998; Administrative Review Council, *Internal Review of Agency Decision Making* (Report No 44, 2000): © Commonwealth of Australia 2000;

Administrative Review Council, *Decision Making: Lawfulness Best Practice Guide 1* (2007); Administrative Review Council, *Best Practice Guide 4 – Decision Making: Reasons* (2007): © Commonwealth of Australia 2007. Reproduced under Creative Commons Attribution 4.0 International (CC BY 4.0) licence: https://creativecommons.org/licenses/by/4.0/.

Extract from Administrative Review Council, *Federal Judicial Review in Australia* (Report No 50, 2012): © Commonwealth of Australia 2012. Licenced under a CC BY 3.0 licence: https://creativecommons.org/licenses/by/3.0/au/.

Extract from Australian Law Reform Commission, *Traditional Rights and Freedoms – Encroachments by Commonwealth Laws* (Report No 129, 2015): © Commonwealth of Australia.

Extracts from Commonwealth, *Commonwealth Administrative Review Committee Report* (Parl Paper No 144, 1971): Reproduced courtesy of the National Archives of Australia.

Extract from Commonwealth Ombudsman, *Automated Decision-making: Better Practice Guide* (2019): © Commonwealth of Australia. Reproduced under Creative Commons Attribution 3.0 Australia (CC BY 3.0) licence: https://creativecommons.org/licenses/by/3.0/au/.

Extracts from Commonwealth Parliamentary Debates (Hansard) are reproduced from the Parliament of Australia website with the kind permission of the Commonwealth of Australia (Department of Parliamentary Services). The Hansards can be downloaded for free from https://www.aph.gov.au/Parliamentary_Business/Hansard, subject to copyright conditions.

Extract from Office of the Australian Information Commissioner ('OAIC'), *Department of Immigration and Border Protection: Own Motion Investigation Report* (November 2014) and *FOI Agency Resource 5: Exemptions and Conditional Exemptions Under the Freedom of Information Act 1982* (September 2011): © Office of the Australian Information Commissioner website. Licenced under a CC BY 3.0 licence: https://creativecommons.org/licenses/by/3.0/au/.

Extracts from *Royal Commission into the Home Insulation Program* (Report, 2014) © Commonwealth of Australia 2014. Licenced under a CC BY 3.0 licence: https://creativecommons.org/licenses/by/3.0/au/.

Extracts from *Commonwealth Law Reports, Federal Court Reports, Federal Law Reports* and *Australian Law Journal Reports*: Reproduced with permission of Thomson Reuters (Professional) Australia Limited: https://legal.thomsonreuters.com.au.

Extracts from *Administrative Law Decisions* and *Australian Law Reports*: Originally published by LexisNexis.

Extract from *Liversidge v Anderson* [1942] AC 206: © Incorporated Council of Law Reporting for England and Wales. Reproduced with permission.

Extract from Dawn Oliver, 'Accountability and the Foundations of British Democracy – the Public Interest and Public Service Principles' in Nicholas Bamforth and Peter Leyland (eds), *Accountability in the Contemporary Constitution* (Oxford University Press, 2013): © Oxford University Press. Reproduced with permission.

Extract from Janina Boughey, 'Executive Power in Emergencies: Where is the Accountability?' (2020) 45(3) *Alternative Law Journal* 168: © Janina Boughey, SAGE Publications. Reproduced by permission of SAGE Publications and the author.

Extract from *Farrugia v Secretary, Department of Social Services* [2022] AATA 11: © Administrative Appeals Tribunal. Reproduced with permission.

Extract from *King v Ombudsman* (2020) 137 SASR 18: Reproduced with permission from the Attorney-General for the State of South Australia and the South Australian Courts Administration Authority.

Extracts from Council of Australasian Tribunals, Tribunal Independence in Appointments: A Best Practice Guide (2016) and Practice Manual for Tribunals (5th ed, 2020): © Council of Australasian Tribunals. Reproduced with permission.

Extract from IDF Callinan, *Section 4 of the Tribunals Amalgamation Act 2015 (Cth)* (Report, 19 December 2018): © Commonwealth of Australia. Reproduced under Creative Commons Attribution 4.0 International (CC BY 4.0) licence: https://creativecommons.org/licenses/by/4.0/.

Every effort has been made to trace and acknowledge copyright. The publisher apologises for any accidental infringement and welcomes information that would redress this situation.

CHAPTER

1

INTRODUCTION

An introduction to this book 2

Why accountability? 3

AV Dicey, *Introduction to the Study of the Law of the Constitution* (Macmillan, 1915) (first published 1885) 3

Charles de Secondat, Baron de Montesquieu, *The Spirit of Laws* (Thomas Nugent trans, G Bell and Sons, 1914) (first published 1748) 4

Church of Scientology Inc v Woodward (1982) 154 CLR 25 5

A v Hayden (No 2) (1984) 156 CLR 532 6

Accountability for what? Administrative law values 7

Dawn Oliver, 'Accountability and the Foundations of British Democracy – the Public Interest and Public Service Principles' in Nicholas Bamforth and Peter Leyland (eds), *Accountability in the Contemporary Constitution* (Oxford University Press, 2013) 289 7

Chief Justice James Allsop, 'Values in Public Law' (2017) 91 *Australian Law Journal* 118 9

Administrative law and statutory interpretation 11

SZTAL v Minister for Immigration and Border Protection (2017) 262 CLR 362 11

Modern accountability: some challenges 12

Janina Boughey, 'Executive Power in Emergencies: Where is the Accountability?' (2020) 45(3) *Alternative Law Journal* 168 12

An introduction to this book

The cases and materials in this book complement the introduction to administrative law provided in *Government Accountability: Australian Administrative Law*, third edition ('the textbook'). It is assumed that readers of this book will also have access to the textbook. The chapters in this book mirror those in the textbook. We envisage that readers will begin their study of a topic by reading the relevant section of the textbook and will turn to this book to study key cases and concepts in greater depth. For this reason, this book contains very limited commentary on the cases and materials.

There are two primary reasons for supplementing the textbook with a book of cases and materials. First, as every student and practitioner of law knows, cases and legislation are authoritative sources of law; a textbook can only provide the authors' non-authoritative description of that law. Therefore, any serious student of administrative law will be sure to read the leading cases and relevant legislation for themselves. This book makes that task easier by presenting key extracts from those primary materials in a relatively accessible format.

Second, we use this book to explore topics beyond the explanation provided in the textbook. For selected topics, we provide case studies demonstrating how administrative law principles and mechanisms work in practice and interact with one another. Where space permits, we have included materials that reveal multiple dimensions of a single issue. Dissenting judgments and contrasting opinions are presented in order to encourage critical thinking about the status quo.

In selecting and editing the extracts in this book, we seek to balance these objectives: providing an accessible collection of leading cases and key statutory provisions while also embracing the complexities of administrative law principles and practice. (Of course, readers who wish to understand an area of law in depth must go further than reading the extracts in this book; they must read the cases and statutes in their entirety and undertake further research.) Where possible, we have included not only those portions of judgments that lay down authoritative statements of principle, but also those portions that explain how those principles apply to the facts of the case. This provides the reader with the tools to develop a thorough understanding of how the legal rules and principles operate.

Statutory interpretation is a central element of contemporary administrative law (and, indeed, of most areas of Australian law). Accordingly, many of the case extracts in this book are structured in a way that emphasises statutory interpretation. The statutory provisions that are key to the reasoning in the case are set out in full at the beginning of the extract (as they stood at the relevant time; subsequent amendments have not been incorporated). Space permitting, judicial engagement with the application of the rules of statutory interpretation to those provisions is included. Not only does this approach present an accurate picture of what was decided in each case, it also gives the reader opportunities to examine the interplay between the rules of statutory interpretation and the common law in specific fact situations.

It has not been possible to include every important case, nor to provide the extensive extracts we might have if accessibility had not been a high priority. We hope this book provides the reader with a sophisticated introduction to Australian administrative law, and with the interest and ability to further develop their understanding.

This introductory chapter provides a range of perspectives on the relationship between administrative law and the rule of law, and introduces the overarching concept that we use to explain administrative law principles and mechanisms: the idea of accountability.

Why accountability?

AV Dicey, *Introduction to the Study of the Law of the Constitution* (Macmillan, 1915) (first published 1885)

The work of the famous English legal scholar, AV Dicey, has been hugely influential in the development of common law legal systems and legal thinking. In this extract, Dicey provides a seminal description of the concept of the rule of law.

> ***183*** When we say that the supremacy or the rule of law is a characteristic of the English constitution, we generally include under one expression at least three distinct though kindred conceptions.
>
> We mean, in the first place, that no man is punishable or can be lawfully made to suffer in body or goods except for a distinct breach of law established in the ordinary legal manner before the ordinary Courts ***184*** of the land. In this sense the rule of law is contrasted with every system of government based on the exercise by persons in authority of wide, arbitrary, or discretionary powers of constraint.
>
> ... ***189*** We mean in the second place, when we speak of the 'rule of law' as a characteristic of our country, not only that with us no man is above the law, but (what is a different thing) that here every man, whatever be his rank or condition, is subject to the ordinary law of the realm and amenable to the jurisdiction of the ordinary tribunals.
>
> In England the ideal of legal equality, or of the universal subjection of all classes to one law administered by the ordinary Courts, has been pushed to its utmost limit. With us every official, from the Prime Minister down to a constable or a collector of taxes, is under the same responsibility for every act done without legal justification as any other citizen.
>
> ...
>
> ***191*** There remains yet a third and a different sense in which the 'rule of law' or the predominance of the legal spirit may be described as a special attribute of English institutions. We may say that the constitution is pervaded by the rule of law on the ground that the general principles of the constitution (as for example the right to personal liberty, or the right of public meeting) are with us the result of judicial decisions determining the rights of private persons in particular cases brought before the Courts; whereas under many foreign constitutions the security (such as it is) given to the rights of individuals results, or appears to result, from the general principles of the constitution or the 'administrative tribunals' (*tribunaux administratifs*) of France. The notion which lies at the bottom of the 'administrative law' known to foreign countries is, that affairs or disputes in which the government or its servants are concerned are beyond the sphere of the civil Courts and must be dealt with by special and more or less official bodies. This idea is utterly unknown to the law of England, and indeed is fundamentally inconsistent with our traditions and customs.

The 'rule of law,' lastly, may be used as a ***199*** formula for expressing the fact that with us the law of the constitution, the rules which in foreign countries naturally form part of a constitutional code, are not the source but the consequence of the rights of individuals, as defined and enforced by the Courts; that, in short, the principles of private law have with us been by the action of the Courts and Parliament so extended as to determine the position of the Crown and of its servants ...

Charles de Secondat, Baron de Montesquieu, *The Spirit of Laws* (Thomas Nugent trans, G Bell and Sons, 1914) (first published 1748)

The concept of the separation of powers, which is central to administrative law, is strongly associated with the work of the French political philosopher, Montesquieu. In the extract below, Montesquieu explains the link between the separation of powers and individual liberty.

Book XI: Of the laws which establish political liberty with regard to the constitution

162 In every government there are three sorts of power: the legislative; the executive in respect to things dependent on the law of nations; and the executive in regard to matters that depend on the civil law.

By virtue of the first, the prince or magistrate enacts temporary or perpetual laws, and amends or abrogates those that have been already enacted. By the second, he ***163*** makes peace or war, sends or receives embassies, establishes the public security, and provides against invasions. By the third, he punishes criminals, or determines the disputes that arise between individuals. The latter we shall call the judiciary power, and the other simply the executive power of the state.

The political liberty of the subject is a tranquillity [sic] of mind arising from the opinion each person has of his safety. In order to have this liberty, it is requisite the government be so constituted as one man need not be afraid of another.

When the legislative and executive powers are united in the same person, or in the same body of magistrates, there can be no liberty; because apprehensions may arise, lest the same monarch or senate should enact tyrannical laws, to execute them in a tyrannical manner.

Again, there is no liberty, if the judiciary power be not separated from the legislative and executive. Were it joined with the legislative, the life and liberty of the subject would be exposed to arbitrary control; for the judge would be then the legislator. Were it joined to the executive power, the judge might behave with violence and oppression.

There would be an end of everything, were the same man or the same body, whether of the nobles or of the people, to exercise those three powers, that of enacting laws, that of executing the public resolutions, and of trying the causes of individuals. ...

[Citations omitted]

Church of Scientology Inc v Woodward (1982) 154 CLR 25

Facts

The Church of Scientology was concerned that the Australian Security Intelligence Organisation ('ASIO') had collected intelligence about the Church and had continued to do so even after establishing that the Church was not a security risk. The Church and one of its members commenced proceedings in the High Court, seeking declarations that ASIO's investigations into the Church were unlawful and prohibiting it from continuing those investigations. ASIO applied to have the statement of claim struck out on the ground that the legislation establishing ASIO shielded its conduct from judicial review.

The High Court granted ASIO's application to strike out the statement of claim, albeit because of the particular form in which the Church framed its action rather than any general immunity of ASIO from judicial review. Brennan J, who dissented, made some observations that are now recognized as classic statements on the relationship between the executive, the courts, legislation, and the rule of law in Australia.

Brennan J (dissenting)

> ***70*** The jurisdiction of this Court to give relief compelling compliance with the Act is not in question. It was conceded that the activities of the Organization [(ASIO)] were subject to judicial review, and the concession was rightly made. As the law which sustains the Organization in existence limits its functions, it would mock the will of Parliament to deny that the functions which it has defined may be exceeded without restraint by the courts. Judicial review is neither more nor less than the enforcement of the rule of law over executive action; it is the means by which executive action is prevented from exceeding the powers and functions assigned to the executive by law and the interests of the individual are protected accordingly.
>
> ***71*** It is submitted, however, that the Act commits to the Organization the determination of what activities it will undertake within its charter, and that a decision to engage in a particular activity is not open to review merely because a mistake is made as to whether that activity is within its charter. Bad faith apart, it is said, mistakes in making decisions are necessarily incidental to or part of the Organization's function of deciding whether to undertake a particular activity and mistaken decisions, honestly made, are not amenable to judicial review.
>
> The submission cannot be accepted. The Organization's functions are not defined in terms of what the Organization believes them to be. The provisions of the Act, not the Organization's opinion, furnish the measure of its legitimate functions. No doubt it is necessary for the Organization to decide whether a particular activity is within its functions but such a decision is merely the ***72*** administrative step taken to ensure compliance with the Act. What Fullagar J said with respect to the constitutional validity of administrative acts in *Australian Communist Party v The Commonwealth* [(1951) 83 CLR 1, 258] applies equally to the statutory validity of an executive act undertaken in reliance upon a statutory power:

> The validity of a law or of an administrative act done under a law cannot be made to depend on the opinion of the law-maker, or the person who is to do the act, that the law or the consequence of the act is within the constitutional power upon which the law in question itself depends for its validity.

[Citations omitted]

A v Hayden (No 2) (1984) 156 CLR 532

Facts

On 30 November 1983, a group of people employed by various Commonwealth agencies took part in a training exercise organised by the Australian Secret Intelligence Service ('ASIS'). The objective of the exercise was to rescue a 'hostage' being held by 'captors' on the tenth floor of the Sheraton Hotel in Melbourne. ASIS did not seek the hotel's permission to carry out the exercise; nor did it inform hotel staff or patrons that the exercise would take place. The exercise went awry (Mason J described it as having 'the appearance of a law school moot based on an episode taken from the adventures of Maxwell Smart': *A v Hayden (No 2)* (1984) 156 CLR 532, 550). It began with participants battering in a hotel room door using sledgehammers, and culminated in them making a hasty exit through the hotel lobby, wearing masks and brandishing pistols and submachine guns (for further details, see *Royal Commission on Australia's Security and Intelligence Agencies: Report on the Sheraton Hotel Incident* (Report, 1984)).

The Chief Commissioner of Police for Victoria requested that the Commonwealth provide the names of the individuals involved in the exercise, so that Victorian police could make inquiries with a view to commencing prosecutions for offences committed in the course of the training exercise. The participants sought to prevent the Commonwealth from disclosing their identities, arguing that they were protected by a confidentiality clause in their employment contracts with the Commonwealth, and that disclosing their identities would be a national security risk. For its part, the Commonwealth had reached an agreement with the Victorian Government under which both governments passed legislation that would permit Victorian courts to sit in private if and when hearing any criminal charges arising from the Sheraton Hotel incident.

The procedural history of the proceedings is complex. For present purposes, the judgments are significant for their invocation of rule of law principles to explain the limits on executive power.

Gibbs CJ

> ***540*** The fact that this foolish exercise was carried out under the authority of the Commonwealth would in itself provide no reason in law why the Commonwealth should not disclose the identities of the plaintiffs to the Chief Commissioner. It is fundamental to our legal system that the executive has no power to authorize a breach of the law and that it is no excuse for an offender to say that he acted under the orders of a superior officer.

Mason J

550 The Commonwealth has a legitimate concern with the administration of the criminal law in its application to the events recorded in the stated case. However, the emphasis which the Commonwealth seeks to give to this responsibility should not be allowed to obscure its responsibility for what occurred. It is possible that the promise [of confidentiality] was given, and the arrangements for the training exercise made, in the belief that executive orders would provide sufficient legal authority or justification for what was done. It is very difficult to believe that this was the Commonwealth's view – superior orders are not and never have been a defence in our law – though it is conceivable that the plaintiffs may have had some such belief. I mention these aspects of the case lest concentration on the legal questions presented by the stated case should divert attention away from the primary role played by the Commonwealth in this enterprise, a primary role which should be kept steadily in mind if the criminal law ever comes to be set in motion against the plaintiffs. For the future, the point needs to be made loudly and clearly, that if counterespionage activities involve breaches of the law they are liable to attract the consequences that ordinarily flow from breaches of the law.

Murphy J

562 The executive power of the Commonwealth must be exercised in accordance with the Constitution and the laws of the Commonwealth. The Governor-General, the federal Executive Council and every officer of the Commonwealth are bound to observe the laws of the land. If necessary, constitutional and other writs are available to restrain apprehended violations and to remedy past violations. I restate these elementary principles because astonishingly one of the plaintiffs asserted through counsel that it followed from the nature of the executive government that it is not beyond the executive power, even in a situation other than war, to order one of its citizens to kill another person. Such a proposition is inconsistent with the rule of law. It is subversive of the Constitution and the laws. It is, in other countries, the justification for death squads.

Accountability for what? Administrative law values

Dawn Oliver, 'Accountability and the Foundations of British Democracy – the Public Interest and Public Service Principles' in Nicholas Bamforth and Peter Leyland (eds), *Accountability in the Contemporary Constitution* (Oxford University Press, 2013) 289

In the following extract, Emeritus Professor Dawn Oliver, University College London, discusses the purposes of public accountability mechanisms as they operate in the United Kingdom, and broader principles that are relevant throughout western democracies.

289 Discussion of accountability commonly revolves around ways in which public officeholders (including Members of the two Houses of Parliament and of the government, and other elected people – for instance in the devolved bodies and in local authorities, civil servants, local authority officers, police officers and others exercising public functions) are answerable to public bodies of various kinds or to the electorate: officials to the courts; ministers to Parliament and the electorate; civil servants to ministers; public authorities to ombudsmen; local authorities to their electorates. I take accountability to entail, in this context, a legal, political, social or moral duty on the part of an accountor to explain and justify his or her action or inaction to particular bodies demanding explanations – accountees – according to standards set by or associated with the role of the accountee. If the courts are involved, the standards will be legal; if the ombudsman, the standard will be whether there has been maladministration resulting in injustice, and so on. If the accountee considers that mistakes or errors have been made, the accountor may be required – whether by law or other social norms – to put matters right by meeting the requirements of the accountee, for instance by apologizing, making amends, ensuring that similar errors are not made in future, resigning or submitting to punishment.

We do not often ask exactly why a web of accountability mechanisms exists in a democracy such as the UK; what good the mechanisms are supposed to achieve; ***290*** what evils they are supposed to avoid; or whether the wide range of established and approved accountability mechanisms have anything in common.

We know that election of members of the legislature and the executive is not enough to produce and maintain a well-functioning democratic system in which the rule of law is observed, human rights and civil and political liberties are respected, and it is accepted that no party or government has a monopoly of wisdom; ie that authority is not enough and justifications for action may be expected – these being the essential elements of a liberal democracy, in my view. Without appropriate (and appropriateness is crucial) accountability mechanisms, election alone could produce imprudent, partisan, sectarian, discriminatory, illegitimate, corrupt government that would be inconsistent with the very concepts of democracy and the rule of law. And access to the courts alone cannot protect us from bad government. Further mechanisms of accountability are required. I shall suggest that what most accountability arrangements in the UK have in common is recognition of the need to uphold two important constitutional principles: public bodies should seek to promote the general or public interest and not sectional or partisan interests (the public interest principle); thus, they should serve, altruistically, the public and not their own interests (the public service principle). ... While I am focusing on the UK system ... in fact these principles are commonly included in the constitutional texts of western democracies.

Some concepts need to be clarified before we can proceed. First: accountability. I have sketched the meaning of accountability in the first paragraph. ... In exploring the workings of accountability mechanisms in the context of the British constitution and the public service and public interests principles, we need to be aware that 'accountees' vary widely: many of them are expected, and consider their role to be, to promote public interests rather than sectional or sectoral interests. Ministers are 'responsible' – nowadays 'accountable' is a better term – to the two Houses of Parliament: they are supposed to be concerned about public interest in, among other things, the competence and integrity of ministers. Ministers are required to explain and justify their own or their officials' actions to Parliament in terms of public interest standards and not, for instance, in terms of partisan standards that they know conflict with public interests.

Of course, politicians are liable to focus on short-term rather than long-term problems and their solutions, or on winning or retaining votes in the next election. They may lack expertise where it is needed and they may panic in emergencies or when faced by heavy public pressure. The system in the UK therefore involves many non-party political or expert bodies – executive agencies and quasi-autonomous non-governmental organisations (Quangos) – which work under mandates (framework documents in ***291*** the case of executive agencies, statutory or other legal mandates in the case of many Quangos) which spell out the public interests and how they should be weighed against one another, or against sectional interests. Given the inevitability of differences of opinion as to how conflicting public interests are to be weighed in particular instances, safeguards are to be found in the public servant's duties ... and their 'enforcement' via, for instance, rights of access to information under the *Freedom of Information Act 2000*, the possibility of judicial review ..., and a whole range of other accountability mechanisms. ...

The votes of the electorate at election time respond to the record of the incumbent government: elections are accountability moments. Individuals may exercise their votes in accordance with their own interests, but the assumption is that the aggregate of individuals' votes will reflect or promote the general interest and the public service principle. And – very importantly – sections of the public to whom information about the work of officials is disclosed, whether by the press or on freedom of information requests or in other ways – will articulate the standards they expect of public bodies: criticisms may well result in resignations.

[Citations omitted]

Chief Justice James Allsop, 'Values in Public Law' (2017) 91 *Australian Law Journal* 118

This is the published version of Chief Justice Allsop's 2015 James Spigelman Oration, delivered in Sydney on 27 October 2015.

118 [T]he values about which I wish to speak inhere in the fabric of our law and have done for centuries. This is not best understood by the process of tracing the course of the words of charters and bills of rights, or the course of precedent or by comparing the terms of statutes of different eras, alone. It is to be understood, first, by recognising that public law is concerned with power – state power: its organisation, distribution, exercise and control; and secondly, by identifying the public values that inhere in those complex relationships of organisation, distribution, exercise and control. It is this identification of the values that assists in understanding the features of our legal system that are timeless.

Power, and its control, is not only the domain of public law; private law sees the control of power, and the protection of the vulnerable, as central themes. This is reason for questioning any strictness, or clarity of division, in the public/private taxonomy. Power is power, it might be said. Yet there is something super-added, something meaningful, sometimes something menacing in the presence of state authority. By way of example only, this can be seen in the distinction between torture and private brutality. In the former, a special repugnance to the brutality (worthy of raising the status of the law prohibiting it towards a *ius cogens*) is brought by its infliction in the name of a polity, a political system, a people. The distinction between public and private law is real, if not linear in its boundaries, if not logical in its form and content, if not always consistent in its application. For these reasons, the distinction is worth making.

...

120 A little more should be said at this point about power and law. It is a mistake to view law and legitimate power as based on command alone. Law is comprised not only of command from a legitimate source, but it is also the expression and recognition of natural human and societal bonds of conduct. Ultimately, a legal system, to be just and to work effectively, must be derived from the consent or acceptance of the governed. By consent, I do not mean the individual willingness in each case to accept the particular exercise of power, rather I mean the underlying acceptance of the legitimacy of the organs and mode of the exercise of societal authority. This may involve, but does not require, central command; it rests, ultimately, upon reciprocal acceptance and shared values. An examination of the lucid analysis by Finn J of the laws and customs of the Torres Strait Islander peoples in [*Akiba v Queensland (No 2)* (2010) 204 FCR 1, 58–79 [177]-[264]] reveals law as social bonds steeped in reciprocity, and consent.

But power is real. It and its exercise are often based on compulsion, and may be of such a character as to change the lives and fortunes of those subject to it, for the worse. Governmental power is given to those in different branches of government by the operation of an organised political process, being our system of national and state responsible and representative government, resting on the sovereignty of the Australian people ...

121 An organised political system with a foundation of the sovereignty of the governed provides the constitutional framework in which to view power as reciprocal, consensual and as serving the people. It also provides the framework for the values of the governed, of the people, to inform how governmental power is wielded (on their behalf).

Let us, in that context, examine then the values that inform the understanding and exercise of public law. Drawing together the above general remarks, at least five values or groups of values can be posited. They are not meant to be crisp in definition. I would begin with a value or feature that may be seen as prosaic, but it is the product of

> other features, and is essential to any system of government or organisation of power: *reasonable certainty,* so power can be understood, known and exercised, and branches of government take responsibility for its exercise, in a workably efficient and fair way. Secondly: *honesty and fidelity to the Constitution,* and to the freedoms and free society that it assumes, reflecting the constant of a principle of legality. Thirdly: *a rejection of unfairness, unreasonableness and arbitrariness.* Fourthly: *equality.* Fifthly: *humanity, and the dignity and autonomy of the individual,* as the recognition of, and respect for, the reciprocal human context of the exercise of power and the necessary humanity of the process; in many contexts this translates as the recognition of mercy. ...
>
> Power is not only to be appreciated or understood by debates about who is to wield it: Parliament, Minister, civil servant, judge or private individual, or about who has the last say in approving (or not) how power has been wielded; it is about people – how people should be treated in the exercise of power in a just and decent society. This is not about being nice. Rather, it is about how those who are the subject of the exercise of power in a free democracy, should be entitled to expect that the lawful exercise of power involves attributes or characteristics that recognise and reinforce human dignity and decency, and that reflect the high trust that society has placed in those with public power to exercise it lawfully and for the common good.

[Citations omitted]

Administrative law and statutory interpretation

SZTAL v Minister for Immigration and Border Protection (2017) 262 CLR 362

In this case, High Court judges explain the contemporary Australian approach to statutory interpretation.

Kiefel CJ, Nettle and Gordon JJ

> ***368*** [14] The starting point for the ascertainment of the meaning of a statutory provision is the text of the statute whilst, at the same time, regard is had to its context and purpose. Context should be regarded at this first stage and not at some later stage and it should be regarded in its widest sense. This is not to deny the importance of the natural and ordinary meaning of a word, namely how it is ordinarily understood in discourse, to the process of construction. Considerations of context and purpose simply recognise that, understood in its statutory, historical or other context, some other meaning of a word may be suggested, and so too, if its ordinary meaning is not consistent with the statutory purpose, that meaning must be rejected.

Gageler J

> ***374*** [37] ... The task of construction begins, as it ends, with the statutory text. But the statutory text from beginning to end is construed in context, and an understanding of context has utility 'if, and in so far as, it assists in fixing the meaning of the statutory text'.
>
> ***375*** [38] The constructional choice presented by a statutory text read in context is sometimes between one meaning which can be characterised as the ordinary or grammatical meaning and another meaning which cannot be so characterised. More commonly, the choice is from 'a range of potential meanings, some of which may be less immediately obvious or more awkward than others, but none of which is wholly ungrammatical or unnatural', in which case the choice 'turns less on linguistic fit than on evaluation of the relative coherence of the alternatives with identified statutory objects or policies'.
>
> [39] Integral to making such a choice is discernment of statutory purpose. The unqualified statutory instruction that, in interpreting a provision of a Commonwealth Act, 'the interpretation that would best achieve the purpose or object of the Act (whether or not that purpose or object is expressly stated in the Act) is to be preferred to each other interpretation' [*Acts Interpretation Act 1091* (Cth) s 15AA] 'is in that respect a particular statutory reflection of a general systemic principle'.

[Citations omitted]

Modern accountability: some challenges

Janina Boughey, 'Executive Power in Emergencies: Where is the Accountability?' (2020) 45(3) *Alternative Law Journal* 168

In this article, Boughey considers how traditional accountability mechanisms have fared in the COVID-19 pandemic.

> ***169* What powers have been exercised by Australian governments in response to COVID-19?**
>
> The Commonwealth, state and territory governments have each exercised a wide range of emergency powers which were granted to them by their respective parliaments. For the most part, the Commonwealth government has exercised powers in relation to migration, customs, the economy (including social security payments), and medical services and pharmaceuticals, while state and territory governments have made orders restricting people's movement and activities, requiring people to isolate and maintain 'social distance', and closing businesses, schools, public spaces and community facilities. This reflects the division of powers between the Commonwealth and states under the *Constitution* although, of course, there are overlaps, as the blame shifting over the handling of the Ruby Princess has demonstrated.

The rules, orders and decisions that governments have made in response to COVID-19 have taken a number of legal forms. The new National Cabinet – a body comprised of the first ministers of the Commonwealth, state and territory governments and advised by a Committee of chief medical officers from those jurisdictions – has made many of the major decisions restricting the movement and activities of Australians and determining when those restrictions should be eased. For example, on 12 June 2020, National Cabinet agreed to replace the 100-person limit on non-essential indoor gatherings with a 4-square-metre rule. Many of these National Cabinet decisions have required legislation or delegated legislation in order to be implemented. The easing of restrictions on indoor gatherings, for instance, required states and territories to issue new orders reflecting the new rules. A large portion of the new emergency laws have been implemented via delegated legislation, including those with significant impacts on the rights and freedoms of Australians. Commonwealth Ministers and health officials have made delegated legislation banning travel, banning cruise ships, taking over hotels to quarantine returning travellers, making it illegal to 'price gouge' when selling personal protective equipment and regulating the use of data collected from the COVID tracing app, among many other things. The form that other rules have taken is not clear … or take the form of 'soft law'. Responsibility for enforcing many of these rules has been given to police forces, who have been given discretionary powers to issue fines and, in extreme cases, arrest and charge people with breaching public health orders. There are accountability challenges arising from the ways in which each of these types of power have been used during COVID.

(Avoiding) parliamentary oversight

One of the major strengths of the Australian government response to COVID-19 has been the level of cooperation between governments, which has been achieved via the establishment of the National Cabinet. The National Cabinet has been described as a 'peacetime war cabinet' and has allowed Australian governments to share information and coordinate an effective national response to the emergency.

However, the National Cabinet is not accountable in the same way that federal, state and territory cabinets are. As an intergovernmental body, it is not responsible to a single parliament, but to nine separate parliaments. This complicates the way responsible government functions in practice. Leaders will be able to answer any questions of their respective parliaments and parliamentary committees by simply explaining that the jurisdiction is committed to a particular course of action through the intergovernmental agreement. This tends to curtail any opportunity for parliamentary input or debate.

The Prime Minister has also declared that National Cabinet meetings have 'the status of a cabinet meeting' ***170*** with respect to confidentiality protocols and exemptions from Freedom of Information legislation. Without access to information, there is no accountability through any means: political, legal or administrative.

…

A second way in which ordinary parliamentary oversight processes have been limited is via the use of non-disallowable delegated legislation. As noted above, a significant portion of the new rules needed to respond effectively to the pandemic have been implemented via delegated legislation, which is usually subject to parliamentary oversight. There are different rules about how parliaments oversee delegated legislation, and what powers they have in each Australian jurisdiction and in relation to different types of instruments. The Commonwealth Parliament has the power to disallow most delegated legislation; state and territory parliaments can all disallow regulations and usually some other forms of delegated legislation; and there are parliamentary committees in each jurisdiction which scrutinise and report to their respective parliament on whether delegated legislation is lawful, appropriate and proportionate.

Not all delegated legislation is subject to these parliamentary oversight mechanisms. ...

A large proportion of the COVID-19 powers which have been exercised via delegated legislation are ... exempt from parliamentary disallowance. So while a parliamentary committee might read them, investigate them and report on them to parliament, there is nothing parliament can do if it thinks that the determinations go beyond the scope of what the Minister is authorised to do or that rules are disproportionate or unsuitable.

...

***172* Are the rules binding and enforceable?**

... [A]nother difficulty with many of the state orders is how difficult they are to find, and how frequently they have changed. Ordinary people (ie, people who are not law academics!) are unlikely to spend hours searching government gazettes for the most recent COVID rules in order to figure out what their rights and obligations are. This means that the public is heavily reliant on the governments' explanations as to the meaning and content of its rules.

Indeed, some of the rules that governments have told us we must follow do not seem to be sourced in law at all. In NSW, for example, physical distancing rules in public places appear largely to take the form of government advice or guidelines, rather than enforceable orders. ...

Government guidelines, advice and interpretations of the law which do not have legally binding force are often called 'soft law'. The term conveys the fact that, despite their lack of force, these informal instruments are commonly 'treated like law' and are 'immensely effective as a means of regulating conduct'. This is a great benefit of soft law; people believe it is law so tend to comply with it, without the need for heavy-handed government enforcement.

But, in Australia, there are significant accountability gaps in relation to governments' use of soft law. ...

In practical terms, this means that a person might rely on government advice about what the law is and conduct their business accordingly. But if that government advice turns out to be wrong, the person may still be able to be penalised for having breached the law ... and will not usually have any remedy for losses they have suffered in following what they thought were the rules.

Police discretion

Police have been given a range of new, extraordinary powers to enforce many of the COVID-19 rules. In many cases, this involves police exercising discretion in deciding whether a person's conduct is 'reasonable' (eg, whether their excuse for leaving the house is reasonable), and if it is not, exercising discretion as to whether or not to issue a penalty (usually a fine). There have been numerous reports of these powers being used in ways that are discriminatory, inconsistent, disproportionate and potentially exceed police powers.

173 The big problem with discretions to issue fines, from an accountability perspective, is the lack of cheap, independent, merits review of the decision to issue the fine. While there are internal review processes through which fines can be challenged without going to court, the grounds on which a fine can be challenged tend to be extremely limited. ... Police can withdraw fines, but this is a non-reviewable discretionary power. The only other option for challenging an infringement notice is to go to court. Thus, there is a strong incentive to pay fines, even if they have been issued unlawfully or unfairly.

...

Judicial review

... Courts are able to review the lawfulness of delegated legislation and administrative decisions made by governments in response to COVID-19. ... However, there are several limitations which mean that the courts alone are not an adequate accountability mechanism.

First, courts are limited to reviewing the lawfulness of government actions. Unlike parliaments and executive oversight agencies, they have no power to assess whether the actions of governments were proportionate or well directed.

Second, court proceedings tend to be expensive and time-consuming. ...

Third, courts only have jurisdiction where a party with standing brings the matter before them. This usually requires a person to have been directly affected by government action (eg, a fine having been issued, or a decision made about their circumstances). Australian courts cannot rule on the general validity of government action or delegated legislation. ...

Fourth, there are limits on what courts can and will review when it comes to government action, and courts have rightly tended to be particularly cautious, or deferential, in their review of government actions taken during emergencies.

Finally, even where they do have jurisdiction, and are willing to decide a matter, courts are limited in the remedies they can issue. ...

174 Different forms of government accountability are appropriate in different circumstances. Emergencies probably necessitate a decrease in certain formal accountability mechanisms, particularly those that delay or diminish a government's ability to effectively respond to the emergency. However, there must be alternative ways through which governments explain themselves, and in which they can ultimately be judged for their handling of the emergency. Any limits on formal accountability should be justifiable, and it is not clear whether the exclusion of parliamentary disallowance or use of soft law is necessary. And limits to government accountability must not become permanent features of the way governments make rules. We should retain the good features of the governments' approach to this emergency – like their willingness to explain their decisions and answer media questions. But we should be careful to ensure that ordinary accountability measures resume as quickly as possible.

[Citations omitted]

PART I

ADMINISTRATIVE DECISION-MAKING

CHAPTER

2

ORGANISATION AND STRUCTURE OF GOVERNMENT

Introduction 20

The Crown and the executive: terminology and constitutional framework 20

Constitution 20

Sue v Hill (1999) 199 CLR 462 21

Executive entities 22

Public Service Act 1999 (Cth) 22

Private bodies in the public sphere 24

Plaintiff M68/2015 v Minister for Immigration and Border Protection (2016) 257 CLR 42 24

NEAT Domestic Trading Pty Ltd v AWB Ltd (2003) 216 CLR 277 29

Administrative Review Council, *The Contracting Out of Government Services* (Report No 42, 1998) 34

Crown immunity 35

Bropho v Western Australia (1990) 171 CLR 1 35

Introduction

This chapter complements Chapter 2 of *Government Accountability: Australian Administrative Law,* third edition. It contains a cross-section of material relating to the entities that make up the executive, including relevant constitutional provisions, values and terminology. The complex contemporary question of outsourcing and privatisation is explored in-depth through two High Court cases and a 1998 Administrative Review Council report that foreshadows issues that continue to present challenges for administrative law principles and mechanisms.

The Crown and the executive: terminology and constitutional framework

Constitution

Chapter II—The Executive Government

61 Executive Power

The executive power of the Commonwealth is vested in the Queen and is exercisable by the Governor-General as the Queen's representative, and extends to the execution and maintenance of this Constitution, and of the laws of the Commonwealth.

62 Federal Executive Council

There shall be a Federal Executive Council to advise the Governor-General in the government of the Commonwealth, and the members of the Council shall be chosen and summoned by the Governor-General and sworn as Executive Councillors, and shall hold office during his pleasure.

63 Provisions referring to Governor-General

The provisions of this Constitution referring to the Governor-General in Council shall be construed as referring to the Governor-General acting with the advice of the Federal Executive Council.

64 Ministers of State

The Governor-General may appoint officers to administer such departments of State of the Commonwealth as the Governor-General in Council may establish.

Such officers shall hold office during the pleasure of the Governor-General. They shall be members of the Federal Executive Council, and shall be the Queen's Ministers of State for the Commonwealth.

After the first general election no Minister of State shall hold office for a longer period than three months unless he is or becomes a senator or a member of the House of Representatives.

Sue v Hill (1999) 199 CLR 462

Facts

Heather Hill was elected to the Senate in the 1998 federal election. She was a dual citizen of Australia and the United Kingdom. Section 44 of the *Constitution* prevents a person from being a senator if the person is a 'citizen of a foreign power'. The major issue in this case was whether the United Kingdom is a 'foreign power' within the meaning of s 44. The High Court held that the United Kingdom was a 'foreign power' and, therefore, Ms Hill had not been properly elected to the Senate. In the course of their reasoning, Gleeson CJ, Gummow and Hayne JJ reflected on the various meanings of the term 'the Crown'.

Gleeson CJ, Gummow and Hayne JJ

The meaning of 'the Crown' in constitutional theory

497 [83] [I]t is necessary to say a little as to the senses in which the expression 'the Crown' is used in constitutional theory derived from the United Kingdom. In its oldest and most specific meaning, 'the Crown' is part of the regalia which is 'necessary to support the splendour and dignity of the Sovereign for the time being', is not devisable and descends from one sovereign to the next. The writings of constitutional lawyers at the time show that it was well understood in 1900, at the time of the adoption of the Constitution, ***498*** that the term 'the Crown' was used in several metaphorical senses.

...

[84] The first use of the expression 'the Crown' was to identify the body politic. ... The Constitution, in identifying the new body politic which it established, did not use the term 'the Crown' in this way ...

[85] The second usage of 'the Crown' is related to the first and identifies that office, the holder of which for the time being is the incarnation of the international personality of a body politic, by whom and to whom diplomatic representatives are accredited and by whom and with whom treaties are concluded. The Commonwealth of Australia, as such, had assumed international personality at some date well before the enactment of the *Australia Act* [in 1986] ...

...

499 [87] Thirdly, the term 'the Crown' identifies what Lord Penzance in *Dixon* called 'the Government' [*Dixon v London Small Arms Co* (1876) 1 App Cas 632, 651], being the executive as distinct from the legislative branch of government, represented by the Ministry and the administrative bureaucracy which attends to its business. As has been indicated, under the Constitution the executive functions bestowed upon 'the Queen' are exercised upon Australian advice.

[88] The fourth use of the term 'the Crown' arose during the course of colonial development in the nineteenth century. It identified the paramount powers of the United Kingdom, the parent state, in relation to its dependencies.

500 [89] [T]he 'Home Government' ceased before 1850 to contribute to the expenses of the colonial government of New South Wales. On the grant of responsible government, certain prerogatives of the Crown in the colony, even those of a proprietary nature, became vested 'in the Crown in right of the colony', as Jacobs J put it in *New South Wales v The Commonwealth* [(1975) 135 CLR 337, 494]. Debts might be payable to the exchequer of one government but not to that of another and questions of disputed priority could arise. ...

501 [90] The expression 'the Crown in right of ...' the government in question was used to identify these newly created and evolving political units. With the formation of federations in Canada and Australia it became more difficult to continue to press 'the Crown' into service to describe complex political structures. Harrison Moore identified 'the doctrine of unity and indivisibility of the Crown' as something 'not persisted in to the extent of ignoring that the several parts of the Empire are distinct entities' ['The Crown as Corporation' (1904) 20 *Law Quarterly Review* 351, 358]. He pointed to the 'inconvenience and mischief' which would follow from rigid adherence to any such doctrine where there were federal structures ...

[91] Whilst formally they may not be juristic persons, [the States and the Commonwealth] are conceived as politically organised bodies having mutual legal relations and are amenable to the ***502*** jurisdiction of courts exercising federal jurisdiction. The employment of the term 'the Crown' to describe the relationships inter se between the United Kingdom, the Commonwealth and the States was described by Latham CJ in 1944 [*Minister for Works (WA)* v *Gulson* (1944) 69 CLR 338, 350–1] as involving 'verbally impressive mysticism' ...

[Citations omitted]

Executive entities

Public Service Act 1999 (Cth)

[As at 1 December 2022]

The *Public Service Act 1999* (Cth) regulates the Australian Public Service ('APS'), which carries out many of the functions of the Australian Government. The APS's *Values and Code of Conduct* are one mechanism for internalising a culture of accountability, integrity, impartiality and other desirable values.

Part 3—The Australian Public Service

9 Constitution of the APS

The Australian Public Service consists of Agency Heads and APS employees.

10 APS Values

Committed to service

(1) The APS is professional, objective, innovative and efficient, and works collaboratively to achieve the best results for the Australian community and the Government.

Ethical

(2) The APS demonstrates leadership, is trustworthy, and acts with integrity, in all that it does.

Respectful

(3) The APS respects all people, including their rights and their heritage.

Accountable

(4) The APS is open and accountable to the Australian community under the law and within the framework of Ministerial responsibility.

Impartial

(5) The APS is apolitical and provides the Government with advice that is frank, honest, timely and based on the best available evidence.

...

13 The APS Code of Conduct

(1) An APS employee must behave honestly and with integrity in connection with APS employment.

(2) An APS employee must act with care and diligence in connection with APS employment.

(3) An APS employee, when acting in connection with APS employment, must treat everyone with respect and courtesy, and without harassment.

(4) An APS employee, when acting in connection with APS employment, must comply with all applicable Australian laws

...

(6) An APS employee must maintain appropriate confidentiality about dealings that the employee has with any Minister or Minister's member of staff.

(7) An APS employee must:

  (a) take reasonable steps to avoid any conflict of interest (real or apparent) in connection with the employee's APS employment; and

  (b) disclose details of any material personal interest of the employee in connection with the employee's APS employment.

(8) An APS employee must use Commonwealth resources in a proper manner and for a proper purpose.

(9) An APS employee must not provide false or misleading information in response to a request for information that is made for official purposes in connection with the employee's APS employment.

(10) An APS employee must not improperly use inside information or the employee's duties, status, power or authority:

  (a) to gain, or seek to gain, a benefit or an advantage for the employee or any other person; or

  (b) to cause, or seek to cause, detriment to the employee's Agency, the Commonwealth or any other person.

(11) An APS employee must at all times behave in a way that upholds:

(a) the APS Values and APS Employment Principles; and

(b) the integrity and good reputation of the employee's Agency and the APS.

(12) An APS employee on duty overseas must at all times behave in a way that upholds the good reputation of Australia.

(13) An APS employee must comply with any other conduct requirement that is prescribed by the regulations.

Private bodies in the public sphere

Plaintiff M68/2015 v Minister for Immigration and Border Protection (2016) 257 CLR 42

Migration Act 1958 (Cth)

[As at relevant date]

198AHA Power to take action etc. in relation to arrangement or regional processing functions of a country

(1) This section applies if the Commonwealth enters into an arrangement with a person or body in relation to the regional processing functions of a country.

(2) The Commonwealth may do all or any of the following:

(a) take, or cause to be taken, any action in relation to the arrangement or the regional processing functions of the country;

(b) make payments, or cause payments to be made, in relation to the arrangement or the regional processing functions of the country;

(c) do anything else that is incidental or conducive to the taking of such action or the making of such payments.

(3) To avoid doubt, subsection (2) is intended to ensure that the Commonwealth has capacity and authority to take action, without otherwise affecting the lawfulness of that action.

(4) Nothing in this section limits the executive power of the Commonwealth.

(5) In this section:

action includes:

(a) exercising restraint over the liberty of a person; and

(b) action in a regional processing country or another country.

arrangement includes an arrangement, agreement, understanding, promise or undertaking, whether or not it is legally binding.

regional processing functions includes the implementation of any law or policy, or the taking of any action, by a country in connection with the role of the country as a regional processing country, whether the implementation or the taking of action occurs in that country or another country.

Facts

The Minister had designated Nauru as a 'regional processing country' under s 198AB(1) of the *Migration Act 1958* (Cth): that is, a country where 'unauthorised maritime arrivals' (asylum seekers who had attempted to reach Australia by boat) would remain while their claims to asylum were assessed. After a person's claim was assessed, there was a possibility the Minister would consider whether to allow the person to apply for an Australian visa. The governments of Australia and Nauru entered into an agreement under which Nauru agreed to accept the asylum seekers for processing, while Australia would bear the costs of transferring them to, and accommodating them in, Nauru.

Pursuant to this agreement, the Australian Government entered into contracts with private companies to build a Regional Processing Centre in Nauru. The Australian Government paid for the construction and maintenance of the Centre's buildings. The Australian Government was to engage contractors to assess the asylum seekers' refugee claims under Nauruan law. Nauru was to provide merits review of the decisions on refugee status, but Australia was to fund the merits review.

Nauru passed the *Asylum Seekers (Regional Processing Centre) Act 2012* (Nauru) ('*RPC Act*') to regulate regional processing arrangements. Section 18C of this Act prohibited detainees in the Regional Processing Centre from leaving the Centre without approval. Nauru also created a special class of visa, the Regional Processing Centre visa ('RPC visa'), which authorised asylum seekers to enter and remain in Nauru while their claims were being processed. An RPC visa could only be granted on the application of an officer of the Australian Government, and Australia paid the fee for the RPC visa.

Further details on the operation of the regional processing arrangements, including the 'Administrative Arrangements' upon which Australia and Nauru agreed, appear in the judgments extracted below.

Plaintiff M68, a Bangladeshi asylum seeker, attempted to come to Australia by boat. Australian migration officials intercepted the boat and took Plaintiff M68 first to Christmas Island and then to Nauru. She was detained in the Regional Processing Centre in Nauru for just over four months while her claim to refugee status was assessed. She was then taken to Australia temporarily for medical treatment. While she was in Australia, the government of Nauru announced it would adopt an 'open centre policy' under which asylum seekers would be free to come and go from the Regional Processing Centre at any time.

Plaintiff M68 commenced proceedings in the High Court under ss 75(iii) and (v) of the *Constitution,* seeking a declaration that the Minister had procured, imposed or enforced her detention, and that this conduct had not been authorised by law. The issues arising in the case were put to the High Court as a 'Special Case': that is, a series of questions of law for the Court to answer. One of her arguments was that her detention had breached the constitutional prohibition, recognised in *Chu Kheng Lim v Minister for Immigration* (1992) 176 CLR 1, on punitive detention by the Commonwealth executive. *Lim* only restricts the powers of the Commonwealth Government (and not the government of Nauru); it was therefore important to consider the extent of the Commonwealth's involvement in detaining Plaintiff M68.

The High Court dismissed Plaintiff M68's claim by 6:1 (Gordon J dissenting). For present purposes, the facts of the case provide an insight into the respective roles of the Australian

Government, the Nauru Government, and private contractors in the tasks of detaining asylum seekers and determining their claims to asylum. The differing views taken by French CJ, Kiefel and Nettle JJ on the one hand and Gordon J on the other hand to the issue of whether Plaintiff M68 was detained by the Australian Government illustrate the complexity of bringing the exercise of power to account when governments 'outsource' their functions.

French CJ, Kiefel and Nettle JJ

> ***62*** [10] Pursuant to the Administrative Arrangements, it was agreed that the Government of Nauru would appoint an operational manager, to be in charge of the day-to-day management of the Centre; and that the Government of Australia would appoint an officer as a programme coordinator, to be responsible for managing all Commonwealth officers and service contracts in relation to the Centre, including the contracting of a service provider to provide services at the Centre for transferees and to provide for their security and safety. A Joint Committee and a Joint Working Group were to be established.
>
> [11] A Ministerial Forum was established to oversee the implementation of the regional partnership between Australia and Nauru and to provide updates on the delivery of projects in Nauru, including the operation of the Centre, and was co-chaired by the Commonwealth Minister and by the Nauru Minister for Justice and Border Control. The Joint Committee, comprised of representatives of the respective governments, met regularly to discuss the operation of the Centre. The ***63*** Joint Working Group, chaired by the Nauru Minister, met each week to discuss matters relating to the Centre, including regional processing issues.
>
> [12] Transfield Services (Australia) Pty Ltd ('Transfield') has been a service provider at the Centre pursuant to a contract with the Commonwealth, represented by the Department of Immigration and Border Protection ('the Transfield Contract'), since March 2014. Transfield undertook to provide 'garrison and welfare services' to transferees and personnel at the regional processing centres. 'Garrison services' include security, cleaning and catering services. As service provider it was required to ensure that the security of the perimeter of the site was maintained. The Department provides fencing, lighting towers and other security infrastructure.
>
> [13] Transfield subcontracted the Transfield Contract to Wilson Security Pty Ltd ('Wilson Security'). Representatives of the two companies attend regular meetings with, and report to, the Department of Immigration and Border Protection and to the Government of Nauru. The Commonwealth occupies an office at [the Regional Processing Centre] at which officers of the Australian Border Force carry out functions in relation to the Centre or transferees at the Centre, including managing service provider contracts, Commonwealth- funded projects, such as construction projects, and relationships and communications between the Commonwealth, the service providers and the Government of Nauru.
>
> ...
>
> ***67*** [29] The central question identified by the plaintiff is whether the Commonwealth's involvement in her detention was authorised by a valid Commonwealth statute.

[30] It is necessary at the outset to be clear about who detained the plaintiff on Nauru. 'Detention' in this context is detention in the custody of the State and involves the exercise of governmental power.

...

[32] The plaintiff ... was detained in custody under the laws of Nauru, administered by the Executive government of Nauru. The *Immigration Act 2014* (Nauru) requires that a person who is not a citizen must have a valid visa to enter or remain in Nauru. Even if the plaintiff was taken to Nauru without her consent, the *Immigration Act* applied to her. The plaintiff was obliged to remain at the Centre under supervision and was not free to leave it, because of the residency requirements of the RPC visa issued by the Government of Nauru, the prohibition on leaving the Centre in s 18C(1) of the RPC Act, which applies to the plaintiff because she has the status of a 'protected person', and the offence provision in s 18C(2).

68 [33] The only exception to the prohibition in s 18C(1) is where prior approval is given to a resident of the Centre by an authorised officer, an operational manager of the Centre or other authorised persons. The Secretary of the Department of Justice and Border Control of Nauru appoints authorised officers and must declare the appointment of an operational manager by notice in the Government Gazette. No Commonwealth officers were appointed as authorised officers by the Secretary for the purposes of the RPC Act. Staff of Wilson Security were appointed by the Secretary as authorised officers and were therefore authorised by the law of Nauru to exercise powers under the RPC Act.

[34] Contrary to the plaintiff's submissions, it is very much to the point that the restrictions applied to the plaintiff are to be regarded as the independent exercise of sovereign legislative and executive power by Nauru. The recognition that it was Nauru that detained the plaintiff is important, for it is central to the plaintiff's case that the legislative authority which the Commonwealth required, and which it is argued was not provided, is an authority to detain the plaintiff, with the concomitant power to authorise others to effect that detention.

...

69 [39] Clearly the Commonwealth sought the assistance of Nauru with respect to the processing of claims by persons such as the plaintiff. It may be accepted that the Commonwealth was aware that Nauru required the plaintiff to be detained. In order to obtain Nauru's agreement to receive the plaintiff, the Commonwealth funded the Centre and the services provided there in accordance with the Administrative Arrangements. The Commonwealth concedes the causal connection between its conduct and the plaintiff's detention. It may be accepted that its involvement was materially supportive, if not a necessary condition, of Nauru's physical capacity to detain the plaintiff. But, for the reasons given above, it cannot be said that the Commonwealth thereby authorised or controlled the plaintiff's detention.

Gordon J (dissenting)

152 [352] A premise of many of the questions in the Special Case is that the conduct of the Commonwealth 'facilitated, organised, caused, imposed, procured, or resulted in the detention of the plaintiff at [the Regional Processing Centre]'. In argument, the Plaintiff contended that the detention had been 'funded, authorised, caused, procured and effectively controlled by, and was at the will of, the Commonwealth'. The effect of this, according to the Plaintiff, was that as a matter of substance the Commonwealth detained the Plaintiff. That contention should be accepted. The Commonwealth detained the Plaintiff on Nauru. This part of the reasons will explain why that is so.

The Commonwealth, by its acts and conduct, detained the Plaintiff outside Australia, and after the Commonwealth had exercised its undoubted power to expel the Plaintiff (an alien) from Australia or prevent entry by the Plaintiff into Australia. Those acts and conduct were or at the least included:

(1) making ... directions ... pursuant to s 198AD(5) of the Migration Act, with respect to regional processing countries to which particular classes of unauthorised maritime arrivals must be taken and stipulating that Nauru was such a country;

(2) signing the [memorandum of understanding ('MOU')] with Nauru, whereby the Commonwealth could decide to transfer unauthorised maritime arrivals to Nauru, would bear all costs incurred under or incidental to the MOU, would put in place and participate in the Administrative Arrangements and the day-to-day practical arrangements for the implementation of the MOU on Nauru and would assist ***153*** Nauru in removing Transferees not found to be in need of international protection;

(3) removing the Plaintiff from Christmas Island to Nauru pursuant to s 198AD(2) of the Migration Act on 22 January 2014 and, for the purposes of effecting that removal, exercising powers in s 198AD(3) of the Migration Act;

(4) applying to the Nauruan Justice Secretary, without the consent of the Plaintiff, for the grant of a RPC Visa to the Plaintiff and paying to Nauru the fee payable for the grant of the RPC Visa to the Plaintiff, whilst knowing that the RPC Visa specified that the Plaintiff had to reside at the Nauru RPC [Regional Processing Centre] and that the RPC Act also required the Plaintiff to reside at the Nauru RPC;

(5) on the Plaintiff's arrival on Nauru, first the Service Providers contracted by the Commonwealth (with the assistance of Nauruan officials) escorting the Plaintiff to transport and taking her to the Nauru RPC and, then, the Commonwealth officials providing all the relevant documentation relating to the Plaintiff to Staff Members at the Nauru RPC;

(6) having the power to contract with, contracting with, and paying for, Transfield to provide the Nauru RPC;

(7) providing the 'security infrastructure' at the Nauru RPC, which includes 'perimeter fencing, lighting towers and an entry gate';

(8) having the power to contract with, contracting with, and paying for, Transfield to ensure that the security of the perimeter of the Nauru RPC is maintained at all times in accordance with policies and procedures as notified from time to time by the Commonwealth;

(9) 'requiring' Transfield to 'exercise use of force' within the Nauru RPC in certain circumstances;

(10) having significant governance responsibilities and control at the Nauru RPC, including participation in the Joint Committee, participation in the Joint Working Group, the power to appoint the Operational Manager responsible for the day-to-day operation of the Nauru RPC, the power to appoint the Programme Coordinator responsible for managing all Australian officers and services contracts in relation to the Nauru RPC and the power to appoint the provider of the Nauru RPC;

(11) ***154*** having contracted for, and having, the power to terminate (at its own discretion) the contract for the provision of the Nauru RPC and to 'Step In' and take over the Nauru RPC; and

(12) having contracted for, and having, the power to control the content of and compliance with the OPC Guidelines.

[354] The Plaintiff could not leave Nauru. The Plaintiff was confined to the Nauru RPC. The acts and conduct of the Commonwealth just set out demonstrate that her detention in the Nauru RPC was 'facilitated, organised, caused, imposed [or] procured' by the Commonwealth. The Commonwealth asserted the right by its servants (or Transfield as its agent) to apply force to persons detained in the Nauru RPC for the purpose of confining those persons within the bounds of the place identified as the place of detention, the Nauru RPC. To that end, the Commonwealth asserted the right by its servants or agents to assault detainees and physically restrain them.

[355] Put another way, there could be no dispute that the Commonwealth took the Plaintiff to a place outside Australia (namely Nauru). But, on Nauru, the Commonwealth did not discharge the Plaintiff from its detention. Despite having removed the Plaintiff to a place outside Australia, the Commonwealth intended to and did exercise restraint over the Plaintiff's liberty on Nauru, if needs be by applying force to her. Notwithstanding that there is no explicit mention of detention in the MOU or the Administrative Arrangements, the Commonwealth detained the Plaintiff on Nauru by its acts and conduct.

[Citations omitted]

NEAT Domestic Trading Pty Ltd v AWB Ltd (2003) 216 CLR 277

Wheat Marketing Act 1989 (Cth)

[As at relevant date]

57 Control of export of wheat

(1) A person shall not export wheat unless:

(a) the [Wheat Export] Authority has given its written consent to the export of the wheat; and

(b) the export of the wheat is in accordance with the terms of that consent.

Penalty:

(a) in the case of a natural person - $60,000; or

(b) in the case of a body corporate - $300,000.

(1A) The prohibition in subsection (1) does not apply to nominated company B.

...

(3) The Authority's consent to the export of wheat may be limited to the export of the wheat in specified circumstances, in accordance with specified requirements or by a specified person.

(3A) Before giving a consent, the Authority must consult nominated company B.

(3B) The Authority must not give a bulk-export consent without the prior approval in writing of nominated company B.

Facts

The Australian Wheat Board was a Commonwealth body established by statute in 1939, with the function of regulating the wheat market. Until 1999, the Board operated as a 'single desk'; that is, it was the only entity permitted to export wheat from Australia. Wheat growers sold their wheat to the Board, which marketed and sold the wheat overseas.

In 1999, the *Wheat Marketing Act 1989* (Cth) was amended, fundamentally changing the wheat marketing system by reducing government involvement. The Wheat Board was privatised, becoming a grower-owned corporation (AWB Ltd) and a wholly owned subsidiary (AWB International Ltd ('AWBI')). A new statutory authority, the Wheat Export Authority, was created to regulate exports. AWBI became the 'nominated company B' for the purposes of s 57 of the *Wheat Marketing Act 1989* (Cth). This meant AWBI had a right to export wheat without seeking permission from the Wheat Export Authority. Other producers required written consent from the Wheat Export Authority before exporting wheat. Before giving written consent, the Wheat Export Authority was required to consult with AWBI and could not give consent unless AWBI also consented.

NEAT Domestic Trading applied to the Wheat Export Authority for consent to export durum wheat to Italy and Morocco. AWBI refused consent and, consequently, the Wheat Export Authority withheld its consent.

NEAT sought review of AWBI's decision under the *Administrative Decisions (Judicial Review) Act 1977* (Cth) ('*AD(JR) Act*'), seeking a declaration that AWBI's refusal to grant consent was unlawful. Section 5 of the *AD(JR) Act* allowed review of 'a decision of an administrative character made ... under an enactment'. Therefore, one of the major issues was whether AWBI's decision fitted this description.

McHugh, Hayne and Callinan JJ

296 [47] AWBI does not owe its existence to the Act; it is a company limited by shares incorporated under the *Corporations Law.* To a very great extent, its powers, and the powers and obligations of its organs, are regulated by the applicable companies legislation.

...

297 [48] [U]nder s 57 of the 1989 Act, a company incorporated under ordinary companies legislation for the pursuit of commercial purposes is given a role to play in connection with permitting what otherwise is conduct (exporting wheat) forbidden by federal statute on pain of penalty. And the company given this role is itself exempted from the operation of this prohibition.

[49] At the least, then, there is an intersection between the private and the public. A private corporation is given a role in a scheme of public regulation. The parties could point to no other federal legislation in which there was a similar intersection. If processes of privatisation and corporatisation continue, it may be that an intersection of this kind will be encountered more frequently. At its most general this presents the question whether public law remedies may be granted against private bodies. More particularly, do public law remedies lie where AWBI fulfils the role which it plays under the 1989 Act?

[50] We would answer this second, more particular question, 'No'. That answer depends in important respects upon the particular structure of the legislation in question. It is not to be understood as an answer to the more general question we identified.

[51] There are three related considerations which lead us to give that answer. First, there is the structure of s 57 and the roles which the 1989 Act gives to the two principal actors — the Authority and AWBI. Secondly, there is the 'private' character of AWBI as a company incorporated under companies legislation for the pursuit of the objectives stated in its constituent document: here, maximising returns to those who sold wheat through the pool arrangements. Thirdly, it is not possible to impose public law obligations on AWBI while at the same time accommodating pursuit of its private interests.

The roles of the Authority and AWBI

[52] Section 57 gives the Authority, not AWBI, the power to give the consent to export without which an offence is committed. It is the Authority's decision to give its consent which is the operative and determinative decision which the 1989 Act requires or authorises.

....

298 [54] Unlike the Authority, AWBI needed no statutory power to give it capacity to provide an approval in writing. As a company, AWBI had power to create such a document. No doubt the production of such a document was given statutory significance by s 57(3B) but that subsection did not, by implication, confer statutory authority on AWBI to make the decision to give its approval or to express that decision in writing. ...

[55] On that understanding of s 57(3B) AWBI's determination to approve the Authority's giving consent was not a decision under an enactment for the purposes of the AD(JR) Act. The approval was a condition precedent to the Authority considering whether to give its consent to export.

...

AWBI

[57] The two other considerations we have mentioned (the 'private' character of AWBI and accommodating public law obligations with AWBI's private interests) are

conveniently dealt with together. AWBI, not only does not owe its existence to the 1989 Act, it, and its organs, had ... various obligations ... Chief among those was, and is, the pursuit of its private objectives. So far as its constituent documents and applicable companies law principles are concerned, reference to any wider 'public' considerations would be irrelevant.

[58] Because the 1989 Act did not expressly or impliedly require or ***299*** authorise AWBI to decide whether to approve the issue of a bulk export permit, AWBI could not be compelled, by mandamus or otherwise, to decide whether to grant or not grant its approval. It was under no statutory, or other, obligation to consider that question.

[59] It follows that s 57(3B) is not to be read as imposing on AWBI a duty to consider those matters that we have described as 'public' considerations when deciding whether or not to grant approval. That is, s 57(3B) is not to be read as requiring AWBI to consider matters of the kind which the Authority should take into account in forming its decision whether to grant its consent. Nor should it be read as shifting to AWBI the obligation to take account of matters derived from the subject matter, scope or purpose of the Act which bear upon a decision whether a particular export should be permitted. The subsection did not require AWBI to consider those matters to the exclusion of consideration of its own commercial interests; it did not require AWBI to give preference to those matters over its own commercial interests.

.....

[61] Under the 1989 Act AWBI could export without consent. It could, indeed it should, have been seeking to maximise returns to those who sold wheat through the pool arrangements. One way of doing that was to remain the *sole* bulk exporter of wheat.

[62] If remaining the sole bulk exporter of wheat was a consideration that might legitimately be taken into account by AWBI when deciding whether to give approval to the Authority consenting to bulk export of wheat ... it is a consideration which could outweigh *any* countervailing consideration which an applicant for consent could advance. ...

300 [63] That being so, there is no sensible accommodation that could be made between the public and the private considerations which would have had to be taken to account if the 1989 Act were read as obliging AWBI to take account of public considerations.

[64] For these reasons, neither a decision of AWBI not to give approval to a consent to export, nor a failure to consider whether to give that approval, was open to judicial review under the AD(JR) Act or to the grant of relief in the nature of prohibition, certiorari or mandamus.

Kirby J (dissenting)

300 [66] In *Gerlach v Clifton Bricks Pty Ltd* (2002) 209 CLR 478, 503–4 [70], Callinan J and I said:

> All repositories of public power in Australia, certainly those exercising such power under laws made by an Australian legislature, are confined in the

> performance of their functions to achieving the objects for which they have been afforded such power. No Parliament of Australia could confer absolute power on anyone ... [T]here are legal controls which it is the duty of courts to uphold when their jurisdiction is invoked for that purpose.

Although we were in dissent as to its application to the circumstances of that case, the general principle so stated was not questioned.

[67] This appeal presents an opportunity for this Court to reaffirm that principle in circumstances, now increasingly common, where the exercise of public power, contemplated by legislation, is 'outsourced' to a body having the features of a private sector corporation. The question of principle presented is whether, in the performance of a function provided to it by federal legislation, a private corporation is accountable according to the norms and values of public law or is cut adrift from such mechanisms of accountability and is answerable only to its shareholders and to the requirements of corporations law or like rules.

[68] Given the changes in the delivery of governmental services in recent times, performed earlier and elsewhere by ministries and public agencies, this question could scarcely be more important for the future of administrative law. It is a question upon which this Court should not take a wrong turning.

...

308 [95] As with so many legal questions in Australia, the starting point for analysis must be the Constitution. It sets the ultimate boundaries within which the exercise of public or governmental power must take place in this country. ...

[96] The character of the decisions of bodies assigned important public functions is not determined conclusively by the structure of such bodies (for instance as private or statutory corporations), still less by arguments about the merits or demerits, advantages or disadvantages of privatisation or private sector management. In so far as such decisions derive their necessity or effectiveness, and the bodies making them derive their existence or particular functions, from federal legislation, they may involve the exercise of public power. In so far as they do this, under the Constitution, a Minister must be accountable to the Parliament in respect of such exercise. In turn, through the Parliament, the Minister, and the government of which he or she is part, are responsible to the electors. This appeal was argued as if the Constitution was silent on the issues for decision. In my view, ***309*** the Constitution cannot be ignored ... It is a critical matter of context.

...

310 [103] ... AWBI holds, in effect, a veto over the statutory consent of the Authority, which is without doubt a public body. To that extent, a private corporation to a large degree controls the conduct of an independent statutory agency of the Commonwealth made up of officers of the ***311*** Commonwealth answerable to this Court, amongst other ways, under the Constitution [s 75(v)]. That constitutionally entrenched power of judicial review is one of the limits on the extent to which corporatisation and privatisation of federal administrative action in Australia may escape the disciplines of judicial scrutiny.

[104] Further, the interests involved in and affected by AWBI's decisions to grant or withhold the approval required by the Act are much wider than the private interests of an ordinary corporation. The Act not only grants AWBI the privileged position of a statutory monopoly, but it involves that corporation in the scheme of regulation established. The presence of either, and certainly of both of those elements imposes upon AWBI obligations in the proper exercise of those of its functions that were relevant to the operation of the statutory regulatory scheme, and that had a substantial effect on growers ...

[Citations omitted]

[Editors' note: Kirby J held that AWBI's decisions in this case were reviewable under the *AD(JR) Act*.]

Administrative Review Council, *The Contracting Out of Government Services* (Report No 42, 1998)

The Administrative Review Council provided advice to the Attorney-General regarding the administrative law system from 1976 until 2015. The Council published research reports on administrative law and also a series of best practice guidelines for primary decision-makers and tribunal members.

Does the community have sufficient or effective avenues of redress where services are contracted out?

28 [3.53] When government activities and services are contracted out, neither existing public law nor private law remedies may be adequate to solve problems experienced by service recipients or other members of the community who are affected by the contractor's actions. For example, a service recipient who has no contractual relationship with the contractor will not be able to enforce the contractor's contractual obligations to the agency, will not be able to complain to the Ombudsman about poor service and will not be able to seek access under the FOI Act to information held by the contractor that would show how the service had in fact been delivered.

[3.54] Nor do private law remedies provide the same type of feedback and enhancement of government decision making and accountability that is provided by administrative law remedies. There is a potential loss of accountability where administrative law remedies are not available and private law remedies may not fill that void. If, for example, there is no ability for service recipients to make complaints about poor service, the agency may lose valuable information about the standard of service being delivered. Further, service recipients may find that neither the agency nor the contractor will remedy a problem because each considers that it is the other's responsibility under the terms of their contractual arrangements. The benefits of administrative law, not only for individuals but also for the community ***29*** in general, may be lost unless they are extended by legislation and enhanced by the use of private law remedies.

Tendency for public and private law to merge

[3.55] The traditional view of administrative law is that its mechanisms apply only to public sector agencies, leaving private law remedies, including tort law, contract and consumer protection legislation to govern activities outside the public sector. That view has already been challenged. Mechanisms originally developed in administrative law have been adopted by the private sector, for example, industry specific ombudsmen and other complaint-handling schemes.

[3.56] A number of commentators and government studies have referred to the blurring of traditional distinctions between what is 'public' and 'private'. In addition to the adoption of administrative law type remedies in the private sector, governments are increasingly looking to corporate models for reform of the public sector. The increasing reliance on contracting out is one of the changes occurring in the way government is operating.

[Citations omitted]

Crown immunity

Bropho v Western Australia (1990) 171 CLR 1

Aboriginal Heritage Act 1972 (WA)

[As at relevant date]

5 Application to places

This Act applies to -

(a) any place of importance and significance where persons of Aboriginal descent have, or appear to have, left any object, natural or artificial, used for, or made or adapted for use for, any purpose connected with the traditional cultural life of the Aboriginal people, past or present;

(b) any sacred, ritual or ceremonial site, which is of importance and special significance to persons of Aboriginal descent; ...

6 Application to objects

(1) This Act applies to all objects, whether natural or artificial and irrespective of where found or situated in the State, which are or have been of sacred, ritual or ceremonial significance to persons of Aboriginal descent, or which are or were used for, or made or adapted for use for, any purpose connected with the traditional cultural life of the Aboriginal people past or present.

10 Duty of the Minister and of the Trustees

(1) It is the duty of the Minister to ensure that so far as is reasonably practicable all places in Western Australia that are of traditional or current sacred, ritual

or ceremonial significance to persons of Aboriginal descent should be recorded on behalf of the community, and their relative importance evaluated so that the resources available from time to time for the preservation and protection of such places may be coordinated and made effective.

17 Offences relating to Aboriginal sites

A person who—

(a) excavates, destroys, damages, conceals or in any way alters any Aboriginal site; or

(b) in any way alters, damages, removes, destroys, conceals, or who deals with in a manner not sanctioned by relevant custom, or assumes the possession, custody or control of, any object on or under an Aboriginal site, commits an offence unless he is acting with ... the consent of the Minister under section 18.

Facts

The Western Australian Development Corporation ('the Corporation') was a corporation established under the *Western Australian Development Corporation Act 1983* (WA). Under s 4(3) of that Act, the Corporation was an agent of the Crown in right of Western Australia, and enjoyed the status, immunities and privileges of the Crown. The Corporation proposed to conduct a major development on a site owned by the Western Australian Government.

Robert Bropho, an Aboriginal person, believed the development would damage places of significance to Aboriginal people. He commenced proceedings seeking a declaration that the site was a place to which the *Aboriginal Heritage Act 1972* (WA) applied, and an injunction restraining any development that would damage the significant sites. The Corporation argued it was not bound by the provisions of the *Aboriginal Heritage Act 1972* (WA). As well as being the leading Australian authority on the presumption that legislation does not bind the Crown, the case provides an example of a situation in which that presumption was rebutted.

Mason CJ, Deane, Dawson, Toohey, Gaudron and McHugh JJ

16 The problem of principle in relation to the rule [that statutes worded in general terms are to be construed as inapplicable to the Crown] lies in judicial statements of its content and operation which have tended to discount the significance of its character as an aid to statutory construction and to treat it as if it were an inflexible principle which, in the absence of express reference to the Crown, precludes a statute from binding the Crown unless a test of 'necessary implication', which 'is not easily satisfied', is applied and satisfied ...

17 One can point to other 'rules of construction' which require clear and unambiguous words before a statutory provision will be construed as displaying a legislative intent to achieve a particular result. ... ***18*** The rationale of all such rules lies in an assumption that the legislature would, if it intended to achieve the particular effect, have made its intention in that regard unambiguously clear. ... If such an assumption be shown to be or to have become ill-founded, the foundation upon which the particular presumption rests will necessarily be weakened or removed ...

For so long as 'the Crown' encompassed little more than the Sovereign, his or her direct representatives and the basic organs of government, there may well have been convincing reasons for an assumption that a legislative intent that general statutory provisions should bind the Crown and those who represent it would be either stated in express terms or made 'manifest from the very terms of the statute'. The basis of an assumption to that effect lay in a mixture of considerations: regard for the dignity and majesty of the Crown; concern to ensure that any proposed statutory derogation from the authority of the Crown was made plain in the legislative provisions submitted for the royal assent; and, the general proposition that, since laws are made by rulers for subjects, a general description of those bound by a statute is not to be read as including the Crown.

19 Whatever force such considerations may continue to have in relation to legislative provisions which would deprive the Crown 'of any part of [the] ancient prerogative, or of those rights which are ... essential to [the] regal capacity', they would seem to have little relevance, at least in this country, to the question whether a legislative provision worded in general terms should be read down so that it is inapplicable to the activities of any of the employees of the myriad of governmental commercial and industrial instrumentalities covered by the shield of the Crown. So to say is ... simply to point to the fact that the historical considerations which gave rise to a presumption that the legislature would not have intended that a statute bind the Crown are largely inapplicable to conditions in this country where the activities of the executive government reach into almost all aspects of commercial, industrial and developmental endeavour and where it is a commonplace for governmental commercial, industrial and developmental instrumentalities and their servants and agents, which are covered by the shield of the Crown either by reason of their character as such or by reason of specific statutory provision to that effect, to compete and have commercial dealings on the same basis as private enterprise. It is in that contemporary context that the question must be asked whether it is possible to justify the preservation in our law of an inflexible rule which, in the absence of express reference, requires a reading down of the general words of a statute to exclude the Crown (and its instrumentalities and agents) unless it is 'manifest from the very terms of the statute' that it was the legislative intent that the Crown should be bound and which, in ascertaining whether such a legislative intent is manifest, allows account to be taken of the purpose of the statute only if it is possible to affirm that that purpose must be 'wholly frustrated' unless the Crown is bound.

20 There seems to us to be but one real argument of substance favouring the preservation of such an inflexible and stringent rule. It lies in the weight of authority ... On the other hand, there has been a growing tendency to question the appropriateness of the rule to modern circumstances and to confine its applicability. That tendency is not surprising in the context of the range of modern governmental activities and of recent developments in the approach to statutory construction. Indeed, the contemporary approach to statutory construction, with its added emphasis on legislative purpose and permitted reference to a range of extrinsic materials for the ascertainment of that purpose, has added an element of anachronism to a judicial confinement of the permissible basis for discerning a legislative intent that the Crown be bound to what is 'manifest from the very terms of the statute' ...

22 It follows from what has been said above that considerations of principle preclude recognition of an inflexible rule that a statute is not to be construed as binding the Crown or Crown instrumentalities or agents unless it manifests a legislative intent so to do either by express words or by 'necessary implication' in the limited and stringent sense explained above. If such a legislative intent appears when the relevant legislative provision is construed in a context which includes the presumption against the Crown and its instrumentalities or agents being so bound, that legislative intent must, as a matter of principle, prevail ...

23 In the case of legislative provisions enacted subsequent to this decision, the strength of the presumption that the Crown is not bound by the general words of statutory provisions will depend upon the circumstances, including the content and purpose of the particular provision and the identity of the entity in respect of which the question of the applicability of the provision arises. If, for example, the question in issue is whether the general words of a statute should be construed in a way which would make the Sovereign herself or himself in the right of the Commonwealth or of a State liable to prosecution and conviction for a criminal offence, the presumption against a legislative intent to that effect would be extraordinarily strong. On the other hand, if the question in issue is of the kind involved in the present case, namely, whether the employees of a governmental corporation engaged in commercial and developmental activities are bound by general provisions designed to safeguard places or objects whose preservation is of vital significance to a particular section of the community, the presumption against the applicability of general words to bind such employees will represent little more than the starting point of the ascertainment of the relevant legislative intent. Implicit in that is acceptance of the propositions that, notwithstanding the absence of express words, an Act may, when construed in context, disclose a legislative intent that one of its provisions will bind the Crown while others do not and that a disclosed legislative intent to bind the Crown may be qualified in that it may, for example, not apply ***24*** directly to the Sovereign herself or to a Crown instrumentality itself as distinct from employees or agents. Always, the ultimate questions must be whether the presumption against the Crown being bound has, in all the circumstances, been rebutted, and, if it has, the extent to which it was the legislative intent that the particular Act should bind the Crown and/or those covered by the prima facie immunity of the Crown.

... [T]here can be discerned in the [*Aboriginal Heritage Act 1972* (WA)] a clear legislative intent that the general words of s 17 should apply to employees and agents of governmental instrumentalities such as the Corporation in the course of their duties as such. We turn to explain why that is so.

There is no difficulty in discerning in the provisions of the Act a legislative intent that those provisions apply generally to Crown land and to objects on such land. The duty of the Minister to ensure that 'all places in Western Australia' that are of Aboriginal significance be recorded was clearly intended to extend to all land, regardless of its ownership. Section 6 of the Act makes explicit the legislative intent that the Act applies to all objects 'irrespective of where found or situated in the State' ... Indeed, in a context where ninety-three per cent of Western Australian land is Crown land and approximately fifty per cent of Western Australian land is what is described as 'Vacant Crown land', the Act would be extraordinarily ineffective to achieve its stated purpose of preserving Western Australia's Aboriginal sites and objects if it applied only in respect of the comparatively small proportion of the State which is not Crown land. In the context of the clear applicability of the provisions of the ***25*** Act to Crown land, the conclusion that it was the legislative intent that the general words of s 17 should apply indifferently to natural persons in Western Australia, including government employees, is all but inevitable ... [C]onsideration of the subject matter and disclosed policy and purpose of the Act seems to us to make it apparent that it was not the legislative intent that the activities of government employees, be they bulldozer drivers, demolition workers or dynamiters, acting in the course of their duties, should be excluded from s 17's prohibition of destroying or damaging Aboriginal sites or objects without the authorization of the Trustees or the consent of the Minister. Construed in context, the general words of the provisions of s 17 disclose a clear legislative intent that they not be read down so as to be inapplicable to government employees in the course of their duties as such. That being so, a government employee who engages in conduct of the proscribed kind will be guilty of an offence against the section ...

Once the conclusion is reached that the provisions of s 17 are applicable to employees of the Corporation in the course of their duties, it is apparent that the Corporation has no power to authorize its employees or others to carry out activities of the type proscribed by the section. Nor has the Crown in right of the State of Western Australia any such power. That being so, the appellant is entitled, if the facts alleged in the statement of claim are established on the hearing as the only relevant facts, to the declaratory and injunctive relief which he seeks against the respondents.

CHAPTER

3

ADMINISTRATIVE POWERS

Introduction	41
Administrative powers and discretions	41
Administrative Review Council	41
Administrative Review Council, *Decision Making: Lawfulness* (Best Practice Guide 1, 2007)	41
Commonwealth Ombudsman, *Automated Decision-Making: Better Practice Guide* (2019)	43
Statutory powers	47
Coco v The Queen (1994) 179 CLR 427	47
Minister for Immigration and Citizenship v Li (2013) 249 CLR 332	50
The Pilbara Infrastructure Pty Ltd v Australian Competition Tribunal (2012) 246 CLR 379	51
Non-statutory powers	53
Osland v Secretary, Department of Justice (No 1) (2008) 234 CLR 275	53
Minister for Arts, Heritage and Environment v Peko-Wallsend Ltd (1987) 15 FCR 274	54

Introduction

This chapter complements Chapter 3 in *Government Accountability: Australian Administrative Law,* third edition, which investigates the various classes of executive power, both statutory and non-statutory. The vast majority of executive power is conferred by statute. The following extracts emphasise the importance of statutory interpretation when establishing the scope of express and implied powers. The final two extracts consider prerogative power.

Administrative powers and discretions

Administrative Review Council

The Administrative Review Council was a Commonwealth advisory body, established as part of the 'new administrative law' reforms following the 1971 report of the Kerr Committee (this report is introduced in more depth in Chapter 7). The Administrative Review Council provided advice to the Attorney-General regarding the administrative law system from 1976 until 2015 (www.ag.gov.au/legal-system/administrative-law/administrative-review-council-publications). The Council published research reports on administrative law and also a series of best practice guidelines for primary decision-makers and tribunal members. The extract below discusses the nature of statutory power and the role of discretion.

Administrative Review Council, *Decision Making: Lawfulness* (Best Practice Guide 1, 2007)

Power to make a decision

2 It is important that a decision maker is clear about the decision to be made and about the source of power for that decision. The most common source of power is legislation - either an Act of Parliament (a statute) or a subordinate law made by a person or body to whom Parliament has delegated law-making power. Examples of subordinate laws are regulations, statutory rules and ordinances. It is the decision maker's responsibility to know the legislation being relied on and to keep abreast of any amendments.

Not every decision made by a government agency needs to be authorised by legislation. As well as statutory powers, many agencies possess executive powers to perform their normal administrative functions. Among these executive powers are the common legal powers of an ordinary person or organisation — for example, the power to enter into contracts, to acquire and manage property, to publish guides or advice to the public, and to conduct lawsuits. An agency established as a statutory corporation is often given such powers by legislation or the powers can be incidental to the agency's express powers.

Other laws can regulate the use of statutory and executive powers; for example, when an agency enters into a contract of employment it must abide by the general laws relating to employment contracts.

The extent of power

Powers accorded through legislation are always of limited scope. In some cases, though, their scope might go beyond what is expressly authorised by the words of the legislation. Sometimes an additional power can be implied where it is reasonably necessary to make an express power effective; for example, a statute authorising an agency to grant licences implicitly authorises the agency to develop forms and procedures for licence applications.

Legislation often authorises action that is detrimental to individuals. Examples are statutes that impose taxes, fines and other penalties, authorise compulsory acquisition of land or confiscation of property, or empower police or other officials to detain people. Provisions of this type are interpreted narrowly: they authorise only those actions expressly mentioned.

Statutes are not read as implicitly authorising actions that are contrary to the fundamental human rights recognised by the common law. Among such rights are freedom of speech, freedom of movement, freedom to assemble, freedom from arbitrary detention, search and seizure, freedom to practise one's religion, freedom from arbitrary deprivation of one's property, and the right of access to the courts ...

The decision maker

3 A statute will always state who has authority to exercise the powers conferred by statute. The designated person may be the Minister, agency head, governing board of the agency or other officer.

Another way a statute can distribute a power is to assign the power to an 'authorised officer' – usually somebody who has been appointed in writing by a particular person, such as the Minister or the secretary of a department ...

The judgments or choices that must be made

6 The legislation providing authority for a decision might stipulate the decision to be made if certain facts exist. For example, an Act could stipulate that an application be refused if the applicant does not meet specified criteria. A duty to decide in a particular way is often expressed by the use of words such as 'shall' or 'must'.

Decision-making powers given to administrative agencies are often discretionary powers. These powers involve an element of judgment about the decision. A discretionary power is often expressed using the word 'may'. For example, if an Act says 'The Secretary may grant the application unconditionally, or grant it subject to such conditions, or refuse the application' the decision maker has a choice.

Legislation might also require a decision maker to exercise judgment about whether certain conditions are met—for example, whether a person has 'reasonable grounds' for failing to do something or is a 'fit and proper person' to hold a particular licence or permit. To make these discretionary judgments, it is essential to examine the facts of the case and assess whether they meet the legislative criteria.

Exercising discretion

If an authorised officer has power to make a decision that involves discretionary power or a discretionary judgment, only that officer can exercise that power or make that judgment. They can take into account the advice or recommendations of others, but it is their responsibility to exercise the discretion and make the decision. Further, their decision must not be made solely so as to accord with the wishes or views of any other person — including a supervisor, the agency head or the Minister. The agency or the Minister can provide general guidelines, but they may not direct the officer in relation to the decision or prevent them exercising their discretion.

Commonwealth Ombudsman, *Automated Decision-Making: Better Practice Guide* (2019)

[Editors' note: In 2004, the Administrative Review Council ('ARC') considered automated (computerised) decision-making in its *Automated Assistance in Administrative Decision Making* (Report No 46). The ARC guide was updated in 2007 by a cross agency working group, and again in 2019 by the Commonwealth Ombudsman, the Office of the Australian Information Commissioner and the Attorney-General's Department <www.ombudsman.gov.au/publications/better-practice-guides/automated-decision-guide>.]

***5* What is an automated system?**

Automated systems range from traditional rules-based systems (for example a system which calculates a rate of payment in accordance with a formula set out in legislation) through to more specialised systems which use automated tools to predict and deliberate, including through the use of machine learning.

The term automated system is used in this guide to describe a computer system that automates part or all of an administrative decision-making process. The key feature of such systems is the use of pre-set logical parameters to perform actions, or make decision[s] without the direct involvement by a human being at the time of decision.

Automated systems can be used in different ways in administrative decision-making. For example:

- They can make a decision.
- They can recommend a decision to the decision-maker.
- They can guide a decision-maker through relevant facts, legislation and policy, closing off irrelevant paths as they go.
- They may include decision-support systems, such as useful commentary about relevant legislation, case law and policy for the decision-maker at relevant points in the decision-making process.
- They can provide preliminary assessments for individuals or internal decision-makers.

- They can automate aspects of the fact finding process which may influence subsequent decisions, for example by applying data:
  - from other sources (e.g. data matching information)
  - directly entered or uploaded to the system by an individual.

***6* Guiding principles for automated systems**

Automated systems must comply with administrative law principles of legality, fairness, rationality and transparency. They must also comply with privacy requirements and human rights obligations. As a matter of good public administration, they should be efficient, accessible, accurate and consider the needs of any vulnerable and non-digital ready users.

The legal frameworks of administrative law, privacy and human rights will assist agencies in designing automated systems to ensure that key risks in automation are avoided, such as algorithmic bias, inaccurate (or less accurate) decisions being produced by an automated system and unclear reasons for decisions.

Administrative law, privacy requirements and human rights obligations should be integrated into the design of an automated system through appropriate planning and assessment. The same principles apply when automated systems are reviewed by agencies.

Big data analytics, Artificial Intelligence (AI) and Machine Learning have become an increasingly utilised feature of automated systems. Agencies must also be mindful of the international standards relating to the use of AI. In May 2019, the Australia Government signed up to the Organisation for Economic Co-operation and Development Principles on Artificial Intelligence (the OECD AI principles). Under the OECD AI principles, an AI system is:

> a machine-based system that can, for a given set of human-defined objectives, make predictions, recommendations, or decisions influencing real or virtual environments. AI systems are designed to operate with varying levels of autonomy.

...

***8* Is an automated system suitable?**

Automation of any part of a process is not suitable where it would:

- Contravene administrative law requirements of legality, fairness, rationality and transparency.
- Contravene privacy, data security or other legal requirements (including human rights obligations).
- Compromise accuracy in decision-making.
- Significantly undermine public confidence in government administration

This guide sets out some of the considerations when assessing the suitability of an automated system. Agencies should consider what steps they need to take in determining the suitability of an automated system depending on the possible impact of the decisions to be made by the automated system. For example, decisions that will have a significantly detrimental and irreversible impact on individuals will require more scrutiny compared to a decision with short term impact that is easily reversible.

...

***9* Administrative law and automated systems**

Legislative authority for automated decisions

It is possible for an automated system to make decisions by using pre-programmed decision-making criteria without the use of human judgement at the point of decision. The authority for making such decisions will only be beyond doubt if specifically enabled by legislation. The construction of such an authorisation should nominate a position or title of a person with ultimate responsibility for the decision, such as the Secretary of the relevant department.

Discretion and automated systems

In 2004, the Administrative Review Council developed best practice principles for automated assistance in administrative decision-making. At that time, the Council was of the view that automated systems that make decisions, as opposed to helping a decision-maker make a decision, are generally only suitable for decisions involving non-discretionary elements.

Automation of decisions is an evolving area, and there is not yet clear and definitive guidance from the courts about whether it is necessary for all discretions to be exercised personally by a decision-maker. For example, it is unclear:

- whether it is acceptable for discretions to be automated if they are set to apply beneficially to the person affected, or
- the extent to which a discretion may be automated (if at all) in circumstances where a person affected is:
- provided with advance notice of the decision to be made and matters potentially adverse to their interests
- permitted to make submissions regarding relevant matters of fact and law
- able to ask for the decision to be made, or reviewed, by a human decision-maker.

Agencies considering automated systems for administrative decision-making must therefore pay particular attention to decision-making paths involving the exercise of judgement or discretion, to ensure that elements of decision-making involving the use of discretion or judgement uphold the administrative law values of legality and fairness.

What is discretion?

Discretion will generally exist in statutory provisions which:

- Provide the decision-maker with a range of options to choose between.
- Include words such as 'the decision-maker may' or 'the Secretary may'.
- Require the decision-maker to exercise broad judgment where a statutory standard is to be applied, for instance, that the person is a 'fit and proper person' or concerning the 'public interest'.
- Require the decision-maker to consider whether they have reached a 'state of satisfaction' that any legislative pre-conditions have been met before a decision is made.

Different outcomes can be reached in discretionary decisions, because different weight may be attached by the decision-maker to the relevant factors leading to a decision.

10 There are inherent challenges in administering broad discretions, which can include additional cost and the risk of inconsistency in decision-making. However, discretions ensure legislative frameworks are sufficiently flexible. They are a tool to avoid unfair or unjust outcomes that might otherwise result from inflexible application of a particular statutory provision and can help ensure decision-making is consistent with broader legislative and policy intent. For example, a discretion to provide an exemption to a requirement, based on an individual's circumstances, can ensure hardship relief and fairness in administration of the statute.

Supporting discretionary decision-makers

When properly designed and modelled, automated systems may enhance the exercise of decision-making discretion and judgement by the following measures:

- only permitting the use of human discretion and judgement where it is relevant
- outlining and/or breaking down the factors decision-makers should consider when making their judgement
- providing links to relevant support materials and guides
- requiring that decision-makers clearly state and record reasons for decisions, as a statement of reasons or other official (and auditable) output.

...

***17* Governance and design**

Automated systems projects must establish appropriate governance frameworks and ensure that legal, policy and program areas are involved during the system's development.

In developing automated systems projects, agencies should apply high standard information technology project methodologies and techniques and the Digital Service Standard14. Additionally, the Australian Government privacy framework requires agencies have privacy project planning and governance mechanisms in place. ...

Enabling scrutiny of the development of an automated system is as important as the transparency and accountability characteristics of the system itself. Whatever governance arrangements are appropriate to the project and the agency environment, agencies should ensure that project decisions regarding automated systems and/or exercise of discretion or judgement are adequately documented.

There are potentially many inputs to the decision as to which areas are suitable for automated decision-making. Scoping for an automated system project should include an examination of the relevant legislation, policies or procedures, and the specific clauses and/or parts that an agency seeks to automate.

Authorised decision-making

As authority to act is a fundamental tenet of administrative decision-making, it is important that the verification process for an automated system is able to test whether the nominated decision-maker is authorised to act. As a consequence, the audit facility should be able to report user access and decisions against delegations.

Verification and quality assurance processes are particularly important where a decision-maker is exercising delegations under multiple Acts, on behalf of another agency or under contract. In these instances, an automated system should be designed to allow functionality privileges or access commensurate with users' delegations. Quality assurance is addressed further below.

Any approach taken to deal with discretion or judgement within an automated system should have the capacity to capture and record the decision-maker's reasoning. This capacity should preferably be built into the system itself, to ensure that the automated system's audit trail clearly sets out each of the decision points involving discretion or judgement.

[Citations omitted]

Statutory powers

Coco v The Queen (1994) 179 CLR 427

Invasion of Privacy Act 1971 (Qld)

[As at relevant date]

43 Prohibition on use of listening devices

(1) A person is guilty of an offence against this Act if he uses a listening device to overhear, record, monitor or listen to a private conversation and is liable on conviction on indictment to a penalty not exceeding $2000 or to imprisonment for not more than two years or to both such penalty and imprisonment.

(2) Subsection (1) of this section does not apply—

...

(c) to or in relation to the use of any listening device by—

(i) a member of the police force acting in the performance of his duty if he has been authorized in writing to use a listening device by—

(a) the Commissioner of Police;

(c) an Assistant Commissioner of Police; or an officer of police of or above the rank of Inspector who has been appointed in writing by the Commissioner to authorize the use of listening devices,

under and in accordance with an approval in writing given by a judge of the Supreme Court in relation to any particular matter specified in the approval;

...

(3) In considering any application for approval to use a listening device pursuant to subparagraph (i) of paragraph (c) of subsection (2) of this section a judge of the Supreme Court shall have regard to—

(a) the gravity of the matters being investigated;

(b) the extent to which the privacy of any person is likely to be interfered with; and

(c) the extent to which the prevention or detection of the offence in question is likely to be assisted,

and the judge may grant his approval subject to such conditions, limitations and restrictions as are specified in his approval and as are in his opinion necessary in the public interest.

Facts

A judge of the Supreme Court of Queensland approved the use of listening devices under s 43 of the *Invasion of Privacy Act 1991* (Qld). The judge's order purported to authorise police officers to enter onto private premises owned by Cosco Holdings Pty Ltd in order to install the listening devices. Members of the Australian Federal Police gained access to these premises by posing as Telecom workers and pretending that they were investigating a fault in a telephone line. They installed listening devices under cover of this disguise. Santo Coco was subsequently convicted of offering to bribe a Commonwealth officer, with evidence gathered from the listening devices being used in his trial. Mr Coco appealed his conviction to the Queensland Court of Appeal and then to the High Court.

The issue was whether s 43 conferred power on a judge to authorise entry on to the premises for the purpose of installing and maintaining a listening device.

The case has become a seminal authority on one of the most influential principles of statutory interpretation in administrative law: the 'principle of legality' (that is, the presumption that parliament would not intend to override fundamental rights and freedoms, unless indicated by express words or through necessary implication).

Mason CJ, Brennan, Gaudron and McHugh JJ

436 Statutory authority to engage in what otherwise would be tortious conduct must be clearly expressed in unmistakable and unambiguous language. Indeed, it has been said that the presumption is that, in the absence of express provision to the contrary, the legislature did not intend to authorize what would otherwise have been tortious conduct. But the presumption is rebuttable and will be displaced if there is a clear implication that authority to enter or remain upon private property was intended. Such an implication may be made, in some circumstances, if it is necessary to prevent the statutory provisions from becoming inoperative or meaningless. However, as Gaudron and McHugh JJ observed in *Plenty v Dillon* [(1991) 171 CLR 654]:

> [I]nconvenience in carrying out an object authorized by legislation is not a ground for eroding fundamental common law rights. ...

437 The insistence on express authorization of an abrogation or curtailment of a fundamental right, freedom or immunity must be understood as a requirement for some manifestation or indication that the legislature has not only directed its attention to the question of the abrogation or curtailment of such basic rights, freedoms or immunities but has also determined upon abrogation or curtailment of them. The courts should not impute to the legislature an intention to interfere with fundamental rights. Such an intention must be clearly manifested by unmistakable and unambiguous language. General words will rarely be sufficient for that purpose if they do not specifically deal with the question because, in the context in which they appear, they will often be ambiguous on the aspect of interference with fundamental rights.

So long as the requirement for express statutory authorization is understood in the sense explained above, we would accept the requirement as a correct statement of principle. At the same time, in our view, the principle was expressed more simply by Brennan J in *Re Bolton; Ex parte Beane* [(1987) 162 CLR 514, 523] in these terms:

> Unless the Parliament makes unmistakably clear its intention to abrogate or suspend a fundamental freedom, the courts will not construe a statute as having that operation.
>
> In *Bropho* v *Western Australia* [(1990) 171 CLR 1, 18] Mason CJ, Deane, Dawson, Toohey, Gaudron and McHugh JJ pointed out that the rationale against the presumption against the modification or abrogation of fundamental rights is to be found in the assumption that it is:
>
>> in the last degree improbable that the legislature would overthrow fundamental principles, infringe rights, or depart from the general system of law, without expressing its intention with irresistible clearness; and to give any such effect to general words, simply because they have that meaning in their widest, or usual, or natural sense, would be to give them a meaning in which they were not really used [*Potter* v *Minahan* (1908) 7 CLR 277, 304].

At the same time, curial insistence on a clear expression of an unmistakable and unambiguous intention to abrogate or curtail a fundamental freedom will enhance the parliamentary process by ***438*** securing a greater measure of attention to the impact of legislative proposals on fundamental rights.

The need for a clear expression of an unmistakable and unambiguous intention does not exclude the possibility that the presumption against statutory interference with fundamental rights may be displaced by implication. Sometimes it is said that a presumption about legislative intention can be displaced only by necessary implication but that statement does little more than emphasize that the test is a very stringent one. As we remarked earlier, in some circumstances the presumption may be displaced by an implication if it is necessary to prevent the statutory provisions from becoming inoperative or meaningless. However, it would be very rare for general words in a statute to be rendered inoperative or meaningless if no implication of interference with fundamental rights were made, as general words will almost always be able to be given some operation, even if that operation is limited in scope.

Section 43 of the Queensland Act does not contain express words conferring power upon a Supreme Court judge to authorize conduct which would otherwise be tortious and involve interference with a fundamental common law right. In this case, the installation of the listening device in the premises of Cosco Holdings Pty Ltd ('Cosco') infringed the fundamental right of a person to exclude others from his

> or her property. Section 43 authorizes an invasion of privacy by allowing, in certain circumstances, the monitoring and recording of private conversations. The question is whether it also allows a judge to authorize members of the police force to enter on to premises in such a way as would otherwise amount to a trespass in order to install the devices. ...
>
> The respondent argued that, in the context of s 43(3), authorization 'to use a listening device' extends to installation of a listening device where it is necessary to enter on to premises in order to listen to a private conversation. One answer to that argument is that the word 'use' has a narrower meaning ... ***439***
>
> The other and more compelling answer is that there is no clear expression in the legislation of an unmistakable and unambiguous intention to confer such a power. In our view, it cannot be said that there is to be implied in s 43 power in a judge to authorize conduct which otherwise would amount to a trespass.

[Citations omitted]

[Editors' note: The Court held that the evidence gathered from the listening device was inadmissible. Mr Coco's conviction was quashed and a new trial ordered.]

Minister for Immigration and Citizenship v Li (2013) 249 CLR 332

Facts

This case is extracted in Chapter 14, concerning the unreasonableness ground of judicial review and the facts are set out in that Chapter. In the context of statutory powers in this chapter, French CJ explains the concept of discretion and its limits.

French CJ

> ***348*** Every statutory discretion, however broad, is constrained by law. As Dixon J said in *Shrimpton v The Commonwealth* [(1945) 69 CLR 613, 629–630]:
>
>> [C]omplete freedom from legal control, is a quality which cannot ... be given under our Constitution to a discretion, if, as would be the case, it is capable of being exercised for purposes, or given an operation, which would or might go outside the power from which the law or regulation conferring the discretion derives its force.
>
> Every statutory discretion is confined by the subject matter, scope and purpose of the legislation under which it is conferred. Where the ***349*** discretion is conferred on a judicial or administrative officer without definition of the grounds upon which it is to be exercised then: 'the real object of the legislature in such cases is to leave scope for the judicial or other officer who is investigating the facts and considering the general purpose of the enactment to give effect to his view of the justice of the case.' That view, however, must be reached by a process of reasoning.

Every discretion has to be exercised, as Kitto J put it in *R v Anderson; Ex parte Ipec-Air Pty Ltd* [(1965) 113 CLR 177], according to 'the rules of reason'. His Honour, paraphrasing *Sharp v Wakefield* [[1891] AC 173, 179] said: 'a discretion allowed by statute to the holder of an office is intended to be exercised according to the rules of reason and justice, not according to private opinion; according to law, and not humour, and within those limits within which an honest man, competent to discharge the duties of his office, ought to confine himself'. Mason J in *FAI Insurances Ltd v Winneke* [(1982) 151 CLR 342, 368] quoted Kitto J and linked his words to the general rule 'that the extent of ... discretionary power is to be ascertained by reference to the scope and purpose of the statutory enactment'.

[Citations omitted]

The Pilbara Infrastructure Pty Ltd v Australian Competition Tribunal (2012) 246 CLR 379

Trade Practices Act 1974 (Cth)

[As at relevant date]

[Editors' note: Part IIIA allowed the Minister to 'declare' privately owned infrastructure (such as roads, railway lines and communications systems), thus allowing third parties to access the infrastructure in order to improve competition.]

44H Designated Minister may declare a service

(1) On receiving a declaration recommendation [from the National Competition Council], the designated Minister must either declare the service or decide not to declare it.

...

(2) In deciding whether to declare the service or not, the designated Minister must consider whether it would be economical for anyone to develop another facility that could provide part of the service....

...

(3) The designated Minister cannot declare a service unless he or she is satisfied of all of the following matters:

(a) that access (or increased access) to the service would promote competition in at least one market (whether or not in Australia), other than the market for the service;

(b) that it would be uneconomical for anyone to develop another facility to provide the service;

(c) that the facility is of national significance, having regard to:

(i) the size of the facility; or

(ii) the importance of the facility to constitutional trade or commerce; or

(iii) the importance of the facility to the national economy;

(d) that access to the service can be provided without undue risk to human health or safety;

(e) that access to the service is not already the subject of an effective access regime;

(f) that access (or increased access) to the service would not be contrary to the public interest.

Facts

A mining company applied for access to railway lines owned by third parties to carry the company's iron ore. The National Competition Council ('NCC') recommended that access be granted. The Minister declared access to three of the four services sought, and was deemed to have decided not to declare the fourth. The railway facility providers applied to the Australian Competition Tribunal for review of that decision. The Tribunal set aside the Minister's decision to declare one of the lines, varied the time period for the declaration on another line, and affirmed the Minister's decisions on the other two lines. The railway facility providers and the mining company applied for judicial review of the Tribunal's decisions in the Federal Court. The Full Court of the Federal Court rejected the mining company's argument that the Tribunal had misinterpreted the public interest criterion in s 44H(4)(f) of the *Trade Practices Act 1974* (Cth). The mining company appealed that decision to the High Court and also argued that the Tribunal had misconceived its task in the review process. The High Court allowed the appeal, ordered that the Tribunal's decision be quashed, and remitted the matter to the Tribunal to be determined again following the High Court's interpretation of the scope of its powers.

In the context of statutory powers in this chapter, the following excerpt considers the nature of discretion when considering the public interest.

French CJ, Gummow, Hayne, Crennan, Kiefel and Bell JJ

The significance of the six mandatory criteria

400 [41] It is next necessary to consider whether the content of the criteria of which both the NCC and the Minister had to be satisfied before recommending declaration of a service and deciding to declare a service sheds any light on the tasks that the Act required the NCC, the Minister and the Tribunal to perform ...

[42] Criterion (f) was 'that access (or increased access) to the service would not be contrary to the public interest'. It is well established that, when used in a statute, the expression 'public interest' imports a ***401*** discretionary value judgment to be made by reference to undefined factual matters. As Dixon J pointed out in *Water Conservation and Irrigation Commission (NSW)* v *Browning* [(1947) 74 CLR 492, 505] when a discretionary power of this kind is given, the power is 'neither arbitrary nor completely unlimited' but is 'unconfined except in so far as the subject matter and the scope and purpose of the statutory enactments may enable the Court to pronounce given reasons to be definitely extraneous to any objects the legislature could have had in view'. It follows that the range of matters to which the NCC and, more particularly, the Minister may have regard when considering whether to be satisfied that access (or increased access) would *not* be contrary to the public interest is very wide indeed. And conferring the power to *decide* on the Minister

(as distinct from giving to the NCC a power to *recommend)* is consistent with legislative recognition of the great breadth of matters that can be encompassed by an inquiry into what is or is not in the public interest and with legislative recognition that the inquiries are best suited to resolution by the holder of a political office.

[43] Another criterion of which the NCC and the Minister must be satisfied (criterion (c)) may also direct attention to matters of broad judgment of a generally political kind. It required the NCC and the Minister to be satisfied that the facility in question is of *national* significance having regard to its size, or the importance of the facility to constitutional trade or commerce, or the importance of the facility to the *national* economy...

[Citations omitted]

Non-statutory powers

Osland v Secretary, Department of Justice (No 1) (2008) 234 CLR 275

Facts

Heather Osland was convicted of the murder of her husband in a highly publicised case involving claims of battered woman syndrome. After unsuccessful appeals [*Osland v The Queen* (1998) 197 CLR 316], Mrs Osland petitioned the Governor of Victoria for mercy seeking a pardon - an exercise of prerogative power. The petition for mercy was refused. The Victorian Attorney-General issued a press release referring to a joint advice from three Queen's Counsel that had recommended that her petition be denied. Mrs Osland sought access under freedom of information to documents relating to her petition, including the joint advice and other legal advice. After the Department of Justice refused access to the documents, Mrs Osland sought review in the Victorian Civil and Administrative Tribunal. The Tribunal granted access to the documents but the Victorian Court of Appeal overturned this decision. Mrs Osland appealed to the High Court.

The freedom of information aspect of the case, and further detail on the case, is discussed in Chapter 6. For present purposes, the case is important for its explanation of the way in which multiple members of the executive can be involved in a decision ultimately made by the Crown's representative in the exercise of the prerogative.

Gleeson CJ, Gummow, Heydon and Kiefel JJ

282 [8] Having exhausted her rights of appeal, the appellant invoked the power of the Governor of Victoria to grant a pardon. Morris J [President of the Victorian Civil and Administrative Tribunal] gave the following account of the legal basis of that power, and the practice that is followed in matters where the power is invoked. This account was not disputed in argument, and may be accepted as accurate and sufficient for present purposes.

A petition for the exercise of the prerogative of mercy is a request made to the Crown by an individual seeking release from the effects of a conviction in circumstances where all avenues of appeal to the courts have been exhausted or where the courts have no jurisdiction. The Governor of Victoria has the power to exercise the prerogative of mercy as a representative of Her Majesty the Queen. The power derives from section 7 of the *Australia Act 1986* (Cth) which provides that the powers and functions of the Queen in respect of a State are exercisable only by the Governor of the State (subject to exceptions which are not presently relevant). Section 7(5) of that Act provides that advice to the Queen (and her representative) in relation to the exercise of the powers and functions of the Queen in respect of a State shall be tendered by the Premier of the State.

On 14 February 1986 the Queen issued Letters Patent relating to the Office of the Governor of Victoria. Clause III of the Letters Patent states, among other things, that the Premier shall tender advice to the Governor in relation to the exercise of powers and ***283*** functions of the Governor not permitted or required to be exercised in Council. By convention, the accepted practice is and has been that the Premier seeks the advice of the Attorney-General in relation to whether the prerogative should be exercised. In turn, when the advice of the Attorney-General is sought, it is practice for the Attorney-General to ask his or her department to consider, evaluate and make recommendations in relation to the petition. Sometimes the advice of the Victorian Government Solicitor is sought. To the extent that a petition of mercy raises non-legal grounds (for example, compassionate grounds, meritorious conduct grounds, or other special grounds) the assessment of the petition on those other grounds is usually conducted within the department. Clearly enough, though, there will often be an overlap between what might be described as legal grounds and what might be described as non-legal grounds.

Before tendering his advice to the Premier, the Attorney-General may wish to follow up the advice he or she has received in relation to the matter. Generally the Attorney- General advises the Premier and it is then a matter for the Premier to proffer advice to the Governor. On rare occasions the Attorney-General's advice may be considered by Cabinet before the Premier makes a recommendation to the Governor. However this did not apply in the present case.

Minister for Arts, Heritage and Environment v Peko-Wallsend Ltd (1987) 15 FCR 274

Facts

The case involved a challenge to a decision by the Cabinet to nominate Stage 2 of Kakadu National Park for inclusion on the World Heritage List. The case is discussed in Chapter 10 in relation to justiciability. For the purposes of this chapter, the Court accepted that the decision was made by Cabinet in the exercise of a prerogative power.

Bowen CJ

The Executive

276 Under our Constitution the executive power of the Commonwealth is exercisable by the Governor-General. There is a Federal Executive Council to advise the Governor- General, the members of the Council being chosen by the Governor-General and sworn in as Executive Councillors (ss 61–62). When the Constitution refers to the Governor-General in Council it is construed as referring to the Governor-General acting with the advice of the Federal Executive Council. The Governor-General may appoint officers to administer such departments of State as the Governor-General in Council may establish. They are members of the Executive Council and are the Ministers of State for the Commonwealth (ss 63–64).

The Governor-General, except in very limited instances, acts on the advice of his Minister or Ministers conveyed to him in Executive Council. Often the advice flows from a decision of Cabinet. However, Cabinet is not mentioned in the Constitution and is not in any formal legal sense the Executive. I mention this because the declaration of the learned primary Judge which is challenged on this appeal was a declaration that 'the decision of the Executive made on the 16 September 1986 to nominate Stage 2 of Kakadu National Park for inclusion on the World Heritage List is void'.

The only decision was a decision of Cabinet. The matter did not come before the Executive, that is the Governor-General in Council. The parties to the appeal agreed that the reference to the Executive in his Honour's declaration was to be taken as a reference to Cabinet. The learned primary Judge is, of course, as familiar as anyone with the distinction. Indeed, he was conscious of the fact that although formal decision-making power rests with the Governor-General in Council the real decision-making power rests with the Cabinet. The decision dealt with by the declaration was not, and did not have to be, referred to the Governor-General in Council. Under the Convention for the Protection of the World Cultural and Natural Heritage ('the Convention') the relevant State Party was the Commonwealth of Australia.

277 In the past it has been customary in Australia for Parliament to pass Acts which impose duties or confer powers or discretions upon Ministers and not unusual to impose duties or confer powers or discretions upon the Governor-General in Council. I am not aware of any Act of Parliament which imposes a duty or confers powers or discretions on Cabinet.

Cabinet

279 As I have said Cabinet is not mentioned in the Constitution. It is a body which functions according to convention. The number of departments of State and, in consequence, the number of Ministers may vary from Government to Government. Until 1956 it was the practice for all Members of the Ministry, including Ministers without portfolio, to sit as members of Cabinet. Beginning with the Menzies Ministry sworn in on 11 January 1956 the practice was introduced of a Cabinet comprising some but not all Members of the Ministry. Since then this inner circle of Ministers has generally been referred to as the Cabinet. When Cabinet meets it is customary for particular members of the outer Ministry to attend when matters concerning or affecting their particular departments are before Cabinet for discussion.

...

It is to Cabinet that the highest decisions of policy affecting Australia are brought. Often the questions arising involve intense conflict of interests or of opinion in the community. In Cabinet these conflicts have to be resolved. Decisions have to be taken in the public interest, notwithstanding that the lives, interests and rights of some individual citizens may be adversely affected by the decision.

This is not to say that Cabinet should decide matters without considering all relevant material. But there are recognized channels for communicating arguments or submissions. Each Minister has the support and advice of a department of State. Representations may be made to the relevant department or in appropriate cases to the Minister. Every citizen has access to a local Member of Parliament or a Senator in the particular State, who can assist in the advancement of the individual citizen's point of view. The prospect of Cabinet itself, even by delegation, having to accord a hearing to individuals who may be adversely affected by its decisions, is a daunting one. It could bring the proceedings of Cabinet to a grinding halt.

After a decision of Cabinet is made it may require for its implementation an Act of the Parliament or a decision of a particular Minister or of the Governor-General in Council. There is generally further scope for submissions or representations at some stage even after a Cabinet decision and always scope for political action ...

CHAPTER

4

DELEGATED LEGISLATION

Introduction 58

Executive exercise of legislative power 58

Australian Law Reform Commission, *Traditional Rights and Freedoms – Encroachments by Commonwealth Laws* (Report No 129, 2015) 58

Distinguishing acts of legislative and administrative character 62

R G Capital Radio Ltd v Australian Broadcasting Authority (2001) 113 FCR 185 62

Types of delegated legislation 68

Legislation Act 2003 (Cth) 68

Legislative regulation and parliamentary review of delegated legislation 70

Case study: Disallowance of *Aboriginal Land Rights (Northern Territory) Amendment (Delegation) Regulation 2013* (Cth) 70

Judicial review of delegated legislation 76

Minister for Primary Industries and Energy v Austral Fisheries Pty Ltd (1993) 40 FCR 381 76

Plaintiff M47/2012 v Director-General of Security (2012) 251 CLR 1 78

Attorney-General v Corporation of the City of Adelaide (2013) 249 CLR 1 81

Introduction

This chapter complements Chapter 4 of *Government Accountability: Australian Administrative Law,* third edition. The chapter contains several case extracts on the issue of judicial review of delegated legislation. However, judicial review cases provide only a small part of the picture of the practical and substantive issues surrounding delegated legislation. The other material in this chapter fills in the picture. An extract from the Australian Law Reform Commission's report, *Traditional Rights and Freedoms,* highlights the problems with overreliance on delegated, rather than primary, legislation. A case study of delegated legislation being disallowed has been included to show how the process of parliamentary scrutiny works.

Executive exercise of legislative power

Australian Law Reform Commission, *Traditional Rights and Freedoms – Encroachments by Commonwealth Laws* (Report No 129, 2015)

Delegating legislative power

447 [17.1] Under the constitutional doctrine of the separation of powers, parliaments make law, the executive administers and enforces the law, and the judiciary adjudicates disputes about the law. The doctrine is reflected in the structure of the Australian Constitution. [Chapter I of the *Constitution* is entitled 'The Parliament'; Chapter II, 'The Executive Government'; and Chapter III, 'The Judicature'.] But the separation between legislative and executive power is not as clear as some might imagine. For one thing, in Australia, members of the executive (the Cabinet and other government ministers) are also members of the legislature.

[17.2] From the separation of powers doctrine, and from the principle that it is Parliament's role to make laws on important matters of policy, may be derived the principle that legislative power should not be inappropriately delegated to the executive.

[17.3] Laws that have a significant impact on rights and liberties, and laws creating offences with high penalties, should usually be in primary, not delegated, legislation. More generally, wide and vague delegations of legislative power undermine the separation of powers doctrine by allowing those who enforce the law to also make the law.

[17.4] Delegating legislative power to the executive is now commonplace and is said to be essential for an efficient and effective government. Parliament delegates such power not only to government ministers, but also government agencies such as the Australian Taxation Office and the Australian Securities and Investments Commission (ASIC).

448 [17.5] Given the quantity of delegated law in Australia, careful and ongoing scrutiny—built into the law making process—may be the most suitable way to limit inappropriate delegations of legislative power. ...

Examples of laws that delegate legislative power

453 [17.34] There are thousands of legislative instruments currently in force in Australia, covering a wide range of subject matter, including laws about food standards, fisheries, civil aviation, corporations, superannuation, taxation and migration, to name only a few.

[17.35] Acts that include delegations of legislative power often do so in terms similar to this provision, from the *Atomic Energy Act 1953* (Cth) [s 65]:

> The Governor-General may make regulations, not inconsistent with this Act, prescribing matters:
>
> (a) required or permitted by this Act to be prescribed; or
>
> (b) necessary or convenient to be prescribed for carrying out or giving effect to this Act.

[17.36] Some provisions like this will set out more fully the types of regulations that may be made. For example, there is considerable detail about what the relevant regulations may do in s 63 of the *Therapeutic Goods Act 1989* (Cth).

[17.37] Sometimes a provision in an Act delegating legislative power is expressed broadly and there is little substantive law in the primary legislation. This is sometimes called 'skeleton' legislation—the bare bones are in the primary legislation, but most of the law is in the delegated legislation. [Editors' note: This is also called 'coat-hanger' or 'framework' legislation.] This arrangement has often been criticised ... The Senate Standing Committee for the Scrutiny of Bills (Scrutiny of Bills Committee) said in 2012 that 'framework' bills were becoming increasingly prevalent and that 'important information' should be included in the primary legislation, 'unless there is a principled reason for including it in delegated legislation'.

454 [17.38] Important questions of policy, particularly when they affect individual rights, are often considered inappropriate subject matter for delegated legislation. The Law Council expressed concern about a new provision to be inserted into the *Migration Act 1958* (Cth), under which a person may be required to provide 'personal identifiers' for any purposes under the Act or the *Migration Regulations 1994* (Cth). The Law Council said that significant matters such as this should instead be set out in primary legislation, not in regulations:

> the power to prescribe both a purpose for which personal identifiers may be collected and the collection of biometric data via regulation raises the potential for the scheme to go beyond the initial intention of the Bill and the Migration Act, without adequate parliamentary scrutiny. Permitting changes to the purposes of collection of biometric data by regulation can result in significant incursions into privacy, while escaping general public awareness [Law Council of Australia, Submission 140].

[17.39] Offence provisions generally belong in primary legislation, particularly where the penalties for infringement are high. For example, s 30B of the *National*

Credit Code [National Consumer Credit Protection Act 2009 (Cth) sch 1, s 30B(2)] allows for the making of certain regulations concerning credit card contracts, including for offences and civil penalties against the regulations. Although there are limits in the Act on the offences and penalties, the Scrutiny of Bills Committee said the 'penalties which may be imposed by regulation are significant and it is unclear why the offences and requirements cannot adequately be specified in the legislation which will be considered in detail by Parliament'.

[17.40] 'Henry VIII clauses' are another type of delegation of legislative power that is considered inappropriate. These allow delegated legislation to amend the primary legislation. The Scrutiny of Bills Committee often comments on such provisions. In 2009, for example, the Committee noted the large number of Henry VIII clauses in the National Consumer Credit Protection Bill 2009—so many in fact that it was 'not possible to provide commentary in relation to all of them'. The relevant Minister defended the arrangement, telling the Committee that the Government needed to ensure that there was 'adequate flexibility in the new arrangements to ensure the smooth ***455*** transition to a national credit regime'. Section 35A of the *Fair Work Act 2009* (Cth), which relates to the geographical application of the Act, is another example.

[17.41] Government agencies and regulators will sometimes be given the power to make delegated legislation. The Commissioner of Taxation and ASIC, for example, both have statutory powers to make certain rules and regulations. For example, under the *Income Tax Assessment Act 1936* (Cth), the Commissioner of Taxation may determine by legislative instrument which taxpayers are required to lodge an income tax return. Under *A New Tax System (Goods and Services Tax) Act 1999* (Cth), the Commissioner of Taxation may make certain determinations in relation to how much Goods and Services Tax is payable on taxable importations ...

Safeguards

456 [17.44] Some concerns about delegated legislation may be addressed by the procedures that must be followed in making the legislation, particularly since the enactment of the *Legislative Instruments Act 2003* (Cth) [now *Legislation Act 2003* (Cth)]. These safeguards are designed to allow Parliament to oversee the making of delegated legislation, to scrutinise it through committees, and to repeal laws that Parliament considers should not have been made.

[17.45] The requirement that legislative instruments be published on a public register was a major development introduced by the *Legislative Instruments Act,* and helps make the process of making delegated legislation more open and accountable. Another important safeguard is the automatic repeal or 'sunsetting' of legislative instruments, usually after ten years.

...

[17.47] Parliamentary scrutiny, particularly by committees, is also an important safeguard. The Scrutiny of Bills Committee and the Senate Standing Committee on

Regulations and Ordinances (Regulations and Ordinances Committee) both consider whether an Act of Parliament inappropriately delegates legislative power to the executive. Established in 1932, the Regulations and Ordinances Committee in particular scrutinises delegated legislation to ensure 'that it does not contain matter more appropriate for parliamentary enactment'. The legislative scrutiny process and the role of the parliamentary committees have been called the 'key mechanisms for ensuring that the Executive does the right thing'.

457 [17.48] Common law principles may also provide additional safeguards. For example, unless the statute provides for the sub-delegation of legislative power, a delegate generally cannot sub-delegate power ...

458 [17.51] Grants of delegated power ought not to be so expressed that it becomes impossible in practice for courts to review the limits of the power. For example, provisions should not give ministers powers to do that which is, in their opinion, 'requisite or expedient for a broadly framed statutory purpose'.

[17.52] The tabling, disallowance, and committee scrutiny of delegated legislation are important safeguards and practical ways for Parliament to control executive law making. If it were thought that legislative power were being inappropriately delegated, consideration might be given to the adequacy of these safeguards, and perhaps to whether the safeguards are ever inappropriately avoided. For example, some statutes exempt legislative instruments from the disallowance or sunsetting provisions in the *Legislative Instruments Act 2003* (Cth).

[17.53] Further measures designed to limit inappropriate delegations of legislative power were suggested by PIAC [Public Interest Advocacy Centre], which described parliamentary scrutiny of delegated legislation as, in practice, minimal. For example, it recommended that the Regulations and Ordinances Committee should have a stronger role and that legislative instruments be subject to judicial review under the *Administrative Decisions (Judicial Review) Act 1977* (Cth). It also suggested that the *Legislative Instruments Act* be amended to include a non-exhaustive list of powers and matters which should not be delegated, unless there is a public interest in doing so.

Conclusion

[17.54] Although delegating legislative power to the executive is necessary for an efficient and effective government, some laws are more properly made by Parliament—for example, laws that have a signifcant impact on individual rights and laws creating serious criminal offences. Given the quantity of delegated law in Australia, robust safeguards and ongoing scrutiny appear to be suitable ways to limit inappropriate delegations of legislative power.

[Some citations omitted]

Distinguishing acts of legislative and administrative character

R G Capital Radio Ltd v Australian Broadcasting Authority (2001) 113 FCR 185

Broadcasting Services Act 1992 (Cth)

[As at relevant date]

Part 3—Planning of the broadcasting services bands

23 Planning criteria

In performing functions under this Part, the ABA [Australian Broadcasting Authority] is to promote the objects of this Act including the economic and efficient use of the radiofrequency spectrum, and is to have regard to:

(a) demographics; and

(b) social and economic characteristics within the licence area, within neighbouring licence areas and within Australia generally; and

(c) the number of existing broadcasting services and the demand for new broadcasting services within the licence area, within neighbouring licence areas and within Australia generally; and

(d) developments in technology; and

(e) technical restraints relating to the delivery or reception of broadcasting services; and

(f) the demand for radiofrequency spectrum for services other than broadcasting services; and

(g) such other matters as the ABA considers relevant.

24 ABA to determine priorities

(1) Before preparing frequency allotment plans or licence area plans, the ABA must, by notice in writing, determine priorities, as between particular areas of Australia and as between different parts of the broadcasting services bands, for the preparation of those plans. ...

25 Preparation of frequency allotment plans

(1) Where the Minister has, under section 31 of the *Radiocommunications Act 1992*, referred a part of the radiofrequency spectrum to the ABA for planning, the ABA must prepare in writing a frequency allotment plan that determines the number of channels that are to be available in particular areas of Australia to provide broadcasting services using that part of the radiofrequency spectrum. ...

26 Preparation of licence area plans

(1) The ABA is to prepare in writing licence area plans that determine the number and characteristics, including technical specifications, of broadcasting services

that are to be available in particular areas of Australia with the use of the broadcasting services bands, and those plans must be consistent with the relevant frequency allotment plan.

...

27 Processes to be public

(1) In performing its functions under sections 24, 25 and 26, the ABA must make provision for wide public consultation.

(2) The ABA is to keep a record of, and make available for public inspection, all advice received by the ABA, and all assumptions made by the ABA, in performing its functions under sections 24, 25 and 26.

Facts

The case concerned a determination by the Australian Broadcasting Authority ('ABA') to make available an additional commercial radio service in Gosford. The ABA prepared in writing licence area plans as required under the *Broadcasting Services Act 1992* (Cth) s 26(1). R G Capital Radio, who operated an existing commercial radio station in Gosford, challenged the decision under the *Administrative Decisions (Judicial Review) Act 1977* (Cth) ('*AD(JR) Act*'). *AD(JR) Act* review is only available for a decision 'of an administrative character' (*AD(JR) Act* s 5(1); see Chapter 9). Therefore, the Federal Court had to determine whether preparing these licence plans was an action of an administrative or legislative character.

Wilcox, Branson and Lindgren JJ

194 [40] There is no simple rule for determining whether a decision is of an administrative or a legislative character. As long ago as 1932, the *Report of the Committee on Ministers' Powers* (the Donoughmore Committee) (HMSO Cmd 4060) stated (at 19):

> It is indeed difficult in theory and impossible in practice to draw a precise dividing line between the legislative on the one hand and the purely administrative on the other; administrative action so often partakes of both legislative and executive characteristics.

In the decided cases, various factors have been referred to as supporting an administrative or a legislative characterisation. ...

[42] It is convenient to deal seriatim with the considerations discussed in the decided cases or raised by counsel in argument before us. However, it must be emphasised that the task of the Court, at the end of the day, is to make a judgment on the critical issue that takes into account all of these considerations. No one consideration is decisive of the issue.

Determining content of a general rule as distinct from the application of a rule to particular facts

Perhaps the most commonly stated distinction between the two types of decision is that legislative decisions determine the content of rules of general, usually prospective, application whereas administrative decisions apply rules of that kind to particular cases ...

[44] In *Tooheys* [*Minister for Industry and Commerce v Tooheys Ltd* (1982) 60 FLR 325] a Full Court of this Court stated (at 331):

> The distinction is essentially between the creation or formulation of new rules of law having general application and the application of those general rules to particular cases. In *Commonwealth* v *Grunseit [Commonwealth v Grunseit* (1943) 67 CLR 58] Latham CJ expressed [at 82] the distinction in these terms: 'The general distinction between legislation and the execution of legislation is that legislation determines the content of ***195*** a law as a rule of conduct or a declaration as to power, right or duty, whereas executive authority applies the law in particular cases'.

[45] In its Report to the Attorney-General, *Rule Making by Commonwealth Agencies* (Report No 35, 1992) the Administrative Review Council stated as follows (at pars 3.2 to 3.4):

> 3.2 In broad terms, legislative action involves the formulation of general rules of conduct, usually operating prospectively. Executive or administrative action, by contrast, applies general rules to particular cases.
>
> 3.3 While this distinction is a useful starting point, it does not hold in all cases. Thus, a recent Act of the Victorian Parliament was directed to 'the care or treatment and the management' of a named individual [*Community Protection Act 1990* (Vic)]. It was unquestionably legislative in character because it altered pre-existing law. Similarly, executive action may have a wider effect than the particular case for which it was originally made. An example is the power under the *Customs Act 1901* to make a Commercial Tariff Concession Order at the request of an importer for a particular act of importation. The order can then be applied to other like cases.
>
> 3.4 Three characteristics might be used to distinguish legislative action from executive action - determination of the content of the law; the binding quality of the rules; and the generality of their application. The first is likely to be conclusive. The presence of the second and third in combination is also a very strong indicator that an instrument is legislative in nature.
>
> ...

196 [49] The licence area plans which the ABA is required by s 26(1) to prepare determine the number and characteristics of broadcasting services that are to be available in particular geographical areas of Australia. The considerations to which the ABA is required to have regard are the general ones identified in s 23 of the *BS Act* ... A licence area plan may be prepared for a geographical area in which there are not yet broadcasting services, or it may, as in the present case, be prepared for an area where such services already exist. Preparation of the plan may (as in the present case) or may not have implications for an existing licensee. Either way, the licence area plan lays down general parameters within which takes place the decision-making process (the allocation of licences) for which Pt 4 of the *BS Act* provides.

[50] This first criterion for distinguishing between the legislative and the administrative points to determinations under s 26(1) of the *BS Act* being of a legislative character, not an administrative one ...

Parliamentary control

198 [56] The absence of any provision for disallowance by Parliament points against characterisation of a decision under s 26(1) of the *BS Act* as legislative. However, although persuasive, the absence is not fatal to such a characterisation. No case declares provision for disallowance to be a litmus test of legislative character. Its absence is to be taken into account as a factor pointing against that character, but that is all. Ultimately, we feel, it is outweighed by other considerations.

Publication of making of licence area plan

[57] [T]he making of a licence area plan must be notified in the *Gazette.* The notice must also state where copies of the instrument can be purchased. In [*SAT FM Pty Ltd v Australian Broadcasting Authority* (1997) 75 FCR 604] Sundberg J observed (at 608) that a requirement of publication has been seen as suggesting the legislative character of the subject of the publication.

[58] We do not find the publicity requirement to be a compelling indication of the legislative character of the decision. Some decisions which are clearly administrative must be notified in the *Gazette:* for example, a Ministerial declaration which effects the acquisition of land by compulsory process: *Lands Acquisition Act 1989* (Cth) s 41. Nonetheless, the requirement of publication is consistent with the decision having a legislative character.

Wide public consultation

[59] ... It will be recalled that s 27(1) provides that, in performing its functions under ss 24, 25 and 26 of the *BS Act,* the ABA 'must make provision for wide public consultation'. Similarly, s 27(2) requires that the ABA keep a record of, and make available for public inspection, all advice received by it, and assumptions made by it, in performing its functions under ss 24, 25 and 26. RGC submits that the obligation of wide public consultation is directed to natural justice considerations and is therefore a pointer to the decision being one of an administrative nature. In SATFM, on the other hand, Sundberg J (at 608) treated this ***199*** obligation as endowing a decision to make a licence area plan with 'a legislative rather than an administrative character'.

[60] In our view, the obligation of wide public consultation does not arise out of a natural justice concern to give a hearing opportunity to interests which might be adversely affected by the making of a licence area plan. Rather, it seems to us, the obligation is directed to ensuring that the ABA will 'promote the objects of [the BS] *Act'* and 'have regard to' the considerations identified in s 23. The objects of the *BS Act* are stated in broad terms. The considerations identified in s 23 include 'the demand for new broadcasting services within the licence area, within neighbouring licence areas and

within Australia generally'. A proper appreciation of these matters is likely to be facilitated by 'wide public consultation'. The Explanatory Memorandum for the Broadcasting Services Bill 1992 (Cth) stated of the provision which became s 27(2) (at 32):

> This is one of the many provisions in this Act which are intended to make the ABA accountable in the exercise of its powers and performance of its function.

[61] It seems to us that, if anything, the requirement of wide public consultation emphasises the general nature of a licence area plan, and so adds weight to the first consideration dealt with at [43] to [50] above. The accountability to which s 27(2) is directed does not indicate that the decision to make a licence area plan is of an administrative character.

The wide policy considerations

[62] In preparing a licence area plan the ABA must: (i) promote the objects of the *BS Act* including the economic, and efficient use of the radiofrequency spectrum, and (ii) have regard to the broad considerations listed in s 23... ; and perform its functions consistently with the regulatory policy described in s 4 of the *BS Act*, any general policies of the Government notified by the Minister under s 28 of the *Commonwealth Authorities and Companies Act 1997* (Cth) and any directions given by the Minister in accordance with the *BS Act*: see s 160 of the *BS Act* ...

200 [66] The breadth of the considerations which the ABA is required to take into account in making a licence area plan does not alone compel a conclusion this is not an administrative act. More persuasive are the nature and impact of the resulting decision. Nonetheless, the present consideration is consistent with a legislative result.

Absence of executive variation or control

[71] We think the absence of provision for executive variation or control is an indicator that a decision of the ABA under s 26(1) has a legislative character. The ABA itself can vary a licence area plan (s 26(2)) and the Minister is empowered to give other directions to the ABA (cf ss 31(1), 160(c), 162, 163), but the Minister cannot control the ABA in formulating a licence area plan (s 163).

Absence of merits review of decisions under s 26(1) of the BS Act

...

201 [76] ... In s 204 of the *BS Act*, the legislature specified what decisions under that Act should be reviewable by the Tribunal. The legislature did not include a decision under s 26(1). With one exception, all the decisions mentioned in s 204 are decisions under provisions occurring in Parts of the *BS Act* subsequent to Pt 3. (The exception is a declaration by the ABA under s 6(3) that a drama program is not an 'Australian drama program'.) They are all decisions of a kind apt to impact directly on private interests. Although not conclusive, the omission from s 204 of the more general 'planning' decisions of the ABA, for which Pt 3 provides, is a further indication that the legislature did not consider those decisions (including a decision under s 26(1)) to be of an administrative character.

***202* Binding legal effect of licence area plans**

[77] In *SAT FM* Sundberg J stated (at 608–609):

> A plan has binding legal effect once prepared, in the sense that various statutory provisions are only enlivened following its preparation. Thus, before allocating a new broadcasting services bands licence, the Authority must designate one of the areas referred to in s 26 as its licence area: s 29.
>
> The 'areas referred to in section 26' are areas in plans in fact prepared by the Authority. A person may not exercise control of more than two commercial radio broadcasting licences in the same licence area: s 54. The Authority may determine the licence area population of the licence area (s 30), and this determines the number of television licences a person can control: s 53. The fact that a plan has this 'carry-on' effect supports its characterisation as a legislative measure ...

We agree this consideration is a further indication that a decision under s 26(1) is of a legislative character. A licence area plan under s 26, like a determination of priorities under s 24 and a frequency allotment plan under s 25, is a general measure of a kind one might expect to find contained in the statute, if this were practicable, constituting the legislative background against which applications for, and allocations of, licences are enabled to take place.

Summary

[78] It is necessary to take into account all of the considerations discussed ... above; no single feature is decisive. Taking them all into account, we are of the opinion that the determination of a licence area plan under s 26(1) of the *BS Act* is a decision of a legislative, not an administrative, character. The considerations we find most persuasive are the following:

- The licence area plan is of general application as distinct from being a determination which affects only particular individuals or is made with particular individuals in contemplation;
- Notwithstanding the power of variation given by s 26(2), a licence area plan is obviously expected to have a moderately long term application and to lay down parameters within which decisions affecting individuals will be taken;
- There is a clear distinction between the planning concerns of Pt 3 of the Act and the Pt 4 provisions regarding allocation of licences which more directly affect the interests of individuals; and
- Section 204 of the Act provides for review by the Tribunal of a wide range of decisions for which the *BS Act* provides, including decisions under Pt 4 and subsequent Parts of the Act, but omits review of the preparation of a licence area plan under s 26(1).

[Citations omitted]

Types of delegated legislation

Legislation Act 2003 (Cth)

[Compilation date: As at 1 December 2022]

8 Definition of *legislative instrument*

(1) A ***legislative instrument*** is an instrument to which subsection (2), (3), (4) or (5) applies.

Note: Instruments that can be legislative instruments may be described by their enabling legislation in different ways, for example as regulations, rules, ordinances or determinations.

Primary law provides for something to be done by legislative instrument

(2) If a primary law gives power to do something by legislative instrument, then:

(a) if the thing is done, it must be done by instrument; and

(b) that instrument is a ***legislative instrument***.

Example 1: A primary law provides that 'The Minister may, by legislative instrument, determine licence conditions for the purposes of this section.'.

Example 2: A primary law provides as follows:

'(1) The Chief Executive may, by instrument, determine licence conditions.

(2) The Chief Executive may, by instrument, exempt a person from the requirement under this Act to hold a licence.

(3) An instrument made by the Chief Executive under subsection (1) or (2) is a legislative instrument.'.

Instruments registered on the Federal Register of Legislation

(3) An instrument made under a power delegated by the Parliament is a ***legislative instrument*** if it is registered as a legislative instrument.

Note: An instrument made under a power delegated by the Parliament may be a legislative instrument because it is registered as a legislative instrument, whether or not it is a legislative instrument because of another provision of this section.

Instruments that determine or alter the law etc.

(4) An instrument is a ***legislative instrument*** if:

(a) the instrument is made under a power delegated by the Parliament; and

(b) any provision of the instrument:

(i) determines the law or alters the content of the law, rather than determining particular cases or particular circumstances in which the law, as set out in an Act or another legislative instrument or provision, is to apply, or is not to apply; and

(ii) has the direct or indirect effect of affecting a privilege or interest, imposing an obligation, creating a right, or varying or removing an obligation or right.

Instruments declared to be legislative instruments

(5) An instrument is a *legislative instrument* if it is declared by section 10 or 57A to be a legislative instrument.

Note: Section 10 declares regulations and some other instruments to be legislative instruments. Section 57A declares some instruments to be legislative instruments that were made under a power delegated by the Parliament before 1 January 2005, when the substantive provisions of this Act commenced.

Instruments that are not legislative instruments

(6) Despite subsections (4) and (5), an instrument is not a *legislative instrument* if it is:

(a) declared by an Act not to be a legislative instrument; or

(b) prescribed by regulation for the purposes of this paragraph.

(7) However, subsection (6) does not apply to an instrument that is a legislative instrument under subsection (3) by registration.

(8) Despite anything else in this section, the following are not legislative instruments, and cannot become legislative instruments under subsection (3) (by being registered as legislative instruments):

(a) an instrument that is a notifiable instrument because of subsection 11(1) (primary law gives power to do something by notifiable instrument);

(b) a commencement instrument;

(c) a compilation of a legislative instrument or notifiable instrument;

(d) rules of court or a compilation of rules of court;

(e) an explanatory statement for a legislative instrument, or rules of court mentioned in paragraph (d).

Note: Rules of court may, however, be registered under this Act, and may be otherwise treated as if they were legislative instruments by their enabling legislation.

...

38 Tabling of legislative instruments

(1) The Office of Parliamentary Counsel must arrange for a copy of each registered legislative instrument to be delivered to each House of the Parliament to be laid before each House within 6 sitting days of that House after the registration of the instrument.

(3) If a copy of a legislative instrument is not laid before each House of the Parliament in accordance with this section, the legislative instrument is repealed immediately after the last day for it to be so laid.

...

42 Disallowance of legislative instruments

(1) If:

(a) notice of a motion to disallow a legislative instrument or provision of a legislative instrument is given in a House of the Parliament within 15 sitting days of that House beginning on the first sitting day after a copy of the instrument was laid before that House; and

(b) within 15 sitting days of that House beginning on the first sitting day after the giving of that notice, the House passes a resolution, in pursuance of the motion, disallowing the instrument or provision;

the instrument or provision so disallowed is repealed immediately after the passing of that resolution.

(2) If:

(a) notice of a motion to disallow a legislative instrument or a provision of a legislative instrument is given in a House of the Parliament within 15 sitting days of that House beginning on the first sitting day after a copy of the instrument was laid before that House; and

(b) at the end of 15 sitting days of that House beginning on the first sitting day after the giving of that notice of motion:

(i) the notice has not been withdrawn and the motion has not been called on; or

(ii) the motion has been called on, moved and (where relevant) seconded and has not been withdrawn or otherwise disposed of;

the instrument or provision specified in the motion is then taken to have been disallowed and is repealed at that time.

Legislative regulation and parliamentary review of delegated legislation

Case study: Disallowance of *Aboriginal Land Rights (Northern Territory) Amendment (Delegation) Regulation 2013* (Cth)

Background

Section 78 of the *Aboriginal Land Rights (Northern Territory) Act 1976* (Cth) grants the Governor-General the power to make regulations. Regulations were promulgated under the Act in 2007: *Aboriginal Land Rights (Northern Territory) Regulations 2007* (Cth). On 12 December 2013, the Governor-General, acting with the advice of the Federal Executive Council, made amending regulations: *Aboriginal Land Rights (Northern Territory) Amendment (Delegation) Regulation 2013* (Cth). The 2013 amending regulations dealt with provisions in the Act that enable an Aboriginal and Torres Strait Islander corporation to make an application to a Land Council seeking delegation of certain powers held by the Council (s 28(3) of the Act).

The 2013 amending regulations prescribed information that must be included in applications for delegation made by an Aboriginal and Torres Strait Islander corporation and set a three-month period for a Land Council to make a decision on applications. If that three-month period was not met, there would be a deemed refusal of the application.

A major area of concern for the Senators supporting the disallowance was the three-month time frame and degree to which there had been consultation with the relevant stakeholders about the proposed amendments to the regulations; views differed on the extent of the consultation that had taken place. The Senate disallowed the regulations on 20 March 2014.

This case study shows how the process of parliamentary disallowance of delegated legislation works.

Aboriginal Land Rights (Northern Territory) Act 1976 (Cth)

[As at relevant date]

An Act providing for the granting of Traditional Aboriginal Land in the Northern Territory for the benefit of Aboriginals, and for other purposes

28 Delegation ...

Delegation to Aboriginal and Torres Strait Islander corporation

...

(3) A Land Council may, in writing under its common seal, delegate to an Aboriginal and Torres Strait Islander corporation that has made an application in accordance with section 28A, the Council's functions or powers under the following provisions:

- (a) section 11A (about agreements concerning land under claim);
- (b) section 19 (about dealings with interests in land by Land Trusts);
- (ba) section 19A (about grant of township leases);
- (c) Part IV (about mining);
- (d) section 67B (about granting estates or interests while land is subject to a traditional land claim).

28A Delegation of a Land Council's functions or powers to Aboriginal and Torres Strait Islander corporation Application

(1) An Aboriginal and Torres Strait Islander corporation may, in writing, apply to a Land Council to have the Council delegate to the corporation some or all of the Council's functions or powers that are delegable to the corporation if a majority of the members of the corporation are either:

- (a) the traditional Aboriginal owners of land in the [relevant area]; or
- (b) Aboriginals who live in that part.

(2) An application must:

...

- (c) contain any other information prescribed by the regulations; ...

Deemed refusal

(1) If the Council has neither made nor refused to make the delegation within the period worked out in accordance with the regulations, or such longer period as is agreed by the Minister, the Council is taken, at the end of that period, to have refused to make the delegation.

28B Variation or revocation of a delegation to Aboriginal and Torres Strait Islander corporation.

...

(2) If the Council has neither varied nor refused to vary the delegation within the period worked out in accordance with the regulations, or such longer period as

is agreed by the Minister, the Council is taken, at the end of that period, to have refused to vary the delegation.

78 Regulations

The Governor-General may make regulations, not inconsistent with this Act, prescribing all matters required or permitted by this Act to be prescribed, or necessary or convenient to be prescribed for carrying out or giving effect to this Act and, in particular, prescribing penalties, not exceeding a fine of 6 penalty units, for offences against the regulations.

Aboriginal Land Rights (Northern Territory) Amendment (Delegation) Regulation 2013 (Cth)

[No longer in force]

Select Legislative Instrument No. 272, 2013

I, Quentin Bryce AC CVO, Governor-General of the Commonwealth of Australia, acting with the advice of the Federal Executive Council, make the following regulation under the *Aboriginal Land Rights (Northern Territory) Act 1976*.

Dated 12 December 2013
Quentin Bryce
Governor-General

SCHEDULE 1—AMENDMENTS

Aboriginal Land Rights (Northern Territory) Regulations 2007

Insert:

…

8 Application for delegation—deemed refusal period

For subsection 28A(5) of the Act, the period is 3 months from the day the Land Council receives an application for the delegation of functions or powers.

8A Application to vary delegation—deemed refusal period

For subsection 28B(6) of the Act, the period is 3 months from the day the Land Council receives an application to vary a delegation of functions or powers.

Explanatory statement

EXPLANATORY STATEMENT

Select Legislative Instrument No 272, 2013

Issued by the authority of the Minister for Indigenous Affairs

Aboriginal Land Rights (Northern Territory) Act 1976

Aboriginal Land Rights (Northern Territory) Amendment (Delegation) Regulation 2013

General outline

The Aboriginal *Land Rights (Northern Territory) Act 1976* (the Act) provides for the granting of Traditional Aboriginal land in the Northern Territory for the benefit of Aboriginal people.

Land is granted under the Act to Aboriginal Land Trusts to hold title to the land for the benefit of Aboriginal people entitled by Aboriginal tradition to the use or occupation of the land. Aboriginal Land Councils are established under the Act to carry out a range of functions and powers in relation to Aboriginal land. Land Trusts may only deal with the land in accordance with directions given to it by the Land Council for the area in which the land is situated.

...

Consultation

The Northern Land Council, the Central Land Council, the Tiwi Land Council, the Anindilyakwa Land Council, the Northern Territory Government, the Minerals Council of Australia and the Northern Territory Cattlemen's Association have been consulted in relation to the preparation of the Regulation. The consultation included circulation of an exposure draft of the Regulation. Responses to the Regulation exposure draft were considered in the finalisation of the Regulation.

A number of Aboriginal corporations were also approached regarding consultations on issues relevant to the Regulation. Consultative meetings were held with those Aboriginal corporations that were interested and available.

Commonwealth, *Parliamentary Debates*, Senate, 5 March 2014

Senator MCLUCAS [an Opposition Senator] to move:

That the Aboriginal Land Rights (Northern Territory) Amendment (Delegation) Regulation 2013, as contained in Select Legislative Instrument 2013 No 272 and made under the *Aboriginal Land Rights (Northern Territory) Act 1976*, be disallowed [F2013L02122].

Fifteen sitting days remain, including today, to resolve the motion or the instrument will be deemed to have been disallowed.

Commonwealth, *Parliamentary Debates*, Senate, 19 March 2014

REGULATIONS AND DETERMINATIONS

Aboriginal Land Rights (Northern Territory) Amendment (Delegation)
Regulation 2013
Disallowance

***1559* Senator MOORE** (Queensland):

At the request of Senator McLucas, I move:

That the Aboriginal Land Rights (Northern Territory) Amendment (Delegation) Regulation 2013, as contained in Select Legislative Instrument 2013 No 272 and made under the *Aboriginal Land Rights (Northern Territory) Act 1976*, be disallowed.

This will lead into the debate we are having about a disallowance motion for a range of regulations that are being put forward by the Minister. Before I commence, I want to acknowledge—and draw the attention of the Senate to—the Deputy Chair and the CEO of the Northern Land Council and the Chair of the Central Land Council, who are in the gallery and are sharing this discussion with us today.

The Opposition will be seeking to disallow these motions. We believe that in this area—a most sensitive area of activity that has been regulated and looked at by a series of governments and inquiries over so many years—there are two key points which I think we need to enshrine in all actions we take in this area. One of course must be effective, responsive and engaging consultation with the people who are involved and who will be affected by any form of change. We have heard this so many times. Commitments have been made by a series of governments that where there is any change to Aboriginal legislation there must be—there has to be—effective consultation. We put forward that that effective consultation has not taken place in this case.

The process outlined in the regulations includes a three-month turnaround for decisions which must involve careful scrutiny of the proposal for a corporation to take over key functions—and that scrutiny would be expected and must occur. But this is not a workable expectation: Aboriginal land councils have a clear schedule of meeting times, which we all know; when and where these councils meet is public and transparent. Their people know when they meet; we know when they meet. Not one of them would be able to turn around a decision of this nature within a three-month period. To put that forward in this regulation just does not make it workable. And the thing that comes behind that, of course, is that if there is not a decision made—and a response given back—by one of the land councils about a proposed devolution of authority to a corporation, the expectation is that the Minister will step in immediately ...

***1564* Senator PERIS (Northern Territory): ...**

I support the disallowance, and I call on both the Prime Minister and the Minister for Indigenous Affairs to ensure that, next time they intend to make changes that affect Aboriginal people, they do the right thing and have the decency to properly consult with them. I thank the land councils for coming here today and for the work they continue to do in protecting our land and for standing up for Aboriginal Territorians.

Senator SIEWERT (Western Australia—Australian Greens Whip) (18:16): From the outset I indicate that the Greens will be supporting this disallowance.

1566 We need to remember where this power came from. It was about gaining control of decision making over land. I am not suggesting that Minister Scullion is trying to concentrate that power. I am saying, however, that in the future these regulations could be used to enable more concentration of ministerial control over decisions that rightly sit with the traditional owners. The Greens will not support that further concentration of power in the executive. We believe that decision making should be with the traditional owners.

On behalf of the Greens, I [sic] very willing to say that, if there is another proposal which deals more appropriately with the time frame of decision making and with the questions and issues that have been raised by the land councils, we will be very happy to look at that alternative approach but we will not support the approach that is currently outlined in this regulation. We did raise very serious concerns when these amendments were first made, and we still hold those very serious concerns. I am not about to agree to a regulation that in fact concentrates those decision-making powers outside of the processes of land councils.

Having said that, we will agree to look at an alternative approach. We are very happy to consider that, but we will not support this regulation. We will support the disallowance.

Senator XENOPHON (South Australia) (18:26): Can I indicate that I take a contrary position. I will not support the disallowance. I have listened very carefully to what the contributors have put in relation to this debate, and I note particularly the comments made by Senator Siewert in relation to looking at alternative approaches. I have approached this issue by looking at some of the procedural aspects of the regulations, which I thought had some merit, but I do acknowledge the contributions made by other senators ...

***1568* Senator SCULLION** (Northern Territory—Minister for Indigenous Affairs and Leader of The Nationals in the Senate) (18:30): ...

Just in terms of a correction, Senator. This regulation—and I do not have time to just make up regulation, to just slip in here and throw a few regulations around—was the subject of a significant consultation process with all the land councils and with Aboriginal corporations. There were a series of consultations, and the reason those consultations were had was that there was mischief afoot. Certainly, the land councils in that consultation had indicated a whole range of things, and in response to that we made some changes. On the basis of that very clear advice, we put the regulations forward ...

Commonwealth, *Parliamentary Debates*, Senate, 20 March 2014

***1632* Senator MOORE** (Queensland) (12:07): ... [W]e continue to disapprove of these regulations as now presented to the chamber. I want to restate what was said by this side of the chamber last night, which is that we are not closing down any further discussion on the need for change. There is no intention of that. What we said clearly last night, I hope, was that on two basic issues we reject these regulations as they now stand. One was the issue of consultation. Despite the Minister for Indigenous Affair's efforts last night, talking about the wide range of consultation that took place, we submit that there was a short period of time in which the land councils were able to respond, as they did, to the issues around regulations which are going to impact very seriously on their operations but, more particularly, on the way the process was going to operate across the Northern Territory.

...

The PRESIDENT: The question is that the motion moved by Senator Moore be agreed to.

DIVISION

DIVISION

Ayes 33

Noes...........28

Majority........5

After the disallowance

Sections 28A(5) and 28B(6) of the *Aboriginal Land Rights (Northern Territory) Act 1976* (Cth) were later amended by the *Aboriginal Land Rights (Northern Territory) Amendment Act 2015* (Cth) (No 175 of 2015) to introduce a requirement that a Land Council take all reasonable steps to ensure that a decision is made on a delegation application within six months of receiving it, or a longer period if agreed in writing by the Aboriginal and Torres Strait Islander corporation. If an agreement was made for a longer period, the Minister had to be notified in writing (ss 28A(6) and 28B(7)).

Judicial review of delegated legislation

Minister for Primary Industries and Energy v Austral Fisheries Pty Ltd (1993) 40 FCR 381

Fisheries Act 1952 (Cth)

[As at relevant date]

7B Management plans

(1) The Minister may, by instrument in writing, determine a plan of management for a fishery in proclaimed waters.

...

(5) Where, in a plan of management for a fishery, the Minister determines the fishing capacity permitted for the fishery, then ... the plan of management may make provision for and in relation to -

...

(b) the allocation to persons of units of fishing capacity in the fishery;

Facts

The case concerned calculation and allocation of units of fishing capacity for a fishery management plan under s 7B(5)(b) of the *Fisheries Act 1952* (Cth). Austral Fisheries Pty Ltd, whose fishing activities were affected by the plan, applied to the Federal Court for judicial review under s 39B of the *Judiciary Act 1903* (Cth). The judge at first instance (O'Loughlin J) held that the formula that had been adopted for the allocation of catch quotas was based on a 'statistical fallacy' and produced an absurd result [*Austral Fisheries Pty Ltd v Minister for Primary Industries and Energy* (1992) 37 FCR 463]. The Full Court (Lockhart, Beaumont, and Hill JJ) dismissed the appeal.

Lockhart J

381 Subordinate legislative bodies can make laws which Parliament has expressly empowered them to make. I respectfully agree with Diplock L J in *Mixnam's Properties Ltd v Chertsey Urban District Council* [1964] 1 QB 214 at 237–238 that:

> The various special grounds upon which subordinate legislation has ***382*** sometimes been said to be void - for example, because it is unreasonable; because it is uncertain; because it is repugnant to the general law or to some other statute - can, I think, today be properly regarded as being particular applications of the general rule that subordinate legislation, to be valid, must be shown to be within the powers conferred by the statute....

384 Delegated legislation may be declared to be invalid on the ground of unreasonableness if it leads to manifest arbitrariness, injustice or partiality; but the underlying rationale is that legislation of this offending kind cannot be within the scope of what Parliament intended when authorising the subordinate legislative authority to enact laws.

It is with these principles in mind that I approach the question whether cl 11 of the South East Fishery (Individual Transferable Quota) Management Plan 1991 (the Plan) is invalid. It is obvious that the application of cl 11 of the Plan creates unreasonableness between fishermen who fish in the South Eastern Fishery and leads to the irrational result referred to in the judgments of the learned primary judge (O'Loughlin J). His Honour said:

> In order to explain the mistake that was made in the formula, it is necessary to bear in mind that its primary objective was to assess, over a specified period, the involvement of an individual in the particular fishery by having regard to his catch history and financial involvement. This could have best been done by adding the annual factors and expressing the individual's total as a percentage of the industry's total for the same period. Instead a percentage was struck in respect of each year; thereafter those annual percentages were totalled and divided by the number of years that were involved in the exercise.

Why the market share of each fisherman was taken for each of the five years in question, totalling the annual percentages and dividing the result by five; rather than simply adopting an averaging method, whereby each fisherman's total catch over the whole five- year period is expressed as a percentage of the industry's total fleet catch over the same period, is unclear from the evidence. By taking the percentage of each fisherman year by year plainly results in anomalies, especially with respect to low catch years. I am mindful of the fact that any quota system introduced by government will necessarily interfere with the operation of free market forces and will almost certainly create some kind of injustice as between the players in the market, and I take that into account. But cl 11 is so artificial and creates such extraordinary results that I cannot accept it as being within the scope of the statutory powers conferred by the *Fisheries Act 1952* (Cth), in particular s 7B.

It is plain that the Department of Primary Industries and Energy, when formulating the quota allocation process under the Plan, purported to apply three principles in determining the quota allocation process for the individual transferable quota system, namely:

(a) the process should be as fair and as equitable as possible;

(b) it should most effectively reflect market share for a species over the catch history period; and

(c) it should minimise disruption to the fishery.

These are permissible and worthy objectives, but they were not achieved by cl 11. The adoption of option 25 appears to have taken place very late in the stage of settling the final details of the Plan.

It is only in an extreme case that the court takes the step of declaring invalid delegated legislation of the kind with which this case is concerned, but in my view this is such a case.

Plaintiff M47/2012 v Director-General of Security (2012) 251 CLR 1

Migration Act 1958 (Cth)

[As at relevant date]

31 Classes of visas

(1) There are to be prescribed classes of visas.

...

(3) The regulations may prescribe criteria for a visa or visas of a specified class ...

498 Exercise of powers under Act

(1) The powers conferred by or under this Act shall be exercised in accordance with any applicable regulations under this Act ...

504 Regulations

(1) The Governor-General may make regulations, not inconsistent with this Act, prescribing all matters which by this Act are required or permitted to be prescribed or which are necessary or convenient to be prescribed for carrying out or giving effect to this Act

...

505 Regulations about visa criteria

To avoid doubt, regulations for the purpose of prescribing a criterion for visas of a class may provide that the Minister, when required to decide whether an applicant for a visa of the class satisfies the criterion:

(a) is to get a specified person or organisation, or a person or organisation in a specified class, to:

(i) give an opinion on a specified matter; or

(ii) make an assessment of a specified matter; or

(iii) make a finding about a specified matter; or

(iv) make a decision about a specified matter; and

(b) is:

(i) to have regard to that opinion, assessment, finding or decision in; or

(ii) to take that opinion, assessment, finding or decision to be correct for the purposes of;

deciding whether the applicant satisfies the criterion.

Migration Regulations 1994 (Cth)

[As at relevant date]

SCHEDULE 4—PUBLIC INTEREST CRITERIA AND RELATED PROVISIONS

Part 1—Public interest criteria

4002 The applicant is not assessed by the Australian Security Intelligence Organisation to be directly or indirectly a risk to security, within the meaning of section 4 of the *Australian Security Intelligence Organisation Act 1979.*

Facts

Plaintiff M47 was a refugee from Sri Lanka who sought a protection visa in Australia. A delegate of the Minister for Immigration and Citizenship refused to grant a visa on the basis that Plaintiff M47 had received an adverse security assessment from the Australian Security Intelligence Organisation (ASIO) and so he did not satisfy the public interest criterion prescribed in the regulations made under the *Migration Act 1958* (Cth). The Refugee Review Tribunal affirmed the delegate's decision. Plaintiff M47 applied to the High Court for certiorari to quash the visa decision or the adverse security assessment finding.

Although the case raised several administrative law issues, the extracts below concern the decision by the High Court majority that the public interest criterion 4002 was beyond power.

French CJ

The regulation-making power

41 [54] Regulations made under s 504 must be 'not inconsistent with' the *Migration Act.* Even without that expressed constraint delegated legislation cannot be repugnant to the Act which confers the power to make it. Repugnancy or inconsistency may be manifested in various ways. An important consideration in judging inconsistency for present purposes is 'the degree to which the legislature has disclosed an intention of dealing with the subject with which the statute is concerned'. A grant of power to make regulations in terms conferred by s 504 does not authorise regulations which will 'extend the scope or general operation of the enactment but [are] strictly ancillary'. In considering whether there has been a valid ***42*** exercise of the regulation-making power '[t]he true nature and purpose of the power must be determined'.

[55] The plaintiff relied upon those general propositions in support of his submission that public interest criterion 4002 is repugnant to the *Migration Act* and its

scheme. Before considering the regulatory framework under which the criterion was prescribed it is necessary to say something about s 498 of the *Migration Act*.

[56] Section 498(1) ... does not authorise the making of regulations which abrogate, modify or qualify the scope of the powers conferred by the *Migration Act*. Nor does s 498 provide a gateway for construction of the *Migration Act* by reference to regulations made under it. Generally speaking an Act, which does not provide for its own modification by operation of regulations made under it, is not to be construed by reference to those regulations. That would be a case of the tail wagging the dog. ...

Regulations – the public interest criteria

42 [57] The Regulations provide for classes of visa which are set out in Sch 1 to the Regulations and are in addition to the classes of visa created by the *Migration Act* itself. The criteria prescribed by the Regulations, for each class of visa, are in addition to those prescribed by the Act. They are to be found in Sch 2 to the Regulations. ...

[58] One of the primary criteria [for the class of visa for which Plaintiff M47 applied] is in cl 866.225, which provides:

> The applicant:
>
> **(a)** satisfies public interest criteria 4001, 4002 and 4003A; and
>
> **(b)** if the applicant had turned 18 at the time of application - satisfies public interest criterion 4019.
>
> ....

44 [59] ... Public interest criterion 4002 does not create a mechanism, of the kind contemplated by s 505, for third party assessment informing the Minister's decision. It is itself a criterion. As a matter of construction, the term 'is not assessed' in public interest criterion 4002 must be taken to refer to the absence of any current adverse assessment by ASIO that a person is directly or indirectly a risk to security. That is to say, if ASIO has made such an assessment at one time and thereafter made a fresh assessment that the applicant is not a risk to security, the applicant will, while that later assessment stands, satisfy the criterion in public interest criterion 4002.

[60] Criteria similar, but not identical, to public interest criteria 4001 and 4002 were prescribed when the Regulations were first made in 1994 ... That criterion was replaced with the present criterion in 2005. ...

Whether public interest criterion 4002 is invalid

46 [65] The *Migration Act* creates a statutory scheme, the purpose of which is to give effect to Australia's obligations under the [Refugee] Convention and to provide for cases in which those obligations are limited or qualified. It provides, in ss 36 and 65, for the grant of protection visas to persons to whom Australia owes protection obligations. It provides for the refusal or cancellation of such visas in respect of persons to whom Australia owes obligations where:

- the person may nevertheless be expelled from the country for 'compelling reasons of national security' pursuant to Art 32;

- the person may be removed from the country where 'there are reasonable grounds for regarding [the person] as a danger to the security of the country in which [the person] is' pursuant to Art 33(2).

[66] The Act provides procedural protection by way of merits review of decisions to refuse or cancel a visa relying on Arts 32 or 33(2). That protection is not available in those 'national interest' cases in which the Minister makes a decision personally to refuse or cancel a visa pursuant to s 501 and issues a certificate under s 502. That is the statutory scheme by reference to which the validity of public interest criterion 4002 is to be judged.

...

48 [71] ... [T]he relationship between public interest criterion 4002 and the provisions of ss 500–503 of the *Migration Act* spells invalidating inconsistency. That is primarily because the condition sufficient to support the assessment referred to in public interest criterion 4002 subsumes the disentitling national security criteria in Arts 32 and 33(2). It is wider in scope than those criteria and sets no threshold level of threat necessary to enliven its application. The public interest criterion requires the Minister to act upon an assessment which leaves no scope for the Minister to apply the power conferred by the Act to refuse the grant of a visa relying upon those Articles. It has the result that the effective decision-making power with respect to the disentitling condition which reposes in the Minister under the Act is shifted by cl 866.225 of the Regulations into the hands of ASIO. Further, and inconsistently with the scheme for merits review provided in s 500, no merits review is available in respect of an adverse security assessment under the ASIO Act made for the purposes of public interest criterion 4002. Public interest criterion 4002 therefore negates important elements of the statutory scheme relating to decisions concerning protection visas and the application of criteria derived from Arts 32 and 33(2). It is inconsistent with that scheme. In my opinion cl 866.225 of the Regulations is invalid to the extent that it prescribes public interest criterion 4002.

[72] Because public interest criterion 4002 is invalid, the refusal of the plaintiff's application for a protection visa was affected by jurisdictional error. As a result there has, at this time, been no valid decision on the plaintiff's application for a protection visa.

[Citations omitted]

Attorney-General v Corporation of the City of Adelaide (2013) 249 CLR 1

Local Government Act 1934 (SA)

[As at relevant date]

667 By-laws

(1) Subject to this Act, a council may make by-laws for all or any of the following purposes:

...

9 Miscellaneous

XVI generally for the good rule and government of the area, and for the convenience, comfort and safety of its inhabitants.

City of Adelaide By-laws

[As at relevant date]

BY-LAW NO 4

2. No person shall without permission on any road:

...

2.3 Preaching and canvassing

preach, canvass, harangue, tout for business or conduct any survey or opinion poll provided that this restriction shall not apply to [a] designated area as resolved by the Council known as a 'Speakers Corner' and any survey or opinion poll conducted by or with the authority of a candidate during the course of a Federal, State or Local Government Election or during the course and for the purpose of a Referendum;

...

2.8 Distribute

give out or distribute to any bystander or passer-by any handbill, book, notice, or other printed matter, provided that this restriction shall not apply to any handbill or leaflet given out or distributed by or with the authority of a candidate during the course of a Federal, State or Local Government Election or to a handbill or leaflet given out or distributed during the course and for the purpose of a Referendum.

Facts

Jacob and Samuel Corneloup, members of an unincorporated association known as 'Street Church', wanted to preach and distribute religious material in various prominent locations in Adelaide's central business district. They applied for a declaration that paragraphs 2.3 and 2.8 of By-law No 4 were invalid. They argued that the By-laws were beyond the grant of power in s 667 of the *Local Government Act 1934* (SA) and also breached the constitutional implied freedom of political communication. The High Court held the By-laws were valid.

In the following extract, French CJ considers reasonableness and proportionality in relation to the making of delegated legislation.

French CJ

Reasonableness and reasonable proportionality

34 [47] The third respondent [Samuel Corneloup] ... asserted that the impugned provisions of By-law No 4 were 'an unreasonable exercise' of the by-law making power and 'not a reasonably proportionate or proportionate exercise of the power'. Those grounds invoke criteria of invalidity which have overlapping histories and applications. They define limits on the by-law making power.

[48] A high threshold test for unreasonableness invalidating delegated legislation was set by the Privy Council in *Slattery v Naylor* [(1888) LR 13 App Cas 446]. Their Lordships spoke of a 'merely fantastic and capricious bye-law, such as reasonable men could not make in good faith' [at 452]. That criterion did not invite judicial merits review of delegated legislation. Nor has unreasonableness ever been so regarded in this Court. As their Lordships said, a by-law would not be treated as unreasonable 'merely because it does not contain qualifications which commend themselves to the minds of judges' [at 453] ...

[49] The high threshold approach to invalidating unreasonableness was reflected early in the life of this Court in *Widgee Shire Council v Bonney* [(1907) 4 CLR 977], where Griffith CJ, ... said [at 982–983]:

> The existence of a power and the expediency of its exercise are quite different matters. The question of the existence of the power can always be determined by a Court of law. But, in my opinion, the expediency of the exercise of a power is not a matter for determination by a Court.

... All ***35*** the Justices treated unreasonableness, so understood, as going to power. The point was made plainly by Higgins J [at 989]:

> Questions as to the validity of by-laws really come under the ordinary principles applicable to powers; and when it is said that a by-law is unreasonable, and therefore invalid, what is really meant is that the provisions in the by-law cannot reasonably be regarded as being within the scope or ambit or purpose of the power. The language used in Courts of equity with regard to powers seems to me to be more appropriate, and to conduce to greater clearness of thought.

...

36 [53] In *Shanahan v Scott* [(1957) 96 CLR 245], the Court considered limitations on a very general power to make regulations 'providing for all or any purposes ... necessary or expedient for the administration of the Act or for carrying out the objects of the Act' [Dixon CJ, Williams, Webb and Fullagar JJ at 250]. Such a power, it was said, would not support 'attempts to widen the purposes of the Act, to add new and different means of carrying them out or to depart from or vary the plan which the legislature has adopted to attain its ends' [at 250]. In *Minister for Resources v Dover Fisheries Pty Ltd* [(1993) 43 FCR 565], Gummow J, considering a similarly worded regulation-making power, said of the indicia of invalidity identified in *Shanahan v Scott* that [at 578]:

> These are indicia which assist in deciding the general question of whether the regulations in question are a reasonable means of attaining the ends of the legislative delegation of power.

37 The text of the regulation-making powers considered in *Shanahan v Scott* and in *Dover Fisheries* expressly raised the requirement that regulations made under them have a rational connection to the statutory purpose. Nevertheless, as the approach adopted by Gummow J suggested, the analysis in those cases is applicable to the general question whether a regulation is invalid for unreasonableness.

[54] Applying the general approach to 'unreasonableness' set out in the preceding cases, and accepting its subsistence as a limit on delegated legislative power, the impugned provisions of By-law No 4 could not be said to have been invalid on that ground. Paragraphs 2.3 and 2.8 provided a rational mechanism for the regulation by proscription, absent permission, of conduct on roads which involves unsolicited communication to members of the public. They were not, on their face, capricious or oppressive. Nor did they represent a gratuitous interference with the rights of those affected by them. They provided a mechanism for protecting members of the public from gratuitous interference with their freedom to choose whether and, if so, when and where they would be the subject of proselytising communications. They were directed to modes and places of communication, rather than content. It was not necessary to the application of the high threshold test of unreasonableness to consider possible alternative modes of regulation. The criterion is not confined to purposive powers. Paragraphs 2.3 and 2.8 were not invalid on account of unreasonableness.

[55] The difficulties of making out a challenge to validity on the basis of unreasonableness no doubt explain the focus in the third respondent's written submissions on the ground of contention asserting lack of reasonable proportionality. Proportionality is not a legal doctrine. In Australia it designates a class of criteria used to determine the validity or lawfulness of legislative and administrative action by reference to rational relationships between purpose and means, and the interaction of competing legal rules and principles, including qualifications of constitutional guarantees, immunities or freedoms. Proportionality criteria have been applied to purposive and incidental law-making powers derived from the *Constitution* and from statutes. They have also been applied in determining the validity of laws affecting constitutional guarantees, immunities and freedoms, including the implied freedom of political communication which is considered later in these reasons.

[56] A high threshold test, which falls into the class of proportionality criteria, was applied to determine the validity of delegated legislation by Dixon J in *Williams v Melbourne Corporation.* His Honour, speaking of unreasonableness in the context of a purposive bylaw ***38*** making power, pointed out that although there might, on the face of it, be a sufficient connection between the subject of the power and that of the by-law [(1933) 49 CLR 142, 155, see also 150 (Starke J), 158 (Evatt J), 159 (McTiernan J)]:

> the true character of the by-law may then appear to be such that it *could not* reasonably have been adopted as a means of attaining the ends of the power. In such a case the by-law will be invalid, not because it is inexpedient or misguided, but because it is not a real exercise of the power (emphasis added).
>
> ...

39 [58] In *South Australia v Tanner* [(1989) 166 CLR 161], which concerned the validity of delegated legislation, the majority noted, without demur, that the parties had accepted 'the reasonable proportionality test of validity ... namely, whether the regulation is capable of being considered to be reasonably proportionate to the pursuit of the enabling purpose' [(1989) 166 CLR 161, 165]. Their Honours equated that test with the test enunciated by Dixon J in *Williams* and added that it was [(1989) 166 CLR 161, 165] 'in substance, whether the regulation goes beyond any restraint which could be reasonably adopted for the prescribed purpose'. The test sets an appropriate limit on the exercise of purposive powers entrusted to a public authority to make delegated legislation. It gives due respect to the authority entrusted by the parliament in the law-making body. Historically, it can be regarded as a development of the high threshold 'unreasonableness' test derived from the nineteenth century English authorities. It requires a rational relationship between the purpose for which the power is ***40*** conferred and the laws made in furtherance of that purpose, whether it be widely or narrowly defined.

[59] The high threshold test for reasonable proportionality should be accepted as that applicable to delegated legislation made in furtherance of a purposive power.

[Citations omitted]

PART

II

PUBLIC ACCOUNTABILITY MECHANISMS

CHAPTER

5

PUBLIC INVESTIGATORY BODIES

Introduction 90

Investigation and scrutiny through parliament 90

Williams v Commonwealth (No 1) (2012) 248 CLR 156 90

Egan v Willis (1998) 195 CLR 424 92

New South Wales Legislative Council, *Order for the Production of Documents* (Standing Order 52, May 2004) 95

Auditors-General 96

Auditor-General Act 1997 (Cth) 96

Public Governance, Performance and Accountability Act 2013 (Cth) 98

Auditor-General Performance Audit, *Offshore Processing Centres in Nauru and Papua New Guinea: Contract Management of Garrison Support and Welfare Services* (ANAO Report No 32 2016–17, 17 January 2017) 102

Ombudsmen 106

Ombudsman Act 1976 (Cth) 106

Chairperson, Aboriginal and Torres Strait Islander Commission v Commonwealth Ombudsman (1995) 63 FCR 163 111

King v Ombudsman (2020) 137 SASR 18 115

Royal commissions 119

Royal Commissions Act 1902 (Cth) 119

Royal Commission into the Home Insulation Program (Report, 2014) 119

Introduction

This chapter complements Chapter 5 in *Government Accountability: Australian Administrative Law*, third edition, which investigates the role of parliament and other bodies, such as auditors-general and ombudsmen, in scrutinising and investigating the actions of government.

Investigation and scrutiny through parliament

Williams v Commonwealth (No 1) (2012) 248 CLR 156

Constitution

53 Powers of the houses in respect of legislation

Proposed laws appropriating revenue or moneys, or imposing taxation, shall not originate in the Senate. But a proposed law shall not be taken to appropriate revenue or moneys, or to impose taxation, by reason only of its containing provisions for the imposition or appropriation of fines or other pecuniary penalties, or for the demand or payment or appropriation of fees for licences, or fees for services under the proposed law.

The Senate may not amend proposed laws imposing taxation, or proposed laws appropriating revenue or moneys for the ordinary annual services of the Government. The Senate may not amend any proposed law so as to increase any proposed charge or burden on the people.

The Senate may at any stage return to the House of Representatives any proposed law which the Senate may not amend, requesting, by message, the omission or amendment of any items or provisions therein. And the House of Representatives may, if it thinks fit, make any of such omissions or amendments, with or without modifications. Except as provided in this section, the Senate shall have equal power with the House of Representatives in respect of all proposed laws.

54 Appropriation Bills

The proposed law which appropriates revenue or moneys for the ordinary annual services of the Government shall deal only with such appropriation.

...

83 Money to be appropriated by law

No money shall be drawn from the Treasury of the Commonwealth except under appropriation made by law.

Facts

Ron Williams – a Toowoomba father of six children – challenged the Commonwealth's funding of the Darling Heights State School's chaplaincy service under the National School Chaplaincy Program ('NSCP'). Under the NSCP, the Commonwealth funded chaplaincy services at schools. The NSCP had no statutory backing: it relied on an annual parliamentary appropriation and the Commonwealth's executive power to enter into contracts with each provider of chaplaincy services. Mr Williams successfully challenged the scheme on the ground that the Commonwealth lacked the executive power to enter into the funding agreement with the Scripture Union of Queensland to provide chaplaincy services to the Darling Heights State School. The High Court found that parliament must not only authorise government expenditure through the appropriations process, but the constitutional structures of federalism and responsible government also required parliament to provide legislative authorisation for government funding schemes and contracts, with some exceptions; for example, those required in the ordinary course of running a government department. In the following extract, Crennan J discusses responsible government and the role of parliament in the scrutiny of expenditure.

After *Williams (No 1)*, the Financial Framework Legislation Amendment Bill (No 3) 2012 (Cth) was rushed through the Commonwealth Parliament. This legislation aimed to provide legislative support for approximately 400 Commonwealth spending programs. In a second High Court challenge, Ron Williams successfully challenged the provision supporting the NSCP on the constitutional law basis that it was not supported by a head of Commonwealth legislative power.[1]

Crennan J

350 [510] Prior to Federation, it was appreciated that the sharing of political power was an important mechanism for avoiding arbitrary government and thereby maintaining civil order. That appreciation underpinned the principle of responsible government and the idea that a democratic representative assembly would give qualified persons a 'stake' in government, both of which are sourced in the constitutional history of Britain and Australia in the nineteenth century. The same appreciation also underpinned the doctrine of the separation of powers, sourced in the constitutional history of America in the eighteenth century.

[511] The relationship between Ch I and Ch II of the *Constitution*, between the Parliament and the Executive, between ss 1 and 61, between representative and responsible government, can be discerned in numerous constitutional requirements. For the purposes of the present action, relevant requirements in Ch I include the requirement that there be a yearly session of Parliament (s 6), that both Houses of Parliament be democratically elected (ss 7 and 24), that Parliament makes laws (s 51), including in respect of taxation (s 51(ii)), and that appropriation from the Consolidated Revenue Fund be undertaken as required by ss 53, 54 and 56 ...

[512] Chapter II of the *Constitution* (ss 61–70) deals with 'The Executive Government'. As well as s 61, Ch II contains provision for a Federal Executive Council to advise the Governor-General (s 62). Further, Ministers administering 'departments of State of the Commonwealth' cannot hold office for longer than three months without being or becoming a member of one of the Houses of Parliament (s 64), thus ensuring their accountability to Parliament. Section 67 governs the appointment of civil servants, who are officers of the Executive.

351 [513] Section 83, in Ch IV, secures Parliament's control over supply.

[514] Section 96, dealing with financial relations between the Commonwealth and the States, has been referred to already and s 97 imposes audit requirements.

1 *Williams v Commonwealth (No 2)* (2014) 252 CLR 416.

[515] Accountability of the Executive arises not only from the requirements under the *Constitution* affecting the Executive mentioned above, but also from various conventions of Parliament, the established mechanisms of parliamentary debate and question time, and the requirement that members of the Executive provide information to Select Committees of both Houses of Parliament. Leaving aside appropriation legislation, Bills are conventionally introduced to Parliament, and their purposes explained, by the Minister responsible for their initiation in the House of which the Minister is a member, or by a delegate in the House of which the Minister is not a member. They are then the subject of parliamentary scrutiny and debate. The ultimate passage of a Bill into law may involve a number of compromises along the way, reflected in amendments which secure the Bill's final acceptance. Parliament's control over expenditure is effected through the legislative process.

[516] The practical workings of a system of government which is both responsible and democratically representative are not static, and have given rise to a more general and flexible sense of 'responsible government' to indicate a government which is responsive to public opinion and answerable to the electorate. The mechanisms and layers of accountability described above permit the ventilation, accommodation, and effective authorisation of political decisions. The notion of a government's mandate to pass laws and to spend money rests both on democratic representative government and on the relationship between Parliament and the Executive, involving, as it does, both scrutiny and responsibility. Whilst the Executive has the power to initiate new policy and to implement such policy when authorised to do so, either by Parliament or otherwise under the *Constitution*, Parliament has the power to scrutinise and authorise such policy (if it is not otherwise authorised by the *Constitution*), and the exclusive power to grant supply in respect of it and control expenditure. The principles of accountability of the Executive to Parliament and Parliament's control over supply and expenditure operate inevitably to constrain the Commonwealth's capacities to ***352*** contract and to spend. Such principles do not constrain the common law freedom to contract and to spend enjoyed by non-governmental juristic persons.

[517] Although the practice of responsible government varies over time, most particularly as the party system results in close identification of Parliament and the Executive, the scope of s 61 to encompass *any* expenditure by the Commonwealth Executive is limited by the system of government under the *Constitution.*

[Citations omitted]

Egan v Willis (1998) 195 CLR 424

Facts

In 1996, the New South Wales Legislative Council ordered the Treasurer, Michael Egan, to produce documents relating to the government's response to a commission of inquiry into the environmental impact of a proposed goldmine in Lake Cowal and the government's subsequent consent to the project. The Treasurer refused to do so and the Council found him in contempt, suspended him for the remainder of the day, and ordered him to be removed from the chamber by the parliamentary officer known as the 'Usher of the Black Rod'. Mr Egan took the matter to court, seeking a declaration that the resolution suspending him from the House was invalid, and also a declaration of trespass to the person against the Usher. The trespass claim was on the basis that parliament did not have the power to order him to produce documents and therefore the Usher was not authorised (justified) to physically escort him from the building.

The New South Wales Court of Appeal [*Egan v Willis* (1996) 40 NSWLR 650] refused to declare that the resolution suspending him was invalid, but did declare that the defendants had committed an unlawful trespass by going beyond what was justified. Mr Egan was not merely taken from the Chamber but had been forcibly taken out into the street.

On appeal from the Supreme Court of New South Wales, the High Court confirmed the power of the New South Wales Parliament to order the production of documents and its power to find a minister in contempt and suspend him or her from the Chamber. That justified his removal from the Chamber. The trespass issue, that came to be known as the 'footpath point', was not appealed.

Gaudron, Gummow and Hayne JJ

Standing orders

441 [14] Part V of the Standing Rules and Orders of the Legislative Council ('the Standing Orders') is headed 'PAPERS'. It comprises Standing Orders 18–22. Standing Order 18 states:

> Any Papers may be ordered to be laid before the House and the Clerk shall communicate to the Premier's Department any such order.

Standing Order 20 provides:

> All Papers and Documents laid upon the Table of the House by a Minister shall be considered public, and may be ordered to be printed on motion without notice ...

442 [15] In the Court of Appeal, Gleeson CJ said that the context shows that Standing Order 18 'refers to what are sometimes called State papers, that is to say, papers which are created or acquired by ministers, office-holders, and public servants by virtue of the office they hold under, or their service to, the Crown in right of the State of New South Wales' [*Egan* (1996) 40 NSWLR 650, 654].

[16] Part VIII of the Standing Orders is headed 'QUESTIONS SEEKING INFORMATION FROM THE GOVERNMENT OR PRIVATE MEMBERS' and comprises Standing Orders 29-32A. Standing Order 29 deals with Question Time. It states:

> Questions may be put to Ministers of the Crown relating to public affairs; and to other Members, relating to any Bill, Motion, or other public matter connected with the business of the House, in which such Members may be concerned, and the Clerk shall enter upon the Minutes of Proceedings the Questions of which formal notice shall have been given, with the answers returned to the same.

...

451 [42] A system of responsible government traditionally has been considered to encompass 'the means by which Parliament brings the Executive to account' so that 'the Executive's primary responsibility in its prosecution of government is owed to Parliament'. The point was made by Mill, writing in 1861, who spoke of the task of the legislature 'to watch and control the government: to throw the light of publicity on its acts'. It has been said of the contemporary position in Australia that, whilst 'the primary role of Parliament is to pass laws, it also has important functions to question and criticise government on behalf of the people' and that 'to secure accountability of government activity is the very essence of responsible government'. In *Lange v Australian Broadcasting Corporation* [(1997) 189 CLR 520, 561], reference was made to those provisions of the Commonwealth Constitution which prescribe the system of responsible government as necessarily implying 'a limitation on legislative and executive power to deny the electors and their representatives information concerning the conduct of the executive branch of ***452*** government throughout the life of a federal Parliament'. The Court added [*Lange* (1997) 189 CLR 520, 561]:

> Moreover, the conduct of the executive branch is not confined to Ministers and the public service. It includes the affairs of statutory authorities and public utilities which are obliged to report to the legislature or to a Minister who is responsible to the legislature.

In Australia, s 75(v) of the *Constitution* and judicial review of administrative action under federal and State law, together with freedom of information legislation, supplement the operation of responsible government in this respect.

...

453 [45] One aspect of responsible government is that Ministers may be members of either House of a bicameral legislature and liable to the scrutiny of that chamber in respect of the conduct of the executive branch of government. Another aspect of responsible government, perhaps the best known, is that the ministry must command the support of the lower House of a bicameral legislature upon confidence motions. The circumstance that Ministers are not members of a chamber in which the fate of administration is determined in this way does not have the consequence that the first aspect of responsible government mentioned above does not apply to them. Nor is it a determinative consideration that the political party or parties, from members of which the administration has been formed, 'controls' the lower but not the upper chamber. Rather, there may be much to be said for the view that it is such a state of affairs which assists the attainment of the object of responsible government of which Mill spoke in 1861.

...

454 [49] The primary function of the Legislative Council is indicated by s 5 of the *Constitution Act* [*1902* (NSW)]. This is the exercise by the Legislative Council, as an element of the legislature, of its power, subject to the provisions of the Commonwealth Constitution, to make laws for the peace, welfare and good government of New South Wales in all cases whatsoever. As has been pointed out, subject to restrictions with respect to money Bills, a Bill may originate in the Legislative Council. Further, the Legislative Council has, in general, equal power of disallowance of delegated legislation.

[50] In addition, the long practice since 1856 with respect to the production to the Council of State papers, together with the provision in Standing Order 29 for the putting to Ministers of questions relating to public affairs and the convention and parliamentary practice with respect to the representation in the Legislative Council by a Minister in respect of portfolios held by members in the Legislative Assembly, are significant.

...

[53] ... Reduced to its essentials, what happened in the present case involved the determination by the ***455*** Legislative Council to seek the provision to it by a member, who is a Minister and who 'represented' another Minister in the Legislative Assembly, of State papers which, as Gleeson CJ described them, related 'to matters of government business which the Council wished to debate' [*Egan* (1996) 40 NSWLR 650, 653]. The appellant had in his custody and control certain documents which fell within the description of those sought in the relevant resolution. The Minister chose not to produce the papers, claiming, consistently with the position taken by the Cabinet, that the Legislative Council had no power to call for them. He was then suspended for the balance of the day's sitting.

[54] If a member will not produce documents sought by the House ... one of the steps that the House may undoubtedly take is to resolve that the member be suspended for a limited time from the service of the House, and that is what happened here.

[Citations omitted]

New South Wales Legislative Council, *Order for the Production of Documents* (Standing Order 52, May 2004)

Background

After *Egan v Willis* (1998) 195 CLR 424 (extracted above), the New South Wales Treasurer, Michael Egan, refused to comply with another request for documents on the basis of legal professional privilege and public interest immunity.[2] As a result of the controversy caused by these cases, the New South Wales Legislative Council established a system of independent arbitration to determine the legitimacy of government privilege claims. This shows how parliaments may respond to challenges to their accountability role by strengthening the mechanisms by which they perform that role.

Standing Order No 52

Order for the production of documents

(1) The House may order documents to be tabled in the House. The Clerk is to communicate to the Premier's Department, all orders for documents made by the House.

(2) When returned, the documents will be laid on the table by the Clerk.

(3) A return under this order is to include an indexed list of all documents tabled, showing the date of creation of the document, a description of the document and the author of the document.

(4) If at the time the documents are required to be tabled the House is not sitting, the documents may be lodged with the Clerk, and unless privilege is claimed, are deemed to be have been presented to the House and published by authority of the House.

(5) Where a document is considered to be privileged:

2 *Egan v Chadwick* (1999) 46 NSWLR 563.

(a) a return is to be prepared showing the date of creation of the document, a description of the document, the author of the document and reasons for the claim of privilege,

(b) the documents are to be delivered to the Clerk by the date and time required in the resolution of the House and:

(i) made available only to members of the Legislative Council,

(ii) not published or copied without an order of the House.

(6) Any member may, by communication in writing to the Clerk, dispute the validity of the claim of privilege in relation to a particular document or documents. On receipt of such communication, the Clerk is authorised to release the disputed document or documents to an independent legal arbiter, for evaluation and report within seven calendar days as to the validity of the claim.

(7) The independent legal arbiter is to be appointed by the President and must be a Queen's Counsel, a Senior Counsel or a retired Supreme Court Judge.

(8) A report from the independent legal arbiter is to be lodged with the Clerk and:

(a) made available only to members of the House,

(b) not published or copied without an order of the House.

(9) The Clerk is to maintain a register showing the name of any person examining documents tabled under this order.

Auditors-General

As well as financial auditing of government departments and agencies the Auditor-General also has the power to conduct general performance auditing of departments and agencies.

Auditor-General Act 1997 (Cth)

[As at 1 December 2022]

PART 3—THE AUDITOR-GENERAL

7 Auditor-General

(1) There is to be an Auditor-General for the Commonwealth.

(2) Whenever a vacancy occurs in the office of Auditor-General, an appointment must be made to the office as soon as practicable.

8 Independence of the Auditor-General

(1) The Auditor-General is an independent officer of the Parliament.

(2) The functions, powers, rights, immunities and obligations of the Auditor-General are as specified in this Act and other laws of the Commonwealth. There are no implied functions, powers, rights, immunities or obligations arising from the Auditor-General being an independent officer of the Parliament.

(3) The powers of the Parliament to act in relation to the Auditor-General are as specified in or applying under this Act and other laws of the Commonwealth.

For this purpose, ***Parliament*** includes:

(a) each House of the Parliament; and

(b) the members of each House of the Parliament; and

(c) the committees of each House of the Parliament and joint committees of both Houses of the Parliament.

There are no implied powers of the Parliament arising from the Auditor-General being an independent officer of the Parliament.

(4) Subject to this Act and to other laws of the Commonwealth, the Auditor-General has complete discretion in the performance or exercise of his or her functions or powers. In particular, the Auditor-General is not subject to direction from anyone in relation to:

(a) whether or not a particular audit is to be conducted; or

(b) the way in which a particular audit is to be conducted; or

(c) the priority to be given to any particular matter.

PART 4—MAIN FUNCTIONS AND POWERS OF THE AUDITOR-GENERAL

11 Annual financial statements of Commonwealth entities, Commonwealth companies and subsidiaries

The Auditor-General's functions include auditing the:

(a) annual financial statements of Commonwealth entities in accordance with the *Public Governance, Performance and Accountability Act 2013;* and

(b) annual financial statements of Commonwealth companies in accordance with that Act; and

(c) annual financial statements of subsidiaries of corporate Commonwealth entities and Commonwealth companies in accordance with that Act.

DIVISION 2—PERFORMANCE AUDITS

17 Performance audits of Commonwealth entities, Commonwealth companies and subsidiaries

(1) The Auditor-General may at any time conduct a performance audit of:

(a) a Commonwealth entity; or

(b) a Commonwealth company; or

(c) a subsidiary of a corporate Commonwealth entity or a Commonwealth company.

(2) However, the Auditor-General may only conduct such an audit on request by the Joint Committee of Public Accounts and Audit if the audit is of:

(a) a corporate Commonwealth entity that is a GBE [Government Business Enterprise], or of any of its subsidiaries; or

(b) a wholly-owned Commonwealth company that is a GBE, or any of its subsidiaries.

(3) Nothing prevents the Auditor-General from asking the Joint Committee of Public Accounts and Audit to make a particular request under subsection (2).

(4) As soon as practicable after completing the report on an audit under this section, the Auditor-General must:

- (a) cause a copy of the report to be tabled in each House of the Parliament; and
- (b) give a copy of the report to the responsible Minister; and
- (c) give a copy of the report:
  - (i) if the audit is of a Commonwealth entity—to an official who is, or is a member of, the accountable authority of the entity; or
  - (ii) if the audit is of a Commonwealth company—to a director of the company; or
  - (iii) if the audit is of a subsidiary of a corporate Commonwealth entity or Commonwealth company—to a person who is, or is a member of, the governing body of the subsidiary; and
- (d) to the extent that the report relates to the operations of a Commonwealth partner—give a copy of the report to a person who is, or is a member of, the governing body of the Commonwealth partner.

(5) The Auditor-General may give a copy of, or an extract from, the report to any person (including a Minister) who, or any body that, in the Auditor-General's opinion, has a special interest in the report or the content of the extract.

Public Governance, Performance and Accountability Act 2013 (Cth)

[As at 1 December 2022]

CHAPTER 1—INTRODUCTION

DIVISION 2—OBJECTS OF THIS ACT

5 Objects of this Act

The objects of this Act are:

- (a) to establish a coherent system of governance and accountability across Commonwealth entities; and
- (b) to establish a performance framework across Commonwealth entities; and
- (c) to require the Commonwealth and Commonwealth entities:
  - (i) to meet high standards of governance, performance and accountability; and
  - (ii) to provide meaningful information to the Parliament and the public; and
  - (iii) to use and manage public resources properly; and
  - (iv) to work cooperatively with others to achieve common objectives, where practicable; and

(d) to require Commonwealth companies to meet high standards of governance, performance and accountability.

CHAPTER 2—Commonwealth entities and the Commonwealth

12 Accountable authorities

(1) Each Commonwealth entity has an accountable authority.

(2) The following table sets out the person or body that is the *accountable authority* of a Commonwealth entity:

ITEM	ACCOUNTABLE AUTHORITIES	
	If the Commonwealth entity is:	**then the accountable authority of the entity is:**
1	a Department of State	the Secretary of the Department.
2	a Parliamentary Department	the Secretary of the Department.
3	a listed entity	the person or group of persons prescribed by an Act or the rules to be the accountable authority of the entity.
4	a body corporate	the governing body of the entity, unless otherwise prescribed by an Act or the rules.

[Editors' note: a *listed entity* is defined in s 8 as:

(a) any body (except a body corporate), person, group of persons or organisation (whether or not part of a Department of State); or

(b) any combination of bodies (except bodies corporate), persons, groups of persons or organisations (whether or not part of a Department of State);

that is prescribed by an Act or the rules to be a listed entity.]

13 Officials

(1) Each Commonwealth entity has officials.

Officials of Commonwealth entities (other than listed entities)

(2) An ***official*** of a Commonwealth entity (other than a listed entity) is a person who is in, or forms part of, the entity.

(3) Without limiting subsection (2), an ***official*** of a Commonwealth entity (other than a listed entity) includes:

(a) a person who is, or is a member of, the accountable authority of the entity; or

(b) a person who is an officer, employee or member of the entity; or

(c) a person, or a person in a class, prescribed by an Act or the rules to be an official of the entity.

(4) Despite subsections (2) and (3), each of the following is not an *official* of a Commonwealth entity (other than a listed entity):

(a) a Minister;

(b) a judge;

- (c) a consultant or independent contractor of the entity (other than a consultant or independent contractor of a kind prescribed by an Act or the rules for the purposes of paragraph (3)(c));
- (d) a person, or a person in a class, prescribed by an Act or the rules not to be an official of the entity.

Officials of listed entities

(5) An ***official*** of a Commonwealth entity that is a listed entity is a person who is prescribed by an Act or the rules to be an official of the entity.

PART 2-2—ACCOUNTABLE AUTHORITIES AND OFFICIALS

DIVISION 2—ACCOUNTABLE AUTHORITIES

15 Duty to govern the Commonwealth entity

(1) The accountable authority of a Commonwealth entity must govern the entity in a way that:

- (a) promotes the proper use and management of public resources for which the authority is responsible; and
- (b) promotes the achievement of the purposes of the entity; and
- (c) promotes the financial sustainability of the entity.

(2) In making decisions for the purposes of subsection (1), the accountable authority must take into account the effect of those decisions on public resources generally.

16 Duty to establish and maintain systems relating to risk and control

The accountable authority of a Commonwealth entity must establish and maintain:

- (a) an appropriate system of risk oversight and management for the entity; and
- (b) an appropriate system of internal control for the entity;

including by implementing measures directed at ensuring officials of the entity comply with the finance law.

17 Duty to encourage cooperation with others

The accountable authority of a Commonwealth entity must encourage officials of the entity to cooperate with others to achieve common objectives, where practicable.

18 Duty in relation to requirements imposed on others

When imposing requirements on others in relation to the use or management of public resources for which the accountable authority of a Commonwealth entity is responsible, the accountable authority must take into account:

- (a) the risks associated with that use or management; and
- (b) the effects of imposing those requirements.

19 Duty to keep responsible Minister and Finance Minister informed

(1) The accountable authority of a Commonwealth entity must do the following:

- (a) keep the responsible Minister informed of the activities of the entity and any subsidiaries of the entity;

(b) give the responsible Minister or the Finance Minister any reports, documents and information in relation to those activities as that Minister requires;

(c) notify the responsible Minister as soon as practicable after the accountable authority makes a significant decision in relation to the entity or any of its subsidiaries;

(d) give the responsible Minister reasonable notice if the accountable authority becomes aware of any significant issue that may affect the entity or any of its subsidiaries;

(e) notify the responsible Minister as soon as practicable after the accountable authority becomes aware of any significant issue that has affected the entity or any of its subsidiaries.

...

21 Non-corporate Commonwealth entities

The accountable authority of a non-corporate Commonwealth entity must govern the entity in accordance with paragraph 15(1)(a) in a way that is not inconsistent with the policies of the Australian Government.

DIVISION 3—OFFICIALS

25 Duty of care and diligence

(1) An official of a Commonwealth entity must exercise his or her powers, perform his or her functions and discharge his or her duties with the degree of care and diligence that a reasonable person would exercise if the person:

(a) were an official of a Commonwealth entity in the Commonwealth entity's circumstances; and

(b) occupied the position held by, and had the same responsibilities within the Commonwealth entity as, the official.

...

26 Duty to act honestly, in good faith and for a proper purpose

An official of a Commonwealth entity must exercise his or her powers, perform his or her functions and discharge his or her duties honestly, in good faith and for a proper purpose.

27 Duty in relation to use of position

An official of a Commonwealth entity must not improperly use his or her position:

(a) to gain, or seek to gain, a benefit or an advantage for himself or herself or any other person; or

(b) to cause, or seek to cause, detriment to the entity, the Commonwealth or any other person.

28 Duty in relation to use of information

A person who obtains information because they are an official of a Commonwealth entity must not improperly use the information:

(a) to gain, or seek to gain, a benefit or an advantage for himself or herself or any other person; or

(b) to cause, or seek to cause, detriment to the Commonwealth entity, the Commonwealth or any other person.

29 Duty to disclose interests

(1) An official of a Commonwealth entity who has a material personal interest that relates to the affairs of the entity must disclose details of the interest.

...

PART 2-3—PLANNING, PERFORMANCE AND ACCOUNTABILITY

DIVISION 3—PERFORMANCE OF COMMONWEALTH ENTITIES

40 Audit of annual performance statements for Commonwealth entities

(1) The responsible Minister for a Commonwealth entity or the Finance Minister (the ***requesting Minister***) may request the Auditor-General to examine and report on the entity's annual performance statements.

Note: The Auditor-General may at any time conduct a performance audit of a Commonwealth entity: see Division 2 of Part 4 of the *Auditor-General Act 1997.*

(2) If, under a request under subsection (1), the Auditor-General examines and reports on the entity's annual performance statements, the Auditor-General must give a copy of the report to the requesting Minister.

(3) The requesting Minister must cause a copy of the Auditor-General's report to be tabled in each House of the Parliament as soon as practicable after receipt. The copy that is tabled must be accompanied by a copy of the entity's annual performance statements.

Auditor-General Performance Audit, *Offshore Processing Centres in Nauru and Papua New Guinea: Contract Management of Garrison Support and Welfare Services* (ANAO Report No 32 2016–17, 17 January 2017)

[Editors' note: In 2016, the Auditor-General conducted a performance audit to assess whether the Department of Immigration and Border Protection had appropriately established and managed the contracts for services provided by private companies at offshore processing centres in Nauru and Papua New Guinea.]

1 BACKGROUND

Introduction

21 [1.1] On 28 June 2012 the Prime Minister and Minister for Immigration and Citizenship announced that an expert panel would provide a report on the best way forward to prevent asylum seekers risking their lives on boat journeys to Australia. The expert panel's report, released on 13 August 2012, included a range of disincentives, including the establishment of offshore processing centres in the Republic of Nauru (Nauru) and Papua New Guinea (PNG).

[1.2] The centres were subsequently established with the agreement of the Nauruan and PNG Governments. The Australian Government was to bear all costs associated with the construction and operation of the centres. Transfers of asylum seekers to Nauru commenced on 14 September 2012 and to PNG on Manus Island on 21 November 2012.

[1.3] To underpin operations at the centres, the Department of Immigration and Border Protection (DIBP or the department) entered into contractual arrangements for the delivery of garrison support and/or welfare services. These services are essential to the operation of the offshore processing centres. Garrison support includes security, cleaning and catering services. Welfare services include individualised care to maintain health and well-being such as recreational and educational activities.

[1.4] The number of asylum seekers held in offshore processing centres has varied over time, as has each centre's demographic profile. In August 2013 Manus Island became a single adult male facility when the women and children held on Manus Island were transferred to Nauru. At its peak there were 300 women held and 208 children held in Nauru. As at 31 August 2016 there was a total of 1233 people housed in the offshore processing centres. In Nauru there were 410 asylum seekers made up of 306 men, 55 women and 49 children. On Manus Island there were 823 men.

...

Garrison Support and Welfare Service Contracts

22 [1.5] The department has engaged four contractors to deliver garrison support and welfare services in Nauru and on Manus Island. The total combined value of the contracts, as reported on AusTender, was $3,386 million at 6 December 2016 ...

Commonwealth procurement and contracting

26 [1.8] The Australian Government is a significant purchaser of goods and services and has in place resource management legislation and related policies that establish the framework for procurement. The Commonwealth Procurement Rules (CPRs) state that:

> *Procurement* encompasses the whole process of procuring *goods* and services. It begins when a need has been identified and a decision has been made on the procurement requirement. *Procurement* continues through the processes of risk assessment, seeking and evaluating alternative solutions, the awarding of a *contract*, the delivery of and payment for the *goods* and services and, where relevant, the ongoing management of the *contract* and consideration of disposal of *goods*.

[1.9] Achieving value for money is the core rule of the CPRs. Effective contract management requires a focus, in all contracting decisions and actions, on the outcomes that entities are seeking to achieve and cost-effective delivery approaches. In practical terms, value for money is achieved where contractors deliver all goods and services procured to the standard required and at the agreed price. Effective contract management also requires an active focus on the management of risks throughout the life of a contract. The CPRs:

... enable entities to design procurement processes that are robust and transparent while permitting innovative solutions that reflect the scale, scope and risk of the desired outcome.

27 [1.10] The *Public Governance, Performance and Accountability Act 2013* (PGPA Act) requires entities to promote the proper use and management of public resources. Entities determine their own contract management practices, consistent with the PGPA Act, through Accountable Authority Instructions (AAIs) and, if appropriate, supporting operational guidelines. Central procurement units (CPUs) and other advisers may also provide specific expertise and advice to entity officials undertaking procurement processes, including contract management.

[1.11] During the period covered by this audit, DIBP's Secretary issued a number of AAIs and supplementary guidance updating departmental requirements on matters such as delegations, contract management and making payments. The department's CPU also issued several updates to the contract management manual. The manual identified a range of key issues to be addressed in contract management including: provisions, terms and conditions which address legal and policy requirements; a clear statement of work; establishing a performance management regime; and planning for transition in and transition out. The manual also identified key tasks such as reviewing and updating risks, agreeing roles and responsibilities, arranging appropriate delegations and approvals, and setting up record keeping arrangements.

...

Audit approach

28 [1.14] The objective of the audit was to assess whether DIBP had appropriately established and managed the contracts for garrison support and welfare services at offshore processing centres in Nauru and Papua New Guinea (Manus Island); and whether the processes adopted met the requirements of the Commonwealth Procurement Rules (CPRs) including consideration and achievement of value for money.

[1.15] The audit examined contracts entered into in 2012, when the arrangements were first put into place, through to the current contract which is due to expire in October 2017.

...

Audit methodology

[1.17] The ANAO [Australian National Audit Office] reviewed DIBP and service provider records; and interviewed relevant DIBP officers and stakeholders including service providers, tenderers and government officials from Nauru and Papua New Guinea. The audit team also visited the centres in Nauru and on Manus Island during August and September 2015. Fieldwork was conducted between March 2015 and October 2016.

SUMMARY AND RECOMMENDATIONS

...

8 [7] This is a companion audit to ANAO Performance Audit Report No 16 2016–17, *Offshore Processing Centres in Nauru and Papua New Guinea: Procurement of Garrison Support and Welfare Services.* As in the earlier audit, the ANAO's review of departmental records was, due to shortcomings in DIBP's record keeping system, based on the available records. DIBP was not able to provide the ANAO with assurance that it provided all departmental records relevant to the audit.

CONCLUSION

[8] The Department of Immigration and Border Protection's management of the garrison support and welfare services contracts at the offshore processing centres in Nauru and Papua New Guinea (Manus Island) has fallen well short of effective contract management practice.

[9] The garrison support and welfare contracts were established in circumstances of great haste to give effect to government policy decisions and the department did not have a detailed view of what it wanted to purchase or the standards to apply. These are key considerations in achieving value for money. While the department took between 20 to 43 weeks (depending on the contract) to enter into final 2013 contracts, there remained significant shortcomings in the contractual framework. Many of the shortcomings persisted in the 2014 contracts, indicating that the 2014 contract consolidation process was not informed by lessons learned from the department's management and operation of the 2013 contracts.

[10] The department did not put in place effective mechanisms to manage the contracts. Other than the contracts, there was no documentation of the means by which the contract objectives would be achieved. In the absence of a plan, assurance processes such as the inspection and audit of services delivered, has not occurred in a systematic way and risks were not effectively managed. In addition, the department has not maintained appropriate records of decisions and actions taken in the course of its contract management. As a consequence, the department has not been well placed to assess whether its service strategies were adequate or fully met government objectives.

[11] The department developed a comprehensive and risk based performance framework for the contracts to help it assess provider performance. However, development of the framework was delayed and in applying the framework the department was not consistent in its treatment of different providers. Performance measurement under the framework relied heavily on ***9*** self-assessments by providers and the department performed limited independent checks. Delays in the department's review of self-assessments and the provision of feedback on contractor performance eroded the link between actual performance and contract payments. Risk assessment was a key component of the performance reporting processes and while risk assessments were conducted, DIBP did not review risk ratings or

determine if controls and mitigations were in place and working. Risks materialised in both the 2013 and 2014 contracts.

[12] An appropriate framework of controls was in place for payments under the contracts, including the authorisation of actual payments by a delegate. This control was intended to provide additional assurance over payments under the contracts but did not always operate as intended. In respect to $2.3 billion in payments made between September 2012 and April 2016, delegate authorisations were not always secured or recorded: an appropriate delegate provided an authorisation for payments totalling $80 million; $1.1 billion was approved by DIBP officers who did not have the required authorisation; and for the remaining $1.1 billion there was no departmental record of who authorised the payments.

[13] In addition, this audit highlighted further weaknesses in the department's management of procurement. Substantial contract variations totalling over $1 billion were made without a documented assessment of value for money.

[14] Contract management is core business for Australian Government entities, and the department has managed detention contracts since 1997. Previous ANAO audits of the department's contract management have found that: its contracting framework had not established clear expectations of the level and quality of services to be delivered; and its ability to monitor the performance of contractors was compromised by a lack of clarity in standards and performance measures and reliance on incident reporting to determine when standards were not being met. This audit has identified a recurrence of these (and other) deficiencies, which have resulted in higher than necessary expense for taxpayers and significant reputational risks for the Australian Government and the department. The audit recommendations are intended to address the significant weaknesses observed in DIBP's contract management practices.

...

[Citations omitted]

Ombudsmen

Ombudsman Act 1976 (Cth)

[As at 1 December 2022]

4 Establishment of offices of Ombudsman and Deputy Ombudsman

(1) For the purposes of this Act, there shall be:

(a) a Commonwealth Ombudsman; and

(b) at least one, and not more than 3, Deputy Commonwealth Ombudsmen.

(2) The functions of the Commonwealth Ombudsman are to investigate complaints made to him or her under this Act and to perform such other functions as are conferred on him or her by:

(a) this Act or the regulations; or

(b) another Act or regulations made under another Act; or

(c) an ACT enactment or regulations made under an ACT enactment.

(3) The Commonwealth Ombudsman, in performing his or her functions in relation to immigration (including immigration detention), may, if he or she so chooses, be called the Immigration Ombudsman.

(4) The Commonwealth Ombudsman, in performing his or her functions in relation to the Australian Federal Police, may, if he or she so chooses, be called the Law Enforcement Ombudsman.

....

5 Functions of Ombudsman

(1) Subject to this Act, the Ombudsman:

(a) shall investigate action, being action that relates to a matter of administration, taken either before or after the commencement of this Act by a Department, or by a prescribed authority, and in respect of which a complaint has been made to the Ombudsman; and

(b) may, of his or her own motion, investigate any action, being action that relates to a matter of administration, taken either before or after the commencement of this Act by a Department or by a prescribed authority; and

(c) with the consent of the Minister, may enter into an arrangement under which the Ombudsman will perform functions of an ombudsman under an ombudsman scheme established in accordance with the conditions of licences or authorities granted under an enactment.

(2) The Ombudsman is not authorized to investigate:

(a) action taken by a Minister; or

(aa) action that constitutes proceedings in Parliament for the purposes of section 16 of the *Parliamentary Privileges Act 1987*; or

(b) action taken by a Justice or Judge of a court created by the Parliament; or

(ba) action by chief executive officer, in relation to a court, or by a person who, for the purposes of this Act, is to be taken to be a member of the staff of a court:

(i) when exercising a power of the court; or

(ii) when performing a function, or exercising a power, of a judicial nature; or

(c) action taken by:

(i) a magistrate or coroner for the Australian Capital Territory, Norfolk Island, the Territory of Christmas Island or the Territory of Cocos (Keeling) Islands; or

(ii) a person who holds office as a magistrate in a State or the Northern Territory in the performance of the functions of a magistrate conferred on him or her by or under an Act; or

(d) action taken by any body or person with respect to persons employed in the Australian Public Service or the service of a prescribed authority, being action taken in relation to that employment, including action taken with respect to the promotion, termination of appointment or discipline of a person so employed or the payment of remuneration to such a person; or

(g) action taken by a Department or by a prescribed authority with respect to the appointment of a person to an office or position established by or under an enactment, not being an office or position in the Australian Public Service or an office in the service of a prescribed authority.

...

8 Investigations

Ombudsman must inform of investigation

(1) The Ombudsman shall, before commencing an investigation under this Act of action taken by a Department or by a prescribed authority, inform the principal officer of the Department or of the authority that the action is to be investigated.

(1A) The Ombudsman may from time to time make with the principal officer of a Department or of a prescribed authority an arrangement with respect to the manner in which, and the period within which, the Ombudsman is to inform that principal officer that he or she proposes to investigate action taken by the Department or authority, being action included in a class or classes of actions specified in the arrangement.

Investigation to be in private

(2) An investigation under this Act shall be conducted in private and, subject to this Act, in such manner as the Ombudsman thinks fit.

....

Ombudsman may obtain information

(3) Subject to this Act, the Ombudsman may, for the purposes of this Act, obtain information from such persons, and make such inquiries, as he or she thinks fit.

Rights to appear

(4) Subject to subsection (5), it is not necessary for the complainant or any other person to be afforded an opportunity to appear before the Ombudsman or any other person in connexion with an investigation by the Ombudsman under this Act.

(5) The Ombudsman shall not make a report in respect of an investigation under this Act in which he or she sets out opinions that are, either expressly or impliedly, critical of a Department, prescribed authority or person unless, before completing the investigation, he or she has:

(a) if the opinions relate to a Department or prescribed authority—afforded the principal officer of the Department or authority and the officer principally concerned in the action to which the investigation relates opportunities to appear before him or her, or before an authorized person, and to make such submissions, either orally or in writing, in relation to that action as they think fit; and

(b) if the opinions relate to a person—afforded that person an opportunity to appear before him or her, or before an authorized person, and to make such submissions, either orally or in writing, in relation to the action to which the investigation relates as he or she thinks fit.

....

Breaches of duty etc.

(10) Where the Ombudsman forms the opinion, either before or after completing an investigation under this Act, that there is evidence that a person, being an officer of a Department or of a prescribed authority, has been guilty of a breach of duty or of misconduct and that the evidence is, in all the circumstances, of sufficient force to justify his or her doing so, the Ombudsman shall bring the evidence to the notice of:

(a) if the person is the Secretary of the Department—the Minister administering the Department; or

(b) if the person is an officer of a Department but not the Secretary of that Department—the Secretary of that Department;

...

15 Reports by Ombudsman

(1) Where, after an investigation under this Act into action taken by a Department or prescribed authority has been completed, the Ombudsman is of the opinion:

(a) that the action:

(i) appears to have been contrary to law;

(ii) was unreasonable, unjust, oppressive or improperly discriminatory;

(iii) was in accordance with a rule of law, a provision of an enactment or a practice but the rule, provision or practice is or may be unreasonable, unjust, oppressive or improperly discriminatory;

(iv) was based either wholly or partly on a mistake of law or of fact; or

(v) was otherwise, in all the circumstances, wrong;

(b) that, in the course of the taking of the action, a discretionary power had been exercised for an improper purpose or on irrelevant grounds; or

(c) in a case where the action comprised or included a decision to exercise a discretionary power in a particular manner or to refuse to exercise such a power:

(i) that irrelevant considerations were taken into account, or that there was a failure to take relevant considerations into account, in the course of reaching the decision to exercise the power in that manner or to refuse to exercise the power, as the case may be; or

(ii) that the complainant in respect of the investigation or some other person should have been furnished, but was not furnished, with particulars of the reasons for deciding to exercise the power in that manner or to refuse to exercise the power, as the case may be;

this section applies to the decision, recommendation, act or omission constituting that action.

(2) Where the Ombudsman is of the opinion:

(a) that a decision, recommendation, act or omission to which this section applies should be referred to the appropriate authority for further consideration;

(b) that some particular action could be, and should be, taken to rectify, mitigate or alter the effects of, a decision, recommendation, act or omission to which this section applies;

(c) that a decision to which this section applies should be cancelled or varied;

(d) that a rule of law, provision of an enactment or practice on which a decision, recommendation, act or omission to which this section applies was based should be altered;

(e) that reasons should have been, but were not, given for a decision to which this section applies; or

(f) that any other thing should be done in relation to a decision, recommendation, act or omission to which this section applies;

the Ombudsman shall report accordingly to the Department or prescribed authority concerned.

(3) The Ombudsman:

(a) shall include in a report under subsection (2) his or her reasons for the opinions specified in the report; and

(b) may also include in such a report any recommendations he or she thinks fit to make.

(4) The Ombudsman may request the Department or prescribed authority to which the report is furnished to furnish to him or her, within a specified time, particulars of any action that it proposes to take with respect to the matters and recommendations included in the report.

(5) Where the Ombudsman reports under subsection (2) to a Department or prescribed authority, the Department or authority may furnish to the Ombudsman such comments concerning the report as it wishes to make.

(6) The Ombudsman shall furnish a copy of a report made by him or her under subsection to the Minister concerned.

16 Reports where appropriate action not taken on Ombudsman's report

(1) Where action that is, in the opinion of the Ombudsman, adequate and appropriate in the circumstances is not taken with respect to the matters and recommendations included in a report to a Department or to a prescribed authority under section 15 within a reasonable time after the Ombudsman furnished the report to the Department or to the prescribed authority, the Ombudsman may inform the Prime Minister accordingly in writing.

(2) Where the Ombudsman furnishes information to the Prime Minister in accordance with subsection (1) in relation to a report, the Ombudsman shall furnish to the Prime Minister with the information:

- (a) if a copy of the report has not previously been forwarded to the Prime Minister under subsection 15(6)—a copy of the report; and
- (b) if the Department or prescribed authority to which the report was made has furnished comments concerning the report to the Ombudsman—a copy of those comments.

(3) In considering whether to furnish information in relation to a report to the Prime Minister in accordance with subsection (1), the Ombudsman shall have regard to any comments furnished to him or her by the Department or prescribed authority to which the report was made.

...

17 Special reports to Parliament

Where the Ombudsman has acted under subsection 16(1) in relation to a report concerning an investigation made by him or her, the Ombudsman may also forward to the President of the Senate and the Speaker of the House of Representatives, for presentation to the Senate and the House of Representatives, respectively, copies of a report prepared by him or her concerning the investigation for presentation to both Houses of the Parliament, being a report that sets out a copy of any comments furnished to the Ombudsman under subsection 15(5) by the Department or prescribed authority concerned.

Chairperson, Aboriginal and Torres Strait Islander Commission v Commonwealth Ombudsman (1995) 63 FCR 163

Facts

The Commonwealth Ombudsman investigated a complaint made by New Burnt Bridge Aboriginal Corporation ('NBBAC') about the Aboriginal and Torres Strait Islander Commission ('ATSIC') and two of the Commission's senior managers concerning procurement and funding of consultants for an Aboriginal housing project. The Ombudsman prepared a draft report that criticised ATSIC and the managers. After receiving submissions from ATSIC, the Ombudsman's final report remained critical and recommended disciplinary proceedings. The Chairperson of ATSIC applied to the Federal Court for judicial review of the Ombudsman's investigation and report on the basis that the Ombudsman did not have the power to report findings of guilt or make disciplinary recommendations. ATSIC also argued that the Ombudsman had failed to provide adequate reasons and failed to accord procedural fairness.

The following extracts consider the powers and duties of the Ombudsman, including whether the statute could be interpreted to imply that the Ombudsman had the power to make 'findings'. Einfeld J held that the Ombudsman did not have the power to make definitive findings of guilt of an individual, but did have the express power to report her opinions, including disciplinary recommendations. In this case, in all but a few instances, the Ombudsman had lawfully expressed her opinions.

Einfeld J

2.3 Publication of the report

168 The Ombudsman has no power to put her recommendations into action, or compel any action on the part of the relevant individual, department or authority. However, there are at her disposal a number of quite persuasive mechanisms to gain the desired results, including the option to make public various aspects of the investigation.

...

3.2 The attack on the report

171 The applicant submitted that the report was ultra vires on a number of grounds. Firstly, it was said to contain findings that certain individuals were or may have been guilty of a criminal or disciplinary offence when the Ombudsman is not authorised to make such findings. Secondly, the applicant submitted that the report may not contain disciplinary recommendations. Thirdly, it was alleged that elements of procedural fairness were not adequately complied with. Finally, certain reasons provided by the Ombudsman in accordance with s 15(3) were said to be insufficient.

4 REPORTING ADVERSELY

Insinuations of personal culpability by a major public investigative body carry great stigma and have the potential to do serious harm to reputations. Given the nature of the claims and the forum in which they are being made ***172*** here, such reputations may never have the opportunity of being vindicated at a trial. Additionally it is not at all unlikely that such conclusions could interfere with any disciplinary process.

4.1 Findings of individual guilt

The applicant said that because of the intention that the report become public, any findings of unlawfulness or administrative misconduct could cause reputations to suffer in circumstances where the protection mechanisms and avenues of redress of the court system are not available.

[Editors' note: Einfeld J considered the common law duty of procedural fairness.]

...

4.1.2 Statutory construction

In the present case the central question is somewhat different. Rather than a question of the nature and extent of the general requirements of procedural fairness, it concerns, first, whether or not the powers of the Ombudsman extend to making findings of individual guilt and, then, whether or not the demands of procedural fairness outlined by the Act were followed.

[Editors' note: Einfeld J rejected the applicants' argument, based upon an alleged clash between two statutory provisions, that once the Ombudsman formed the opinion that there was evidence of a breach of duty or of misconduct and brought that to the attention of the relevant authority, the Ombudsman could make no further use of that information in the report.]

...

4.1.3 Implied power

174 The applicant's second argument for excluding findings of guilt was broader in that it relied on one of the fundamental principles of protection of common law rights - if the statute does not expressly provide for the Ombudsman to report findings, then a power to do so should not be read in.

Nowhere in the *Ombudsman Act* is there an express power to make 'findings', the legislature having several times specifically employed the word 'opinion'. Furthermore, the fact that the Ombudsman's principal function is investigative and not determinative suggests that she does not need and is not intended to make findings. This intention of the legislature may also be gleaned ***175*** from the Second Reading Speech on the legislation [Australia, House of Representatives, *Debates,* 29th Parliament, 1st session, 2nd period, pp 1184, 1185]:

> The existing methods of checking deficiencies in administration are many and varied ... The duties of the Minister of the Crown are such that he cannot effectively exercise responsibility for all the many activities of departments under his administration. For these reasons the existing remedies need to be supplemented by an institution for investigating complaints which is independent and thorough, which can go behind the screen hiding the department or authority from the citizen. The Ombudsman will be able to go behind that screen and report on what he finds.

I do not ascribe a special meaning to the last of those words. In the context, what the Ombudsman 'finds' was used loosely and did not intend to convey 'findings' in the legal sense. The Attorney-General (The Hon K E Enderby QC) further told Parliament:

> The Ombudsman will not be confined to making a report. He will be able to exercise a personal influence with departments and authorities and he will have the status to do that. In the grievance field he can act as a conciliator, and he can make suggestions to departments in an informal way.

The intention is that the Ombudsman investigate, report and make suggestions, not make determinations on the issues identified. I believe that the power to make findings in that sense should not be read into this statute.

4.2 Difference between 'findings' and 'opinions'

On one view 'opinions' are 'findings'. The applicant submitted that a 'finding' is a conclusion that someone 'has' committed a wrong, whereas an 'opinion' is a conclusion that someone 'may have' or 'appears to have' committed a wrong. It was also said that in common legal parlance, the word 'findings' is often linked with facts and 'opinions' with law. But such formulae cannot be the guidepost - juries and judges sitting without juries regularly make 'findings' for or against litigants which are statements of both law and fact. Perhaps to some extent the words take their character from the office and powers of the speaker. A first instance or trial judge setting out opinions is in substance making findings, whatever the nomenclature. On the other hand, the administrative nature of the office of Ombudsman and the statutory prescription of her duties preclude her from making findings in any final sense, to the extent that what she purports to do is in fact to express opinions, highly regarded and often far-reaching opinions certainly, but opinions nonetheless.

The greatest risk to the two individuals concerned here, presumably the reason this case is before the Court, is the risk to their reputations from the Ombudsman's public produce. It was therefore submitted that a statement dressed up as a 'finding' may carry more risk of damage to the individual than the expression of the same statement couched as an 'opinion'. But semantics cannot solve this problem. Whatever the ruminations of lawyers, the interested public may not understand the legal differences between an 'opinion' and a 'finding' and who has the power to make which. It is sufficient to say that the Ombudsman is empowered to report her opinions, which includes the reasons for the opinions. The opinions will ordinarily state ***176*** that if the evidence upon which they are based is accepted, certain stated conclusions will or may be seen to follow.

That formulation of the Ombudsman's charter is not intended to consign her to prefacing every sentence with the words 'In my view' or the like. Perhaps a bold and obvious disclaimer at the beginning of each of her reports, with a direction that they not be reproduced without the disclaimer, would assist. But even this course will only be satisfactory if the Ombudsman is in truth reporting her opinions and is not seeking to dress up as opinions what are in substance findings.

4.3 Opinions of individual guilt

I have concluded that the Ombudsman may not report findings of individual guilt. What of opinions?

...

The provision in s 8(5) of the Act that reports containing adverse opinions may not be made 'unless' the procedural fairness guidelines are followed does not mean that the Ombudsman may not report opinions that are critical of an individual. In fact the subsection clearly infers that she may. Whilst there are many opinions critical of a person that stop short of suggesting the guilt of an offence, it was expressly contemplated that both implied and express criticisms would be made. Given the difficulty of defining the differences between 'opinions' and 'findings', it seems clear that the legislature intended not to fetter the range of opinions open to the Ombudsman. Moreover, the Act balances the protection of the reputation of the individuals concerned through the entitlement to procedural fairness against the obvious public importance of ***177*** investigating misconduct and unlawfulness in the public sector and the Ombudsman's statutory duty to report her opinions on such investigations accompanied by reasons. Accordingly, it is my opinion that the Ombudsman may report opinions touching individual guilt.

4.4 Summary of conclusions

(a) The Act does not empower the Ombudsman to make definitive findings of guilt of an individual and this power should not be implied.

(b) The Ombudsman is expressly empowered to report her opinions on action that should be taken to deal with the matters revealed by her investigations. The reasons for these opinions, which must be supplied, may include opinions on what the evidentiary material appeared or might be found to disclose.

(c) In that sense properly reasoned opinions on the issue of individual guilt may be reported. Similarly reasoned recommendations may be made.

King v Ombudsman (2020) 137 SASR 18

Ombudsman Act 1972 (SA)

[As at relevant date]

18 Procedure on investigations

(1) Notwithstanding any other provision of this Part, the Ombudsman may make a preliminary investigation of an administrative act to determine whether to proceed with a full investigation of that act.

(1a) The Ombudsman must, before proceeding with a full investigation of an administrative act, inform the principal officer of the relevant agency of the decision to proceed with such an investigation.

(2) Every investigation under this Act must be conducted in private.

(3) The Ombudsman—

  (a) is not required to hold a hearing for the purposes of an investigation;

  (b) may obtain information from such persons and in such manner as the Ombudsman thinks fit;

  (c) may determine whether any person to whom an investigation relates may have legal or other representation.

(4) Before making a report affecting an agency to which this Act applies the Ombudsman must allow the principal officer of the agency a reasonable opportunity to comment on the subject matter of the report.

(5) The Ombudsman must report any evidence of breach of duty or misconduct on the part of a member, officer or employee of an agency to which this Act applies to the principal officer of the agency.

(6) Subject to this Act, the procedure to be adopted in relation to an investigation will be as determined by the Ombudsman.

...

25 Proceedings on the completion of an investigation

...

(2) In the case of an investigation to which this section applies in which the Ombudsman is of the opinion—

- (a) that the subject matter of the investigation should be referred back to the appropriate agency for further consideration; or
- (b) that action can be, and should be, taken to rectify, or mitigate or alter the effects of, the administrative act to which the investigation related; or
- (c) that the practice in accordance with which the administrative act was done should be varied; or
- (d) that any law in accordance with which or on the basis of which the action was taken should be amended or repealed; or
- (e) that the reason for any administrative act should be given; or
- (f) that any other steps should be taken,

the Ombudsman must report that opinion and the reasons for it to the principal officer of the relevant agency and may make such recommendations as the Ombudsman thinks fit.

(3) The Ombudsman must send a copy of any report or recommendation made under subsection (2) to the responsible Minister and, in the case of a report or recommendation relating to the sheriff, to the State Courts Administration Council.

(4) The principal officer of an agency in relation to which a recommendation is made under subsection (2) must, at the request of the Ombudsman, report to the Ombudsman within a time allowed in the request on what steps have been taken to give effect to the recommendation and, if no such steps have been taken, the reason for the inaction.

(5) If it appears to the Ombudsman that appropriate steps have not been taken to give effect to a recommendation made under this section, the Ombudsman may make a report on the matter (containing a copy of the earlier report and the recommendation) to the Premier.

(6) Where the Ombudsman reports to the Premier under subsection (5), the Ombudsman may forward copies of the report to the Speaker of the House of

Assembly and the President of the Legislative Council with a request that they be laid before their respective Houses.

...

28 Determination of the Ombudsman's jurisdiction

Where—

(a) an investigation has been commenced or is proposed under this Act; and

(b) a question arises as to whether the Ombudsman has jurisdiction to conduct the investigation,

the Supreme Court may, on the application of the Ombudsman, an agency to which this Act applies or the principal officer of such an agency, determine the question and make any orders necessary to give effect to the determination.

Facts

The case concerned judicial review proceedings commenced by Mr King in his capacity as General Manager of the Anangu Pitjantjatjara Yankunytjatjara (APY). The APY is a body corporate established by the *Anangu Pitjantjatjara Yankunytjatjara Land Rights Act 1981* (SA) and is an agency under the *Ombudsman Act 1972* (SA). The Ombudsman had investigated Mr King in response to complaints made by the then Chairperson of the APY Executive Board. The Ombudsman had reported on one concluded investigation in 2016 and a further investigation was being considered. At first instance, Kelly J found that the Ombudsman had made no jurisdictional errors and dismissed the judicial review proceedings.[3] The Full Court of the South Australian Supreme Court (Doyle J, Parker J and Tilmouth AJ) dismissed the appeal. Justice Doyle discussed the amenability of the Ombudsman's reporting function to judicial review in the following passages.

Doyle J

*** 51*** *Amenability of Ombudsman's reporting function to judicial review*

[140] Having considered the statutory framework for the exercise of the Ombudsman's functions and powers, and having surveyed the relevant authorities, it is my view that relief in the nature of certiorari will not ordinarily be available to quash an Ombudsman's report. I consider that the nature of the reporting power, and in particular the absence of any direct legal consequence flowing from its exercise, will ordinarily be fatal to the availability of that form of relief. However, I do not think that it follows that there are no constraints upon the Ombudsman's powers to investigate and report that might warrant judicial intervention.

[141] Judicial intervention will be available in circumstances where the Ombudsman does not have jurisdiction to conduct the relevant investigation (for example, pursuant to the Court's jurisdiction under s 28 of the Ombudsman Act), or where the Ombudsman has acted in excess of his coercive powers during the conduct of the investigation. Intervention in such circumstances might result in declaratory or injunctive relief, or perhaps relief in the nature of prohibition.

3 *King v Ombudsman* [2019] SASC 107.

[142] Further, given the potentially significant practical and reputational consequences of reports of the type contemplated by s 25(2) … I consider that the formation and expression of at least those opinions contemplated by [the relevant statutory provisions] will be conditioned by the usual implied constraints. Parliament has expressly made the power to report under s 25(2) subject to the provision of a level of procedural fairness through the obligation to provide an opportunity for comment under s 18(4), and subject to an obligation to provide reasons under s 25(2). There being no exclusion by plain words of necessary intendment, I see no reason why the conferral of power to report in accordance with s 25(2) … should not also be conditioned by the usual implied constraints upon lawful administrative decision-making and ***52*** action. Relevantly for the purposes of the present case, that would include a requirement that the opinions be based upon relevant considerations, and not be legally unreasonable.

[143] That said, given the broad and general terms in which the matters set out in [the relevant statutory provisions] are expressed, and the absence of any expressly mandated relevant considerations, as a matter of practical reality there may be only limited scope for judicial intervention. Further, given the general unavailability of certiorari to quash an Ombudsman's report, the relief that will be available in respect of jurisdictional error in the formation of opinions contained in a report will likely be confined to declaratory relief.

[144] Returning to my view as to the general unavailability of certiorari, I have relied in this respect upon a combination of the features of the Ombudsman's functions, and the statutory scheme within which they exist, as detailed in the preceding section of these reasons. By way of general summary, I have relied upon the nature of the Ombudsman's investigation and reporting functions; the political context in which these functions are exercised; the fact that they exist for the purpose of investigation, recommendation and persuasion, rather than determination or adjudication; and the fact that reports under s 25(2) do not directly affect the rights of the agencies or persons the subject of the investigation and report.

[145] As to the last of these matters, I do not think a report prepared by the Ombudsman (or the opinions or recommendations contained therein) is properly characterised as a precondition to a course of action, or a step in a process, capable of altering rights or interests in the sense contemplated by *Ainsworth v Criminal Justice Commission* or *Hot Holdings Pty Ltd v Creasy*. It is true that a report from the Ombudsman is required to be provided to both the principal officer of the relevant agency (s 25(2)), and the responsible Minister (s 25(3)). And, as such, there will often be a realistic prospect that some action may follow which may affect a person's rights or interests. This prospect is enhanced by the obligation upon the principal officer to report back to the Ombudsman as to what steps have been taken to give effect to the Ombudsman's recommendations (s 25(4)), and the Ombudsman's power to then refer the matter to the Premier and have it laid before Parliament in the event that appropriate steps have not been taken (s 25(5) and (6)).

[146] However, consistently with the views expressed by the Court in *Kaldas v Barbour*, I do not consider that this supports a conclusion any higher than that as a result of the contents of a report, the principal officer of the relevant agency or the responsible Minister may take some (unidentified) action which may affect the legal rights of an agency or person. On the authorities, this would not be enough for certiorari to lie to quash the report. It would not give the report, or the opinions and recommendations contained therein, a sufficient status to enliven the discretion to grant relief in the nature of certiorari.

...

53 [148] However, even assuming certiorari will not ordinarily lie to quash an Ombudsman's report, it does not follow that the Ombudsman's power to investigate, and then form opinions, make recommendations and provide a report under s 25(2) are immune from judicial review. As recognised by the High Court in *Ainsworth v Criminal Justice Commission*, potential prejudice to a person's reputational interests may suffice to sustain an entitlement to procedural fairness, and declaratory relief in vindication of that entitlement.

[Citations omitted]

Royal commissions

Royal Commissions Act 1902 (Cth)

[As at 1 December 2022]

1A Power to issue Royal Commission

Without in any way prejudicing, limiting, or derogating from the power of the King, or of the Governor-General, to make or authorise any inquiry, or to issue any commission to make any inquiry, it is hereby enacted and declared that the Governor-General may, by Letters Patent in the name of the King, issue such commissions, directed to such person or persons, as he or she thinks fit, requiring or authorising him or her or them or any of them to make inquiry into and report upon any matter specified in the Letters Patent, and which relates to or is connected with the peace, order, and good government of the Commonwealth, or any public purpose or any power of the Commonwealth.

Royal Commission into the Home Insulation Program (Report, 2014)

Background

In 2009–2010, the Labor Government pursued a policy of subsidising home insulation as part of its larger stimulus response to the global financial crisis. The scheme was implemented by the Department of Environment, Water, Heritage and the Arts ('DEWHA') and the lack of regulation and oversight in its rollout led to four deaths, fires, electrified roofs, fraud, and rorting of the subsidy system. In 2014, the Coalition Government established a royal commission to investigate the home insulation program and the deaths associated with it. The Royal Commission identified a number of systemic failures and shortcomings in senior management of the Department, and called for clearer identification of roles and responsibilities in the future.

Letters Patent

ELIZABETH THE SECOND, by the Grace of God Queen of Australia and Her other Realms and Territories, Head of the Commonwealth:

TO

Mr Richard Ian Hanger AM QC

GREETING

WHEREAS a measure, known as the 'Energy Efficient Homes Package', was announced by former Prime Minister Kevin Rudd on 3 February 2009.

AND a component of that Package was the 'Homeowner Insulation Program', which was replaced on 1 July 2009 by the 'Home Insulation Program' (both of which form the *Program*).

AND it is claimed that the deaths of Matthew Fuller, Rueben Barnes, Mitchell Sweeney and Marcus Wilson may have arisen from the implementation of the Program.

AND it is important in the public interest that claims that deaths, serious injuries, financial loss or damage to pre-existing home insulation businesses, effects on families and other matters arising from the implementation of the Program be fully explored.

NOW THEREFORE We do, by these Our Letters Patent issued in Our name by Our Governor-General of the Commonwealth of Australia on the advice of the Federal Executive Council and under the Constitution of the Commonwealth of Australia, the *Royal Commissions Act 1902* and every other enabling power, appoint you to be a Commission of inquiry, and require and authorise you, to inquire into the matters that may have arisen from the development and implementation of the Program, and related matters, and in particular, without limiting the scope of your inquiry, the following matters:

a. the processes by which the Australian Government made decisions about the establishment and implementation of the Program, and the bases of those decisions, including how workplace health and safety and other risks relating to the Program were identified, assessed and managed;

b. whether the Australian Government was given, or sought, any advice, warnings or recommendations by or from industry representatives, regulatory authorities or other agencies of the Commonwealth, a State or a Territory during the establishment and implementation of the Program, and what action the Australian Government took in response to any such advice, warnings or recommendations;

c. whether, in establishing or implementing the Program, the Australian Government:
   i. failed to have sufficient regard to workplace health and safety or other risks relating to the Program; or
   ii. failed to have sufficient regard to advice, warnings or recommendations mentioned in paragraph (b); or
   iii. failed to deal adequately with the risks, advice, warnings or recommendations; and, if so, why sufficient regard was not had to the risks, advice, warnings or recommendations, or why they were not dealt with adequately;

d. whether the death of:
   i. Matthew Fuller; or
   ii. Rueben Barnes; or
   iii. Mitchell Sweeney; or
   iv. Marcus Wilson;

   could have been avoided by the appropriate identification, assessment or management, by the Australian Government, of workplace health and safety and other risks relating to the Program;

e. whether the Australian Government should have taken action, in relation to the identification, assessment or management of workplace health and safety and other risks relating to the Program, that you consider would or may have avoided the deaths of the persons named in paragraph (d);

f. the effects of the Program on:
   i. the families of the persons named in paragraph (d); and
   ii. pre-existing home insulation businesses;

g. whether the Australian Government should change its laws, policies, practices, processes, procedures or systems for the purpose of seeking to prevent the recurrence of any failure identified by your inquiry.

AND, without limiting the scope of your inquiry or the scope of any recommendations arising out of your inquiry that you may consider appropriate, We direct you to consider:

h. all relevant matters occurring during the period:
   i. starting at the commencement of the policy development that led to the introduction of the Program; and
   ii. ending at the termination of the Program; and

i. all remedial measures undertaken by the Australian Government after the Program was terminated.

AND, without limiting the scope of your inquiry or the scope of any recommendations arising out of your inquiry that you may consider appropriate, We declare that you may:

j. consider:
   i. damage to property claimed to have arisen from the implementation of the Program; and
   ii. the effects on pre-existing home insulation businesses resulting from the damage; and

k. make findings or recommendations about those matters;

but you are not required by these Our Letters Patent to do so.

AND We further declare that you are not required by these Our Letters Patent to inquire, or to continue to inquire, into a particular matter to the extent that you are satisfied that the matter has been, is being, or will be, sufficiently and appropriately dealt with by any of the following:

l. the inquests in Queensland and New South Wales into the deaths of the persons named in paragraph (d);

m. the findings of any court or tribunal inquiring into serious injuries, or loss or damage, claimed to have arisen from the Program;

n. inquiries by State or Territory governments, police forces or other agencies into the deaths of the persons named in paragraph (d) or into serious injuries, or loss or damage, claimed to have arisen from the Program;

o. the findings of the Report by the Australian National Audit Office into the Program;

p. the findings of the Review of the Administration of the Program;

q. any other relevant inquiry, proceeding or finding.

AND We direct you to make any recommendations arising out of your inquiry that you consider appropriate.

AND We declare that you are a relevant Commission for the purposes of sections 4 [Search warrants] and 5 [Application by telephone for search warrants] of the *Royal Commissions Act 1902.*

AND We declare that in these Our Letters Patent:

pre-existing home insulation business means a business of installing insulation in domestic premises that was in existence before 3 February 2009.

AND We:

r. require you to begin your inquiry as soon as practicable; and

s. require you to make your inquiry as expeditiously as possible; and

t. authorise you to submit to Our Governor-General any interim report that you consider appropriate; and

u. require you to submit to Our Governor-General a report of the results of your inquiry, and your recommendations, not later than 30 June 2014.

IN WITNESS, We have caused these Our Letters to be made Patent.

WITNESS Quentin Bryce, Governor-General of the Commonwealth of Australia.

Dated 12/12/2013

Report by Ian Hanger AM QC

14 THE FUTURE: AVOIDING REPETITION OF FAILURES

14.1 Introduction

299 14.1.1 When failures occur of the kind that I have set out in this Report, there is often a tendency to see them as arising only within a specific set of circumstances and to conclude that these are unlikely to be repeated. Views of this kind do not inspire an examination of events to draw conclusions about what might be done in the future.

14.1.2 I do not think that the deficiencies I have identified are ones that could only have occurred in the specific circumstances of the Home Insulation Program (HIP). Several systemic or fundamental shortcomings can be identified which not only are capable of repetition (of course in different circumstances) but which might be avoided through diligence and the taking of some additional measures.

14.1.3 My focus in this Chapter is on those matters and what might be offered in a forward-looking or constructive sense to complete and complement the detailed discussion in this report about the failings in the particular circumstances of the HIP. Many of these observations relate to the work and practices of the Australian Public Service (APS) in designing and implementing policies, but I also make suggestions about options to improve the safety of persons working in roof cavities in Australia.

14.2 Capacity of Commonwealth agencies and staff to undertake projects and programs

14.2.1 The Department of the Environment, Water, Heritage and the Arts (DEWHA) was inexperienced in designing and implementing a program of the nature, size and scale of the HIP—it had next to no project management expertise ... Its Secretary, Ms Kruk, initiated a review when she commenced there, but had insufficient time to complete it before the HIP was due to start. DEWHA lacked the capacity to achieve the tasks which it had been given.

...

14.3 Role of senior management

302 14.3.1 The role of senior managers is to oversee staff and to have overall responsibility for the delivery of the agency's responsibilities, often in the form of projects or programs. In the public service, senior managers have particular roles in serving the political executive, by providing advice, warnings and guidance.

14.3.2 Many of the shortcomings in the HIP are failures of senior managers. In general terms, I would summarise the shortcomings of senior APS management involved with the HIP as:

14.3.2.1 a failure to provide candid advice to Ministers. This was most exemplified by a failure to warn candidly that the 1 July 2009 commencement date was unachievable if the HIP were to be accompanied by the usual protections and terms (including an adequate audit and compliance regime);

30314.3.2.2 similarly, a lack of candour in the briefings to Minister Garrett concerning the effect and significance of the decision to relax the requirements for training in June 2009;

14.3.2.3 a lack of subject-matter expertise in relation to the environment in which the HIP operated, which resulted in advice being inaccurate, based on false assumptions or poorly targeted;

14.3.2.4 a failure to provide leadership of the HIP, by which I mean to assume responsibility for the program as a whole and do what was necessary with the staff working under them to ensure that their time and efforts were efficiently directed.

...

14.4 Clearer articulation of roles and responsibilities

304 14.4.1 Committees are not well-suited to making decisions and taking action, yet they are common in the Public Service. The Project Control Group (PCG) is a clear example in the case of the HIP.

14.4.2 Most PCG members were extremely passive participants. Decisions were routinely taken by exception—that is, in the absence of debate or dissent, it was assumed that there was consensus. Dissent or debate seems to have been rare. In this regard, 'groupthink' might have prevailed in certain meetings of the PCG, such as in respect of the 8 May 2009 decision with respect to the relaxation of training and competencies in particular.

14.4.3 The PCG did not discharge its function of, among other things, providing oversight and strategic direction to the insulation programs and ensuring high standards of governance were met. The existence of the PCG (like many such committees) was conducive to decision makers (albeit as part of a collective body) avoiding taking personal responsibility for decisions. Its mere existence seems to have been treated as having satisfied some substantive purpose when its establishment was merely a means by which to achieve steps of substance. The obsession with process at the expense of substance is a particular failing that the HIP reveals.

14.4.4 There is a further problem with collective bodies in the public service.

14.4.5 In the case of the HIP, there was a strong emphasis on seeing the members of the PCG as a 'team', rather than any other form of collective body. This attitude concerns me, because this manner of thinking saw DEWHA prioritise concurrence and cooperation at the expense of robust debate. When such a mentality prevails, any person that challenges the group was perceived as not being a team player, or as somehow unreasonably blocking the will of the majority.

...

14.6 Frank and fearless advice

306 14.6.1 ... It is an obligation of public servants that they provide the political Executive with advice that is frank and fearless. It falls to the political Executive to make the most important and difficult of decisions, and to suffer the harsh consequences at the ballot box, in the party room or in Parliament itself if those decisions are unpopular, clearly wrong or otherwise imprudent.

> ***307*** 14.6.2 It has been a long-standing principle that public servants had security of tenure giving them both longstanding experience in the field of public administration, a great depth of knowledge about that art and the workings of various portfolios. Security of tenure has another important consequence: public servants could, if warranted, advise their Minister against certain courses of action, and in trenchant terms if necessary. The Minister, in turn, was free to act contrary to the advice given, but could of course suffer criticism and censure if that contrary advice was later vindicated.
>
> 14.6.3 However, these circumstances have changed in recent decades—the public service is no longer automatically a lifetime career, nor does it, for many, offer the security of tenure it once did. The changes have not been all bad: security of tenure tends to protect persons who perform poorly at work or who are, or grow to be, unsuited to the job. But on the other hand, without some security, public servants might reasonably feel less able to give advice to a Minister who, if he or she finds it unpalatable, might take action which threatens that person's employment. More insidiously, Ministers and Department heads might procure written briefings that contain only that information which supports a particular result, premised on the view that for a senior public official to receive advice contrary to the manner in which they wish to act is undesirable and exposes that senior official to criticism. To act in this manner threatens the independence of the public service and the role we require them to fulfill.

[Citations omitted]

CHAPTER

6

INFORMATION DISCLOSURE

Introduction 127

The duties of public servants 127

Archives Act 1983 (Cth) 127

Hocking v Director-General of the National Archives of Australia (2020) 271 CLR 1 131

Public Service Act 1999 (Cth) 133

Public Service Regulations 1999 (Cth) 133

Confidential information 134

Commonwealth v John Fairfax & Sons Ltd (1980) 147 CLR 39 134

Information security – personal information 137

Office of the Australian Information Commissioner ('OAIC'), *Department of Immigration and Border Protection: Own Motion Investigation Report* (November 2014) 137

Minister for Immigration and Border Protection v SZSSJ (2016) 259 CLR 180 141

Public interest disclosure (whistleblowers) 143

Public Interest Disclosure Act 2013 (Cth) 143

Freedom of information 148

Freedom of Information Act 1982 (Cth) 148

Office of the Australian Information Commissioner ('OAIC'), *FOI Agency Resource 5: Exemptions and Conditional Exemptions Under the Freedom of Information Act 1982* (September 2011) 156

Case study: *Osland v Secretary, Department of Justice (No 1) & (No 2)* 159

Freedom of Information Act 1982 (Vic) 159
Introduction 160
Osland v Secretary, Department of Justice (No 1) (2008) 234 CLR 275 160
Osland v Secretary, Department of Justice (No 2) (2010) 241 CLR 320 164
Reasons for decisions 165
Public Service Board of New South Wales v Osmond (1986) 159 CLR 656 165
Administrative Review Council, *Best Practice Guide 4 – Decision Making: Reasons* (2007) 168
Administrative Review Council, *Federal Judicial Review in Australia* (Report No 50, 2012) 170
Ombudsman Act 1976 (Cth) 172
Administrative Appeals Tribunal Act 1975 (Cth) 172
Administrative Decisions (Judicial Review) Act 1977 (Cth) 173

Introduction

This chapter complements Chapter 6 in *Government Accountability: Australian Administrative Law*, third edition. Information disclosure is fundamental to all areas of administrative law. Whether a request for information comes from a superior court, a parliamentary committee, a royal commissioner, an ombudsman, a journalist, or an individual questioning a government decision, access to information is essential when holding governments to account. The sources in this chapter consider secrecy, unofficial disclosures by leaks and whistleblowers, statutory obligations of the executive to publish information, and the rights of individuals to apply for access to government-held information and reasons for decisions.

The duties of public servants

Government agencies are subject to a range of legal obligations to maintain and preserve records, keep them secure and confidential, and comply with legal obligations to give public access.

Archives Act 1983 (Cth)

[As at 1 December 2022]

3 Interpretation

(1) In this Act, unless the contrary intention appears: ...

Commonwealth institution means:

(a) the official establishment of the Governor-General;

(b) the Executive Council;

(c) the Senate;

(d) the House of Representatives;

(e) a Department;

(f) a Federal court or a court of a Territory other than the Northern Territory or Norfolk Island;

(g) an authority of the Commonwealth; or

(h) the Administration of an external Territory

Commonwealth record means:

(a) a record that is the property of the Commonwealth or of a Commonwealth institution; or

(b) a record that is to be deemed to be a Commonwealth record ...

but does not include a record that is exempt material.

[Editors' note: Exempt material includes material included in library, gallery and museum collections.]

...

record means a document, or an object, in any form (including any electronic form) that is, or has been, kept by reason of:

(a) any information or matter that it contains or that can be obtained from it; or

(b) its connection with any event, person, circumstance or thing.

Note: For the definition of *document,* see section 2B of the *Acts Interpretation Act 1901*.

...

(2) For the purposes of this Act, the archival resources of the Commonwealth consist of such Commonwealth records and other material as are of national significance or public interest and relate to:

(a) the history or government of Australia;

(b) the legal basis, origin, development, organization or activities of the Commonwealth or of a Commonwealth institution;

(c) a person who is, or has at any time been, associated with a Commonwealth institution;

(d) the history or government of a Territory; or

(e) an international or other organization the membership of which includes, or has included, the Commonwealth or a Commonwealth institution;

...

DIVISION 2—DEALINGS WITH COMMONWEALTH RECORDS

24 Disposal, destruction etc. of Commonwealth records

(1) Subject to this Part, a person must not engage in conduct that results in:

(a) the destruction or other disposal of a Commonwealth record; or

(b) the transfer of the custody or ownership of a Commonwealth record; or

(c) damage to or alteration of a Commonwealth record.

Penalty: 20 penalty units.

...

(2) Subsection (1) does not apply to anything done:

(a) as required by any law;

(b) with the permission of the Archives or in accordance with a practice or procedure approved by the Archives;

(c) in accordance with a normal administrative practice, other than a practice of a Department or authority of the Commonwealth of which the Archives has notified the Department or authority that it disapproves; or

...

(5) For the purposes of the application of subsection (1) to a record of a kind used by means of any mechanical or electronic device or equipment, including a computer, any treatment or modification of the record that would prevent the obtaining from the record of information or matter that could previously have been obtained from the record shall be deemed to be destruction of the record.

...

31 Records in open access period to be publicly available

(1A) This section applies to a Commonwealth record that:

(a) is in the open access period; and

(b) is in the care of the Archives or in the custody of a Commonwealth institution; and

(c) is not an exempt record.

(1) Subject to this Part, the Archives must cause the record to be made available for public access.

...

(2) If the record is in the custody of a Commonwealth institution, the institution must make such arrangements with the Archives as will enable the Archives to meet its obligations under subsection (1) in relation to the record.

...

33 Exempt records

(1) For the purposes of this Act, a Commonwealth record is an exempt record if it contains information or matter of any of the following kinds:

(a) information or matter the disclosure of which under this Act could reasonably be expected to cause damage to the security, defence or international relations of the Commonwealth;

(b) information or matter:

(i) that was communicated in confidence by, or on behalf of, a foreign government, an authority of a foreign government or an international organisation (the ***foreign entity***) to the Government of the Commonwealth, to an authority of the Commonwealth or to a person who received the communication on behalf of the Commonwealth or an authority of the Commonwealth (the ***Commonwealth entity***); and

(ii) which the foreign entity advises the Commonwealth entity is still confidential; and

(iii) the confidentiality of which it would be reasonable to maintain;

(c) information or matter the disclosure of which under this Act would have a substantial adverse effect on the financial or property interests of the Commonwealth or of a Commonwealth institution and would not, on balance, be in the public interest;

(d) information or matter the disclosure of which under this Act would constitute a breach of confidence;

(e) information or matter the disclosure of which under this Act would, or could reasonably be expected to:

(i) prejudice the conduct of an investigation of a breach, or possible breach, of the law, or a failure, or possible failure, to comply with a law relating to taxation or prejudice the enforcement or proper administration of the law in a particular instance;

(ii) disclose, or enable a person to ascertain, the existence or identity of a confidential source of information in relation to the enforcement or administration of the law; or

(iii) endanger the life or physical safety of any person;

(f) information or matter the disclosure of which under this Act would, or could reasonably be expected to:

(i) prejudice the fair trial of a person or the impartial adjudication of a particular case;

(ii) disclose lawful methods or procedures for preventing, detecting, investigating, or dealing with matters arising out of, breaches or evasions of the law the disclosure of which would, or would be reasonably likely to, prejudice the effectiveness of those methods or procedures; or

(iii) prejudice the maintenance or enforcement of lawful methods for the protection of public safety;

(g) information or matter the disclosure of which under this Act would involve the unreasonable disclosure of information relating to the personal affairs of any person (including a deceased person);

(h) information or matter relating to trade secrets, or any other information or matter having a commercial value that would be, or could reasonably be expected to be, destroyed or diminished if the information or matter were disclosed;

(j) information or matter (other than information or matter referred to in paragraph (h)) concerning a person in respect of his or her business or professional affairs or concerning the business, commercial or financial affairs of an organization or undertaking, being information or matter the disclosure of which would, or could reasonably be expected to, unreasonably affect that person adversely in respect of his or her lawful business or professional affairs or that organization or undertaking in respect of its lawful business, commercial or financial affairs.

Hocking v Director-General of the National Archives of Australia (2020) 271 CLR 1

Facts

Historian Professor Jenny Hocking sought access to records that had been lodged with the Archives in 1978 by the Official Secretary to the Governor-General. The records, known as the 'Palace Letters', were correspondence between the Governor-General, Sir John Kerr, or his official Secretary, and the Queen by means of her Private Secretary, over the period 15 August 1974 to 5 December 1977; notably covering the dismissal of the Whitlam government on 11 November 1975. Professor Hocking's application to the Archives for access was refused on the grounds that the letters were not Commonwealth records. She sought judicial review of that decision.[1] The Federal Court at first instance, and on appeal, held that the correspondence was the personal property of the former Governor-General, Sir John Kerr, not Commonwealth records.[2] Special access restrictions had been imposed; if the letters were Commonwealth records then access was governed by *Archives Act 1983* (Cth) s 31. Professor Hocking appealed to the High Court, which held that the letters were the 'property' of the official establishment of the Governor-General (a Commonwealth institution), and so were Commonwealth records. The passages below demonstrate how the meaning of 'property' within the context of the *Archives Act* is to be purposively construed to enable the Archives 'to preserve and make publicly available the archival resources of the Commonwealth'.

The High Court issued a writ of mandamus to compel the Director-General of the Archives to reconsider Professor Hocking's request for access. The letters were released by the Archives online in 2020.[3]

Kiefel CJ, Bell, Gageler and Keane JJ

***39* Four issues of construction**

[70] To address the ultimate question of whether each item of the deposited correspondence is properly characterised as 'a record that is the property of the Commonwealth or of a Commonwealth institution' within the meaning of the Archives Act, it is necessary to determine the proper construction of the four principal statutory terms which combine to give that composite expression its relevant content. The four statutory terms are 'record', 'the Commonwealth' as distinct from 'a Commonwealth institution', 'the official establishment of the Governor-General' as a Commonwealth institution, and perhaps most importantly, 'property'.

...

***45* 'property'**

[89] Property is not 'a monolithic notion of standard content and invariable intensity'; it is not 'a term of art with one specific and precise meaning'. It is 'a term that can be, and is, applied to many different kinds of relationship with a subject matter'. The

1 Under *Judiciary Act 1903* (Cth) s 39B.

2 *Hocking v Director-General of the National Archives of Australia* (2018) 255 FCR 1; *Hocking v Director-General of the National Archives of Australia* (2019) 264 FCR 1,

3 The Kerr Palace Letters <www.naa.gov.au/explore-collection/kerr-palace-letters>

relationship with a subject matter is in some contexts best understood in terms of a 'bundle of rights'. In other contexts, it is best understood in terms of a 'legally endorsed concentration of power'.

...

46 [92] The question, however, is not as to the content of the common law concepts of 'possession' or 'possessory title' but as to the meaning of 'property' within the context of the Archives Act. The two are not the same.

[93] Within the definition of 'Commonwealth record', 'property' obviously connotes a relationship between a record – a tangible thing – on the one hand and either the Commonwealth as a body politic or a Commonwealth institution as a functional unit of government on the other hand. The nature and intensity of the requisite relationship is a question of statutory construction the resolution of which is informed by the statutory context.

[94] Despite the focus of those involved in the early stages of the drafting of the Archives Act on the 'ownership' of a record, the inclusion within the definition of 'Commonwealth institution' of Departments of State of the Commonwealth and of other functional units of government which lack legal personality necessarily means that the connoted relationship cannot be confined to the holding of rights. Much less can it be confined to the holding of rights corresponding to ownership or possession at common law. The relationship connoted can only be understood in terms of a legally endorsed concentration of power. The question becomes as to the nature and intensity of the requisite concentration of power.

[95] Purposively construed in the context of the *Archives Act*, the relationship between a record and either the Commonwealth as a body politic or a Commonwealth institution as a functional unit of government connoted by 'property' is best understood as a legally endorsed concentration of power to control the physical custody of the record. The power might arise from a capacity to exercise a common law or statutory right arising from ownership or possession. But it need not so arise. The power might be exclusive. But it need not be.

47 [96] The paradigm of a Department of State of the Commonwealth rather indicates that the concentration of power can arise from a capacity to control the physical custody of the record that is conferred and is exercisable as a matter of management or administration rather than as a matter of the recognition and vindication of rights of ownership or possession at common law. The *Archives Act* is not concerned to vindicate the incidents of ownership or possession at common law such as the right to destroy or the right to alienate the property. A record which is kept in the control of a Department in the course of the management and administration of the affairs of the Commonwealth is sensibly described as property of the Commonwealth for the purposes of the *Archives Act* whether or not another person – such as the author of the record – may have a claim to ownership or possession of the record under the general law.

[97] The paradigm of a Department of State of the Commonwealth also indicates that the power to control the physical custody of the record need not depend on the capacity to assert any right of ownership or possession at common law given that the Department is not an entity capable of bearing or enforcing legal rights. Nor need the power of control

extend to the ultimate power to dispose of the record. The power can be constrained, including by rights of ownership or possession vested in the Commonwealth as a body politic or in another legal person. The exercise of the power can be subject to a power of direction in another – in the case of a Department, most obviously its Minister.

[98] That contextual understanding of the statutory reference to 'property' furthers the legislative purpose of enabling the Archives to preserve and make publicly available the archival resources of the Commonwealth. It does so by ensuring that the Archives is able to assume the custody of a Commonwealth record of national significance or public interest without needing to concern itself with questions of the ultimate ownership or possessory title.

[99] Underlying the legislative scheme is an expectation that a record the physical custody of which is within the lawful power of control of the Commonwealth as a body politic or of a Commonwealth institution as a functional unit of government will in the regular course of administration be kept in the actual physical custody of a Commonwealth institution. Within the Commonwealth institution there will be a 'person responsible for the custody of the record'. That person will be compelled to transfer the record to the Archives if the record is determined by the Director-General to be part of the archival resources of the Commonwealth. The circumstance that a record is in fact kept in the actual physical custody of a Commonwealth institution lacking in legal personality makes it highly likely that the true owner ***48*** of the record will be the Commonwealth as a body politic. But the circumstance cannot exclude the possibility that the true owner of the document is some other person.

[Citations omitted]

Public Service Act 1999 (Cth)

[As at 1 December 2022]

13 The APS Code of Conduct

...

(13) An APS employee must comply with any other conduct requirement that is prescribed by the regulations.

Public Service Regulations 1999 (Cth)

[As at 1 December 2022]

PART 2—THE AUSTRALIAN PUBLIC SERVICE

DIVISION 2.1—THE CODE OF CONDUCT

2.1 Duty not to disclose information (Act s 13)

(1) This regulation is made for subsection 13(13) of the Act.

(2) This regulation does not affect other restrictions on the disclosure of information.

(3) An APS employee must not disclose information which the APS employee obtains or generates in connection with the APS employee's employment if it is reasonably foreseeable that the disclosure could be prejudicial to the effective working of government, including the formulation or implementation of policies or programs.

(4) An APS employee must not disclose information which the APS employee obtains or generates in connection with the APS employee's employment if the information:

(a) was, or is to be, communicated in confidence within the government; or

(b) was received in confidence by the government from a person or persons outside the government;

whether or not the disclosure would found an action for breach of confidence.

(5) Subregulations (3) and (4) do not prevent a disclosure of information by an APS employee if:

(a) the information is disclosed in the course of the APS employee's duties; or

(b) the information is disclosed in accordance with an authorisation given by an Agency Head; or

(c) the disclosure is otherwise authorised by law; or

(d) the information that is disclosed:

(i) is already in the public domain as the result of a disclosure of information that is lawful under these Regulations or another law; and

(ii) can be disclosed without disclosing, expressly or by implication, other information to which subregulation (3) or (4) applies.

(6) Subregulations (3) and (4) do not limit the authority of an Agency Head to give lawful and reasonable directions in relation to the disclosure of information.

Confidential information

Commonwealth v John Fairfax & Sons Ltd (1980) 147 CLR 39

Facts

In 1980, journalists and publishers Richard Walsh and George Munster attempted to publish a book of leaked government documents titled *Documents on Australian Defence and Foreign Policy 1968–1975.* Pre-publication publicity for the book, and newspaper articles containing extracts from the book, alerted the Commonwealth Government to the imminent publication. It contained Commonwealth foreign affairs and defence documents, including memoranda, assessments, briefings and cables on matters such as the East Timor crisis, and the re-negotiations of the agreements for United States military bases in Australia. The Commonwealth sought injunctions to restrain publication of the book and newspaper extracts on three bases: that publication of the documents would involve the commission of an offence under the *Crimes Act 1914* (Cth); that it would disclose confidential information; and that it would infringe the Crown's copyright in the documents.

The Commonwealth failed on two of the three bases: Mason J would not restrain by injunction a threatened breach of the criminal law, nor disclosure of confidential information. However, the Commonwealth succeeded in obtaining an injunction by relying on its copyright in the documents. The following extracts concern the confidential information claim, and the special approach to be adopted when considering government information.

Mason J

Disclosure of confidential information

...

50 The plaintiff had within its possession confidential information comprised in the documents published in the book. The probability is that a public servant having access to the documents, in breach of his duty and contrary to the security classifications, made copies of the documents available to Messrs ***51*** Walsh and Munster or to an intermediary who handed them to Messrs Walsh and Munster. In drawing this inference I am mindful that no claim is made that copies of the documents came into the possession of Messrs Walsh and Munster with the authority of the plaintiff.

No attempt has been made to suggest that the defendants were unaware of the classified nature of the documents or of the plaintiff's claim that it had not authorized publication. The book records the security classification of many of the documents. ...

Basic to the plaintiff's argument is the proposition that information which is not 'public property and public knowledge', in the words of Lord Greene MR in *Saltman Engineering Co Ltd v Campbell Engineering Co Ltd* [(1948) 65 RPC 20, 215], is protected by the principle [of equity that a court will restrain the publication of confidential information]. Even unclassified government information would fall within the protection claimed, so long as it is not publicly known. According to the plaintiff, no relevant distinction is to be drawn between the Government and a private person. A citizen is entitled to the protection by injunction of the secrets of his or her private life, as well as trade secrets. So, with the government, it is entitled to protect information which is not public property, even if no public interest is served by maintaining confidentiality.

However, the plaintiff must show, not only that the information is confidential in quality and that it was imparted so as to import an obligation of confidence, but also that there will be 'an unauthorised use of that information to the detriment of the party communicating it' [*Coco v AN Clark (Engineers) Ltd* [1969] RPC 41, 47]. The question then, when the executive government seeks the protection given by equity, is: What detriment does it need to show?

The equitable principle has been fashioned to protect the personal, private and proprietary interests of the citizen, not to protect the very different interests of the executive government. It acts, or is supposed to act, not according to standards of private interest, but in the public interest. This is not to say that equity will not protect information in the hands of the government, but it is to say that when equity protects government information it will look at the matter through different spectacles.

52 It may be a sufficient detriment to the citizen that disclosure of information relating to his affairs will expose his actions to public discussion and criticism. But it can scarcely be a relevant detriment to the government that publication of material concerning its actions will merely expose it to public discussion and criticism. It is unacceptable in our democratic society that there should be a restraint on the publication of information relating to government when the only vice of that information is that it enables the public to discuss, review and criticize government action.

Accordingly, the court will determine the government's claim to confidentiality by reference to the public interest. Unless disclosure is likely to injure the public interest, it will not be protected.

The court will not prevent the publication of information which merely throws light on the past workings of government, even if it be not public property, so long as it does not prejudice the community in other respects. Then disclosure will itself serve the public interest in keeping the community informed and in promoting discussion of public affairs. If, however, it appears that disclosure will be inimical to the public interest because national security, relations with foreign countries or the ordinary business of government will be prejudiced, disclosure will be restrained. There will be cases in which the conflicting considerations will be finely balanced, where it is difficult to decide whether the public's interest in knowing and in expressing its opinion, outweighs the need to protect confidentiality.

...

53 How, then, does the claim for an injunction to restrain disclosure of confidential information stand? ...

The contents of some documents possibly suggest that disclosure of them would embarrass Australia's relations with other countries and consequently affect their willingness to make available defence and diplomatic information on a confidential basis.

I have given particular attention to Ch 6 of the book and to ten passages in it identified by Mr Henderson. In some passages overseas political and diplomatic personalities are mentioned, information and attitudes are ascribed to them and comments, ***54*** some critical, are made about them. Some confidential reports or opinions of ambassadors of foreign countries are set out. Some of the ten passages appear in the East Timor material which the defendants intended to publish.

However, I am not persuaded that the degree of embarrassment to Australia's foreign relations which will flow from disclosure is enough to justify interim protection of confidential information. In any event, the question whether an injunction should be granted on this ground is resolved against the plaintiff by the publication that has taken, and is likely to take, place.

> The sales of the book already made, including those made to Indonesia and the United States, the countries most likely to be affected by its contents, and the publication of the first instalment in the two newspapers, indicate that the detriment which the plaintiff apprehends will not be avoided by the grant of an injunction. In other circumstances the circulation of about 100 copies of a book may not be enough to disentitle the possessor of confidential information from protection by injunction, but in this case it is likely that what is in the book will become known to an ever-widening group of people here and overseas, including foreign governments.

[Citations omitted]

Information security – personal information

Governments must protect the private information they hold relating to citizens and comply with privacy principles under the *Privacy Act 1988* (Cth) and state equivalents that regulate the collection, storage, security and accuracy of personal records.

The consequences of failure to ensure data security can be seen in the following case concerning a data breach by the Department of Immigration and Border Protection that disclosed information about asylum seekers in detention. The Department commissioned KPMG to report on the breach; the Office of the Australian Information Commissioner (OAIC) also undertook a separate investigation of breaches under the *Privacy Act 1988* (Cth). Two individuals whose personal information was disclosed by the breach brought a judicial review action in the courts seeking access to the full KPMG report on the grounds of procedural fairness.

Office of the Australian Information Commissioner ('OAIC'), *Department of Immigration and Border Protection: Own Motion Investigation Report* (November 2014)[4]

Overview

On 21 February 2014, the Australian Information Commissioner opened an own motion investigation into the Department of Immigration and Border Protection ('DIBP') following a media report that a database containing the personal information of approximately 10,000 asylum seekers was available on DIBP's website. DIBP confirmed this was the case.

The investigation, led by the Australian Privacy Commissioner ('the Commissioner'), on behalf of the Office of the Australian Information Commissioner ('OAIC'), focused on whether DIBP had reasonable security safeguards in place to protect the asylum seekers' information, and whether DIBP had disclosed the information in accordance with the *Privacy Act 1988* (Cth) *(Privacy Act).*

4 Available at: <www.oaic.gov.au/privacy/privacy-decisions/investigation-reports/department-of-immigration-and-border-protection-own-motion-investigation-report>

After considering the facts of the case, submissions from DIBP, and the relevant provisions of the *Privacy Act*, the Commissioner came to the view that DIBP had breached the *Privacy Act* by failing to put in place reasonable security safeguards to protect the personal information it held against loss, unauthorised access, use, modification or disclosure and against other misuse. The Commissioner also found that DIBP had unlawfully disclosed personal information.

BACKGROUND

On 19 February 2014, the OAIC received information that a database containing the personal information of 'almost 10,000' asylum seekers was available on DIBP's website ('the data breach').

Each month, DIBP publishes a document titled *Immigration Detention and Community Statistics Summary* on its website (www.immi.gov.au). The document includes statistics about asylum seekers. For accessibility reasons, DIBP publishes the document in Adobe PDF and Microsoft Word versions.

On 10 February 2014, DIBP published the Microsoft Word version of the January 2013 issue of the *Immigration Detention and Community Statistics Summary,* dated 31 January 2014 ('the Detention report').

In preparing the Microsoft Word version of the Detention report for web publication, DIBP embedded the Microsoft Excel spreadsheet that had been used to generate the statistics used in the Detention report. The spreadsheet included the personal information of approximately 9250 asylum seekers ('the listed individuals') and was accessible through the Detention report.

DIBP was notified about the breach by the Guardian Australia at 9.15am on 19 February 2014. DIBP removed the Detention report from its website by 10.00am on that date. The Detention report was available on DIBP's website for about eight-and-a-half days.

DIBP also identified that the Detention report was also available on The Internet Archive (Archive.org) from 11 February 2014. DIBP wrote to Archive.org on 24 February, seeking removal of the report. Archive.org complied with this request on 27 February. The Detention report was available on Archive.org for about 16 days.

The categories of personal information compromised in the data breach consisted of:

a. full names
b. gender
c. citizenship
d. date of birth
e. period of immigration detention
f. location
g. boat arrival details
h. reasons why the individual was deemed to be unlawful.

The Commissioner was particularly concerned about this information being publicly available due to the vulnerability of the listed individuals.

Relevant provisions of the *Privacy Act*

Until 11 March 2014, agencies covered by the *Privacy Act* were required to comply with 11 Information Privacy Principles ('IPPs'), contained in Division 2 of Part III of the *Privacy Act.* The IPPs were replaced by the Australian Privacy Principles ('APPs') on 12 March 2014. DIBP was subject to the IPPs at the time of the data breach (February 2014).

The IPPs applied to the handling of 'personal information', which the *Privacy Act* defined as: information or an opinion (including information or an opinion forming part of a database), whether true or not, and whether recorded in a material form or not, about an individual whose identity is apparent, or can reasonably be ascertained, from the information or opinion.

The *Privacy Act* provisions relevant to this data breach are: IPP 4 (storage and security of personal information) and IPP 11 (limits on the disclosure of personal information).

In particular:

- IPP 4(a) – an agency must ensure that records containing personal information are protected by such security safeguards as are reasonable in the circumstances against loss, unauthorised access, use, modification or disclosure or other misuse.
- IPP 11.1 – an agency must not disclose personal information about an individual unless a listed exception applies.

Findings

Security of personal information (IPP 4(a))

To assess whether DIBP had reasonable security safeguards in place, in accordance with IPP 4(a), the Commissioner considered information from DIBP and the report on the data breach by KPMG ('the KPMG report') about the security safeguards in place prior to the data breach, and what security safeguards would have been reasonable in the circumstances to protect the personal information held. This included considering DIBP's particular circumstances, such as:

- the sensitivity of the personal information held
- the risk to the individuals concerned if the personal information is not secure
- its information handling practices
- the ease with which a security measure can be implemented.

The Commissioner also had regard to the guidance set out in the OAIC's *Guide to Information Security.*

Where there is a known risk to data security, IPP 4 would generally have required that reasonable steps be taken to mitigate that risk.

The Commissioner found that the data breach was caused by the failure of a number of Departmental policy documents to adequately mitigate against the known risk of embedded data. This included the failure of DIBP to make Departmental staff aware of the risk of embedded data. These failures led to the errors by Departmental staff who created and cleared the Detention report.

Further, this data breach may also have been avoided if DIBP had processes in place to de-identify data where particular areas of the agency do not require access to the full data set.

...

De-identification of information

Given the sensitivity of the data in question and the number of people involved in compiling, clearance and publication of the Detention report, the Commissioner found that a reasonable security safeguard in this situation would be to de-identify the information at an early stage in the process of compiling the Detention report.

Such a process would have removed the possibility of the identifying data inadvertently being disclosed at a later stage, and would have limited access to the personal information only to those employees that required access to enable DIBP to carry out the functions and activities for which the information is held.

...

Disclosure of personal information (IPP 11)

As part of the investigation, the Commissioner considered whether there had been a breach of IPP 11. IPP 11 regulated the disclosure of personal information and states that an agency shall not disclose personal information to a person, body or agency unless an exception applies.

In general terms, an agency '*discloses*' personal information when it makes the information accessible to others outside the agency and releases the subsequent handling of the personal information from its effective control. The release may be an accidental release or an unauthorised release by an employee.

The Commissioner found that DIBP 'disclosed' the compromised information within the meaning of IPP 11, as it made the personal information accessible to the general public by publishing it on its website.

...

Conclusion

The Commissioner found that:

- DIBP breached IPP 4 by failing to put in place reasonable security safeguards to protect the personal information that it held against loss, unauthorised access, use, modification or disclosure and against other misuse; and
- the publication of the personal information of the listed individuals was an unauthorised disclosure, in contravention of IPP 11.

This data breach demonstrates the difficulties of effectively containing a breach where information has been published online, and highlights the importance of taking steps to minimise the risk of data breaches occurring, rather than relying on steps to attempt to contain them after they have occurred.

The Commissioner found that DIBP took some steps to contain the data breach and put in place processes to assess and respond to the data breach. However, there are areas where the execution of these processes could have been improved.

The Commissioner expressed concern about the length of time it took DIBP to detect the cached copy of the Detention report on Archive.org and effect its removal.

The personal information involved in this data breach was disclosed in the context of DIBP voluntarily publishing statistical information on its website. Public sector information is a national resource, and the Commissioner encourages agencies to proactively make public sector information publicly available. However, this data breach demonstrates the importance of agencies implementing appropriate information handling practices to facilitate open access to public sector information while also protecting the personal information that they hold.

The Commissioner noted that the OAIC has received a large number of individual complaints about this incident. This investigation focused on the systems failures that led to the breaches of the *Privacy Act* and the measures to be taken to prevent future breaches rather than the impact on individuals affected by the breach, as this will be dealt with as part of the complaints process. The Commissioner's finding in this own motion investigation that DIBP breached IPP 4 and IPP 11 will be taken into account when investigating individual complaints.

Based on DIBP's remediation activities, DIBP's ongoing implementation of recommendations made by KPMG, and its intention to engage an auditor confirm its remediation steps, the Commissioner decided to close the investigation.

[Citations omitted]

Minister for Immigration and Border Protection v SZSSJ (2016) 259 CLR 180

Facts

In February 2014, a data breach by the Department of Immigration and Border Protection released information to the internet on approximately 9250 asylum seekers. Details of the breach are outlined in the OAIC report above. The Department commissioned KPMG to investigate. People affected by the breach were advised and given an abridged version of KPMG report. The full KPMG report included internet protocol ('IP') addresses that had accessed the data. Departmental officers conducted International Treaties Obligations Assessments ('ITOAs') to assess the effect of the data breach on all individuals whose data had been disclosed, and to consider Australia's non-refoulement obligations under international law. (Non-refoulement is a principle of international law that prohibits the expulsion or return of asylum seekers to a country where their life or freedom would be threatened.)[5] It was not possible to determine the true extent of disclosure of the information, and who might have had accessed it. Officers conducting the ITOAs were instructed to assume that applicants' personal information may have been accessed by government authorities in their country of origin.

5 *Convention Relating to the Status of Refugees,* opened for signature 28 July 1951, 189 UNTS 150 (entered into force 22 April 1954) art 33.

A Bangladeshi national ('SZSSJ') and Chinese national ('SZTZI') affected by the breach sought access to a full copy of the KPMG report. The Full Court of the Federal Court[6] held that the Department's failure to adequately explain the ITOA process and provide an unabridged version of the KPMG report was a breach of procedural fairness. The Full Court held that, in these particular circumstances, the Department was obliged to go beyond what would normally be required and 'show its full hand subject to any proper (and curially supervisable) consideration of confidentiality'.[7]

The High Court reversed that decision on appeal. The High Court held that while the Department owed the applicants a duty of procedural fairness,[8] that duty had not been breached in this case. The circumstances of data breach did not expand the duty to give the person affected notice and an opportunity to be heard into a broader obligation to disclose all information the Department held about the data breach.

French CJ, Kiefel, Bell, Gageler, Keane, Nettle and Gordon JJ

> ***207*** [83] Ordinarily, affording a reasonable opportunity to be heard in the exercise of a statutory power to conduct an inquiry requires that a person whose interest is apt to be affected be put on notice of: the nature and purpose of the inquiry; the issues to be considered in conducting the inquiry; and the nature and content of information that the repository of power undertaking the inquiry might take into account as a reason for coming to a conclusion adverse to the person. Ordinarily, there is no requirement that the person be notified of information which is in the possession of, or accessible to, the repository but which the repository has chosen not to take into account at all in the conduct of the inquiry.
>
> [84] Extraordinary as they are, the circumstances of the Data Breach do not warrant a departure from those ordinary requirements. That the Department was responsible for its occurrence is regrettable. That the Department was responsible for its occurrence nevertheless provides no foundation for apprehending that an officer of the Department tasked with assessing the consequences of the Data Breach for an individual applicant would not bring an impartial and unprejudiced mind to the conduct of an assessment. Nor does that circumstance provide a principled foundation for converting the ordinary requirement of procedural fairness that an affected person be given notice into a duty that the Department reveal 'all that it knows' about the Data Breach.
>
> ...
>
> ***209*** [92] SZSSJ and SZTZI were not deprived of any opportunity to submit evidence or to make submissions relevant to the subject matter of the ITOA process as a result of not having such further information as might be inferred to have been contained in the unabridged version of the KPMG report. Exactly how and why the Data Breach occurred was simply not relevant to the question of whether one or more of Australia's non-refoulement obligations were engaged in respect of them. And irrespective of what the unabridged KPMG report might have to say about the identities of the 104 IP addresses from which the document had been accessed during the 14 day period of the Data Breach, the fact would remain that once the document was

6 *SZSSJ v Minister for Immigration and Border Protection* (2015) 234 FCR 1.

7 Ibid 32 [121].

8 See Chapter 12.

downloaded the personal information of SZSSJ and SZTZI could have been accessed by anyone. Even if the unabridged KPMG report might have allowed SZSSJ and SZTZI to prove by reference to the report that one or more of those IP addresses were associated with persons or entities from whom they feared harm, that proof would advance their cases for engagement of Australia's nonrefoulement obligations no further than the assumption already made in their favour.

[Citations omitted]

Public interest disclosure (whistleblowers)

Public interest disclosures by whistleblowers are a particular kind of disclosure that occurs from within an organisation by current or former staff and is made without permission from their employer. Statutory schemes offer some protection to whistleblowers from reprisals and legal liabilities when they disclose information about misconduct and wrongdoing.

Public Interest Disclosure Act 2013 (Cth)

[As at 1 December 2022]

PART 2—PROTECTION OF DISCLOSERS

DIVISION 1—PROTECTIONS

9 Simplified outline

The following is a simplified outline of this Division:

An individual is not subject to any civil, criminal or administrative liability for making a public interest disclosure.

It is an offence to take a reprisal, or to threaten to take a reprisal, against a person because of a public interest disclosure (including a proposed or a suspected public interest disclosure).

The Federal Court or Federal Circuit and Family Court of Australia (Division 2) may make orders for civil remedies (including compensation, injunctions and reinstatement of employment) if a reprisal is taken against a person because of a public interest disclosure (including a proposed or a suspected public interest disclosure). It is an offence to disclose the identity of an individual who makes a public interest disclosure.

SUBDIVISION A—IMMUNITY FROM LIABILITY

10 Protection of disclosers

(1) If an individual makes a public interest disclosure:

(a) the individual is not subject to any civil, criminal or administrative liability (including disciplinary action) for making the public interest disclosure; and

(b) no contractual or other remedy may be enforced, and no contractual or other right may be exercised, against the individual on the basis of the public interest disclosure.

(2) Without limiting subsection (1):

(a) the individual has absolute privilege in proceedings for defamation in respect of the public interest disclosure; and

(b) a contract to which the individual is a party must not be terminated on the basis that the public interest disclosure constitutes a breach of the contract.

11 Liability for false or misleading statements etc. unaffected

(1) Section 10 does not apply to civil, criminal or administrative liability (including disciplinary action) for knowingly making a statement that is false or misleading.

...

SUBDIVISION B—PROTECTION FROM REPRISALS

13 What constitutes taking a reprisal

(1) A person (the ***first person***) *takes a reprisal* against another person (the ***second person***) if:

(a) the first person causes (by act or omission) any detriment to the second person; and

(b) when the act or omission occurs, the first person believes or suspects that the second person or any other person made, may have made or proposes to make a public interest disclosure; and

(c) that belief or suspicion is the reason, or part of the reason, for the act or omission.

(2) ***Detriment*** includes any disadvantage, including (without limitation) any of the following:

(a) dismissal of an employee;

(b) injury of an employee in his or her employment;

(c) alteration of an employee's position to his or her detriment;

(d) discrimination between an employee and other employees of the same employer.

(3) Despite subsection (1), a person does not take a reprisal against another person to the extent that the person takes administrative action that is reasonable to protect the other person from detriment ....

[Editors' note: Sections 14–16 deal with compensation orders and reinstatement for reprisals.]

19 Offences

Taking a reprisal

(1) A person commits an offence if the person takes a reprisal against another person. Penalty: Imprisonment for 2 years or 120 penalty units, or both.

(2) In a prosecution for an offence against subsection (1), it is not necessary to prove that the other person made, may have made or intended to make a public interest disclosure.

Threatening to take a reprisal

(3) A person (the ***first person***) commits an offence if:

(a) the first person makes a threat to another person (the ***second person***) to take a reprisal against the second person or a third person; and

(b) the first person:

(i) intends the second person to fear that the threat will be carried out; or

(ii) is reckless as to the second person fearing that the threat will be carried out.

Penalty: Imprisonment for 2 years or 120 penalty units, or both.

(4) For the purposes of subsection (3), the threat may be:

(a) express or implied; or

(b) conditional or unconditional.

(5) In a prosecution for an offence under subsection (3), it is not necessary to prove that the person threatened actually feared that the threat would be carried out.

...

SUBDIVISION C—PROTECTING THE IDENTITY OF DISCLOSERS

20 Use or disclosure of identifying information

Disclosure of identifying information

(1) A person (the ***first person***) commits an offence if:

(a) another person (the ***second person***) has made a public interest disclosure; and

(b) the first person discloses information (***identifying information***) that:

(i) was obtained by any person in that person's capacity as a public official; and

(ii) is likely to enable the identification of the second person as a person who has made a public interest disclosure; and

(c) the disclosure is to a person other than the second person.

Penalty: Imprisonment for 6 months or 30 penalty units, or both.

Use of identifying information

(2) A person (the ***first person***) commits an offence if the person uses identifying information.

Penalty: Imprisonment for 6 months or 30 penalty units, or both.

[Editors' note: Subsections (1) and (2) are subject to exceptions under sub-s (3) relevant to certain statutory purposes or functions, when the person has consented, or the information had previously been lawfully published].

DIVISION 2—PUBLIC INTEREST DISCLOSURES

25 Simplified outline

The following is a simplified outline of this Division:

The protections in Division 1 apply to public interest disclosures.

Broadly speaking, a public interest disclosure is a disclosure of information, by a public official, that is:

- a disclosure within the government, to an authorised internal recipient or a supervisor, concerning suspected or probable illegal conduct or other wrongdoing (referred to as 'disclosable conduct'); or
- a disclosure to anybody, if an internal disclosure of the information has not been adequately dealt with, and if wider disclosure satisfies public interest requirements; or
- a disclosure to anybody if there is substantial and imminent danger to health or safety; or
- a disclosure to an Australian legal practitioner for purposes connected with the above matters.

However, there are limitations to take into account the need to protect intelligence information.

SUBDIVISION A—PUBLIC INTEREST DISCLOSURES

26 Meaning of public interest disclosure

(1) A disclosure of information is a ***public interest disclosure*** if:

(a) the disclosure is made by a person (the ***discloser***) who is, or has been, a public official; and

(b) the recipient of the information is a person of the kind referred to in column 2 of an item of the following table; and

(c) all the further requirements set out in column 3 of that item are met:

PUBLIC INTEREST DISCLOSURES

Item	Column 1 Type of disclosure	Column 2 Recipient	Column 3 Further requirements
1	Internal disclosure	An authorised internal recipient, or a supervisor of the discloser	The information tends to show, or the discloser believes on reasonable grounds that the information tends to show, one or more instances of disclosable conduct.
2	External disclosure	Any person other than a foreign public official	(a) The information tends to show, or the discloser believes on reasonable grounds that the information tends to show, one or more instances of disclosable conduct. (b) On a previous occasion, the discloser made an internal disclosure of information that consisted of, or included, the information now disclosed. (c) Any of the following apply: (i) a disclosure investigation relating to the internal disclosure was conducted under Part 3, and the discloser believes on reasonable grounds that the investigation was inadequate;

PUBLIC INTEREST DISCLOSURES			
Item	Column 1 Type of disclosure	Column 2 Recipient	Column 3 Further requirements
			(ii) a disclosure investigation relating to the internal disclosure was conducted (whether or not under Part 3), and the discloser believes on reasonable grounds that the response to the investigation was inadequate; (iii) this Act requires an investigation relating to the internal disclosure to be conducted under Part 3, and that investigation has not been completed within the [prescribed] time limit ... (e) The disclosure is not, on balance, contrary to the public interest. (f) No more information is publicly disclosed than is reasonably necessary to identify one or more instances of disclosable conduct. (h) The information does not consist of, or include, intelligence information. (i) None of the conduct with which the disclosure is concerned relates to an intelligence agency.
3	Emergency disclosure	Any person other than a foreign public official	(a) The discloser believes on reasonable grounds that the information concerns a substantial and imminent danger to the health or safety of one or more persons or to the environment. (b) The extent of the information disclosed is no greater than is necessary to alert the recipient to the substantial and imminent danger. (c) If the discloser has not previously made an internal disclosure of the same information, there are exceptional circumstances justifying the discloser's failure to make such an internal disclosure. (d) If the discloser has previously made an internal disclosure of the same information, there are exceptional circumstances justifying this disclosure being made before a disclosure investigation of the internal disclosure is completed. (f) The information does not consist of, or include, intelligence information.

PUBLIC INTEREST DISCLOSURES			
Item	**Column 1 Type of disclosure**	**Column 2 Recipient**	**Column 3 Further requirements**
4	Legal practitioner disclosure	An Australian legal practitioner	(a) The disclosure is made for the purpose of obtaining legal advice, or professional assistance, from the recipient in relation to the discloser having made, or proposing to make, a public interest disclosure. (b) If the discloser knew, or ought reasonably to have known, that any of the information has a national security or other protective security classification, the recipient holds the appropriate level of security clearance. (e) The information does not consist of, or include, intelligence information.

[Editors' note: Under s 29, 'disclosable conduct' is conduct of a Commonwealth government agency, public official, or contracted service provider. It must be of a kind listed in the s 29 table and includes: conduct that is illegal or perverts the course of justice; maladministration; abuse of public trust; falsification of scientific research; wastage of public money; and conduct that endangers public health or safety or the environment.

Part 3 imposes obligations on agencies to investigate public interest disclosures.]

Freedom of information

Freedom of Information Act 1982 (Cth)

[As at 1 December 2022]

3 Objects—general

(1) The objects of this Act are to give the Australian community access to information held by the Government of the Commonwealth, by:

(a) requiring agencies to publish the information; and

(b) providing for a right of access to documents.

(2) The Parliament intends, by these objects, to promote Australia's representative democracy by contributing towards the following:

(a) increasing public participation in Government processes, with a view to promoting better-informed decision-making;

(b) increasing scrutiny, discussion, comment and review of the Government's activities.

(3) The Parliament also intends, by these objects, to increase recognition that information held by the Government is to be managed for public purposes, and is a national resource.

(4) The Parliament also intends that functions and powers given by this Act are to be performed and exercised, as far as possible, to facilitate and promote public access to information, promptly and at the lowest reasonable cost.

3A Objects—information or documents otherwise accessible

Scope

(1) This section applies if a Minister, or an officer of an agency, has the power to publish, or give access to, information or a document (including an exempt document) apart from under this Act.

Publication and access powers not limited

(2) The Parliament does not intend, by this Act, to limit that power, or to prevent or discourage the exercise of that power:

- (a) in the case of the power to publish the information or document—despite any restriction on the publication of the information or document under this Act; and
- (b) in the case of the power to give access to the information or document—whether or not access to the information or document has been requested under section 15.

4 Interpretation

In this Act, unless the contrary intention appears:

...

document includes:

- (a) any of, or any part of any of, the following things:
  - (i) any paper or other material on which there is writing;
  - (ii) a map, plan, drawing or photograph;
  - (iii) any paper or other material on which there are marks, figures, symbols or perforations having a meaning for persons qualified to interpret them;
  - (iv) any article or material from which sounds, images or writings are capable of being reproduced with or without the aid of any other article or device;
  - (v) any article on which information has been stored or recorded, either mechanically or electronically; or
  - (vi) any other record of information; or
- (b) any copy, reproduction or duplicate of such a thing; or
- (c) any part of such a copy, reproduction or duplicate;

but does not include:

(d) material maintained for reference purposes that is otherwise publicly available; or

(e) Cabinet notebooks.

document of an agency: a document is ***a document of an agency*** if:

(a) the document is in the possession of the agency, whether created in the agency or received in the agency;

...

exempt document means:

(a) a document that is exempt for the purposes of Part IV (exempt documents) (see section 31B); or

(b) a document in respect of which, by virtue of section 7, an agency, person or body is exempt from the operation of this Act; or

(c) an official document of a Minister that contains some matter that does not relate to the affairs of an agency or of a Department of State.

...

official document of a Minister or ***official document of the Minister*** means a document that is in the possession of a Minister, or that is in the possession of the Minister concerned, as the case requires, in his or her capacity as a Minister, being a document that relates to the affairs of an agency or of a Department of State and, for the purposes of this definition, a Minister shall be deemed to be in possession of a document that has passed from his or her possession if he or she is entitled to access to the document and the document is not a document of an agency.

...

PART III—ACCESS TO DOCUMENTS

11 Right of access

(1) Subject to this Act, every person has a legally enforceable right to obtain access in accordance with this Act to:

(a) a document of an agency, other than an exempt document; or

(b) an official document of a Minister, other than an exempt document.

(2) Subject to this Act, a person's right of access is not affected by:

(a) any reasons the person gives for seeking access; or

(b) the agency's or Minister's belief as to what are his or her reasons for seeking access.

11A Access to documents on request

Scope

(1) This section applies if:

(a) a request is made by a person, in accordance with subsection 15(2) [requests for access], to an agency or Minister for access to:

(i) a document of the agency; or

(ii) an official document of the Minister; and

(b) any charge that, under the regulations, is required to be paid before access is given has been paid.

(2) This section applies subject to this Act.

Mandatory access—general rule

(3) The agency or Minister must give the person access to the document in accordance with this Act, subject to this section.

Exemptions and conditional exemptions

(4) The agency or Minister is not required by this Act to give the person access to the document at a particular time if, at that time, the document is an exempt document.

(5) The agency or Minister must give the person access to the document if it is conditionally exempt at a particular time unless (in the circumstances) access to the document at that time would, on balance, be contrary to the public interest.

(6) Despite subsection (5), the agency or Minister is not required to give access to the document at a particular time if, at that time, the document is both:

(a) a conditionally exempt document; and

(b) an exempt document:

(i) under Division 2 of Part IV (exemptions); or

(ii) within the meaning of paragraph (b) or (c) of the definition of *exempt document* in subsection 4(1).

11B Public interest exemptions—factors

Scope

(1) This section applies for the purposes of working out whether access to a conditionally exempt document would, on balance, be contrary to the public interest under subsection 11A(5).

(2) This section does not limit subsection 11A(5).

Factors favouring access

(3) Factors favouring access to the document in the public interest include whether access to the document would do any of the following:

(a) promote the objects of this Act (including all the matters set out in sections 3 and 3A);

(b) inform debate on a matter of public importance;

(c) promote effective oversight of public expenditure;

(d) allow a person to access his or her own personal information.

Irrelevant factors

(4) The following factors must not be taken into account in deciding whether access to the document would, on balance, be contrary to the public interest:

(a) access to the document could result in embarrassment to the Commonwealth Government, or cause a loss of confidence in the Commonwealth Government;

(b) access to the document could result in any person misinterpreting or misunderstanding the document;

(c) the author of the document was (or is) of high seniority in the agency to which the request for access to the document was made;

(d) access to the document could result in confusion or unnecessary debate.

Guidelines

(5) In working out whether access to the document would, on balance, be contrary to the public interest, an agency or Minister must have regard to any guidelines issued by the Information Commissioner for the purposes of this subsection under section 93A.

...

15 Requests for access

Persons may request access

(1) Subject to section 15A, a person who wishes to obtain access to a document of an agency or an official document of a Minister may request access to the document.

[Editors' note: Section 15A concerns request for access to personnel records.]

Requirements for request

(2) The request must:

(a) be in writing; and

(aa) state that the request is an application for the purposes of this Act; and

(b) provide such information concerning the document as is reasonably necessary to enable a responsible officer of the agency, or the Minister, to identify it; and

(c) give details of how notices under this Act may be sent to the applicant (for example, by providing an electronic address to which notices may be sent by electronic communication).

...

Agency required to assist

(3) Where a person:

(a) wishes to make a request to an agency; or

(b) has made to an agency a request that does not comply with this section;

it is the duty of the agency to take reasonable steps to assist the person to make the request in a manner that complies with this section.

...

20 Forms of access

(1) Access to a document may be given to a person in one or more of the following forms:

(a) a reasonable opportunity to inspect the document;

(b) provision by the agency or Minister of a copy of the document;

(c) in the case of a document that is an article or thing from which sounds or visual images are capable of being reproduced, the making of arrangements for the person to hear or view those sounds or visual images;

(d) in the case of a document by which words are recorded in a manner in which they are capable of being reproduced in the form of sound or in which words are contained in the form of shorthand writing or in codified form, provision by the agency or Minister of a written transcript of the words recorded or contained in the document.

...

22 Access to edited copies with exempt or irrelevant matter deleted

Scope

(1) This section applies if:

(a) an agency or Minister decides:

(i) to refuse to give access to an exempt document; or

(ii) that to give access to a document would disclose information that would reasonably be regarded as irrelevant to the request for access; and

(b) it is possible for the agency or Minister to prepare a copy (an *edited copy)* of the document, modified by deletions, ensuring that:

(i) access to the edited copy would be required to be given under section 11A (access to documents on request); and

(ii) the edited copy would not disclose any information that would reasonably be regarded as irrelevant to the request; and

(c) it is reasonably practicable for the agency or Minister to prepare the edited copy, having regard to:

(i) the nature and extent of the modification; and

(ii) the resources available to modify the document; and

(d) it is not apparent (from the request or from consultation with the applicant) that the applicant would decline access to the edited copy.

Access to edited copy

(2) The agency or Minister must:

(a) prepare the edited copy as mentioned in paragraph (1)(b); and

(b) give the applicant access to the edited copy.

...

23 Decisions to be made by authorised persons

(1) Subject to subsection (2) a decision in respect of a request made to an agency may be made, on behalf of the agency, by the responsible Minister or the principal officer of the agency or, subject to the regulations, by an officer of the agency acting within the scope of authority exercisable by him or her in

accordance with arrangements approved by the responsible Minister or the principal officer of the agency.

...

[Editors' note: Subsection (2) concerns requests to courts, tribunals or bodies specified in sch 1.]

24 Power to refuse request—diversion of resources etc.

(1) If an agency or Minister is satisfied, when dealing with a request for a document, that a practical refusal reason exists in relation to the request (see section 24AA), the agency or Minister:

(a) must undertake a request consultation process (see section 24AB); and

(b) if, after the request consultation process, the agency or Minister is satisfied that the practical refusal reason still exists—the agency or Minister may refuse to give access to the document in accordance with the request.

(2) For the purposes of this section, the agency or Minister may treat 2 or more requests as a single request if the agency or Minister is satisfied that:

(a) the requests relate to the same document or documents; or

(b) the requests relate to documents, the subject matter of which is substantially the same.

24AA When does a practical refusal reason exist?

(1) For the purposes of section 24, a ***practical refusal reason*** exists in relation to a request for a document if either (or both) of the following applies:

(a) the work involved in processing the request:

(i) in the case of an agency—would substantially and unreasonably divert the resources of the agency from its other operations; or

(ii) in the case of a Minister—would substantially and unreasonably interfere with the performance of the Minister's functions;

(b) the request does not satisfy the requirement in paragraph 15(2)(b) (identification of documents).

(2) Subject to subsection (3), but without limiting the matters to which the agency or Minister may have regard, in deciding whether a practical refusal reason exists, the agency or Minister must have regard to the resources that would have to be used for the following:

(a) identifying, locating or collating the documents within the filing system of the agency, or the office of the Minister;

(b) deciding whether to grant, refuse or defer access to a document to which the request relates, or to grant access to an edited copy of such a document, including resources that would have to be used for:

(i) examining the document; or

(ii) consulting with any person or body in relation to the request;

(c) making a copy, or an edited copy, of the document;

(d) notifying any interim or final decision on the request.

(3) In deciding whether a practical refusal reason exists, an agency or Minister must not have regard to:

(a) any reasons that the applicant gives for requesting access; or

(b) the agency's or Minister's belief as to what the applicant's reasons are for requesting access; or

(c) any maximum amount, specified in the regulations, payable as a charge for processing a request of that kind.

...

26 Reasons and other particulars of decisions to be given

(1) Where, in relation to a request, a decision is made relating to a refusal to grant access to a document in accordance with the request or deferring provision of access to a document, the decision-maker shall cause the applicant to be given notice in writing of the decision, and the notice shall:

(a) state the findings on any material questions of fact, referring to the material on which those findings were based, and state the reasons for the decision; and

(aa) in the case of a decision to refuse to give access to a conditionally exempt document—include in those reasons the public interest factors taken into account in making the decision; and

(b) where the decision relates to a document of an agency, state the name and designation of the person giving the decision; and

(c) give to the applicant appropriate information concerning:

(i) his or her rights with respect to review of the decision;

(ii) his or her rights to make a complaint to the Information Commissioner in relation to the decision; and

(iii) the procedure for the exercise of the rights referred to in subparagraphs (i) and (ii);

including (where applicable) particulars of the manner in which an application for internal review (Part VI) and IC review (Part VII) may be made.

(1A) Section 13 of the *Administrative Decisions (Judicial Review) Act 1977* does not apply to a decision referred to in subsection (1).

(2) A notice under this section is not required to contain any matter that is of such a nature that its inclusion in a document of an agency would cause that document to be an exempt document.

...

PART IV—EXEMPT DOCUMENTS

31B Exempt documents for the purposes of this Part

A document is ***exempt*** for the purposes of this Part if:

(a) it is an exempt document under Division 2; or

(b) it is conditionally exempt under Division 3, and access to the document would, on balance, be contrary to the public interest for the purposes of subsection 11A(5).

Office of the Australian Information Commissioner ('OAIC'), *FOI Agency Resource 5: Exemptions and Conditional Exemptions Under the Freedom of Information Act 1982* (September 2011)

[Editors' note: The following table is a summary of exemptions published by the OAIC. Refer to the relevant sections of the *Freedom of Information Act 1982* (Cth) for the specific wording of exemptions.]

EXEMPTIONS

s 33	Exempts documents if their disclosure would, or could reasonably be expected to, cause damage to Australia's **national security**, **defence** or **international relations**, or would divulge information communicated in confidence to the Commonwealth by a foreign government or an international organisation. This includes information communicated pursuant to a treaty or formal instrument on protection of classified information.
s 34	Exempts **Cabinet documents**, which are Cabinet submissions, official records of the Cabinet, briefings to a minister on a Cabinet submission, and drafts of Cabinet submissions, official records and Cabinet briefings. A Cabinet submission must have been created for the dominant purpose of being submitted for Cabinet's consideration and must have actually been submitted or be proposed by a sponsoring minister to be submitted (s 34(1)). Includes a document that is a copy, part of or an extract from an exempt document (s 34(2)), and a document that contains information which would reveal a Cabinet deliberation or decision (except where the deliberation or decision has been officially disclosed) (s 34(3)). A document is not exempt merely because it is an attachment to an exempt document (s 34(4)). A document by which a Cabinet decision is officially published (such as a media release) is not an exempt document (s 34(5)). Information in a Cabinet document is not exempt matter if the information consists of purely factual information, unless disclosure would reveal a Cabinet deliberation or decision whose existence has not been officially disclosed (s 34(6)).
s 37	Exempts documents if their disclosure would or could reasonably be expected to affect the **enforcement of law and protection of public safety**, including by: • prejudicing the conduct of an investigation of a breach relating to taxation or proper administration of the law • revealing the existence or identity of a confidential informant (see s 37(2A) for confidential sources) • endangering any person's life or physical safety • prejudicing a fair trial • disclosing lawful methods of investigation or prejudicing methods for protecting public safety.
s 38	Exempts documents to which **secrecy provisions apply** under a provision of another Act and either: • that provision is specified in Schedule 3 of the FOI Act, or • s 38 is expressly applied to the document or information in the document, by that secrecy provision, or by another provision of that or any other enactment (s 38(1)(b)).

	There are two limitations to this exemption. An applicant has a right of access to a document that is exempt if the relevant secrecy provision does not prohibit disclosure to that applicant. The exemption does not apply if the applicant requests a document which contains their own personal information, except if disclosure is prohibited under the *Migration Act* 1958.
s 42	Exempts documents subject to **legal professional privilege** (LPP). The dominant purpose test and the independent legal adviser and client relationship are determinative when considering LPP. Documents are not exempt if the person entitled to claim LPP waives the claim (s 42(3)(a)). Section 42 does not apply to an agency's operational information (as defined in s 8A).
s 45	Exempts documents containing **material obtained in confidence**, where the person who provided the confidential information would be able to bring an action under the general law for breach of confidence to prevent disclosure, or to seek compensation for loss or damage arising from disclosure.
s45A	Exempts Parliamentary Budget Office documents.
s 46	Exempts documents if their disclosure would, apart from the FOI Act and any immunity of the Crown, **be in contempt of court or infringe the privileges of the Parliament.** A contempt of court is an action which interferes with the due administration of justice. The term 'parliamentary privilege' refers to the privileges or immunities of the Houses of the Parliament and the powers of the Houses to protect the integrity of their processes.
s 47	Exempts documents **disclosing trade secrets or commercially valuable information** whose value would be, or could reasonably be expected to be, destroyed or diminished if the information were disclosed. See also the business or professional affairs conditional exemption (s 47G).
s 47A	Exempts **electoral rolls**, including: • print, microform and digital copies of electoral rolls • documents that set out particulars of individual electors that were used to prepare electoral rolls or were derived from electoral roll data.

Conditional exemptions: Application of the public interest test to conditional exemptions

An agency or minister must give access to a conditionally exempt document unless, at the time, disclosure would, on balance, be contrary to the public interest (ss 11A(5)). The *Freedom of Information Act 1982* (Cth) sets out certain factors that favour access and some that must not be taken into account (s 11B(3) and (4)).

s 47B	Conditionally exempts documents if their disclosure would or could reasonably be expected to damage **Commonwealth-State relations or relations with Norfolk Island** or disclose information communicated in confidence by or on behalf of a government or authority of a State to the Commonwealth or the Government of Norfolk Island.
s 47C	Conditionally exempts documents if their disclosure would disclose **deliberative processes.** Deliberative matter includes opinions, advices or recommendations that have been obtained, prepared or recorded, and consultations or deliberation that have taken place, as part of the deliberative processes relating to the functions of an agency, a minister or the Government of the Commonwealth or Norfolk Island. Operational information (as defined in s 8A) and purely factual material are not deliberative matter.

	Does not apply to: • reports of scientific or technical experts • reports of a body or organisation established within an agency • records of a final decision given in the exercise of a power or of an adjudicative function (s 47C(3)).
s 47D	Conditionally exempts documents if their disclosure would have a substantial adverse effect on the **financial or property interests of the Commonwealth or Norfolk Island.** Relates both to expenditure and revenue-generating activities, including intellectual property and the Crown's interests in natural resources.
s 47E	Conditionally exempts documents if their disclosure would reasonably be expected to affect **certain operations of agencies** on one or more of the following grounds: • prejudice to the effectiveness of procedures or methods for the conduct of tests, examinations or audits • prejudice to the attainment of the objects of particular tests, examinations or audits • a substantial adverse effect on the management or assessment of personnel • a substantial adverse effect on the proper and efficient conduct of operations.
s 47F	Conditionally exempts documents if their disclosure would involve the unreasonable disclosure of **personal information about any person** (including a deceased person). An agency or minister must take into account: • the extent to which the information is well known • whether the person to whom the information relates is known to be associated with the matters dealt with in the document • the availability of the information from publicly accessible sources • any other relevant matters (s 47F(2)). Access can be given to a qualified person nominated by the applicant if it would be detrimental to the applicant's health or well-being to be given direct access to the documents. The qualified persons include medical practitioners, psychiatrists, psychologists, counsellors and social workers.
s 47G	Conditionally exempts documents if their release would disclose information about a person's **business or professional affairs**, or the business, commercial or financial affairs of an organisation or undertaking, and the disclosure: • would or could reasonably be expected to unreasonably affect those lawful affairs, or • could reasonably be expected to prejudice the supply of information to the Commonwealth, Norfolk Island or an agency. Consider also the trade secrets or commercially valuable information exemption (s 47).
s 47H	Conditionally exempts documents containing information about **research** being undertaken by an agency officer if its disclosure would be likely unreasonably to expose the agency or officer to disadvantage. Only applies to CSIRO and Australian National University (ANU) (see Schedule 4).
s 47J	Conditionally exempts documents if their disclosure would reasonably be expected to have a substantial adverse effect on **Australia's economy** (including on a particular sector of the economy or the economy of a particular region), by: • influencing a decision or action, or • giving a person or class of persons an undue benefit or detriment in relation to their business by providing premature knowledge of an action or inaction. Documents include those containing matter relating to currency or exchange rates, interest rates, taxes, financial regulation and foreign investment.

Case study: *Osland v Secretary, Department of Justice (No 1) & (No 2)*

Freedom of Information Act 1982 (Vic)

[As at relevant date]

PART III—ACCESS TO DOCUMENTS

13 Right of access

Subject to this Act, every person has a legally enforceable right to obtain access in accordance with this Act to—

(a) a document of an agency, other than an exempt document; or

(b) an official document of a Minister, other than an exempt document.

....

PART IV—EXEMPT DOCUMENTS

...

32 Documents affecting legal proceedings

(1) A document is an exempt document if it is of such a nature that it would be privileged from production in legal proceedings on the ground of legal professional privilege.

...

PART VI – REVIEW OF DECISIONS

...

50 Applications for review

(2) Subject to sections 51 and 51A [concerning internal review and health records] ... , an applicant may apply to the Tribunal for review of—

(a) a decision refusing to grant access to a document in accordance with a request;

(b) a decision deferring the provision of access to a document;

...

(3) On the hearing of an application for review the Tribunal shall have, in addition to any other power, the same powers as an agency or a Minister in respect of a request, including power to decide that access should be granted to an exempt document (not being a document referred to in section 28 [Cabinet documents], section 29A [national security], section 31(3) [certain law enforcement documents], or in section 33 [personal privacy]) where the Tribunal is of opinion that the public interest requires that access to the document should be granted under this Act.

Introduction

The *Freedom of Information Act 1982* (Vic) grants a power to the Civil and Administrative Tribunal to disclose some exempt documents when the Tribunal is of the opinion that disclosure is in the public interest (s 50(4)). There are numerous public interest tests in freedom of information statutes in other Australian jurisdictions, but no equivalent override granted to a Tribunal. The application of a public interest override to a legal professional privilege exemption in this way may not be relevant in other jurisdictions. Nevertheless, the High Court's consideration of accountability through public scrutiny, and the concept of 'public interest', in the following *Osland* cases has broader relevance.

Osland v Secretary, Department of Justice (No 1) (2008) 234 CLR 275

Facts

Heather Osland was convicted of the murder of her husband in 1996 and sentenced to 14 years gaol in a highly publicised Victorian case involving claims of battered woman syndrome. The case became a catalyst for changes to the Victorian law on defences to homicide involving family violence.[9] After unsuccessful appeals,[10] Ms Osland petitioned the Governor of Victoria for mercy seeking a pardon – an exercise of prerogative power. The petition for mercy was refused. She served 9.5 years of her 14-year sentence and was released in 2005.

In response to the petition for mercy, the Victorian Attorney-General issued a press release referring to a joint advice from three Queen's Counsel that recommended it be denied. Ms Osland sought access under freedom of information to documents relating to her petition, including the joint advice and other legal advice. The Victorian Department of Justice refused access under s 32 (legal professional privilege) and she sought review in the Victorian Civil and Administrative Tribunal (VCAT). Ms Osland argued throughout the Tribunal and later court proceedings that by issuing the press release the Attorney-General had waived legal professional privilege in the joint advice. That argument failed at every level in the legal proceedings.

Despite the legal professional privilege exemption, which had no specific public interest test, the Tribunal granted access to the documents on the basis of a public interest override in the Victorian legislation (*Osland v Department of Justice* (2005) 23 VAR 378). Morris J in the Tribunal thought it was particularly relevant to the public interest analysis that other legal advices had been obtained, while only one (joint) advice had been cited by the Attorney-General in the press release. He expressed the view that '[i]n order to clear the air and properly inform the public it would be necessary for the whole of these documents, not just the conclusions, to be made available' (at 393 [53]).

9 The Osland case was cited by the Victorian Law Reform Commission in its report on defences to homicide that led to law reform: Victorian Law Reform Commission, Defences to Homicide: Final Report (2004). For a discussion of the impact of the Osland case see: Kellie Toole, 'Self-defence and the reasonable woman: equality before the new Victorian law' (2012) 36 *Melbourne University Law Review* 250, 258–60.

10 *Osland v The Queen* (1998) 197 CLR 316.

The Department of Justice appealed the Tribunal decision and the Victorian Court of Appeal held that there was no basis for disclosure of the documents in the public interest (*Department of Justice v Osland* (2007) 26 VAR 425). In contrast to the Tribunal, Bongiorno AJA in the Court of Appeal, saw the possibility of differing legal opinions as a public interest basis for refusing access. The Court of Appeal did not inspect the documents. Heather Osland successfully appealed to the High Court in the first of two High Court cases dealing with the FOI application (*Osland v Secretary, Department of Justice (No 1)* (2008) 234 CLR 275). The majority judges held that the Court of Appeal ought to have examined the documents.

In the first of the extracts below from the joint judgment, Gleeson CJ, Gummow, Heydon and Kiefel JJ consider whether possible differences between the legal advices was a relevant public interest factor for, or against, disclosure, and the importance of public accountability.

In the second of the extracts below, Kirby J discusses the history of secrecy in Australian public administration and the objectives underlying the 'radical' reform of freedom of information.

Gleeson CJ, Gummow, Heydon and Kiefel JJ

> ***300*** [55] Bongiorno A-JA, with whom Ashley JA agreed, took up the point [about possible differences between the advices] directly, although without looking at the documents to see whether there was any factual foundation for it. He dealt with the matter by saying that, if the opinions received by the Attorney-General were in some material respects different, then that was a reason against, rather than in favour of, releasing them. On that factual hypothesis, 'the release of those opinions would enable a political collateral attack on the exercise of the prerogative of mercy which would have the effect of changing its fundamental nature'.
>
> [56] Regardless of whether the advice given by the Attorney-General to the Governor was legally unexaminable, the conduct of the Attorney-General was not unaccountable. The very exercise in which the Attorney-General was engaged in putting out his press release assumed political accountability. Political attack on a decision not to exercise the prerogative of mercy in a particular case, or at least on the process leading to such a decision, is not alien to the process. That does not mean abrogating legal professional privilege and other statutorily recognised grounds of confidentiality. What it means, however, is that the risk of political criticism is not of itself a public interest argument against disclosure. This aspect of the reasoning of two members of the Court of Appeal was erroneous.
>
> [57] There are obvious difficulties in giving the phrase 'public interest' as it appears in s 50(4) a fixed and precise content. It is sufficient to say here that the assumption by the Attorney-General of political accountability by the putting out of the press release may, in the circumstances, enliven s 50(4). If there were nothing more to it than that Morris J was saying that the very existence of a number of advices meant that, in order to 'clear the air' and dispel any speculation about possible inconsistency, they should all be released then the Court of Appeal should have rejected that reasoning. If, however, there were some material difference in the advices, or the facts on which they were based, then, depending on the nature and extent of that difference, it is not impossible that an aspect of the public interest could require its

revelation. If Morris J had said nothing about the matter, there was no particular reason why the Court of Appeal should have set out itself to look for such a problem. However, in the light of what Morris J said, the Court of Appeal should have looked at the documents. Its failure to ***301*** do so was an error of principle in the exercise of a discretion. It could not be said that, as a matter of principle, no inconsistency between the various advices could possibly have required the disclosure of all or any of them. The Attorney-General, in his press release, referred, for an obvious and legitimate purpose, to certain legal advice as recommending the course that was finally taken. If it had been the case that the Government had received other and materially different legal advice then, depending on the nature and extent of the difference, it is possible that this could have been a relevant consideration in deciding the requirements of the public interest under s 50(4). This is not to say that the existence of differences would necessarily require disclosure. Rather, the existence of such differences as might require disclosure, having been raised obliquely by Morris J, could not be disregarded as legally impossible.

Kirby J

301 [60] The *Freedom of* Information *Act 1982* (Vic) (the FOI Act) introduced to Victoria (as like statutes have introduced elsewhere) an important change in public administration. Australian public administration inherited a culture of secrecy traceable to the traditions of the counsellors of the Crown dating to the Norman Kings of England. Those traditions were reinforced in later dangerous Tudor times by officials such as Sir Francis Walsingham. They were then strengthened by the enactment throughout the British Empire of official ***302*** secrets legislation. A pervasive attitude developed 'that government "owned" official information'. This found reflection in a strong public service convention of secrecy. The attitude behind this convention was caricatured in the popular television series *Yes Minister* in an aphorism ascribed to the fictitious Cabinet Secretary, Sir Arnold Robinson: 'Open Government is a contradiction in terms. You can be open—or you can have government.' The ensuing laughter has helped to break the spell of the tradition by revealing its presumption when viewed in the contemporary age with its more democratic values.

[61] In Australia, the culture of governmental secrecy was sustained both by statute and by common law. In 1966, inspired by the example of legislation in Scandinavian countries, the Congress of the United States of America adopted a *Freedom of Information Act.* This, in turn, enlivened discussion about reform elsewhere. In 1982, an Australian federal *Freedom of Information Act* was enacted. This stimulated initiatives in the state sphere, where, because the public service dated to colonial times, it was sometimes more traditional and more secretive in its procedures than the federal service, dating as it did only to 1901.

[62] The basic purpose of the introduction of freedom of information ('FOI') legislation is the same in all jurisdictions. It is to reinforce 'the three basic principles of democratic government, namely, openness, accountability and responsibility'.

The central objective is to strengthen constitutional principles of governance not always translated into reality because of a lack of material information available to electors. Fundamentally, the idea behind such legislation is to flesh out the constitutional provisions establishing the system of representative government; to increase citizen participation in government beyond a fleeting involvement on election days; and to reduce the degree of apathy and cynicism sometimes arising from a lack of real elector knowledge about, or influence upon, what is going on in government ...

303 [65] The starting point for resolving the issues presented by the present appeal is an appreciation of the duty of this Court, in this context, to do what we are constantly instructing other courts to do in giving effect to legislation. This is to read the legislative text in its context (including against the background of the significant change that the legislation introduces) and, so far as the text and context permit, to give effect to the legislative purpose.

[66] In the present setting, that purpose is a radical one. It assigns very high importance to a public interest in greater openness and transparency in public administration. Given the historical background, the attitudinal shift that FOI legislation demanded of Ministers, departments, agencies and the public service is nothing short of revolutionary. The courts ought not to obstruct that shift. On the contrary, they should strive to interpret FOI legislation in a manner harmonious with its objectives, doing so to the fullest extent that the text allows.

...

305 [73] ... [T]he object and purpose of the FOI Act are central to the resolution of the present appeal. In part, these may be derived from the overall design of that Act, read against the background of what preceded it. But, in part, they are evident from the short and long titles of the FOI Act and from s 3.

[74] The long title of the FOI Act declares that it is: 'An Act to give the Members of the Public Rights of Access to Official Documents of the Government of Victoria and of its Agencies and for other purposes.' Section 3(1) is worth reproducing in full:

> The object of this Act is to extend as far as possible the right of the community to access to information in the possession of the Government of Victoria and other bodies constituted under the law of Victoria for certain public purposes by —
>
> **(a)** making available to the public information about the operations of agencies and, in particular, ensuring that rules and practices affecting members of the public in their dealings with agencies are readily available to persons affected by those rules and practices; and
>
> **(b)** creating a general right of access to information in documentary form in the possession of Ministers and agencies limited only by exceptions and exemptions necessary for the protection of essential public interests and the private and business affairs of persons in respect of whom information is collected and held by agencies.

> [75] Apparently concerned that Ministers, departments, agencies and courts might conceivably adhere, or return, to the old ways of governmental secrecy, the Victorian Parliament spoke directly to all of those actors. It declared its intention as to how the FOI Act should be interpreted. Section 3(2) of that Act states that such interpretation is to be adopted as would 'further the object set out in sub-section (1) [of s 3]'. It further requires any discretions conferred by the Act to be ***306*** exercised 'as far as possible so as to facilitate and promote ... the disclosure of information'.
>
> [76] It is difficult to know how the Parliament of Victoria could have been more emphatic, forthright or clear in indicating the commencement of a new legal era. Courts that construe an Act such as the FOI Act, attentive to preserve the status quo ante, avid to find exceptions, and generous in discerning documents exempt from disclosure, are not being faithful to Parliament's purposes and the declared objects of the Act. An approach hostile to the disclosure of information in documentary form will frustrate the imputed intention of Parliament. To the extent that past rules deriving from the royal prerogative, the common law or earlier inconsistent legislation suggest otherwise, those rules must now be adapted to the provisions, objects and realities of the FOI Act. The duty of the courts, including this Court, is to ensure that this occurs.

[Citations omitted]

Osland v Secretary, Department of Justice (No 2) (2010) 241 CLR 320

Facts

The facts of the case are outlined above in *Osland (No 1)*. After the first High Court decision the matter was remitted from the High Court to the Victorian Court of Appeal, which affirmed its earlier decision to refuse the request for access (*Secretary, Department of Justice v Osland (No 2)* (2009) 25 VR 490). The decision of the Victorian Court of Appeal was, in turn, reversed by the High Court because the Court of Appeal had gone beyond its limited role of reviewing for error of law and had substituted its own decision on whether the public interest required disclosure of the documents. (Extracts concerning review for legal error are included in Chapter 9 of this book.) The High Court set aside the orders in the second Court of Appeal decision and reinstated the Victorian Civil and Administrative Tribunal's original order granting access to the documents. It was after this second High Court appeal decision that Mrs Osland was entitled to release of the documents.

In the extract below, French CJ, Gummow and Bell JJ consider the concept of the 'public interest'.

French CJ, Gummow and Bell JJ

> ***329*** [13] The FOI Act neither defines nor expressly limits the range of matters relevant to the 'public interest' which may require that access should be granted. As was said in the joint judgment in this Court on the first appeal, '[t]here are obvious

difficulties in giving the phrase 'public interest' as it appears in s 50(4) a fixed and precise content'. The nature of 'public interest' determinations in the exercise of statutory powers was described in *O'Sullivan v Farrer* [(1989) 168 CLR 210, 216 (Mason CJ, Brennan, Dawson and Gaudron JJ) quoting Dixon J in *Water Conservation and Irrigation Commission (NSW) v Browning* (1947) 74 CLR 492, 505]:

> the expression 'in the public interest', when used in a statute, classically imports a discretionary value judgment to be made by reference to undefined factual matters, confined only 'in so far as the subject matter and the scope and purpose of the statutory enactments may enable ... given reasons to be [pronounced] definitely extraneous to any objects the legislature could have had in view'.

[Citations omitted]

Reasons for decisions

Public Service Board of New South Wales v Osmond (1986) 159 CLR 656

Facts

Mr Osmond was employed in the New South Wales public service when he applied for a promotion to a vacant position. Another applicant who was also eligible was appointed and Mr Osmond appealed to the Board. After the Board advised Mr Osmond orally that his appeal had been dismissed, he requested reasons for the decision but the Board refused. Mr Osmond applied to the Supreme Court of New South Wales for a declaration that the Board was obliged to provide reasons. He was unsuccessful at first instance, but a majority of the New South Wales Court of Appeal (Kirby P and Priestley J A, Glass JA dissenting) held that there was such a duty.[11] That decision was reversed by the High Court, which held that at common law there is no general obligation to provide reasons, while leaving open the possibility of such a duty in a special case or exceptional circumstances.

Gibbs CJ

662 Kirby P based his conclusion that the Board was bound to give reasons for its decision on the broad principle that the common law requires those entrusted by statute with the discretionary power to make decisions which will affect other persons to act fairly in the performance of their statutory functions. He said: [1984] 3 NSWLR 447, 467]

> The overriding duty of public officials who are donees of statutory powers is to act justly, fairly and in accordance with their statute. Normally, this will

11 *Osmond v Public Service Board of New South Wales* [1984] 3 NSWLR 447.

> require, where they have a power to make discretionary decisions affecting others, an obligation to state the reasons for their decisions. That obligation will exist where, to do otherwise, would render nugatory a facility, however limited, to appeal against the decision. It will also exist where the absence of stated reasons would diminish a facility to have the decision otherwise tested by judicial review to ensure that it complies with the law and to ensure that matters have been taken into account which should have been taken into account or that matters have not been taken into account which ought not to have been taken into account.

He recognized exceptions to the obligation to state reasons, eg where it would be otiose to do so, or where it was clear by inference or otherwise what the reasons were, or where the giving of reasons would disclose confidential information or invade privacy. However he said that the present case did not fall within any exception to the rule. Priestley JA expressed a more guarded view and declined to lay down any general propositions about the right to reasons where such a right is not given by statute. He held that the rules of natural justice applied to the appeal to the Board and that those rules, in the circumstances of the present case, required that reasons be given for the decision of the Board on the appeal.

With the greatest respect to the learned Judges in the majority in the Court of Appeal, the conclusion which they have reached is opposed to overwhelming authority. There is no general rule of the common law, or principle of natural justice, that requires reasons to be given for administrative decisions, even decisions which have been made in the exercise of a statutory discretion and which may adversely affect the interests, or defeat the legitimate or reasonable expectations, of other persons.

...

670 It remains to consider whether, notwithstanding that there is no general obligation to give reasons for an administrative decision, the circumstances make this a special case in which natural justice required reasons to be given. The rules of natural justice are designed to ensure fairness in the making of a decision and it is difficult to see how the fairness of an administrative decision can be affected by what is done after the decision has been made. However, assuming that in special circumstances natural justice may require reasons to be given, the present is not such a case. The issues before the Board were simple and well defined: which of the two officers had the greater efficiency, and if neither of them had greater efficiency than the other, which was the senior? ... Neither the provisions of the Act nor the circumstances of the case justified the conclusion that the rules of natural justice required the Board to communicate the reasons for its decision.

I have dealt with this question at what may be regarded as tedious length in deference to the judgments of the majority of the Court of Appeal. In truth, however, I regard the law as clear. There was no rule of common law, and no principle of natural justice, requiring the Board to give reasons for its decision, however desirable it might be thought that it should have done so.

Deane J

675 There was a time when the ordinary prescript of prudence for an administrative decision-maker who was anxious to avoid litigation was to decline to give reasons for the discretionary exercise of a statutory power in a manner which would adversely affect the property or rights of another ... that approach is no longer, if it ever was, acceptable as a general prescript to be observed by all administrative decision-makers. That is a good thing since the exercise of a decision-making power in a way which adversely affects others is less likely to be, or to appear to be, arbitrary if the decision-maker formulates and provides reasons for his decision. Nonetheless, the stage has not been reached in this country where it is a general prima facie requirement of the common law rules of natural justice or procedural fair play that the administrative decision-maker, having extended to persons who might be adversely affected by a decision an adequate opportunity ***676*** of being heard, is bound to furnish reasons for the exercise of a statutory decision-making power. To the contrary, the ordinary common law position remains that established by the authorities referred to by the Chief Justice in his judgment, namely, that where, as a matter of ordinary construction, the relevant statutory provisions do not impose an obligation to give reasons, the rules of natural justice will not remedy the omission.

...

On the other hand, it is trite law that the common law rules of natural justice or procedural fair play are neither standardized nor immutable. The procedural consequences of their application depend upon the particular statutory framework within which they apply and upon the exigencies of the particular case. Their content may vary with changes in contemporary practice and standards. That being so, the statutory developments referred to in the judgments of Kirby P and Priestley JA in the Court of Appeal in the present case are conducive to an environment within which the courts should be less reluctant than they would have been in times past to discern in statutory provisions a legislative intent that the particular decision-maker should be under a duty to give reasons or to accept that special circumstances might arise in which contemporary standards of natural justice or procedural fair play demand that an administrative decision-maker provide reasons for a decision to a person whose property, rights or legitimate expectations are adversely affected by it. Where such circumstances exist, statutory provisions conferring the relevant decision-making power should, in the absence of a clear intent to the contrary, be construed so as to impose upon the decision-maker an implied statutory duty to provide such reasons. As has been said however, the circumstances in which natural justice or procedural fair play requires that an administrative decision-maker give reasons for his decision are special, that is to say, exceptional.

677 ... [T]he circumstances of the present case were not such as to give rise to a duty on the part of the respondent Public Service Board to provide reasons for its decision to dismiss Mr Osmond's appeal against the appointment of another applicant to the position of Chairman of Local Lands Boards.

[Citations omitted]

Administrative Review Council, *Best Practice Guide 4 – Decision Making: Reasons* (2007)

Introduction

1 Providing a statement of the reasons, evidence and facts for a decision is a fundamental part of administrative review.

A statement of reasons affords a person affected by a decision the opportunity to have the decision explained. The person can then decide whether to exercise their rights of review and appeal, and, if they decide to do so, they are then able to act in an informed manner.

Describing the reasoning process can also help decision makers think more carefully about their task and be more careful in their decision making. Further, the preparation of statements of reasons can help agencies identify relevant principles and create standards to guide future decision making.

Bodies that review government decisions—courts, tribunals, ombudsmen and other oversight bodies—pay close attention to reasons for decisions when deciding whether a decision should be set aside, a new decision made, or other remedial action taken. A decision maker is likely to face criticism when the reasons for a decision are deficient or do not provide a full or accurate account of why the decision was made.

Providing reasons for a decision should not be treated as an obligation that is separate from other principles of good decision making. It is good administrative practice to make a note of every decision at the time the decision is made. This makes it easier to provide a statement of reasons if asked to do so. A documentary record of the decision-making process also helps others understand when, why and by whom a decision was made.

...

The decision

7 A statement of reasons should refer to the legislation that authorised the decision. It is better to quote, rather than summarise, the relevant statutory provisions and then note which aspects need to be resolved or answered, as well as the decision reached on those matters.

Paraphrasing the legislation is unwise because the meaning might be inadvertently changed. For example, if the decision to be made is whether an applicant for a pension or benefit is living in a 'marriage-like relationship' it would be erroneous to say that the question is whether the person is in a 'de facto relationship'.

The name and position of the decision maker should be made clear, as well as that person's legal authority to make the decision. If the person is a delegate this too should be noted.

The findings on material facts

A statement of reasons must contain the findings on all material facts. If a finding is not set out a court might conclude that it was not taken into account and that the decision is invalid as a consequence.

8 A material fact is a fact that can affect the outcome of a decision. Consequently, the findings on material facts are those that support the decision, based on the consideration of all relevant evidence.

The legislation might expressly provide that a fact is material—for example, by making the exercise of power depend on its existence or non-existence. Material facts can also be implied by the subject matter or the scope or purpose of the legislation.

A finding of fact will sometimes be established directly by the evidence—for example, a person's age or nationality. At other times a material fact might be inferred from other facts; for example, a finding that a person was in a 'marriage-like relationship' could be inferred from things such as living arrangements and personal relationships. When a finding of fact is inferred, the statement should set out the primary facts and the process of inference.

The evidence on which the findings were based

A statement of reasons must refer to the evidence on which each material finding of fact is based. It is not sufficient simply to list all the documents that were considered in reaching the decision. The statement should identify the evidence that was considered relevant, credible and significant in relation to each material finding of fact.

When referring to evidence it is not necessary to quote it or to provide a copy, so long as the evidence can be readily identified. The evidence might be identified by stating its source or nature, whichever is more intelligible and informative—for example, 'the medical report from Dr X dated 20 June'.

The statement should demonstrate that each finding of fact is rationally based on evidence. If the evidence was conflicting, the statement should say which evidence was preferred and why ....

The reasons for the decision

The actual reasons relied upon by the decision maker at the time of making the decision must be stated. Every decision should be amenable to logical explanation. The statement must detail all steps in the reasoning process that led to the decision, linking the facts to the decision. The statement should enable a reader to understand exactly how the decision was reached; they should not have to guess at any gaps.

9 The statement must go further than merely expressing conclusions: it must give reasons for those conclusions. This might necessitate mention of the legislation, relevant principles of case law, and policy statements or guidelines or other agency practices that were taken into account. The criteria and other factors considered in making the decision and why material facts were accepted should be noted.

Appeal rights

A statement should also include appeal rights. In particular, details of any right to seek internal review or review by an administrative tribunal (such as the Administrative Appeals Tribunal) should be provided. Time limits for seeking review should also be given.

...

***10* Record keeping**

At the time of making a decision it is good administrative practice to prepare a record that can form the basis for a statement of reasons if one is requested. In particular, it is prudent to make a contemporaneous note of the assessment of evidence, findings of fact and reasons.

Administrative Review Council, *Federal Judicial Review in Australia* (Report No 50, 2012)

9 REASONS FOR DECISIONS

Summary

152 [9.1] The provision of reasons is of central importance to administrative law. The benefits of providing reasons to those affected by administrative decision making include:

- preventing disputes from occurring and from escalating;
- satisfying the requirements of natural justice and assisting in applications for review or appeal;
- providing evidence about the reason for a decision to assist tribunals and courts in performing merits and judicial review;
- improving the quality and consistency of primary decision making; and
- promoting public confidence in the administrative process through transparency.

....

When should reasons be recorded and conveyed?

158 [9.28] If reasons are not provided at the time of the decision, it is possible that the statement of reasons provided in response to [a later] request may not accurately record the basis for the decision. This is more likely in cases where one or more of the following apply:

- the actual reasons for the decision have not been recorded;
- the statement of reasons is prepared by a legal adviser;
- the original decision maker is no longer available; and
- the decision maker is a Minister who has made a decision on the basis of a recommendation which does not clearly disclose the findings and the reasons for the decision.

Timing of the recording and giving of reasons

[9.29] The Council considers that the timing of the recording of reasons is particularly important, noting the important distinction between the right to be given reasons and the obligation to record reasons.

...

Encouraging contemporaneous recording of reasons

161 [9.40] The Council considers that the contemporaneous recording of reasons by decision makers has a number of significant advantages. First, reasons recorded at the time of making are more likely to reflect a decision maker's actual reasons. Secondly, contemporaneous reasons can be provided at the time notice of the decision is given, improving overall communication. Thirdly, the process of writing reasons materially assists decision-makers during the process—facilitating the detailed consideration of all necessary issues. The process of providing for reasons disciplines a decision maker's thinking.

[9.41] The Council's view is that the contemporaneous recording of reasons is a principle of good administration, which should be reflected in agency best practice and in any Charters of Good Administration.

Recommendation 11

All Australian Government agencies should endeavour to record reasons at the time of making decisions.

Statement of reasons not prepared by the decision maker

[9.42] Statements of reasons that are not prepared by the decision maker raise more significant issues than reasons prepared by the decision maker at a later time. Stephen Lloyd SC and Donald Mitchell have noted the issue of legal practitioners 'settling' ***162*** draft reasons to remove legal errors [Stephen Lloyd and Donald Mitchell, 'Statements of the decision maker's actual reasons' (2010) 59 Admin Review 56]. There are risks associated with this practice. While it removes the error from the record, the decision may still be affected by the legal error. Lloyd and Mitchell also point out that such advice would be protected by legal professional privilege and not subject to scrutiny by the courts. They suggested that the Council could provide directions to Government officials on the kind of advice that should and should not be sought from legal practitioners about reasons.

[9.43] The absence of the original decision maker is a particular instance where not providing contemporaneous reasons or records of a decision is problematic. Lloyd and Mitchell suggest that when this is the case, the person currently responsible for the area should give their own reasons for the decision, and remake the decision if they consider it is incorrect. This would ensure that the reasons are the actual reasons for the decision.

[9.44] Evidentiary problems have arisen in relation to Ministerial decisions where the only reasons available are either a submission to the Minister from an agency recommending a particular approach, or ex post facto reasons prepared by the agency. As a matter of practice, Lloyd and Mitchell suggest that, where appropriate, agencies could provide a statement of reasons with a submission for the Minister to sign, which he/she can alter as necessary.

[Some citations omitted]

Ombudsman Act 1976 (Cth)

[As at 1 December 2022]

DIVISION 2—REPORTS

15 Reports by Ombudsman

(1) Where, after an investigation under this Act into action taken by a Department or prescribed authority has been completed, the Ombudsman is of the opinion:

...

(c) in a case where the action comprised or included a decision to exercise a discretionary power in a particular manner or to refuse to exercise such a power:

...

(ii) that the complainant in respect of the investigation or some other person should have been furnished, but was not furnished, with particulars of the reasons for deciding to exercise the power in that manner or to refuse to exercise the power, as the case may be;

this section applies to the decision, recommendation, act or omission constituting that action.

(2) Where the Ombudsman is of the opinion:

...

(e) that reasons should have been, but were not, given for a decision to which this section applies;

...

the Ombudsman shall report accordingly to the Department or prescribed authority concerned.

(3) The Ombudsman:

(a) shall include in a report under subsection (2) his or her reasons for the opinions specified in the report; and

(b) may also include in such a report any recommendations he or she thinks fit to make.

Administrative Appeals Tribunal Act 1975 (Cth)

[As at 1 December 2022]

28 Person affected by decision may obtain reasons for decision Request for statement of reasons

(1) Subject to subsection (1AAA), if a person makes a decision in respect of which an application may be made to the Tribunal for a review, any person (in this section referred to as the ***applicant***) who is entitled to apply to the Tribunal for a review of the decision may, by notice in writing given to the person who made the decision, request that person to give to the applicant a statement in writing setting out the findings on

material questions of fact, referring to the evidence or other material on which those findings were based and giving the reasons for the decision, and the person who made the decision shall, as soon as practicable but in any case within 28 days after receiving the request, prepare, and give to the applicant, such a statement.

Exceptions

(1AAA) Subsection (1) does not apply in relation to:

(a) a decision that is reviewable in the Security Division; or

(b) a decision that is a decision on AAT first review within the meaning of any of the following:

(i) the *A New Tax System (Family Assistance) (Administration) Act 1999;*

(ii) the *Child Support (Registration and Collection) Act 1988;*

(iii) the *Social Security (Administration) Act 1999;*

(iv) the *Student Assistance Act 1973;*

(v) the *Paid Parental Leave Act 2010.*

...

Inadequate statement of reasons

(5) An applicant who has been given a statement under subsection (1) may apply to the Tribunal for a declaration that the statement does not contain one or more of the following:

(a) adequate particulars of findings on material questions of fact;

(b) an adequate reference to the evidence or other material on which those findings were based;

(c) adequate particulars of the reasons for the decision.

(6) If the Tribunal makes the declaration, the person to whom the request for the statement was made must, as soon as practicable and no later than 28 days after the day the declaration was made, give the applicant an additional statement containing further and better particulars in relation to the matters specified in the declaration.

[Editors' note: Subsections 28(1AA)–(4) concern what happens if a decision-maker contests an applicant's entitlement to reasons, and circumstances in which a decision-maker may refuse to give reasons, or the applicant is otherwise not entitled. As this book went to press it was announced that the Administrative Appeals Tribunal would be *abolished* and replaced with a new federal administrative review body.]

Administrative Decisions (Judicial Review) Act 1977 (Cth)

[As at 1 December 2022]

13 Reasons for decision may be obtained

(1) Where a person makes a decision to which this section applies, any person who is entitled to make an application to the Federal Court or the Federal Circuit and Family Court of Australia (Division 2) under section 5 [Editors' note: s 5 is set out in Chapter 9 of this book] in relation to the decision may, by notice in writing given to the person who made the decision, request him or her to furnish a statement in writing setting out the findings on material questions of fact, referring to the evidence or other material on which those findings were based and giving the reasons for the decision.

(2) Where such a request is made, the person who made the decision shall, subject to this section, as soon as practicable, and in any event within 28 days, after receiving the request, prepare the statement and furnish it to the person who made the request.

...

(7) If the Federal Court or the Federal Circuit and Family Court of Australia (Division 2), upon application for an order under this subsection made to it by a person to whom a statement has been furnished in pursuance of a request under subsection (1), considers that the statement does not contain adequate particulars of findings on material questions of fact, an adequate reference to the evidence or other material on which those findings were based or adequate particulars of the reasons for the decision, the court may order the person who furnished the statement to furnish to the person who made the request for the statement, within such time as is specified in the order, an additional statement or additional statements containing further and better particulars in relation to matters specified in the order with respect to those findings, that evidence or other material or those reasons.

...

(11) In this section, *decision to which this section applies* means a decision that is a decision to which this Act applies, but does not include:

(a) a decision in relation to which section 28 of the *Administrative Appeals Tribunal Act 1975* applies;

(b) a decision that includes, or is accompanied by a statement setting out, findings of facts, a reference to the evidence or other material on which those findings were based and the reasons for the decision; or

(c) a decision included in any of the classes of decision set out in Schedule 2.

[Editors' note: Subsections 13(3)–(6) and (8)–(10) concern what happens if a decision-maker is of the opinion that the applicant is not entitled to reasons, and circumstances in which reasons may be refused or the applicant is otherwise not entitled. Sections 13A and 14 provide that certain information is not required to be disclosed in a statement of reasons.]

PART

III

MERITS REVIEW

CHAPTER

7

REVIEW ON THE MERITS

Introduction	178
Why merits review?	178
Commonwealth, *Commonwealth Administrative Review Committee Report* (Parl Paper No 144, 1971)	178
Internal review	180
Administrative Review Council, *Internal Review of Agency Decision Making* (Report No 44, 2000)	180
A New Tax System (Family Assistance) (Administration) Act 1999 (Cth)	183
Examples of merits review decisions	187
Farrugia v Secretary, Department of Social Services [2022] AATA 11	187
Tipungwuti v Director – Crime Victims Services Unit (No 2) [2016] NTCAT 191	190

Introduction

This chapter complements Chapter 7 of *Government Accountability: Australian Administrative Law*, third edition. These chapters introduce the concept of merits review in Australia. An important point is that merits review is a creature of statute. The availability of merits review, the authority responsible for conducting review, the nature of review, the process to be followed and the remedies available in a given case can only be determined by careful examination of the relevant statutory provisions. For this reason, this chapter is not a collection of canonical authorities on merits review; few, if any, such authorities exist.

The first two sections of this chapter ('Why merits review?' and 'Internal review') provide government perspectives on the need for, aims of, and potential drawbacks of, merits review. The third section consists of two case studies of merits review. These cases are chosen to show how a merits review application might proceed; how merits review arguments are constructed; and the possible outcomes of merits review.

Why merits review?

Commonwealth, *Commonwealth Administrative Review Committee Report* (Parl Paper No 144, 1971)

Many features of modern Australian administrative law owe their existence to the 1971 report of the Commonwealth Administrative Review Committee ('Kerr Committee'). The Committee was chaired by Sir John Kerr (then a Judge of the Commonwealth Industrial Court, later Chief Justice of the Supreme Court of New South Wales and, subsequently, Governor-General) and its other members were Sir Anthony Mason (then a Judge of Appeal of the Supreme Court of New South Wales; later Chief Justice of the High Court), Bob Ellicott QC (then Commonwealth Solicitor-General; later Commonwealth Attorney-General and subsequently a Federal Court judge) and Professor Harry Whitmore (Dean of Law at the Australian National University). The Committee's terms of reference were:

1. To consider what jurisdiction (if any) to review administrative decisions made under Commonwealth law should be exercised by the proposed [Federal Court], by some other Federal Court or by some other Court exercising federal jurisdiction.
2. To consider the procedures whereby review is to be obtained.
3. To consider the substantive grounds for review.
4. To consider the desirability of introducing legislation along the lines of the United Kingdom *Tribunals and Inquiries Act 1958* (UK).
5. To report to the government the conclusions of the Committee.

One of the Committee's major contributions was to highlight the importance of merits review in addition to judicial review, and to recommend the establishment of the Commonwealth merits review tribunal that became the Administrative Appeals Tribunal. Throughout the report, the Committee emphasised that different administrative law mechanisms complement each other; judicial review, for example, cannot fully be understood without also considering merits review. Although the framework of Australian administrative law has changed enormously since 1971 (largely as a result of the Kerr Committee Report), the Committee's observations on the respective roles of judicial review and merits review remain valid today.

> ***1*** [4] We have taken the view that it was not intended by the terms of reference to confine the work of the Committee to an examination of any particular aspect of the review of administrative decisions and that the Committee should examine all aspects of the review of administrative decisions ...
>
> [5] The subject of administrative review is one which requires to be considered in its entirety because it has been universally accepted that judicial review by the courts standing alone, by the prerogative writs, declaration or injunction under the existing law, cannot provide for an adequate review of administrative decisions. ***2*** It has been the uniform experience of the common law countries, including the United Kingdom, the United States of America and New Zealand, that the traditional supervision by the courts of the administrative process must be supplemented by provision for review on questions of law or on the merits of administrative decisions affecting the rights and property of the citizen ... We have therefore considered in detail, in arriving at our recommendations on the first term of reference, the question whether jurisdiction to review administrative decisions on the merits should as a general rule be conferred on a court, or whether such jurisdiction should be exercised by some other tribunal and, if so, what type of tribunal. This in turn has raised the question whether the true function of the courts in relation to administrative review is to be complementary either to a system of general administrative review by a single review authority existing apart from the courts, or to a system of specialized review tribunals existing apart from the courts, or to a combination of both systems.
>
> [6] We have found that it is neither correct nor practicable to examine in isolation judicial review in the traditional sense; it must be seen and examined in the total context of review of administrative decisions. The adequacy of any system of judicial review can be assessed and judged only in the light of such other provision for administrative review as does, or should, exist at the same time. Further, it must be kept in mind that a question of importance which can arise in relation to some functions is whether they are better suited to judicial or non-judicial review.
>
> ...
>
> ***9*** [20] A person aggrieved by a decision of a Commonwealth official or tribunal will generally feel that the decision was wrong on the facts or merits of the matter. Sometimes there is an appeal on the merits to an administrative tribunal or to the courts, but generally such a person has no way of appealing against a decision on the facts or merits. The courts are, in most cases, not open to him for this purpose and he is driven, if he wishes to upset a decision, to find some way of attacking it in the courts upon legal grounds. The legal grounds are, however, limited and the means, or remedies, complicated. He has to select his court, his ground of attack, and his procedure or remedy. If, being driven to seek in the courts an invalidating judgment, he succeeds in having a decision set aside, he is, in effect, in many cases back where he started with the administrative process to be faced again before the same administrative officer or body. An attempt is often made to have a decision upset, not so much

because of the legal flaws involved but because a person aggrieved by it thinks that it is wrong on the merits and success in the courts in many cases involves the risk of the same decision on the merits being reached, after the previous judicial decision has been given, by the same administrative body and by processes which can no longer be attacked in the courts.

...

20 [58] It is generally accepted that this complex pattern of rules as to appropriate courts, principles and remedies [in judicial review] is both unwieldy and unnecessary. The pattern is not fully understood by most lawyers; the layman tends to find the technicalities not merely incomprehensible but quite absurd .. The basic fault of the entire structure is, however, that review cannot as a general rule, in the absence of special statutory provisions, be obtained 'on the merits' - and this is usually what the aggrieved citizen is seeking.

[Citations omitted]

Internal review

Administrative Review Council, *Internal Review of Agency Decision Making* (Report No 44, 2000)

In this extract, the Administrative Review Council discusses the effect of internal review on primary decision-making. The research for this report included interviews with 92 agency officers, consisting of primary decision-makers, internal reviewers, supervisors and managers. While the research was conducted more than 20 years ago, the report still contains useful insights into the dynamics of merits review.

Factors limiting internal review's ability to improve primary decision making

The potential for the existence of internal review to have negative impacts on primary decision making

51 [7.3] A criticism of internal review, and of the merits review system in general, is that it can encourage primary decision makers to exercise 'soft' options in order to avoid the likelihood of a review of the decision; for example, by deciding to grant a benefit, against better judgment, to a claimant who might otherwise appeal.

[7.4] ... There was some anecdotal evidence gleaned from the surveys which suggests this practice is not unknown.

> Some people don't like making adverse decisions—the customer gets mad, it creates more work, and an internal review officer may become involved. It is easier to just not make an adverse decision. (Primary decision-maker)

52 [7.5] Conversely, another commentator has stated that there are very few areas where primary decision makers are directly influenced by concern that their decision will be overturned by a review body. In his opinion, the directions and guidance given to decision makers are emphatically to the effect that they should not try to second-guess what will happen if a decision is taken on review [D Volker, 'The Effect of Administrative Law Reforms - Primary Level Decision Making' (1989) 58 *Canberra Bulletin of Public Administration* 112, 113].

[7.6] The survey tested the 'soft options' theory by asking primary decision makers whether the prospect of internal review affected the way they make decisions. The results lend some weight to the above view, since around two-thirds considered that there was no effect.

[7.7] Of the minority that considered that there was an effect, only positive effects were mentioned. For example, taking a beneficial view of the facts if the case was close, and being more thorough in their work, were each mentioned by three respondents.

[7.8] Managers were also asked about the same issue. Unlike primary decision makers, slightly more than half did consider that the prospect of internal review had an effect on primary decision making. The most commonly mentioned effect was that there was more of an incentive to make the right decision. Disappointingly, the next most commonly mentioned effect was that the existence of internal review provided an easy option in suggesting an appeal to a client.

[7.9] Two of the effects mentioned by managers ... that internal review provided an easy option in suggesting an appeal to a client, and that it eases pressure on the primary decision maker, suggest the emergence of a different effect than that concentrated on by commentators. This is backed up by the comments of some internal review officers, which suggested that, rather than primary decision makers making more generous decisions because of the availability of internal review, the availability of internal review was sometimes used as ***53*** an excuse for less than thorough work or failure to deal properly with a dissatisfied client (for example, by thoroughly explaining the decision or offering to re-examine the case).

> The system is flawed from the initial stages because the primary decision makers use the internal review officers to pass hard decisions to. Sometimes the customer is encouraged to challenge a decision even when they know the internal review officer will confirm the decision. It gives a false hope to the customer. (Internal review officer)
>
> ...
>
> Explanations of how decisions are reached is done poorly at primary decision maker level. The main role of the internal review officer is to explain how decisions are reached. (Internal review officer)

[7.10] In particular, the responses above indicate strong anecdotal evidence of a problem in relation to primary decision makers' lack of personal contact with clients, and their ability and willingness to provide proper explanations of decisions to clients. The surveys indicated that the vast majority of primary decision makers surveyed informed applicants of their decisions by letter, and that these letters contain information on internal review rights. Internal review may therefore occur simply because the client has not had personal contact with the decision maker and has not had the decision properly explained.

To the extent this occurs, systems of internal review risk failure in meeting their aims of improving decision making and providing natural justice for clients. Efficiency aims are also jeopardised if cases are referred unnecessarily to internal review.

...

Survey results about contact between internal review officers and primary decision makers
[7.17] Both internal review officers and primary decision makers were asked about contact between them. The majority of primary decision makers indicated that they knew when their decisions were being reviewed. Around two-thirds of the internal review officers indicated that they contacted primary decision makers before reviewing the decision either always or regularly.

...

> ***56*** If I am going to set aside a decision, but have reservations, I will discuss the case with the primary decision maker. Then next time the primary decision maker might seek out the internal review officer's thoughts. I won't discuss details of the particular case, just encourage a generic issues discussion. I also explain that if the case comes on review, my view might change. The decision should be better as a result of the discussion, but still might be changed. Geography is not the issue. The issue is building up confidence in the decision making process. (Internal review officer)

....

Using internal review to detect problems in administration and policy
58 [7.33] [I]nternal review can be used in an agency to detect problems in policy and its administration ...

59 [7.34] ... [T]wo-thirds of managers surveyed for this Report kept statistics of internal review reversal rates. These statistics were used, among other purposes, to monitor trends, identify problems in policy and legislation, and identify training needs. It is clear that such statistics, if collected and analysed in a sufficiently detailed fashion, are a useful tool that can be used by agencies to maximise the normative impact of internal review.

...

[7.36] Managers, internal review officers and primary decision makers participating in the survey were all asked what sorts of problems were identified through internal review mechanisms.

[7.37] Among managers and internal review officers, the most commonly mentioned problems were lack of evidence, investigation and fact finding by primary decision makers to support their decisions, and lack of understanding among primary decision makers of the legal requirements or policy applying to decisions.

[7.38] Primary decision makers were more likely than internal review officers or managers to identify that internal review uncovered problems with the legislation or policy (rather than with the processes of decision making).

[7.39] Other problems identified by all respondents included:

- bias on the part of primary decision makers;
- carelessness or not listening properly;
- customers not informed of appeal rights properly;
- poor documentation;
- ... inexperience; and
- requests for internal review that were really complaints about service.

A New Tax System (Family Assistance) (Administration) Act 1999 (Cth)

[As at relevant date]

An example of legislation conferring a right of internal review (the *Paid Parental Leave Act 2010* (Cth)) has been provided in *Government Accountability: Australian Administrative Law*, third edition. Here, we set out a more complex system of internal review in greater detail. This example shows how a statute may provide multiple avenues of review. In such a case, it is important to understand when each form of review is available.

The *A New Tax System (Family Assistance) (Administration) Act 1999* (Cth) governs claims for the family tax benefit and other forms of family tax assistance. Division 1 of pt 5 of the Act provides for two forms of internal review: review by the Secretary of the Department on the Secretary's own motion, and review by the Secretary or Child Support Registrar initiated by a person affected by a decision. Division 2 of pt 5 provides for review by the Administrative Appeals Tribunal ('AAT').[1]

Subdivision A of pt 5 div 1 provides for review on the Secretary's own motion. Section 104 identifies decisions that the Secretary may review on the Secretary's own motion:

> **104 Decisions that may be reviewed by Secretary on own initiative**
>
> Under section 105, the Secretary may review any decision of an officer under the family assistance law except:
>
> (a) a decision under section 67EB to pay an amount; or
>
> (b) a decision to give a person a notice under section 199E (notice about effect of non-compliance by provider on eligibility for CCS or ACCS); or
>
> (c) a decision under section 205A (business continuity payments—reports not given); or
>
> (d) a decision under section 85GA of the Family Assistance Act (funding agreements) in relation to an agreement.

The 'family assistance law' referred to in s 104 is defined in s 3 to include the *A New Tax System (Family Assistance) (Administration) Act 1999* (Cth) itself, the *A New Tax System (Family Assistance) Act 1999* (Cth), and certain other Acts.

1 In December 2022, the Commonwealth Attorney-General announced that the Administrative Appeals Tribunal would be abolished and replaced with a new merits review body. The legislation in this extract remains a useful example of a complex system of merits review.

While s 104 identifies decisions the Secretary may review, s 105 confers power on the Secretary to conduct that review:

> **105 Secretary may review certain decisions on own initiative**
>
> (1) If:
>
> (a) a decision (the ***original decision***) is a decision that, under section 104, the Secretary may review under this section; and
>
> (b) the Secretary is satisfied that there is sufficient reason to review the decision;
>
> the Secretary may review the decision.
>
> *Secretary may review decision even if application has been made to the AAT*
>
> (2) The Secretary may review the original decision even if an application has been made to the AAT for review in relation to the decision.
>
> *Secretary must not review decision if review under section 109A occurring*
>
> (3) The Secretary must not review the original decision under this section while any review of the decision is taking place under section 109A.
>
> *Secretary may make decisions in respect of an original decision*
>
> (4) The Secretary may decide (the ***review decision***) to:
>
> (a) affirm the original decision; or
>
> (b) vary the original decision; or
>
> (c) set the original decision aside and substitute a new decision.
>
> ...

Note that there is no obligation on the Secretary to review a decision to which s 105 applies; the Secretary may review a decision if 'the Secretary is satisfied that there is sufficient reason to review the decision'.[2] The power, under s 105(4), to affirm, vary or set aside and substitute a decision indicates that review under s 105 is a de novo review.

Section 105 sets out the relationship between review by the Secretary and other forms of merits review under this Act: the Secretary may review a decision on their own motion even if an application for review has been made to the Administrative Appeals Tribunal in respect of the decision,[3] but not if review under s 109A is underway.[4] As we will see, review under s 109A is review by the Secretary or Child Support Registrar on the application of a person affected by a decision (as opposed to review on the Secretary's own motion).

Subdivision B of pt 5 div 1 creates a scheme for review of decisions on the application of persons affected. The decisions that may be reviewed on application of a person affected are identified in s 108. These are not exactly the same as the decisions that may be reviewed on the Secretary's own motion:

2 Section 105(1)(b).
3 Section 105(2).
4 Section 105(3).

108 Decisions that may be reviewed under section 109A

Decisions that may and may not be reviewed under section 109A

(1) A decision of any officer under the family assistance law must be reviewed on application under section 109A unless an exception set out in subsection (2), (5) or (6) applies to the decision.

(2) The exceptions to the rule in subsection (1) are:

(a) a decision made by:

(i) the Secretary personally; or

(ii) another agency head himself or herself in the exercise of a delegated power; or

(iii) the Chief Executive Centrelink in the exercise of a delegated power; or

(iv) the Chief Executive Medicare in the exercise of a delegated power; or

(b) decision under section 67EB to pay an amount; ...

[Paragraphs (c) to (h), and subsections (2A) to (5), specify certain other categories of decision that may not be reviewed under s 109A.]

Section 109A requires the Secretary (and, in some cases, the Child Support Registrar) to review decisions on application:

109A Review of certain decisions may be initiated by applicant

(1) A person affected by a decision (the ***original decision***):

(a) that is not a care percentage decision; and

(b) that is not a decision under Part 8 (approval of providers of child care services); and

(c) that, under section 108, must be reviewed under this section;

may apply to the Secretary for review of the original decision.

(1A) A person affected by a decision (the ***original decision***):

(a) that is a care percentage decision; and

(b) that, under section 108, must be reviewed under this section;

may apply to the Secretary, or the Child Support Registrar, for review of the original decision.

(1B) If a decision (the ***original decision***):

(a) is made under Part 8 (approval of providers of child care services) in relation to a provider; and

(b) under section 108, must be reviewed under this section;

the provider may apply to the Secretary for review of the original decision.

(2) If the person makes an application under subsection (1), (1A) or (1B), the Secretary must either:

(a) review the original decision and decide (the ***review decision***) to:

(i) affirm it; or

(ii) vary it; or

(iii) set it aside and substitute a new decision; or

(b) arrange for an authorised review officer (see section 109C) to do so.

...

As with review under s 105, the power to affirm, vary, or set aside and substitute a decision indicates that review under s 109A is de novo review.

Note two differences between review under s 105 and review under s 109A. First, the Secretary has power to refer a review application to an authorised officer rather than reviewing the application personally. Second, if an application is made under s 109A, the Secretary must either review the decision or arrange for an authorised officer to do so,[5] while there is no compulsion for the Secretary to review a decision on their own motion.

Division 2 of pt 5 provides for review of decisions by the AAT – that is, for external merits review:

111 Application for AAT first review

(1) If the decision reviewer has affirmed, varied or set aside a decision under Subdivision B of Division 1, application may be made to the AAT for review (***AAT first review***) of the decision as affirmed or varied or, if it has been set aside and another decision substituted, the decision so substituted.

(1A) If a decision has been made by:

(a) the Secretary personally; or

(b) another agency head himself or herself in the exercise of a delegated power; or

(c) the Chief Executive Centrelink in the exercise of a delegated power; or

(d) the Chief Executive Medicare in the exercise of a delegated power;

application may be made to the AAT for review (also ***AAT first review***) of the decision.

...

(3) In this section:

decision reviewer means a person who, in accordance with subsection 109A(2), reviewed a decision that was the subject of an application under section 109A.

Section 111 provides for external merits review of decisions made on internal review;[6] and of decisions made by senior officeholders.[7] If the 'first review' decision proves unsatisfactory, a person may apply for a 'second review' by the AAT under pt 5 div 2 sub-div D:

128 Application for AAT second review

(1) Application may be made to the AAT for review (***AAT second review***) of a decision made by the AAT under subsection 43(1) of the AAT Act on AAT first review.

Section 43(1) of the *Administrative Appeals Tribunal Act 1975* (Cth) provides for de novo merits review:

(1) For the purpose of reviewing a decision, the Tribunal may exercise all the powers and discretions that are conferred by any relevant enactment on the person who made the decision and shall make a decision in writing:

5 Sections 108(1) and 109A(2).
6 Section 111(1).
7 Section 111(1A).

(a) affirming the decision under review;

(b) varying the decision under review; or

(c) setting aside the decision under review and:

(i) making a decision in substitution for the decision so set aside; or

(ii) remitting the matter for reconsideration in accordance with any directions or recommendations of the Tribunal.

Examples of merits review decisions

The two case studies in this section are not high-profile decisions; nor are they of any great significance to anybody other than the parties. They are included in this book as straightforward examples of merits review.

Farrugia v Secretary, Department of Social Services [2022] AATA 11

This is an example of de novo merits review in a generalist tribunal, following internal review and a First Review by the AAT under the *A New Tax System (Family Assistance) (Administration) Act 1999* (Cth) (relevant provisions of which are set out above). The case demonstrates how a matter progresses through a multi-level merits review system.

In addition, *Farrugia* illustrates the scope of a de novo merits review hearing to examine a matter afresh. Here, the AAT considers a wide range of material (some of which may not have been admissible as evidence in a court hearing), including material provided at the AAT's request after the hearing, to determine a highly contested factual question. The dispute was purely about that factual question; there was no dispute about the applicable law.

A New Tax System (Family Assistance) Act 1999 (Cth)

[As at relevant date]

35B Determination of percentage of care—child is in the adult's care

Initial determination

(1) If:

(a) the Secretary is satisfied that there has been, or will be, a pattern of care for a child over a period (the ***care period***) such that, for the whole, or for parts (including different parts), of the care period, the child was or will be, under subsection 22(2), (3) or (4), an FTB child of more than one individual; and

(b) one of those individuals (the ***adult***), or the partner of the adult, makes or has made a claim under Part 3 of the *A New Tax System (Family Assistance) (Administration) Act 1999* for payment of family tax benefit in respect of the child for some or all of the days in the care period; and

(c) the adult is not a partner of at least one of the other individuals referred to in paragraph (a);

the Secretary must determine the adult's percentage of care for the child during the care period.

...

Percentage of care

(3) The percentage determined under subsection (1) ... must be a percentage that corresponds with the actual care of the child that the Secretary is satisfied that the adult has had, or will have, during the care period.

...

Facts

This matter concerned the entitlement of a 16-year-old girl's separated parents (referred to as 'the Father' and 'the Mother') to the Family Tax Benefit for a period between January and October 2020. The amount of Family Tax Benefit to which each parent was entitled depended on the percentage of time their daughter had spent in that parent's care.

Until January 2020, the daughter lived with the Father, with occasional visits from the Mother. In January 2020, conflict arose between the daughter and the Father's partner. This led to a change in the daughter's living arrangements. From October 2020, the parents shared the care of the daughter 50/50.

There was, however, a dispute about how the daughter's care was shared between January and October 2020. The Father contended he had 100 per cent care of his daughter during this time, while the Mother contended she had 80 per cent care for the same period.

In January 2020, the Mother informed Services Australia that she had 80 per cent care of her daughter. A change of care decision to that effect was made. This decision was then subject to a series of reviews under the provisions of the *A New Tax System (Family Assistance) (Administration) Act 1999* (Cth) (set out above).[8] On internal review, an Authorised Review Officer varied the decision to 72 per cent care of the Father and 28 per cent care of the Mother. The Mother applied to the AAT for a First Review of the Authorised Review Officer's decision. The Father did not appear at that hearing (and would later explain he did not appreciate the consequences of failure to appear). The AAT varied the care decision to 72 per cent care to the Mother and 28 per cent to the Father.

The Father applied for a Second Review by the AAT. At this hearing, both the Mother and the Father gave evidence, as did witnesses for both parents. The Secretary was represented by a lawyer. Because the hearing took place during the COVID-19 pandemic (in October 2021), an audio-visual hearing was facilitated via Microsoft Teams. Due to technical difficulties, the Mother attended via audio link only. The AAT received various forms of evidence including verbal evidence, written witness statements, photographs, text messages, letters and a receipt for school fees. The witnesses included friends and family members who gave evidence about the time the daughter had spent in the care of each parent.

Prior to the hearing, each parent provided a 'care calendar' recording the time the daughter had spent with them in the relevant period. The Father's calendar indicated that the daughter had been in his care for 55 per cent of the time while the Mother's calendar indicated that she

8 At pp 183–7.

had been in her care for 96 per cent of the time. After the hearing, the AAT invited each parent to provide a second care calendar with direct evidence to support assertions that the daughter was in their care on any given day. The Mother did not provide a second care calendar. The Father provided a calendar with some supporting evidence (such as text messages) which, the Tribunal concluded, showed the daughter had been in his care for 47 per cent of the time.[9]

The reasons of the AAT attempt to reconcile this body of vague and inconsistent evidence.

Member P Ranson

> [6] At its heart, this case is all about entitlement to Family Tax Benefit (FTB), that is, how much FTB is the Father entitled to and how much is the Mother entitled to during the period January 2020 to October 2020.
>
> [7] Throughout this matter ... the evidence of the Father and the Mother has been highly conflicted and in some cases of limited reliability. ... The Father contends he had 100% care yet his evidence, at best, suggests around 50% care. The Mother contends she had 80% care of the daughter during the period from January 2020 to October 2020. Clearly, they can't both be correct.

[Editors' note: Member P Ranson considered the reliability of the witness statements provided by each parent:]

> [32] The statement by [the Father's former partner] does not state when she and the Father lived together and therefore when she saw the daughter full-time in his care. The statement of Ms Halcrow does not state how she knows the daughter was in the full-time care of the Father and in any event it is undated. Mr RF and Ms AH are siblings of the Father and their witness statements appear to rely on statements made by the Father and the daughter during visits to Melbourne three months after the end of the Care Period and other times during visits to Cairns the timing of which was not identified.
>
> [33] For the Mother, the witness statement by Ms HM again does not state how she knows the daughter moved back in with her mother. Ms ED does provide what appears to be contemporaneous evidence of witnessing the daughter staying overnight at her mother's house however her comment is that it occurred 'more and more' and lately over 85% of the time. Since this statement was made in July 2020 and is vague as to dates it hardly supports the assertion of the Mother the daughter was full-time or even 80% in her care throughout the Care Period. The statement by Dr WD appears to be based on hearsay as she also does not specify how she knows where the daughter stays overnight. Neither Ms HM, nor Dr WD were called to answer the gaps in their evidence.
>
> ...
>
> [37] The difficulty for the Tribunal in making this decision is ... the hugely conflicting evidence of the Father and the Mother and the largely hearsay evidence of their witnesses. Sifting through the inconsistencies in the evidence and in particular the calendars of care, it seems clear to the Tribunal a change of care did occur on or

9 At [24].

about 12 January 2020 so a care decision must be made. From then on, the daughter appears to have spent some time each week with each parent despite the assertion of the Mother there were five months during the Care Period in which the daughter had no contact whatsoever with her father. The question is how many nights she was overnight with each parent.

[38] The Father and the Mother agree two nights a week the daughter was overnight with each of them. It is apparent each parent provided care and supervision of the daughter when she was with them. Whilst the daughter may have spent from one to three nights per week staying with friends, she was still in the care of one or the other of her parents when she did so. That said, in 2020 the daughter was 16 and as a late teen she no doubt made up her own mind as to where she would stay and who she was in contact with.

[39] There is insufficient evidence to support the assertion by the Mother she had 80% or more overnight care of the daughter during the Care Period. There is also no evidence the Father had 100% care of the daughter during the Care Period. For the reasons above and on the evidence before the Tribunal for the relevant care period, it finds each parent had equal shared care of the daughter. This is the only possible decision the Tribunal considers that could be made with any reliability.

Conclusion

[40] As such, the Tribunal sets aside the decision of [the First Review] 2021 and in substitution finds the care of the daughter during the period 12 January 2020 to 10 October 2020 was 50% to the Father and 50% to the Mother.

Tipungwuti v Director – Crime Victims Services Unit (No 2) [2016] NTCAT 191

Victims of Crime Assistance Act 2006 (NT)

[As at relevant date]

30 Application to Director for award

An eligible victim of a violent act may apply to the Director for an award of financial assistance.

31 Time limit for lodging application

(1) An application for an award must be made:

(a) for an application relating to a compensable violent act – within 2 years after the occurrence of the violent act; ...

(2) However, the Director may accept an application made after the expiry of the time limit (a *late application)* if the Director considers the circumstances justify it.

(3) In deciding whether to accept a late application, the Director must have regard to the following matters:

(a) whether the injury or death occurred as a result of sexual assault, domestic violence or child abuse;

(b) the age of the applicant at the time of the violent act;

(c) whether the offender was in a position of power, influence or trust in relation to the applicant;

(d) any mental incapacity of the applicant;

(e) whether the delay in making the application will affect the assessor's ability to make a proper decision;

(f) whether the violent act was reported to a police officer within a reasonable time after it occurred or at any time before the application is made.

...

48 Decisions that may be reviewed

(1) An applicant for an award may apply to the [Northern Territory Civil and Administrative] Tribunal for review of the following decisions:

(a) a decision of the Director to refuse to accept a late application notified under section 31(4) ...

Northern Territory Civil and Administrative Tribunal Act 2014 (NT)

[As at relevant date]

45 Rehearing

The Tribunal must review a reviewable decision by way of rehearing.

46 Proceeding for review of reviewable decision

(1) The objective of the Tribunal exercising its review jurisdiction is to produce the correct or preferable decision.

(2) A proceeding in the Tribunal's review jurisdiction will include:

(a) an examination of the evidence or the material before the decision maker; and

(b) a consideration of any further evidence or material that the Tribunal decides, in the circumstances of the particular case, to admit for a rehearing.

(3) The reasons for decision provided by the decision maker, or any grounds for review set out in the application, do not limit the Tribunal in conducting a proceeding in the Tribunal's review jurisdiction.

Facts

This case is included as an example of merits reviews where the statute (ss 45 and 46 of the *Northern Territory Civil and Administrative Tribunal Act 2014* (NT)) provides for something slightly less than de novo merits review. In this example, the Tribunal's power to receive fresh evidence was crucial to the process and outcome.

In 2001, Graham Tipungwuti was hit with a stick by his younger brother, suffering a badly broken arm. In 2014, Mr Tipungwuti applied for financial assistance under the *Victims of Crime*

Assistance Act 2006 (NT). Steve Wheelhouse, the Director of the Crime Victims Services Unit ('CSVU') refused to accept the application because it was 11 years out of time. The reasons given for refusing to grant an extension of time included that Mr Tipungwuti had failed to report the incident to police; and that the passage of time had affected the ability to make a proper decision. Mr Tipungwuti applied to the Northern Territory Civil and Administrative Tribunal for review.

In order to help understand how the delay might affect the CSVU assessor's ability to make the appropriate decision, the Tribunal ordered CSVU to provide additional material about its processes for assessing claims for financial assistance.

In addition, Mr Tipungwuti provided an unsworn declaration explaining his circumstances. This document had not been available to CSVU when making the decision; however, the Tribunal exercised its discretion under s 46(2)(b) of the *Northern Territory Civil and Administrative Tribunal Act 2014* (NT) to receive fresh material on the rehearing.

Declaration by Mr Tipungwuti

Background

I am a 53 year old Tiwi man from Wurrumiyanga, Tiwi Islands. I was born in Wurrumiyanga and have lived here my whole life.

I speak Tiwi and English. Tiwi is my first language and my best language. When I speak to people I prefer to speak in Tiwi because it's my language and I can understand them better and can talk better in Tiwi.

I went to school at Wurrumiyanga until year 10.

I can't read and write very well.

...

I am ... on the disability pension. I have had a disability for all my life. I am not sure what the name of this disability is, but it makes me walk with a limp and makes it hard for me to walk long distances.

Awareness of CVSU scheme

I don't read the newspaper. Sometimes I listen to the radio. I listen to FM radio. I also watch TV. I usually watch movies and the news.

I don't know much about the law. I know about getting in trouble with Police, and the Police lock you up. I know a lot about Tiwi law. In Tiwi law, it's kind of the same and you can get in trouble culture way for bad behaviour.

I only recently found out about compensation.

My sisters, Flora Tipungwuti and Jane Puautjimi, told me about compensation. They told me I should go and see the doctor about the scar that I have on my arm and the plate that the doctors put in my arm because my bone had cracked. They also told me I should go see NAAJA [North Australian Aboriginal Justice Agency] mob to make a report. They told me that I might be able to get some money for what happened. That's all they said.

I went to see NAAJA about two or three months after my sisters told me about this compensation.

NAAJA helped me fill in the forms to claim compensation, and talked to me and helped me with my compensation claim.

Violent act

My little brother, Andre Tipungwuti, hit me with a stick on my left arm, when I was about 39, or about 10 years ago.

...

I went to Nguiu hospital, and then they flew me into the Royal Darwin Hospital. I had x-ray and the doctors had a good look at my arm and the bone was cracked. I had to have surgery to get a plate in my arm. I have a big scar now on my arm. I was in hospital for about two months.

Report to police

I did not report what happened to the Police.

I didn't report to the Police because in Tiwi culture way, I had shame about it. I couldn't talk to the Policeman because of the shame of it. It was a big shame for my younger brother to do this to me. All my extended family members were not happy about this and felt shame too. It was a shame on my brother for doing this to me, using a weapon on me and causing a serious injury. In Tiwi culture, the younger brother should always respect the older brothers and sisters, not hurt them.

I was also worried and frightened that my brother might hurt me again if I reported him to the Police, or that he might hurt me even more next time. I thought it was likely he would hurt me again if I reported him to Police because this would make him even more angry.

Use of interpreter

I made this statement with the help of Tiwi interpreter, Richard Tungatalum. Richard works for the Aboriginal Interpreter Service. Richard was with me when I talked to my lawyer about this statement over the phone. Richard spoke to me in Tiwi and spoke to my lawyer in English.

President Bruxner SM

[41] In considering the question whether the applicant's late application ought to be accepted it is convenient to first have regard to the matters listed in section 31(3).

[42] It will be seen the listed matters tend by their nature to pull in different directions.

Section 31(3)(a) – domestic violence

...

[47] [T]he fact the applicant's injuries resulted from domestic violence must be taken to militate in favour of acceptance of a late application. That said, it must also be acknowledged that the weight of this factor is affected by the relatively technical sense in which the applicant's injuries were domestic violence related.

Section 31(3)(b) – age

[48] The applicant was aged about 40 at the time of his injuries.

[49] Although youth or old age might be factors that some circumstances favour acceptance of a late application, the applicant's age must be taken to be something that counts against him.

Section 31(3)(c) – offender's power or influence over applicant

[50] The respondent considered there was no evidence that the applicant's brother was in a position of power or influence over the applicant.

[51] Having regard to what was submitted on the applicant's behalf ... I am not sure this is correct.

[52] In any case, having regard to the applicant's unattested declaration, there is evidence that the applicant's failure to report the offence was partly explained by his fear of reprisals from his brother and I consider that this carries some weight in favour of late acceptance of the application.

Section 31(3)(d) – mental incapacity

[53] It is not suggested that the applicant relevantly suffers from any mental incapacity.

Section 31(3)(e) – effect of delay on the assessor's ability to make a proper decision

[54] The respondent concluded that the applicant's delay adversely affected the assessor's ability to make a proper decision on the application because 'there is limited evidence in relation to the details of the alleged assault and any behaviour by the applicant that may have contributed to his injury'. (The possible relevance of contributing behaviour on the part of the applicant is that it is a basis upon which an award of financial assistance may be reduced - see section 41(1)(a) of the *VOCA Act.)*

...

[58] The applicant's application for financial assistance is based upon events that occurred more than 10 years ago. To the extent evidence regarding those events does not already exist, there is obvious potential for proper consideration of the application - in the sense of consideration that produces a reliable outcome - to be impeded.

[59] It is important, however, for the impacts of the delay to be real rather than hypothetical.

[60] First, the contemporaneous medical records contain considerable detail of the assault upon him and the injuries he suffered as a result.

[61] Secondly, having carefully considered the unattested declarations of Mr Wheelhouse, I am not persuaded that the applicant's delay has had the effects described in the respondent's decision. This is especially the case having regard to Mr Wheelhouse's evidence regarding the steps that would in fact have been taken had the application been made on time.

...

[63] Although I am prepared to accept that the applicant's delay in making the application for financial assistance will inevitably have some impacts ...., I do not consider that those impacts will be so substantial as to be decisive.

Section 31(3)(f) – non-reporting to police

[64] Section 31(3)(f) requires consideration of 'whether the violent act was reported to a police officer within a reasonable time after it occurred or at any time before the application is made'.

[65] As already noted, the applicant has made no report to police regarding the alleged assault in December 2001.

[66] Plainly this is a circumstance that weighs against acceptance of the applicant's late application.

...

[69] Had the applicant had not offered an explanation for his failure to report the assault to police then this might have been a telling factor against accepting his late application. The applicant has, however, offered an explanation - namely fear of reprisals and cultural (shaming) considerations - and the explanation is neither fanciful nor inherently improbable.

[70] ... Mr Wheelhouse has offered the view that the explanation would likely be considered 'unsatisfactory' by an assessor.

[71] In my opinion that question is properly to be considered by an assessor in the context of a thorough assessment of an application for assistance. It is worth noting here that it will remain a matter for the applicant to satisfy the assessor of the existence of circumstances preventing the making of a report.

Conclusion

[73] Although I consider the relevant factors closely balanced, it is my view that the correct or preferable decision (section 46(1) of the *NTCAT Act*) is for the applicant's late application to be accepted under section 31(2) of the *VOCA Act.*

...

[75] The unchallenged evidence of the applicant is that he made the application for financial assistance within a few months of learning for the first time of the existence of the crime victims assistance scheme.

[76] Although the substantial passage of time since December 2001 will likely have some impacts upon the investigation and assessment of his application, I do not consider that those impacts are sufficient that the applicant should be denied the opportunity of making a claim.

[77] In any such claim the applicant will need to overcome the hurdle presented by sections 43(b) and (c) of the *VOCA Act.*

...

[78] Accordingly I order that:

1. The respondent's decision notified to the applicant on 26 August 2015 not to accept the applicant's late application dated 4 October 2014 for an award of financial assistance is set aside; and
2. In substitution, the late application is accepted under section 31(2) of the *Victims of Crime Assistance Act 2006.*

CHAPTER

8

ADMINISTRATIVE REVIEW TRIBUNALS

Introduction 197

Issues of tribunal design 197

Council of Australasian Tribunals, *Tribunal Independence in Appointments: A Best Practice Guide* (2016) 197

Council of Australasian Tribunals, *Practice Manual for Tribunals* (5th ed, 2020) 199

Re Drake and Minister for Immigration and Ethnic Affairs (No 2) (1979) 2 ALD 634 200

The Australian administrative tribunal framework 206

Commonwealth, *Commonwealth Administrative Review Committee Report* (Parl Paper No 144, 1971) 206

Administrative Appeals Tribunal Act 1975 (Cth) 207

IDF Callinan, *Review: Section 4 of the Tribunals Amalgamation Act 2015* (Cth) (Report, 19 December 2018) 212

Robin Creyke, 'Australian Tribunals: Impact of Amalgamation' (2020) 26(4) *Australian Journal of Administrative Law* 206 213

Drake v Minister for Immigration and Ethnic Affairs (1979) 46 FLR 409 215

Shi v Migration Agents Registration Authority (2008) 235 CLR 286 218

Frugtniet v Australian Securities and Investments Commission (2019) 266 CLR 250 223

Introduction

This chapter complements Chapter 8 of *Government Accountability: Australian Administrative Law,* third edition. Together, these chapters introduce the system of administrative tribunals that has become one of the most salient features of Australian administrative law.

In this chapter, the section 'Issues of tribunal design' provides perspectives on tribunal independence and the relationship of tribunals to primary decision-makers. These perspectives give readers the tools to understand and evaluate the characteristics of individual tribunals, as well as the strengths and weaknesses of merits review by a tribunal. The second section of the chapter, 'Australia's Administrative Tribunal Framework', highlights pivotal moments in the development of Australia's system of administrative tribunals at the Commonwealth and state/territory level respectively. Key government reports – starting with the Kerr Committee's seminal 1971 contribution – and commentary provide snapshots of how tribunals have been considered at their inception, during their operation, and after amalgamation. The chapter concludes with extracts from landmark High Court cases explaining the role of merits review tribunals.

Issues of tribunal design

Council of Australasian Tribunals, *Tribunal Independence in Appointments: A Best Practice Guide* (2016)

The Council of Australasian Tribunals is a 'body through which tribunals can come together to examine and compare ideas, working methods, organisation and management, member trainings and support programs.'[1] In this publication, the Council highlights the importance of tribunal independence and the ways in which the appointment process can support or jeopardise independence.

> ***1*** Adjudication, whether undertaken by courts or by tribunals, must be performed impartially. An impartial adjudicator has no personal stake in the case and is free of any improper influence to decide in a particular way. To ensure that adjudicators are impartial, they must be independent of any source of improper influence or pressure. A Tribunal's impartiality must be safeguarded by arrangements which ensure its independence. Impartiality is a state of mind, while independence refers to the objective conditions which enable tribunals to adjudicate impartially.
>
> Like all justice institutions, tribunals can operate effectively only so long as the public has confidence in their independence. For this reason, the International Framework for Tribunal Excellence, developed under the Council's leadership, identifies 'Independence' as one of the eight areas for measurement of tribunal excellence. The Framework defines independence as 'the degree of separation from the

1 'Home', *Council of Australasian Tribunals* (Web Page) <https://coat.asn.au/>.

Executive'. The Executive includes the Ministers and Cabinet, departments or ministries of state and other administrative agencies of government.

...

2 The process for appointing Heads and members is of particular significance for the independence of tribunals. In Australia and New Zealand, appointments are made by the Executive. In most jurisdictions, the appointment is made by the Governor or Governor-General in Council or the Executive Council on the nomination of a Minister and with the approval of Cabinet.

While the system of appointment by the Executive confers high authority on tribunal members, it also gives Ministers the power to determine the makeup of the tribunal's membership and to affect the interests of members in a direct, individual and concrete way. If the power is exercised improperly, the independence of tribunals may be impaired. The risk is greater for tribunals which review government decisions or adjudicate disputes in which a Minister or government body is a party or has a policy interest in the outcome. For example, a Minister may be responsible for recommending appointments to a tribunal which determines appeals from decisions of the Minister or the Minister's department.

The system of Executive appointments is not necessarily inconsistent with tribunal independence. The system serves the public well when Ministers take care to appoint applicants who are best qualified for the position by their skills, knowledge and personal attributes. Threats to independence can arise where irrelevant considerations or improper purposes are taken into account in appointment decisions, as in the following scenarios:

- A Minister recommends a person for appointment in order to show favour to a relative, friend or associate (nepotism), or because the person is politically aligned to the Minister or the Minister's party (political patronage), or because the Minister or the Cabinet believes the person will be disposed to decide cases favourably to the Minister's policy interests or opinions.
- The Minister fails to nominate an outstanding candidate, or the Cabinet fails to approve a nomination, because of a personal attribute which is protected under anti-discrimination or human rights legislation, such as the candidate's gender, religion, marital status or political beliefs.

3

- The Minister fails to recommend a member for reappointment because of the member's record in making decisions which, although lawful and proper, are contrary to the views or interests of the Minister, the Minister's department, or members of the Minister's party.
- The Member fails to nominate a current member for reappointment, or Cabinet fails to approve the nomination, because the member was previously appointed by an Executive led by another political party.

[Citations omitted]

Council of Australasian Tribunals, *Practice Manual for Tribunals* (5th ed, 2020)

This manual, intended for use by tribunal members, identifies typical characteristics of procedure in tribunal hearings.

> ***100*** Proceedings before tribunals are generally described as *inquisitorial*. The following characteristics have been identified as typical of tribunal proceedings, as against those of courts:
>
> - the 'parties' are not necessarily adversaries
> - there is likely to be inequality of power and legal skills between the parties
> - administrative review on the merits aids good government
> - the interests of good administration require that the correct or preferable decision be made, not only for the parties but to provide guidance for the future
> - good administration requires just, efficient and effective determination.
>
> These characteristics have an impact upon how tribunal hearings are conducted, and distinguish tribunal hearings in important respects from those of courts. While tribunals have a duty to act 'judicially', this does not mean that they should model their procedures on those of the courts.
>
> ***101*** Tribunals have, by virtue of statute, specific inquisitorial powers which 'enable the adjudicator to take the initiative in eliciting evidence and formulating legal arguments, and to control the way in which a case is presented'. These include:
>
> - discretion over procedure and the freedom to frame their own procedures in a less formal way
> - the power to inform themselves on any matter and to undertake proactive investigations
> - utilising their own knowledge and making their own inquiries without necessarily being fettered by the technical rules of evidence and procedure which apply to courts.
>
> An aspect of the informal character of tribunals is that, from time to time, it is appropriate for tribunal members to obtain information additional to what is formally provided to them by parties. However, when this takes place, parties must be advised of the information obtained, and given a proper opportunity to respond to it. This is an example of the obligation for tribunals to extend procedural fairness to parties...
>
> Depending upon the powers given to it by its enabling legislation, a tribunal may be able to:
>
> - summon a person to attend to give evidence or produce documents, at the request of a party or on the tribunal's own motion
> - ***102*** request or require an administering agency to exercise any powers it has to require a person to give information or give documents
> - question witnesses
> - authorise a person to take evidence on behalf of the tribunal

- arrange a medical examination or commission a report, or require an administering agency to do so
- require an administering agency to investigate a matter and report to the tribunal
- enter and inspect premises or authorise a person to do so or
- refer a question of fact to an expert, expert panel or special referee empowered to advise or give an opinion, or, possibly, even to decide a question.

[Citations omitted]

Re Drake and Minister for Immigration and Ethnic Affairs (No 2) (1979) 2 ALD 634

Migration Act 1958 (Cth)

[As at relevant date]

12 Aliens convicted of crimes

Where ... an alien has been convicted in Australia of a crime of violence against the person or of extorting any money or thing by force or threat, or of an attempt to commit such a crime, or has been convicted in Australia of any other offence for which he has been sentenced to imprisonment for one year or longer, the Minister may, upon the expiration of, or during, any term of imprisonment served or being served by that alien in respect of the crime, order the deportation of that alien.

Facts

Daniel Drake was born in Los Angeles. In 1968, at the age of 31, he moved to Australia with his six-year-old son, Mark. Over the next ten years, Mr Drake lived in Australia, formed a relationship with an Australian woman, and became a successful dealer in antique bottles. Mark went to school in Australia. At no time during this period did Mr Drake apply for Australian citizenship, apparently because he wanted to retain his American citizenship. In 1978, he was convicted of using and possessing marijuana, was fined a total of $550, and sentenced to 12 months imprisonment (although he was released on a good behaviour bond after three months).

Following Mr Drake's conviction, the Minister considered whether he should exercise his discretion to deport Mr Drake under s 12 of the *Migration Act 1958* (Cth). In doing so, the Minister considered a policy he had issued to guide the exercise of this power:

Deportation of criminals

4.01 A decision by the Minister to order the deportation of a person from Australia is made after consideration by the Minister of all the material facts and circumstances relating to that person. Every case is decided upon the basis of its individual circumstances.

4.02 The basic question considered by the Minister is whether in all the circumstances it is in the best interests of the Commonwealth of Australia that the person be deported.

...

4.07 The following matters are taken into account when a decision is being made whether to order the deportation of a person from Australia;

- The nature of the offence;
- The circumstances of the commission of the offence;
- The view of the offence expressed by the Court before which the offender appeared;
- The nature of the penalty;
- The extent of rehabilitation of the offender;
- The prospects of recidivism;
- The necessity to prevent or inhibit the commission of like offences by other persons;
- The previous criminal history of the offender;
- The public interest;
- The circumstances of the offender;
- The circumstances of the family of or other persons having a relationship with the offender;
- The obligations of the Commonwealth under the Convention Relating to the Status of Refugees.

After applying this policy, the Minister decided to deport Drake. The Administrative Appeals Tribunal affirmed that decision (*Re Drake and Minister for Immigration and Ethnic Affairs* [1978] AAT 111) but the Federal Court allowed an appeal (*Drake v Minister for Immigration and Ethnic Affairs* (1979) 46 FLR 409, extracted below) and remitted the matter to the Administrative Appeals Tribunal. On remittal, Brennan J, sitting as President of the AAT, delivered reasons that have become a seminal statement of the role of policy in administrative decision-making and have influenced conceptualisations of the relationship between the three branches of government in Australia.

Brennan J

638 The multiplicity of factors for consideration in each case evidently precluded the Parliament, as it precludes the Minister, from defining principles of universal application to govern the exercise of the power [in s 12] in every case. In the absence of such principles, the exercise of the power must depend ***639*** upon the circumstances of each case and the weight then to be accorded to the relevant factors ...

When such a power is conferred upon more than one decision-maker, a tendency to inconsistency in making decisions may appear ... [T]o some degree, each decision-maker will vary from another in his perception of Australia's interests, the effect of offending conduct, and the effect of a decision, one way or another, upon those interests. These are not generally matters of logical proof or evidentiary demonstration. After allowing for the variations in the facts of particular cases, the degree of inconsistency in decision-making will depend upon the extent of the disparity in the respective decision-makers' perceptions of Australia's best interests and the way in which those interests are affected.

... [T]he possibility of a ... member of this Tribunal attributing to a particular kind of offending conduct a gravity different from the gravity attributed to the same conduct by another ... member, or by the Minister, adds to the prospect of inconsistency in decision-making ... The Minister and each ... member may perceive Australia's interests differently and may differ in their perception of the way in which offending conduct adversely affects those interests. Such differences will lead to inconsistency in making decisions.

Inconsistency is not merely inelegant; it brings the process of deciding into disrepute, suggesting an arbitrariness which is incompatible with commonly accepted notions of justice. In matters of deportation, which so profoundly affect the interests of the deportee and his family and which are of relevance to the community at large, inconsistency born of the application of differing standards and values should be reduced as far as it is possible to do so.

...

640 There are powerful considerations in favour of a Minister adopting a guiding policy. It can serve to focus attention on the purpose which the exercise of the discretion is calculated to achieve, and thereby to assist the Minister and the others to see more clearly, in each case, the desirability of exercising the power in one way or another. Decision-making is facilitated by the guidance given by an adopted policy, and the integrity of decision-making in particular cases is the better assured if decisions can be tested against such a policy. By diminishing the importance of individual predilection, an adopted policy can diminish the inconsistencies which might otherwise appear in a series of decisions, and enhance the sense of satisfaction with the fairness and continuity of the administrative process.

Of course, a policy must be consistent with the statute. It must allow the Minister to take into account the relevant circumstances, it must not require him to take into account irrelevant circumstances, and it must not serve a purpose foreign to the purpose for which the discretionary power was created ... [I]t would be inconsistent with [s 12] ... of the Migration Act if the Minister's policy sought to preclude consideration of relevant arguments running counter to an adopted policy which might be reasonably advanced in particular cases. The discretions reposed in the Minister by these sections cannot be exercised according to broad and binding rules. The Minister must decide each of the cases under [s 12] ... on its merits. His discretion cannot be so truncated by a policy as to preclude consideration of the merits of specified classes of cases. A fetter of that kind would be objectionable, even though it were adopted by the Minister on his own initiative. A Minister's policy, formed for the purposes of [s 12] ... ***641*** must leave him free to consider the unique circumstances of each case, and no part of a lawful policy can determine in advance the decision which the Minister will make in the circumstances of a given case.

That is not to deny the lawfulness of adopting an appropriate policy which guides but does not control the making of decisions, a policy which is informative of the standards and values which the Minister usually applies. There is a distinction between an unlawful policy which creates a fetter purporting to limit the range of discretion conferred by a statute, and a lawful policy which leaves the range of discretion intact while guiding the exercise of the power. Lord Denning referred to the distinction in *Sagnata Investments Ltd v Norwich Corporation* [1971] 2 QB 614 at 626, where he said:

> I take it to be perfectly clear now that an administrative body ... which may have to consider numerous applications of a similar kind, is entitled to lay down a general policy which it proposed to follow in coming to its individual decisions, provided always that it is a reasonable policy which it is fair and just to apply. Once laid down, the administrative body is entitled to apply the policy in the individual cases which come before it. The only qualification is that the administrative body must not apply the policy so rigidly as to reject an applicant without hearing what he has to say. It must not 'shut its ears to an application': see [*British Oxygen Co v Board of Trade]* [1971] AC 610, 625 per Lord Reid. The applicant is entitled to put forward reasons urging that the policy should be changed, or saying that in any case it should not be applied to him. But, so long as the administrative body is ready to hear him and consider what he has to say, it is entitled to apply its general policy to him as to others.

Subject to these limits the Minister may arrive at his decisions by reference to a policy of his own devising ...

642 The Minister's policy ... does not go beyond the limits charted by the authorities. It merely identifies factors to which the Minister refers, and the kinds of conduct which he regards as more gravely affecting Australia's interests; it does not accord a determinative effect to any factor, or deny the ability of countervailing factors to lead the Minister in particular cases to decline to order deportation. The Minister thus maintains the discretionary power intact, specifying merely the weight which he ordinarily gives to convictions of the stated kind.

...

Not only is it lawful for the Minister to form a guiding policy; its promulgation is desirable, for reasons stated above.

...

Application of a policy of this kind does not mean an unquestioning adoption of its standards and values, but rather an assumption that, in the absence of any reason to the contrary, its standards and values are appropriate to guide the decision in cases falling within its terms. It is in this sense that I use the term 'apply' hereafter with reference to the Minister's stated policy.

It is one thing for the Minister to apply his own policy in deciding cases; it is another thing for the Tribunal to apply it. In point of law, the Tribunal is as free as the Minister to apply or not to apply that policy. The Tribunal's duty is to make the correct or preferable decision in each case on the material before it, and the Tribunal is at liberty to adopt whatever policy it chooses, or no policy at all, in fulfilling its statutory function.

....

643 If the Tribunal applies Ministerial policy, it is because of the assistance which the policy can furnish in arriving at the preferable decision in the circumstances of the case as they appear to the Tribunal. One of the factors to be considered in arriving at the preferable decision in a particular case is its consistency with other decisions in comparable cases, and one of the most useful aids in achieving consistency is a guiding policy. An appropriate guiding policy should thus be applied, but what policy should it be?

Counsel for the appellant submitted that it would sap the independence of the Tribunal if it were to apply Ministerial policy, and that submission no doubt grows out of the long and essential resistance of the courts to the attempts of the executive to influence the course of judicial decisions ... [T]here is a material difference between the nature of a decision of the Tribunal reviewing the exercise of a discretionary administrative power, and the nature of a curial decision. The judgment of a court turns upon the application of the relevant law to the facts as found; a decision of the Tribunal, reviewing a discretionary decision of an administrative character, takes into account the possible application of an administrative policy.

The policy which guides the exercise of a discretionary administrative power may rightly seek to achieve an objective of public significance, and a balance may have to be struck between the achieving of that objective and the interests of an individual. In this respect, the making of a discretionary administrative decision is to be distinguished from the making of a curial decision. Generally speaking, a discretionary administrative decision creates a right in or imposes a liability on an individual; a curial decision declarers and enforces a right or liability antecedently created or imposed. The distinction is too simply stated, but it suffices to show that the adjudication of rights and liabilities by reference to governing principles of law is a different function from the function of deciding what those rights or liabilities should be. The former function rightly ignores the policies of the executive government; the latter should not. In the course of making their decisions, courts have formulated rules of law ... but it does not follow that, at the present time, general administrative policy should be formulated by an adjudicative tribunal. The detachment which is desirable for adjudication is not in sympathy with the purposiveness of policy formation.

...

Under the Westminster system of government, a Minister is politically responsible to the Parliament ***644*** for the policy adopted to guide the exercise of his discretionary power, and he should be left to formulate that policy in whatever manner he thinks appropriate from time to time. Administrative policies are necessarily amenable to revocation or alteration on political grounds, and they are best formed and amended in a political context.

....

On some occasions, reasons may be shown to warrant departure from ministerial policy; for example, where the intervention of new circumstances has clearly made a policy statement obsolete.

But in general, it would be manifestly imprudent for the Tribunal to override a ministerial policy and to adopt a general administrative policy of its own. Although the practice of giving reasons for decisions inevitably spins out threads of policy from the facts of the cases, the policy developed in this way originates in the need to ensure that justice is done in individual cases, and it is a different development from a ministerial declaration of broad policy relating to the generality of cases ... [T]he laying down of a broad policy on deportation is essentially a political function, to be performed by the Minister who is responsible to the Parliament for the policy he adopts. The very independence of the Tribunal demands that it be apolitical ... The Tribunal is not linked into the chain of responsibility from Minister to Government to Parliament, its membership is not appropriate for the formulation of broad policy and it is unsupported by a bureaucracy fitted to advise upon broad policy. It should therefore be reluctant to lay down broad policy ...

If consistency in decision-making is sought, as it ought to be, the standards and values which a Minister expresses in a statement of lawful policy can be a constant reference point for each of the ... members of the Tribunal in exercising the discretion in particular cases. Ministerial policy can be an aid to consistency among Tribunal decisions, and to consistency between the decisions of the Tribunal and those of the Minister. Decisions made under a ***645*** statutory power and reviewed by the Tribunal are but a proportion of the decisions made under that power, and it would be a regrettable anomaly if the decisions which were not reviewed revealed different standards and values from those made on review.

These considerations warrant the Tribunal's adoption of a practice of applying lawful ministerial policy, unless there are cogent reasons to the contrary. If it were shown that the application of ministerial policy would work an injustice in a particular case, a cogent reason would be shown, for consistency is not preferable to justice. Injustice, in the context of [s 12], must mean a disproportion between the detriment suffered by those affected by the execution of a deportation order and the benefit which might reasonably be expected to result to the community at large or to particular individuals in the community if the order were affirmed.

In my view, the Tribunal, being entitled to determine its own practice in respect of the part which ministerial policy plays in the making of Tribunal decisions, should adopt the following practice.

When the Tribunal is reviewing the exercise of a discretionary power reposed in a Minister, and the Minister has adopted a general policy to guide him in the exercise of the power, the Tribunal will ordinarily apply that policy in reviewing the decision, unless the policy is unlawful or unless its application tends to produce an unjust decision in the circumstances of the particular case. Where the policy would ordinarily be applied, an argument against the policy itself or against its application in the particular case will be considered, but cogent reasons will have to be shown against its application, especially if the policy is shown to have been exposed to Parliamentary scrutiny.

[Editors' note: After considering the facts of the case and applying the legislation and policy, Brennan J concluded that the Minister's decision was the preferable one and affirmed the Minister's decision to deport Mr Drake.]

The Australian administrative tribunal framework

Commonwealth, *Commonwealth Administrative Review Committee Report* (Parl Paper No 144, 1971)

The Kerr Committee Report was introduced in Chapter 7. As the extracts in that chapter demonstrate, the Committee emphasised the importance of merits review in any system of administrative law. The Committee recommended that the Commonwealth respond by establishing a Commonwealth merits review tribunal. This recommendation led to the creation of the Administrative Appeals Tribunal.

Chapter 14: An Administrative Review Tribunal

...

86 [289] We have already recommended that the Court exercise a supervisory jurisdiction only, partly for constitutional reasons and partly because we do not regard a court as being the most appropriate body to review administrative decisions on the merits ... However, our decision that such review be not conferred on the proposed Administrative Court does not in any way imply a view that it is unnecessary to provide further for the review, on the merits, of administrative decisions ...

[290] We have made our recommendation as to the jurisdiction, procedures and grounds of review in relation to the Court having in mind the role which we see the Court playing in a comprehensive system of administrative law in Australia. ...

[291] Stated broadly, our view is that the work of the Court should be complementary to a system of administrative review on the merits. As we have already, we are disposed to the view that, as part of any comprehensive system of administrative law in Australia, there should be a general Administrative Review Tribunal.

[292] If an Administrative Review Tribunal of the type we suggest were set up we would have in mind that the Chairman be one of a panel of the Administrative Court allocated to preside over the Tribunal from time to time. In addition, we would envisage that there would be two other members of the Tribunal. One could be an officer of the Commonwealth Department or authority responsible for administering the decision under review. This would, of course, be a shifting membership but it would ensure that particular knowledge of the area of administration which produced the decision under review would be available to the Tribunal. The other member would be a layman drawn preferably ***87*** from a panel of persons chosen for their character and experience in practical affairs. ...

Chapter 21: General conclusions and main recommendations and proposals

...

115 [17] A general policy of providing for a review of administrative decisions on the merits should be adopted on a much broader basis than now exists.

[18] It is expected that amongst the many discretions conferred by Commonwealth law there are sufficient to justify the establishment of a general Administrative Review Tribunal and if this expectation is fulfilled ... we propose that ... there should ... be established an Administrative Review Tribunal to review administrative decisions in those cases thought suitable to be reviewed by such a general review tribunal rather than by a specialist review tribunal.

[Citations omitted]

[Editors' note: The 'Administrative Court' referred to here was a proposed specialist federal judicial review court.]

On 16 December 2022, the Commonwealth Attorney-General announced that the Administrative Appeals Tribunal would be abolished and replaced with a new merits review body. At the time of writing, the legislation establishing this body was not publicly available.

Because the Administrative Appeals Tribunal was the model for most Australian merits review tribunals, the provisions of the *Administrative Appeals Tribunal Act 1975* (Cth) remain worthy of study.

Administrative Appeals Tribunal Act 1975 (Cth)

[As at 1 December 2022]

PART 1—PRELIMINARY

2A Tribunal's objective

In carrying out its functions, the Tribunal must pursue the objective of providing a mechanism of review that:

(a) is accessible; and

(b) is fair, just, economical, informal and quick; and

(c) is proportionate to the importance and complexity of the matter; and

(d) promotes public trust and confidence in the decision-making of the Tribunal.

3 Interpretation

(1) In this Act, unless the contrary intention appears:

...

enactment means:

(a) an Act;

(b) an Ordinance of a Territory other than the Northern Territory, the Australian Capital Territory or Norfolk Island; or

(c) an instrument (including rules, regulations or by-laws) made under an Act or under such an Ordinance;

and includes an enactment as amended by another enactment.

...

(3) Unless the contrary intention appears, a reference in this Act to a decision includes a reference to:

(a) making, suspending, revoking or refusing to make an order or determination;

(b) giving, suspending, revoking or refusing to give a certificate, direction, approval, consent or permission;

(c) issuing, suspending, revoking or refusing to issue a licence, authority or other instrument;

(d) imposing a condition or restriction;

(e) making a declaration, demand or requirement;

(f) retaining, or refusing to deliver up, an article; or

(g) doing or refusing to do any other act or thing.

PART IV—REVIEWS BY THE TRIBUNAL OF DECISIONS

DIVISION 1—APPLICATIONS FOR REVIEW OF DECISIONS

25 Tribunal may review certain decisions

Enactment may provide for applications for review of decisions

(1) An enactment may provide that applications may be made to the Tribunal:

(a) for review of decisions made in the exercise of powers conferred by that enactment;

...

(3) Where an enactment makes provision in accordance with subsection (1) or (2), that enactment:

(a) shall specify the person or persons to whose decisions the provision applies;

(b) may be expressed to apply to all decisions of a person, or to a class of such decisions; and

(c) may specify conditions subject to which applications may be made.

...

Enactment may add to, exclude or modify operation of certain provisions

(6) If an enactment provides for applications to the Tribunal:

(a) that enactment may also include provisions adding to, excluding or modifying the operation of any of the provisions of this Act relation to such applications; and

(b) those sections and subsections have effect subject to any provisions so included.

...

27 Persons who may apply to Tribunal

(1) Where this Act or any other enactment (other than the *Australian Security Intelligence Organisation Act 1979*) provides that an application may be made to the Tribunal for a review of a decision, the application may be made by or on behalf of any person or persons (including the Commonwealth or an authority of the Commonwealth or Norfolk Island or an authority of Norfolk Island) whose interests are affected by the decision.

...

(2) An organization or association of persons, whether incorporated or not, shall be taken to have interests that are affected by a decision if the decision relates to a matter included in the objects or purposes of the organization or association.

(3) Subsection (2) does not apply in relation to a decision given before the organization or association was formed or before the objects or purposes of the organization or association included the matter concerned.

28 Person affected by decision may obtain reasons for decision

Request for statement of reasons

(1) Subject to subsection (1AAA) [which creates exceptions for certain decisions], if a person makes a decision in respect of which an application may be made to the Tribunal for a review, any person (in this section referred to as the *applicant)* who is entitled to apply to the Tribunal for a review of the decision may, by notice in writing given to the person who made the decision, request that person to give to the applicant a statement in writing setting out the findings on material questions of fact, referring to the evidence or other material on which those findings were based and giving the reasons for the decision, and the person who made the decision shall, as soon as practicable but in any case within 28 days after receiving the request, prepare, and give to the applicant, such a statement.

...

30 Parties to proceeding before Tribunal

...

Parties

(1) Subject to paragraph 42A(2)(b), the parties to a proceeding before the Tribunal for a review of a decision are:
   (a) any person who, being entitled to do so, has duly applied to the Tribunal for a review of the decision;
   (b) the person who made the decision;
   (c) if the Attorney-General intervenes in the proceeding under section 30A—the Attorney-General; and
   (d) any other person who has been made a party to the proceeding by the Tribunal on application by the person in accordance with subsection (1A).

...

Person whose interests are affected may apply to be a party

(1A) Where an application has been made by a person to the Tribunal for a review of a decision, any other person whose interests are affected by the decision may apply, in writing, to the Tribunal to be made a party to the proceeding, and the Tribunal may, in its discretion, by order, make that person a party to the proceeding.

...

33 Procedure of Tribunal

(1) In a proceeding before the Tribunal:

(a) the procedure of the Tribunal is, subject to this Act and the regulations and to any other enactment, within the discretion of the Tribunal;

(b) the proceeding shall be conducted with as little formality and technicality, and with as much expedition, as the requirements of this Act and of every other relevant enactment and a proper consideration of the matters before the Tribunal permit; and

(c) the Tribunal is not bound by the rules of evidence but may inform itself on any matter in such manner as it thinks appropriate.

Decision-maker must assist Tribunal

(1AA) In a proceeding before the Tribunal for a review of a decision, the person who made the decision must use his or her best endeavours to assist the Tribunal to make its decision in relation to the proceeding.

Parties etc. must assist Tribunal

(1AB) A party to a proceeding before the Tribunal, and any person representing such a party, must use his or her best endeavours to assist the Tribunal to fulfil the objective in section 2A.

...

DIVISION 6—TRIBUNAL'S DECISION ON REVIEW

43 Tribunal's decision on review

...

Tribunal's decision on review

(1) For the purpose of reviewing a decision, the Tribunal may exercise all the powers and discretions that are conferred by any relevant enactment on the person who made the decision and shall make a decision in writing:

(a) affirming the decision under review;

(b) varying the decision under review; or

(c) setting aside the decision under review and:

(i) making a decision in substitution for the decision so set aside; or

(ii) remitting the matter for reconsideration in accordance with any directions or recommendations of the Tribunal.

Tribunal must give reasons for its decision

(2) Subject to this section and to sections 35 and 36D, the Tribunal shall give reasons either orally or in writing for its decision.

...

Tribunal must give copies of its decision to parties

(3) The Tribunal shall cause a copy of its decision to be given to each party to the proceeding.

...

Tribunal's decision taken to be decision of decision-maker

(6) A decision of a person as varied by the Tribunal, or a decision made by the Tribunal in substitution for the decision of a person, shall, for all purposes (other than the purposes of applications to the Tribunal for a review or of appeals in accordance with section 44), be deemed to be a decision of that person and, upon the coming into operation of the decision of the Tribunal, unless the Tribunal otherwise orders, has effect, or shall be deemed to have had effect, on and from the day on which the decision under review has or had effect.

44 Appeals to Federal Court of Australia from decisions of the Tribunal

Appeal on question of law

(1) A party to a proceeding before the Tribunal may appeal to the Federal Court of Australia, on a question of law, from any decision of the Tribunal in that proceeding.

Note 1: This Part does not apply to certain migration proceedings (see section 43C).

Note 2: A party to a child support first review may in some instances appeal instead to the Federal Circuit and Family Court of Australia (Division 2).

(1A) Subsection (1) does not apply in relation to a proceeding in the Social Services and Child Support Division [with certain exceptions].

...

Powers of Federal Court

(4) The Federal Court of Australia shall hear and determine the appeal and may make such order as it thinks appropriate by reason of its decision.

(5) Without limiting by implication the generality of subsection (4), the orders that may be made by the Federal Court of Australia on an appeal include an order affirming or setting aside the decision of the Tribunal and an order remitting the case to be heard and decided again, either with or without the hearing of further evidence, by the Tribunal in accordance with the directions of the Court.

...

Federal Court may make findings of fact

...

(7) If a party to a proceeding before the Tribunal appeals to the Federal Court of Australia under subsection (1), the Court may make findings of fact if:

 (a) the findings of fact are not inconsistent with findings of fact made by the Tribunal (other than findings made by the Tribunal as the result of an error of law); and

(b) it appears to the Court that it is convenient for the Court to make the findings of fact, having regard to:

(i) the extent (if any) to which it is necessary for facts to be found; and

(ii) the means by which those facts might be established; and

(iii) the expeditious and efficient resolution of the whole of the matter to which

(iv) the proceeding before the Tribunal relates; and

(v) the relative expense to the parties of the Court, rather than the Tribunal, making the findings of fact; and

(vi) the relative delay to the parties of the Court, rather than the Tribunal, making the findings of fact; and

(vii) whether any of the parties considers that it is appropriate for the Court, rather than the Tribunal, to make the findings of fact; and

(viii) such other matters (if any) as the Court considers relevant.

(8) For the purposes of making findings of fact under subsection (7), the Federal Court of Australia may:

(a) have regard to the evidence given in the proceeding before the Tribunal; and

(b) receive further evidence.

(9) Subsection (7) does not limit the Federal Court of Australia's power under subsection (5) to make an order remitting the case to be heard and decided again by the Tribunal.

...

IDF Callinan, *Review: Section 4 of the Tribunals Amalgamation Act 2015* (Cth) (Report, 19 December 2018)

The *Tribunals Amalgamation Act 2015* (Cth) (*TA Act*) effected the amalgamation of several specialist tribunals into the AAT. Section 4 of the *TA Act* required a review of these changes to be undertaken after three years. Former High Court judge IDF Callinan was appointed to conduct that review.

161 [10.3] The *TA Act* has not achieved the full purpose for which it was enacted. Having said that, I would point out that the purpose was ambitious, perhaps excessively or unnecessarily so. I will explain why I think this to be the case.

[10.4] The AAT that came into existence in 1976 was novel, small and free standing. The *Original Act* which created it contained few indications of the processes that it should follow: its conception was effectively contemporaneous with the establishment of a Commonwealth Ombudsman, other executive offices, and the new, Chapter III, Federal Court. Some of the 'jurisdictions' were similar in intent and bound to overlap. The borders between them could only be drawn over time and experience. ... Many of the departments, agencies and other bodies whose decisions are reviewable by the AAT did not exist. ... The population of Australia grew between 1976 and 2015 from some 14 million people to almost 24 million people. Many additional – and highly complex – social security benefits (with differing criteria for access to them) have become available to Australians under Commonwealth law since 1976.

[10.5] A National Disability Insurance Scheme of the current kind was not remotely on the horizon in 1976. It is improbable that anyone then would have foreseen that the ***162*** AAT, in the space of four decades, would be called upon to review many thousands of decisions made by officials and other members of the Executive under more than 400 Commonwealth laws annually.

...

[10.7] No one could doubt the good intentions that moved the Parliament to enact the *TA Act*. Perhaps what may, however, have been underestimated, are the increasing volume of matters to be reviewed and the divergences in practices, legislative or otherwise, of the different Tribunals and Divisions which came to constitute the amalgamated AAT. Not only were the practices and procedures different, but, also, the organisation and presentation of files by Departments whose decisions are reviewable were different. As desirable as complete harmonisation may theoretically be, it is difficult and probably undesirable to impose upon the respective Divisions, identical, or even very similar practices and procedures.

...

164 [10.15] The AAT does not operate as a truly amalgamated body. "Levels" of separation are not necessary and appropriate but some degree of process and procedures is dictated by the legislation under which decisions are reviewed.

[Citations omitted]

Robin Creyke, 'Australian Tribunals: Impact of Amalgamation' (2020) 26(4) *Australian Journal of Administrative Law* 206

This article reports the results of a survey of amalgamated Australian tribunals (the Administrative Appeals Tribunal ('AAT'), ACT Civil and Administrative Tribunal ('ACAT'), NSW Civil and Administrative Tribunal ('NCAT'), Northern Territory Civil and Administrative Tribunal ('NTCAT'), Queensland Civil and Administrative Tribunal ('QCAT'), South Australian Civil and Administrative Tribunal ('SACAT'), Victorian Civil and Administrative Tribunal ('VCAT') and the WA State Administrative Tribunal) about the effects of amalgamation.

231 As VCAT pointed out 'a citizen is more likely to be involved in a VCAT matter over their lifetime than any other element of the justice system'. This fact alone justifies attention to administrative justice by tribunals. Whether amalgamation has contributed to the achievement of this end has been explored in this article.

Overall, the responses to the survey have been positive. Many of the key objectives of amalgamation, particularly those relating to accessibility, efficiency and effectiveness, have been realised. This should not obscure the fact that the positive findings ... are not uniformly applicable, nor mask some of the concerns this survey has exposed. At the same time, it is acknowledged that some advantages of amalgamation have not yet been fully explored. As the Bleby review [of SACAT] noted of the variable adoption of less formal processes among SACAT members, this is 'due largely to lack of opportunity on the part of members to talk about and exchange ideas on such matters'. Hopefully this will occur in time.

A key finding is that successful amalgamation correlates with the size of the amalgamated tribunal. The smaller and more contained is the amalgamated tribunal, the more likely is it to achieve the benefits of consolidation. That was demonstrated by the smaller tribunals involved in the survey. They have generally been able to introduce uniform procedures, deploy their staff across all the tribunal's jurisdiction, and achieve the cohesion and unified rules and modes of operations which were the aims of amalgamation.

The evidence that size matters comes not only from the smaller tribunals. The larger tribunals too such as VCAT and QCAT referred to their concerns that if the tribunal takes on too many jurisdictions, those objectives will increasingly not be met. The example of the pressures and reputational impact on the AAT of the increasing backlog of migration cases reinforces this finding.

...

Servicing regional areas remains a challenge for all the tribunals, ACAT excepted. Although, as NCAT indicated, amalgamation may have enhanced the ability to extend dispute resolution services to non-metropolitan regions, for most tribunals, problems of providing appropriate members, locations for hearings, and offering the administrative support required for effective applications in the regions continue to pose problems. ...

Whether an amalgamated tribunal costs less for government than the previous fragmented systems is not possible to assess. Information about pre-existing costs does not exist. There is anecdotal evidence from some tribunals that operating costs have reduced. That is supported by the reduction in the number of leases for buildings, combined administrative services, and other reductions in management costs.

For governments to conclude, however, that this means there have been savings, and these are likely to continue would be to adopt a complacency which is unwarranted. The QCAT example that from 2009 to 2019 the sessional members did not receive any wages or salary increases illustrates the dangers of such an attitude.

232 There are warning signs of concern about costs which were expressed more generally. The survey illustrates that there is an urgent need for infrastructure costs to upgrade the tribunals' technology if efficiencies expected of an amalgamated tribunal are to be realised. In addition, ensuring that tribunal members and some staff receive appropriate training to improve their skill levels, is a pressing need to enable the more widespread availability of [alternative or facilitative dispute resolution].

A finding with particular relevance to the AAT is that the benefits of amalgamation can be undermined when the procedural or other features of a particular jurisdiction are cemented by legislation. The AAT's experience graphically illustrates this barrier and it is pleasing that this has been recognised by the Callinan review. The statutory injunction for the tribunals that they operate with flexibility is a sufficient means, coupled with strong leadership, to ensure the preservation of different modes of procedures without resorting to legislative support.

...

Generally speaking, choice of the tribunals for inclusion in an amalgamated body has been felicitous. Nonetheless, the survey responses by the States and Territories do indicate a degree of unease about the inclusion of guardianship and possibly the mental health jurisdictions under the amalgamated tribunal umbrella. Some tribunals were comfortable with the inclusion; others had reservations, not least because of the impact on the availability of specialist members if their time is fully occupied on guardianship or mental health matters, or where more complex legislative requirements may be imposed. Overall, however, as NCAT pointed out, 'people prefer not to have to go to court' and would rather the jurisdiction be given to the tribunals.

The AAT experience in accommodating the migration jurisdictions, although it may not have had any swamping effect, does indicate that governments need to respond promptly with appointments when there are insufficient members for a particular jurisdiction if adverse publicity for the tribunal's operations is to be avoided. Although the Callinan review concluded that 'The objectives of the TA Act (Tribunals Amalgamation Act) have not yet been achieved', and 'the AAT is not operating as a truly amalgamated body' this summation may be too harsh given the peculiar difficulties attending that amalgamation and the steps towards harmonisation which the AAT has managed to achieve.

The reviews of the tribunals which have already occurred are a salutary reminder of the need for the tribunals to establish benchmarks against which to measure achievement of their statutory objectives.

Overall, the benefits of amalgamation outweigh the developmental issues. These findings are a tribute to the wisdom and foresight of the governments in Australia which have pursued this next developmental step in the story of tribunals in this country. The outcomes offer the public enhanced opportunities to have their applications for a minor civil remedy, or a dispute with government, decided by an impartial body which is independent of government, using alternative methods of dispute resolution which can minimise the stress, and procedures which can be tailored to the particular matter, and which imposes less costs on the individual than would an equivalent process before a court. This is a signal achievement.

Drake v Minister for Immigration and Ethnic Affairs (1979) 46 FLR 409

Facts

Detailed facts and legislation are set out in the extract of *Re Drake and Minister for Immigration and Ethnic Affairs (No 2)* (1979) 2 ALD 634, extracted above on page pp 200–6.

The Minister ordered that Mr Drake be deported due to his criminal convictions. The AAT affirmed that decision (*Re Drake and Minister for Immigration and Ethnic Affairs* [1978] AAT 111). Mr Drake appealed to the Federal Court under s 44 of the *Administrative Appeals Tribunal Act 1975* (Cth). This extract is from the Federal Court's decision on that appeal.

This case is significant for several reasons, including establishing that it was constitutionally permissible for a Federal Court judge to sit on the AAT. In the extract below, Bowen CJ and Deane J consider the task of the AAT in merits review. This judgment is still accepted as one of the leading statements of the role of the AAT on merits review, and can be applied to de novo merits review tribunals more generally. The judgment of Smithers J demonstrates how those principles apply to a fact situation.

One of Mr Drake's grounds of appeal from the Tribunal was that the AAT member (Deputy President Davies) placed so much weight on the Minister's policy that he failed to exercise his own independent judgment.

The Court unanimously allowed the appeal on this point and remitted the matter to the AAT, where it was heard by Brennan J. The reasons for Brennan J's decision are above (*Re Drake and Minister for Immigration and Ethnic Affairs (No 2)* (1979) 2 ALD 634).

Bowen CJ and Deane J

> ***419*** The function of the Tribunal is, as we have said, an administrative one. It is to review the administrative decision that is under attack before it. In that review, the Tribunal is not restricted to consideration of the questions which are relevant to a judicial determination of whether a discretionary power allowed by statute has been validly exercised ...
>
> The question for the determination of the Tribunal is not whether the decision which the decision maker made was the correct or preferable one on the material before him.
>
> The question for the determination of the Tribunal is whether that decision was the correct or preferable one on the material before the Tribunal. The Act offers little general guidance on the criteria and rules which the Tribunal is to apply in the performance of its task of reviewing administrative decisions which are subjected to its surveillance. Even in a case such as the present where the legislation under which the relevant decision was made fails to specify the particular criteria or considerations which are relevant to the decision, the Tribunal is not, however, at large. In its proceedings, it is obliged to act judicially, that is to say, with judicial fairness and detachment. In its review of an administrative decision, it is subject to the general constraints to which the administrative officer whose decision is under review was subject ...

[Editors' note: Their Honours considered the role of policy in the AAT's reasoning, concluding that it was permissible for the AAT to take policy into account.]

> ***420*** In a matter such as the present where it was permissible for the decision maker to take relevant government policy into account in making his decision, but where the Tribunal is not under a statutory duty to regard itself as being bound by that policy, the Tribunal is entitled to treat such government policy as a relevant factor in the determination of an application for review of that decision ... On the other hand, the Tribunal is not, in the absence of specific statutory provision, entitled to abdicate its function of determining whether the decision made was, on the material before the Tribunal, the correct or preferable one in favour of a function of merely determining whether the decision made conformed with whatever the relevant general government policy might be.

[Editors' note: Their Honours agreed with Smithers J's reasons for concluding that the Tribunal failed to make 'an independent assessment and independent determination and that, in the result, it failed properly to perform its function of reviewing the Minister's decision' (at 422).]

Smithers J

429 It might be thought that it would be open to the Administrative Appeals Tribunal not to decide for itself whether a decision made by an administrator was the right decision which ought to have been made in the circumstances but rather to satisfy itself that the decision of the administrator was one which an administrator acting reasonably might have made. But to do this would be to review the reasons for the decision rather than the decision itself. It is the actual decision which by virtue of s 25(1) and (4) of the *Administrative Appeals Tribunal Act* the Tribunal is authorized and required to review. The duty of the Tribunal is to satisfy itself ***430*** whether a decision in respect of which an application for review is duly instituted is a decision which in its view, was objectively, the right one to be made. Merely to examine whether the administrator acted reasonably in relation to the facts, either as accepted by him or as found by the Tribunal may not reveal this ... It is to permit implementation of the function of the Tribunal, as so understood, that there has been conferred upon the Tribunal extensive powers of investigation. Those powers are conferred so that the Tribunal may equip itself to make an appropriate recommendation or affirm the decision: see s 43 of the *Administrative Appeals Tribunal Act* ...

[T]he [Tribunal's] reasons for decision ... induce an impression that what the Tribunal was really engaged in doing was acting in a supervisory role. In this role it was necessary for the Tribunal to form judgments as to the validity of views which the Minister had taken with respect to various matters considered by him. The Tribunal did this. And it is a question whether having done so the Tribunal applied its own views to decide whether the Minister's decision was arrived at by a reasonable or justifiable application by him of ministerial policy and if so should be affirmed, or applied its own views to decide objectively for itself whether according to the standard of good government the Minister's decision was the right one.

If the former then the Tribunal was acting in a supervisory role according to which it would tend to affirm the ministerial decision not because the Tribunal considered it to be the right one but because it considered that it was a decision which might reasonably and rationally be made in the application of ministerial policy. There are persuasive indications in the reasons that the supervisory role was the role adopted by the Tribunal in this case.

...

431 Features of the reasons which support the view that the role adopted by the Tribunal was the supervisory role may be indicated as follows: first the acceptance of ministerial policy as determinative, secondly the strict application thereof, thirdly the arrangement of the fourth part of the reasons according to the headings adopted in par 4.07 of the policy statement by the Minister, fourthly the investigation as a matter of importance of whether the Minister had misdirected himself in law as to the nature of his discretion in reaching his decision, fifthly, the intensive investigation of the matters to which the Minister had adverted and the weight allotted by him to various considerations, sixthly, the reconciliation with ministerial reasonableness of those views of the Minister with which the Tribunal disagreed, seventhly the literal application of par 4.07 of the policy statement, eighthly, the exclusion from consideration of subject matters other than those which were referred to in par 4.07 and other than those which the Minister himself had considered, and lastly, the absence from the reasons of any firm and unambiguous statement that the Tribunal itself was satisfied that the decision to deport the applicant was the right decision in the best interests of Australia.

[Editors' note: After considering other aspects of the Tribunal's reasoning, Smithers J reached the following conclusion.]

> ***432*** [T]he Tribunal acted on the basis that the function of the Tribunal was only to satisfy itself that the Minister had applied his policy as stated in par. 4.07 to the facts as he understood them in a way which whilst not always in harmony with that which the Tribunal itself would have adopted, was nevertheless reasonable. It would appear that the Tribunal did not approach the matter a new ***433*** but accepted the Minister's policy as determinative with all the limitations that that involved.

[Citations omitted]

Shi v Migration Agents Registration Authority (2008) 235 CLR 286

Migration Act 1958 (Cth)

[As at relevant date]

PART 3—MIGRATION AGENTS AND IMMIGRATION ASSISTANCE

DIVISION 3—REGISTRATION OF MIGRATION AGENTS

303 Disciplining registered migration agents

(1) The Migration Agents Registration Authority may:

- (a) cancel the registration of a registered migration agent by removing his or her name from the register; or
- (b) suspend his or her registration; or
- (c) caution him or her;

if it becomes satisfied that:

- (d) the agent's application for registration was known by the agent to be false or misleading in a material particular; or
- (e) the agent becomes bankrupt; or
- (f) the agent is not a person of integrity or is otherwise not a fit and proper person to give immigration assistance; or

(g) an individual related by employment to the agent is not a person of integrity; or

(h) the agent has not complied with the Code of Conduct prescribed under section 314

...

306 Review by the Administrative Appeals Tribunal

Subject to the *Administrative Appeals Tribunal Act 1975*, application may be made to the Administrative Appeals Tribunal for review of a decision by the Migration Agents Registration Authority made under this Division.

Facts

Nelson Shi was registered as a migration agent in 1995. In July 2003, the Migration Agents Registration Authority found that Mr Shi had breached the Code of Conduct multiple times, including by failing to keep adequate office and financial records, failing to keep clients informed, failing to supervise his staff, and failing to maintain his knowledge of migration law. The Authority cancelled his registration, acting under ss 303(1)(f) and (h) of the *Migration Act 1958* (Cth).

Mr Shi applied to the Administrative Appeals Tribunal for review of this decision. On 31 July 2003, before hearing Mr Shi's substantive application, the Tribunal stayed the Authority's decision to cancel Mr Shi's registration, but imposed a condition that Mr Shi was to be supervised by another migration agent. The Tribunal also required Mr Shi to give an undertaking that he would not do any work relating to protection visas.

The Tribunal finally heard Mr Shi's application in April 2005, and handed down its decision in September 2005. The Tribunal found that Mr Shi had committed some, but not all, of the breaches of the Code of Conduct that the Authority had identified. The Tribunal member also explained (in *Re Shi and Migration Agents Registration Authority* [2005] AAT 851, [24]):

> I take into account that [Mr Shi] has had a supervising migration agent for over two years who is a knowledgeable and experienced migration agent and who holds Mr Shi in high regard. There has been no evidence of breaches since the first decision was made in 2003 and his rate of success has been very high in recent years. Most of the non-compliances with the Code related to protection visas which he has not dealt with since early in 2003.

The Tribunal set aside the Authority's decision and substituted a decision to caution Mr Shi (subject to further supervision and a condition that he not do work relating to protection visas).

The Authority appealed to the Federal Court under s 44 of the *Administrative Appeals Tribunal Act 1975* (Cth). One of the questions of law on which the Authority appealed was whether the Tribunal had erred in considering whether Mr Shi was a fit and proper person to be a migration agent *at the time of the Tribunal's decision* in 2005, rather than at the time of the Authority's decision in 2003. The primary judge in the Federal Court upheld the appeal, and the Full Court of the Federal Court dismissed an appeal from the primary judge's decision. Mr Shi appealed to the High Court. The High Court allowed the appeal, thus reinstating the Tribunal's decision.

The High Court's analysis of the role of the Tribunal is one of the leading statements on the nature of de novo merits review in Australia.

Kirby J

The proper approach of the Tribunal

295 [25] *Focusing on the legislation:* To resolve the question of whether the Tribunal has exceeded or mistaken its jurisdiction and powers a court must give close attention to the enabling legislation. It is undesirable to attempt universal or unqualified propositions. Here, the issue is how to define the jurisdiction and powers of the Tribunal in conducting a review of a decision of the Authority, having regard both to the general provisions of the AAT Act, affording the power of review, and to the more specific provisions of the Migration Act, defining the characteristics of the decision that is subject to review. Only when all of the relevant features of the two inter-related statutes are understood can a correct decision be arrived at as to the ambit of the review in question and the manner in which it should be conducted.

[26] The starting point is a recognition that the Parliament has not spelt out in explicit terms an answer to the first question in this appeal. There is nothing in s 43 of the AAT Act to indicate whether, '[f]or the purpose of reviewing a decision', the Tribunal is to have regard to the facts and circumstances at the time the 'decision under review' was made or at the time of the Tribunal's making of a 'decision in writing'. It is this silence that necessitates examination of the inter-related legislation relevant to the particular case. The inter-relationship determines the character of the 'decision' that is under review and the 'powers and discretions' that the Tribunal is to exercise pursuant to s 43(1) of the AAT Act.

....

296 [29] ... [T]he preferable conclusion on the jurisdiction and powers of the Tribunal, and on the manner in which it should discharge its functions in cases of the present kind, is that [the Tribunal was right to consider the facts as at the time of its decision.] There are five factors, of varying degrees of significance, that combine to produce this conclusion.

[30] *Nature of the Tribunal:* First, it is essential to appreciate the radical objectives that lay behind the enactment of the AAT Act. That Act grew out of a series of official reports directed towards a major change in federal administrative law and practice. The first (and possibly the most significant) of these reports was that delivered in 1971 by the Commonwealth Administrative Review Committee.

...

[Editors' note: Kirby J quoted the Committee's observations, extracted in Chapter 7 of this book, about the complexity of judicial review and the inability of judicial review to provide aggrieved citizens with what they really want: review on the merits.]

297 [31] It was for this reason that the Committee recommended the establishment of what it called an 'administrative review tribunal'. Describing the jurisdiction and powers that should be given to such a general federal tribunal for administrative appeals, it proposed:

> [S]uch a Tribunal could be given jurisdiction to review on the merits certain administrative decisions made under Commonwealth law. The jurisdiction

> should be to hear and determine an application by a person who is aggrieved or adversely affected by a decision on the ground that the decision was erroneous on the facts and merits of the case. If such an application is made the Tribunal should also have power to deal with all questions of law necessary for its decision.

[32] The proposal to create such a tribunal, with the power to make decisions 'on the merits', represented a bold departure from the pre-existing law, with its focus on constitutional and statutory 'prerogative' remedies of judicial review. In so far as those remedies were invoked it was, and still is, commonly insisted that the court performing the review is not concerned, as such, with the factual merits of the matter, but only with legal merits, and then often only with any errors of a jurisdictional kind shown to exist at the time of the initial decision. But given the nature of the Tribunal, it is important to approach particular questions concerning its jurisdiction and powers with the history and purpose of its creation at the forefront of attention.

[33] *Function of the Tribunal:* Secondly, in the earliest days of the operation of the Tribunal, questions naturally arose as to how, under s 43 of the AAT Act (not relevantly altered since), the Tribunal should proceed with its function of review ...

[Editors' note: Kirby J reviewed some of the early authorities, including *Drake v Minister for Immigration and Ethnic Affairs* (1979) 46 FLR 409 and *Collector of Customs (New South Wales) v Brian Lawlor Automotive Pty Ltd* (1979) 41 FLR 338.]

298 [36] Responding to a submission [in *Re Control Investment Pty Ltd and Australian Broadcasting Tribunal (No 2)* (1981) 3 ALD 88] that the word 'may' in s 43 of the AAT Act implied an element of discretion such as to authorise the Tribunal to limit its function as it saw fit, Davies J concluded [at 92]:

> [T]he provision 'For the purpose of reviewing a decision, the Tribunal may exercise all the powers and discretions that are conferred by any relevant enactment on the person who made the decision ...' is not concerned to confer upon the Tribunal authority to limit its function but rather to confer upon it an amplitude of powers so that the Tribunal may exercise, if it is convenient and useful to do so, not only the decision-making power upon which the decision-maker relied, but all relevant powers and discretions which were conferred by the enactment upon the decision-maker. The provision extends the authority of the Tribunal so that it may more adequately exercise its function of reviewing on the merits the subject decision.

299 [37] Davies J acknowledged that regard might be had to the decision of the primary decision-maker as part of the 'material before the Tribunal', particularly where it involved special expertise or knowledge [at 92–3]. But ultimately, it was for the Tribunal to reach its own decision upon the relevant material including any new, fresh, additional or different material that had been received by the Tribunal as relevant to its decision. In effect, this was no more than a consequence of the Tribunal's obligation to conduct a true merits review.

[38] There was no error in this analysis. On the contrary, it represents the correct and preferable view of the legislation establishing the functions and powers of the Tribunal.

[39] *Purpose of s 43 of the AAT Act:* Thirdly, a conclusion that, ordinarily, the Tribunal might have regard to new, fresh, additional or different evidence in reaching its own decision is reinforced by the apparent purpose of s 43 of the AAT Act. Under that section, when the Tribunal decides to set the decision under review aside, it must consider whether to remit the decision to the Tribunal for reconsideration (with or without directions or recommendations) or whether to make a fresh decision 'in substitution for the decision so set aside'.

[40] Of necessity, any such fresh decision replaces the decision of the primary administrative decision-maker within the Executive Government of the Commonwealth. In law, and in effect, it becomes the decision of the Executive Government. Many days, weeks, months or even a year or more might have passed since the original decision was made by the primary decision-maker. It would be theoretically conceivable that the Tribunal might make a decision which ought to have been made years, months, weeks or many days earlier, leaving it to the primary decision-maker then to update or alter that decision if any new facts and circumstances required, or warranted, that course. However, given the obvious purpose of having the Tribunal (as it is commonly put) 'step into the shoes' of the primary decision-maker, so as to make the decision that ought to have been made 'on the merits', this would appear to ascribe to the Tribunal an artificial function. It would not be the natural and appropriate function, given the role, purpose and powers of the Tribunal, viewed in its administrative setting.

[41] When making a decision, administrative decision-makers are generally obliged to have regard to the best and most current information available. This rule of practice is no more than a feature of good public administration. When, therefore, the Tribunal elects to make 'a decision in substitution for the decision so set aside', as the ***300*** Act permits, it would be surprising in the extreme if the substituted decision did not have to conform to such a standard.

...

[43] *Nature of the decision under review:* Fourthly, although the foregoing considerations lead to a conclusion that the Tribunal is not ordinarily confined to material that was before the primary decision-maker, or to consideration of events that had occurred up to the time of its decision, the fact that the review contemplated by s 43 of the AAT Act is one addressed to a 'decision', inferentially arising under a different federal enactment, makes it necessary in each case to identify the precise nature and incidents of the decision that is the subject of the review.

[44] Sometimes, it may be inherent in the nature of a particular decision at review of that decision is confined to identified past events. If, for example, under federal legislation, a pension is payable at fortnightly rests, by reference to particular qualifications that may themselves alter over time, a 'review' of an administrative 'decision' to grant or refuse such a pension, by reference to statutory qualifications, may necessarily be limited to the facts at the particular time of the decision.

...

301 [47] The nature and incidents of the decision under review in the present case do not support a contention that the review was limited to the particular time in the past when the decision was made by the Authority. The present was not a case where, of its nature, a decision was made falling to be determined by reference to the state of evidence at a particular time. Both the language of s 303 of the Migration Act and its purpose suggest otherwise.

[48] Section 303 of the Migration Act directs the Authority's attention, amongst other things, to whether an agent 'becomes bankrupt'; whether he or she 'is not a person of integrity' or 'otherwise not a fit and proper person'; and whether 'an individual related by employment to the agent is not a person of integrity'. Each of these grounds is ***302*** expressed in the present tense. Necessarily, the circumstances to which each is addressed could be altered by supervening events. Thus, the language in s 303 of the Migration Act clearly contemplates the possibility that circumstances may change between an initial decision of the Authority and a subsequent decision of the Tribunal, performing the 'review' which s 306 of the Migration Act contemplates and for which s 43 of the AAT Act provides.

...

[50] This reasoning is further strengthened by an appreciation that the fundamental object of the exercise of the Authority's power to cancel or suspend the registration of an agent under the Migration Act is the protection of the section of the public that deals with migration agents. It is not, as such, the punishment of agents. This object is best achieved by the Tribunal making its decision upon the most up to date material available to it at the time of its own decision.

...

[52] *Errors in the reasoning below:* Fifthly, there are a number of particular defects in the reasoning of the majority in the Full Court ...

303 [55] *Conclusion: the appellant succeeds:* For the foregoing reasons, the majority of the Full Court erred in their construction of the powers of the Tribunal. The reasons of [the primary judge] are to be preferred, in respect of the approach that it was proper for the Tribunal to take and the materials upon which it was entitled and required to rely.

[Citations omitted]

Frugtniet v Australian Securities and Investments Commission (2019) 266 CLR 250

National Consumer Credit Protection Act 2009 (Cth)

[As at relevant date]

80 ASIC's power to make a banning order

(1) ASIC may make a banning order against a person:

...

(f) if ASIC has reason to believe that the person is not a fit and proper person to engage in credit activities; ...

Crimes Act 1914 (Cth)

[As at relevant date]

PART VIIC—PARDONS, QUASHED CONVICTIONS AND SPENT CONVICTIONS

DIVISION 3—SPENT CONVICTIONS

85ZV Spent convictions

...

(2) Subject to Division 6, but despite any other Commonwealth law or any Territory law, if a person's conviction of a State offence or a foreign offence is spent, the person is not required:

...

(b) in any State or foreign country—to disclose to any Commonwealth authority in that State or country, for any purpose, the fact that the person has been charged with, or convicted of, the offence.

...

85ZW Effect of right of non-disclosure

Subject to Division 6, but despite any other Commonwealth law, or any State law or Territory law, where, under section 85ZV, it is lawful for a person not to disclose, in particular circumstances, or for a particular purpose, the fact that he or she was charged with, or convicted of, an offence:

(a) it is lawful for the person to claim, in those circumstances, or for that purpose, on oath or otherwise, that he or she was not charged with, or convicted of, the offence; and

(b) anyone else who knows, or could reasonably be expected to know, that section 85ZV applies to the person in relation to the offence shall not:

(i) without the person's consent, disclose the fact that the person was charged with, or convicted of, the offence to any other person, or to a Commonwealth authority or State authority, where it is lawful for the first-mentioned person not to disclose it to that other person or that authority; or

(ii) in those circumstances, or for that purpose, take account of the fact that the person was charged with, or convicted of, the offence.

85ZZH Exclusions

Division 3 does not apply in relation to the disclosure of information to or by, or the taking into account of information by a person or body referred to in one of the following paragraphs for the purpose specified in relation to the person or body:

...

(c) a court or tribunal established under a Commonwealth law, a State law or a Territory law, for the purpose of making a decision, including a decision in relation to sentencing;

Facts

In 1978, Rudy Frugtniet was convicted, in the United Kingdom, of various offences of dishonesty. In 1997, in New South Wales, Mr Frugtniet was found to have omitted an offence of obtaining property by deception, but no conviction was entered for that offence. At the time of these proceedings, these offences were 'spent convictions' under s 85ZM of the *Crimes Act 1914* (Cth): the UK convictions because the 'waiting period' for those convictions had expired, and the NSW conviction because no conviction was entered.

In 2014, Mr Frugtniet was engaging in various credit activities, including through a business that provided mortgages. The Australian Securities and Investments Commission (ASIC) made a banning order, under s 80 of the *National Consumer Credit Protection Act 2009* (Cth), against Mr Frugtniet, based on a pattern of dishonest conduct over a long period. The banning order prevented Mr Frugtniet from engaging in credit activities. Because s 85ZW of the *Crimes Act 1914* (Cth) precluded it from doing so, ASIC did *not* consider Mr Frugtniet's spent convictions.

Mr Frugtniet applied to the AAT for review of ASIC's decision. The AAT took the view that s 85ZZH of the *Crimes Act 1914* (Cth) meant the AAT was entitled to take the spent convictions into account. The AAT affirmed ASIC's decision. The Federal Court dismissed an appeal under s 44 of the *Administrative Appeals Tribunal Act 1975* (Cth). On appeal, the High Court held unanimously that the AAT was *not* entitled to consider the spent convictions. In reaching this conclusion, the High Court reflected on the AAT's merits review function.

Kiefel CJ, Keane and Nettle JJ

***256* The nature of administrative merits review**

[14] The enactment of the AAT Act established a new and substantially unprecedented regime of administrative merits review, distinguished principally by the AAT's jurisdiction to re-exercise the ***257*** functions of original administrative decision-makers. The question for determination by the AAT on the review of an administrative decision under s 25 of the AAT Act is thus whether the decision is the correct or preferable decision. That question is required to be determined on the material before the AAT, not on the material as it was when before the original decision-maker. As Bowen CJ and Deane J held in *Drake v Minister for Immigration and Ethnic Affairs* [(1979) 24 ALR 577, 589], however, and has since been affirmed by this Court in *Shi v Migration Agents Registration Authority* [(2008) 235 CLR 286], the AAT is not at large. It is subject to the same general constraints as the original decision-maker and should ordinarily approach its task as though it were performing the relevant function of the original decision-maker in accordance with the law as it applied to the decision-maker at the time of the original decision.

[15] Depending on the nature of the decision the subject of review, the AAT may sometimes take into account evidence that was not before the original decision-maker, including evidence of events subsequent to the original decision. But subject to any clearly expressed contrary statutory indication, the AAT may do so only if and to the extent that the evidence is relevant to the question which the original decision-maker was bound to decide; really, as if the original decision-maker were deciding the matter at the time that it is before the AAT. The AAT cannot take into account

matters which were not before the original decision-maker where to do so would change the nature of ***258*** the decision or, put another way, the question before the original decision-maker. As Kiefel J observed in *Shi* [(2008) 235 CLR 286, 327 [142]], identifying the question raised by the statute for consideration will usually determine the facts that may be taken into account in connection with the decision. The issue is one of relevance, to be determined by reference to the elements of the question necessary to be addressed in reaching a decision.

Bell, Gageler, Gordon and Edelman JJ

271 [51] [T]he jurisdiction conferred on the AAT by ss 25 and 43 of the AAT Act, where application is made to it under an enactment, is to stand in the shoes of the decision-maker whose decision is under review so as to determine for itself on the material before it the decision which can, and which it considers should, be made in the exercise of the power or powers conferred on the primary decision-maker for the purpose of making the decision under review. The AAT exercises the same power or powers as the primary decision-maker, subject to the same constraints. The primary decision, and the statutory question it answers, marks the boundaries of the AAT's review. The AAT must address the same question the primary decision-maker was required to address, and the question raised by statute for decision by the primary decision-maker determines the considerations that must or must not be taken into account by the AAT in reviewing that decision. A consideration which the primary decision-maker must take into account in the exercise of statutory power to make the decision under review must be taken into account by the AAT. Conversely, a consideration which the primary decision-maker must not take into account must not be taken into account by the AAT.

[Citations omitted]

PART IV

JUDICIAL REVIEW

CHAPTER

9

INTRODUCTION TO JUDICIAL REVIEW

Introduction	230
Stephen Gageler, 'The Legitimate Scope of Judicial Review' (2001) 21(3) *Australian Bar Review* 279	231
Statutory review on a question of law	231
Osland v Secretary, Department of Justice (No 2) (2010) 241 CLR 320	232
Administrative Appeals Tribunal Act 1975 (Cth)	234
Judicial review – review of legality	235
Attorney-General (NSW) v Quin (1990) 170 CLR 1	236
Statutory construction	238
Project Blue Sky Inc v Australian Broadcasting Authority (1998) 194 CLR 355	238
Sources of judicial review jurisdiction	241
Constitution	241
Judiciary Act 1903 (Cth)	241
State Supreme Courts	242
Supreme Court Act 1970 (NSW)	242
Supreme Court Act 1935 (SA)	243
Administrative Law Act 1978 (Vic)	244

Origins of common law and constitutional judicial review 246
Re Refugee Review Tribunal; Ex parte Aala (2000) 204 CLR 82 246
Kirk v Industrial Court of New South Wales (2010) 239 CLR 531 247
Statutory judicial review 249
Administrative Decisions (Judicial Review) Act 1977 (Cth) 249
Kioa v West (1985) 159 CLR 550 253
Australian Broadcasting Tribunal v Bond (1990) 170 CLR 321 254
Griffith University v Tang (2005) 221 CLR 99 256
The concepts of jurisdictional error and error of law on the face of the record 258
Craig v South Australia (1995) 184 CLR 163 258
Minister for Immigration and Multicultural Affairs v Yusuf (2001) 206 CLR 323 261
Kirk v Industrial Court of New South Wales (2010) 239 CLR 531 263
Probuild Constructions (Aust) Pty Ltd v Shade Systems Pty Ltd (2018) 264 CLR 1 268
Hossain v Minister for Immigration and Border Protection (2018) 264 CLR 123 272
MZAPC v Minister for Immigration and Border Protection (2021) 95 ALJR 441 275
Nathanson v Minister for Home Affairs (2022) 96 ALJR 737 276
What is the face of the record? 278
Craig v South Australia (1995) 184 CLR 163 278
Supreme Court Act 1970 (NSW) 280
Administrative Law Act 1978 (Vic) 280

Introduction

This chapter complements Chapter 9 of *Government Accountability: Australian Administrative Law,* third edition. It introduces the concepts of statutory appeal on questions of law, statutory construction, and judicial review. The sources set out the framework for judicial review at state and Commonwealth level. The sources consider the foundations of the courts' jurisdiction to review the decision-making processes of inferior courts and the executive government, and the concepts of jurisdictional error and error of law on the face of the record.

Stephen Gageler, 'The Legitimate Scope of Judicial Review' (2001) 21(3) *Australian Bar Review* 279

279 There is in Australian legal theory a bright line between judicial review and merits review. The theory is rooted less in the nature of administrative decision-making than in the nature of judicial power which under Ch III of the Australian Constitution is separated from legislative power and executive power and reposed in a separate branch of government. In that branch of government is reposed the final determination of legal truth. The same conception of the unique role of the constitutionally separated judiciary that justifies and sustains the judicial review of an exercise of legislative power justifies and sustains the judicial review of an exercise of executive power. ...

Judicial review on the approach now accepted by the High Court is therefore an aspect of the rule of law which has itself been identified as an ***280*** assumption against which the Constitution was framed. Judicial review is justified and sustained by one consideration alone: the declaration and enforcement of the legal rules which determine the limits and govern the exercise of a repository's powers. That is the duty and jurisdiction of the courts.

For present purposes of equal importance is that that is the *sole* duty and jurisdiction of the courts. The judicial review of administrative action is in this respect no different from the exercise by a court of any other jurisdiction.

The merits of an administrative decision on this analysis are wholly beyond the scope of judicial review. This is not because the merits constitute a separate or distinct field into which the judiciary ought not trespass as a matter of institutional competence or public policy. It is because the merits are simply outside the subject-matter of judicial inquiry. The merits are the residue of administrative decision-making that in any given case lies beyond any question of legality.

That is the theory. The practice is somewhat blurred. The distinction between judicial review and merits review is not always so clear. This is in part because the theory is not always observed. It is in part because the applicable legal rules are uncertain or in a state of development. There is a raging debate as to whether the courts in discerning or developing or applying those legal rules have overstepped a line which in the interests of public administration they should observe.

[Citations omitted]

Statutory review on a question of law

A statutory appeal on a question of law is, in many ways, similar to judicial review proceedings: it involves a court searching for legal error in the decision under review. Many statutes establishing tribunals provide for an appeal (from the tribunal to a court) on a question of law. In this part, the nature of an appeal under s 148 of the *Victorian Civil and Administrative Tribunal Act 1998* (Vic) and the orders that can be made are considered in the context of the *Osland* freedom of information case.

Osland v Secretary, Department of Justice (No 2) (2010) 241 CLR 320

Victorian Civil and Administrative Tribunal Act 1998 (Vic)

[As at relevant date]

148 Appeals from the Tribunal

(1) A party to a proceeding may appeal, on a question of law, from an order of the Tribunal in the proceeding –

(a) to the Court of Appeal, if the Tribunal was constituted for the purpose of making the order by the President or a Vice President, whether with or without others; or

(b) to the Trial Division of the Supreme Court in any other case – if the Court of Appeal or the Trial Division, as the case requires, gives leave to appeal.

...

(7) The Court of Appeal or the Trial Division, as the case requires, may make any of the following orders on an appeal –

(a) an order affirming, varying or setting aside the order of the Tribunal;

(b) an order that the Tribunal could have made in the proceeding;

(c) an order remitting the proceeding to be heard and decided again, either with or without the hearing of further evidence, by the Tribunal in accordance with the directions of the court;

(d) any other order the court thinks appropriate.

Facts

The facts of *Osland (No 1)* and *Osland (No 2)* are outlined in Chapters 3 and 6. Heather Osland was convicted of the murder of her husband and petitioned the Governor of Victoria for mercy seeking a pardon. In response to the petition for mercy, the Victorian Attorney-General issued a press release referring to a joint advice from three Queen's Counsel that had recommended that the petition be denied. Mrs Osland sought access under freedom of information to documents relating to her petition, including the joint advice and other legal advice. The Victorian Department of Justice refused access to the documents and a long battle before tribunal and courts ensued.

In this, the second of two High Court appeals relating to the freedom of information application, the Court discussed the nature of an appeal under s 148 of the *Victorian Civil and Administrative Tribunal Act 1998* (Vic).

French CJ, Gummow and Bell JJ

331 [18] Section 148 confers 'judicial power to examine for legal error what has been done in an administrative tribunal'. Despite the ***332*** description of proceedings under the section as an 'appeal', it confers original not appellate jurisdiction; the proceedings are 'in the nature of judicial review'.

[19] The jurisdiction conferred by s 148(1) is confined to appeals on questions of law. Section 148(7) does not enlarge that jurisdiction. It confers powers on the court in aid of its exercise. That feature of s 148 resembles s 44 of the *Administrative Appeals Tribunal Act 1975* (Cth) (the *Commonwealth AAT Act*), which defines the analogous jurisdiction of the Federal Court to hear appeals on questions of law against decisions of the Administrative Appeals Tribunal (AAT). Under s 44(4) of the *Commonwealth AAT Act,* the Federal Court, in determining an appeal, may 'make such order as it thinks appropriate by reason of its decision'. But wide as that power may be, the Court 'should not usurp the fact-finding function of the AAT'. Those observations turn upon the text of s 44. They do not depend upon the separation of judicial and executive powers, which limits the functions that can be conferred upon federal courts. They have application to the jurisdiction conferred upon the Court of Appeal by s 148 of the *VCAT Act,* which is, in concept and in terms, modelled on, although not identical to, s 44.

[20] The Court of Appeal, in the exercise of its jurisdiction under s 148 of the *VCAT Act,* may make substitutive orders where only one conclusion is open on the correct application of the law to the facts found by the Tribunal. Such a case arises when no other conclusion ***333*** could reasonably be entertained. In that event, the Court can make the order that the Tribunal should have made. The language of s 148(7) is also wide enough to allow the Court of Appeal to make substitutive orders in other circumstances. But its powers must, as with the equivalent powers of the Federal Court in relation to the AAT, be exercised having regard to the limited nature of the appeal. Absent such restraint, a question of law would open the door to an appeal by way of rehearing. Where there is a factual matter that has to be determined as a consequence of the appeal, it may be that it is able conveniently to be determined by the Court of Appeal upon uncontested evidence or primary facts already found by the Tribunal. When the outstanding issue involves the formation of an opinion which is, as in this case, based upon considerations of public interest, then it should in the ordinary case be remitted to the body established for the purpose of making that essentially factual, evaluative and ministerial judgment.

[Citations omitted]

On 16 December 2022, the Commonwealth Attorney-General announced that the Administrative Appeals Tribunal would be abolished and replaced with a new merits review body. At the time of writing, the legislation establishing this body was not publicly available.

Because the Administrative Appeals Tribunal was the model for most Australian merits review tribunals, the provisions of the *Administrative Appeals Tribunal Act 1975* (Cth) remain worthy of study.

Administrative Appeals Tribunal Act 1975 (Cth)

[As at 1 March 2018]

44 Appeals to Federal Court of Australia from decisions of the Tribunal

Appeal on question of law

(1) A party to a proceeding before the Tribunal may appeal to the Federal Court of Australia, on a question of law, from any decision of the Tribunal in that proceeding.

...

Appeal about standing

(2) Where a person has applied to the Tribunal for a review of a decision, or has applied to be made a party to a proceeding before the Tribunal for a review of a decision, and the Tribunal decides that the interests of the person are not affected by the decision, the person may appeal to the Federal Court of Australia from the decision of the Tribunal.

...

Jurisdiction

(3) The Federal Court of Australia has jurisdiction to hear and determine appeals instituted in that Court in accordance with subsections (1) and (2) and that jurisdiction:
- (a) may be exercised by that Court constituted as a Full Court;
- (b) shall be so exercised if:
  - (i) the Tribunal's decision was given by the Tribunal constituted by a member who was, or by members at least one of whom was, a Deputy President who is not a Judge; and
  - (ii) after consulting the President, the Chief Justice of that Court considers that it is appropriate for the appeal from the decision to be heard and determined by that Court constituted as a Full Court; and
- (c) shall be so exercised if the Tribunal's decision was given by the Tribunal constituted by a member who was, or by members at least one of whom was, a Judge.

Powers of Federal Court

(4) The Federal Court of Australia shall hear and determine the appeal and may make such order as it thinks appropriate by reason of its decision.

(5) Without limiting by implication the generality of subsection (4), the orders that may be made by the Federal Court of Australia on an appeal include an order affirming or setting aside the decision of the Tribunal and an order remitting the case to be heard and decided again, either with or without the hearing of further evidence, by the Tribunal in accordance with the directions of the Court.

Constitution of Tribunal if Federal Court remits case etc.

(6) If the Federal Court of Australia makes an order remitting a case to be heard and decided again by the Tribunal:

(a) the Tribunal need not be constituted for the hearing by the person or persons who made the decision to which the appeal relates; and

(b) whether or not the Tribunal is reconstituted for the hearing—the Tribunal may, for the purposes of the proceeding, have regard to any record of the proceeding before the Tribunal prior to the appeal (including a record of any evidence taken in the proceeding), so long as doing so is not inconsistent with the directions of the Court.

Federal Court may make findings of fact

(7) If a party to a proceeding before the Tribunal appeals to the Federal Court of Australia under subsection (1), the Court may make findings of fact if:

(a) the findings of fact are not inconsistent with findings of fact made by the Tribunal (other than findings made by the Tribunal as the result of an error of law); and

(b) it appears to the Court that it is convenient for the Court to make the findings of fact, having regard to:

(i) the extent (if any) to which it is necessary for facts to be found; and

(ii) the means by which those facts might be established; and

(iii) the expeditious and efficient resolution of the whole of the matter to which the proceeding before the Tribunal relates; and

(iv) the relative expense to the parties of the Court, rather than the Tribunal, making the findings of fact; and

(v) the relative delay to the parties of the Court, rather than the Tribunal, making the findings of fact; and

(vi) whether any of the parties considers that it is appropriate for the Court, rather than the Tribunal, to make the findings of fact; and

(vii) such other matters (if any) as the Court considers relevant.

(8) For the purposes of making findings of fact under subsection (7), the Federal Court of Australia may:

(a) have regard to the evidence given in the proceeding before the Tribunal; and

(b) receive further evidence.

(9) Subsection (7) does not limit the Federal Court of Australia's power under subsection to make an order remitting the case to be heard and decided again by the Tribunal.

(10) The jurisdiction of the Federal Court of Australia under subsection (3) includes jurisdiction to make findings of fact under subsection (7).

Judicial review – review of legality

When engaging in judicial review, courts perform the function of ensuring the executive acts lawfully. In the following case, Brennan J explains the scope and purpose of judicial review.

Attorney-General (NSW) v Quin (1990) 170 CLR 1

Facts

This case concerned the restructuring of the New South Wales magistrates' courts in 1982. Courts of Petty Sessions were abolished by statute and replaced by Local Courts, with the new magistrates appointed by the Governor on the recommendation of the Attorney-General. Ninety-five of the 100 former magistrates who applied for positions in the new courts were appointed. The policy was that former magistrates would be appointed unless they were considered unfit for judicial office. Eris Quin was not appointed and obtained from the Supreme Court of New South Wales a declaration that the Attorney-General's decision was void on the ground of breach of natural justice (procedural fairness). In a second action brought by Mr Quin that was removed into the New South Wales Court of Appeal, the Court of Appeal made another declaration. The effect of that declaration was that the decision about Mr Quin's appointment should be made by the Attorney-General according to the original policy and not in competition with subsequent applicants.

The Attorney-General (NSW) successfully appealed to the High Court and the decision of the New South Wales Court of Appeal was reversed. The declaration made by the Court of Appeal had gone beyond the role of the court and intruded into the merits or exercise of discretion by the Attorney-General. The following extract from Brennan J has become a frequently cited statement about the scope of judicial review.

Brennan J

> ***35*** Judicial review provides no remedies to protect interests, falling short of enforceable rights, which are apt to be affected by the lawful exercise of executive or administrative power. If it were otherwise, the courts would be asserting a jurisdiction, in protection of individual interests, to override the law by which a power to affect those interests is conferred on the repository.
>
> Judicial review has undoubtedly been invoked, and invoked beneficially, to set aside administrative acts and decisions which are unjust or otherwise inappropriate, but only when the purported exercise of power is excessive or otherwise unlawful ...
>
> The essential warrant for judicial intervention is the declaration and enforcing of the law affecting the extent and exercise of power: that is the characteristic duty of the judicature as the third branch of government. In *Victoria v The Commonwealth and Hayden* [(1975) 134 CLR 338, 380], Gibbs J said that the duty of the courts extends to pronouncing on the validity of executive action when challenged on the ground that it exceeds constitutional power, but the duty extends to judicial review of administrative action alleged to go beyond the power conferred by statute or by the prerogative or alleged to be otherwise in disconformity with the law. The duty and the jurisdiction of the courts are expressed in the memorable words of Marshall CJ in *Marbury v Madison* [(1803) 1 Cranch 137, 177]:
>
> > It is, emphatically, the province and duty of the judicial department to say what the law is.
>
> The duty and jurisdiction of the court to review administrative ***36*** action do not go beyond the declaration and enforcing of the law which determines the limits and governs the exercise of the repository's power. If, in so doing, the court avoids

administrative injustice or error, so be it; but the court has no jurisdiction simply to cure administrative injustice or error. The merits of administrative action, to the extent that they can be distinguished from legality, are for the repository of the relevant power and, subject to political control, for the repository alone.

The consequence is that the scope of judicial review must be defined not in terms of the protection of individual interests but in terms of the extent of power and the legality of its exercise. In Australia, the modern development and expansion of the law of judicial review of administrative action have been achieved by an increasingly sophisticated exposition of implied limitations on the extent or the exercise of statutory power, but those limitations are not calculated to secure judicial scrutiny of the merits of a particular case.

...

37 If it be right to say that the court's jurisdiction in judicial review goes no further than declaring and enforcing the law prescribing the limits and governing the exercise of power, the next question immediately arises: what is the law? And that question, of course, must be answered by the court itself. In giving its answer, the court needs to remember that the judicature is but one of the three coordinate branches of government and that the authority of the judicature is not derived from a superior capacity to balance the interests of the community against the interests of an individual. The repository of administrative power must often balance the interests of the public at large and the interests of minority groups or individuals. The courts are not equipped to evaluate the policy considerations which properly bear on such decisions, nor is the adversary system ideally suited to the doing of administrative justice: interests which are not represented as well as interests which are represented must often be considered. Moreover, if the courts were permitted to review the merits of administrative action whenever interested parties were prepared to risk the costs of litigation, the exercise of administrative power might be skewed in favour of the rich, the powerful, or the simply litigious.

Some advocates of judicial intervention would encourage the courts to expand the scope and purpose of judicial review, especially to provide some check on the Executive Government which nowadays exercises enormous powers beyond the capacity of the Parliament to supervise effectively. Such advocacy is misplaced. If the courts were to assume a jurisdiction to review administrative acts or decisions which are 'unfair' in the opinion of the court not the product of procedural unfairness, but unfair on the merits – the courts would be assuming a jurisdiction to do the very thing which is to be done by the repository of an administrative power, namely, choosing among the courses of action upon which reasonable minds might differ ... The courts – above all other institutions of government – have a duty to uphold and apply the law which ***38*** recognizes the autonomy of the three branches of government within their respective spheres of competence and which recognizes the legal effectiveness of the due exercise of power by the Executive Government and other repositories of administrative power. The law of judicial review cannot conflict with recognition of the legal effectiveness of the due exercise of power by the other branches of government.

If judicial review were to trespass on the merits of the exercise of administrative power, it would put its own legitimacy at risk.

[Citations omitted]

Statutory construction

This focus on review of legality means that, in relation to powers that are conferred by statute, statutory construction is central to judicial review. The following case, *Project Blue Sky Inc v Australian Broadcasting Authority*, is a routinely cited authority that explains the duty of the courts to give meaning to the words of a statute as the legislature intended. Further extracts from the case concerning whether failure to comply with a condition regulating the exercise of a statutory power are in Chapter 15.

Project Blue Sky Inc v Australian Broadcasting Authority (1998) 194 CLR 355

Broadcasting Services Act 1992 (Cth)

[As at relevant date]

122 Program standards for children's programs and Australian content

(1) The ABA must, by notice in writing:

(a) determine standards that are to be observed by commercial television broadcasting licensees; and

(b) determine standards that are to be observed by community television broadcasting licensees.

(2) Standards under subsection (1) for commercial television broadcasting licensees are to relate to:

(a) programs for children; and

(b) the Australian content of programs.

(3) Standards under subsection (1) for community television broadcasting licensees are to relate to programs for children.

(4) Standards must not be inconsistent with this Act or the regulations.

158 Primary functions of the [Australian Broadcasting Authority]

The primary functions of the ABA are:

...

(h) to assist broadcasting service providers to develop codes of practice that, as far as possible, are in accordance with community standards; and

(i) to monitor compliance with those codes of practice; and

(j) to develop program standards relating to broadcasting in Australia; and

(k) to monitor compliance with those standards;

...

160 General obligations of the ABA

The ABA is to perform its functions in a manner consistent with:

(a) the objects of this Act and the regulatory policy described in; and

(b) any general policies of the Government notified by the Minister under section 161; and

(c) any directions given by the Minister in accordance with this Act; and

(d) Australia's obligations under any convention to which Australia is a party or any agreement between Australia and a foreign country.

Facts

The Australian Broadcasting Authority ('ABA') made a program standard requiring television stations to broadcast a minimum amount of Australian content. Project Blue Sky, a company that aimed to promote the growth of the New Zealand film and television industry, argued this standard was inconsistent with a free trade agreement between Australia and New Zealand, under which each country agreed to grant the other access to local markets equal to that afforded to local traders. The High Court held that Clause 9 of the Australian Content Standard was inconsistent with the trade agreement and in breach of the Act.

Further extracts appear in Chapter 15 concerning the consequences of a failure to comply with a statutory provision.

McHugh, Gummow, Kirby and Hayne JJ

Conflicting statutory provisions should be reconciled so far as is possible

381 [69] The primary object of statutory construction is to construe the relevant provision so that it is consistent with the language and purpose of all the provisions of the statute. The meaning of the provision must be determined 'by reference to the language of the instrument viewed as a whole'. In *Commissioner for Railways (NSW) v Agalianos* [(1955) 92 CLR 390, 397], Dixon CJ pointed out that 'the context, the general purpose and policy of a provision and its consistency and fairness are surer guides to its meaning than the logic with which it is constructed'. Thus, the process of construction must always begin by examining the context of the provision that is being construed.

[70] A legislative instrument must be construed on the prima facie basis ***382*** that its provisions are intended to give effect to harmonious goals. Where conflict appears to arise from the language of particular provisions, the conflict must be alleviated, so far as possible, by adjusting the meaning of the competing provisions to achieve that result which will best give effect to the purpose and language of those provisions while maintaining the unity of all the statutory provisions. Reconciling conflicting provisions will often require the court 'to determine which is the leading provision and which the subordinate provision, and which must give way to the other'. Only by determining the hierarchy of the provisions will it be possible in many cases to give each provision the meaning which best gives effect to its purpose and language while maintaining the unity of the statutory scheme.

[71] Furthermore, a court construing a statutory provision must strive to give meaning to every word of the provision. In *The Commonwealth v Baume* [(1905) 2 CLR 405, 414] Griffith CJ cited *R v Berchet* to support the proposition that it was 'a known rule in the interpretation of Statutes that such a sense is to be made upon the whole as that no clause, sentence, or word shall prove superfluous, void, or insignificant, if by any other construction they may all be made useful and pertinent'.

...

The legal meaning of s 122

384 [78] ... [T]he duty of a court is to give the words of a statutory provision the meaning that the legislature is taken to have intended them to have. Ordinarily, that meaning (the legal meaning) will correspond with the grammatical meaning of the provision. But not always. The context of the words, the consequences of a literal or grammatical construction, the purpose of the statute or the canons of construction may require the words of a legislative provision to be read in a way that does not correspond with the literal or grammatical meaning. In *Statutory Interpretation* [3rd ed (1997) 343–4], Mr Francis Bennion points out:

> The distinction between literal and legal meaning lies at the heart of the problem of statutory interpretation. An enactment consists of a verbal formula. Unless defectively worded, this has a grammatical meaning in itself. The unwary reader of this formula (particularly if not a lawyer) may mistakenly conclude that the grammatical meaning is all that is of concern. If that were right, there would be little need for books on statutory interpretation. Indeed, so far as concerns law embodied in statute, there would scarcely be a need for law books of any kind. Unhappily this state of being able to rely on grammatical meaning does not prevail in the realm of statute law; nor is it likely to. In some cases the grammatical meaning, when applied to the facts of the instant case, is ambiguous. Furthermore there needs to be brought to the grammatical meaning of an enactment due consideration of the relevant matters drawn from the context (using that term in its widest sense). Consideration of the enactment in its context may raise factors that pull in different ways. For example the desirability of applying the clear literal meaning may conflict with the fact that this does not remedy the mischief that Parliament intended to deal with.

[79] The express words of s 160 require the ABA to carry out its functions in accordance with the directions given by that section. Section 160 therefore provides the conceptual framework in which the functions conferred by s 158 are to be carried out. The function specified in s 158(j) encompasses the direction in s 122 to 'determine standards' to be observed by commercial and community television broadcasting licensees. The carrying out of the directions in s 122 is therefore one of the functions of the ABA.

385 [80] If s 122(1) and (2) were given their grammatical meaning, without regard to the provisions of s 160, they would authorise the making of standards which were inconsistent with Australia's obligations under international conventions or under its agreements with foreign countries. However, the express words of s 122(4) and the mandatory direction in s 160 show that the grammatical meaning of s 122(1) and (2) is not the legal meaning of those sub-sections. When s 122 is read with s 160, the legal meaning of s 122 is that the ABA must determine standards relating to the Australian content of programs but only to the extent that those standards are consistent with the directions in s 160. If, by reason of an obligation under a convention or agreement with a foreign country, it is impossible to make an Australian content standard that is consistent with that obligation, the ABA is precluded by s 160 from making the standard, notwithstanding the literal command of s 122(1) and (2). Accordingly, in making the Australian Content Standard in December 1995, the ABA was under an obligation to ensure that the Standard was not inconsistent with the Trade Agreement or the Protocol.

[81] The majority judges in the Full Court in the present case were therefore in error in holding that the relationship of s 160 and s 122 is that of a general and a special provision. They are interlocking provisions, with s 160 – the dominant provision – directing how the function conferred by s 122 is to be carried out. The power conferred by s 122 must therefore be exercised within the framework imposed by s 160.

[Citations omitted]

Sources of judicial review jurisdiction

Constitution

75 Original jurisdiction of High Court

In all matters:

...

(iii) in which the Commonwealth, or a person suing or being sued on behalf of the Commonwealth, is a party;

...

(v) in which a writ of Mandamus or prohibition or an injunction is sought against an officer of the Commonwealth;

the High Court shall have original jurisdiction.

Judiciary Act 1903 (Cth)

[As at 1 December 2022]

39B Original jurisdiction of Federal Court of Australia

Scope of original jurisdiction

(1) Subject to subsections (1B), (1C) and (1EA), the original jurisdiction of the Federal Court of Australia includes jurisdiction with respect to any matter in which a writ of mandamus or prohibition or an injunction is sought against an officer or officers of the Commonwealth.

(1A) The original jurisdiction of the Federal Court of Australia also includes jurisdiction in any matter:

(a) in which the Commonwealth is seeking an injunction or a declaration; or

(b) arising under the Constitution, or involving its interpretation; or

(c) arising under any laws made by the Parliament, other than a matter in respect of which a criminal prosecution is instituted or any other criminal matter.

[Editors' note: Subsections (1B) and (1C) concern criminal prosecutions, and sub-s (1EA) concerns civil proceedings before the Federal Circuit and Family Court of Australia or a court of a State or Territory.]

State Supreme Courts

In each state, the Supreme Court has judicial review jurisdiction in respect of the decisions of that state's inferior courts and administrative decision-makers. The various state statutes establishing the Supreme Courts of each state confer jurisdiction in different ways. As the following extracts of the relevant New South Wales, South Australian and Victorian Acts show, the legislation may be more or less explicit in relation to judicial review jurisdiction.

Supreme Court Act 1970 (NSW)

[As at 1 December 2022]

22 Continuance

The Supreme Court of New South Wales as formerly established as the superior court of record in New South Wales is hereby continued.

23 Jurisdiction generally

The Court shall have all jurisdiction which may be necessary for the administration of justice in New South Wales.

...

65 Order to fulfil duty

(1) The Court may order any person to fulfil any duty in the fulfilment of which the person seeking the order is personally interested.

(2) The Court may, on terms, make an interlocutory order under subsection (1) in any case where it appears to the Court just or convenient so to do.

(3) The powers of the Court under this section are in addition to any other powers of the Court.

...

69 Proceedings in lieu of writs

(1) Where formerly:

(a) the Court had jurisdiction to grant any relief or remedy or do any other thing by way of writ, whether of prohibition, mandamus, certiorari or of any other description, or

(b) in any proceedings in the Court for any relief or remedy any writ might have issued out of the Court for the purpose of the commencement or conduct of the proceedings, or otherwise in relation to the proceedings, whether the writ might have issued pursuant to any rule or order of the Court or of course,

then, after the commencement of this Act:

(c) the Court shall continue to have jurisdiction to grant that relief or remedy or to do that thing; but

(d) shall not issue any such writ, and

(e) shall grant that relief or remedy or do that thing by way of judgment or order under this Act and the rules, and

(f) proceedings for that relief or remedy or for the doing of that thing shall be in accordance with this Act and the rules.

(2) Subject to the rules, this section does not apply to:

(a) the writ of habeas corpus ad subjiciendum,

(b) any writ of execution for the enforcement of a judgment or order of the Court, or

(c) any writ in aid of any such writ of execution.

(3) It is declared that the jurisdiction of the Court to grant any relief or remedy in the nature of a writ of certiorari includes jurisdiction to quash the ultimate determination of a court or tribunal in any proceedings if that determination has been made on the basis of an error of law that appears on the face of the record of the proceedings.

(4) For the purposes of subsection (3), the face of the record includes the reasons expressed by the court or tribunal for its ultimate determination.

(5) Subsections (3) and (4) do not affect the operation of any legislative provision to the extent to which the provision is, according to common law principles and disregarding those subsections, effective to prevent the Court from exercising its powers to quash or otherwise review a decision.

Supreme Court Act 1935 (SA)

[As at 1 December 2022]

17 General jurisdiction

(1) The court shall be a court of law and equity.

(2) There shall be vested in the court—

(a) the like jurisdiction, in and for the State, as was formerly vested in, or capable of being exercised by, all or any of the courts in England, following:
   (i) The High Court of Chancery, both as a common law court and as a court of equity:
   (ii) The Court of Queen's Bench:
   (iii) The Court of Common Pleas at Westminster:
   (iv) The Court of Exchequer both as a court of revenue and as a court of common law:
   (v) The courts created by commissions of assize:

(b) such other jurisdiction, whether original or appellate, as is vested in, or capable of being exercised by the court:

(c) such other jurisdiction as is in this Act conferred upon the court.

Administrative Law Act 1978 (Vic)

[As at 1 December 2022]

2 Definitions

In this Act unless the context or subject-matter otherwise requires—

decision means a decision operating in law to determine a question affecting the rights of any person or to grant, deny, terminate, suspend or alter a privilege or licence and includes a refusal or failure to perform a duty or to exercise a power to make such a decision;

person affected in relation to a decision, means a person whether or not a party to proceedings, whose interest (being an interest that is greater than the interest of other members of the public) is or will or may be affected, directly or indirectly, to a substantial degree by a decision which has been made or is to be made or ought to have been made by the tribunal;

tribunal means a person or body of persons who, in arriving at the decision in question, is or are by law required, whether by express direction or not, to act in a judicial manner to the extent of observing one or more of the rules of natural justice, but does not include—

(a) a court of law or a tribunal constituted or presided over by a Judge of the Supreme Court; or

(b) a Royal Commission, Board of Inquiry or Formal Review within the meaning of the *Inquiries Act 2014*.

3 Tribunal decisions may be reviewed

Any person affected by a decision of a tribunal may make application (hereinafter called an application for review) to the Supreme Court for an order calling on the tribunal or the members thereof (hereinafter called an order for review) and also any party interested in maintaining the decision to show cause why the same should not be reviewed.

7 Powers of court

Upon the return of the order for review, the Court may discharge the order or may exercise all or any of the jurisdiction or powers and grant all or any of the remedies which upon the material adduced and upon the grounds stated in the order might be exercised or granted in proceedings for relief or remedy in the nature of certiorari, mandamus, prohibition or quo warranto or in proceedings for a declaration of invalidity in respect of the decision or for an injunction to restrain the implementation thereof and may extend the period limited by statute for the making of the decision but shall not exercise any other jurisdiction or power or grant any other remedy.

8 Reasons for decision to be furnished by tribunal on request by party concerned

(1) A tribunal shall, if requested to do so by any person affected by a decision made or to be made by it, furnish him with a statement of its reasons for the decision.

...

(3) The statement of reasons shall be in writing and furnished within a reasonable time.

(4) The Supreme Court, upon being satisfied by the person making the request that a reasonable time has elapsed without any such statement of reasons for the decision having been furnished or that the only statement furnished is not adequate to enable a Court to see whether the decision does or does not involve any error of law, may order the tribunal to furnish, within a time specified in the order, a statement or further statement of its reasons and if the order is not complied with the Court, in addition to or in lieu of any order to enforce compliance by the tribunal or any member thereof, may make any such order as might have been made if error of law had appeared on the face of the record.

(5) Notwithstanding anything in this section a tribunal shall not be bound to furnish a statement of reasons, and the Court shall not be bound to order it to do so, where to furnish the reasons would, in the opinion of the Court, be against public policy, or the person making the request is not a person primarily concerned with the decision and to furnish the reasons would, in the opinion of the Court, be against the interests of a person primarily concerned.

...

11 As to who may seek prerogative writ declaration or injunction

Any person affected by the decision of a tribunal or inferior court shall have sufficient standing to maintain proceedings for relief or remedy in the nature of certiorari, mandamus or prohibition or in proceedings for a declaration of invalidity or an injunction in relation to the decision but nothing in this section shall take away or impair any right to relief otherwise existing or the discretion to refuse any such relief.

Origins of common law and constitutional judicial review

Re Refugee Review Tribunal; Ex parte Aala (2000) 204 CLR 82

Facts

The case was brought before the High Court under s 75(v) of the *Constitution*. An Iranian citizen, Mansour Aala, arrived in Australia in 1991 and sought a protection visa. The Refugee Review Tribunal refused to grant a visa because it was not satisfied that Mr Aala had a well-founded fear of persecution. When it made its decision, the Tribunal did not have some information that had previously been provided by Mr Aala, but he had been led to believe during the hearing that the Tribunal Member had 'all of those files'. Mr Aala sought certiorari to quash the decision of the Tribunal on the ground of breach of procedural fairness, and mandamus to direct the Tribunal to consider his application for a protection visa according to law. Mr Aala also sought prohibition to prevent the Minister from acting upon the Tribunal's decision. He argued that in making the decision in breach of procedural fairness the Tribunal had made a jurisdictional error. The High Court granted all three writs. Extracts considering the concept of jurisdictional error are set out later in this chapter. The extracts below consider the origins of the prerogative writs and their constitutional expression.

Gaudron and Gummow JJ

92 [18] Section 75(v) may not add to the jurisdiction conferred by s 75(iii). It appears that s 75(v) was included as a safeguard against the possibility that the provision in s 75(iii) respecting matters in which a person being sued on behalf of the Commonwealth is a party would be read down by reference to decisions construing Art III of the United States Constitution.

[19] Nevertheless, in *R v Federal Court of Australia; Ex parte WA National Football League* [(1979) 143 CLR 190, 201], Barwick CJ referred to the term 'prohibition' in s 75(v) as importing 'the law appertaining to the grant of prohibition by the King's Bench'. However, in the operation of s 75(v) of the Constitution, terms such as 'prohibition' and 'jurisdiction' are not simply institutions or concepts of the general law. They are constitutional expressions.

[20] The term 'prerogative writ' came to be used in England with respect to prohibition and other writs because they were conceived as being intimately connected with the rights of the Crown and to ensure that the prerogative was not encroached upon by disobedience to the prescribed structure for the administration of justice. In Australia, the Parliament consists of the Queen, the Senate and the House of Representatives *(Constitution*, s 1) and the executive power of the Commonwealth is vested by s 61 in the Queen and is exercisable by the Governor-General as the Queen's representative. However, save perhaps provision in s 72(i) for appointment of judges by the Governor-General in Council, the Crown is not an element in the Judicature established by Ch III. In *Deputy Commissioner of Taxation v Richard Walter Pty Ltd* [(1995) 183 CLR 168, 204–5], Deane and Gaudron JJ said that, taken together, s 75(iii) and s 75(v) had the effect of ensuring 'that there is available, to a relevantly affected citizen, a Ch III court with jurisdiction to grant relief against an invalid purported

exercise of Commonwealth legislative power or an unlawful exercise of, or refusal to exercise, Commonwealth executive authority'.

[21] What is thereby enforced is the fidelity required by covering cl 5 to the Constitution itself rather than any fidelity owed to the Crown as a particular element in the constitutional structure. The term ***93*** 'prerogative writ' has been used as a convenient shorthand, particularly to differentiate in s 75(v) writs of mandamus and prohibition from an injunction. But it is an inapt description of any remedy granted by a court exercising the judicial power of the Commonwealth. If any shorthand expression is to be used, 'constitutional writ' would be preferable.

[22] Prohibition goes against officers of the Commonwealth in circumstances not contemplated by the Court of King's Bench and not within the expression 'excess of jurisdiction' as understood in England. Thus, an officer of the Commonwealth may be restrained by prohibition in respect of activity under an invalid law of the Parliament or of activity beyond the executive power of the Commonwealth identified in s 61 of the Constitution. Further, the common law did not have to take into account the errors of a superior federal court in determining the constitutional limits of its own jurisdiction ... Hence the force of the statement by Mason, Brennan and Dawson JJ in *Re Grimshaw; Ex parte Australian Telephone and Phonogram Officers' Association* [(1986) 60 ALJR 588, 594]:

> The jurisdiction of this Court to grant prohibition under s 75(v) of the Constitution directed to a non-judicial tribunal is not necessarily governed by the same principles as those which govern the common law jurisdiction of a superior court to grant prohibition to an inferior court.

[23] Nevertheless, in considering the particular relationship between prohibition, excess of jurisdiction and denial of procedural fairness, some assistance is derived from considering the state of affairs in the administration of prohibition both in England and in the Australian colonies at the time of the commencement of the Constitution, and thereafter.

[Citations omitted]

Kirk v Industrial Court of New South Wales (2010) 239 CLR 531

Constitution

CHAPTER III—THE JUDICATURE

71 Judicial power and Courts

The judicial power of the Commonwealth shall be vested in a Federal Supreme Court, to be called the High Court of Australia, and in such other federal courts as the Parliament creates, and in such other courts as it invests with federal jurisdiction. The High Court shall consist of a Chief Justice, and so many other Justices, not less than two, as the Parliament prescribes.

...

73 Appellate jurisdiction of High Court

The High Court shall have jurisdiction, with such exceptions and subject to such regulations as the Parliament prescribes, to hear and determine appeals from all judgments, decrees, orders, and sentences:

(i) of any Justice or Justices exercising the original jurisdiction of the High Court;

(ii) of any other federal court, or court exercising federal jurisdiction; or of the Supreme Court of any State, or of any other court of any State from which at the establishment of the Commonwealth an appeal lies to the Queen in Council;

...

Facts

The case concerned criminal liability under the *Occupational Health and Safety Act 1983* (NSW) of a farm owner, Graeme Kirk, for the death of a farm manager in a workplace incident when an all-terrain vehicle the manager was driving overturned. The Industrial Court of New South Wales convicted and sentenced Mr Kirk. The High Court held that the Industrial Court had made jurisdictional errors (discussed further below) by misconstruing the *Occupational Health and Safety Act 1983* (NSW) and failing to comply with the rules of evidence. The case deals with a privative clause in the *Industrial Relations Act 1996* (NSW) which attempted to prevent judicial review of decisions of the Industrial Court; this is covered in Chapter 10. The privative clause did not prevent review for jurisdictional error. Extracts concerning jurisdictional error are below at pp 263–68. The following extract describes the supervisory jurisdiction of the State Supreme Courts to undertake judicial review.

French CJ, Gummow, Hayne, Crennan, Kiefel and Bell JJ

580 [97] At federation, each of the Supreme Courts referred to in s 73 of the *Constitution* had jurisdiction that included such jurisdiction as the Court of Queen's Bench had in England.

[98] The supervisory jurisdiction of the Supreme Courts was at federation, and remains, the mechanism for the determination and the enforcement of the limits on the exercise of State executive and judicial power by persons and bodies other than the Supreme Court. ***581*** That supervisory role of the Supreme Courts exercised through the grant of prohibition, certiorari and mandamus (and habeas corpus) was, and is, a defining characteristic of those courts. And because, 'with such exceptions and subject to such regulations as the Parliament prescribes', s 73 of the *Constitution* gives this Court appellate jurisdiction to hear and determine appeals from all judgments, decrees, orders and sentences of the Supreme Courts, the exercise of that supervisory jurisdiction is ultimately subject to the superintendence of this Court as the 'Federal Supreme Court' in which s 71 of the *Constitution* vests the judicial power of the Commonwealth.

[99] There is but one common law of Australia. The supervisory jurisdiction exercised by the State Supreme Courts by the grant of prerogative relief or orders in the nature of that relief is governed in fundamental respects by principles established as part of the common law of Australia. That is, the supervisory jurisdiction exercised by

the State Supreme Courts is exercised according to principles that in the end are set by this Court. To deprive a State Supreme Court of its supervisory jurisdiction enforcing the limits on the exercise of State executive and judicial power by persons and bodies other than that Court would be to create islands of power immune from supervision and restraint. It would permit what Jaffe described as the development of 'distorted positions' [(1957) 70 *Harvard Law Review* 953, 963]. And as already demonstrated, it would remove from the relevant State Supreme Court one of its defining characteristics.

[Citations omitted]

Statutory judicial review

Administrative Decisions (Judicial Review) Act 1977 (Cth)

[As at 1 December 2022]

3 Interpretation

(1) In this Act, unless the contrary intention appears:

...

decision to which this Act applies means a decision of an administrative character made, proposed to be made, or required to be made (whether in the exercise of a discretion or not and whether before or after the commencement of this definition):

(a) under an enactment referred to in paragraph (a), (b), (c) or (d) of the definition of ***enactment***; or

(b) by a Commonwealth authority or an officer of the Commonwealth under an enactment referred to in paragraph (ca) or (cb) of the definition of ***enactment***;

other than:

(c) a decision by the Governor-General; or

(d) a decision included in any of the classes of decisions set out in Schedule 1.

...

enactment means:

(a) an Act, other than:

(i) the *Commonwealth Places (Application of Laws) Act 1970*; or

(ii) the *Northern Territory (Self Government) Act 1978*; or

(iii) an Act or part of an Act that is not an enactment because of section 3A (certain legislation relating to the ACT); or

(b) an Ordinance of a Territory other than the Australian Capital Territory or the Northern Territory; or

(c) an instrument (including rules, regulations or by-laws) made under an Act or part of an Act covered by paragraph (ca); or (ca) an Act of a State, the Australian Capital Territory or the Northern Territory, or a part of such an Act, ... ; or

(cb) an instrument (including rules, regulations or by-laws) made under an Act or part of an Act covered by paragraph (ca); or

(d) any other law, or a part of a law, of the Northern Territory declared by the regulations, in accordance with section 19A, to be an enactment for the purposes of this Act;

and, for the purposes of paragraph (a), (b), (c), (ca) or (cb), includes a part of an enactment.

failure, in relation to the making of a decision, includes a refusal to make the decision.

...

(2) In this Act, a reference to the making of a decision includes a reference to:

(a) making, suspending, revoking or refusing to make an order, award or determination;

(b) giving, suspending, revoking or refusing to give a certificate, direction, approval, consent or permission;

(c) issuing, suspending, revoking or refusing to issue a licence, authority or other instrument;

(d) imposing a condition or restriction;

(e) making a declaration, demand or requirement;

(f) retaining, or refusing to deliver up, an article; or

(g) doing or refusing to do any other act or thing;

and a reference to a failure to make a decision shall be construed accordingly.

(3) Where provision is made by an enactment for the making of a report or recommendation before a decision is made in the exercise of a power under that enactment or under another law, the making of such a report or recommendation shall itself be deemed, for the purposes of this Act, to be the making of a decision.

(4) In this Act:

(a) a reference to a person aggrieved by a decision includes a reference:

(i) to a person whose interests are adversely affected by the decision; or

(ii) in the case of a decision by way of the making of a report or recommendation – to a person whose interests would be adversely affected if a decision were, or were not, made in accordance with the report or recommendation; and

(b) a reference to a person aggrieved by conduct that has been, is being, or is proposed to be, engaged in for the purpose of making a decision or by a failure to make a decision includes a reference to a person whose interests are or would be adversely affected by the conduct or failure.

(5) A reference in this Act to conduct engaged in for the purpose of making a decision includes a reference to the doing of any act or thing preparatory to the making of the decision, including the taking of evidence or the holding of an inquiry or investigation.

5 Applications for review of decisions

(1) A person who is aggrieved by a decision to which this Act applies ... may apply to the Federal Court or the Federal Circuit and Family Court of Australia (Division 2) for an order of review in respect of the decision.

[Editors' note: The section goes on to list grounds – see Chapter 11.]

6 Applications for review of conduct related to making of decisions

(1) Where a person has engaged, is engaging, or proposes to engage, in conduct for the purpose of making a decision to which this Act applies, a person who is aggrieved by the conduct may apply to the Federal Court or the Federal Circuit and Family Court of Australia (Division 2) for an order of review in respect of the conduct ...

[Editors' note: The section goes on to list grounds.]

7 Applications in respect of failures to make decisions

(1) Where:

(a) a person has a duty to make a decision to which this Act applies;

(b) there is no law that prescribes a period within which the person is required to make that decision; and

(c) the person has failed to make that decision;

a person who is aggrieved by the failure of the first-mentioned person to make the decision may apply to the Federal Court or the Federal Circuit and Family Court of Australia (Division 2) for an order of review in respect of the failure to make the decision on the ground that there has been unreasonable delay in making the decision.

(2) Where:

(a) a person has a duty to make a decision to which this Act applies;

(b) a law prescribes a period within which the person is required to make that decision; and

(c) the person failed to make that decision before the expiration of that period;

a person who is aggrieved by the failure of the first-mentioned person to make the decision within that period may apply to the Federal Court or the Federal Circuit and Family Court of Australia (Division 2) for an order of review in respect of the failure to make the decision within that period on the ground that the first-mentioned person has a duty to make the decision notwithstanding the expiration of that period.

8 Jurisdiction of Federal Circuit and Federal Family Court of Australia (Division 2)

(1) The Federal Court has jurisdiction to hear and determine applications made to the Federal Court under this Act.

(2) The Federal Circuit and Family Court of Australia (Division 2) has jurisdiction to hear and determine applications made to the Federal Circuit and Family Court of Australia (Division 2) under this Act.

...

12 Application to be made a party to a proceeding

(1) A person interested in a decision, in conduct that has been, is being, or is proposed to be, engaged in for the purpose of making a decision, or in a failure

to make a decision, being a decision, conduct or failure in relation to which an application has been made to the Federal Court or the Federal Circuit and Family Court of Australia (Division 2) under this Act, may apply to the court to be made a party to the application.

(2) The court may, in its discretion:

(a) grant the application either unconditionally or subject to such conditions as it thinks fit; or

(b) refuse the application.

13 Reasons for decision may be obtained

(1) Where a person makes a decision to which this section applies, any person who is entitled to make an application to the Federal Court or the Federal Circuit and Family Court of Australia (Division 2) under section 5 in relation to the decision may, by notice in writing given to the person who made the decision, request him or her to furnish a statement in writing setting out the findings on material questions of fact, referring to the evidence or other material on which those findings were based and giving the reasons for the decision ...

...

16 Powers of the Federal Court and the Federal Circuit and Family Court of Australia (Division 2) in respect of applications for order of review

(1) On an application for an order of review in respect of a decision, the Federal Court or the Federal Circuit and Family Court of Australia (Division 2) may, in its discretion, make all or any of the following orders:

(a) an order quashing or setting aside the decision, or a part of the decision, with effect from the date of the order or from such earlier or later date as the court specifies;

(b) an order referring the matter to which the decision relates to the person who made the decision for further consideration, subject to such directions as the court thinks fit;

(c) an order declaring the rights of the parties in respect of any matter to which the decision relates;

(d) an order directing any of the parties to do, or to refrain from doing, any act or thing the doing, or the refraining from the doing, of which the court considers necessary to do justice between the parties.

(2) On an application for an order of review in respect of conduct that has been, is being, or is proposed to be, engaged in for the purpose of the making of a decision, the Federal Court or the Federal Circuit and Family Court of Australia (Division 2) may, in its discretion, make either or both of the following orders:

(a) an order declaring the rights of the parties in respect of any matter to which the conduct relates;

(b) an order directing any of the parties to do, or to refrain from doing, any act or thing the doing, or the refraining from the doing, of which the court considers necessary to do justice between the parties.

(3) On an application for an order of review in respect of a failure to make a decision, or in respect of a failure to make a decision within the period within which the decision was required to be made, the Federal Court or the Federal Circuit and Family Court of Australia (Division 2) may, in its discretion, make all or any of the following orders:

(a) an order directing the making of the decision;

(b) an order declaring the rights of the parties in relation to the making of the decision;

(c) an order directing any of the parties to do, or to refrain from doing, any act or thing the doing, or the refraining from the doing, of which the court considers necessary to do justice between the parties.

(4) The Federal Court or the Federal Circuit and Family Court of Australia (Division 2) may at any time, of its own motion or on the application of any party, revoke, vary, or suspend the operation of, any order made by it under this section.

Kioa v West (1985) 159 CLR 550

Facts

This case is discussed in detail in Chapter 12 in relation to procedural fairness. The case concerned an order by a delegate of the Minister to deport Mr Kioa who had overstayed on a temporary entry permit. Mr Kioa argued that the decision had been made in breach of the rules of procedural fairness. In the following extract, Mason J considered the then relatively new *Administrative Decisions (Judicial Review) Act 1977* (Cth). His Honour concluded that the primary object of the legislation was to effect procedural reform, rather than to introduce a radical substantive change to the common law grounds of review.

Mason J

576 The statutory grounds of review enumerated in s 5(1) are not new – they are a reflection in summary form of the grounds on which administrative decisions are susceptible to challenge at common law. The section is therefore to be read in the light of the common law and it should not be understood as working a challenge to common law grounds of review, except in so far as the language of the section requires it – see, for example, s 5(1). It is in this respect that s 5(1) makes every decision to which it applies subject to review on the grounds stated and in so doing it may give a number of grounds a wider reach than they would have at common law. But it is not the primary object of the section to amend or alter the common law content of the various grounds. ...

577 The language does not manifest an intention to work a radical substantive change in the law by attaching to every decision to which s 5 applies an obligation to comply with the rules of natural justice.

The appellants rely on extrinsic materials in the form of the Minister's Second Reading Speech, the Report of the Commonwealth Administrative Review Committee (Parliamentary Paper No 144 of 1971) and the Report of the Committee of Review of Prerogative Writ Procedures (Parliamentary Paper No 56 of 1973) – see the *Acts Interpretation Act 1901* (Cth) s 15AB. These materials do not support the appellants' submission. Instead they reinforce the view that the primary object of the *AD(JR) Act* was to achieve procedural reform and not to work a radical substantive change in the grounds on which administrative decisions are susceptible to challenge at common law.

Australian Broadcasting Tribunal v Bond (1990) 170 CLR 321

Broadcasting Act 1942 (Cth)

[As at relevant date]

88 Suspension and revocation of commercial licence

...

(2) The Tribunal may suspend or revoke a commercial licence if it appears to the Tribunal that it is advisable in the public interest to do so, having regard only to the following matters or circumstances:

...

(b) the Tribunal is satisfied that the licensee

(i) is no longer a fit and proper person to hold the licence; ...

Facts

The Australian Broadcasting Tribunal ('ABT') was considering whether to revoke or suspend broadcast licences held by companies under *Broadcasting Act 1942* (Cth). The companies were effectively controlled by Alan Bond through his shareholdings. At the relevant time, the ABT had not yet decided whether to revoke any licence. Rather, it had made and published findings that Mr Bond and – because Mr Bond controlled them – the companies were not fit and proper persons to hold licences. Mr Bond's conduct had been impugned because of allegations that he had made inappropriate payments to the then Premier of the State of Queensland, Sir Joh Bjelke-Petersen, under the guise of settling defamation proceedings. There were also allegations that he had threatened to use television station staff to gather information about a business competitor. The ABT indicated that it was going to consider whether the licences should be revoked. At that point, Mr Bond sought review of various findings and rulings by the ABT. A central question was whether the findings and rulings were reviewable 'decisions' or 'conduct' for the purposes of the *Administrative Decisions (Judicial Review) Act 1977* (Cth). Extracts from the case are also included in Chapter 14 in relation to the ground of no evidence.

Mason CJ

335 The fact that the *AD(JR) Act* is a remedial statute providing for a review of administrative action rather than some form of appeal from final decisions disposing of issues between parties indicates that no narrow view should be taken of the word ***336*** 'decision'. In this respect it is significant that s 5 does not speak of 'final decision'. ...

Nonetheless other considerations point to the word having a relatively limited field of operation. First, the reference in the definition in s 3(1) to 'a decision of an administrative character made ... under an enactment' indicates that a reviewable decision is a decision which a statute requires or authorizes rather than merely a step taken in the course of reasoning on the way to the making of the ultimate decision. Secondly, the examples of decision listed in the extended definition contained in s 3(2) are also indicative of a decision having the character or quality of finality, an outcome reflecting something in the nature of a determination of an application, inquiry or dispute or, in the words of Deane J, 'a determination effectively resolving an actual substantive issue'. Thirdly, s 3(3), in extending the concept of 'decision' to include 'the making of a report or recommendation before a decision is made in the exercise of a power', to that extent qualifies the characteristic of finality. Such a provision would have been unnecessary had the Parliament intended that 'decision' comprehend every decision, or every substantive decision, made in the course of reaching a conclusive determination. Finally, s 3(5) suggests that acts done preparatory to the making of a 'decision' are not to be regarded as constituting 'decisions' for, if they were, there would be little, if any, point in providing for judicial review of 'conduct' as well as of a 'decision'.

The relevant policy considerations are competing. On the one hand, the purposes of the *AD(JR) Act* are to allow persons aggrieved by the administrative decision-making processes of government a convenient and effective means of redress and to enhance those processes. On the other hand, in so far as the ambit of the concept of 'decision' is extended, there is a greater risk that the efficient administration of government will be impaired. ... ***337*** To interpret 'decision' in a way that would involve a departure from the quality of finality would lead to a fragmentation of the processes of administrative decision-making and set at risk the efficiency of the administrative process.

The policy arguments do not, in my opinion, call for an answer different from that dictated by the textual and contextual considerations. That answer is that a reviewable 'decision' is one for which provision is made by or under a statute. That will generally, but not always, entail a decision which is final or operative and determinative, at least in a practical sense, of the issue of fact falling for consideration. A conclusion reached as a step along the way in a course of reasoning leading to an ultimate decision would not ordinarily amount to a reviewable decision, unless the statute provided for the making of a finding or ruling on that point so that the decision, though an intermediate decision, might accurately be described as a decision under an enactment.

Another essential quality of a reviewable decision is that it be a substantive determination. With the exception of s 3(2)(g), the instances of decision mentioned in s 3(2) are all substantive in character. ...

If 'decision' were to embrace procedural determinations, then there would be little scope for review of 'conduct', a concept which appears to be essentially procedural in character. To take an example, the refusal by a decision-maker of an application for an adjournment in the course of an administrative hearing would not constitute a reviewable decision, being a procedural matter not resolving a substantive issue and lacking the quality of finality. Then it is the 'conduct' of the hearing in refusing an adjournment that is the subject of review. To treat the refusal of the adjournment

338 in this way is more consistent with the concept of 'conduct' than with the notion of 'decision under an enactment'.

...

341 The distinction between reviewable decisions and conduct engaged in for the purpose of making such a decision is somewhat elusive. However, once it is accepted that 'decision' connotes a determination for which provision is made by or under a statute, one that generally is substantive, final and operative, the place of 'conduct' in the statutory scheme of things becomes reasonably clear. In its setting in s 6 the word 'conduct' points to action ***342*** taken, rather than a decision made, for the purpose of making a reviewable decision. In other words, the concept of conduct looks to the way in which the proceedings have been conducted, the conduct of the proceedings, rather than decisions made along the way with a view to the making of a final determination. Thus, conduct is essentially procedural and not substantive in character.

[Citations omitted]

Griffith University v Tang (2005) 221 CLR 99

Facts

Ms Tang was a PhD candidate at Griffith University. She was accused of academic misconduct by falsifying results of her research and was consequently excluded from the University. Ms Tang sought judicial review of that decision under the *Judicial Review Act 1991* (Qld) – the Queensland equivalent of the *Administrative Decisions (Judicial Review) Act 1977* (Cth) ('*AD(JR) Act*'). Like the *AD(JR) Act*, the *Judicial Review Act 1991* (Qld) provided for review of decisions 'of an administrative character made ... under an enactment'. The issue in this case was whether the decision to exclude Ms Tang was made 'under' an enactment. The majority of the High Court held that it was not.

Gummow, Callinan and Heydon JJ

128 [79] The decision so required or authorised must be 'of an administrative character'. This element of the definition casts some light on the force to be given by the phrase '*under* an enactment'. What is it, in the course of administration, that flows from or arises out of the decision taken so as to give that significance which has merited the legislative conferral of a right of judicial review upon those aggrieved?

[80] The answer in general terms is the affecting of legal rights and obligations. Do legal rights or duties owe in an immediate sense their existence to the decision, or depend upon the presence of the decision for their enforcement? To adapt what was said by Lehane J in *Lewins* [(1996) 68 FCR 87, 103], does the decision in question derive from the enactment the capacity to affect legal rights and obligations? Are legal rights and obligations affected not under the general law but by virtue of the statute?

[81] If the decision derives its capacity to bind from contract or some other private law source, then the decision is not 'made under' the enactment in question ...

129 [82] For these reasons, a statutory grant of a bare capacity to contract does not suffice to endow subsequent contracts with the character of having been made under that enactment. A legislative grant of capacity to contract to a statutory body will not, without more, be sufficient to empower that body unilaterally to affect the rights or liabilities of any other party. The power to affect the other party's rights and obligations will be derived not from the enactment but from such agreement as has been made between the parties. A decision to enter into a contract would have no legal effect without the consent of the other party; the agreement between the parties is the origin of the rights and liabilities as between the parties.

Kirby J (dissenting)

153 [154] ... [T]he *Review Act* is one that has been adopted to enlarge, and not to restrict, judicial remedies. The provision of remedies against legally flawed decisions by public authorities (some of which, on legal analysis, may be no 'decision' at all) is, after all, simply the application to such authorities of the requirement fundamental to our system of government, namely accountability to the rule of law. It renders the recipients of public power and public funds answerable, through the courts, to the people from whom the power is ultimately derived and the funds ordinarily raised by taxation, and for whose interests such recipients are, in a sense, public fiduciaries.

[155] Moreover, relief by way of judicial review is ordinarily discretionary. A court is not, as such, concerned with the factual merits but with observance of legality. Sometimes, the complainant will have remedies otherwise. These are still further reasons why it is inappropriate ***154*** for this Court to struggle to confine the operation of the remedial provisions of the *Review Act* in a way that is not fully sustained by that Act's language, structure and purposes. In my respectful opinion, the conclusion reached in the joint reasons offends all of these requirements. The *Review Act* is not concerned only with affection of a complaining party's 'legal rights and obligations'. It is concerned as well with affection of that party's 'interests' — a much broader notion, and deliberately so.

[156] ... If, therefore, the phrase 'made ... under an enactment' is approached by reference to the test that I favour, in order to identify the competing possibilities of the legal source of the 'decision' concerning the respondent, those possibilities in the present case are (1) the University Act [*Griffith University Act 1998* (Qld)]; or (2) legal powers that the University has derived outside the University Act.

...

[158] ... [W]hereas the University, as a corporation with 'all the powers of an individual', could enter contracts and do any other thing an individual could do, its power to provide university education and confer higher degrees derived, and derived only, from a source in the *University Act.* Necessarily, the power of the University to withdraw the provision of education at university standard to an admitted candidate and to deny access by such a candidate to a higher education award, had likewise to find a source in the University Act. The power to withhold is included in the power to grant ...

> ***155*** [159] ... The source of the University's power to make the 'decision' that it did in relation to the respondent was, and was only, the University Act. The 'decisions' affecting the 'interests' of the respondent were not made 'under' some other legal source of power. They were made 'under' the Act or they were unlawful.

[Citations omitted]

The concepts of jurisdictional error and error of law on the face of the record

Craig v South Australia (1995) 184 CLR 163

Facts

Anthony Craig was charged with larceny of a motor car (or, in the alternative, receiving stolen goods) and arson of that car. His trial was set down for hearing in the South Australian District Court. Mr Craig had no legal representation. He applied for a stay of proceedings until he could be provided with representation at public expense. The judge ordered the stay, relying on the High Court decision in *Dietrich v The Queen* (1992) 177 CLR 292. That decision held that in a criminal trial for a serious offence the jurisdiction to stay proceedings if the accused will not otherwise receive a fair trial extends to ordering a stay when a defendant is unrepresented by counsel. The Crown applied to the Full Court of the Supreme Court for certiorari to quash the District Court order and mandamus to direct the judge to remake the order according to law, on the basis that the District Court had misapplied *Dietrich.* The Full Court made the orders sought, but the High Court overturned the decision on appeal.

The High Court held that if the District Court had made an error of law, that error had been made 'within jurisdiction'. The High Court drew a distinction between the more limited kinds of errors that amounted to jurisdictional error for inferior courts, and the wider range of errors an administrative tribunal (and by extension other administrative decision-makers) might make that would be characterised as jurisdictional. In the following extracts, the High Court discusses the concept of jurisdictional error and the separate basis for certiorari – error of law on the face of the record – and the continued relevance of a distinction between the two in Australia. Further extracts below at pp 278–80 consider what 'the record' is at common law.

Brennan, Deane, Toohey, Gaudron and McHugh JJ

> **Scope of certiorari**
>
> ***175*** Where available, certiorari is a process by which a superior court, in the exercise of original jurisdiction, supervises the acts of an inferior court or other tribunal. It is not an appellate procedure enabling either a general review of the order or decision of the inferior court or tribunal or a substitution of the order or decision which the superior court thinks should have been made. Where the writ runs, it merely enables the quashing of the impugned order or decision upon one or more of a number of distinct established

grounds, most importantly, jurisdictional error, failure to observe some applicable requirement ***176***of procedural fairness, fraud and 'error of law on the face of the record'. Where the writ is sought on the ground of jurisdictional error, breach of procedural fairness or fraud, the superior court entertaining an application for certiorari can, subject to applicable procedural and evidentiary rules, take account of any relevant material placed before it. In contrast, where relief is sought on the ground of error of law on the face of the record, the superior court is restricted to the 'record' of the inferior court or tribunal and the writ will enable the quashing of the impugned order or decision only on the ground that it is affected by some error of law which is disclosed by that record.

The above summary identification of the grounds upon which the prerogative writ of certiorari may properly issue glosses over a number of difficulties about the content of those grounds. Two of those difficulties are of direct relevance in the present case where it is argued that the alleged error on the part of the trial judge was either 'jurisdictional error' or 'error of law on the face of the record' for the purposes of certiorari. The first relates to what relevantly constitutes 'jurisdictional error'. The second is what constitutes 'the record' for the purpose of determining whether there is 'error of law on the face of the record'.

Jurisdictional error

In considering what constitutes 'jurisdictional error', it is necessary to distinguish between, on the one hand, the inferior courts which are amenable to certiorari and, on the other, those other tribunals exercising governmental powers which are also amenable to the writ. Putting to one side some anomalous exceptions, the inferior courts of this country are constituted by persons with either formal legal qualifications or practical legal training. They exercise jurisdiction as part of a hierarchical legal system entrusted with the administration of justice under the Commonwealth and State Constitutions. In contrast, the tribunals other than courts which are amenable to certiorari are commonly constituted, wholly or partly, by persons without formal legal qualifications or legal training. While normally subject to administrative review procedures and prima facie bound to observe the requirements of procedural fairness, they are not part of ***177*** the ordinary hierarchical judicial structure. In what follows, the anomalous courts or tribunals which fall outside the above broad descriptions can be ignored. Since the District Court of South Australia is undoubtedly a court, the primary focus of discussion will be upon what constitutes jurisdictional error on the part of an inferior court.

An inferior court falls into jurisdictional error if it mistakenly asserts or denies the existence of jurisdiction or if it misapprehends or disregards the nature or limits of its functions or powers in a case where it correctly recognises that jurisdiction does exist. Such jurisdictional error can infect either a positive act or a refusal or failure to act. Since certiorari goes only to quash a decision or order, an inferior court will fall into jurisdictional error for the purposes of the writ where it makes an order or decision (including an order or decision to the effect that it lacks, or refuses to exercise, jurisdiction) which is based upon a mistaken assumption or denial of jurisdiction or a misconception or disregard of the nature or limits of jurisdiction.

Jurisdictional error is at its most obvious where the inferior court purports to act wholly or partly outside the general area of its jurisdiction in the sense of entertaining a matter or making a decision or order of a kind which wholly or partly lies outside the theoretical limits of its functions and powers. An inferior court would, for example, act wholly outside the general area of its jurisdiction in that sense if, having jurisdiction strictly limited to civil matters, it purported to hear and determine a criminal charge. Such a court would act partly outside the general area of its jurisdiction if, in a matter coming within the categories of civil cases which it had authority to hear and determine, it purported to make an order of a kind which it lacked power to make, such as an order for specific performance of a contract when its remedial powers were strictly limited to awarding damages for breach. Less obviously, an inferior court can, while acting wholly within the general area of its jurisdiction, fall into jurisdictional error by doing something which it lacks authority to do. If, for example, it is an essential condition of the existence of jurisdiction with respect to a particular matter that a certain event or requirement has in fact occurred or been satisfied, as distinct from the inferior court's own conclusion that it has, there will be jurisdictional error if the court or tribunal purports to act in circumstances where that event has not in fact occurred or that requirement has not in fact been satisfied even though the matter is the kind of matter which the court has jurisdiction to entertain. Similarly, jurisdictional error will occur where an inferior court disregards or takes account of some matter in circumstances where the statute or other instrument establishing it and conferring its jurisdiction requires that that particular matter be taken into account or ignored as a pre-condition of the existence of any authority to make an order or decision in the circumstances of the particular case. Again, an inferior court will exceed its authority and fall into jurisdictional error if it misconstrues that statute or other ***178*** instrument and thereby misconceives the nature of the function which it is performing or the extent of its powers in the circumstances of the particular case. In the last-mentioned category of case, the line between jurisdictional error and mere error in the exercise of jurisdiction may be particularly difficult to discern.

It was submitted on behalf of the respondent State of South Australia that an inferior court commits jurisdictional error whenever it addresses the wrong issue or asks itself the wrong question. Particular reliance was placed, in support of that submission, upon the well known passage in Lord Reid's speech in *Anisminic Ltd v Foreign Compensation Commission* [[1969] 2 AC 147, 171] ...

...

Lord Reid's comments were subsequently suggested by Lord Diplock [*O'Reilly v Madman* [1983] 2 AC 237, 278] and held by the Divisional Court to be also applicable to an inferior court with the result that the distinction between jurisdictional error and error within ***179*** jurisdiction has been seen as effectively abolished in England. That distinction has not, however, been discarded in this country and, for the reasons which follow, we consider that Lord Reid's comments should not be accepted here as an authoritative statement of what constitutes jurisdictional error by an inferior court for the purposes of certiorari. In that regard, it is important to bear in mind a critical distinction which exists between administrative tribunals and courts of law.

At least in the absence of a contrary intent in the statute or other instrument which established it, an administrative tribunal lacks authority either to authoritatively determine questions of law or to make an order or decision otherwise than in accordance with the law. ... If such an administrative tribunal falls into an error of law which causes it to identify a wrong issue, to ask itself a wrong question, to ignore relevant material, to rely on irrelevant material or, at least in some circumstances, to make an erroneous finding or to reach a mistaken conclusion, and the tribunal's exercise or purported exercise of power is thereby affected, it exceeds its authority or powers. Such an error of law is jurisdictional error which will invalidate any order or decision of the tribunal which reflects it.

In contrast, the ordinary jurisdiction of a court of law encompasses authority to decide questions of law, as well as questions of fact, involved in matters which it has jurisdiction to determine. The identification of relevant issues, the formulation of relevant questions ***180*** and the determination of what is and what is not relevant evidence are all routine steps in the discharge of that ordinary jurisdiction. Demonstrable mistake in the identification of such issues or the formulation of such questions will commonly involve error of law which may, if an appeal is available and is pursued, be corrected by an appellate court and, depending on the circumstances, found an order setting aside the order or decision of the inferior court. Such a mistake on the part of an inferior court entrusted with authority to identify, formulate and determine such issues and questions will not, however, ordinarily constitute jurisdictional error. Similarly, a failure by an inferior court to take into account some matter which it was, as a matter of law, required to take into account in determining a question within jurisdiction or reliance by such a court upon some irrelevant matter upon which it was, as a matter of law, not entitled to rely in determining such a question will not ordinarily involve jurisdictional error.

[Citations omitted]

Minister for Immigration and Multicultural Affairs v Yusuf (2001) 206 CLR 323

Facts

Ms Yusuf sought a protection visa, claiming she had a well-founded fear of persecution on the ground of race if she returned to Somalia. Her application was refused by a delegate of the Minister and she sought review by the Refugee Review Tribunal. She provided a statement to the Tribunal claiming that her home in Somalia had been attacked by a rival clan. The Tribunal dismissed her application and in doing so made no finding in relation to her claim that her home had been attacked. The *Migration Act 1958* (Cth) set out grounds under which decisions of the Tribunal were judicially reviewable by the Federal Court. Ms Yusuf successfully sought review by the Federal Court and the Minister's appeal to the Full Court of the Federal Court was dismissed.

The matter came before the High Court (along with another brought by an Armenian asylum seeker, Mr Israelian) as an appeal by the Minister. Ms Yusuf and Mr Israelian also brought separate applications in the High Court's original jurisdiction under s 75(iii) and (v) of the *Constitution*, arguing that the Tribunal had made a jurisdictional error, which could be reviewed in the exercise of that jurisdiction, even if the error was not of a kind within the (then) more limited grounds on which the Federal Court could review the decision.

The High Court considered in detail the kinds of errors that were reviewable errors under the specific provisions set out in the *Migration Act 1958* (Cth). The Minister's appeal in Ms Yusuf's case was allowed and the application for s 75 relief was dismissed. The majority held that the Tribunal had not made a reviewable error under the Act or a jurisdictional error for the purposes of s 75 of the *Constitution*. In the following passage McHugh, Gummow and Hayne JJ discuss the concept of jurisdictional error.

McHugh, Gummow and Hayne JJ

> ***351*** [82] It is necessary, however, to understand what is meant by 'jurisdictional error' under the general law and the consequences that follow from a decision-maker making such an error. As was said in *Craig v South Australia* [(1995) 184 CLR 163, 179], if an administrative tribunal (like the Tribunal)
>
> > falls into an error of law which causes it to identify a wrong issue, to ask itself a wrong question, to ignore relevant material, to rely on irrelevant material or, at least in some circumstances, to make an erroneous finding or to reach a mistaken conclusion, and the tribunal's exercise or purported exercise of power is thereby affected, it exceeds its authority or powers. Such an error of law is jurisdictional error which will invalidate any order or decision of the tribunal which reflects it.
>
> 'Jurisdictional error' can thus be seen to embrace a number of different kinds of error, the list of which, in the passage cited from *Craig*, is not exhaustive. Those different kinds of error may well overlap. The circumstances of a particular case may permit more than one characterisation of the error identified, for example, as the decision-maker both asking the wrong question and ignoring relevant material. What is important, however, is that identifying a wrong issue, asking a wrong question, ignoring relevant material or relying on irrelevant material in a way that affects the exercise of power is to make an error of law.
>
> Further, doing so results in the decision-maker exceeding the authority or powers given by the relevant statute. In other words, if an error of those types is made, the decision-maker did not have authority to make the decision that was made; he or she did not have jurisdiction to make it. Nothing in the Act suggests that the Tribunal is given authority to authoritatively determine questions of law or to make a decision otherwise than in accordance with the law

[Citations omitted]

Kirk v Industrial Court of New South Wales (2010) 239 CLR 531

Occupational Health and Safety Act 1983 (NSW)

[As at relevant date]

15 Employers to ensure health, safety and welfare of their employees

(1) Every employer shall ensure the health, safety and welfare at work of all the employer's employees.

(2) Without prejudice to the generality of subsection (1), an employer contravenes that subsection if the employer fails:

(a) to provide or maintain plant and systems of work that are safe and without risks to health,

(b) to make arrangements for ensuring safety and absence of risks to health in connection with the use, handling, storage or transport of plant and substances,

(c) to provide such information, instruction, training and supervision as may be necessary to ensure the health and safety at work of the employer's employees,

(d) as regards any place of work under the employer's control:

(i) to maintain it in a condition that is safe and without risks to health, or

(ii) to provide or maintain means of access to and egress from it that are safe and without any such risks,

(e) to provide or maintain a working environment for the employer's employees that is safe and without risks to health and adequate as regards facilities for their welfare at work, or

(f) to take such steps as are necessary to make available in connection with the use of any plant or substance at the place of work adequate information:

(i) about the use for which the plant is designed and about any conditions necessary to ensure that, when put to that use, the plant will be safe and without risks to health, or

(ii) about any research, or the results of any relevant tests which have been carried out, on or in connection with the substance and about any conditions necessary to ensure that the substance will be safe and without risks to health when properly used.

...

Maximum penalty: 5000 penalty units in the case of a corporation or 500 penalty units in any other case.

...

53 Defence

It shall be a defence to any proceedings against a person for an offence against this Act or the regulations for the person to prove that:

(a) it was not reasonably practicable for the person to comply with the provision of this Act or the regulations the breach of which constituted the offence, or

(b) the commission of the offence was due to causes over which the person had no control and against the happening of which it was impracticable for the person to make provision.

Facts

The case deals with a privative clause in the *Industrial Relations Act 1996* (NSW) which attempted to limit judicial review of decisions of the Industrial Court of New South Wales. (Privative clauses are covered in Chapter 10.) Properly construed, the privative clause did not prevent review for jurisdictional error. The following extract considers the concept of jurisdictional error.

The case concerned criminal liability of a farm owner, Graeme Kirk, following a workplace incident that resulted in the death of a farm manager. The Industrial Court of New South Wales convicted and sentenced Mr Kirk. The High Court held that the Industrial Court had made jurisdictional errors by misconstruing the *Occupational Health and Safety Act 1983* (NSW) ('*OH&S Act*') and failing to comply with the rules of evidence. Section 15 of the *OH&S Act* imposed an obligation on the employer to ensure the health, safety and welfare of employees at work. There was a defence (s 53) and to rely upon that defence an employer needed to establish that it was not reasonably practicable to comply with the provisions. The charges needed to state how the employer was alleged to have contravened the provisions by identifying specific acts or omissions. It was not, as had happened in this case, sufficient to simply state that Mr Kirk had 'failed to ensure the health, safety and welfare at work of its employees'. The High Court held that the Industrial Court had wrongly construed the Act so that the prosecutor was not required to identify what particular measures the employer should have taken but did not.

French CJ, Gummow, Hayne, Crennan, Kiefel and Bell JJ

570 [64] ... [I]t is important to recognise the use to which the principles expressed in terms of 'jurisdictional error' and its related concept of 'jurisdictional fact' are put. The principles are used in connection with the control of tribunals of limited jurisdiction on the basis that a 'tribunal of limited jurisdiction should not be the final judge of its exercise of power; it should be subject to the control of the courts of more general jurisdiction'. Jaffe expressed the danger, against which the principles guarded, as being that 'a tribunal preoccupied with special problems or staffed by individuals of lesser ability is likely to develop distorted positions. In its concern for its administrative task it may strain just those limits with which the legislature was most concerned' [Louis L Jaffe, 'Judicial Review: Constitutional and Jurisdictional Fact' (1957) 70 *Harvard Law Review* 953, 963]. It is not useful to examine whether Jaffe's explanation of why distorted positions may develop is right. What is important is that the development of distorted positions is to be avoided. And because that is so, it followed, in that author's opinion, that denominating some questions as 'jurisdictional'

> is almost entirely functional: it is used to validate review when review is felt to be necessary ... If it is understood that the word ***571*** 'jurisdiction' is not a metaphysical absolute but simply expresses the gravity of the error, it would seem that this is a concept for which we must have a word and for which use of the hallowed word is justified.

[65] In England, the difficulties presented by classification of some errors as jurisdictional and others as not were ultimately understood as requiring the conclusion that *any* error of law by a decision-maker (whether an inferior court or a tribunal) rendered the decision ultra vires. But that is a step which this Court has not taken.

Jurisdictional error in Australia

[66] In *Craig v South Australia,* this Court recognised [(1995) 184 CLR 163, 177–80] the difficulty of distinguishing between jurisdictional and non-jurisdictional errors, but maintained the distinction. As was pointed out in *Re Refugee Review Tribunal; Ex parte Aala* [(2000) 204 CLR 82, 141 [163]]:

> The difficulty of drawing a bright line between jurisdictional error and error in the exercise of jurisdiction should not be permitted, however, to obscure the difference that is illustrated by considering clear cases of each species of error. There is a jurisdictional error if the decision maker makes a decision outside the limits of the functions and powers conferred on him or her, or does something which he or she lacks power to do. By contrast, incorrectly deciding something which the decision maker is authorised to decide is an error within jurisdiction. (This is sometimes described as authority to go wrong, that is, to decide matters within jurisdiction incorrectly.) The former kind of error concerns departures from limits upon the exercise of power. The latter does not.

As was also pointed out in *Aala,* there can be no automatic transposition to Australia of the principles that developed in England in relation to the availability of certiorari and prohibition. The ***572*** constitutional context is too different to permit such a transposition. At the federal level, allowance must be made for the evident constitutional purposes of s 75(v) of the *Constitution;* at a State level, other constitutional considerations are engaged.

...

[67] The drawing of a distinction between errors within jurisdiction and errors outside jurisdiction was held, in *Craig,* to require different application as between 'on the one hand, the inferior courts which are amenable to certiorari and, on the other, those other tribunals exercising governmental powers which are also amenable to the writ' [*Craig* (1995) 184 CLR 163, 176.]

...

573 [69] Behind these conclusions lies an assumption that a distinction can readily be made between a court and an administrative tribunal. At a State level that distinction may not always be drawn easily, for there is not, in the States' constitutional arrangements, that same separation of powers that is required at a federal level by Ch III of the Constitution. No less importantly, behind the conclusions expressed in *Craig* lie premises about what is meant by jurisdictional error. Unexpressed premises about what is meant by jurisdictional error give content to the notion of 'authoritative' when it is said, as it was in *Craig*, that tribunals cannot 'authoritatively' determine questions of law, but that courts can.

[70] When certiorari is sought, there is often an issue about whether the decision is open to review. If 'authoritative' is used in the sense of 'final', a decision could be described as 'authoritative' only if certiorari will not lie to correct error in the decision. To observe that inferior courts generally have authority to decide questions of law 'authoritatively' is not to conclude that the determination of any particular question is not open to review by a superior court. Whether a particular decision reached is open to review is a question that remains unanswered. The 'authoritative' decisions of inferior courts are those decisions which are not attended by jurisdictional error. That directs attention to what is meant in this context by 'jurisdiction' and 'jurisdictional'. It suggests that the observation that inferior courts have authority to decide questions of law 'authoritatively' is at least unhelpful.

Jurisdictional error – this case

[71] It is neither necessary, nor possible, to attempt to mark the metes and bounds of jurisdictional error. Professor Aronson has collected authorities recognising some eight categories of jurisdictional error [Aronson, 'Jurisdictional Error without the Tears', in Groves and Lee (eds), *Australian Administrative Law: Fundamentals, Principles and Doctrines* (2007) 330, 335-336]. It is necessary, however, to make good the proposition stated earlier in these reasons that the two errors that have been identified as made by the Industrial Court at first instance (and not corrected on appeal to the Full Bench) were jurisdictional errors. The Court in *Craig* explained the ambit of jurisdictional error in the case of an inferior court in reasoning that it is convenient to summarise as follows.

[72] First, the Court [in *Craig*] stated, as a general description of what is jurisdictional error by an inferior court, that an inferior court falls into jurisdictional error 'if it mistakenly asserts or denies the existence of ***574*** jurisdiction or if it *misapprehends* or disregards the nature or *limits* of its *functions or powers* in a case where it correctly recognises that jurisdiction does exist' (emphasis added). Secondly, the Court pointed out that jurisdictional error 'is at its most obvious where the inferior court purports to act wholly or partly outside the general area of its jurisdiction in the sense of *entertaining a matter or making a decision* or order *of a kind* which wholly or partly lies *outside the theoretical limits of its functions and powers*' (emphasis added). (The reference to '*theoretical* limits' should not distract attention from the need to focus upon the limits of the body's functions and powers. Those limits are real and are to be identified from the relevant statute establishing the body and regulating its work.) Thirdly, the Court amplified what was said about an inferior court acting beyond jurisdiction by entertaining a matter outside the limits of the inferior court's functions or powers by giving three examples: (a) the absence of a jurisdictional fact; (b) disregard of a matter that the relevant statute requires be taken to account as a condition of jurisdiction (or the converse case of taking account of a matter required to be ignored); and (c) misconstruction of the relevant statute thereby misconceiving the nature of the function which the inferior

court is performing or the extent of its powers in the circumstances of the particular case. The Court said of this last example that 'the line between jurisdictional error and mere error in the exercise of jurisdiction may be particularly difficult to discern'.

[73] As this case demonstrates, it is important to recognise that the reasoning in *Craig* that has just been summarised is not to be seen as providing a rigid taxonomy of jurisdictional error. The three examples given in further explanation of the ambit of jurisdictional error by an inferior court are just that - examples. They are not to be taken as marking the boundaries of the relevant field. So much is apparent from the reference in *Craig* to the difficulties that are encountered in cases of the kind described in the third example.

[74] The first of the errors in question in this case - the errors of construction of s 15 of the *OH&S Act* - can be identified as a jurisdictional error of the third kind identified in *Craig*. That is, it can be identified as the Industrial Court misapprehending the limits of its functions and powers. Misconstruction of s 15 of the *OH&S Act* led the Industrial Court to make orders convicting and sentencing Mr Kirk ***575*** and the Kirk company where it had no power to do so. It had no power to do that because no particular act or omission, or set of acts or omissions, was identified at *any* point in the proceedings, up to and including the passing of sentence, as constituting the offences of which Mr Kirk and the Kirk company were convicted and for which they were sentenced. And the failure to identify the particular act or omission, or set of acts or omissions, alleged to constitute the contravening conduct followed from the misconstruction of s 15. By misconstruing s 15 of the *OH&S Act*, the Industrial Court convicted Mr Kirk and the Kirk company of offences when what was alleged and what was established did not identify offending conduct.

[75] The explanation just offered also demonstrates that the error made by the Industrial Court was not only an error about the limits of its functions or powers. It was an error which led to it making orders convicting Mr Kirk and the Kirk company where it had no power to do so. The Industrial Court had no power to do that because an offence against the *OH&S Act* had not been proved. It follows that the Industrial Court made orders beyond its powers to make.

[76] In addition to the error just considered, the Industrial Court misapprehended a limit on its powers by permitting the prosecution to call Mr Kirk at the trial. The Industrial Court's power to try charges of criminal offences was limited to trying the charges applying the laws of evidence. The laws of evidence permit many forms of departure from the rules that are stated. Many, perhaps most, departures from the strict rules of evidence can be seen as agreed to by parties at least implicitly. But calling the accused as a witness for the prosecution is not permitted, even if the accused consents to that course. The joint trial of Mr Kirk and the Kirk company was not a trial conducted in accordance with the laws of evidence. The Industrial Court thus conducted the trial of Mr Kirk and the Kirk company in breach of the limits on its power to try charges of a criminal offence.

[77] For these reasons, putting aside consideration of the privative provisions of s 179 of the *IR Act*, certiorari would lie in this case for jurisdictional error in both of the respects identified. It is necessary, however, before dealing directly with the

construction and application of those privative provisions to say something further about error of law on the face of the record.

Error of law on the face of the record

[78] Ordinarily, the conclusion that jurisdictional error is shown makes consideration of whether there is an error of law on the face of the record superfluous. But in order to understand the extent to which privative provisions may validly deprive a State Supreme Court of the supervisory jurisdiction exercised by the grant of relief in the nature of prohibition and certiorari, something more must be said here about error of law on the face of the record.

[79] The continued vitality of the principle that certiorari will lie for error of law on the face of the record may seem incongruous. Why should ***576*** the availability of the remedy turn to any extent upon a question of form, if the motive for allowing the remedy is the marking and maintenance of boundaries of power?

[80] These reasons will explain that there is continued utility in maintaining the distinction between certiorari for error of law on the face of the record and certiorari for jurisdictional error. The utility of the distinction lies in constitutional considerations. Before identifying those constitutional considerations, it is necessary to say something further about error of law on the face of the record and, in particular, about what constitutes the 'record' ...

577 [84] In *Craig*, the Court rejected a more expansive approach to certiorari which would include both the reasons for decision and the complete transcript of proceedings in the 'modern record' of an inferior court ...

[85] No application in the present proceedings was made to reconsider the decision in *Craig*. However, the conclusion that the record of a court does not include its reasons certainly confines the availability of certiorari. Some but not all errors of law made by a court will found the grant of relief. And the availability of certiorari is confined for the stated purpose of not providing a 'discretionary general appeal for error of law'.

[Some citations omitted]

Probuild Constructions (Aust) Pty Ltd v Shade Systems Pty Ltd (2018) 264 CLR 1

Building and Construction Industry Security of Payment Act 1999 (NSW)

[As at relevant date]

8 Rights to progress payments

(1) On and from each reference date under a construction contract, a person:

(a) who has undertaken to carry out construction work under the contract, or

(b) who has undertaken to supply related goods and services under the contract, is entitled to a progress payment.

...

22 Adjudicator's determination

(1) An adjudicator is to determine:

(a) the amount of the progress payment (if any) to be paid by the respondent to the claimant (the adjudicated amount), and

(b) the date on which any such amount became or becomes payable, and

(c) the rate of interest payable on any such amount.

(2) In determining an adjudication application, the adjudicator is to consider the following matters only:

(a) the provisions of this Act,

(b) the provisions of the construction contract from which the application arose,

(c) the payment claim to which the application relates, together with all submissions (including relevant documentation) that have been duly made by the claimant in support of the claim,

(d) the payment schedule (if any) to which the application relates, together with all submissions (including relevant documentation) that have been duly made by the respondent in support of the schedule,

(e) the results of any inspection carried out by the adjudicator of any matter to which the claim relates.

Facts

The *Building and Construction Industry Security of Payment Act 1999* (NSW) ('Security of Payment Act') is one of a number of equivalent state Acts that grant to builders and suppliers doing work under construction contracts an entitlement to progress payments, and sets out procedures for recovering those payments. A person claiming to be entitled to a progress payment serves a claim on a respondent who may respond with a payment schedule. If the payment schedule amount is less than the claimed amount, or if the respondent does not pay by the due date, the claimant can apply for adjudication of the dispute.

In this case, Shade Systems agreed to supply and install external louvres for apartments being built by Probuild Constructions. Shade Systems served a payment claim on Probuild and Probuild responded with a claim for liquidated damages that it said was owing because work had not been completed by a 'date for practical completion' in the subcontract. Shade Systems took its progress payment claim to adjudication. The adjudicator rejected Probuild's liquidated damages claim and determined that the full progress payment was payable to Shade Systems. Probuild sought certiorari to quash the adjudicator's determination in the New South Wales Supreme Court under s 69 of the *Supreme Court Act 1970* (NSW). The primary judge granted certiorari for error of law on the face of the record.[1] On appeal, the Court of Appeal of the Supreme Court of New South Wales held that the Supreme Court did not have jurisdiction to grant certiorari to quash the adjudicator's determination because the Security of Payment Act ousted certiorari for error of law on the face of the record. The appeal to the High Court was dismissed. Whilst the Act contained no express privative (ouster) clause, the High Court held that it 'evinces a clear

1 *Probuild Constructions (Aust) Pty Ltd v Shade Systems Pty Ltd* [2016] NSWSC 770, [74].

legislative intention to exclude the jurisdiction'.[2] Privative clauses are covered in Chapter 10 of this book. In the following extracts, the joint judgment explains the object of the legislation and the interim nature of the adjudicator's progress payment determination; Gageler J explains why Probuild had correctly conceded that any error by the adjudicator was not jurisdictional.

Kiefel CJ, Bell, Keane, Nettle and Gordon JJ

258 [36] First, it is to be recalled that the Security of Payment Act was enacted 'to reform payment behaviour in the construction industry' [New South Wales, Legislative Assembly, *Parliamentary Debates* (Hansard), 8 September 1999, 104] by seeking to ensure that a person who undertakes to carry out ***259*** construction work under a construction contract is entitled to receive, and is able to recover, progress payments promptly in relation to the carrying out of that work. In particular, it was designed to 'stamp out the practice of developers and contractors delaying payment to subcontractors and suppliers'. And it achieves that objective by setting up a scheme, including a 'unique form of adjudication of disputes over the amount due for payment', which is, as Basten JA observed in the Court of Appeal, 'coherent, expeditious and self-contained' [*Shade Systems* (2016) 344 ALR 355, 369 [59]]. The intended result is that 'each party knows precisely where they stand at any point of time' [*Chase Oyster Bar Pty Ltd v Hamo Industries Pty Ltd* (2010) 78 NSWLR 393, 406 [47]].

[37] Second, it is important to appreciate the subject matter of the Security of Payment Act. The Security of Payment Act is not concerned with finally and conclusively determining the entitlements of parties to a construction contract. Section 8 confers an entitlement to a progress payment, which may be the final payment, a single or one-off payment or what is described as a 'milestone payment'. Part 3 of the Security of Payment Act creates a distinct procedure for enforcing that statutory entitlement, which includes the making of a payment claim, the provision of a payment schedule in response and the determination of a payment claim by an adjudicator (at the option of the claimant).

[38] The statutory entitlement to a progress payment and the procedure for recovery of a progress payment are separate from, and in addition to, a contractor's entitlement under a construction contract to receive payment for completed work. The statutory entitlement is predicated upon the existence of a construction contract, but the entitlement and the means available for its enforcement stand apart from the parties' rights under that contract. Indeed, the Security of Payment has effect despite any contractual provision to the contrary: any purported derogation is void. Moreover, the Security of Payment Act acknowledges and preserves parties' contractual entitlements. Importantly, the Security of Payment Act provides that in any proceedings before a court or tribunal in relation to any matter arising under a contract, the court or tribunal must allow for, and may make such orders as it considers appropriate for the restitution of, any amount paid under or for the purposes of Pt 3.

[39] ... [T]he Security of Payment Act was the subject of substantial amendments in 2002. Introducing the Bill for the *Building and Construction Industry Security of Payment Amendment Act 2002* (NSW), the responsible Minister stated:

2 *Probuild Constructions (Aust) Pty Ltd v Shade Systems Pty Ltd* (2018) 264 CLR 1, 15 [35] (Kiefel CJ, Bell, Keane, Nettle and Gordon JJ).

> [The Security of Payment Act] was designed to ensure prompt payment and, for that purpose, [the Security of Payment Act] set up a unique form of adjudication of disputes over the amount due for payment. Parliament intended that a progress payment, on account, should be made promptly and that any disputes over the amount finally due should be decided separately. The final determination could be by a court or by an agreed alternative dispute resolution procedure. But meanwhile the claimant's entitlement, if in dispute, would be decided on an interim basis by an adjudicator, and that interim entitlement would be paid.

The Security of Payment Act does not speak of 'interim' entitlements and payments, but the label aptly reflects how the statutory entitlement interacts with any underlying contractual liability.

260 [40] Third, underpinning the 'interim' statutory entitlement is an understanding that '[c]ash flow is the lifeblood of the construction industry'. Put another way, any interruption to the cash flow of a person carrying out construction work is apt to create the risk of financial failure. Consistent with that understanding, the procedure in Pt 3 is designed to operate quickly. So much is apparent from the detailed time limits that apply at each stage. ... These time limits are 'carefully calibrated'. The time limits have been rightly described as imposing 'brutally fast' deadlines on the claimant, the respondent and the adjudicator to ensure the prompt resolution of payment disputes.

Gageler J

268 [79] ... Probuild conceded before the Court of Appeal and in its appeal to this Court that the error of law made by the adjudicator in the interpretation of the construction contract was a non-jurisdictional error.

[80] Probuild's concession was undoubtedly correct. The authority that s 22(1) of the Security of Payment Act confers on an adjudicator to determine the amount and timing of a progress payment is an authority to determine (in the event of the recovery procedure prescribed in Pt 3 being regularly invoked) the amount and timing of a progress payment a statutory entitlement to which exists by operation of s 8 separately and in parallel to such common law or other statutory rights as the parties to the construction contract may have under or in respect of that contract. The adjudicator's making of the determination is explicitly conditioned by the requirement of s 22(1) which is expressed in terms no higher than that the adjudicator 'is to consider' enumerated 'matters', one of which is 'the provisions of the construction contract'. The adjudicator's authority to make the determination is required by s 21 to be exercised 'as expeditiously as possible', and in any event within no more than ten business days of the adjudicator notifying the parties of his or her acceptance of the application, and without the parties having an entitlement to legal representation in any conference which the adjudicator might choose to call. If the adjudicated amount is not promptly paid, a certificate of the determination is then permitted by s 25 to be filed as a judgment for a debt in any court of competent jurisdiction and to be enforced accordingly without the adjudicator's determination being able to be challenged in any proceeding to have the judgment set aside. The principal statutory object stated in s 3(1), to ensure that a person undertaking to carry out construction work under a construction contract 'is

entitled to receive, and is able to recover, progress payments in relation to the carrying out of that work', would be thwarted were mere error of law made by the adjudicator in the interpretation of the contract to vitiate the determination and thereby to render it liable to be quashed or declared invalid by the Supreme Court.

[81] But it is important to be clear about exactly what Probuild's concession necessarily involved. The concession involved acceptance that, despite the common law presumption that a statutory conferral of decision-making authority on a person or body other than a court is impliedly conditioned by a requirement that the authority be exercised only on a correct understanding of the applicable law, the textual and contextual indications are sufficiently ***269*** strong to compel the conclusion that s 22(1) is properly interpreted within the totality of the statutory scheme of which it forms part as conferring authority on an adjudicator to make a determination based on the adjudicator's own interpretation of the construction contract irrespective of whether that interpretation be right or wrong in law.

[Citations omitted]

Hossain v Minister for Immigration and Border Protection (2018) 264 CLR 123

Facts

Mr Hossain, a citizen of Bangladesh, applied for a partner visa. A delegate of the Minister refused to grant the visa. Mr Hossain applied to the Administrative Appeals Tribunal for merits review of the delegate's decision. The Tribunal was not satisfied that two of the prescribed criteria for the visa had been met. The first such criterion was that the application be made within 28 days of the applicant ceasing to hold a previous visa 'unless the Minister is satisfied that there are compelling reasons for not applying [that criterion]'. The second criterion was that the visa applicant 'does not have outstanding debts to the Commonwealth unless the Minister is satisfied that appropriate arrangements have been made for payment'. The Tribunal found that it was not satisfied that either criterion was met, and so affirmed the decision of the delegate. The Tribunal wrongly addressed the question of whether there were compelling reasons for not applying the criterion *as at the time of the application for the visa* rather than *as at the time of its own decision*. The Minister conceded that this was an error of law, but argued that it was not a jurisdictional error because it could not have affected the ultimate decision, since the visa could only be granted if both criteria were satisfied, and there was no error affecting the Tribunal's assessment of the second criterion.

Kiefel CJ, Gageler and Keane JJ

133 [27] Just as identification of the preconditions to and conditions of an exercise of decision-making power conferred by statute turns on the construction of the statute, so too does discernment of the extent of non-compliance which will result in an otherwise compliant decision lacking the characteristics necessary to be given force and effect by the statute ***134*** turn on the construction of the statute. The question of whether a particular failure to comply with an express or implied statutory condition in purporting to make a particular decision is of a magnitude which has resulted in taking the decision outside the jurisdiction conferred by the statute cannot be answered except by reference to the construction of the statute.

[28] The common law principles which inform the construction of statutes conferring decision-making authority reflect longstanding qualitative judgments about the appropriate limits of an exercise of administrative power to which a legislature can be taken to adhere in defining the bounds of such authority as it chooses to confer on a repository in the absence of affirmative indication of a legislative intention to the contrary. Those common law principles are not derived by logic alone and cannot be treated as abstractions disconnected from the subject matter to which they are to be applied. They are not so delicate or refined in their operation that sight is lost of the fact that '[d]ecison-making is a function of the real world'.

[29] That a decision-maker 'must proceed by reference to correct legal principles, correctly applied' is an ordinarily (although not universally) implied condition of a statutory conferral of decision-making authority. Ordinarily, a statute which impliedly requires that condition or another condition to be observed in the course of a decision-making process is not to be interpreted as denying legal force and effect to every decision that might be made in breach of the condition. The statute is ordinarily to be interpreted as incorporating a threshold of materiality in the event of non-compliance.

[30] Whilst a statute on its proper construction might set a higher or lower threshold of materiality, the threshold of materiality would not ordinarily be met in the event of a failure to comply with a condition if complying with the condition could have made no ***133*** difference to the decision that was made in the circumstances in which that decision was made. The threshold would not ordinarily be met, for example, where a failure to afford procedural fairness did not deprive the person who was denied an opportunity to be heard of 'the possibility of a successful outcome', or where a decision-maker failed to take into account a mandatory consideration which in all the circumstances was 'so insignificant that the failure to take it into account could not have materially affected' the decision that was made.

133 [34] Formation of the Minister's state of satisfaction or of non-satisfaction is in each case conditioned by a requirement that the Minister or his or her delegate, or the Tribunal forming its own conclusion on review, must proceed reasonably and on a correct understanding and application of the applicable law, which includes the criteria prescribed by the *Migration Act* and the *Migration Regulations* for the visa in question.

[35] Here the Tribunal breached that implied condition by misconstruing and misapplying the criterion which related to the timing of the making of the application. The breach, however, could have made no difference to the decision which the Tribunal in fact made to affirm the decision of the delegate. That was because the Tribunal was not satisfied that the public interest criterion was met, and, on the findings which the Tribunal made, the Tribunal could not reasonably have been satisfied that the public interest criterion was met. The Tribunal in those circumstances had no option but to affirm the decision of the delegate.

...

[37] The Tribunal's error in construing and applying the criterion relating to the timing of the making of the application did not rise to the level of a jurisdictional error.

Edelman J

145 [66] In *Attorney-General (NSW) v Quin* [(1990) 170 CLR 1, 36], Brennan J said that in Australia the development and expansion of judicial review had 'been achieved by an increasingly sophisticated exposition of implied limitations on the extent or the exercise of statutory power'. The broad test for determining whether an implied legislative condition is jurisdictional was set out by McHugh, Gummow, Kirby and Hayne JJ in *Project Blue Sky Inc v Australian Broadcasting Authority* [(1998) 194 CLR 355, 390 [93]]. Their Honours said that it was necessary to 'ask whether it was a purpose of the legislation that an act done in breach of the provision should be invalid'.

146 [67] A close examination of legislation will usually have the effect that not every express or implied condition must be construed in a binary way. A legislative condition need not be construed as (i) always depriving a decision maker of power, or (ii) never doing so, no matter how it is breached. The question is always one of construction of the legislation: which breaches of a provision does the legislation, either expressly or, more commonly, impliedly, treat as depriving the decision maker of power? Just as it is unlikely to be concluded that Parliament intended to authorise an unreasonable exercise of power, so too it is unlikely to be an intention that the legislature is taken to have that a decision be rendered invalid by an immaterial error.

[68] An illustration of this point is the decision of this Court in *Minister for Immigration and Citizenship v SZIZO* [(2009) 238 CLR 627]. In that case, the Refugee Review Tribunal failed to comply with the requirements of ss 441A and 441G of the *Migration Act* because it sent notice of the hearing to the first applicant only, instructing him to inform the other applicants of the hearing. All of the applicants attended the hearing and had the opportunity to participate. This Court said [at 640 [35]] that the 'admitted absurdity of the outcome is against acceptance of the conclusion that the legislature intended that invalidity be the consequence of departure from *any* of the procedural steps leading up to the hearing' (emphasis added).

...

147 [72] In summary, although the issue will always be one of construction of the express or implied terms of the statute, an error will not usually be material, in this sense of affecting the exercise of power, unless there is a possibility that it could have changed the result of the exercise of power. In other words, materiality will generally require the error to deprive a person of the possibility of a successful outcome. There may be unusual circumstances where an error is so fundamental that it will be material whether or not a person is deprived of the possibility of a successful outcome. One circumstance, for reasons that could ***147*** include respect for the dignity of the individual, may be an extreme case of denial of procedural fairness. Another may be ... where a decision maker fails to exercise jurisdiction to decide a question according to the applicable criterion. No such circumstances arise on this appeal.

[Citations omitted]

MZAPC v Minister for Immigration and Border Protection (2021) 95 ALJR 441

Facts

This case concerned the question of which party bears the onus in relation to questions of materiality. In the High Court, the applicant accepted that an error which was not material, in the sense that it could not realistically have made a difference to the outcome, would not be a jurisdictional error, but argued that, once the existence of a relevant error was established by the applicant, the *respondent* (here, the Minister for Immigration and Border Protection) should then bear the burden of showing that the error was *not* material. The following extract sets out key parts of the reasoning of the majority for holding that an applicant for judicial review bears the onus of demonstrating that an error could realistically have resulted in the decision-maker having made a different decision.

Kiefel CJ, Gageler, Keane and Gleeson JJ

> ***449*** [1] This appeal raises issues concerning the content and proof of the element of materiality identified in *Hossain v Minister for Immigration and Border Protection* [(2018) 264 CLR 123] as ordinarily required to exist for a breach of an express or implied condition of a conferral of statutory decision-making authority to result in jurisdictional error.
>
> [2] Materiality was subsequently explained in *Minister for Immigration and Border Protection v SZMTA* [(2019) 264 CLR 421] to involve a realistic possibility that the decision in fact made could have been different had the breach of the condition not occurred. Existence or non-existence of a realistic possibility that the decision could have been different was explained to be a question of fact in respect of which the plaintiff in an application for judicial review of the decision on the ground of jurisdictional error bears the onus of proof.
>
> [3] The explanation in *SZMTA* is sound in principle and consistent with precedent. *SZMTA* ought not to be revisited.
>
> ...
>
> ***454*** [38] The counterfactual question of whether the decision that was in fact made could have been different had there been compliance with the condition that was in fact breached cannot be answered without determining the basal factual question of how the decision that was in fact made was in fact made. Like other historical facts to be determined in other civil proceedings, the facts as to what occurred in the making of the decision must be determined in an application for judicial review on the balance of probabilities by inferences drawn from the totality of the evidence. And like other counterfactual questions in civil proceedings as to what could have occurred – as distinct from what would have occurred – had there been compliance with a legal obligation that was in fact breached, whether the decision that was in fact made could have been different had the condition been complied with falls to be determined as a matter of reasonable conjecture within the parameters set by the historical facts that have been determined on the balance of probabilities.

[39] Bearing the overall onus of proving jurisdictional error, the plaintiff in an application for judicial review must bear the onus of proving on the balance of probabilities all the historical facts necessary to sustain the requisite reasonable conjecture. The burden of the plaintiff is not to prove on the balance of probabilities that a different decision would have been made had there been compliance with the condition that was breached. But the burden of the plaintiff is to prove on the balance of probabilities the historical facts necessary to enable the court to be satisfied of the realistic possibility that a different decision could have been made had there been compliance with that condition.

[40] There is no reason to consider that the burden placed on the plaintiff of proving on the balance of probabilities the historical facts necessary to enable the court to be satisfied of the realistic possibility that a different decision could have been made had there been compliance with the condition that has been breached is significantly more onerous than the burden indisputably borne by the plaintiff of proving on the balance of probabilities the historical facts necessary to enable the court to be satisfied that the condition has in fact been breached. ... ***455*** [T]here is no reason to consider that the burden would more fittingly be borne by the active defendant in a proceeding for judicial review to prove the historical facts necessary to enable the court to be satisfied that a different decision could not have been made.

...

457 [51] Just as a court called upon to determine whether a new trial should be ordered must be careful not to assume the function of the primary trier of fact (whether it be a judge or a jury), so a court called upon to determine whether jurisdictional error has occurred must be careful not to assume the function of the decision-maker. Faced with a procedural irregularity having been shown to have occurred in a decision-making process, the court is nevertheless in each case charged with the responsibility of determining for itself whether the result in fact arrived at by the decision-maker in the decision-making process could realistically have been different had that procedural irregularity not occurred.

[Citations omitted]

Nathanson v Minister for Home Affairs (2022) 96 ALJR 737

Facts

Narada Nathanson was a citizen of New Zealand who had been living in Australia since 2010. In 2018, a delegate of the Minister for Home Affairs cancelled Mr Nathanson's visa. The delegate was required to cancel the visa pursuant to s 501(3A) of the *Migration Act 1958* (Cth) because Mr Nathanson had been convicted of an offence for which he had been sentenced to imprisonment for 12 months or more, and was serving his sentence on a full-time basis in a custodial institution. Mr Nathanson made representations as to why the visa cancellation should be revoked. A delegate of the Minister declined to revoke the cancellation decision. Mr Nathanson then appealed to the Administrative Appeals Tribunal against that decision. The Tribunal affirmed the decision not to revoke the visa cancellation decision. In reaching that decision, the Tribunal took into account, adversely to Mr Nathanson, certain allegations of family violence contained in police reports that were before the Tribunal. The Tribunal relied upon the evidence of family violence to inform its assessment of the protection of the Australian community and the expectations of the Australian community. In the High Court, it was not disputed that the Tribunal had failed to accord procedural fairness to Mr Nathanson in using the evidence in that way without adequate notice to him that it might do so. The issue was whether Mr Nathanson had established that the breach of procedural fairness was material.

Kiefel CJ, Keane and Gleeson JJ

> ***741*** [1] ... [T]he Tribunal's error in failing to afford the appellant procedural fairness will have involved jurisdictional error only if that failure was material to the Tribunal's decision. Materiality is established if the error deprived the appellant of a realistic possibility of a different outcome. The appellant bore the onus of demonstrating that the denial of procedural fairness was material in this sense.
>
> ...
>
> ***748*** [33] There will generally be a realistic possibility that a decision-making process could have resulted in a different outcome if a party was denied an opportunity to present evidence or make submissions on an issue that required consideration. The standard of 'reasonable conjecture' is undemanding. It recognises that a fundamental purpose of affording procedural fairness is to afford an opportunity to raise relevant matters which are not already obvious, or not liable to be advanced by the apparently persuasive 'story' of the opposing party. Where a Tribunal errs by denying a party a reasonable opportunity to present their case, 'reasonable conjecture' does not require demonstration of how that party might have taken advantage of that lost opportunity. ... To the contrary, the standard of 'reasonable conjecture', correctly applied, proceeds on assumptions that are derived from the rationale for procedural fairness, namely that, if given a fair opportunity to present their case, a party will take advantage of that opportunity and that, by doing so, the party could achieve a favourable outcome.
>
> ...
>
> ***749*** [39] ... [I]t is necessary to consider how the Tribunal's decision was in fact made. That decision was made by weighing the range of considerations in [the relevant Ministerial Direction] that were of relevance to the appellant, following an evaluation of the appellant's history, relevant circumstances and prospects as appropriate, in order to make findings about each of those considerations. In that context, additional evidence and submissions directed to mitigating the significance of the evidence of domestic violence could realistically have affected the Tribunal's evaluative fact finding concerning the nature and seriousness of the appellant's conduct and, ultimately, the outcome of the Tribunal's review. There was no need for the appellant to establish the nature of any additional evidence or submission that might have been presented at the Tribunal hearing, had that hearing been procedurally fair. As a matter of reasonable conjecture, ... the appellant may have been able to present evidence on his own behalf or from his wife, and to make submissions that could have led to a different characterisation by the Tribunal of the nature of the appellant's offending.

[Citations omitted]

What is the face of the record?

The distinction between jurisdictional error and error of law on the face of the record has been discussed in the sources above. In the extracts from *Craig v South Australia* (1995) 184 CLR 163 below, the High Court discusses what 'the record' is at common law. Following that case are two examples, from New South Wales and Victoria, of statutory expansion of the record to include a decision-maker's reasons.

Craig v South Australia (1995) 184 CLR 163

Facts

The facts of this case are set out above at p 258.

Brennan, Deane, Toohey, Gaudron and McHugh JJ

The face of the record

180 The history of the writ of certiorari can be traced back to at least the fourteenth century. That history provides part of the context in which questions of the ambit of the writ must be resolved. Resort to medieval history should not, however, be permitted to allow either a transformation of certiorari into a general appeal or a side-stepping of the nineteenth century legislative reforms aimed at curbing the excessive availability of the writ which had given rise to undesirable technicality. Those legislative reforms were directly concerned with challenges to convictions before magistrates. Their practical effect was, however, to bring about a general confinement of the content of an inferior court's 'record' for the purposes of certiorari to the documents initiating and defining the matter in the inferior court and the impugned order or determination.

One finds in some recent cases in this country support for the adoption of an expansive approach to certiorari which would include both the reasons for decision and the complete transcript of proceedings in the 'modern record' of an inferior court ... ***181*** [That approach] should, on balance, be rejected. For one thing, it is inconsistent with the weight of authority in this Court which supports the conclusion that, in the absence of some statutory provision to the contrary, the record of an inferior court for the purposes of certiorari does not ordinarily include the transcript, the exhibits or the reasons for decision. More importantly, the approach that the transcript of proceedings and the reasons for decision constitute part of 'the record' would, if accepted, go a long way towards transforming certiorari into a discretionary general appeal for error of law upon which the transcript of proceedings and the reasons for decision could be scoured and analysed in a search for some internal error. It is far from clear that policy considerations favour such an increase in the availability of certiorari to correct non-jurisdictional error of law. In particular, a situation in which any proceeding in an inferior court which involved a disputed question of law could be transformed into superior court proceedings notwithstanding immunity from ordinary appellate procedures would represent a significant increase in the financial hazards to which those involved in even minor litigation in this country are already exposed. On balance, it appears to us that the question whether there should be such an increase in the availability of certiorari, or of orders in the nature of certiorari, is one that is best left to the responsible legislature.

The fact that the transcript of proceedings and reasons for decision do not, of themselves, constitute part of 'the record' does not preclude incorporation of them by reference. That was recognised in *Public Service Board (NSW) v Osmond* [(1986) 159 CLR 656, 667] where Gibbs CJ [at 671] in a judgment which represented the judgment of the Court, referred to 'the rule, well established at common law ... that reasons do not form part of the record, for the purposes of certiorari', and added the qualification 'unless the tribunal chooses to incorporate them'. [T]hat qualification has been accepted in other judgments in ***182*** this Court. As so accepted, however, it should not be understood as having the effect that a merely introductory or incidental reference to the reasons for decision produces the consequence that the whole or part of the reasons somehow become part of both the formal order and 'the record' of the particular court. As Mahoney JA has pointed out [*Commissioner for Motor Transport v Kirkpatrick* (1988) 13 NSWLR 368, 378], such a result would mean the question of what constitutes 'the record' would 'be determined by accidents of whether particular words were used in the judgment of the body concerned'. The qualification should be understood as referring only to so much of the reasons or transcript of proceedings as is referred to in the formal order in a way which brings about its incorporation as an integral part of that order and 'the record'. If, for example, the formal order incorporates undertakings given by a party 'as set out in' a particular designated document or is said to be made 'in terms of proposed orders set out in the reasons for judgment', the order and the record will incorporate only those parts of the particular document or the reasons for judgment which set out, qualify or otherwise affect the content of those undertakings or proposed orders. Conversely. A merely introductory or incidental reference will not suffice to incorporate, in either the formal order or the record, reasons given for making the formal order which do not in fact constitute part of it. Thus, for example, an introductory remark such as the phrase 'for the reasons given' or the word 'accordingly' will not, of itself, have the effect of incorporating the whole or any part of the reasons for decision in either the formal order or 'the record'.

The determination of the precise documents which constitute 'the record' of the inferior court for the purposes of a particular application for certiorari is ultimately a matter for the court hearing the application. The effect of the foregoing is that '[o]rdinarily, in the absence of statutory prescription, the record will comprise no more than the documentation which initiates the proceedings and thereby grounds the jurisdiction of the tribunal, the pleadings (if any) and the adjudication'. Where the inferior court or tribunal has prepared a formal record, the court hearing the application may amend it by discarding material which should not have been included. Where the inferior court or tribunal has not prepared a formal record or the formal record prepared is incomplete, the court hearing the application ***183*** can, if the material placed before it is adequate for the purpose, construct or complete the record.

In the present case where no formal order has been taken out and no complete record had been prepared by the District Court, the record included the information, the transcript record of the appellant's statement to the effect that he made what he called 'a *Dietrich* application', the orders made by the trial judge on 22 June 1993 and the challenged stay order which the trial judge finally made on 28 July 1993. The fact that, on 28 July, Judge Russell said, 'For the reasons that I have already published and given in relation to this matter', before indicating that there would be an order staying the proceedings, did not have the consequence that the record for the purposes of certiorari included the reasons for decision given by his Honour on 22 June.

[Some citations omitted]

Supreme Court Act 1970 (NSW)

[As at 1 December 2022]

69 Proceedings in lieu of writs

...

(3) It is declared that the jurisdiction of the Court to grant any relief or remedy in the nature of a writ of certiorari includes jurisdiction to quash the ultimate determination of a court or tribunal in any proceedings if that determination has been made on the basis of an error of law that appears on the face of the record of the proceedings.

(4) For the purposes of subsection (3), the face of the record includes the reasons expressed by the court or tribunal for its ultimate determination.

(5) Subsections (3) and (4) do not affect the operation of any legislative provision to the extent to which the provision is, according to common law principles and disregarding those subsections, effective to prevent the Court from exercising its powers to quash or otherwise review a decision.

Administrative Law Act 1978 (Vic)

[As at 1 December 2022]

10 Reasons to be part of record

Any statement by a tribunal or inferior court whether made orally or in writing, and whether or not made pursuant to a request or order under section 8, of its reasons for a decision shall be taken to form part of the decision and accordingly to be incorporated in the record.

CHAPTER

10

LIMITS ON JUDICIAL REVIEW

Introduction 282

Justiciability 282

R v Toohey; Ex parte Northern Land Council (1981) 151 CLR 170 282

Minister for Arts, Heritage and Environment v Peko-Wallsend Ltd (1987) 15 FCR 274 285

Standing to commence judicial review proceedings 288

Australian Conservation Foundation v Commonwealth (1980) 146 CLR 493 288

Onus v Alcoa of Australia Ltd (1981) 149 CLR 27 291

Administrative Decisions (Judicial Review) Act 1977 (Cth) 293

Argos Pty Ltd v Corbell (2014) 254 CLR 394 294

Privative clauses 298

Plaintiff S157/2002 v Commonwealth (2003) 211 CLR 476 298

Kirk v Industrial Court of New South Wales (2010) 239 CLR 531 304

No-invalidity clauses 308

Commissioner of Taxation (Cth) v Futuris Corporation Ltd (2008) 237 CLR 146 308

Restricting access to information before the courts 311

Graham v Minister for Immigration and Border Protection (2017) 263 CLR 1 311

Introduction

This chapter complements Chapter 10 of *Government Accountability: Australian Administrative Law,* third edition. The supervisory role of the courts is powerful and constitutionally entrenched. However, any system that enables one arm of government to supervise the actions of another requires a certain level of restraint to balance the separate powers appropriately. The exclusions built into the statutory judicial review schemes and the focus in common law and constitutional judicial review cases upon jurisdictional error impose limitations on the scope of judicial review. These concepts were covered in Chapter 9. This chapter considers further limits on judicial review, specifically justiciability, standing, and attempts by parliament to impose statutory limits.

Justiciability

R v Toohey; Ex parte Northern Land Council (1981) 151 CLR 170

Facts

The Northern Land Council made a land rights claim over a substantial part of the Cox Peninsula in the Northern Territory under Commonwealth legislation. Under that Commonwealth legislation, a claim could not apply to 'town' land. The meaning of 'town' land was determined by Northern Territory planning law. Regulation 5 of the Planning Regulations made by the Administrator of the Northern Territory provided that most of the land in the Cox Peninsula was town land. Toohey J, sitting as an Aboriginal Land Commissioner, decided that the part of the Peninsula that was specified as 'town' land was not available to be claimed. The High Court granted an order (mandamus) directing the Aboriginal Land Commissioner to proceed to deal with the land rights application.

The case is also extracted Chapter 14 concerning the improper purpose ground of judicial review. The extract below relates to justiciability. Mason J discusses the evolution of judicial review cases to a point where the courts are now prepared to review the exercise of prerogative and statutory powers by representatives of the Crown.

Mason J

> ***217*** In my view the rule that the acts of the Crown or its representative cannot be impugned has no application to the exercise of a statutory discretion by the Crown in Council or by a Crown representative. The general rule, to the extent to which it now has any application at all, is confined to the exercise of prerogative powers.
>
> The proposition that the acts of the Crown or its representative cannot be impugned, though limited in ambit, has, as might be expected, ancient authority to support it. It reflected the position of the Sovereign as the head and representative of the English state in the seventeenth century. It was only natural that it should be accepted and applied by the King's courts which evolved the doctrine that the King

can do no wrong from the earlier rule that the ***218*** Sovereign could not be sued in his own courts. Needless to say, the authorities related to the exercise of prerogative powers, the conferring of power on the Crown and its representatives by statute being of comparatively recent origin.

For the most part the rule was expressed in absolute or very wide terms. Blackstone, in his *Commentaries on the Laws of England* (1809) Bk 1, p 251, states 'In the exertion therefore of those prerogatives, which the law has given him, the king is irresistible and absolute, according to the forms of the constitution.' Chitty on *Prerogatives of the Crown* (1820), p 6, says 'in the exercise of his lawful prerogatives an unbounded discretion is, generally speaking, left to the King'.

Even so, as de Smith points out in his *Judicial Review of Administrative Action*, 4th ed (1980), p 286, the courts in earlier times took it upon themselves to decide whether a particular prerogative power existed, what was its extent, whether it had been exercised in appropriate form and how far, if at all, it had been superseded by statute.

There was no doubt that an exercise of prerogative power was considered to be immune from attack for mala fides. Likewise, although the grounds on which exercise of a discretionary power might be set aside had not been fully elaborated and refined at that time, there is no doubt that an attack on the exercise of a prerogative power for improper purpose and inadequacy of grounds was regarded as inconsistent with accepted doctrine. So much at least emerges from the authorities which Gibbs J and I discussed in *Barton* v *The Queen* (1980) 147 CLR 75. According to these authorities the prerogative discretions of the Attorney-General to enter a nolle prosequi, to grant or refuse a fiat in relator actions and to file an ex officio information are not subject to curial review ...

219 Generally speaking the discussion in [the cited] and other cases proceeds on the footing that the exercise of prerogative power by the Attorney-General is unexaminable as such, without assigning any particular ground therefor ... As we shall see, the view that the counsels of the Crown are secret is no longer an acceptable basis for excluding acts or decisions of the Crown from judicial review, but for the moment this question may be put to one side. Other bases which have been suggested for the rule, but not generally accepted, are the need to protect the administrative process from unnecessary judicial intervention and the sufficiency of the doctrine of ministerial responsibility.

There is, as the commentators have noted, a contrast between the readiness of the courts to review a statutory discretion and their reluctance to review the prerogative. The difference in approach is none the less soundly based. The statutory discretion is in so many instances readily susceptible to judicial review for a variety of reasons. Its exercise very often affects the right of the citizen; there may be a duty to exercise the discretion one way or another; the discretion may be precisely limited in scope; it may be conferred for a specific or an ascertainable purpose; and it will be exercisable by reference to criteria or considerations express or implied. The prerogative powers lack some or all of these characteristics. Moreover, they are in some instances by reason of their very nature not susceptible of judicial review ... [The cited authorities] suggest that the refusal of the courts to review the exercise of the royal prerogatives relating to war and the ***220*** armed services is based on the view that they are not, by reason of their character and their subject matter, susceptible of judicial review ...

The foundations of the old rule have been undermined. Procedural reforms have overcome the Sovereign's immunity from suit which in turn was the source of the principle that the King can do no wrong. Appropriate as it is that this principle should apply to personal acts of the Sovereign, it is at least questionable whether it should now apply to acts affecting the rights of the citizen which, though undertaken in the name of the Sovereign or his representative, are in reality decisions of the executive government. In the exercise of the prerogative as in other matters the Sovereign and her representatives act in accordance with the advice of her Ministers. This has been one of the important elements in our constitutional development. The continued application of the Crown immunity rule to the exercise of prerogative power is a legal fiction.

An examination of the cases in which the courts have refused to examine the exercise of prerogative powers reveals that most, if not all, of the decisions, can be justified on the ground that the prerogative power in question was not, owing to its nature and subject matter, open to challenge for the reason put forward. The willingness, recently enunciated, of the courts to overrule a Minister's certificate in support of a claim of Crown privilege is an indication that the old rule has been eroded and that the ground stated above should now be recognized as the true basis of the cases on prerogative powers. Crown privilege was formerly regarded as an instance of the prerogative. It is now well settled that the Minister's claim is subject to judicial review and that the courts may look behind the certificate [*Sankey v Whitlam* (1978) 142 CLR 1].

The force of the rule that the acts of the Crown or its representative cannot be impugned has been compromised by the modern authorities indorsing judicial review of the exercise of statutory discretions by the Crown, especially by Ministers of the Crown ... [T]here is much to be said for the view expressed by Lord Denning MR in *Laker Airways Ltd* v *Department of Trade* [1977] QB 643, at p 705 that the exercise of a discretionary prerogative power 'can be ***221*** examined by the courts just as any other discretionary power which is vested in the executive'. The question would then remain whether the exercise of a particular prerogative power is susceptible of review and on what grounds.

In these circumstances should the old rule be extended so as to apply to the exercise of statutory discretions? There are powerful reasons for saying 'No'. As we have seen, the foundations on which the legal fiction was built have crumbled. It has ceased to serve a useful purpose and it is out of harmony with the current approach of the courts to the review of statutory discretions.

[Citations omitted]

Minister for Arts, Heritage and Environment v Peko-Wallsend Ltd (1987) 15 FCR 274

Facts

A group of mining companies (collectively known as 'Peko-EZ') held mineral leases over portions of Kakadu National Park, and had conducted various exploration activities with a view to mining in that area. On 16 September 1986, the federal Cabinet decided to nominate an area of Kakadu National Park, known as 'Stage II', for World Heritage Listing under the *Convention for the Protection of the World Cultural and National Heritage,* opened for signature 16 November 1972, 1037 UNTS 151 (entered into force 17 December 1975). A place nominated for World Heritage Listing could become the subject of a proclamation by the Governor-General under s 6 of the *World Heritage Properties Conservation Act 1983* (Cth), which could prohibit specified activities at the place. Since Peko-EZ's mineral leases fell within Stage II, such a proclamation had the potential to prevent Peko-EZ from going ahead with further exploration or mining.

Peko-EZ commenced proceedings in the Federal Court, seeking an injunction to prevent the Commonwealth from proceeding with the nomination. It argued that the Cabinet decision had been made in breach of the rules of procedural fairness.

At first instance, a judge of the Federal Court issued a declaration 'that the decision of the Executive made on the 16 September 1986 to nominate Stage II of the Kakadu National Park for inclusion on the World Heritage List is void'. The Full Court allowed the appeal, holding that the matter was not justiciable.

Bowen CJ

The prerogative

...

277 The question whether the courts will review a decision made not under a statute but by virtue of the prerogative has not so far been decided in this country. In the United Kingdom in [*Council of Civil Service Unions v Minister for the Civil Service* [1985] AC 374 ('*CSSU* Case')] their Lordships took the view that Executive action was not immune from judicial review merely because it was carried out in pursuance of a power derived from the common law or prerogative rather than a statutory source. A Minister acting under a prerogative power might, depending upon the subject-matter, be under the same duty to act fairly as in the case of his acting under a statutory power. The words 'depending on its subject-matter' were designed to cover matter which were regarded as not justiciable in the courts. Examples given included national security; the making of treaties; the defence of the country; the prerogative of mercy; the grant of honours; the dissolution of Parliament and the appointment of Ministers.

278 ... In my opinion, subject to the exclusion of non-justiciable matters, the courts of this country should now accept responsibility for reviewing the decisions of Ministers or the Governor-General in Council notwithstanding the decisions is carried out in pursuance of a power derived not from statute but from the common law or the prerogative ...

Whether the subject-matter of the decision of 16 September, 1986 is justiciable

The decision of Cabinet on 16 September, 1986 to nominate Stage II of Kakadu National Park for inclusion on the World Heritage List is said to be immune from judicial review because it is a decision made under the prerogative being an act done towards a nation or body under an international treaty.

The decision taken was not taken under the treaty-making power of the Commonwealth.

Nor do I consider it was a decision taken in accordance with an internationally binding obligation flowing from the convention ... I have some doubt whether by reason only of its relationship to the Convention it was non-justiciable.

However, the whole subject matter of the decision involved complex ***279*** policy questions relating to the environment, the rights of Aborigines, mining and the impact on Australia's economic position of allowing or not allowing mining as well as matters affecting private interests ... It appears to me that the subject-matter of the decision in conjunction with its relationship to the terms of the Convention placed the decision beyond review by the court.

Cabinet

... Cabinet is not mentioned in the *Constitution.* It is a body which functions according to convention.

It is to Cabinet that the highest decisions of policy affecting Australia are brought. Often the questions arising involve intense conflict of interests or of opinion in the community. In Cabinet these conflicts have to be resolved. Decisions have to be taken in the public interest, notwithstanding that the lives, interests and rights of some individual citizens may be adversely affected by the decision.

This is not to say that Cabinet should decide matters without considering all relevant material. But there are recognized channels for communicating arguments or submissions. ... Representations may be made to the relevant department or in appropriate cases to the Minister. Every citizen has access to a local Member of Parliament or a Senator in the particular State, who can assist in the advancement of the individual citizen's point of view. The prospect of Cabinet itself ... having to accord a hearing to individuals who may be adversely affected by its decisions, is a daunting one. It could bring the proceedings of Cabinet to a grinding halt.

...

In the present case it would, in my view, be inappropriate for this Court to intervene to set aside a Cabinet decision involving such complex policy considerations as does the decision of 16 September 1986, even if the private interest of the respondents was thought to have been inadequately considered. The matter appears to my mind to lie in the political arena.

Wilcox J

298 The appellants contend that the decision under attack is immune from judicial review; that is, that the legal validity of that decision is not justiciable in a court. They state two reasons, contending that either reason individually is enough; but alternatively relying on the two reasons in combination. Those reasons are, first, the identity of the decision-maker and, secondly, the nature of the decision; namely a decision as to the exercise of the prerogative power of the Crown in connection with an international treaty.

[Editors' note: His Honour discussed the political, non-statutory nature of Cabinet, but then noted that courts could examine the validity of decisions of the Executive Council.]

...

301 The respondents argue that the time has come to equate the position of Cabinet to that of the Executive Council. They point out that the reasons urged in support of the immunity of Cabinet decisions – the doctrine of ministerial responsibility, the fact that decisions often involve policy elements and the general need for confidentiality – are the very same reasons which have ... been held insufficient to exclude the review of Executive Council decisions. I think that there is substance in this. If a case were found in which a statute had reposed in Cabinet – as distinct from a Minister or the Executive Council – the function of making a decision potentially affecting individual rights, it would be difficult to justify a refusal to review that decision.

It is true that difficulties will arise in many cases in which a challenge is made to a Cabinet decision. Not only is there the usual difficulty in relation to a multi-member decisionmaker concerning motives and the matters which were taken into account in making the decision. The rules as to the confidentiality of Cabinet proceedings will sometimes deny to a challenger the material necessary to make out his or her case ... But, with all of these riders, there is no reason of principle to deny relief where the case can be made out ...

[Editors' note: His Honour reviewed the authorities on the justiciability of the exercise of prerogative powers, including the remarks of Mason J in *R v Toohey; Ex parte Northern Land Council* (1981) 151 CLR 170, 219–20, set out earlier in this chapter.]

303 ... [I]n the current state ***304*** of authority, it is not possible to exclude the judicial review of a decision merely because it was one made by the Cabinet, merely because it was a decision taken in the exercise of the prerogative powers of the Crown or merely because the decision combined both these characteristics. The critical matter is the nature and effect of the relevant decision ...

Review in this case, and the application of the rules of natural justice

It is convenient in this case to consider together two questions: whether the subject decision had the characteristics necessary for reviewability and whether it was the type of decision to which the principles of natural justice would apply. ...

305 [I]t is clear that the decision made by Cabinet was disadvantageous to Peko-EZ.

...

But it does not necessarily follow that the decision [was justiciable]. Decisions are made by governments every day which disadvantage individuals, but which are not justiciable ...

Almost every Budget includes decisions to impose direct imposts on individuals within particular classes or who engage in particular activities ... People are advantaged and disadvantaged by decisions to spend, or to refrain from spending, public funds. A Cabinet decision to construct, or not to construct, a public facility in a particular place may have a financially devastating effect upon individuals ...

307 The present case did not relate essentially to the personal circumstances of any individual. It concerned a substantial area of land which the Government regarded as being of national, indeed international, significance and in relation to which many people had concerns of various types.

Having regard to the nature and effect of the decision, the conclusion must be drawn, first, that it was not one having the characteristics of justiciability identified [in the *CCSU Case*] and, secondly, that it did not attract the obligation to accord natural justice to affected persons. Moreover ... although the decision had possible municipal legal significance, the decision primarily involved Australia's international relations. Issues arising out of international relations have widely been regarded as non-justiciable ...

308 In *Koowarta v Bjelke-Petersen* (1982) 153 CLR 168 at 29 Mason J described the possibility of the High Court's reviewing 'the judgment of the Executive and the Parliament that entry into a treaty and its implementation was for Australia's benefit' as 'a course bristling with problems for the Court'. The present case relates to a decision to implement a treaty. It raises the same problem for the courts as a decision to enter into a treaty.

In my opinion it should be concluded that the decision made in this case was not such as to be justiciable or to attract the obligations of natural justice.

[Citations omitted]

Standing to commence judicial review proceedings

Australian Conservation Foundation v Commonwealth (1980) 146 CLR 493

Facts

The Australian Conservation Foundation ('ACF'), an incorporated body, was a national organisation with approximately 6500 members at the time of this litigation. Its principal objects were:

(a) to make every effort to ensure that the air, land and waters of Australia are used with wisdom and foresight and that competing demands upon them are resolved in the best long-term interests of the nation;

(b) to foster the conservation of the distinctive vegetation and fauna and important natural and archaeological features of Australia.

ACF had received grants from, and made submissions to, governments.

Iwasaki Sangyo Company (Australia) Pty Ltd planned a resort and tourist development at Farnborough in central Queensland. Various Commonwealth authorities made decisions that had the effect of approving the development and the foreign exchange transactions associated with it. In the course of the decision-making processes, ACF made submissions to government opposing the development.

ACF sought declarations and injunctive relief against the various decisions in relation to the project. The Commonwealth applied to dismiss the action on the ground that ACF did not have standing. A majority of the High Court (Gibbs, Stephen and Mason JJ, Murphy J dissenting) held that the Council did not have standing, but the Court's explanation of the special interest test has had a major influence on standing cases ever since.

Gibbs J

> ***526*** [T]he action was not brought by the Foundation to assert a private right. It is brought to prevent what is alleged to be a public wrong. The wrong is not one that causes, or threatens to cause, damage to the Foundation, or that affects, or threatens to affect, the interests of the Foundation in any material way. The Foundation seeks to enforce the public law as a matter of principle, as part of an endeavour to achieve its objects and to uphold the values which it was formed to promote. The question is whether, in these circumstances, it has standing to sue.
>
> It is quite clear that an ordinary member of the public, who has no interest other than that which any member of the public has in upholding the law, has no standing to sue to prevent the violation of a public right or to enforce the performance of a public duty ... The assertion of public rights and the prevention of public wrongs by means of [declarations and injunctions] is the responsibility of the Attorney-General, who may proceed either ex officio or on the relation of a private individual. A private citizen who has no special interest is incapable of bringing proceedings for that purpose ...
>
> The rules as to standing are the same whether the plaintiff seeks a declaration or an injunction. In *Boyce* v *Paddington Borough Council* [[1903] 1 Ch 109, 114], Buckley J stated the effect of the earlier authorities as follows:
>
>> A plaintiff can sue without joining the Attorney-General in two cases: first, where the interference with the public right is ***527*** such as that some private right of his is at the same time interfered with ...; and, secondly, where no private right is interfered with, but the plaintiff, in respect of his public right, suffers special damage peculiar to himself from the interference with the public right.
>
> ... The general principle ... that a private person, who is in the same situation as any other member of the public, has no standing to claim either an injunction or a declaration to enforce a public right or duty, has been consistently applied in this Court.
>
> Although the general rule is clear, the formulation of the exceptions to it which Buckley J made in *Boyce* v *Paddington Borough Council* is not altogether satisfactory. Indeed the words which he used are apt to be misleading. His reference to 'special

damage' cannot be limited to actual pecuniary loss, and the words 'peculiar to himself' do not mean that the plaintiff, and no one else, must have suffered damage. However, the expression 'special damage peculiar to himself' in my opinion should be regarded as equivalent in meaning to 'having a special interest in the subject matter of the action' ...

528 Counsel for the Foundation frankly invited us to disregard the existing authorities and devise a new rule of our own, allowing standing to any private citizen to enforce public duties, unless the court in its discretion considered it inadvisable that the action should be allowed to proceed. It is by no means obvious that a rule which leaves it to the Crown (through its representative the Attorney-General) to enforce public duties, and denies standing to a citizen who has no special interest, is a bad one - something can be said on ***529*** both sides of the question. The present case provides an example of the disadvantages entailed by the rule suggested by the Foundation: a decision to approve of an exchange control transaction, the precise nature of which is unknown to the plaintiff, and which, for all the plaintiff knows, has been carried through to completion, might be set aside at the instance of a complete stranger. In any case, if the law is settled, it is our duty to apply it, not to abrogate it. It is for the Parliament, whose members are the elected representatives of the people, to change an established rule if they consider it to be undesirable, and not for judges, unelected and unrepresentative, to determine not what is, but what ought to be, the law.

[Editors' note: His Honour reviewed United States, Canadian and New Zealand authorities.]

530 I would not deny that a person might have a special interest in the preservation of a particular environment. However, an interest, for present purposes, does not mean a mere intellectual or emotional concern. A person is not interested within the meaning of the rule, unless he is likely to gain some advantage, other than the satisfaction of righting a wrong, upholding a principle or winning a contest, if his action succeeds or to suffer some disadvantage, other than a sense of grievance or a debt for costs, if his action fails. A belief, however strongly felt, that the law generally, or a particular law, should be observed, or that conduct of a particular kind should be prevented, does not suffice to give its possessor locus standi. If ***531*** that were not so, the rule requiring special interest would be meaningless. Any plaintiff who felt strongly enough to bring an action could maintain it.

It is quite clear that when the rule is thus understood, the Foundation has no special interest in the preservation of the environment at Farnborough, and of course none in Iwasaki's exchange control transactions. Counsel for the Foundation sought to show an interest in two alternative ways – first, because of the nature of the Foundation and its objects and, secondly, because of the fact that it had sent written comments when the draft environmental impact statement was made available for public comment. The fact that the Foundation is incorporated with particular objects does not strengthen its claim to standing. A natural person does not acquire standing simply by reason of the fact that he holds certain beliefs and wishes to translate them into action, and a body corporate formed to advance the same beliefs is in no stronger position. If it is the fact that some members of the Foundation have a special interest – and it is most unlikely that any would have a special interest to challenge the exchange control transaction - it would not follow that the Foundation has locus standi, for a corporation does not acquire standing because some of its members possess it.

The fact that the Foundation had sent written comments which Iwasaki was required to take into account in revising its draft environmental impact statement did not give the Foundation standing to bring the present action. A person who is concerned enough about proposed action to furnish his comments on it does not necessarily have any interest in the proposed action in the relevant sense. The fact that the Foundation sent the written comments, as permitted by the administrative procedures, is logically irrelevant to the question whether it has a special interest giving it standing. That fact would only have some significance in relation to this question if the administrative procedures revealed an intention that a person who sent written comments thereby acquired further rights. As I have endeavoured to show, that is not the case ...

532 Finally, it was submitted that the question of standing should not be dealt with as a preliminary issue, but should await decision until the merits of the case have been examined. In *Robinson v Western Australian Museum* [(1977) 138 CLR 283, 302], I pointed out that the court has a discretion whether to determine the question of standing immediately or to proceed to deal with the merits without first resolving the ***533*** question of standing. In the present case, in my opinion, it was clearly more convenient to deal with the question of standing ... before proceeding to consider the merits.

[Citations omitted]

Onus v Alcoa of Australia Ltd (1981) 149 CLR 27

Facts

Alcoa of Australia Ltd planned to build an aluminium smelter on land that the company owned at Portland in Victoria. The site contained relics from the settlement of the Gournditch-jmara Aboriginal people. Lorraine Onus and Christina Frankland, who were members of the Gournditch-jmara people, sought injunctions in the Supreme Court of Victoria to restrain Alcoa from carrying out work at the site. They based their claim on the *Archaeological and Aboriginal Relics Preservation Act 1972* (Vic) ('the Relics Act'). The Gournditch-jmara people were the traditional inhabitants of the area, but there was no special provision under the legislation for their involvement. The judge at first instance held that the applicants did not have standing and an appeal to the Full Court of the Supreme Court was dismissed. Ms Onus and Ms Frankland appealed to the High Court. The High Court held that as custodians of the cultural relics, the applicants were able to establish standing. The appeal was allowed and the matter remitted to the Supreme Court of Victoria.

Gibbs CJ

35 The provisions of the Act as a whole show that the Act was passed for the benefit of the public at large, with a view to the conservation of relics which are regarded as being of interest and value not only to Aborigines but also to archaeologists and anthropologists and indeed to Australians generally. It is quite impossible to hold that the Act confers any private rights on Aborigines or any class of them.

The case is therefore one in which two private citizens who cannot show that any right of their own has been infringed bring an action for the purpose of restraining another private citizen (Alcoa) from breaking the criminal law by acting in contravention of ... the *Relics Act.*

The question is whether they have standing to bring the action. If an attempt were made to frame an ideal law governing the standing of a private person to sue for such a purpose, it would be necessary to give weight to conflicting considerations. On the one hand it may be thought that in a community which professes to live by the rule of law the courts should be open to anyone who genuinely seeks to prevent the law from being ignored or violated.

On the other hand, if standing is accorded to any citizen to sue to prevent breaches of the law by another, there exists the possibility, not only that the processes of the law will be abused by busybodies and cranks and persons actuated by malice, but also that persons or groups who feel strongly enough about an issue will be prepared to put some other citizen, with whom they have had no relationship, and whose actions have not affected them except by causing them intellectual or emotional concern, to very great cost and inconvenience in defending the legality of his actions. Moreover, ideal rules as to standing would not fail to take account of the fact that it is desirable, in an adversary system, that the courts should decide only a real controversy between parties each of whom has a direct stake in the outcome of the proceedings. The principle which has been settled by the courts does attempt a reconciliation between these considerations. That principle was recently stated in *Australian Conservation Foundation Inc v The Commonwealth* [(1980) 146 CLR 493]. A plaintiff has no standing to bring an action to prevent the violation of a public right if he has no ***36*** interest in the subject matter beyond that of any other member of the public; if no private right of his is interfered with he has standing to sue only if he has a special interest in the subject matter of the action. The rule is obviously a flexible one since, as was pointed out in that case, the question what is a sufficient interest will vary according to the nature of the subject matter of the litigation.

It seems to me that the appellants have an interest in the subject matter of the present action which is greater than that of other members of the public and indeed greater than that of other persons of Aboriginal descent who are not members of the Gournditch-jmara people. The appellants, and other members of the Gournditch-jmara people, would be more particularly affected than other members of the Australian community by the destruction of the relics. The appellants claim that, in common with other members of the Gournditch-jmara people, they are the custodians of the relics according to the laws and customs of those people. They claim that the relics are of cultural and spiritual importance to them, and that they have used the relics to teach their children the culture of their people.

The main reason advanced in the Supreme Court for denying standing to the appellants was that their interest was entirely emotional and intellectual. Starke J relied upon statements by members of this Court in *Australian Conservation Foundation Inc v The Commonwealth,* [at (1980) 146 CLR, 493, 530, 539, 548] ... ***37*** Of course, a special interest is none the less sufficient if it is accompanied by an emotional or intellectual concern. The present is not a case in which a plaintiff sues in an attempt to give effect to his beliefs or opinions on a matter which does not affect him personally except in so far as he holds beliefs or opinions about it. The appellants claim not only that their relics have a cultural and spiritual significance, but that they are custodians of them according to the laws and customs of their people, and that they actually use them. The position of a small community of Aboriginal people of a particular group living in a particular area which that group has traditionally occupied, and which claims an interest in relics of their ancestors found in that area, is very different indeed from that of a diverse group of white Australians associated by some common opinion on a matter of social policy which might equally concern any other Australian.

[Citations omitted]

Administrative Decisions (Judicial Review) Act 1977 (Cth)

[As at 1 December 2022]

3 Interpretation

...

(4) In this Act:

(a) a reference to a person aggrieved by a decision includes a reference:

(i) to a person whose interests are adversely affected by the decision; or

(ii) in the case of a decision by way of the making of a report or recommendation – to a person whose interests would be adversely affected if a decision were, or were not, made in accordance with the report or recommendation; and

(b) a reference to a person aggrieved by conduct that has been, is being, or is proposed to be, engaged in for the purpose of making a decision or by a failure to make a decision includes a reference to a person whose interests are or would be adversely affected by the conduct or failure.

...

5 Applications for review of decisions

(1) A person who is aggrieved by a decision to which this Act applies that is made after

(2) the commencement of this Act may apply to the Federal Court or the Federal Circuit and Family Court of Australia (Division 2) for an order of review in respect of the decision on any one or more of the following grounds ...[1]

12 Application to be made a party to a proceeding

(1) A person interested in a decision, in conduct that has been, is being, or is proposed to be, engaged in for the purpose of making a decision, or in a failure to make a decision, being a decision, conduct or failure in relation to which an application has been made to the Federal Court or the Federal Circuit and Family Court of Australia (Division 2) under this Act, may apply to the court to be made a party to the application.

(2) The court may, in its discretion:

(a) grant the application either unconditionally or subject to such conditions as it thinks fit; or

(b) refuse the application.

Argos Pty Ltd v Corbell (2014) 254 CLR 394

Administrative Decisions (Judicial Review) Act 1989 (ACT)

[As at relevant date]

3B Meaning of person aggrieved

(1) For this Act, a reference to a person aggrieved by a decision includes a reference to—

(a) a person whose interests are adversely affected by the decision; and

(b) for a decision by way of the making of a report or recommendation—a person whose interests would be adversely affected if a decision were, or were not, made in accordance with the report or recommendation.

...

5 Applications for review of decisions

(1) A person aggrieved by a decision to which this Act applies may apply to the Supreme Court for an order of review in relation to the decision on any 1 or more of the following grounds: ...

Facts

The ACT Minister for the Environment and Sustainable Development approved an application by Nikias Nominees Pty Ltd (referred to in the High Court as 'the second respondent') to develop a shopping centre (including a supermarket) in the Canberra suburb of Giralang.

1 The remainder of s 5, including the grounds, is set out in Chapter 11 at p 319.

Three entities commenced proceedings under the *Administrative Decisions (Judicial Review) Act 1989* (ACT) (referred to by the High Court as the AD(JR) Act), challenging the Minister's decision to approve the development. These were:

- Argos Pty Ltd, which held a lease over Crown Land at Kaleen (a suburb adjacent to Giralang) ('the first appellant');
- The trustees of several trusts that subleased the land at Kaleen, on which they operated a supermarket ('the second appellant'); and
- The Combined Residents Action Association Inc, which operated a supermarket in Evatt, another suburb near Giralang ('the third appellant').

At first instance, an issue arose as to whether the plaintiffs were 'persons aggrieved' for the purposes of the *Administrative Decisions (Judicial Review) Act 1989* (ACT). The trustees and the Combined Residents Action Association Inc argued that the decision to approve the development affected their economic interests because the new supermarket would increase competition and thereby lead to a loss of profits for their existing supermarkets. Argos Pty Ltd argued that the loss of trade at the Kaleen supermarket might force the closure of that supermarket, which might in turn affect the economic interests of Argos Pty Ltd as landlord.

Both at first instance and on appeal, the Supreme Court of the ACT held that none of the plaintiffs had standing, because the effect of the decision on the plaintiffs' interests was too indirect and remote; and mere detriment to a business's economic interests could not give rise to standing. The plaintiffs appealed to the High Court.

The High Court held that the second and third appellants had standing, but the first appellant did not. (Gageler J would have held that all three appellants had standing). The case (without Argos Pty Ltd) was remitted to the ACT Court of Appeal to consider the appeal on its merits. The ACT Court of Appeal's decision on the remitter, *Cavo Pty Ltd v Minister for the Environment and Sustainable Development* (2016) 313 FLR 241, is extracted in Chapter 15 at pp 449–54.

French CJ and Keane J

> ***408*** [35] ... [The relevant planning legislation does not evince] any intention to permit decision-makers to accommodate private traders' desires to be protected from competition per se. In this case, however, the second and third appellants demonstrated, as a matter of fact, that their businesses will suffer a loss in profitability as a result of the decision which they sought to challenge. And if their challenge to the lawfulness of the decision proves to have merit, the consequences of the competitive pressures resulting from the decision they seek to challenge can properly be described as a situation of 'unfair competition', rather than mere competition.
>
> [36] The position of the first appellant is different. There was no finding of fact that the second appellant's business would be likely to fail as a result of increased competition consequent upon the implementation of the Development Proposal. As a result, there was no finding that the first appellant would, in turn, lose the benefit of its lease to the second appellant. Nor was there a finding that, in the event of the

failure of the second appellant, the lettable value of the first appellant's land would be reduced by the implementation of the proposed development. The appeal by the first appellant fails at this point ...

Interests and relevant considerations

409 [41] The first respondent submitted that the standing provision of the *AD(JR) Act* has to be applied with reference to the scope and purpose of the statute under which the decision under review was made. The second and third respondents submitted in similar vein that standing was to be determined by reference to the nature and subject matter of the litigation including the objects of the statute conferring power to make the decision. Those submissions should not be accepted.

[42] The test for standing to apply for review of a decision under the *AD(JR) Act* is expressed in that Act. The applicant must be 'a person aggrieved', a criterion which may be satisfied if the applicant is a person whose interests are adversely affected by the decision. The text of the criterion, on its face, does not allow for its expansion or contraction according to the scope and purpose of the enactment under which the decision is made. It is not to be read or applied with reference to normative considerations based on the policy of the enactment. To do so by reference to individual enactments would undermine an important purpose of the *AD(JR) Act*, which was to simplify judicial review processes.

[43] Consistently with that proposition it will be necessary to have regard to the enactment under which the impugned decision is made and the legal effect and operation of the decision in order to determine how the interests of the applicant for review may be adversely affected or the applicant otherwise a person aggrieved.

...

411 [47] It may be accepted that the public interest in town planning is properly and relevantly served by ensuring that local shopping centres do not become wastelands by excessive competition between traders. ... It may also be accepted that [a criterion in the statute] is concerned with the public interest, and not the interest of individual traders in being protected from competition. But the circumstance that an effect upon a private interest is not a consideration relevant to the making of the decision does not mean that such an interest is not adversely affected by the decision so as to afford an affected person standing to challenge the lawfulness of the decision on grounds that *are* relevant to its validity.

[48] In summary, as Lockhart J said in the *Right to Life Case* [*Right to Life Association (NSW) Inc v Secretary, Department of Human Services and Health* (1995) 56 FCR 50, 65], '[t]he term a "person aggrieved" is not a restrictive one; it is of very wide import'. The courts should not be astute to graft restrictions onto the general language of s 3B(1)(a) of the *AD(JR) Act*. It must be borne in mind that the *AD(JR) Act* is intended to facilitate judicial review of administrative decisions made under a wide range of statutes and having a wide range of practical effects upon members of the community. The availability of judicial review serves to promote the rule of law and to improve the quality of administrative decision making as well as vindicating the

interests of persons affected in a practical way by administrative decision-making. Accordingly, the scope of s 3B(1)(a) of the *AD(JR) Act* should not be artificially narrowed by glosses upon its broad language.

Hayne and Bell JJ

415 [66] The *AD(JR) Act* provides for judicial review of decisions made under many different enactments. It should go without saying that regard must be had to the subject matter, scope and purpose of the *AD(JR) Act* in construing the words of s 3B(1)(a): 'a person whose interests are adversely affected by the decision.' But content cannot be given to that expression, in its application to a particular decision, without regard to the subject matter, scope and purpose of the Act ***416*** under which the decision was made and the proper construction of that Act. Only then can the relationship between the impugned decision and the interests said to be affected adversely be properly identified.

[67] Often, perhaps very often, the connection between decision, interests and asserted effect will be obvious and evidently relevant. But that may not always be so, and in such a case it will be necessary to identify both the interest of the applicant relied on, and whether it is adversely affected by the decision, having regard to the proper construction and application of the Act under which the impugned decision was made.

[68] Reference is not made to the Act under which the decision is made for the purpose of giving some different meaning to the words of s 3B(1)(a) of the *AD(JR) Act.* Rather, reference to the Act under which the decision is made will elucidate whether there is, in the circumstances of the decision in question, a relevant and sufficient connection between the decision, the applicant's interests and the asserted effect on those interests to show that the applicant is a 'person aggrieved' by the decision ...

417 [73] It may well be right to say, as the second and third respondents did, that the *Planning Act* does not have as an object or purpose the 'protection of the commercial interests of [individual] owners of shopping centres or supermarkets, or the protection of existing supermarkets from competition'. But it by no means follows that an individual owner or operator is not adversely affected by a planning decision that will have direct commercial consequences for that owner or operator. As the *Planning Act* makes plain in its statement of objects (s 6), it is concerned with the general commercial health of the Territory. So much appears from the use of the expressions 'the orderly and sustainable development of the ACT', 'the social, environmental and economic aspirations of the people of the ACT', and 'sound financial principles'. Claims of individual adverse effect are not irrelevant to the pursuit of those general objectives.

[Citations omitted]

Privative clauses

Plaintiff S157/2002 v Commonwealth (2003) 211 CLR 476

Migration Act 1958 (Cth)

[As at relevant date]

PART 8—JUDICIAL REVIEW

474 Decisions under Act are final

(1) A privative clause decision:

(a) is final and conclusive; and

(b) must not be challenged, appealed against, reviewed, quashed or called in question in any court; and

(c) is not subject to prohibition, mandamus, injunction, declaration or certiorari in any court on any account.

(2) In this section:

privative clause decision means a decision of an administrative character made, proposed to be made, or required to be made, as the case may be, under this Act or under a regulation or other instrument made under this Act (whether in the exercise of a discretion or not), other than a decision referred to in subsection (4) or (5).

(3) A reference in this section to a decision includes a reference to the following:

(a) granting, making, suspending, cancelling, revoking or refusing to make an order or determination;

(b) granting, giving, suspending, cancelling, revoking or refusing to give a certificate, direction, approval, consent or permission (including a visa);

(c) granting, issuing, suspending, cancelling, revoking or refusing to issue an authority or other instrument;

(d) imposing, or refusing to remove, a condition or restriction;

(e) making or revoking, or refusing to make or revoke, a declaration, demand or requirement;

(f) retaining, or refusing to deliver up, an article;

(g) doing or refusing to do any other act or thing;

(h) conduct preparatory to the making of a decision, including the taking of evidence or the holding of an inquiry or investigation;

(i) a decision on review of a decision, irrespective of whether the decision on review is taken under this Act or a regulation or other instrument under this Act, or under another Act;

(j) a failure or refusal to make a decision.

(4) [Table setting out decisions that are not privative clause decisions] ...

(5) The regulations may specify that a decision, or a decision included in a class of decisions, under this Act, or under regulations or another instrument under this Act, is not a privative clause decision.

Facts

A citizen of Bangladesh applied for a protection visa in Australia. A delegate of the Minister refused the application. The Refugee Review Tribunal affirmed the delegate's decision twice. Section 474 of the *Migration Act 1958* (Cth) appeared to prevent judicial review. The applicant commenced proceedings in the High Court under s 75(v) of the *Constitution* seeking a declaration that s 474 was invalid.

The High Court held that s 474 was valid but did not prevent review for jurisdictional error. A jurisdictional error was not a decision made 'under this Act' and so was not a decision to which s 474 applied.

Gaudron, McHugh, Gummow, Kirby and Hayne JJ

> ***499*** [54] The construction of legislation containing provisions such as s 474 of the Act has a particular, but not entirely satisfactory, history. For the moment, it is necessary to refer only to the decision in *R v Hickman; Ex parte Fox and Clinton* [(1945) 70 CLR 598]. Doubtless because of that decision and, also, because of the terms of s 75(v) of the *Constitution,* the Commonwealth contends that s 474(1) is not to be construed as totally excluding judicial review ...
>
> [56] In *Hickman,* a question arose as to the effect of reg 17 of the *National Security (Coal Mining Industry Employment) Regulations 1941* (Cth), made under the *National Security Act 1939* (Cth) and thus supported by the defence power. ... ***500*** Dixon J said of reg 17:
>
> > The particular regulation is expressed in a manner that has grown familiar. ... [T]he interpretation of provisions of the general nature of reg 17 is well established. They are not interpreted as meaning to set at large the courts or other judicial bodies to whose decision they relate. Such a clause is interpreted as meaning that no decision which is in fact given by the body concerned shall be invalidated on the ground that it has not conformed to the requirements governing its proceedings or the exercise of its authority or has not confined its acts within the limits laid down by the instrument giving it authority, provided always that its decision is a bona fide attempt to exercise its power, that it relates to the subject matter of the legislation, and that it is reasonably capable of reference to the power given to the body.
>
> [57] It should be noted at once that, in the passage last quoted, Dixon J was not speaking of reg 17, but of privative clauses generally. Even so, it is important to appreciate that his Honour's observations were confined to 'decision[s] ... in fact given'. Moreover and as later decisions of this Court have made clear, the expression 'reasonably capable of reference to the power given to the body', has been treated as signifying that it must 'not on its face go beyond ... power'. Thus, even on this general statement, a privative clause cannot protect against a failure to make a decision required by the legislation in which that clause is found or against a decision which, on its face, exceeds jurisdiction.
>
> [58] As to the effect of the privative clause actually considered in *Hickman,* Dixon J first noted that the Parliament could neither 'give power to any judicial or other

authority' in excess of constitutional power nor 'impose limits upon the ... authority of a body ... with the intention that any excess of that authority means invalidity, and ... at ***501*** the same time ... deprive this Court of authority to restrain the invalid action ... by prohibition'. Rather, if legislation purports to impose limits on authority and contains a privative clause, it is, so his Honour said, 'a question of interpretation of the whole legislative instrument whether transgression of the limits, so long as done bona fide and bearing on its face every appearance of an attempt to pursue the power, necessarily spells invalidity'. And in that process, according to his Honour, an attempt should be made to 'reconcile' the apparently conflicting legislative provisions.

...

[60] It follows from *Hickman,* and it is made clear by subsequent cases, that the so- called '*Hickman* principle' is simply a rule of construction allowing for the reconciliation of apparently conflicting statutory provisions. Once this is accepted, as it must be, it follows that there can be no general rule as to the meaning or effect of privative clauses. Rather, the meaning of a privative clause must be ascertained from its terms; and if that meaning appears to conflict with the provision pursuant to which some action has been taken or some decision made, its effect will depend entirely on the outcome of its reconciliation with that other provision.

Privative clauses and the process of reconciling legislative provisions

[61] It was said in *R v Coldham; Ex parte Australian Workers' Union* [(1983) 153 CLR 415, 418 (Mason A-CJ and Brennan J)] that, where there is an inconsistency between a privative clause and other statutory provisions:

> The inconsistency is resolved by reading the two provisions together and giving effect to each. The privative clause is taken into account in ascertaining what the apparent restriction or restraint ***502*** actually signifies in order to determine whether the situation is one in which prohibition lies.

As a general statement, so much may be accepted. However, it provides little guidance as to the manner in which a privative clause is taken into account or the light it sheds on the restriction or restraint in question.

[62] On behalf of the Commonwealth, it was contended that s 474 should first be construed as meaning and intended to mean that decisions are protected so long as there has been a bona fide attempt to exercise the power in question, that they relate to the subject matter of the legislation and are reasonably capable of reference to the power. Then it is said that, being a later provision than those by which particular powers are conferred, s 474 should be construed as impliedly repealing all limitations on those powers leaving only constitutional limitations and those which derive from s 474. In terms, the argument was that s 474 'enlarges the powers of decision-makers so that their decisions are valid so long as they comply with the three *Hickman* provisos'.

...

[64] [It is incorrect to say] that a privative clause is construed as meaning that decisions are protected so long as they conform to 'the three *Hickman* provisos'. Rather,

the position is that the 'protection' which the privative clause 'purports to afford' will be inapplicable unless those provisos are satisfied. And to ascertain what protection a privative clause purports to afford, it is necessary to have regard to the terms of the particular clause in question. Thus, contrary to the submissions for the Commonwealth, it is inaccurate to describe the outcome in a situation where the provisos are satisfied as an 'expansion' or 'extension' of the powers of the decision-makers in question.

[65] There are other difficulties with the argument for the Common- ***503*** wealth. The process of construction for which it contends is not a process of construing the legislation as a whole. It is a process which places a construction on one provision, the privative clause, and asserts that all other provisions may be disregarded. That process ignores what Dixon J said in [*R v Murray; Ex parte Proctor* (1949) 77 CLR 387] was a 'second step in [the process of] interpreting the whole legislative instrument', namely:

> to consider whether particular limitations on power and specific requirements as to the manner in which the tribunal shall be constituted or shall exercise its power are so expressed that they must be taken to mean that observance of the limitations and compliance with the requirements are essential to valid action.
>
> His Honour explained that: a clearly expressed specific intention of [that] kind can hardly give way to the general intention indicated by ... a [privative clause]. ...

[67] So far as it was contended on behalf of the Commonwealth that s 474 effected an implied repeal of statutory limitations on authority or powers conferred by the Act, the argument seeks to give s 474 an effect which ... exceeds anything that was said in *Hickman*.

504 [68] More fundamentally, the method of reconciliation by implied repeal of limitations or restraints in the Act on the exercise of power must be rejected because it seeks to give to s 474 a meaning which its terms cannot bear. It seeks to give to that section a meaning that is descriptive of a recognised limitation on the effectiveness of privative clauses generally and ignores the words of the section which, in terms, limit access to the courts. Accordingly, the argument that s 474 effected an implied repeal of all statutory limitations and restraints must be rejected.

[69] Although s 474 does not purport to effect a repeal of statutory limitations or restraints, it should be noted that it may be that, by reference to the words of s 474, some procedural or other requirements laid down by the Act are to be construed as not essential to the validity of a decision. However, that is a matter that can only be determined by reference to the requirement in issue in a particular case.

[70] Of course, the process of reconciliation ... which may result in some procedural or other requirement being construed as not essential to the validity of an act or decision, is necessary only if there is an apparent conflict between the provisions which impose those requirements and the privative clause in question. Thus, if reliance is placed on a privative clause, the first step must be to ascertain its meaning or, as Dixon J put it in *Murray*, to ascertain 'the protection it purports to afford'.

Construction of s 474 of the Act

[71] There are two basic rules of construction which apply to the interpretation of privative clauses. The first, which applies in the case of privative clauses in legislation enacted by the Parliament of the Commonwealth, is that 'if there is an opposition between the Constitution and any such provision, it should be resolved by adopting [an] interpretation [consistent with the Constitution if] that is fairly open'.

505 [72] The second basic rule, which applies to privative clauses generally, is that it is presumed that the Parliament does not intend to cut down the jurisdiction of the courts save to the extent that the legislation in question expressly so states or necessarily implies. Accordingly, privative clauses are strictly construed.

[73] Quite apart from s 75(v), there are other constitutional requirements that are necessarily to be borne in mind in construing a provision such as s 474 of the Act. A privative clause cannot operate so as to oust the jurisdiction which other paragraphs of s 75 confer on this Court, including that conferred by s 75(iii) ... Further, a privative clause cannot operate so as to allow a non-judicial tribunal or other non-judicial decision-making authority to exercise the judicial power of the Commonwealth. Thus, it cannot confer on a non-judicial body the power to determine conclusively the limits of its own jurisdiction ...

[74] As previously indicated, it was argued on behalf of the plaintiff that s 474(1)(c) of the Act is directly inconsistent with s 75(v) of the *Constitution*. However, s 474(1)(c) cannot be read in isolation from the definition of 'privative clause decision' in s 474(2). That definition relevantly confines 'privative clause decision[s]' to decisions 'made, proposed to be made, or required to be made ... under this Act'.

[75] When regard is had to the phrase 'under this Act' in s 474(2) of the Act, the words of that sub-section are not apt to refer either to ***506*** decisions purportedly made under the Act or, as some of the submissions made on behalf of the Commonwealth might suggest, to decisions of the kind that might be made under the Act. Moreover, if the words of the sub-section were to be construed in either of those ways, s 474(1)(c) would be in direct conflict with s 75(v) of the *Constitution* and, thus, invalid. Further, they would confer authority on a non-judicial decision-maker of the Commonwealth to determine conclusively the limits of its own jurisdiction and, thus, at least in some cases, infringe the mandate implicit in the text of Ch III of the *Constitution* that the judicial power of the Commonwealth be exercised only by the courts named and referred to in s 71.

[76] Once it is accepted, as it must be, that s 474 is to be construed conformably with Ch III of the *Constitution*, specifically, s 75, the expression 'decision[s] ... made under this Act' must be read so as to refer to decisions which involve neither a failure to exercise jurisdiction nor an excess of the jurisdiction conferred by the Act. Indeed so much is required as a matter of general principle. This Court has clearly held that an administrative decision which involves jurisdictional error is 'regarded, in law, as no decision at all'. Thus, if there has been jurisdictional error because, for example, of a failure to discharge 'imperative duties' or to observe 'inviolable limitations or restraints', the decision in question cannot properly be described in the terms used in s 474(2) as 'a decision ... made under this Act' and is, thus, not a 'privative clause decision' as defined in s 474(2) and (3) of the Act.

[77] To say that a decision that involves jurisdictional error is not 'a decision … made under [the] Act' is not to deny that it may be necessary to engage in the reconciliation process earlier discussed to ascertain whether the failure to observe some procedural or other requirement of the Act constitutes an error which has resulted in a failure to exercise jurisdiction or in the decision-maker exceeding its jurisdiction.

…

Constitutional validity of s 474 of the Act

… ***508*** [83] Because, as this Court has held, the constitutional writs of prohibition and mandamus are available only for jurisdictional error and because s 474 of the Act does not protect decisions involving jurisdictional error, s 474 does not, in that regard conflict with s 75(v) of the *Constitution* and, thus, is valid in its application to the proceedings which the plaintiff would initiate. The plaintiff asserts jurisdictional error by reason of a denial to him of procedural fairness and thus s 474, whilst valid, does not upon its true construction protect the decision of which the plaintiff complains. A decision flawed for reasons of a failure to comply with the principles of natural justice is not a 'privative clause decision' within s 474(2) of the Act.

General principles

511 [98] It is important to emphasise that the difference in understanding what has been decided about privative clauses is real and substantive; it is not some verbal or logical quibble. It is real and substantive because it reflects two fundamental constitutional propositions … ***512*** First, the jurisdiction of this Court to grant relief under s 75(v) of the *Constitution* cannot be removed by or under a law made by the Parliament. Specifically, the jurisdiction to grant s 75(v) relief where there has been jurisdictional error by an officer of the Commonwealth cannot be removed. Secondly, the judicial power of the Commonwealth cannot be exercised otherwise than in accordance with Ch III. The Parliament cannot confer on a non-judicial body the power to conclusively determine the limits of its own jurisdiction.

[99] To understand the three *Hickman* provisos as qualifying the powers of those who make privative clause decisions, rather than qualifying the protection which the privative clause affords, either assumes that the Act on its true construction provides no other jurisdictional limitation on the relevant decision making or other power or it assumes that the repository of the power can decide the limits of its own jurisdiction. For the reasons given earlier, the first assumption is wrong. The alternative assumption would contravene Ch III.

…

513 [103] Finally, the issues decided in these proceedings are not merely issues of a technical kind involving the interpretation of the contested provisions of the Act. The Act must be read in the context of the operation of s 75 of the *Constitution*. That section, and specifically s 75(v), introduces into the *Constitution* of the Commonwealth an entrenched minimum provision of judicial review … The provision of the constitutional writs and the conferral upon this Court of an irremovable jurisdiction to issue them to an officer of the Commonwealth constitutes a textual reinforcement for what

Dixon J said about the significance of the rule of law for the Constitution in *Australian Communist Party v The Commonwealth* [(1951) 83 CLR 1, 193]. In that case, his Honour stated that the *Constitution*:

> is an instrument framed in accordance with many traditional conceptions, to some of which it gives effect, as, for example, in separating the judicial power from other functions of government, others of which are simply assumed. Among these I think that it may fairly be said that the rule of law forms an assumption.

[104] The reservation to this Court by the *Constitution* of the jurisdiction in all matters in which the named constitutional writs or an injunction are sought against an officer of the Commonwealth is a means of ***514*** assuring to all people affected that officers of the Commonwealth obey the law and neither exceed nor neglect any jurisdiction which the law confers on them. The centrality, and protective purpose, of the jurisdiction of this Court in that regard places significant barriers in the way of legislative attempts (by privative clauses or otherwise) to impair judicial review of administrative action. Such jurisdiction exists to maintain the federal compact by ensuring that propounded laws are constitutionally valid and ministerial or official action lawful and within jurisdiction. In any written constitution, where there are disputes over such matters, there must be an authoritative decision-maker. Under the *Constitution* of the Commonwealth the ultimate decision-maker in all matters where there is a contest, is this Court. The Court must be obedient to its constitutional function. In the end, pursuant to s 75 of the *Constitution,* this limits the powers of the Parliament or of the Executive to avoid, or confine, judicial review.

[Citations omitted]

Kirk v Industrial Court of New South Wales (2010) 239 CLR 531

Industrial Relations Act 1996 (NSW)

[As at relevant date]

179 Finality of decisions

(1) A decision of the Commission (however constituted) is final and may not be appealed against, reviewed, quashed or called into question by any court or tribunal.

(2) Proceedings of the Commission (however constituted) may not be prevented from being brought, prevented from being continued, terminated or called into question by any court or tribunal.

(3) This section extends to proceedings brought in a court or tribunal in respect of a decision or proceedings of the Commission on an issue of fact or law.

(4) This section extends to proceedings brought in a court or tribunal in respect of a purported decision of the Commission on an issue of the jurisdiction of the Commission, but does not extend to any such purported decision of:

(a) the Full Bench of the Commission in Court Session, or

(b) the Commission in Court Session if the Full Bench refuses to give leave to appeal the decision.

(5) This section extends to proceedings brought in a court or tribunal for any relief or remedy, whether by order in the nature of prohibition, certiorari or mandamus, by injunction or declaration or otherwise.

(6) This section is subject to the exercise of a right of appeal to a Full Bench of the Commission conferred by this or any other Act or law.

(7) In this section:

decision includes any award or order.

Facts

The case concerned liability under the *Occupational Health and Safety Act 1983* (NSW) of a farm owner, Graeme Kirk, for the death of a farm manager in a workplace accident. The Industrial Court of New South Wales convicted and sentenced Mr Kirk. Mr Kirk sought orders in the nature or certiorari to quash the decision of the Industrial Court from the Court of Appeal (New South Wales). The Court of Appeal dismissed the application. On appeal, the High Court held that the Industrial Court (NSW) had made jurisdictional errors by misconstruing the *Occupational Health and Safety Act 1983* (NSW) and failing to comply with the rules of evidence.

Extracts concerning the supervisory jurisdiction of the State Supreme Courts and the concept of jurisdictional error are in Chapter 9 at pp 247–49. The extract below considers the effect of the privative clause in s 179 of the *Industrial Relations Act 1996* (NSW). The High Court held that the privative clause did not prevent review for jurisdictional error by the New South Wales Supreme Court.

French CJ, Gummow, Hayne, Crennan, Kiefel and Bell JJ

579 [93] Finality or privative provisions have been a prominent feature in the Australian legal landscape for many years. The existence and operation of provisions of that kind are important in considering whether the decisions of particular inferior courts or tribunals are intended to be final. They thus bear directly upon the second of the premises that underpin the decision in [*Craig* v *South Australia* (1995) 184 CLR 163] (that finality of decision is a virtue). The operation of a privative provision is, however, affected by constitutional considerations. More particularly, although a privative provision demonstrates a legislative purpose favouring finality, questions arise about the extent to which the provision can be given an operation that immunises the decisions of an inferior court or tribunal from judicial review, yet remain consistent with the constitutional framework for the Australian judicial system.

[94] Understanding the law relating to privative provisions must begin from the proposition, stated by Dixon J in *R v Hickman; Ex parte Fox and Clinton* [(1945) 70 CLR 598, 617], that:

> if in one provision it is said that certain conditions shall be observed, and in a later provision of the same instrument that, notwithstanding they are not observed, what is done is not to be challenged, there then arises a contradiction, and effect must be given to the whole legislative instrument by a process of reconciliation.

But the question presented by a privative provision is not just a conundrum of contrariety requiring a resolution of competing elements of the one legislative instrument.

[Editors' note: Their Honours referred to the constitutional principles applying to privative clauses in legislation, set out in *Plaintiff S157/2002 v Commonwealth* (2003) 211 CLR 476, 512 [98], extracted in this chapter at pp 298–304.]

...

580 [96] In considering State legislation, it is necessary to take account of the requirement of Ch III of the *Constitution* that there be a body fitting the description 'the Supreme Court of a State', and the constitutional corollary that 'it is beyond the legislative power of a State so to alter the constitution or character of its Supreme Court that it ceases to meet the constitutional description'.

[97] At federation, each of the Supreme Courts referred to in s 73 of the *Constitution* had jurisdiction that included such jurisdiction as the Court of Queen's Bench had in England. It followed that each had 'a general power to issue the writ [of certiorari] to any inferior Court' in the State. Victoria and South Australia, intervening, pointed out that statutory privative provisions had been enacted by colonial legislatures seeking to cut down the availability of certiorari. But in *Colonial Bank of Australasia* v *Willan*, the Privy Council said [(1874) LR 5 PC 417, 442] of such provisions that:

> It is, however, scarcely necessary to observe that the effect of [such a privative provision] is not absolutely to deprive the Supreme Court of its power to issue a writ of certiorari to bring up the proceedings of the inferior Court, but to control and limit its action on such writ. *There are numerous cases in the books which establish that, notwithstanding the privative clause in a statute, the Court of Queen's Bench will grant a certiorari;* but some of those authorities establish, and none are inconsistent with, the proposition that in any such case that Court will not quash the order removed, except upon the ground either of a manifest defect of jurisdiction in the tribunal that made it, or of manifest fraud in the party procuring it.

[Emphasis added by French CJ, Gummow, Hayne, Crennan, Kiefel and Bell JJ.]

That is, accepted doctrine at the time of federation was that the jurisdiction of the colonial Supreme Courts to grant certiorari for jurisdictional error was not denied by a statutory privative provision.

[98] The supervisory jurisdiction of the Supreme Courts was at federation, and remains, the mechanism for the determination and the enforcement of the limits on the exercise of State executive and judicial power by persons and bodies other than the Supreme Court. ***581*** That supervisory role of the Supreme Courts exercised

through the grant of prohibition, certiorari and mandamus (and habeas corpus) was, and is, a defining characteristic of those courts. And because, 'with such exceptions and subject to such regulations as the Parliament prescribes', s 73 of the *Constitution* gives this Court appellate jurisdiction to hear and determine appeals from all judgments, decrees, orders and sentences of the Supreme Courts, the exercise of that supervisory jurisdiction is ultimately subject to the superintendence of this Court as the 'Federal Supreme Court' in which s 71 of the *Constitution* vests the judicial power of the Commonwealth.

[99] There is but one common law of Australia. The supervisory jurisdiction exercised by the State Supreme Courts by the grant of prerogative relief or orders in the nature of that relief is governed in fundamental respects by principles established as part of the common law of Australia. That is, the supervisory jurisdiction exercised by the State Supreme Courts is exercised according to principles that in the end are set by this Court. To deprive a State Supreme Court of its supervisory jurisdiction enforcing the limits on the exercise of State executive and judicial power by persons and bodies other than that Court would be to create islands of power immune from supervision and restraint. It would permit what Jaffe described as the development of 'distorted positions' [Louis L Jaffe, 'Judicial Review: Constitutional and Jurisdictional Fact' (1957) 70 *Harvard Law Review* 953, 963]. And as already demonstrated, it would remove from the relevant State Supreme Court one of its defining characteristics.

[100] This is not to say that there can be no legislation affecting the availability of judicial review in the State Supreme Courts. It is not to say that no privative provision is valid. Rather, the observations made about the constitutional significance of the supervisory jurisdiction of the State Supreme Courts point to the continued need for, and utility of, the distinction between jurisdictional and non-jurisdictional error in the Australian constitutional context. The distinction marks the relevant limit on State legislative power. Legislation which would take from a State Supreme Court power to grant relief on account of jurisdictional error is beyond State legislative power. Legislation which denies the availability of relief for non-jurisdictional error of law appearing on the face of the record is not beyond power.

IR Act, s 179

[101] Section 179 of the *IR Act* must be read in a manner that takes account of these limits on the relevant legislative power.

582 [102] Orders in the nature of prohibition, certiorari and mandamus may be directed to the Industrial Court. It is a court subject to the supervisory jurisdiction of the Supreme Court of New South Wales. ...

[104] In its terms, s 179(1), read with s 179(5), could be read in a manner which would speak to the present case. But those provisions could be read as engaged *only* if the expression '[a] decision of the [Industrial Court]' were read as including a decision of the Industrial Court that was attended by jurisdictional error. That is, the provisions could be engaged only if 'decision' includes a decision of the Industrial Court made outside the limits on its power. 'Decision' should not be read in that way.

> [105] ... [T]he contrast between the references in s 179(1) to a 'decision', and in s 179(4) to a 'purported decision', would point away from reading the provisions of s 179(1) as engaged with respect to what purports to be a decision of the Industrial Court but is a decision attended by jurisdictional error ... ***583*** It is, however, not necessary to undertake that task, because even without any internal indication that 'decision' should be read as a decision of the Industrial Court that was made within the limits of the powers given to the Industrial Court to decide questions, that reading of the section follows from the constitutional considerations that have been mentioned. Section 179, on its proper construction, does not preclude the grant of certiorari for jurisdictional error. To grant certiorari on that ground is not to call into question a 'decision' of the Industrial Court as that term is used in s 179(1).

[Citations omitted]

No-invalidity clauses

Commissioner of Taxation (Cth) v Futuris Corporation Ltd (2008) 237 CLR 146

Income Tax Assessment Act 1936 (Cth)

[As at relevant date]

175 Validity of assessment

The validity of any assessment shall not be affected by reason that any of the provisions of this Act have not been complied with.

175A Objections against assessment

A taxpayer who is dissatisfied with an assessment made in relation to the taxpayer may object against it in the manner set out in Part IVC of the *Taxation Administration Act 1953.*

177 Evidence

(1) The production of a notice of assessment, or of a document under the hand of the Commissioner, a Second Commissioner, or a Deputy Commissioner, purporting to be a copy of a notice of assessment, shall be conclusive evidence of the due making of the assessment and, except in proceedings under Part IVC of the *Taxation Administration Act 1953* on a review or appeal relating to the assessment, that the amount and all the particulars of the assessment are correct.

...

Facts

In November 2004, the Commissioner of Taxation issued Futuris Corporation Ltd ('Futuris') with a notice of assessment of Futuris's tax liability. Futuris commenced proceedings in the Federal Court under s 39B of the *Judiciary Act 1903* (Cth) seeking a declaration that the assessment was invalid (this decision was of a type identified in sch 1 of the *Administrative Decisions (Judicial Review) Act 1977* (Cth) as a decision to which that Act did not apply). Futuris sought certiorari to quash the decision, and a declaration that the assessment was invalid because the Commissioner had knowingly 'double counted' almost $20 million of income. The judge at first instance dismissed the application, but the Full Court of the Federal Court allowed an appeal, declared that the assessment was invalid, and quashed the assessment. The Commissioner appealed to the High Court.

The High Court allowed the appeal, holding that any errors made by the Commissioner were, because of s 175 of the *Income Tax Assessment Act 1936* (Cth), not jurisdictional errors.

Gummow, Hayne, Heydon and Crennan JJ

156 [23] The significance of s 175 for the operation of the Act and for the scope of judicial review outside Pt IVC is to be assessed in the manner indicated in *Project Blue Sky Inc* v *Australian Broadcasting Authority* [(1998) 194 CLR 355] ... [C]onsistently with the reasons in *Project Blue Sky* of McHugh, Gummow, Kirby and Hayne JJ, the question for the present case is whether it is a purpose of the Act that a failure by the Commissioner in the process of assessment to comply with provisions of the Act renders the assessment invalid; in determining ***157*** that question of legislative purpose regard must be had to the language of the relevant provisions and the scope and purpose of the statute.

[24] Section 175 must be read with ss 175A and 177(1). If that be done, the result is that the validity of an assessment is not affected by failure to comply with any provision of the Act, but a dissatisfied taxpayer may object to the assessment in the manner set out in Pt IVC of the *Administration Act*; in review or appeal proceedings under Pt IVC the amount and all the particulars of the assessment may be challenged by the taxpayer but with the burden of proof provided in ... the *Administration Act*. Where s 175 applies, errors in the process of assessment do not go to jurisdiction and so do not attract the remedy of a constitutional writ under s 75(v) of the *Constitution* or under s 39B of the *Judiciary Act*.

[25] But what are the limits beyond which s 175 does not reach? The section operates only where there has been what answers the statutory description of an 'assessment'. Reference is made later in these reasons to so-called tentative or provisional assessments which for that reason do not answer the statutory description in s 175 and which may attract a remedy for jurisdictional error. Further, conscious maladministration of the assessment process may be said also not to produce an 'assessment' to which s 175 applies. Whether this be so is an important issue for the present appeal ...

Conclusions with respect to jurisdictional error

...

161 [44] ... The essential point made by Futuris was that the Full Court had correctly differed from the primary judge when it determined that the assessment of taxable income in the second amended assessment was flawed because there had been 'double counting' of the amount of $19,950,088.

[45] In the process of the making of the ... assessment errors by the Commissioner of this nature (if indeed there were errors) fell within the scope of s 175 as explained earlier in these reasons. They could not found a complaint of jurisdictional error attracting the ***162*** exercise of jurisdiction to issue constitutional writs which is conferred by s 75(v) of the *Constitution* on this Court and by s 39B of the *Judiciary Act* upon the Federal Court. If there were errors they occurred within, not beyond, the exercise of the powers of assessment given by the Act to the Commissioner and would be for consideration in the Pt IVC proceedings.

...

[47] ... [P]rinciples of jurisdictional error control the constitutional writs but do not attend the remedy of injunction including that provided in s 75(v) (and thus in s 39B of the *Judiciary Act)*. The same is true of the other equitable remedy, the declaratory order. Nevertheless, the equitable remedies, which are available at the suit of a party with a sufficient interest, operate to declare invalidity and to restrain the implementation of invalid exercises of power. Where s 175 of the Act operates there will be no affectation of the validity of any assessment.

...

164 [52] ... There remains ... the question whether there was a conscious maladministration of the Act and, if so, whether s 175 had any operation in respect of a complaint of jurisdictional error.

The knowledge of the Commissioner

[Editors' note: Their Honours set out the Full Court's finding that the Commissioner knew the assessment involved double counting.]

[54] If this finding as to mental element in the making of the assessment were to withstand the challenge in this Court by the Commissioner, would that, contrary to what has been concluded thus far in these reasons, enliven principles respecting jurisdictional error?

[55] The issue here is whether, upon its proper construction, s 175 of the Act brings within the jurisdiction of the Commissioner when making assessments a deliberate failure to comply with the provisions of the Act. A public officer who knowingly acts in excess of that officer's power may commit the tort of misfeasance in public office ... Members of the Australian Public Service are enjoined by the *Public Service Act* (s 13) to act with care and diligence and to behave with honesty and integrity. This is indicative of what throughout the whole period of the public administration of the laws of the Commonwealth has been the ethos of an apolitical public service which is skilled and efficient in serving the national interest. These considerations point ***165*** decisively against a construction of s 175 which would encompass deliberate failures to administer the law according to its terms.

[56] Such failures manifest jurisdictional error and attract the jurisdiction to issue the constitutional writs ...

[57] It should be added that, with respect to the remedy of injunction, what was said in the joint reasons in *Plaintiff S157/2002 v The Commonwealth* [(2003) 211 CLR

476, 508 [82]] indicates that injunctive relief clearly is 'available for fraud, bribery, dishonesty or other improper purpose'.

[58] However, there was no such failure of due administration with respect to the [assessment in this case].

[Editors' note: Their Honours explained that the evidence showed the Commissioner believed he was acting in accordance with the requirements of the Act.]

[60] Allegations that statutory powers have been exercised corruptly or with deliberate disregard to the scope of those powers are not lightly to be made or upheld. ...

Conclusions

[62] The primary judge was correct to dismiss the s 39B application and the Full Court erred in displacing that outcome. The appeal to this Court should be allowed.

Restricting access to information before the courts

Graham v Minister for Immigration and Border Protection (2017) 263 CLR 1

Migration Act 1958 (Cth)

[As at relevant time]

503A Protection of information supplied by law enforcement agencies or intelligence agencies

(1) If information is communicated to an authorised migration officer by a gazetted agency on condition that it be treated as confidential information and the information is relevant to the exercise of a power under section 501, 501A, 501B, 501BA, 501C or 501CA:

(a) the officer must not divulge or communicate the information to another person, except where:

(i) the other person is the Minister or an authorised migration officer; and

(ii) the information is divulged or communicated for the purposes of the exercise of a power under section 501, 501A, 501B, 501 BA, 501C or 501CA; and

(b) an authorised migration officer to whom information has been communicated in accordance with paragraph (a) or this paragraph must not divulge or communicate the information to another person, except where:

(i) the other person is the Minister or an authorised migration officer; and

(ii) the information is divulged or communicated for the purposes of the exercise of a power under section 501, 501A, 501B, 501BA, 501C or 501CA.

(2) If:

(a) information is communicated to an authorised migration officer by a gazetted agency on condition that it be treated as confidential information and the information is relevant to the exercise of a power under section 501, 501A, 501B, 501BA, 501C or 501CA; or

(b) information is communicated to the Minister or an authorised migration officer in accordance with paragraph (1)(a) or (b);

then:

(c) the Minister or officer must not be required to divulge or communicate the information to a court, a tribunal, a parliament or parliamentary committee or any other body or person; and

(d) if the information was communicated to an authorised migration officer—the officer must not give the information in evidence before a court, a tribunal, a parliament or parliamentary committee or any other body or person.

Facts

New Zealanders Aaron Graham and Mehaka Te Puia were Australian residents who had their visas cancelled on the grounds that they did not pass the character test. The information upon which the decisions to cancel the visas were made was protected from disclosure by s 503A of the *Migration Act 1958* (Cth).

Mr Graham commenced judicial review proceedings in the original jurisdiction of the High Court. He sought the writ of prohibition against the Minister, to prevent him from acting upon the visa cancellation. Mr Te Puia commenced proceedings in the Federal Court under s 476A of the *Migration Act 1958* (Cth), seeking an order to set aside the cancellation of his visa. The Federal Court proceedings were removed to the High Court and both proceedings were heard together.

The High Court held, by majority, that s 503A was constitutionally invalid insofar as it prevented the disclosure of material that had been considered by the Minister when making a visa cancellation decision, to the Federal Court or the High Court hearing judicial review proceedings in relation to that decision.

Kiefel CJ, Bell, Gageler, Keane, Nettle and Gordon JJ

25 [42] [T]he upshot [of the framers' consideration of *Marbury v Madison* 5 US 137 (1803)] was the inclusion within Ch III of the *Constitution* of s 75(v), which confers original jurisdiction on the High Court in all matters in which a writ of mandamus or prohibition or an injunction is sought against an officer of the Commonwealth, and of s 77(i) and (iii) in so far as those provisions empower the Commonwealth Parliament to confer or invest equivalent statutory jurisdiction on or in other courts. The power of a court exercising jurisdiction under, or derived from, s 75(v) to grant a writ of mandamus or prohibition or an injunction against an officer of the Commonwealth is a power to enforce the law that limits and governs the power of that officer.

[43] What follows from the inclusion of s 75(v) in the *Constitution* is that it is 'impossible' for Parliament 'to impose limits upon the quasi-judicial authority of a body which it sets up with the intention that any excess of that authority means invalidity, and yet, at the same time, to deprive this Court of authority to restrain the invalid action of the court or body by prohibition' [*R v Hickman* (1945) 70 CLR 598, 616]. The same is to be said of the impossibility of Parliament imposing a public duty with the intention that the duty must be performed and yet depriving this Court of authority by mandamus to compel performance of the duty imposed and of the impossibility of Parliament imposing a constraint on the manner or extent of exercise of a power with the intention that the constraint must be observed and yet depriving this Court of authority by injunction to restrain an exercise of that power rendered unlawful by reason of being in breach of that constraint.

...

26 [45] Where Parliament enacts a law conferring a decision-making power on an officer and goes on to enact a privative clause, cast in terms that a decision of the officer cannot be called into question in a court, history shows that the privative clause has the potential to be read in different ways. The privative clause might be read as expanding the conferral of decision-making power on the officer, or it might be read as speaking only to what an officer does within the limits of the decision-making power otherwise conferred. On either of those non-literal readings, the privative clause would be valid. The privative clause would be invalid, however, were it to be read literally, so as to deny to a court exercising jurisdiction under or derived from s 75(v) the ability to enforce the legal limits of the decision-making power which Parliament has conferred on the officer.

[46] Where Parliament enacts a law which confers a decision-making power on an officer and goes on to enact some other provision, not cast as a privative clause, that other provision must likewise be invalid if and to the extent that it has the legal or practical operation of denying to a court exercising jurisdiction under, or derived from, s 75(v) the ability to enforce the limits which Parliament has expressly or impliedly set on the decision-making power which Parliament has conferred on the officer.

[47] Parliament can delimit the statutory jurisdiction which it chooses to confer under s 77(i) or invest under s 77(iii) to something less than the full scope of jurisdiction under s 75(v). Parliament can, under s 51(xxxix), regulate the procedure to be followed in the exercise of jurisdiction under s 75(v) or under s 77(i) or s 77(iii), including by defining ***27*** compulsory powers to compel disclosure of relevant information and by limiting admission of relevant evidence.

[48] What Parliament cannot do under s 51(xxxix) or under any other source of legislative power is enact a law which denies to this Court when exercising jurisdiction under s 75(v), or to another court when exercising jurisdiction within the limits conferred on or invested in it under s 77(i) or s 77(iii) by reference to s 75(v), the ability to enforce the legislated limits of an officer's power. The question whether or not a law transgresses that constitutional limitation is one of substance, and therefore of degree. To answer it requires an examination not only of the legal operation of the

law but also of the practical impact of the law on the ability of a court, through the application of judicial process, to discern and declare whether or not the conditions of and constraints on the lawful exercise of the power conferred on an officer have been observed in a particular case.

...

[50] Section 503A(2)(c) of the Act imposes a ... blanket and inflexible limit on obtaining and receiving evidence relevant to the curial discernment of whether or not legislatively imposed conditions of and constraints on the lawful exercise of powers conferred by the Act on the Minister have been observed.

[51] The legal operation of s 503A(2)(c), so far as relevant, is to prevent the Minister from being required to divulge or communicate to any court any information which can be demonstrated objectively to meet the two conditions in s 503A(1). ...

28 [52] The practical impact of that legal operation, so far as relevant, is in the application of s 503A(2)(c) to this Court when exercising jurisdiction under s 75(v) of the *Constitution*, and to the Federal Court when exercising under s 476A(1)(c) and (2) of the Act jurisdiction 'the same as the jurisdiction of the High Court under [s] 75(v) of the *Constitution*', to review a purported exercise of power by the Minister under s 501, s 501A, s 501B or s 501C. The impact is to prevent this Court and the Federal Court from obtaining access to a category of information which, by definition, is relevant to the purported exercise of the power of the Minister that is under review, and which must for that reason be relevant to the determination of whether or not the legal limits of that power and the conditions of the lawful exercise of that power have been observed. This Court and the Federal Court, by the operation of s 503A(2), are denied the ability to require the information to be produced or adduced in evidence by the Minister irrespective of the importance of the information to the determination to be made and irrespective of the importance or continuing importance of the interest sought to have been protected by the gazetted agency when that agency chose to attach to its communication of information to an authorised migration officer the condition that the information be treated as confidential information.

[53] To the extent s 503A(2)(c) operates in practice to deny to this Court and the Federal Court the ability to see the relevant information for the purpose of reviewing a purported exercise of power by the Minister under s 501, 501A, 501B or 501C, s 503A(2) operates in practice to ***29*** shield the purported exercise of power from judicial scrutiny. The Minister is entitled in practice to base a purported exercise of power in whole or in part on information which is unknown to and unknowable by the court, unless the Minister (after consulting with the gazetted agency from which the information originated) chooses to exercise the non-compellable power conferred on the Minister by s 503A(3) to declare that disclosure to the court can occur.

...

32 [65] It is not necessary in this case to further analyse matters of substance and degree which may or may not result in the invalidity of a statutory provision affecting the exercise of a court's jurisdiction under s 75(v). It may be necessary to do so in the future. In this case the effect of s 503A(2) is effectively to deny the court evidence, in the case of the applicant the whole of the evidence, upon which the Minister's decision was based. It strikes at the very heart of the review for which s 75(v) provides.

[66] The Minister and the Attorney-General do not suggest that s 503A(2) might be construed, which is to say read down, so as to save it from invalidity. Section 503A(2) is invalid to the extent that it ***33*** operates as described above, but its invalid application is severable. Applying s 15A of the *Acts Interpretation Act 1901* (Cth), the reference in s 503A(2)(c) to a 'court' must be read to exclude this Court when exercising jurisdiction under s 75(v) of the *Constitution*, and the Federal Court when exercising jurisdiction under s 476A(1)(c) and (2) of the Act, to review a purported exercise of power by the Minister under s 501, 501A, 501B or 501C to which the information is relevant. Section 503A(2) is not otherwise invalid ...

[Citations omitted]

CHAPTER

11

INTRODUCTION TO THE GROUNDS OF REVIEW

Introduction 317

What are the grounds of review? 317

Will Bateman and Leighton McDonald, 'The Normative Structure of Australian Administrative Law' (2017) 45 *Federal Law Review* 153 317

Statutory grounds 319

Administrative Decisions (Judicial Review) Act 1977 (Cth) 319

Administrative Review Council, *Federal Judicial Review in Australia* (Report No 50, 2012) 320

Introduction

This chapter complements Chapter 11 of *Government Accountability: Australian Administrative Law,* third edition. It introduces grounds of review under statutory schemes of judicial review. Later chapters explore grounds of review in specific cases, rather than at a general level. These specific cases will provide the depth and detail necessary to understand grounds of review.

What are the grounds of review?

Will Bateman and Leighton McDonald, 'The Normative Structure of Australian Administrative Law' (2017) 45 *Federal Law Review* 153

In this article, Bateman and McDonald argue there has been a fundamental shift in the way grounds of review are conceptualised in Australian administrative law.

> ***153*** Our chief contention is that over the course of the last 40 (or so) years there has been a profound reorientation of how [the legal norms of Australian administrative law] are conceptualised in Australian law. The shift has been away from an approach which gives prominence to the identification and articulation of 'grounds of review' towards an approach which gives increasing emphasis to statutory interpretation and particulars. We call the first way of thinking about the legal norms of administrative law the 'grounds approach' and the second the 'statutory approach'.
>
> ...
>
> ***155*** Two ways of thinking about legal norms have emerged in Australian administrative law, which are meaningfully distinct. One expresses the legal norms of administrative law as a set of rules and principles described as 'grounds of review' which exist *ex ante* a statute conferring power on an administrator. The other expresses those norms as the product of a parliamentary intention arrived at through a process of statutory interpretation undertaken *ex post* the enactment of a statute conferring administrative power. A degree of juristic abstraction in the statement of legal norms is entailed by the grounds approach, whereas the statutory approach (though not inconsistent with an acceptance of generally applicable presumptions of interpretation) stipulates a focus on the particulars of statutory text and purpose.
>
> The difference between the two approaches can be illustrated by two statements, separated by 20 years, concerning the norms to be applied in discerning the lawfulness of a decision made in violation of natural justice. In *Kioa v West* [(1985) 159 CLR 550, 576–7] Mason J said:
>
> > The statutory grounds of review enumerated in s 5(1) [of the *Administrative Decisions (Judicial Review) Act 1977* (Cth)] are not new – they are a reflection

> in summary form of grounds on which administrative decisions are susceptible to challenge at common law. The section is therefore to be read in the light of the common law and it should not be understood as working a challenge to common law grounds of review, except in so far as the language of the section requires it ... It is in this respect that s 5(1) makes every decision to which it applies subject to review on the grounds stated and in so doing it may give a number of grounds a wider reach than they would have at common law. But it is not the primary object of the section to amend or alter the common law content of the various grounds. ...

In *SAAP v Minister for Immigration and Multicultural and Indigenous Affairs* [(2005) 228 CLR 294, 353–4 [205]], Hayne J said:

> The focus of the inquiry about jurisdictional error must be upon the combined operation of [provisions of the *Migration Act*] ... It is the validity of the act done in purported performance of the obligation to review and decide which is in issue. The question is, having regard to 'the language of the relevant [provisions] and the scope and object of the whole statute', is it 'a purpose of the legislation that an act done in breach ... should be invalid'?

156 Obviously, much happened between 1985 and 2005 and the jolt experienced upon comparing Mason J and Hayne J's statements is not (only) the product of contrasting prose styles or differences in the nature of the particular legal error alleged in each case. Justice Mason speaks of the susceptibility of 'administrative decisions' to 'challenge' on the basis of 'grounds of review' which may be 'statutory' or 'common law' and which 'apply' to 'decisions'. Justice Hayne speaks of the 'validity' of the 'purported performance' of the 'obligation to decide' as determined by a 'legislative intention' discerned by reference to the 'scope and object of the whole statute' through the overarching framework of 'jurisdictional error'.

We style each as 'approaches' to capture the essential point that they represent ways of thinking, rather than doctrinal categories or conceptual dichotomies. The law of judicial review has always reflected a mix of attentiveness to the particulars of statutory context and the application of judicially created doctrine. It is thus not surprising that, in their application, the two approaches have significant points of overlap. Within the grounds approach, statutory interpretation will feature in the application of most grounds of review. There is less transparent overlap within the statutory approach, which involves diminishing, to almost nothing, the grounds of review as norms existing *ex ante* the statute conferring decision-making power. But even where the full force of the statutory approach is evident, the language of the grounds can be found. The admitted overlap between the approaches, and the fact that the move from the grounds to statutory approach has been incremental (not sudden), explains why a significant reorientation of the law has been widely sensed but barely explained or evaluated.

[Citations omitted]

Statutory grounds

Administrative Decisions (Judicial Review) Act 1977 (Cth)

[As at 1 March 2018]

5 Applications for review of decisions

(1) A person who is aggrieved by a decision to which this Act applies that is made after the commencement of this Act may apply to the Federal Court or the Federal Circuit and Family Court of Australia (Division 2) for an order of review in respect of the decision on any one or more of the following grounds:

(a) that a breach of the rules of natural justice occurred in connection with the making of the decision;

(b) that procedures that were required by law to be observed in connection with the making of the decision were not observed;

(c) that the person who purported to make the decision did not have jurisdiction to make the decision;

(d) that the decision was not authorized by the enactment in pursuance of which it was purported to be made;

(e) that the making of the decision was an improper exercise of the power conferred by the enactment in pursuance of which it was purported to be made;

(f) that the decision involved an error of law, whether or not the error appears on the record of the decision;

(g) that the decision was induced or affected by fraud;

(h) that there was no evidence or other material to justify the making of the decision;

(i) that the decision was otherwise contrary to law.

(2) The reference in paragraph (1)(e) to an improper exercise of a power shall be construed as including a reference to:

(a) taking an irrelevant consideration into account in the exercise of a power;

(b) failing to take a relevant consideration into account in the exercise of a power;

(c) an exercise of a power for a purpose other than a purpose for which the power is conferred;

(d) an exercise of a discretionary power in bad faith;

(e) an exercise of a personal discretionary power at the direction or behest of another person;

(f) an exercise of a discretionary power in accordance with a rule or policy without regard to the merits of the particular case;

(g) an exercise of a power that is so unreasonable that no reasonable person could have so exercised the power;

(h) an exercise of a power in such a way that the result of the exercise of the power is uncertain; and

(i) any other exercise of a power in a way that constitutes abuse of the power.

(3) The ground specified in paragraph (1)(h) shall not be taken to be made out unless:

(a) the person who made the decision was required by law to reach that decision only if a particular matter was established, and there was no evidence or other material (including facts of which he or she was entitled to take notice) from which he or she could reasonably be satisfied that the matter was established; or

(b) the person who made the decision based the decision on the existence of a particular fact, and that fact did not exist.

Administrative Review Council, *Federal Judicial Review in Australia* (Report No 50, 2012)

The Administrative Review Council ('ARC') was introduced in Chapter 2 of this book. In this, its last report before it was abolished, the ARC conducted a major review of Australia's system of judicial review at the federal level. The report incorporates submissions made, in response to a consultation paper, by various individuals and groups including government agencies, legal representatives and academics.

Approach to the Grounds of Review

126 [7.6] A question the Council asked in the Consultation Paper was whether there should be a codified list of grounds at all, or whether it is preferable to rely on the courts' development of grounds. As Mason J observed in *Kioa v West*, 'the statutory grounds of review enumerated in s 5(1) are not new—they are a reflection in summary form of the grounds on which administrative decisions are susceptible to challenge at common law'. However, since the ***127*** time the *ADJR Act* grounds were developed, the High Court has placed increasing emphasis on the fact that writs available in the original jurisdiction of the High Court (prohibition and mandamus) only issue where there has been a jurisdictional error.

[7.7] Review under the *ADJR Act* extends beyond the requirement for a jurisdictional error in three respects. First, review under the *ADJR Act* is available for any error of law, whether or not that error is jurisdictional and whether or not the error appears on the face of the record [s 5(1)(f)]. Second, review is available where the decision maker has based the decision on a particular fact, and that fact did not exist—the 'no evidence' ground [ss 5(2)(h) and 5(3)(b)]. This factual error does not have to be a jurisdictional fact or an error of law. Third, review is available where the procedures required by law were not observed [s 5(1)(b)]. This ground appears not to be confined to jurisdictional errors, unlike the common law. Given the evolving concept of jurisdictional error, it is unclear to what extent these grounds go beyond the grounds for constitutional judicial review.

[7.8] Emeritus Professor Mark Aronson argued that repealing the codified grounds of review 'would be the worst of all possible worlds' as it would result in relying on jurisdictional error. He noted that there is 'widespread angst and confusion' over the term, though he believes the 'angst to be greatly over-wrought and the confusion to be quite unnecessary'. The Council agrees that jurisdictional error is a complex concept and reliance solely on jurisdictional error as the basis for review of decisions may be confusing and therefore impede access to review. ... [T]he grounds in the *ADJR Act* cover the key questions which need to be addressed in considering whether a jurisdictional error has been made, both in terms of the statutory scheme and implied limitations on the exercise of the statutory power. While the concept of jurisdictional error may be well understood by expert legal practitioners, particularly barristers, for non-experts the list of grounds in the *ADJR Act* continues to provide a useful tool for framing judicial review applications. Removing the grounds may also create more confusion for practitioners.

[7.9] The grounds of review under the *ADJR Act* have been criticised for a number of reasons. Aronson, for example, has suggested that, while the list approach states the grounds, a person has always needed knowledge of the common law in order to understand them. Kirby J has expressed the view that 'to some extent the development of the common law of ***128*** judicial review in Australia was retarded by the enactment of the *ADJR Act* in 1977'. Stephen Gageler SC [now Gageler J] has noted that the grounds do not have any organising principles, which may make development of the law more difficult. However, it is significant to note that both Aronson and Kirby J ultimately supported a codified list of grounds, with some modifications.

[7.10] It is also true that through the use of the concept of 'jurisdictional error', courts conducting review in the constitutional judicial review jurisdiction focus on the particular statutory scheme rather than general principles. Nonetheless, grounds such as breach of procedural fairness, failing to take into account a relevant consideration, taking into account an irrelevant consideration and other more procedural grounds are almost always implied into the statute. A number of *ADJR Act* grounds address the core concepts of a 'jurisdictional error' relating to the statutory scheme: no jurisdiction to make the decision; the decision was not authorised by the enactment in pursuance of which it was purported to be made; and improper exercise of the power conferred by the enactment. These grounds are extremely broad, and depend upon an interpretation of the particular statutory scheme.

[7.11] The submissions to the Council overwhelmingly supported some form of codification. Drs Billings and Cassimatis stated that codified grounds have 'enhanced accessibility to review, providing both transparency and flexibility to adapt to the evolving administrative state'. The Law Council of Australia noted that the 'clear list' of potential grounds has an 'educative effect by setting out a relatively comprehensive summary of the common law.' The Department of Immigration and Citizenship (DIAC) submitted that simplified and codified grounds of review could assist people to better understand the judicial review process and facilitate them to make better informed decisions. The Australian Crime Commission (ACC) pointed to the usefulness of a codified list of grounds for decision makers, noting that grounds provided 'a structured approach to the assessment process.' Should the list of grounds not be comprehensive, the ACC submitted it would be necessary to supplement the list with principles to guide decision makers to consider all relevant factors. The Council agrees that codified grounds are more transparent and accessible, and that grounds can play a role in explaining judicial review to legal practitioners and other applicants.

[7.12] While there may be some attraction in the idea of leaving the articulation of grounds to the courts—noting the important role the courts play in developing existing grounds—relying solely on case law would almost certainly make framing an application more difficult for practitioners and applicants who were not familiar with administrative law.

129 [7.13] The Council considers that a codified list of grounds should be retained. The codified grounds do continue to play an educative role. They have the potential to educate decision makers about proper decision-making practices, and applicants about their legal rights. Codified grounds are more transparent and accessible than relying solely on principles set out in judicial decisions.

[Citations omitted]

CHAPTER

12

PROCEDURAL FAIRNESS

Introduction 324

The threshold test: when do the rules of procedural fairness apply? 324

Kioa v West (1985) 159 CLR 550 324

Plaintiff S10/2011 v Minister for Immigration and Citizenship (2012) 246 CLR 636 333

Statutory exclusion 336

Re Minister for Immigration and Multicultural Affairs; Ex parte Miah (2001) 206 CLR 57 336

Minister for Immigration and Border Protection v SZMTA (2019) 264 CLR 421 342

BVD17 v Minister for Immigration and Border Protection (2019) 268 CLR 29 344

Plaintiff S10/2011 v Minister for Immigration and Citizenship (2012) 246 CLR 636 347

The hearing rule 349

Re Minister for Immigration and Multicultural and Indigenous Affairs; Ex parte Lam (2003) 214 CLR 1 349

The bias rule 352

Ebner v Official Trustee in Bankruptcy (2000) 205 CLR 337 352

Isbester v Knox City Council (2015) 255 CLR 135 356

Minister for Immigration and Multicultural Affairs v Jia Legeng (2001) 205 CLR 507 359

Introduction

This chapter complements Chapter 12 of *Government Accountability: Australian Administrative Law*, third edition. Many significant administrative law decisions concern the rules of procedural fairness. Space does not permit inclusion of all (or even most) of these decisions. The cases in this chapter have been chosen for their significance in establishing key principles or because they provide striking illustrations of trends in the High Court's approach to procedural fairness. The content of each case extract has been selected to show not only the High Court's exposition of legal principles, but also the application of those principles to factual situations. Although the rules of procedural fairness apply to a wide range of administrative and judicial decisions, many of the leading cases (especially in relation to the hearing rule) have arisen in the context of migration. This is reflected in the subject matter of the cases extracted in this chapter.

The threshold test: when do the rules of procedural fairness apply?

Kioa v West (1985) 159 CLR 550

Migration Act 1958 (Cth)

[As at relevant date]

> **18 Deportation of prohibited immigrants**
>
> The Minister may order the deportation of a person who is a prohibited immigrant under any provision of this Act.

Facts

In September 1981, Jason Kioa, a citizen of Tonga, took leave from his job in Tonga and came to Australia to complete a three-month training course. He entered Australia on a student visa and was granted a temporary entry permit. In November 1981, his wife and two-year-old daughter joined him in Australia, having been granted temporary entry permits. In December 1981, Mr Kioa applied for an extension of his temporary entry permit. However, the initial permit expired before this application had been determined.

The family stayed in Australia after their entry permits expired. At this point, they became 'prohibited immigrants' under the *Migration Act 1958* (Cth). Mr Kioa resigned from his job in Tonga and started working as a machine operator in Melbourne. Migration officials attempted to contact Mr Kioa but were unable to do so, as the family had moved house and Mr Kioa made no attempt to contact the Immigration Department.

In July 1983, Mr Kioa was apprehended at his workplace and taken into custody as a prohibited immigrant. A delegate of the Minister began to consider whether to order that Mr and Mrs Kioa be deported. Mr and Mrs Kioa's lawyer wrote to the Minister indicating that they wished to remain in Australia, and made arguments in support of that position. This included Mr Kioa's active involvement in the Tongan Christian Fellowship in Australia. A departmental officer prepared a briefing paper for the Minister, setting out the relevant circumstances. The briefing paper included the following paragraphs:

> 16. While in Australia Mr Kioa has become active on the council of the Tongan Christian Fellowship, a group affiliated with the Uniting Church. He was elected as a representative on the Executive of this Council with responsibility generally for Tongan youth and the plight of other illegal immigrants. His interest extended to the situation of Tongan persons awaiting deportation.
>
> ...
>
> 21. If Mr Kioa had been genuine in his desire (in Dec 1981) to seek a legitimate extension of his stay, it would have appeared likely that he might have sought a decision on his application rather than change his address without apparently notifying the Department.
>
> ...
>
> 22. Mr Kioa's alleged concern for other Tongan illegal immigrants in Australia and his active involvement with other persons who are seeking to circumvent Australia's immigration laws must be a source of concern.

In November 1983, the Minister's delegate ordered that Mr and Mrs Kioa be deported. In response to a request by Mr Kioa under s 13 of the *Administrative Decisions (Judicial Review) Act 1977* (Cth) (*AD(JR) Act*), the Minister's delegate provided written reasons for the decision. The reasons emphasised Mr Kioa's decision to commence work in Australia (contrary to the provisions of the *Migration Act*) and his lack of effort to communicate his change of address to migration officials even though he knew that his temporary entry permit had expired. The reasons made no mention of Mr Kioa's association with other Tongan immigrants.

Mr and Mrs Kioa sought review of the deportation decision under s 5 of the *AD(JR) Act.* They argued that the decision had been made in breach of the rules of procedural fairness.

The first issue for the High Court was whether the rules of procedural fairness applied to this decision. In two earlier cases (*R v MacKellar; Ex parte Ratu* (1977) 137 CLR 461 and *Salemi v MacKellar (No 2)* (1977) 137 CLR 396) the High Court held that the rules of procedural fairness did *not* apply to a deportation decision under s 18 of the *Migration Act 1958* (Cth). The plaintiffs in *Kioa* argued that amendments to the *Migration Act,* and the enactment of the *AD(JR) Act* had changed the statutory landscape such that *Ratu* and *Salemi* could be distinguished.

The second issue was whether, if the rules of procedural fairness applied, the hearing rule had been breached because the matters raised in the paragraphs of the briefing paper extracted above had not been brought to the plaintiffs' attention prior to the making of the decision. By 4:1 (Mason, Wilson, Brennan and Deane JJ, Gibbs CJ dissenting), the Court held that the rules of procedural fairness did apply, and had been breached.

The judgments of Mason and Brennan JJ have become touchstones for our modern understanding of procedural fairness in Australia. An extract from the dissenting judgment of Gibbs CJ is included to demonstrate the way in which these judgments departed from the previous law.

Gibbs CJ (dissenting)

> ***563*** There were a number of reasons why the Court in *Salemi (No 2)* and *Ratu* held that the Minister is not generally bound to afford a hearing to a prohibited immigrant

> before ordering his deportation ***564*** under s 18, notwithstanding the very serious consequences that deportation may in many cases entail. ... First, there is the nature of the power which s 18 confers. Under that section the Minister is not required to find any fact or form any opinion before he exercises the power. ... If he makes an order against a person who is a prohibited immigrant, no other reason than the fact that the person is a prohibited immigrant is necessary to justify the order; his power is in that case unfettered. Secondly, an order under s 18 does not ordinarily deprive a prohibited immigrant of any right or interest or of the legitimate expectation of any benefit. As Mason J said in *Ratu* [(1977) 137 CLR 461, 478–9]:
>
>> The making of a deportation order under s 18 therefore provides lawful authority for the removal from Australia against his will of a person who has no right to remain here. It is not the case that the order terminates his right to remain; nor can it be said in the ordinary case that it deprives him of a legitimate expectation that he will be allowed to remain here. Deportation, for which the order provides, is then but a consequence of the prohibited immigrant's failure to depart when he has no right to remain.

[Editors' note: Gibbs CJ held that the power conferred by s 18 was not conditioned on an obligation to provide procedural fairness.]

Mason J

[Editors' note: At 578–82, Mason J identified amendments to the *Migration Act 1958* (Cth), and features of the *AD(JR) Act* that provided a basis for distinguishing *Salemi* and *Ratu*.]

> ***582*** It is a fundamental rule of the common law doctrine of natural justice expressed in traditional terms that, generally speaking, when an order is to be made which will deprive a person of some right or interest or the legitimate expectation of a benefit, he is entitled to know the case sought to be made against him and to be given an opportunity of replying to it. The reference to 'right or interest' in this formulation must be understood as relating to personal liberty, status, preservation of livelihood and reputation, as well as to proprietary rights and interests.
>
> The reference to 'legitimate expectation' makes it clear that the doctrine applies in circumstances where the order will not result in ***583*** the deprivation of a legal right or interest. Take, for example, an application for a renewal of a licence where the applicant, though he has no legal right or interest, may nevertheless have a legitimate expectation which will attract the rules of natural justice. ...
>
> It has been said on many occasions that natural justice and fairness are to be equated.
>
> And it has been recognized that in the context of administrative decision-making it is more appropriate to speak of a duty to act fairly or to accord procedural fairness. This is because the expression 'natural justice' has been associated, perhaps too closely associated, with procedures followed by courts of law. The developing application of the doctrine of natural justice in the field of administrative decision-making has been very largely achieved by reference to the presence of characteristics which have

been thought to reflect important characteristics of judicial decision-making. … ***584*** The emphasis given … to the presence and absence of these characteristics diverted attention from the need to insist on the adoption in the administrative process of fair and flexible procedures for decision-making, procedures which do not necessarily take curial procedures as their model.

The law has now developed to a point where it may be accepted that there is a common law duty to act fairly, in the sense of according procedural fairness, in the making of administrative decisions which affect rights, interests and legitimate expectations, subject only to the clear manifestation of a contrary statutory intention. … But the duty does not attach to every decision of an administrative character. Many such decisions do not affect the rights, interests and expectations of the individual citizen in a direct and immediate way. Thus a decision to impose a rate or a decision to impose a general charge for services rendered to ratepayers, each of which indirectly affects the rights, interests or expectations of citizens generally does not attract this duty to act fairly. This is because the act or decision which attracts the duty is an act or decision:

> … which directly affects the person (or corporation) individually and not simply as a member of the public or a class of the public. An executive or administrative decision of the latter kind is truly a 'policy' or 'political' decision and is not subject to judicial review. [*Salemi v MacKellar [No 2]* (1977) 137 CLR 396, 399 (Jacobs J)]

Where the decision in question is one for which provision is made by statute, the application and content of the doctrine of natural justice or the duty to act fairly depends to a large extent on the construction of the statute. … What is appropriate in terms of natural justice depends on the circumstances of the case and they will include, inter alia, the nature of the inquiry, the subject-matter, ***585*** and the rules under which the decision-maker is acting.

In this respect the expression 'procedural fairness' more aptly conveys the notion of a flexible obligation to adopt fair procedures which are appropriate and adapted to the circumstances of the particular case. The statutory power must be exercised fairly, ie, in accordance with procedures that are fair to the individual considered in the light of the statutory requirements, the interests of the individual and the interests and purposes, whether public or private, which the statute seeks to advance or protect or permits to be taken into account as legitimate considerations.

When the doctrine of natural justice or the duty to act fairly in its application to administrative decision-making is so understood, the need for a strong manifestation of contrary statutory intention in order for it to be excluded becomes apparent. The critical question in most cases is not whether the principles of natural justice apply. It is: what does the duty to act fairly require in the circumstances of the particular case? It will be convenient to consider at the outset whether the statute displaces the duty when the statute contains a specific provision to that effect, for then it will be pointless to inquire what the duty requires in the circumstances of the case, unless there are circumstances not contemplated by the statutory provision that may give rise to a legitimate expectation. However, in general, it will be a matter of determining what the duty to act fairly requires in the way of procedural fairness in the circumstances of the case. A resolution of that question calls for an examination of the statutory provisions and the interests which I have already mentioned.

Notwithstanding the characteristics of the power and the elements in the statutory framework which were thought in *Salemi (No 2)* and *Ratu* to indicate an intention to displace the principles of natural justice in relation to s 18, I do not think that it can now be said that the *Migration Act* as it has been amended wholly displaces the duty to act fairly in accordance with the doctrine of natural justice. In one very important respect there has been a radical legislative change. The exercise of the power is susceptible of judicial review and an element in that review is the obligation, on request, to ***586*** furnish a statement setting out material findings of fact, referring to the evidence and other materials, and giving the reasons for the decision. In the light of this it can scarcely be suggested now that the existence of an obligation to comply with the requirements of procedural fairness is inconsistent with the statutory framework or that it will entail administrative inconvenience which is destructive of the statutory objects.

[Editors' note: His Honour next considered what the rules of procedural fairness required in this case.]

587 [R]ecent decisions illustrate the importance which the law attaches to the need to bring to a person's attention the critical issue or factor on which the administrative decision is likely to tum so that he may have an opportunity of dealing with it ...

Of the paragraphs in the submission to the delegate of which the ***588*** appellants complain, it seems to me that there are two matters only in respect of which fairness demands that the applicant should have the chance of replying. The first is the comment in par 21 that had Mr Kioa been genuine in his desire to seek a legitimate extension of his stay in Australia he might have sought a decision on his application 'rather than change his address without apparently notifying the Department'. The second matter is that contained in par 22, namely, the statement that Mr Kioa's concern for other Tongan illegal immigrants and his active involvement with other persons who were seeking to circumvent Australia's immigration laws 'must be a source of concern'. Although the statement of reasons makes no reference to the contents of par 22, it does not disavow them. As the paragraph was extremely prejudicial, the appellants should have had the opportunity of replying to it. ...

In the result I would allow the appeal and quash the deportation order on the ground that a breach of the rules of natural justice occurred in connexion with the making of the decision.

Brennan J

609 At base, the jurisdiction of a court judicially to review a decision made in the exercise of a statutory power on the ground that the decision-maker has not observed the principles of natural justice depends upon the legislature's intention that observance of the principles of natural justice is a condition of the valid exercise of the power. That is clear enough when the condition is expressed; it is seen more dimly when the condition is implied, for then the condition is attributed by judicial construction of the statute. In either case, the statute determines whether the exercise of the power is conditioned on the observance of the principles of natural justice. The statute is construed, as all statutes are construed, against a background of common law notions of justice and fairness and, when the statute does not expressly require that the principles of natural justice be observed, the court construes the statute on the footing that 'the justice of the common law will supply the omission of the legislature': *Cooper v Wandsworth Board of Works* [(1863) 14 CB (NS) 180, 194]. The true intention of the legislature is thus ascertained. When the legislature creates certain powers, the courts presume that the legislature intends the principles of natural justice to be observed in their exercise in the absence of a clear contrary intention ...

611 The question whether a statutory power is conditioned on the observance of the principles of natural justice demands a universal answer for it is a question of construction. Such a condition governs every exercise of the power including every refusal to exercise it. ... [W]hen the exercise of a statutory power is so conditioned, regard must be had to the circumstances of the particular case to ascertain what is needed to satisfy the condition. It is not possible precisely and exhaustively to state what the repository of a statutory power must always do to satisfy a condition that the principles of natural justice be observed. ...

612 Two distinct but closely related questions can be perceived in the cases relating to the exercise of a statutory power: the first, or threshold, question is whether the exercise of the power is conditioned upon observance of the principles of natural justice; the second question, arising when the exercise of the power is so conditioned, is what the principles of natural justice require in the particular circumstances. It is seldom possible to say that the legislature intends to exclude observance of the principles of natural justice in the exercise of a statutory power which is apt to affect individual interests and the more difficult and more frequently addressed question is what the principles of natural justice require in the particular circumstances. ...

The principles of natural justice have a flexible quality which, chameleon-like, evokes a different response from the repository of a statutory power according to the circumstances in which the repository is to exercise the power. ...

614 To ascertain what must be done to comply with the principles of natural justice in a particular case, the starting point is the statute creating the power. By construing the statute, one ascertains ... whether there are any special procedural steps which, being prescribed by statute, extend or restrict what the principles of natural justice would otherwise require. ...

615 An implication that a statutory power is conditioned on observance of the principles of natural justice does not prevent the repository of the power from modifying procedure to meet the particular exigencies of the case. Where the circumstances are such that the purpose for which the power is conferred would be frustrated if notice were given of an intention to exercise it or of the grounds on which it is intended to exercise it, the power may be exercised peremptorily without giving such notice to a person whose interests are likely to be affected. ...

It must therefore be accepted, as one commentator points out [Graeme Johnson, 'Natural Justice and Legitimate Expectation in Australia' (1985) 15 *Federal Law Review* 39, 71], that 'the contents of natural justice range from a full-blown trial into nothingness'. ... [T]he intention to be implied when the statute is silent is that observance of the principles of natural justice conditions the exercise of the power although in some circumstances the content of those principles may be diminished (even to nothingness) to avoid frustrating the purpose for which the power was conferred.

616 ... In *Ridge v Baldwin*, Lord Reid pointed out that the duty to act judicially might be inferred from the nature of the power to be exercised when the power authorized the repository of the power to interfere with an individual's legal rights. But now that qualification has been thought to be unduly restrictive. There are interests beyond legal rights that the legislature is presumed to intend to protect by the principles of natural justice. It is hardly to be thought that a modern legislature when it creates regimes for the regulation of social interests – licensing and permit systems, means of securing opportunities for acquiring legal rights, schemes for the provision of privileges and benefits at the discretion of Ministers or public officials – intends that the interests of individuals which do not ***617*** amount to legal rights but which are affected by the myriad and complex powers conferred on the bureaucracy should be accorded less protection than legal rights. ...

618 In *FAI Insurances* [(1982) 151 CLR 342, 412] I used the term 'interests' rather than 'rights' or 'legitimate expectations' to embrace one of the factors which tend to attract the principles of natural justice, but the 'interests' were qualified:

> The aptitude of the exercise of the power to affect proprietary or financial interests or reputation furnishes a surer ground for implying that the principles of natural justice are to be applied in its exercise.

...

The qualification 'proprietary or financial' reflects what Dixon CJ and Webb J in [*Commissioner of Police v Tanos* (1958) 98 CLR 383, 395] described as 'a deep-rooted principle of the law that before anyone can be punished or prejudiced in his person or property by any judicial or quasi-judicial proceeding he must be afforded an adequate opportunity of being heard'. The reference to reputation reflects the interest protected by the law of defamation. ... ***619*** Although the common law has long been concerned to protect person, property and reputation, it ill accords with modern legislative intention to restrict the application of the presumption to statutory powers which affect only those kinds of interests. It cannot be said that modern legislatures intend that protection should be given only to those kinds of interests, out of the large and increasing variety of interests affected by the exercise of statutory powers. On reflection, my earlier qualification appears erroneous. The presumption that the principles of natural justice condition the exercise of a statutory power may apply to any statutory power which is apt to affect any interest possessed by an individual whether or not the interest amounts to a legal right or is a proprietary or financial interest or relates to reputation. It is not the kind of individual interest but the manner in which it is apt to be affected that is important in determining whether the presumption is attracted.

If a power is apt to affect the interests of an individual in a way that is substantially different from the way in which it is apt to affect the interests of the public at large, the repository of the power will ordinarily be bound or entitled to have regard to the interests of the individual before he exercises the power ... When the repository is bound or is entitled to have regard to the interests of an individual, it may be presumed that observance of the principles of natural justice conditions the exercise of the power, for the legislature can be presumed to intend that an individual whose interests are to be regarded should be heard before the power is exercised. Therefore the presumption applies to any statutory power the exercise of which is apt to affect the interests of an individual alone or apt to affect his interests in a manner which is substantially different from the manner in which its exercise is apt to affect the interests of the public. Of course, the presumption may be displaced by the text of the statute, the nature of the power and the administrative framework created by the statute within which the power is to be exercised. ...

620 The legislature is not likely to intend that a statutory power of a strictly legislative nature be conditioned on the observance of the principles of natural justice for the interests of all members of the public are affected in the same way by the exercise of such a power. ... But the legislature is more likely to intend the exercise of a statutory power of an executive, administrative or quasi-judicial nature to be so conditioned if an exercise of the power singles out individuals by affecting their interests in a manner substantially different from the manner in which the interests of the public at large are affected. ...

623 In the light of these general principles, I turn to the question whether s 18 in the form and context in which it stood when the deportation orders were made confers a power which is conditioned on the observance of the principles of natural justice. That is a question of statutory construction.

[Editors' note: Brennan J then explained that *Salemi* and *Ratu* could be distinguished because amendments to the *Migration Act 1958* (Cth) had changed the nature of the interests affected by s 18. His Honour regarded the enactment of the *AD(JR) Act* as 'an entirely neutral factor' (at 625).]

...

626 [T]he amendments since 1977 are sufficient, in my opinion, to warrant the conclusion that the exercise of [the power conferred by s 18 is] conditioned on the observance of the principles of natural justice. ...

The final and most difficult question on this aspect of the case is whether there has been a failure to observe what the principles of natural justice required in the circumstances. Once the threshold question is resolved and it is established that the exercise of a power is conditioned on the observance of the principles of natural justice, the content of the principles to be observed is determined in the light of the particular circumstances. ...

627 In this case, the letter sent ... on Mr Kioa's behalf was considered by the Minister's delegate. He did not conduct an oral hearing, but a repository of a power who is bound to hear an individual before exercising a power is not necessarily bound to hear him orally. The repository must adopt a fair procedure having regard to the matters he is bound to take into account and ... the matters he proposes to take into account. Subject to one qualification the Minister's delegate gave Mr Kioa the fair hearing the delegate was bound to give him. ...

628 [T]here was one allegation - that contained in par 22 of the Department's submission – which was damaging to the prospects of Mr and Mrs Kioa being allowed to stay in Australia. That information was never put to Mr and Mrs Kioa for their comments. ... Although ... the allegation in par 22 formed no part of the delegate's reasons, it was contained in the material before him which he proposed to consider in coming to a decision.

A person whose interests are likely to be affected by an exercise of power must be given an opportunity to deal with relevant matters adverse to his interests which the repository of the power proposes to take into account in deciding upon its exercise. The person whose interests are likely to be affected does not have to be given an opportunity to comment on every adverse piece of information, irrespective of its credibility, relevance or significance. Administrative decision-making is not to be clogged by inquiries into allegations to which the repository of the power would not give credence, or which are not relevant to his decision or which are of little significance to the decision which is to be made. Administrative decisions are not necessarily to be held ***629*** invalid because the procedures of adversary litigation are not fully observed. ... Nevertheless in the ordinary case where no problem of confidentiality arises an opportunity should be given to deal with adverse information that is credible, relevant and significant to the decision to be made. It is not sufficient for the repository of the power to endeavour to shut information of that kind out of his mind and to reach a decision without reference to it. Information of that kind creates a real risk of prejudice, albeit subconscious, and it is unfair to deny a person whose interests are likely to be affected by the decision an opportunity to deal with the information. He will be neither consoled nor assured to be told that the prejudicial information was left out of account. The allegation in par 22 was apparently credible, relevant and damaging. The failure to give Mr Kioa an opportunity to deal with it before making an order that Mr and Mrs Kioa be deported left a risk of prejudice which ought to have been removed. There was nothing in the circumstances of the ca–e - neither in the administrative framework created by the Act nor in any need for secrecy or speed in making the decision which would have made it unreasonable to have given Mr and Mrs Kioa that opportunity. The failure to give Mr Kioa that opportunity amounts to a non-observance of the principles of natural justice. The result is that the condition governing the power to make the deportation orders was not satisfied and the orders must be set aside.

[Citations omitted]

Plaintiff S10/2011 v Minister for Immigration and Citizenship (2012) 246 CLR 636

Migration Act 1958 (Cth)

[As at relevant date]

48A Non-citizen refused a protection visa may not make further application for protection visa

(1) Subject to section 48B, a non-citizen who, while in the migration zone, has made:

(a) an application for a protection visa, where the grant of the visa has been refused (whether or not the application has been finally determined);

...

may not make a further application for a protection visa while in the migration zone.

...

48B Minister may determine that section 48A does not apply to non-citizen

(1) If the Minister thinks that it is in the public interest to do so, the Minister may, by written notice given to a particular non-citizen, determine that section 48A does not apply to prevent an application for a protection visa made by the non-citizen in the period starting when the notice is given and ending at the end of the seventh working day after the day on which the notice is given.

(2) The power under subsection (1) may only be exercised by the Minister personally.

(3) If the Minister makes a determination under subsection (1), he or she is to cause to be laid before each House of the Parliament a statement that:

(a) sets out the determination; and

(b) sets out the reasons for the determination, referring in particular to the Minister's reasons for thinking that his or her actions are in the public interest.

...

(5) A statement under subsection (3) is to be laid before each House of the Parliament within 15 sitting days of that House after:

(a) if the determination is made between 1 January and 30 June (inclusive) in a year—1 July in that year; or

(b) if the determination is made between 1 July and 31 December (inclusive) in a year—1 January in the following year.

(6) The Minister does not have a duty to consider whether to exercise the power under subsection (1) in respect of any non-citizen, whether he or she is requested to do so by the non-citizen or by any other person, or in any other circumstances.

...

351 Minister may substitute more favourable decision

(1) If the Minister thinks that it is in the public interest to do so, the Minister may substitute for a decision of the [Migration Review] Tribunal under section 349 another decision, being a decision that is more favourable to the applicant, whether or not the Tribunal had the power to make that other decision.

...

(3) The power under subsection (1) may only be exercised by the Minister personally.

(4) If the Minister substitutes a decision under subsection (1), he or she is to cause to be laid before each House of the Parliament a statement that:

(a) sets out the decision of the Tribunal; and

(b) sets out the decision substituted by the Minister; and

(c) sets out the reasons for the Minister's decision, referring in particular to the Minister's reasons for thinking that his or her actions are in the public interest.

...

(6) A statement under subsection (4) is to be laid before each House of the Parliament within 15 sitting days of that House after:

(a) if the decision is made between 1 January and 30 June (inclusive) in a year—1 July in that year; or

(b) if a decision is made between 1 July and 31 December (inclusive) in a year—1 January in the following year.

(7) The Minister does not have a duty to consider whether to exercise the power under subsection (1) in respect of any decision, whether he or she is requested to do so by the applicant or by any other person, or in any other circumstances.

Facts

There were four plaintiffs in this case. All four plaintiffs argued that there had been a denial of procedural fairness in relation to several of the 'dispensing powers' (including ss 48B and 351 of the *Migration Act 1958* (Cth)). For present purposes, it is sufficient to focus on two of them: Plaintiff S10 and Jasvir Kaur.

Plaintiff S10, an asylum seeker from Pakistan, arrived in Australia in August 2007. A delegate of the Minister refused his application for a visa, and Plaintiff S10's applications for merits review and judicial review were dismissed. In October 2009, Plaintiff S10 requested that the Minister exercise his power under s 48B of the *Migration Act 1958* (Cth) to allow Plaintiff S10 to make another application for a protection visa. A departmental officer assessed Plaintiff S10's request, determined it did not meet the guidelines issued by the Minister, and therefore did not refer the request to the Minister.

Ms Kaur came to Australia on a student visa in July 2005. When the visa expired in June 2008, she applied for a further student visa, but a delegate of the Minister refused her visa, and her applications for merits review and then judicial review were dismissed. In December 2010, she requested that the Minister exercise his power under s 351. As with Plaintiff S10, the departmental officer who assessed this request decided not to refer it to the Minister.

Both Plaintiff S10 and Ms Kaur argued that there had been a breach of procedural fairness because the departmental officials who considered their requests did not give them the opportunity to comment on material on which the departmental officials relied.

French CJ and Kiefel J held that the rules of procedural fairness did not apply to the Minister's decision whether or not to consider using the dispensing provisions. In a judgment extracted later in this chapter, Gummow, Hayne, Crennan and Bell JJ held that, although these decisions did attract an obligation to accord procedural fairness, that obligation was impliedly excluded by the statute.

The extracts from this case are included as an example of the operation of the threshold test and the principles of statutory exclusion in a complex statutory context.

French CJ and Kiefel J

647 [28] Each of the dispensing provisions has common features affecting the exercise of the power it confers:

- the Minister must think it is in the public interest to exercise the power;
- the power may only be exercised by the Minister personally;
- the Minister does not have a duty to consider whether to exercise the power, whether he or she is requested to do so by the applicant or by any other person or in any other circumstance;

...

- ***648*** if the Minister does exercise the power the Minister must cause to be laid before each House of Parliament a statement setting out, inter alia, the Minister's decision and the reasons for the Minister's decision and, in particular, the Minister's reasons for thinking that the decision was in the public interest.

[29] ... [Section] 48B cannot be invoked in favour of a non-citizen unless the non-citizen has applied for a protection visa and had that application determined. ... Section 351 only applies to a non-citizen who has made an application for a visa, had the application determined, applied for review before the MRT, and had that application determined. The antecedent processes for application and review attract procedural fairness obligations subject to the specific provisions of the Act relating to its content.

[30] The dispensing provisions and other like provisions in the Act have a distinctive function in its legislative scheme. The Act creates a range of official powers, duties and discretions, particularly in relation to the grant of visas, which are tightly controlled by the Act itself and, under the Regulations, by conditions and criteria to be satisfied before those powers and discretions can be exercised. The dispensing provisions stand apart from the scheme of tightly controlled powers and discretions. They confer upon the Minister a degree of flexibility allowing him or her to grant visas which might not otherwise be able to be granted because of non-satisfaction of substantive or procedural requirements. The powers so conferred are conditioned upon a ministerial judgment of the 'public interest'. That is a term to which it is difficult to give a precise content. It has been described in this Court as 'a discretionary value

judgment to be made by reference to undefined factual matters, confined only "in so far as the subject matter and the scope and purpose of the statutory enactments may enable ... given reasons to be [pronounced] definitely extraneous to any object the legislature could have had in view"'. The dispensing provisions require the Minister to be personally accountable to the ***649*** Parliament for decisions to grant visas made under them. Both the wide purposes for which the powers conferred by the dispensing provisions can be exercised and their non-compellable nature, indicate that they cannot be enlivened by a request for their exercise nor by the existence of circumstances which might be thought, in the public interest, to attract their application.

...

655 [50] The purpose and nature of the powers conferred by each of the dispensing provisions in these proceedings appears from their respective texts. It is clear from their terms that the Minister is under no duty to respond to a request for his or her consideration of the exercise of those powers. Nor is the Minister under a duty, independent of any such request, to consider any class of case for the exercise of those powers. With no statutory duty to consider the exercise of the ***656*** Minister's powers being enlivened by a request or by the occurrence of a case to which the power might apply, no question of procedural fairness arises when the Minister declines to embark upon such a consideration. If, on ministerial instructions, certain classes of request or case are not even to be submitted to him or her for consideration, the position in law is unchanged. There is no exercise of a statutory power under the Act conditioned upon compliance with the requirements of procedural fairness.

[Citations omitted]

Statutory exclusion

Re Minister for Immigration and Multicultural Affairs; Ex parte Miah (2001) 206 CLR 57

Migration Act 1958 **(Cth)**

[As at relevant date]

PART 2—CONTROL OF ARRIVAL AND PRESENCE OF NON-CITIZENS

DIVISION 3—VISAS FOR NON-CITIZENS

Subdivision AB—Code of procedure for dealing fairly, efficiently and quickly with visa applications

54 Minister must have regard to all information in application

(1) The Minister must, in deciding whether to grant or refuse to grant a visa, have regard to all of the information in the application.

...

(3) Without limiting subsection (1), a decision to grant or refuse to grant a visa may be made without giving the applicant an opportunity to make oral or written submissions.

56 Further information may be sought

(1) In considering an application for a visa, the Minister may, if he or she wants to, get any information that he or she considers relevant but, if the Minister gets such information, the Minister must have regard to that information in making the decision whether to grant or refuse the visa.

(2) Without limiting subsection (1), the Minister may invite, orally or in writing, the applicant for a visa to give additional information in a specified way.

57 Certain information must be given to applicant

(1) In this section, ***relevant information*** means information ... that the Minister considers:

(a) would be the reason, or a part of the reason, for refusing to grant a visa; and

(b) is specifically about the applicant or another person and is not just about a class of persons of which the applicant or other person is a member; and

(c) was not given by the applicant for the purpose of the application.

(2) Subject to subsection (3), the Minister must:

(a) give particulars of the relevant information to the applicant in the way that the Minister considers appropriate in the circumstances; and

(b) ensure, as far as is reasonably practicable, that the applicant understands why it is relevant to consideration of the application; and

(c) invite the applicant to comment on it.

...

69 Effect of compliance or non-compliance

(1) Non-compliance by the Minister with Subdivision AA or AB in relation to a visa application does not mean that a decision to grant or refuse to grant the visa is not a valid decision but only means that the decision might have been the wrong one and might be set aside if reviewed.

(2) If the Minister deals with a visa application in a way that complies with Subdivision AA, AB and this Subdivision, the Minister is not required to take any other action in dealing with it.

Facts

Md Ataul Haque Miah came to Australia from Bangladesh and applied for a protection visa. In his application, he claimed to fear persecution if he were to return to Bangladesh because he had publicly declared his opposition to Islamic fundamentalism. His father, who had held similar political views, had been murdered by Islamic fundamentalists. Mr Miah stated, in his application, that the political party in power at the time he submitted his application, BNP, would not protect him because BNP was allied to Islamic fundamentalists.

A delegate of the Minister refused Mr Miah's application. The delegate's reasons explained that, after Mr Miah made his application, there had been a change of government as a result of the recent Bangladeshi elections. The new government (and, by extension, the majority of the Bangladeshi population) was more politically and religiously moderate than BNP. The delegate therefore concluded that Mr Miah did not face a real chance of persecution if he returned to Bangladesh. In the subsequent proceedings, Mr Miah claimed that the new governing party (the Awami League) was also allied to Islamic fundamentalists and was unlikely to protect him from persecution.

In making the decision, the delegate complied with the 'Code of Procedure' in pt 2, div 3, subdiv AB of the *Migration Act 1958* (Cth). The delegate's conclusions about the new Bangladeshi government relied on a US Department of State report. The delegate did not provide Mr Miah with this information, nor tell Mr Miah that it was being considered. This was because it was general 'country information', rather than information specifically about Mr Miah; therefore, s 57(1)(b) did not require it to be disclosed to Mr Miah.

Mr Miah instructed his solicitors to apply for merits review of the delegate's decision. The solicitors prepared an application to the Refugee Review Tribunal, but then misplaced the application. By the time the application was recovered, the time limit for applying for merits review had expired. At that time, the judicial review jurisdiction conferred on the Federal Court did not extend to the review of decisions that could have been the subject of merits review by the Refugee Review Tribunal. Therefore, Mr Miah applied to the High Court under s 75(v) of the *Constitution,* seeking prohibition, certiorari and mandamus. He argued there had been a breach of the hearing rule because he had not been provided with the country information.

By 3:2, the High Court held that the rules of procedural fairness had not been excluded, and that they had been breached. The Court granted writs of certiorari (to quash the delegate's decision), mandamus (requiring the Minister to reconsider Mr Miah's application for a protection visa), and prohibition (restraining the Minister from taking any action based on the delegate's refusal of a visa).

Gleeson CJ and Hayne J (dissenting)

> ***69*** [34] [S]ubdiv AB of Pt 2, Div 3 was described in its heading as a '[c]ode of procedure for dealing fairly, efficiently and quickly with visa applications'. The expression 'code' is not conclusive of the present issue; but it is not to be disregarded as an indication of legislative intention. ... [T]he legislature has been prescriptive as to the steps that a visa applicant and the Minister are obliged or permitted to take in relation to the provision of information about a visa application. ...
>
> [35] The specificity with which the procedure to be followed is prescribed by the legislation is also to be considered in the context of a visa applicant's right to apply for a full merits review, by the [Refugee Review] Tribunal or the Immigration Review Tribunal, of an adverse decision. ... [T]he legal significance of a full right of appeal from an administrative decision in relation to the decision-maker's duty to give a fair hearing may have a number of aspects. It does not require a conclusion that the decision-maker is not bound to accord procedural fairness. But it may be material, both as to that question and as to the question of the practical content of the requirements

of fairness. In the present case, the Act does not dispense with the requirements of fairness. On the contrary, it specifies procedures to be adopted in the interests of fairness, having regard also to what Parliament saw as the interests of efficiency and speed. In considering the procedures set out in the statute, it is material to note both that the delegate was required to give reasons for his decision, and that the prosecutor was entitled to a full merits review of the decision and to a hearing on that review.

...

73 [49] [The provisions of subdiv AB], read in the context of legislation which requires the decision-maker to give reasons, and entitles an unsuccessful applicant to a full review of the decision on the merits, evince an intention on the part of the legislature to prescribe comprehensively the extent to which, and the circumstances in which, the Minister or delegate is to give an applicant an opportunity to make comments or submissions, or provide information, in addition to the information in the original application. ...

75 [54] The provisions of s 54(3), ... read together with s 69, show a clear intention that the decision-maker is not required to invite submissions on a matter regarded as potentially adverse to an applicant's case, whether the matter is based on a change in circumstances since the application or on any other relevant consideration.

McHugh J

93 [126] It is now settled that, when a statute confers on a public official the power to do something which affects a person's rights, interests or expectations, the rules of natural justice regulate the exercise of that power 'unless they are excluded by plain words of necessary intendment'. An intention on the part of the legislature to exclude the rules of natural justice is not to be assumed nor spelled out from 'indirect references, uncertain inferences or equivocal considerations'. Nor is such an intention to be inferred from the presence in the statute of rights which are commensurate with some of the rules of natural justice. As I pointed out in *Theophanous v Herald & Weekly Times Ltd* [(1994) 182 CLR 104, 196]:

> The true meaning of a legal text almost always depends on a background of concepts, principles, practices, facts, rights and duties which the authors of the text took for granted or understood, without conscious advertence, by reason of their common language or culture.

The common law rules of natural justice are part of this background. They are taken to apply to the exercise of public power unless clearly excluded.

[127] Accordingly, the relevant question in the present proceedings is whether the terms of the Act, particularly subdiv AB, display a legislative intention to exclude the common law rules of natural justice. More specifically, the question is whether the Act intended to deny an applicant 'an opportunity to deal with relevant matters ***94*** adverse to his interests which the repository of the power proposes to take into account in deciding upon its exercise'.

[128] It is highly improbable that the legislature intended to exclude all the common law requirements of natural justice from subdiv AB. There are no clear words to that effect. Where Parliament has wanted to exclude common law rules from applying to the administration of the Act, it has not hesitated to do so in clear words. ... Moreover, subdiv AB is headed 'Code of procedure for dealing *fairly,* efficiently and quickly with visa applications'. (Emphasis added) It therefore assumes that the 'code' will operate fairly. The subdivision sets out various formal procedures which the Minister may or must follow to ensure fairness to applicants. But subdiv AB does not declare that they exhaustively define the content of fair procedure. The subject matter of the Act, the fact that it implements Australia's international obligations, and the omission of words unambiguously pointing to an intention to exclude all the common law rules of natural justice indicate that the exercise of power under subdiv AB is conditioned on the observance of those rules except where the provisions of the Act specifically supersede them.

The 'code' argument

95 [131] The respondents contend that the statutory provisions demonstrate an intention to provide a 'code' of procedures for determining applications for refugee status. By necessary implication, they argue, the 'code' excludes any separate or additional incidents of procedural fairness that are not prescribed within it. They point to the wording of the heading of subdiv AB – '*Code* of procedure for dealing fairly, efficiently and quickly with visa applications'. (Emphasis added) But the use of the term 'code' is too weak a reason to conclude that Parliament intended to limit the requirements of natural justice to what is provided in subdiv AB. It is hardly to be supposed, for example, that the Parliament of this nation intended to exclude the common law rules concerning actual bias or corruption of the decision-making process. Instead, the use of the word 'fairly' makes it difficult to extrapolate a manifestly clear intention to exclude rules of natural justice from applying to the procedures set out in the subdivision.

[132] In addition, the respondents point to the Explanatory Memorandum which states that subdiv AB aims to 'replace the uncodified principles of natural justice with clear and fixed procedures which are drawn from those principles'. However, even when a Minister, in introducing legislation, has expressed a view as to the meaning of that legislation, the court will not give the enactment that meaning if such a reading is not justified. The need to act on the text of the enactment and not the Minister's statement is particularly important when the Minister's meaning has serious consequences for an individual.

...

96 [139] The respondents argue that, because the statute establishes a mandatory duty to inform applicants about certain kinds of information, Parliament could not have intended that a similar duty should be imposed in relation to other types of information. But to so argue is to fall into the error of inferring from the presence of some matters concerned with natural justice that Parliament intended to exclude natural justice in all other respects.

[140] A basic principle of the common law rules of natural justice is that a person whose interests are likely to be affected by an exercise of power must be given an opportunity to deal with relevant matters adverse to his or her interests that the repository of the power proposes to take into account in deciding upon its exercise. This does not mean that all material which comes before the decision-maker must be ***97*** disclosed but, 'in the ordinary case ... an opportunity should be given to deal with adverse information that is credible, relevant and significant to the decision to be made'. ... Nothing in the Act... indicates a clear intention to exclude this principle of natural justice.

[141] ... In some cases, exercises of the power, although conditioned by the rules of natural justice, will *not* require that the applicant have an opportunity to comment on the material. Examples of material that would not require comment by the applicant would include non-adverse country information, favourable or corroborative information in the public domain and information based on the circumstances already described in the application. But there are cases where the exercise of this power *does* require that the applicant be given an opportunity to comment on the material. An example is where the delegate proposes to use new material of which the applicant may be unaware and which is or could be decisive against the applicant's claim for refugee status. The need for disclosure by the delegate is even stronger where the material concerns circumstances that have changed since the date of application and is being used after considerable delay. It is stronger still when the material is equivocal or contains information that the applicant could not reasonably have expected to be used in the way the delegate uses it.

[142] Here the new material was undoubtedly decisive of the prosecutor's claim. The material was totally new. The election took place in Bangladesh more than two months after the application was made. ... But over and above these considerations is the fact that it was seemingly irrelevant to [Mr Miah's] fears whether or not the Awami League or the BNP were in government. Both political parties were arguably unable or unwilling to offer the prosecutor protection from the Islamic fundamentalists. ... ***98*** [Mr Miah] could not reasonably have expected this type of information to be used. Certainly, he could not reasonably have been expected to provide information about a matter that he reasonably perceived as irrelevant to his situation. In other words, this is a case where 'the requirements of procedural fairness may be of added importance ... in that they ensure an opportunity of raising for consideration matters which are *not already obvious*' [*Kioa v West* (1985) 159 CLR 550, 633 (Deane J) (emphasis added)].

[143] The rules of natural justice are flexible and adaptable to the particular circumstances of each case. In the particular circumstances outlined above, they required the delegate, in exercising power under subdiv AB, to inform [Mr Miah] that he was contemplating using information about the election results and to offer [Mr Miah] an opportunity to comment. There was, accordingly, a breach of the rules of natural justice.

[Citations omitted]

Minister for Immigration and Border Protection v SZMTA (2019) 264 CLR 421

Migration Act 1958 (Cth)

[As at relevant date]

PART 7—REVIEW OF PART 7-REVIEWABLE DECISIONS

408 Simplified Outline of this Part

This Part provides for the review of Part 7-reviewable decisions by the Administrative Appeals Tribunal in its Migration and Refugee Division.

Part 7-reviewable decisions relate to the grant or cancellation of protection visas in some circumstances. ...

422B Exhaustive statement of natural justice hearing rule

(1) This Division [div 4] is taken to be an exhaustive statement of the requirements of the natural justice hearing rule in relation to the matters it deals with.

(2) Sections 416, 437 and 438 and Division 7A, in so far as they relate to this Division, are taken to be an exhaustive statement of the requirements of the natural justice hearing rule in relation to the matters they deal with.

(3) In applying this Division, the Tribunal must act in a way that is fair and just.

438 Tribunal's discretion in relation to disclosure of certain information etc.

(1) This section applies to a document or information if:

  (a) the Minister has certified, in writing, that the disclosure of any matter contained in the document, or the disclosure of the information, would be contrary to the public interest for any reason specified in the certificate ... that could form the basis for a claim by the Crown in right of the Commonwealth in a judicial proceeding that the matter contained in the document, or the information, should not be disclosed; or

  (b) the document, the matter contained in the document, or the information was given to the Minister, or to an officer of the Department, in confidence.

(2) If, in compliance with a requirement of or under this Act, the Secretary gives to the Tribunal a document or information to which this section applies, the Secretary:

  (a) must notify the Tribunal in writing that this section applies in relation to the document or information; and

  (b) may give the Tribunal any written advice that the Secretary thinks relevant about the significance of the document or information.

(3) If the Tribunal is given a document or information and is notified that this section applies in relation to it, the Tribunal:

  (a) may, for the purpose of the exercise of its powers, have regard to any matter contained in the document, or to the information; and

(b) may, if the Tribunal thinks it appropriate to do so having regard to any advice given by the Secretary under subsection (2), disclose any matter contained in the document, or the information, to the applicant.

(4) If the Tribunal discloses any matter to the applicant, under subsection (3), the Tribunal must give a direction under section 440 in relation to the information.

Facts

The High Court heard three cases together. In each case, an applicant for a protection visa had had their application refused by a delegate of the Minister. Each had applied to the relevant tribunal[1] for merits review and in each instance, the Secretary gave the Tribunal a notification, under s 438, that the Secretary had provided the Tribunal with information to which s 438 applied. The applicants for review were not informed that this notification had been given.

The *Migration Act* did not contain an express requirement that a s 438 notification must be disclosed to an applicant. The applicants argued that the hearing rule placed an obligation on the Tribunal to disclose the fact of the notification (as opposed to the *content* of the information). The Minister submitted that s 422B excluded any such obligation.

Bell, Gageler and Keane JJ

> ***442*** [34] Importantly, s 422B is not framed in a way that excludes procedural fairness, which it refers to as 'the natural justice hearing rule', from the conduct of the review. Rather, the section is framed in a way that is consistent with the implication of an obligation to afford procedural fairness through the operation of a common law principle of interpretation as a condition of the performance by the Tribunal of its duty to conduct the review. The section is also framed in a way which recognises that the precise content of that obligation to afford procedural fairness depends on 'the particular statutory framework').
>
> [35] By providing that specified provisions ... are taken to be an exhaustive statement of the requirements of procedural fairness in relation to the 'matters' with which they deal, s 422B(1) ... operate[s] to ensure that compliance by the Tribunal with the procedures prescribed by those specified provisions ... constitutes compliance with the obligation of the Tribunal to afford procedural fairness in so far as each provision gives specific content to that obligation. The 'matters' to which the sub-sections refer are the discrete subject matters of the provisions. The discrete subject matter of each provision is indicated by, but not limited to, the terms of each provision.
>
> [36] Section 422B(3) reinforces this operation of s 422B(1) and s 422B(2), and complements the general exhortation to the Tribunal to act according to substantial justice and the merits of the case, by requiring the Tribunal's performance of the procedural obligations imposed on it by Div 4 and the Tribunal's exercise of the procedural powers conferred on it by Div 4 to be informed by the same considerations of fairness and justice as those that inform the common law's implication into the statutory scheme of the Tribunal's overall obligation to afford procedural fairness.

1 In two cases, the applicant applied directly to the Administrative Appeals Tribunal. In the other the applicant applied to the Refugee Review Tribunal, prior to its amalgamation with the Administrative Appeals Tribunal. For present purposes, there is no relevant difference in the statutory provisions.

The design of the sub-section in that way guards against 'rigidity' in the application of procedures ***443*** themselves designed to facilitate partial compliance with the overall obligation of the Tribunal to afford procedural fairness.

[37] Section 422B(2) requires s 416 (the subject matter of which is the ability of the Tribunal to have regard to information considered and findings made in earlier proceedings), each provision of Div 7A (the subject matter of which is the manner of giving and receiving documents) and ss 437 and 438 to be treated as an exhaustive statement of the Tribunal's obligation to afford procedural fairness in so far as the subject matter of those provisions relates to the conduct of the Tribunal's review under Div 4. But in so far as the subject matter of s 438 relates to the conduct of the Tribunal's review under Div 4, that subject matter is confined to how the Tribunal is to treat documents and information to which s 438 applies. The section's subject matter does not extend to the prescription of any consequences, for procedural fairness, of the Secretary providing a notification to the Tribunal under the section. In other words, s 438 is not self-referential. The Minister's submission is for that reason to be rejected.

[Citations omitted]

BVD17 v Minister for Immigration and Border Protection (2019) 268 CLR 29

Migration Act 1958 (Cth)

[As at relevant date]

PART 7AA—FAST TRACK REVIEW PROCESS IN RELATION TO CERTAIN PROTECTION VISA DECISIONS

473BA Simplified outline of this Part

This Part provides a limited form of review of certain decisions (***fast track decisions***) to refuse protection visas to some applicants, including unauthorised maritime arrivals who entered Australia on or after 13 August 2012, but before 1 January 2014, and who have not been taken to a regional processing country. These applicants are known as ***fast track review applicants*** and decisions to refuse to grant them protection visas are known as ***fast track reviewable decisions***.

...

Fast track reviewable decisions must be referred by the Minister to the Immigration Assessment Authority as soon as reasonably practicable after a decision is made. ...

DIVISION 3—CONDUCT OF REVIEW

Subdivision A—Natural justice requirements

473DA Exhaustive statement of natural justice hearing rule

(1) This Division, together with sections 473GA and 473GB, is taken to be an exhaustive statement of the requirements of the natural justice hearing rule in relation to reviews conducted by the Immigration Assessment Authority.

...

473GB Immigration Assessment Authority's discretion in relation to disclosure of certain information etc.

(1) This section applies to a document or information if:

(a) the Minister has certified, under subsection (5), that the disclosure of any matter contained in the document, or the disclosure of the information, would be contrary to the public interest for any reason specified in the certificate ... that could form the basis for a claim by the Crown in right of the Commonwealth in a judicial proceeding that the matter contained in the document, or the information, should not be disclosed; or

(b) the document, the matter contained in the document, or the information was given to the Minister, or to an officer of the Department, in confidence.

(2) If, in compliance with a requirement of or under this Act, the Secretary gives to the Immigration Assessment Authority a document or information to which this section applies, the Secretary:

(a) must notify the Authority in writing that this section applies in relation to the document or information; and

(b) may give the Authority any written advice that the Secretary thinks relevant about the significance of the document or information.

(3) If the Immigration Assessment Authority is given a document or information and is notified that this section applies in relation to it, the Authority:

(a) may, for the purpose of the exercise of its powers in relation to a fast track reviewable decision in respect of a referred applicant, have regard to any matter contained in the document, or to the information; and

(b) may, if the Authority thinks it appropriate to do so having regard to any advice given by the Secretary under subsection (2), disclose any matter contained in the document, or the information, to the referred applicant.

(4) If the Immigration Assessment Authority discloses any matter to the referred applicant under subsection (3), the Authority must give a direction under section 473GD in relation to the information.

(5) The Minister may issue a written certificate for the purposes of subsection (1).

Facts

BVD17 was an asylum seeker from Sri Lanka. After a delegate of the Minister refused to grant him a protection visa, the matter was referred to the Immigration Assessment Authority for Fast Track Review. The information provided to the Authority included a departmental file relating to an application for a protection visa by a member of BVD17's family. A delegate of the Secretary gave the Immigration Assessment Authority a notice under s 473GB(2)(a) stating that s 473GB applied to the departmental file. The fact that the notice had been given was not disclosed to BVD17.

Relying on *Minister for Immigration and Border Protection v SZMTA* (2019) 264 CLR 421 (extracted above), BVD17 submitted that the hearing rule obliged the Immigration Assessment Authority to disclose the fact of the notification, and that the obligation was not excluded by s 473DA. The Minister submitted that *SZMTA* was distinguishable because of the difference between pt 7 (in issue in *SZMTA*) and pt 7AA (in issue in *BVD17*) of the *Migration Act 1958* (Cth).

Kiefel CJ, Bell, Gageler, Keane, Nettle and Gordon JJ

42 [30] The prescription in s 473DA(1) has some parallels with the prescriptions in s 422B(1) and (2), the scope and operation of which were considered in *SZMTA*. Like them, the prescription in s 473DA(1) is framed in a way that is consistent with legislative acknowledgement of an obligation to afford procedural fairness which arises as an implied condition of performance of the duty to conduct a review through operation of a common law principle of statutory interpretation. And like them, the prescription in s 473DA(1) ***43*** 'recognises that the precise content of that obligation to afford procedural fairness depends on "the particular statutory framework"'.

[31] Unlike the prescriptions in s 422B(1) and (2) as interpreted in *SZMTA*, however, the prescription in s 473DA(1) is not framed to confine the exhaustiveness of its operation, in defining the content of the obligation to afford procedural fairness which it acknowledges, to the discrete subject matters of the provisions to which it refers. Instead, it extends the exhaustiveness of its operation, in defining the content of the Authority's obligation to afford procedural fairness, to the entirety of the performance of the overriding duty imposed on the Authority ... to review a fast track reviewable decision .... The reasoning in *SZMTA*, that an incident of the obligation of procedural fairness which conditions performance of the overriding duty of the Tribunal to conduct a review under Pt 7 can arise outside the scope of the discrete subject matters of the provisions to which s 422B(1) and (2) refer, can therefore have no application to the Authority.

[32] Recognising that the prescription in s 473DA(1) is broad in its scope, the appellant argued that the effect of its operation on the identification of the incidents of the Authority's obligation to afford procedural fairness is minimal. The appellant argued that the 'exhaustive statement of the requirements of the natural justice hearing rule' to which s 473DA(1) refers encompasses all that is expressed in and implied by the totality of the provisions which s 473DA(1) mentions. If a particular obligation of disclosure arises by implication from construing Div 3 in combination with s 473GA or s 473GB against the background of the common law then, according to the appellant, that implied obligation is itself part of the 'exhaustive statement of the requirements of the natural justice hearing rule' to which s 473DA(1) refers. All that the prescription in s 473DA(1) achieves, according to the appellant, is to prevent recourse to provisions in Pt 7AA other than Div 3 and ss 473GA and 473GB in determining the express or implied incidents of the Authority's obligation of procedural fairness. ...

44 [33] The argument would deprive s 473DA(1) of any meaningful operation. It cannot be accepted. The evident purpose of s 473DA(1) in prescribing that the provisions to which it refers are to be taken to be an 'exhaustive statement of the requirements of the natural justice hearing rule' is to require that those provisions be construed as a codification of the incidents of the Authority's acknowledged obligation of procedural fairness. The prescription does not preclude all implications. Importantly, it does not preclude an implication that a statutory power within the provisions to which s 473DA(1) refers must be exercised only within the bounds of legal reasonableness. What the prescription does preclude is an incident of the Authority's obligation of procedural fairness arising as a matter of implication through the application of the common law principle of statutory interpretation according to which, where the exercise of a power or the performance of a duty is conditioned by a requirement to afford procedural fairness, 'regard must be had to the circumstances of the particular case to ascertain what is needed to satisfy the condition' with the result that '[i]t is not possible precisely and exhaustively to state what the repository of a statutory power must always do to satisfy [the] condition'.

[34] The consequence of the codifying effect of s 473DA(1) ... is that, except to the extent that procedural unfairness overlaps with legal unreasonableness, procedural fairness analysis is not the 'lens' through which the content of the procedural obligations imposed on the Authority in the conduct of a review under Pt 7AA is to be determined.

[35] [T]he entirety of the content of the Authority's obligation of procedural fairness in the context of a notification under s 473GB(2)(a) is to be found in the outworking of the discretions conferred on the Authority by s 473GB(3). Section 473DA(1) leaves no room for an additional obligation of disclosure to arise in the manner recognised in *SZMTA*.

[Citations omitted]

Plaintiff S10/2011 v Minister for Immigration and Citizenship (2012) 246 CLR 636

Facts

The facts and relevant legislation are set out earlier in this chapter at pp 333–5. In the judgment set out above, French CJ and Kiefel J held that the rules of procedural fairness did not apply to the Minister's decision whether or not to consider using the 'dispensing provisions'. In the judgment extracted below, Gummow, Hayne, Crennan and Bell JJ held that, although these decisions did attract an obligation to accord procedural fairness, that obligation was impliedly excluded by the statute.

Gummow, Hayne, Crennan and Bell JJ

658 [64] The defendants' first submission is that the cases may be dismissed on the footing that the relevant dispensing provisions of the Act do not meet the requirement, for attraction of principles of procedural fairness, that the failure to exercise them is not 'apt to have a substantial adverse effect on some identifiable right, interest, privilege or legitimate expectation'.

[65] That submission should not be accepted ...

[66] [T]he issue presented by the first submission of the defendants is to be considered by asking whether the failure by the Minister to consider the exercise and thus to exercise the dispensing powers in question is apt to affect adversely what is the sufficient interest of a party seeking the exercise of those powers in favour of that party.

[Editors' note: Their Honours quoted relevant passages of Brennan J's judgment in *Kioa v West* (1985) 159 CLR 550.]

...

659 ... [69] A non-citizen who is in the position of the plaintiffs and seeks the engagement and favourable exercise of the dispensing powers under the federal statute with which these cases are concerned does so to obtain a measure of relaxation of what otherwise would be the operation upon non-citizens of the visa system; it is the requirements of that system which must be met to lift what otherwise are the prohibitions upon entry and continued presence in Australia. This is sufficient to satisfy the principles just discussed.

[70] The defendants cannot succeed solely upon the ground that the failure to engage the exercise in their favour of the dispensing power is not apt adversely to affect the interests of those seeking to engage the exercise of those powers.

...

667 [98] [T]here are some provisions in the Act which explicitly exclude the operation of the rules of natural justice. That is a matter to be taken into account in deciding whether or not, upon their proper construction, the dispensing provisions with which these cases are concerned are conditioned upon observance of the requirements of natural justice in favour of persons in the position of the plaintiffs.

[99] However, those dispensing provisions also have the following significant characteristics:

(i) The powers they confer may be exercised by the Minister personally and not otherwise; that is to say, unlike many other decisions respecting the issue of visas, the power may not be delegated by the Minister under s 496 of the Act.

(ii) By the tabling requirements the Minister is rendered accountable in an immediate sense to each House of the Parliament for exercises of the dispensing powers.

(iii) The exercise of the powers is not preconditioned by the making of any request by any other person, and, if a request be made there is no requirement to consider it.

(iv) The exercise of the powers is preconditioned by (a) the Minister having decided to consider whether to exercise the power in question, and (b) the Minister thinking that: 'It is in the public interest' to exercise it; but the Minister is not obliged to take either step.

(v) The expression 'in the public interest' can have no fixed and precise content and involves a value judgment often to be made by reference to undefined matters. Here the legislative supposition upon which the dispensing powers are conferred is that there will be cases in which the requirements which otherwise control the administration of the Act are not to dictate a particular outcome.

(vi) Further, as to (iv), while the personal circumstances of an individual may be taken into account, they are not a mandatory relevant consideration.

(vii) Rather, as the Commonwealth Solicitor-General submitted, individual interests and rights are dealt with by provisions of the Act regulating applications and providing for review of decisions concerning visas.

(viii) The premise for the operation of s 48B is that there has been the refusal of a protection visa (with attendant RRT engagement) which will be final unless the Minister lifts the bar upon further applications which is lowered by s 48A; the *668* premise for the engagement of ... s 351 ... is that on a merits review the relevant tribunal has determined that there is no right to the visa sought ...

(ix) Against that background, it is not surprising that the focus of the four dispensation sections is upon the Minister's view of the public interest rather than upon the satisfaction of conditions for the issue of visas.

Conclusions and orders

The cumulative significance of the matters referred to above in (i)–(ix) is to disclose a situation akin to that identified by Brennan J in *South Australia v O'Shea*, namely where a senior official standing at the peak of the administration of the statute is not required to give an opportunity for a hearing in every case affecting an individual who has had an opportunity of a merits review in the course of the administrative process. Upon their proper construction and in their application to the present cases, the dispensing provisions are not conditioned on observance of the principles of procedural fairness ... The use in the provisions of the Act in question here of language emphatic both of the distinctive nature of the powers conferred upon the Minister (as personal, non-compellable, 'public interest' powers), and of the availability of access to the exercise of those powers only to persons who have sought or could have sought, but have not established their right to, a visa is of determinative significance. It reveals the 'necessary intendment' ... that the provisions are not attended by a requirement for the observance of procedural fairness.

[Citations omitted]

The hearing rule

Re Minister for Immigration and Multicultural and Indigenous Affairs; Ex parte Lam (2003) 214 CLR 1

Migration Act 1958 (Cth)

[As at relevant date]

501 Refusal or cancellation of visa on character grounds

...

(2) The Minister may cancel a visa that has been granted to a person if:

(a) the Minister reasonably suspects that the person does not pass the character test; and

(b) the person does not satisfy the Minister that the person passes the character test.

...

(6) For the purposes of this section, a person does not pass the ***character test*** if:

(a) the person has a substantial criminal record ...

Facts

Hieu Trung Lam was born in Vietnam. In 1970, at the age of 13, he came to Australia as a refugee, and settled in Australia under a transitional (permanent) visa. He fathered two children (who were Australian citizens), but his relationship with the mother of the children broke down and she indicated that she did not wish to see the children, leaving them in Mr Lam's care. Mr Lam, meanwhile, was convicted of various crimes, culminating in 1995 with an eight-year sentence for drug trafficking. The children, then aged two and six, went to live with a friend, Huyen Tran, while Mr Lam was in prison.

In September 2000, an officer of the Department of Immigration and Multicultural and Indigenous Affairs wrote to Mr Lam explaining that his visa could be cancelled under s 501(2) of the *Migration Act 1958* (Cth), because he had a substantial criminal record. The letter from the officer set out the matters that would be taken into account in deciding whether to cancel the visa, including 'the best interests of any children with whom you have an involvement', and invited Mr Lam to provide written comments and information. Mr Lam provided a detailed written submission. Among other things, the submission emphasised the bond between Mr Lam and his children, and the hardship they would all suffer if Mr Lam were deported to Vietnam and separated from them. Ms Tran wrote a letter, which Mr Lam annexed to his submissions, detailing the children's circumstances, supporting Mr Lam's arguments, and advocating that it would be in the best interests of the children to be cared for, in the long term, by Mr Lam and his fiancee.

On 7 November 2000, another departmental officer wrote to Mr Lam requesting the contact details of the children's carer, stating that 'The Department wishes to contact [the carer] in order to assess your relationship with the children and the possible effects on them of a decision to cancel your visa'. Mr Lam provided those details. However, for reasons which were not explained, the Department never contacted Ms Tran.

In January 2001, the Minister cancelled Mr Lam's visa. Mr Lam commenced judicial review proceedings in the High Court under s 75(v) of the *Constitution,* seeking certiorari (to quash the decision) and prohibition (to prevent the Minister taking steps to deport him). Mr Lam argued that the Department's failure to contact Ms Tran, without first giving Mr Lam the opportunity to make submissions on that matter, constituted a breach of the hearing rule. The High Court unanimously dismissed Mr Lam's application.

Substantial sections of the judgments in *Lam* focus on explaining the limited reach of the concept of 'legitimate expectations' in procedural fairness. The parts of Gleeson CJ's judgment extracted below discuss that issue in terms that have broader significance for the content of the hearing rule, particularly in their emphasis on the concept of 'practical injustice'.

Gleeson CJ

8 [18] The applicant's complaint is based entirely upon the fact that the Department did not contact Ms Tran ... The procedural unfairness is said to arise from the fact that the decision to cancel the visa was made without the applicant having been told that it had been decided not to contact Ms Tran, and that the Department intended to rely, for the purposes of its assessment of the applicant's relationship with the children, and the possible effects on them of a decision to cancel the applicant's visa, on the information [already provided]. ...

[19] That being what is involved in the complaint, it is also important to note what is not involved. There is no suggestion that the applicant in any way relied to his disadvantage upon the representation that Ms Tran would be contacted ... In argument, any such suggestion was disclaimed. The applicant does not seek, either by evidence or by argument, to make out a case that he was deprived of an opportunity to put any further information or submissions to the respondent, or that he did, or failed to do, anything, because of any belief or understanding that was engendered in his mind by the letter of 7 November.

...

10 [29] ... The [plaintiff's] argument is that ... the letter [of 7 November 2000] created a legitimate expectation that a certain course would be followed, that such a course was not followed, and, although the applicant cannot demonstrate that he was hereby deprived of any opportunity to advance his case, that there was unfairness. It is acknowledged that if, after 7 November, the officers of the Department had told the applicant that they had no longer intended to contact Ms Tran, and the applicant had been given an opportunity to seek to ***11*** persuade them to change their minds, the applicant would have no case. The unfairness is said to lie in failing to notify the applicant that the officers had changed, or were considering changing, their minds about contacting Ms Tran. It is also acknowledged that, if the officers had not told the applicant, in the first place, that they intended to contact Ms Tran, he would have no case.

...

13 [36] The ... fundamental problem facing the applicant ... relates to the matter of unfairness. A statement of intention, made in the course of decision-making, as to a procedural step to be taken, is said to give rise to an expectation of such a kind that the decision-maker, in fairness, must either take that step or give notice of a change in intention. Yet no attempt is made to show that the applicant held any subjective expectation in consequence of which he did, or omitted to do, anything. Nor is it shown that he lost an opportunity to put any information or argument to the decision-maker, or otherwise suffered any detriment.

[37] A common form of detriment suffered where a decision-maker has failed to take a procedural step is loss of an opportunity to make representations. ... A particular example ***14*** of such detriment is a case where the statement of intention has been relied upon and, acting on the faith of it, a person has refrained from putting material before a decision-maker. In a case of that particular kind, it is the existence of a subjective expectation, and reliance, that results in unfairness. Fairness is not an abstract concept. It is essentially practical. Whether one talks in terms of procedural fairness or natural justice, the concern of the law is to avoid practical injustice.

[38] No practical injustice has been shown. The applicant lost no opportunity to advance his case. He did not rely to his disadvantage on the statement of intention. It has not been shown that there was procedural unfairness. And, as I have already

indicated, there is no warrant for a conclusion that there was a failure properly to take into account the interests of the applicant's children.

Conclusion

[39] The application should be dismissed with costs.

[Citations omitted]

The bias rule

Ebner v Official Trustee in Bankruptcy (2000) 205 CLR 337

Facts

The High Court heard two cases together: *Ebner v Official Trustee in Bankruptcy* and *Clenae Pty Ltd v Australia and New Zealand Banking Group Ltd.* Both cases involved judges who had an interest in the ANZ Bank. At the time, the Bank had assets of around $8000 million, and there were more than 1508 million shares in the Bank.

In *Ebner*, the Official Trustee in Bankruptcy applied to the Federal Court for a declaration that a transfer of property from the bankrupt Maxwell Ebner to his wife Ingrid Ebner (the appellant in the High Court) was void. The property was worth between $300,000 and $450,000, but Mr Ebner had sold it to his wife for $150,000. The ANZ Bank was one of Mr Ebner's creditors. At the start of the court proceedings, Goldberg J disclosed that he was the beneficiary, and a director of the trustee, of a family trust that owned 8000–9000 shares in the ANZ Bank. Mrs Ebner objected to Goldberg J continuing to hear the case. However, Goldberg J dismissed the objection and proceeded to hear the case and grant the injunction sought by the Official Trustee. Mrs Ebner's appeal to the Full Court of the Federal Court was unsuccessful. She appealed to the High Court.

Mrs Ebner conceded that there could be no appearance of bias on the part of Goldberg J. Instead, she relied on a line of English cases to the effect that any direct financial interest in the subject matter of a case would be enough to disqualify the decision-maker: a doctrine known as 'deemed bias'.

Clenae was a complex dispute involving issues of contract, equity and negligence. The ANZ Bank sued the defendants in the Supreme Court of Victoria. After an 18-day trial, Mandie J reserved his decision. Before he handed down the judgment, Mandie J's mother died, leaving him 2400 shares in the ANZ Bank. Mandie J did not disclose this inheritance to the parties in *Clenae.*

He handed down judgment in favour of the ANZ Bank. Later, having learned that Mandie J had inherited the shares, the defendants appealed to the Victorian Court of Appeal, arguing that the shares gave rise to an apprehension of bias. The Court of Appeal dismissed the appeal. The defendants appealed to the High Court.

The High Court dismissed both appeals.

Gleeson CJ, McHugh, Gummow and Hayne JJ

343 [3] Fundamental to the common law system of adversarial trial is that it is conducted by an independent and impartial tribunal. Perhaps the deepest historical roots of this principle can be traced to Magna Carta (with its declaration that right and justice shall not be sold) and the *Act of Settlement 1700* (UK) (with its provisions for the better securing in England of judicial independence). It is a principle which could be seen to be behind the confrontation in 1607 between Coke CJ and King James about the supremacy of law. It could be seen to be applied when Bacon was stripped of office and punished for taking bribes from litigants. ... It is unnecessary, however, to explore the historical origins of the principle. It is fundamental to the Australian judicial system.

...

344 [6] Where, in the absence of any suggestion of actual bias, a question arises as to the independence or impartiality of a judge (or other judicial officer or juror), as here, the governing principle is that, subject to qualifications relating to waiver ... or necessity ..., a judge is disqualified if a fair-minded lay observer might reasonably apprehend that the judge might not bring an impartial mind to the resolution of the question the judge is required to decide. That principle gives effect to the requirement that justice should both be done and be seen to be done, a requirement which reflects the fundamental importance of the principle that the tribunal be ***345*** independent and impartial. It is convenient to refer to it as the apprehension of bias principle.

[7] The apprehension of bias principle may be thought to find its justification in the importance of the basic principle, that the tribunal be independent and impartial. So important is the principle that even the appearance of departure from it is prohibited lest the integrity of the judicial system be undermined. There are, however, some other aspects of the apprehension of bias principle which should be recognized. Deciding whether a judicial officer ... *might* not bring an impartial mind to the resolution of a question that has not been determined requires no prediction about how the judge or juror will in fact approach the matter. The question is one of possibility (real and not remote), not probability. Similarly, if the matter has already been decided, the test is one which requires no conclusion about what factors *actually* influenced the outcome. No attempt need be made to inquire into the actual thought processes of the judge or juror.

[8] The apprehension of bias principle admits of the possibility of human frailty. Its application is as diverse as human frailty. Its application requires two steps. First, it requires the identification of what it is said might lead a judge (or juror) to decide a case other than on its legal and factual merits. The second step is no less important. There must be an articulation of the logical connection between the matter and the feared deviation from the course of deciding the case on its merits. The bare assertion that a judge (or juror) has an 'interest' in litigation, or an interest in a party to it, will be of no assistance until the nature of the interest, and the asserted connection with the possibility of departure from impartial decision making, is articulated. Only then can the reasonableness of the asserted apprehension of bias be assessed.

...

348 [19] Judges have a duty to exercise their judicial functions when their jurisdiction is regularly invoked and they are assigned to cases in accordance with the practice which prevails in the court to which they belong. They do not select the cases they will hear, and they are not at liberty to decline to hear cases without good cause.

Judges do not choose their cases; and litigants do not choose their judges. If one party to a case objects to a particular judge sitting, or continuing to sit, then that objection should not prevail unless it is based upon a substantial ground for contending that the judge is disqualified from hearing and deciding the case.

[20] This is not to say that it is improper for a judge to decline to sit unless the judge has affirmatively concluded that he or she is disqualified. In a case of real doubt, it will often be prudent for a judge to decide not to sit in order to avoid the inconvenience that could result if an appellate court were to take a different view on the matter of disqualification. However, if the mere making of an insubstantial objection were sufficient to lead a judge to decline to hear or decide a case, the system would soon reach a stage where, for practical purposes, individual parties could influence the composition of the bench. That would be intolerable.

...

[24] In *Webb v The Queen* [(1994) 181 CLR 41, 74], a case concerning a juror, Deane J identified four distinct, though overlapping, categories of case involving disqualification by reason of the appearance of bias: interest; conduct; association; and extraneous information. It is not necessary to ***349*** decide upon the comprehensiveness of such categorisation, and its utility may depend upon the context in which it is employed. However, it provides a convenient frame of reference.

[25] The concept of 'interest' is protean. Its use in this context has a long history. In the case of *Dimes v Proprietors of the Grand Junction Canal* [(1852) 3 HLC 759, 793; 10 ER 301, 315], in 1852, Lord Campbell said that the maxim that no one is to be a judge in his own cause is not confined to a cause in which he is a party, but applies to a cause in which the judge has an interest. ...

[26] As a matter of principle, in considering whether circumstances are incompatible with the appearance of impartiality, there is no reason to limit the concept of interest to financial interest, and there may be cases where an indirect interest is at least as destructive of the appearance of impartiality as a direct interest. It may be that, at a time when the focus of most civil litigation was some financial claim or right of property, it was easier to confine relevant interests to financial interests, but in modern times, when so much litigation is concerned with the enforcement of non-economic rights, it is difficult to do so. And even at the level of purely financial interests, the variety of arrangements under which persons may order their affairs makes a rigid distinction between direct and indirect interests artificial and unsatisfactory.

...

[28] The concepts of interest and association will overlap in many cases. ... There is no justification for having different principles for interest and association.

[29] The potential forms of association between a judge and a litigant are ***350*** manifold. Banks provide a good illustration. It may be assumed that all Australian judges have some form of relationship with a bank. There are only four major banking groups in the country. Banks are frequent litigants. ...

[30] It is not only association with a party to litigation that may be incompatible with the appearance of impartiality. There may be a disqualifying association with a

party's lawyer, or a witness, or some other person concerned with the case. In each case, however, the question must be how it is said that the existence of the 'association' or 'interest' might be thought (by the reasonable observer) possibly to divert the judge from deciding the case on its merits. As has been pointed out earlier, unless that connection is articulated, it cannot be seen whether the apprehension of bias principle applies. Similarly, the bare fact of an 'association' will not suffice to answer the relevant question. Having a mortgage with a bank, or knowing a party's lawyer, may (and in many cases will) have no logical connection with the disposition of the case on its merits.

[31] Ownership, direct or indirect, of shares in a corporation is but one possible form of association with, and potential interest in, a litigant or a case. In contemporary Australia, ownership of shares in a listed public company is a common form of saving and investment, both amongst members of the community generally, and amongst judges. It is not confined to wealthy individuals. ...

[Editors' note: Their Honours reviewed the English case law on deemed bias and considered its application in Australia.]

356 [54] Having regard to the current state of the common law in Australia on the subject of disqualification for apprehended bias, we do not accept the submission that there is a separate and free-standing rule of automatic disqualification which applies where a judge has a direct pecuniary interest, however small, in the outcome of the case over which the judge is presiding. ... [A] rule of automatic disqualification would be anomalous. It is in some respects too wide, and in other respects too narrow. There is no reason in principle why it should be limited to interests that are pecuniary, or why, if it were so limited, it should be limited to pecuniary interests ***357*** that are direct. ...

358 [58] [W]e accept that, in the practical application of the general test to be applied in cases of apprehended bias, economic conflicts of interest are likely to be of particular significance, and that, allowing for the imprecision of the concept, the circumstance that a judge has a not insubstantial, direct, pecuniary or proprietary interest in the outcome of litigation will ordinarily result in disqualification. That circumstance did not exist in either of the present cases.

...

359 [67] It was argued that Mandie J's failure to disclose his acquisition of shares in the Banks was itself a ground of, or constituted evidence in support of a ground of, disqualification. This argument requires consideration of the matter of disclosure of potentially disqualifying interests or associations. ...

360 [68] It is necessary to distinguish between considerations of prudence and requirements of law.

[69] As a matter of prudence and professional practice, judges should disclose interests and associations if there is a serious possibility that they are potentially disqualifying. It is common, and proper, practice for a judge who owns shares in a company which is involved in a case in which the judge is sitting to inform the parties of that fact and to give them an opportunity to raise an objection should they wish to be heard. In most cases, the outcome is that no objection is raised and, by reason of

waiver, any potential problem disappears. One reason for the practice is that it gives the parties an opportunity to bring to the attention of the judge some aspect of the case, or of its possible consequences, not known to, or fully appreciated by, the judge.

[70] It is, however, neither useful nor necessary to describe this practice in terms of rights and duties. At most, any 'duty' to disclose would be a duty of imperfect obligation. A failure to disclose is relevant (if at all) only because it may be said to cast some evidentiary light on the ultimate question of reasonable apprehension of bias. A failure to disclose has no other legal significance. In particular it does not, of itself, give a litigant any right to have the judge desist from further hearing the matter or to have the ultimate decision in the matter set aside for want of procedural fairness.

[Citations omitted]

Isbester v Knox City Council (2015) 255 CLR 135

Domestic Animals Act 1994 (Vic)

[As at relevant date]

29 Offences and liability relating to dog attacks

...

(4) If a dog that is not a dangerous dog or a restricted breed dog, attacks or bites any person or animal and causes death or a serious injury to the person or animal, the owner of the dog ... is guilty of an offence and liable to a penalty not exceeding 40 penalty units.

84P Further power to destroy dogs

The Council may destroy a dog which has been seized under this Part at any time after its seizure if—

...

(e) the dog's owner has been found guilty of an offence under section 28, 28A or 29 with respect to the dog; ...

Facts

Izzy, a Staffordshire Terrier, was one of three dogs owned by Tania Isbester. In August 2012, two of the dogs, including Izzy, were involved in an attack on another dog. A person who intervened in the attack sustained a wounded finger. The Knox City Council ('the Council') commenced an investigation into the incident.

In 2013, Ms Isbester was charged with several offences relating to other attacks by her dogs (not including the 2012 incident). Kirsten Hughes was the Co-ordinator of Local Laws for the Knox City Council. Her duties included the regulation of domestic animals. While working on the charges against Isbester, Ms Hughes realised that the Council had never completed its investigation into the 2012 attack. She reopened the investigation, reached the view that Izzy was the dog who had inflicted the injury on the person, and decided that six charges should be laid against

Ms Isbester in relation to that attack. Acting on Ms Hughes' instructions, the Council's solicitors prosecuted the charges. Ms Isbester pleaded guilty to the charges (including an offence under s 29(4) of the *Domestic Animals Act 1994* (Vic)) in the Magistrates Court.

Ms Hughes decided that, in accordance with the Council's usual practice, the Council would convene a panel to consider whether to order that Izzy be destroyed under s 84P. The panel consisted of three Council officers, including Ms Hughes. The panel gave Ms Isbester a hearing and considered material including the evidence prepared for the prosecutions. The panel then decided to order that Izzy be destroyed. The order was formally made by the panel's chairperson (Angelo Kourambas), but Ms Hughes was an active participant in deliberations and drafted the panel's reasons.

Ms Isbester commenced judicial review proceedings in the Supreme Court of Victoria, raising several grounds of review and seeking orders in the nature of certiorari and prohibition. She was unsuccessful, both before the primary judge and before the Court of Appeal. She appealed to the High Court, arguing that Ms Hughes' involvement in the panel decision gave rise to apprehended bias.

The High Court allowed the appeal and quashed the Council's decision. The RSPCA took Izzy into care, and she eventually found a new home with a couple in Queensland.

Kiefel, Bell, Keane and Nettle JJ

> ***149*** [34] The interest which the appellant alleges existed in this case is akin to that which a person bringing charges, whether as a prosecutor or other accuser, might be expected to have in the outcome of the hearing of those charges. It is generally expected that a person in this position may have an interest which would conflict with the objectivity required of a person deciding the charges and any consequential matters, whether that person be a judge or a member of some other decision-making body. ...

[Editors' note: Their Honours referred to the present case's factual similarity to *Dickason v Edwards* (1910) 10 CLR 243 and *Stollery v Greyhound Racing Control Board* (1972) 128 CLR 509. In *Dickason,* the High Court held the District Chief Ranger of a society could not sit on a committee of the society that was hearing charges against the plaintiff for insulting the District Chief Ranger. In *Stollery,* the Court held that a Board member who had accused Mr Stollery of attempting to bribe him ought not to have been in the room while the Board was deciding what action to take against Mr Stollery.]

> ***150*** [39] Ms Hughes' position with respect to the charges in the Magistrates' Court is analogous to the positions of the moving parties in *Dickason* and *Stollery.* It can scarcely be doubted that she had a similar interest in the outcome of the charges. However, neither of those cases addressed the issue behind the question which arises here, on the ***151*** council's case, as to whether it could reasonably be apprehended that Ms Hughes also maintained an interest in the outcome of the decision under s 84P(e).
>
> [40] The council places considerable reliance upon the fact that the decision-making process took place in two stages. The charges were heard, and pleas taken, in the Magistrates Court. The council, through the Panel, dealt with the subsequent but separate issue as to the fate of the dog. Ms Hughes' interest, if any, as a prosecutor, on the council's argument, ended when the proceedings in the Magistrates Court came to an end.

[41] It is true that the question for the Panel was different from that with which the Magistrates Court was concerned. ... In the present case the questions for the Panel would include matters directed to the future, such as the dog's propensity to attack and the safety of the public. However, it is also to be expected that much of the evidence relating to the past offence will also be relevant to penalty and this was the case here. This explains why the briefs of evidence from the Magistrates Court proceedings and Ms Hughes' notes of those proceedings were provided to the other Panel members.

[42] It is not realistic to view Ms Hughes' interest in the matter as coming to an end when the proceedings in the Magistrates' Court were completed. A line cannot be drawn at that point of her involvement so as to quarantine the Magistrates Court proceedings from her actions as a member of the Panel. It is reasonably to be expected that her involvement in the prosecution of the charges created an interest in the final outcome of the matter.

...

[43] In any event, it is not accurate to describe Ms Hughes as a person who in fact had no ongoing involvement in advancing the matter after the Magistrates Court proceedings. Having participated in obtaining the conviction for the offence under s 29(4), she organised the Panel hearing and drafted the letter advising the appellant of it. She supplied the Panel with evidence, including further evidence she had obtained as relevant to the future housing of the dog. If Ms Hughes could not actually be described as a prosecutor with respect to the decision under s 84P(e), she was certainly the moving force.

...

152 [45] ... Ms Hughes' role in this matter did not involve her at quite the same personal level as the manager in *Stollery*, who was subjected to, and affronted by, the alleged bribe; nor was she the target of abuse as in *Dickason*, which was directed to the District Chief Ranger. It may be accepted that these factors added another dimension to the level of involvement of those persons. It cannot, however, be said that this dimension accounted for the disqualification in those cases. The interest identified in *Dickason* and *Stollery* as necessitating disqualification was that of a prosecutor, accuser or other moving party. An interest of that kind points to the possibility of a deviation from the true course of decision-making.

[46] A 'personal interest' in this context is not the kind of interest by which a person will receive some material or other benefit. In the case of a prosecutor or other moving party it refers to a view which they may have of the matter, and which is in that sense personal to them. The interest of a prosecutor may be in the vindication of their opinion that an offence has occurred or that a particular penalty should be imposed, or in obtaining an outcome consonant with the prosecutor's view of guilt or punishment. It is not necessary to analyse the psychological processes to which a person in such a position is subject. It is well accepted, as the two cases referred to show, that it might reasonably be thought that the person's involvement in the capacity of prosecutor will not enable them to bring the requisite impartiality to decision-making. ...

[48] The council submitted that ... ***153*** the [two-step *Ebner*] test could not be met because ... the decision was not made by her, but by her superior, Mr Kourambas. ... [T]he participation of others does not overcome the apprehension that Ms Hughes'

interest in the outcome might affect not only her decision-making, but that of others. ... [S]he played a material part in the decision. That is so even if Mr Kourambas was responsible as delegate for the decision.

...

Conclusion and order

[50] A fair-minded observer might reasonably apprehend that Ms Hughes might not have brought an impartial mind to the decision under s 84P(e). This conclusion implies nothing about how Ms Hughes in fact approached the matter. It does not imply that she acted otherwise than diligently, and in accordance with her duties, ... or that she was not in fact impartial. Natural justice required, however, that she not participate in the decision and because that occurred, the decision must be quashed.

[Citations omitted]

Minister for Immigration and Multicultural Affairs v Jia Legeng (2001) 205 CLR 507

Migration Act 1958 (Cth)

[As at relevant date]

501 Special power to refuse or to cancel visa or entry permit

(1) The Minister may refuse to grant a visa to a person, or may cancel a visa that has been granted to a person, if:

(a) subsection (2) applies to the person; ...

(2) This subsection applies to a person if the Minister:

(a) having regard to:

(i) the person's past criminal conduct; or

(ii) the person's general conduct;

is satisfied that the person is not of good character; ...

(3) The power under this section to refuse to grant a visa to a person, or to cancel a visa that has been granted to a person, is in addition to any other power under this Act, as in force from time to time, to refuse to grant a visa to a person, or to cancel a visa that has been granted to a person.

502 Minister may decide in the national interest that certain persons are to be excluded persons

(1) If:

(a) the Minister, acting personally, intends to make a decision:

...

(ii) under section 501; ...

in relation to a person; and

> (b) the Minister decides that, because of the seriousness of the circumstances giving rise to the making of that decision, it is in the national interest that the person be declared to be an excluded person; the Minister may, as part of the decision, include a certificate declaring the person to be an excluded person.
>
> (2) A decision under subsection (1) must be taken by the Minister personally.
>
> (3) If the Minister makes a decision under subsection (1), the Minister must cause notice of the making of the decision to be laid before each House of the Parliament within 15 sitting days of that House after the day on which the decision was made.

Facts

Jia Legeng came to Australia from China in 1991 on a student visa. In February 1995, he was convicted of several offences (including assault causing bodily harm, and sexual penetration without consent) against a woman with whom he had previously been in a relationship. He was sentenced to six years and three months imprisonment.

Later that year, a delegate of the Minister refused to grant Mr Jia a visa to stay in Australia. Mr Jia was successful on merits review before the Administrative Appeals Tribunal ('AAT'), but the Minister appealed to the Federal Court, which allowed the appeal and remitted the decision to the AAT. The AAT again decided that Mr Jia was eligible for a visa and directed the Minister to grant the visa.

On 14 April 1997, one month after the AAT's second decision in favour of Mr Jia, the Minister was interviewed on radio. The topics covered included the character test in general, and Mr Jia's case in particular. The Minister said:

> What we are looking at here is the commission of offences. I don't believe you are of good character if you've committed significant criminal offences involving penal servitude.

When asked what action he intended to take in relation to Mr Jia, the Minister said:

> I'm considering what steps I can take and there are some avenues. One of the suggestions that's been made is that I could in fact grant the visa and then cancel it on character grounds. I have to weigh up whether or not that is a proper course for me to follow and I also have to look at the issue as to what the potential cost might be to the community if it opens up a whole host of other possible appeals to the Federal Court.

On 23 May, the Minister advised Mr Jia that he had been granted a visa (as directed by the AAT) but that the Minister was considering exercising his powers under ss 501 and 502 of the *Migration Act 1958* (Cth). On 10 June 1997, the Minister reached the conclusion that Mr Jia was not of good character, and therefore decided to cancel his visa under s 501 and to declare him an excluded person under s 502.

Mr Jia sought judicial review in the Federal Court. At this time, the *Migration Act* limited review in the Federal Court to several specified grounds, including actual (but not apprehended) bias. Mr Jia argued that the Minister's decisions had been affected by actual bias. The primary judge rejected this argument, but on appeal the Full Court held there had been actual bias. The Minister appealed to the High Court. In the same proceedings, Mr Jia applied to the High Court under s 75(v) of the *Constitution*, arguing there had been apprehended bias.

The High Court allowed the Minister's Appeal and refused to grant relief under s 75(v). By majority, the Court held there was no actual or apprehended bias. In dissent, Kirby J held there was apprehended, but not actual, bias.

Gleeson CJ and Gummow J

> ***528*** [61] ... [T]he powers conferred upon the Minister by ss 501 and 502 form part of a statutory scheme which involves a complex pattern of administrative and judicial power, and differing forms of accountability. The Minister is a Member of Parliament, with political accountability to the electorate, and a member of the Executive Government, with responsibility to Parliament. ... [T]he Minister functions in the arena of public debate, political controversy, and democratic accountability. At the same time, the Minister's exercise of statutory power is subject to the rule of law, and the form of accountability which that entails ...
>
> ...
>
> ***529*** [63] In [*R v Anderson; Ex parte Ipec-Air Pty Ltd* (1965) 113 CLR 177] it was ... said that there is 'a significant difference between a discretion given to a Minister and one given to a departmental head' [at 202 (Menzies J)]. ... [The consequences that flow from the circumstance that a power is vested in, and exercised by, a Minister] include the consideration that the conduct of a Minister may need to be evaluated in the light of his or her political role, responsibility and accountability.
>
> ...
>
> ***531*** [71] ... Decision-makers, including judicial decision-makers, sometimes approach their task with a tendency of mind, or predisposition, sometimes one that has been publicly expressed, without being accused or suspected of bias. The question is not whether a decision-maker's mind is blank; it is whether it is open to persuasion. ...
>
> ...
>
> ***539*** [102] ... [L]awyers usually equate 'bias' with a departure from the standard of even-handed justice which the law requires from those who occupy judicial, or quasijudicial, office. The Minister is in a different position. The statutory powers in question have been reposed in a political official, a member of the Executive Government, who not only has general accountability to the electorate and to Parliament, but who, in s 502, is made is made subject to a specific form of parliamentary accountability. The power given by s 502 requires the Minister to consider the national interest. As Brennan J observed in *South Australia v O'Shea* [(1987) 163 CLR 378, 411]: 'The public interest in this context is a matter of political responsibility.' The powers given by ss 501 and 502 ... enabled the Minister in effect to reverse the practical consequences of decisions of the Tribunal ... even though no new facts or circumstances had arisen; and even though the Minister had been involved in the proceedings before the Tribunal. As the circumstances of the radio interview demonstrate, the Minister himself can be drawn into public debate about a matter in respect of which he may consider exercising his powers. He might equally well have been asked questions about the cases in Parliament. The position of the Minister is substantially different from that of a judge, or quasi-judicial officer, adjudicating in adversarial litigation. It would be wrong to apply to his conduct the standards of detachment which apply to

judicial officers or jurors. There is no reason to conclude that the legislature intended to impose such standards upon the Minister, and every reason to conclude otherwise.

Hayne J

562 [178] Courts in this country make decisions by procedures that are both formal and adversarial. They do so by the application of rules for decision-making which, although not always defined with absolute certainty, are generally discernible before the contest is joined and are set by legislative or judicial processes which are external to the judge. The process of adjudication is generally conducted in open court. The judge must give reasons for the decision that is reached.

[179] Importantly, the rules about natural justice recognise that, subject to questions of judicial notice, judges, unlike administrators, must act only on the evidence adduced by the parties and must not act upon information acquired otherwise. No less importantly, the rules about judicial prejudgment proceed from the fundamental requirement that the judge is neutral. That requirement for neutrality is buttressed by constitutional and statutory safeguards. Those safeguards include not only the provisions for security of terms of office and remuneration but also extend to statutory provisions prohibiting interference with the course of justice. A judge can have no stake of any kind in the outcome of the dispute. The judge must not '[descend] into the arena and ... have his vision clouded by the dust of the conflict'. The central task and, it may be said, the only loyalty, of the judge is to do justice according to law.

[180] Decisions outside the courts are not attended by these features. Reference need only be made to a body like the Refugee Review Tribunal ... to show that this is so. The procedures for decision-making by that body are much less formal than those of a court. There is no provision for any contradictor and the procedures are, therefore, not adversarial. The decision-maker has little security of tenure and, at least to that extent, may be thought to have some real stake in the outcome. The decision-maker, in a body like the Refugee Review Tribunal, will bring to the task of deciding an individual's application a great deal of information and ideas which have been accumulated or ***563*** formed in the course of deciding other applications. A body like the Refugee Review Tribunal, unlike a court, is expected to build up 'expertise' in matters such as country information. Often information of that kind is critical in deciding the fate of an individual's application, but it is not suggested that to take it into account amounts to a want of procedural fairness by reason of prejudgment.

[181] The analogy with curial processes becomes even less apposite as the nature of the decision-making process, and the identity of the decision-maker, diverges further from the judicial paradigm. It is trite to say that the content of the rules of procedural fairness must be 'appropriate and adapted to the circumstances of the particular case'. What is appropriate when decision of a disputed question is committed to a tribunal whose statutorily defined processes have some or all of the features of a court will differ from what is appropriate when the decision is committed to an investigating body. Ministerial decision-making is different again.

[Citations omitted]

CHAPTER

13

GROUNDS ARISING FROM THE STATUTE CONFERRING A POWER

Introduction 364

Misconceiving the scope of a power 364

New South Wales Registrar of Births, Deaths and Marriages v Norrie (2014) 250 CLR 490 364

Jurisdictional facts 367

Corporation of the City of Enfield v Development Assessment Commission (2000) 199 CLR 135 367

Liversidge v Anderson [1942] AC 206 370

Plaintiff M70/2011 v Minister for Immigration and Citizenship (2011) 244 CLR 144 ('*Malaysia Declaration Case*') 373

Procedural error 378

Forrest & Forrest Pty Ltd v Wilson (2017) 262 CLR 510 378

Improper delegation 387

O'Reilly v Commissioners of the State Bank of Victoria (1983) 153 CLR 1 387

Mandatory and prohibited considerations 390

Minister for Aboriginal Affairs v Peko-Wallsend Ltd (1986) 162 CLR 24 390

Tickner v Chapman (1995) 57 FCR 451 396

Murphyores Inc Pty Ltd v Commonwealth (1976) 136 CLR 1 400

Introduction

This chapter complements Chapter 13 of *Government Accountability: Australian Administrative Law*, third edition. The cases extracted in this chapter illustrate the operation of limits on power that can be discerned from the statute conferring the power: misconceiving the nature or scope of the power, jurisdictional facts (both objective and subjective), procedural error, improper delegation, and mandatory and prohibited considerations. The cases in this chapter are worth studying both for their exposition of legal principles, and for the application of those principles to the facts. *O'Reilly v Commissioners of the State Bank of Victoria* (1983) 153 CLR 1, for example, is not only the leading Australian case on improper delegation, but also an excellent example of the reasoning process used to determine whether delegation is permissible in a particular situation.

With one exception, the cases in this chapter are decisions of the High Court of Australia. The exception is *Liversidge v Anderson* [1942] AC 206 – which is included because Lord Atkin's dissenting judgment is one of the most celebrated administrative law judgments.

Misconceiving the scope of a power

New South Wales Registrar of Births, Deaths and Marriages v Norrie (2014) 250 CLR 490

Births, Deaths and Marriages Registration Act 1995 **(NSW)**

[As at relevant date]

PART 5A—CHANGE OF SEX

32A Definitions

In this Part:

sex affirmation procedure means a surgical procedure involving the alteration of a person's reproductive organs carried out:

(a) for the purpose of assisting a person to be considered to be a member of the opposite sex, or

(b) to correct or eliminate ambiguities relating to the sex of the person.

32DA Application to register change of sex

(1) A person who is 18 or above:

(a) who is an Australian citizen or permanent resident of Australia, and

(b) who lives, and has lived for at least one year, in New South Wales, and

(c) who has undergone a sex affirmation procedure, and

(d) who is not married, and

(e) whose birth is not registered under this Act or a corresponding law,

may apply to the Registrar, in a form approved by the Registrar, for the registration of the person's sex in the Register.

32DC Decision to register change of sex

(1) The Registrar is to determine an application under section 32DA by registering the person's change of sex or refusing to register the person's change of sex.

(2) Before registering a person's change of sex, the Registrar may require the applicant to provide such particulars relating to the change of sex as may be prescribed by the regulations.

Facts

Although born with male reproductive organs, Norrie identified as having a non-specific gender identity. In 1989, she[1] underwent sexual reassignment surgery. In 2009, she applied to the Registrar of Births, Deaths and Marriages to register a change of sex to 'not specified'. The Registrar wrote to Norrie informing her that her application was successful, and her gender had been registered as 'not specified'. However, the Registrar later wrote to Norrie again, this time informing her that the registration was invalid because the Registrar did not have power to register a person as having a non-specific gender. Norrie's appeals to the New South Wales Administrative Decisions Tribunal and to the Appeal Panel of the Tribunal were unsuccessful. Each decision-maker interpreted the word 'sex' in s 32DC as having a 'binary' meaning: a person's sex could only be either male or female. On this interpretation, the Registrar did not have the power to register a change to 'not specified'. Norrie appealed the Tribunal's decision under s 113 of the *Administrative Decisions Tribunal Act 1997* (NSW), which provided for an appeal to the Supreme Court on a question of law. The New South Wales Court of Appeal allowed the appeal, ordering that the Appeal Panel's decision be set aside and the matter remitted to the Tribunal for determination. The Registrar appealed to the High Court.

The issue was whether the Registrar's power under s 32DC was restricted to changing a registered sex from 'male' to 'female' and vice versa, or whether the word 'sex' in s 32DC had a broader meaning.

The Court held that the Registrar did have power to record a change to a 'non-specific' sex, and remitted the matter to the Registrar for determination.

French CJ, Hayne, Kiefel, Bell and Keane JJ

495 [16] [Section] 32DC(1) confers a limited and specific decision-making power on the Registrar. While the Registrar may require such particulars 'relating to the change of sex as may be prescribed by the regulations', neither the Act nor the regulations suggest that the Registrar's function extends to the making of any moral or social judgments; it certainly does not extend to the resolution of medical questions or the formation of a view about the outcome of a sex affirmation procedure.

...

[18] ... [T]he 1996 Amending Act, which introduced Pt 5A (but not including ss 32DA–32DD and s 32J) into the Act, also amended the *Anti-Discrimination Act 1977* (NSW) by adding to that Act definitions of 'recognised transgender person' (a person

1 The relevant judgments – and, indeed, Norrie's own submissions to the High Court – use the personal pronouns 'she' and 'her' when referring to Norrie.

'the record of whose sex is altered under Part 5A of the *Births, Deaths and Marriages Registration Act 1995*') and 'transgender person' (which is defined to include a person 'who, being of indeterminate sex, identifies as a member of a particular sex by living as a member of that sex'). These definitions in the 1996 Amending Act are part of the context in which ***496*** Pt 5A of the Act was enacted. Accordingly, the provisions of Pt 5A are to be applied in a context of express legislative recognition of the existence of persons of 'indeterminate sex'.

...

The arguments in this Court

497 [28] The Registrar submitted that the Court of Appeal strayed too far from the text of the Act in reaching its conclusions. It was said that the Act does not contemplate a range of categories of sex, additional to the ***498*** 'opposite' sexes of male and female. In particular, the definition of 'sex affirmation procedure' in s 32A suggests a process of seeking to become male or female, given that s 32A(a) states that the sex affirmation procedure is carried out for the purpose of 'assisting a person to be considered to be a member of the opposite sex'; and to speak of the opposite sex is necessarily to speak only of male or female. Further, the Registrar submitted, it is reasonable to expect that an intention to recognise another category of 'sex' would have been expressly stated in the Act. In this regard, the definition of 'transgender' in Pt 3A of the *Anti-Discrimination Act* does refer to a person being of an indeterminate sex; but, significantly, this language was not used in Pt 5A of the Act.

...

[30] Norrie submitted that the purpose of the Register is to state the truth about matters recorded in the Register to the greatest possible extent. If the Act proceeded on the assumption that every person was male or female, then s 32A(b) would be superfluous because any change of sex would fall within the scope of s 32A(a). A sex affirmation procedure described in s 32A(b) of the Act, the purpose of which is to 'correct or eliminate ambiguities relating to the sex of the person', was said to be predicated upon legislative recognition that not everyone may be classified as male or female. In this case, the sex affirmation procedure, which is a precondition of an application under s 32DA, was carried out, but Norrie's sex remained ambiguous so that it would be to record misinformation in the Register to classify her as male or female. There is evident force in this submission.

...

Additional categories of sex

499 [33] As a matter of the ordinary use of language, to speak of the opposite sex is to speak of the contrasting categories of sex: male and female. Yet given the terms of s 32A(b) and the context in which it is to be construed, the Act recognises that a person's sex may be indeterminate.

...

[35] The Registrar's initial determination of Norrie's application was right. The appropriate record of her change of sex was from 'male' ... to 'non-specific'. To make that record in the Register would be no more than to recognise, as the Act does,

that not everyone is male or female and that the change to be registered was from an assumed registered classification outside of New South Wales as a male to, as Norrie's application put it, non-specific.

Ambiguities and indeterminacy

[36] The Registrar's submission must be rejected at the point at which it insists that the Registrar is required to decide whether he or she is satisfied (let alone that it has been demonstrated objectively) that, despite an application showing persisting ambiguity in the sex of the applicant following a sex affirmation procedure, the applicant's sex should be recorded in the Register as being either male or female. The registration of a change of sex records the facts supplied by the application so long as the application is supported in accordance with s 32DB.

[37] The provision of the Act which acknowledges 'ambiguities' and the context of the 1996 Amending Act, which referred to persons of 'indeterminate sex', are a sufficient indication that the Act recognises that, as this Court observed in *AB v Western Australia* [(2011) 244 CLR 390 at 402 [23]], 'the sex of a person is not ... in every case unequivocally male or female'.

[38] There is nothing in the text of the Act which gives support to the view that the Registrar must initiate, much less resolve, a dispute ***500*** concerning matters of fact and expert opinions presented to the Registrar under ss 32DA and 32DB. Such a role would not be consistent with the provisions of the Act which charge the Registrar with the role of establishing and maintaining the registers by recording information provided by members of the community.

...

[40] It was open to the Registrar, in the exercise of the power conferred by s 32DC, to register Norrie's change of sex by recording the change from classification as male to non-specific. ...

[Citations omitted]

Jurisdictional facts

Corporation of the City of Enfield v Development Assessment Commission (2000) 199 CLR 135

Development Act 1993 (SA)

[As at relevant date]

35 Special provisions relating to assessment against a Development Plan

...

(3) A development that is of a kind described as a *non-complying* development under the relevant Development Plan must not be granted a provisional development plan consent unless —

(a) where the relevant authority is the Development Assessment Commission – the Minister and, if the development is to be undertaken in the area of a council, that council, concur in the granting of the consent; ...

Development Regulations 1993 (SA)

[As at relevant date]

16 Nature of development

...

(1) If an application will require a relevant authority to assess a proposed development against the provisions of a Development Plan, the relevant authority must determine the nature of the development, and proceed to deal with the application according to that determination.

...

Schedule 1

...

special industry means an industry where the processes carried on, the methods of manufacture adopted or the particular materials or goods used, produced or stored, are likely

(a) to cause or create dust, fumes, vapours, smells or gases; or

(b) to discharge foul liquid or blood or other substance or impurities liable to become foul, and thereby -

(c) to endanger, injure or detrimentally affect the life, health or property of any person (other than any person employed or engaged in the industry); or

(d) to produce conditions which are, or may become, offensive or repugnant to the occupiers or users of land in the locality of or within the vicinity of the locality of the land on which (whether wholly or partly) the industry is conducted.

Facts

Collex Waste Management Services Pty Ltd ('Collex') operated a waste treatment plant on its land at Kilburn in South Australia. Collex applied for provisional development plan consent (a form of development approval) to alter and expand the waste treatment plant. Provisional development plan consent involved the 'relevant authority' (in this case, the Development Assessment Commission) assessing the proposed development against the Development Plan that applied to the area. Under the Development Plan, 'special industry' was classified as 'non-complying'. The Development Assessment Commission determined that the development was 'general industry', rather than 'special industry', and therefore was not 'non-complying'. It subsequently granted provisional development plan consent.

The local council, the City of Enfield, commenced judicial review proceedings in the Supreme Court of South Australia seeking a declaration that the provisional development plan consent was void. Enfield argued the development was 'special industry' and, therefore, 'non-complying'. A finding that the land was 'non-complying' would have several consequences. The Commission would have been required to seek Enfield's consent, and the Minister's consent, to the development; notice of the development would have to be given to the general public (as well as to the owners and occupiers of neighbouring land); and the appeal rights available would be less favourable to Collex and more favourable to those who objected to the development.

Enfield argued that whether the development was a 'non-complying' development was a question of jurisdictional fact, and therefore reviewable by a court on judicial review. The primary judge, Debelle J, accepted this argument and found the development was 'special industry'. An appeal to the Full Court of the Supreme Court was allowed, overturning Debelle J's orders. Enfield appealed to the High Court. The High Court allowed the appeal.

Gleeson CJ, Gummow, Kirby and Hayne JJ

> ***148*** [28] The term 'jurisdictional fact' (which may be a complex of elements) is often used to identify that criterion, satisfaction of which enlivens the power of the decisionmaker to exercise a discretion. Used here, it identifies a criterion, satisfaction of which mandates a particular outcome. Section 35(3) forbids the relevant authority granting a provisional development plan consent to a '*non-complying*' development unless, in a case such as the present, the Minister and the Council concur in the granting of the consent. The determination of the question whether Collex proposed a '*non-complying*' development, which turned upon the application of the criterion of 'special industry', was a condition upon the existence of which there operated the obligation that the Commission not grant consent.
>
> ...
>
> ***149*** [33] [T]aken as a whole, the text of s 35 does not suggest that the determination whether, upon the criteria specified in s 35, the responsible authority is or is not obliged to consent rests upon its own classification of the relevant circumstances. Rather, it indicates that it is not for the relevant authority itself to determine, as a matter of its opinion, whether the restriction imposed upon it by s 35(3) applies because the development is a '*non-complying*' development. ***150*** Section 35(3) does not define the criterion of operation as the opinion of the relevant authority as to the classification of the development.
>
> [34] Had s 35(3) been expressed so as to turn upon the satisfaction or opinion of the relevant authority as to a state of affairs, or were it to be so understood, as Collex submitted, further questions would have arisen. In particular, the existence of the opinion or satisfaction would be treated as requiring an opinion or satisfaction formed reasonably upon the material before the decision-maker. But that is not what s 35(3) involves. It stipulates in direct terms a precondition which obliges, without certain concurrences, refusal of a grant of consent.
>
> ...
>
> ***151*** [38] The result is that the Full Court erred in holding that Debelle J was obliged to determine the action before him, not by application of the law to the evidence, but from a standpoint that, whilst the Supreme Court should 'reserve the right to itself to inquire into the relevant facts and to decide the jurisdictional facts', it would defer 'in grey areas of uncertainty to the practical judgment of the planning authority' and that what had to be shown was 'a serious departure (in planning terms) from the requirements of the Act and Regulations'. It should be added that, contrary to the approach taken by the Full Court, in whatever form the proceeding in the Supreme

Court had been cast, it would have been necessary for Debelle J to determine the 'jurisdictional fact' issue upon the evidence before the Supreme Court. Accordingly, the matter will have to be returned to the Full Court for determination of the outstanding issues on the appeal from Debelle J to that Court.

[Citations omitted]

Liversidge v Anderson [1942] AC 206

Defence (General) Regulations 1939 (UK)

[As at relevant date]

18B(1) Detention Orders

(1) If the Secretary of State has reasonable cause to believe any person to be of hostile origin or associations or to have been recently concerned in acts prejudicial to the public safety or the defence of the realm or in the preparation or instigation of such acts and that by reason thereof it is necessary to exercise control over him, he may make an order against that person directing that he be detained.

...

Facts

The Home Secretary, Sir John Anderson, detained Robert Liversidge under reg 18B of the *Defence (General) Regulations 1939* (UK). Mr Liversidge sued the Home Secretary for false imprisonment, arguing the order under reg 18B was invalid. Mr Liversidge applied for further particulars of the grounds that gave the Home Secretary 'reasonable cause to believe' Liversidge had hostile associations, or that it was necessary to exercise control over him. The Home Secretary argued that an order under reg 18B was valid so long as he, the Home Secretary, had a belief that, *to his mind,* was reasonable.

The two speeches in the House of Lords which are extracted here represent different interpretations of a power conditioned on the subjective opinion of a decision-maker. The reasoning in Lord Atkin's dissenting judgment has become accepted as the approach to interpreting subjective opinion clauses in Australia.

Lord Wright

264 In reg 18B the Home Secretary is expressly empowered to make a detention order in the circumstances specified. What are these circumstances? They are a belief or mental state of the minister. Except for the word 'reasonable,' which I shall later discuss, there is no reference to anything but his personal belief, because I think that actual belief is implied by the words 'has reasonable cause to believe.' His belief is something personal to himself. The reasonable cause can only be material in so far as it is an element present to his mind which determines his own belief. The 'cause to believe' is part of the content of his mind. The matters specified, except hostile origin and, perhaps, hostile associations, are matters of opinion or ***265*** judgment, not matters of fact ...

All the circumstances of national safety to which this House adverted in *Rex v Halliday* [[1917] AC 260] are present in this war, only with vastly increased urgency and gravity, because German methods for effecting the poisonous infiltration among British or allied subjects of their purposes and schemes have been immensely more subtle and ingenious than in the last war. Even a judge may be allowed to take notice of the import of words like Fifth Columnists and Quislings and the like. It is the duty of the Secretary to check these underground and insidious activities of the enemy and their consequences, whether they result in sabotage or in anti-British propaganda or in weakening the national effort and endurance ... [Under reg 18B] [t]he Secretary must ... act on his own responsibility if he has reasonable cause to believe, that is, believes that he has in his own mind what he thinks is reasonable cause. If that is his mental state, the duty to act in the national interest attaches. That is a higher duty than the duty to regard the liberty of the subject. I cannot see any ground for holding ***266*** that the performance of that duty is to be subject to the decision of a judge, who cannot possibly have the full information on which the minister has acted or appreciate the full importance in the national interest of what the information discloses ...

268 But against all these arguments the appellant relies on the use of the word 'reasonable' as qualifying the 'cause to believe.' It is said that 'reasonable' necessarily implies an external standard to be applied by someone other than the Secretary, namely, by a judge. I cannot accept that contention, which seems to me to subordinate the whole substance of the enactment to a single word which itself is ambiguous and inconclusive. The word 'reasonable' does indeed imply instructed and intelligent care and deliberation, the choice of the course which reason dictates. But the choice is not necessarily that of an outsider. If I am right in my view of the effect of the regulation, the choice can only be the choice of the minister. All the word 'reasonable,' then, means is that the minister must not lightly or arbitrarily invade the liberty of the subject. He must be reasonably satisfied before he acts, but it is still his decision and not the decision of anyone else. If in ordinary affairs I say that I reasonably believe in the truth of certain facts or in the propriety of certain conduct, I am prima facie adopting as my reason my own judgment. If I mean to refer to some external yardstick I should in general naturally say so expressly unless the contrary was clear from other circumstances.

[Editors' note: Lord Wright concluded that the validity of the order under reg 18B did not depend on the objective reasonableness of the opinion, and therefore Mr Liversidge was not entitled to the further particulars.]

Lord Atkin (dissenting)

226 [The words of reg 18B] are simple words and as it appears to me obviously give only a conditional authority to the minister to detain any person without trial, the condition being that he has reasonable cause for the belief which leads to the detention order. The meaning, however, which for the first time was adopted by the Court of Appeal in [*Greene v Secretary of State for Home Affairs* [1942] 1 KB 284] and appears to have found favour with some of your Lordships is that there is no condition, for the words 'if the Secretary of State has "reasonable cause"' merely mean 'if the Secretary of State thinks that he has reasonable cause.' The result is that the only implied condition is that the Secretary of State acts in good faith. If he does that—and who could dispute it or disputing it prove the opposite?—the minister has been given complete discretion whether he should detain a subject or not. It is an absolute power which, so far as I know, has never been given before to the executive, and I shall not apologize for taking some time to demonstrate that no such power is in fact given to the minister by the words in question ...

227 It is surely incapable of dispute that the words 'if A has "X"' constitute a condition the essence of which is the existence of X and the having of it by A. If it is a condition to a right (including a power) granted to A, whenever the right comes into dispute the tribunal whatever it may be that is charged with determining the dispute must ascertain whether the condition is fulfilled. In some cases the issue is one of fact, in others of both fact and law, but in all cases the words indicate an existing something the having of which can be ascertained. And the words do not mean and cannot mean 'if A thinks that he has.' 'If A has a broken ankle' does not mean and cannot mean 'if A thinks that he has a broken ankle.' 'If A has a right of way' does not mean and cannot mean 'if A thinks that he has a right of way.' 'Reasonable cause' for an action or a belief is just as much a positive fact capable of determination by a third party as is a ***228*** broken ankle or a legal right. If its meaning is the subject of dispute as to legal rights, then ordinarily the reasonableness of the cause, and even the existence of any cause is in our law to be determined by the judge and not by the tribunal of fact, if the functions deciding law and fact are divided. ...

244 I view with apprehension the attitude of judges who on a mere question of construction when face to face with claims involving the liberty of the subject show themselves more executive minded than the executive. Their function is to give words their natural meaning, not, perhaps, in war time leaning towards liberty, but following the dictum of Pollock CB in *Bowditch v Balchin* [(1850) 5 Ex 378] ... 'In a case in which the liberty of the subject is concerned, we cannot go beyond the natural construction of the statute.' In this country, amid the clash of arms, the laws are not silent. They may be changed, but they speak the same language in war as in peace. It has always been one of the pillars of freedom, one of the principles of liberty for which on recent authority we are now fighting, that the judges are no respecters of persons and stand between the subject and any attempted encroachments on his liberty by the executive, alert to see that any coercive action is justified in law. In this case I have listened to arguments which might have been addressed acceptably to the Court of King's Bench in the time of Charles I. I protest, even if I do it alone, against a strained construction put on words with the effect of giving an uncontrolled power of imprisonment to the minister. To recapitulate: The words have only one meaning. They are used with that meaning in statements of the common law and in statutes. They have never been used in the sense now imputed to them. They are used in the *Defence Regulations* in the natural meaning, and, when it is intended to express the meaning now imputed to them, different and apt words are used in the regulations ***245*** generally and in this regulation in particular... I know of only one authority which might justify the suggested method of construction:

> 'When I use a word,' Humpty Dumpty said in rather a scornful tone, 'it means just what I choose it to mean, neither more nor less.'
>
> 'The question is,' said Alice, 'whether you can make words mean so many different things.'
>
> 'The question is,' said Humpty Dumpty, 'which is to be master—that's all.' ('Through the Looking Glass,' c. vi.)

After all this long discussion the question is whether the words 'If a man has' can mean 'If a man thinks he has.' I am of opinion that they cannot, and that the case should be decided accordingly ...

[Citations omitted]

Plaintiff M70/2011 v Minister for Immigration and Citizenship (2011) 244 CLR 144 ('*Malaysia Declaration Case*')

Migration Act 1958 (Cth)

[As at relevant date]

198A Offshore entry person may be taken to a declared country

(1) An officer may take an offshore entry person from Australia to a country in respect of which a declaration is in force under subsection (3).

...

(3) The Minister may:

(a) declare in writing that a specified country:

(i) provides access, for persons seeking asylum, to effective procedures for assessing their need for protection; and

(ii) provides protection for persons seeking asylum, pending determination of their refugee status; and

(iii) provides protection to persons who are given refugee status, pending their voluntary repatriation to their country of origin or resettlement in another country; and

(iv) meets relevant human rights standards in providing that protection.

Facts

In response to concern about the numbers of asylum seekers attempting to travel to Australia by boat, the Australian Government entered into an 'Arrangement' with Malaysia. Under the Arrangement, Australia would send up to 800 asylum seekers to Malaysia, where their claims to refugee status would be processed; and 4000 refugees residing in Malaysia would be sent to Australia for resettlement. The Minister made a declaration in relation to Malaysia under s 198A(3).

Plaintiff M70 and Plaintiff M106, asylum seekers from Afghanistan, arrived at Christmas Island by boat, making them 'offshore entry persons' for the purpose of the *Migration Act.* Both were likely to be sent to Malaysia under the agreement. They sought a declaration that the Minister's declaration under s 198A(3) was invalid.

The central issues were whether the criteria in s 198A(3)(a)(i)–(iv) were jurisdictional facts, or depended on the Minister's opinion that those criteria were satisfied; and, if either of those was the case, whether the precondition to the exercise of power was satisfied. The plaintiffs argued the criteria were not satisfied because Malaysia was under no legal obligation to provide the protections and access mentioned in s 198A(3)(a). Unlike Australia, Malaysia was not a signatory to the *Refugee Convention*;[2] nor did its domestic law, or its agreement with Australia, place it under any binding obligations in relation to these matters.

Gummow, Hayne, Crennan and Bell JJ held that the criteria in s 198A(3)(a)(i)–(iv) were objective jurisdictional facts. In contrast, French CJ held that the Minister's *satisfaction* of those criteria was a subjective jurisdictional fact. All judges held that the precondition to the exercise of power had not been satisfied.

Gummow, Hayne, Crennan and Bell JJ

> ***193*** [106] Section 198A(3) provides that the Minister 'may: (a) declare ... that a specified country' has the four characteristics identified in sub-paras (i)–(iv) of that paragraph. Section 198A(3)(a) does not refer to the Minister being *satisfied* of the existence of those criteria or provide that the Minister's forming of an *opinion* about those matters is a condition for the exercise of the discretion to make a declaration. Rather, the Minister is given a discretion, and thus has power, to declare that a ***194*** specified country *has* the relevant characteristics. On its face, it is not a power to declare that the Minister *thinks* or *believes* or *is satisfied* that the country has those characteristics.
>
> ...
>
> [109] ... [T]he submissions on behalf of the Minister and the Commonwealth that sub-paras (i)–(iv) of s 198A(3)(a) are not jurisdictional facts should not be accepted. To read s 198A(3)(a) in that way would read it as validly engaged whenever the Minister bona fide thought or believed that the relevant criteria were met. So to read the provision would pay insufficient regard to its text, context and evident purpose. Text, context and purpose point to the need to identify the relevant criteria with particularity. ...
>
> ***195*** [117] When s 198A(3)(a) speaks of a country that provides access and protections it uses language that directs attention to the kinds of ***196*** obligation that Australia and other signatories have undertaken under the Refugees Convention and the Refugees Protocol. Reference has already been made to the non-refoulement obligation imposed by Art 33(1) of the Refugees Convention. But signatories undertake other obligations. Those obligations include:
>
> - to apply the provisions of the Convention to refugees without discrimination as to race, religion or country of origin (Art 3);

2 *Convention Relating to the Status of Refugees*, opened for signature 28 July 1951, 189 UNTS 150 (entered into force 22 April 1954) as amended by the *Protocol Relating to the Status of Refugees*, opened for signature 31 January 1967, 606 UNTS 267 (entered into force 4 October 1967).

- to accord to refugees within a signatory's territory treatment at least as favourable as that accorded to its nationals with respect to freedom to practice their religion and freedom as regards the religious education of their children (Art 4);
- to accord to a refugee free access to the courts of law (Art 16(1));
- to accord to refugees lawfully staying in its territory the most favourable treatment accorded to nationals of a foreign country in the same circumstances as regards the right to engage in wage-earning employment (Art 17(1));
- to accord to refugees the same treatment as is accorded to nationals with respect to elementary education (Art 22(1)); and
- to accord to refugees lawfully in its territory the right to choose their place of residence and to move freely within its territory, subject to any regulations applicable to aliens generally in the same circumstances (Art 26).

... What is clear is that signatories to the Refugees Convention and the Refugees Protocol are bound to accord to those who have been determined to be refugees the rights that are specified in those instruments including the rights earlier described.

[118] The references in s 198A(3)(a)(i)–(iii) to a country that provides access to certain procedures and provides protections of certain kinds must be understood as referring to access and protections of the kinds that Australia undertook to provide by signing the Refugees Convention and the Refugees Protocol. In that sense the criteria stated in s 198A(3)(a)(i)–(iii) are to be understood as a reflex of Australia's obligations.

...

199 [125] A country 'provides access' to effective procedures for assessing the need for protection of persons seeking asylum of the kind described in s 198A(3)(a)(i) if its domestic law provides for such procedures or if it is bound, as a matter of international obligation, to allow some third party (such as the United Nations High Commissioner for Refugees – UNHCR) to undertake such procedures or to do so itself. A country does not provide access to effective procedures if, having no obligation to provide the procedures, all that is seen is that it has permitted a body such as UNHCR to undertake that body's own procedures for assessing the needs for protection of persons seeking asylum.

[126] A country does not provide protections of the kind described in s 198A(3)(a)(ii) or (iii) unless its domestic law deals expressly with the classes of persons mentioned in those sub-paragraphs or it is internationally obliged to provide the particular protections. In particular, a country does not provide protection to persons who are given refugee status, pending their voluntary repatriation to their country of origin or resettlement in another country, unless the country in question provides to persons who have been given refugee status rights of the kind mentioned in the Refugees Convention. Not only did the Arrangement not oblige Malaysia to provide any of those rights, no provision was made in the Arrangement that (if carried out) would provide any of those rights.

...

201 [135] As already explained, the references in s 198A(3)(a) to a country that provides access and provides protection are to be construed as references to provision of access or protection in accordance with an obligation to do so. Where, as in the present case, it is agreed that Malaysia: first, does not recognise the status of refugee in its domestic law and does not undertake any activities related to the reception, registration, documentation and status determination of asylum seekers and refugees; secondly, is not party to the Refugees Convention or the Refugees Protocol; and, thirdly, has made no legally binding arrangement with Australia obliging it to accord the protections required by those instruments; it was not open to the Minister to ***202*** conclude that Malaysia provides the access or protections referred to in s 198A(3)(a)(i)–(iii) ... The jurisdictional facts necessary to making a valid declaration under s 198A(3)(a) were not and could not be established.

[136] The Minister's declaration was made beyond power. It follows that s 198A(1) cannot be engaged to take either plaintiff from Australia to Malaysia.

French CJ

179 [57] The term 'jurisdictional fact' applied to the exercise of a statutory power is often used to designate a factual criterion, satisfaction of which is necessary to enliven the power of a decision-maker to exercise a discretion. The criterion may be 'a complex of elements' [*Enfield City Corporation v Development Assessment Commission* (2000) 199 CLR 135, 148 [28] (Gleeson CJ, Gummow, Kirby and Hayne JJ)]. When a criterion conditioning the exercise of statutory power involves assessment and value judgments on the part of the decision-maker, it is difficult to characterise the criterion as a jurisdictional fact, the existence or non-existence of which may be reviewed by a court. The decision-maker's assessment or evaluation may be an element of the criterion or it may be the criterion itself. Where a power is expressly conditioned upon the formation of a state of mind by the decision-maker, be it an opinion, belief, state of ***180*** satisfaction or suspicion, the existence of the state of mind itself will constitute a jurisdictional fact. If by necessary implication the power is conditioned upon the formation of an opinion or belief on the part of the decision-maker then the existence of that opinion or belief can also be viewed as a jurisdictional fact. The primary submission on the part of the plaintiffs, however, looked to the existence of the matters set out in s 198A(3)(a) as conditioning the Minister's power to make a declaration.

[58] The question is one of statutory construction. The considerations advanced by the plaintiffs cannot overcome the language of s 198A(3). Moreover, clear language would be needed to support the primary characterisation for which they contend. The Minister is empowered under s 198A(3) to make a declaration, the content of which is defined by that sub-section. Putting to one side the nature and scope of the 'protection' referred to in each of sub-paras (i)–(iv), their language indicates the need for ministerial evaluative judgment.

As explained below, consideration of the domestic law of the proposed receiving country and its binding commitments and obligations under international law is mandated. That consideration will necessarily be an evaluative task. The words 'provide', 'access', 'effective procedures' and 'meets relevant human rights standards' all point in that direction. The function conferred upon the Minister is an executive function to be carried out according to law. Absent clear words, the sub-section should not be construed as conferring upon courts the power to substitute their judgment for that of the Minister by characterising the matters in sub-paras (i)–(iv) as jurisdictional facts.

[59] On the other hand, the mere fact that it is the Minister who makes the declaration is not enough to secure its validity. The Solicitor-General was correct when he submitted that the Minister is required to form, in good faith, an evaluative judgment based upon the matters set out in s 198A(3)(a), properly construed. That the Minister properly construe them is a necessary condition of the validity of his declaration. Properly construed, they define the content of the declaration which the Parliament has authorised. If the Minister were to proceed to make a declaration on the basis of a misconstrued criterion, he would be making a declaration not authorised by the Parliament. The misconstruction of the criterion would be a jurisdictional error ... ***181*** A declaration under s 198A(3) affected by jurisdictional error is invalid. Another way of approaching the scope of the ministerial power under s 198A(3) is to treat it as being, by necessary implication, conditioned upon the formation of an opinion or belief that each of the matters set out in s 193A(a)(i)–(iv) is true. The requisite opinion or belief is a jurisdictional fact. If based upon a misconstruction of one or more of the matters, the opinion or belief is not that which the sub-section requires in order that the power be enlivened.

[60] The question that then arises is: Did the Minister properly construe the criteria under s 198A(3)(a)(i)–(iv)?

[61] The temporal element of the Minister's judgment under s 198A(3)(a) is important. Each of the matters the subject of a declaration about a 'specified country' is a statement about that country at the time of the declaration. It is, however, not only a snapshot of the present. The provision of access and protection and the meeting of human rights standards in providing protection must be judged by the Minister as more than merely transient. That is because the declaration enlivens a power to undertake future action: the taking of offshore entry persons to the specified country. The judgment required by the criteria is necessarily a judgment that the circumstance described by each of those criteria is a present and continuing circumstance. The temporal element points to the need for a legal framework to support the continuance of the matters the subject of the Minister's assessment.

[62] The declaration must be a declaration about continuing circumstances in the specified country. It cannot therefore be a declaration based upon, and therefore a declaration of, a hope or belief or expectation that the specified country will meet the criteria at some time in the future even if that time be imminent. It is a misconstruction of the criteria to make a declaration of their subsistence based upon an understanding that the executive government of the specified country is 'keen to improve its treatment of refugees and asylum seekers'. Nor could a declaration rest upon a belief that the government of the specified country has 'made a significant conceptual shift in its thinking about how it wanted to treat refugees and asylum seekers' or that it had 'begun the process of improving the protection offered to such persons'. Yet

the Minister's affidavit suggested that, at least in part, this is how he approached the questions he had to ask himself before making the declaration.

...

182 [65] ... The Minister conceded, by way of the written submissions made on his behalf, that if the proper construction of s 198A(3) meant that he was required to focus upon the laws in effect in Malaysia and not upon the 'practical reality', then he would have erred in this case. In my opinion, the Minister was so required and did so err.

[66] ... The questions the Minister must ask himself, about whether the relevant 'access' and 'protection' are provided and 'human rights standards' are met, are questions which cannot be answered without reference to the domestic laws of the specified ***183*** country, including its *Constitution* and statute laws, and the international legal obligations to which it has bound itself. The use of the terms 'provides access ... to effective procedures', 'protection' and 'relevant human rights standards' are all indicative of enduring legal frameworks. Having regard to the Minister's concession and what appears, in any event, from the submissions upon which the Minister acted and his affidavit, it is clear that he did not look to, and did not find, any basis for his declaration in Malaysia's international obligations or relevant domestic laws ...

Conclusion

[68] The ministerial declaration of 25 July 2011 was affected by jurisdictional error. It was not a declaration authorised by s 198A of the *Migration Act*. The plaintiffs cannot therefore be taken to Malaysia pursuant to the power conferred by s 198A(1).

[Citations omitted]

Procedural error

Forrest & Forrest Pty Ltd v Wilson (2017) 262 CLR 510

Mining Act 1978 (WA)

[As at relevant date]

71 Grant of mining lease

Subject to this Act, the Minister may, on the application of any person, after receiving a recommendation of the mining registrar or the warden in accordance with section 75, grant to the person a lease to be known as a mining lease on such terms and conditions as the Minister considers reasonable.

74 Application for mining lease

(1) An application for a mining lease –

(a) shall be in the prescribed form; and

(b) shall be accompanied by the amount of the prescribed rent for the first year of the term of the lease or portion thereof as prescribed; and

(c) shall be accompanied by the prescribed application fee; and

(ca) shall be accompanied by -

(i) a mining proposal; or

(ii) a mineralisation report prepared by a qualified person; and

(d) shall be lodged in the prescribed manner.

(1AA) Instead of accompanying an application for a mining lease under subsection (1)(ca), a mining proposal may be lodged within the prescribed time and in the prescribed manner and, if so lodged, is to be treated for the purposes of this Division as a mining proposal that accompanied the application for the mining lease under section 74(1)(ca).

...

(3) Within the prescribed period the applicant shall serve such notice of the application as may be prescribed on the owner and occupier of the land to which the application relates and on such other persons as may be prescribed.

...

(5) The Director General of Mines shall ensure that –

(a) any document referred to in subsection (1)(ca) that accompanies the application; and

(b) any document furnished by the applicant in response to a request under subsection (2),

are made available for public inspection at reasonable times.

...

(7) In this section –

...

mineralisation report means a report that sets out details of exploration results in respect of a deposit of minerals located in, on or under the land to which the application relates, including details of –

(a) the type of minerals located in, on or under that land;

(b) the location, depth and extent of those minerals and the way in which that extent has been determined; and

(c) analytical results obtained from samples of those minerals.

74A Report on significant mineralisation required for certain applications

(1) If an application for a mining lease is accompanied by the documentation referred to in section 74(1)(ca)(ii), the Director, Geological Survey shall give the Minister a report as to whether or not there is significant mineralisation in, on or under the land to which the application relates.

(2) For the purposes of preparing the report, the Director, Geological Survey may request the applicant to provide further information in relation to matters dealt with in the mineralisation report.

(3) The report shall be based solely on information contained in the mineralisation report and any further information provided by the applicant in response to a request under subsection (2).

(4) The Director, Geological Survey shall give a copy of the report to the mining registrar and the warden.

(5) The Director General of Mines shall ensure that the report is made available for public inspection at reasonable times.

...

(7) In this section –

mineralisation report means the mineralisation report that accompanied the application.

75 Determination of application for mining lease

(1) A person who wishes to object to the granting of an application for a mining lease shall lodge a notice of objection within the prescribed time and in the prescribed manner.

...

(2) Subject to subsection (2a), if no notice of objection is lodged within the prescribed time, or any notice of objection is withdrawn, the mining registrar shall, unless subsection (4)(b) applies, forward to the Minister a report which recommends the grant or refusal of the mining lease and sets out the reasons for that recommendation.

(2a) If the application for the mining lease is accompanied by the documentation referred to in section 74(1)(ca)(ii), the mining registrar shall not forward a report under subsection (2) unless –

  (a) the mining registrar has received a copy of the section 74A report in relation to the application; and

  (b) the section 74A report states that there is significant mineralisation in, on or under the land to which the application relates.

(3) The mining registrar shall –

  (a) recommend the grant of the mining lease if satisfied that the applicant has complied in all respects with the provisions of this Act; or

  (b) recommend the refusal of the mining lease if not so satisfied

(4) Subject to subsection (4a), if a notice of objection –

  (a) is lodged within the prescribed time; or

  (b) is not lodged within the prescribed time but is lodged before the mining registrar has forwarded a report to the Minister under subsection (2) and the warden is satisfied that there are reasonable grounds for late lodgment,

and the notice of objection is not withdrawn, the warden shall hear the application for the mining lease on a day appointed by the warden and may give any person who has lodged such a notice of objection an opportunity to be heard.

(4a) If the application for the mining lease is accompanied by the documentation referred to in section 74(1)(ca)(ii), the warden shall not hear the application unless –

(a) the warden has received a copy of the section 74A report in relation to the application; and

(b) the section 74A report states that there is significant mineralisation in, on or under the land to which the application relates.

(5) The warden shall as soon as practicable after the hearing of the application forward to the Minister for the Minister's consideration –

(a) the notes of evidence;

(b) any maps or other documents referred to in the notes of evidence; and

(c) a report which recommends the grant or refusal of the mining lease and sets out the reasons for that recommendation.

(6) On receipt of a report under subsection (2) or (5), the Minister may, subject to subsection (7), grant or refuse the mining lease as the Minister thinks fit, and irrespective of whether –

(a) the report recommends the grant or refusal of the mining lease; and

(b) the applicant has or has not complied in all respects with the provisions of this Act.

...

(8) In the case of an application for a mining lease that is accompanied by the documentation referred to in section 74(1)(ca)(ii), the Minister shall refuse to grant the mining lease if the section 74A report states that there is no significant mineralisation in, on or under the land to which the application relates.

...

(10) In this section –

section 74A report means the report given to the Minister under section 74A.

Facts

On 28 July 2011, two mining companies lodged applications for mining leases relating to land in the Pilbara region of Western Australia. The applications were not accompanied by the mineralisation reports required by s 74(1)(ca)(ii) of the *Mining Act 1978* (WA). However, the applicants did provide the mineralisation reports several months later. The Director, Geological Survey prepared reports under s 74A for both applications.

Forrest & Forrest Pty Ltd ('Forrest'), which held a pastoral lease over the land that was the subject of the applications for mining leases, lodged objections to the applications. The warden heard the applications, having before him both the s 74A reports and the mineralisation reports, and giving Forrest an opportunity to be heard. Forrest argued that the warden had no jurisdiction to hear the applications because the mineralisation reports had not been provided at the time of the applications. The warden rejected this argument on the basis that the lateness of the mineralisation reports was a mere irregularity. He proceeded to make a recommendation that the Minister grant the applications.

Forrest commenced judicial review proceedings in the Supreme Court of Western Australia, seeking certiorari to quash the warden's recommendation. The primary judge, and the Court of Appeal, held there had been no jurisdictional error. Forrest appealed to the High Court. The Solicitor-General for Western Australia appeared as amicus curiae.

By 4:1 (Nettle J dissenting), the High Court allowed the appeal and issued declarations that the warden's recommendation was invalid, and a writ of certiorari to quash the recommendation.

Kiefel CJ, Bell, Gageler and Keane JJ

526 [56] Forrest submitted that ss 74(1)(ca)(ii), 74A(1) and 75(4a) of the Act expressly contemplated that a mineralisation report was to be one ***527*** lodged with a mining lease application, with the evident purpose of ensuring that non-compliant applications would not proceed to a hearing by the warden or a grant by the Minister. It was said that a non-compliant application should not be allowed to progress as a burden upon the administration of the Act, or work to the disadvantage of stakeholders such as owners and occupiers of land, or miners in competition with applicants. Forrest argued that the Minister was precluded from proceeding to grant a lease where non-compliance with s 74(1)(ca)(ii) was shown because the pre-requisite to the Minister's jurisdiction under ss 71 and 75(6), being the forwarding of a recommendation from the warden after a hearing authorised by sub-ss (4) and (4a) of s 75, could not be met.

[57] The Solicitor-General submitted that whether an Act requires that a particular process be followed is an entirely different question from whether the failure to follow that process will nullify or invalidate that statutory process and the result of it. In this regard, the Solicitor-General relied upon this Court's decision in *Project Blue Sky* [*Project Blue Sky Inc v Australian Broadcasting Authority* (1998) 194 CLR 355] and argued that, while the language of s 74(1)(ca)(ii) may well be 'precise and prescriptive', that does not assist in resolving the issue whether non-compliance results in invalidity.

...

[60] In light of the contentions of Forrest and the Solicitor-General, one may turn to a consideration of the reasoning of the Court of Appeal. That consideration must begin with a discussion of this Court's decision in *Project Blue Sky.*

Project Blue Sky

[61] In *Project Blue Sky,* the majority of the Court said:

> ***528*** An act done in breach of a condition regulating the exercise of a statutory power is not necessarily invalid and of no effect. Whether it is depends upon whether there can be discerned a legislative purpose to invalidate any act that fails to comply with the condition. The existence of the purpose is ascertained by reference to the language of the statute, its subject matter and objects, and the consequences for the parties of holding void every act done in breach of the condition. Unfortunately, a finding of purpose or no purpose in this context often reflects a contestable judgment ... There is no decisive rule that can be applied; there is not even a ranking of relevant factors or categories to give guidance on the issue.

[62] In *Project Blue Sky,* this Court was concerned with whether a statutory requirement that an administrative agency perform its functions in a manner consistent with Australia's obligations under any convention or international agreement to which Australia is a party was intended to invalidate an act done in breach of the requirement. The majority in *Project Blue Sky* were strongly influenced in reaching a conclusion in the negative by the consideration that the requirement in question regulated the exercise of functions already conferred on the agency, rather than imposed essential preliminaries to the exercise of those functions. Their Honours were also influenced by the circumstance that the provisions did not have 'a rule-like quality which [could] be easily identified and applied', many of the obligations relevant in that case being 'expressed in indeterminate language'. Also important to the decision was the consideration that 'public inconvenience would be a result of the invalidity of the act', especially if those affected by non-compliance were neither responsible for, nor aware of, the non-compliance.

[63] The present case is readily distinguishable. A consideration of 'the language of the statute, its subject matter and objects, and the consequences for the parties of holding void' acts done in breach of the Act, reveals that ss 74(1)(ca)(ii), 74A(1) and 75(4a) imposed essential preliminaries to the exercise of the power conferred by s 71 of the Act. That this was so was made clear by both the express terms and the structure of the provisions as sequential steps in an integrated process leading to the possibility of the grant of a mining lease by the Minister. These provisions were not expressed in indeterminate terms: they imposed rules which could be easily identified and applied. In ***529*** addition, any inconvenience suffered by treating the requirements of the Act as conditions precedent to the exercise of the Minister's power would enure only to those with some responsibility for the non-observance, whereas (as will be explained) the contrary view would disadvantage both the public interest and individuals who were within the protection of the Act. Finally, and importantly, *Project Blue Sky* was not concerned with a statutory regime for the making of grants of rights to exploit the resources of a State.

[64] ... [A line of authority] establishes that where a statutory regime confers power on the executive government of a State to grant exclusive rights to exploit the resources of the State, the regime will, subject to provision to the contrary, be understood as mandating compliance with the requirements of the regime as essential to the making of a valid grant. ...

[65] This approach to statutory construction had its origin in colonial times in legislation which vested the disposition of land not already disposed of by the Crown in the legislatures of the Australian colonies. Adherence to this approach supports parliamentary control of the disposition of lands held by the Crown in right of the State. It gives effect to an abiding appreciation that the public interest is not well served by allowing non-compliance with a legislative regime to be overlooked or excused by the officers of the executive government charged with its administration. To permit such a state of affairs might imperil the honest and efficient enforcement of the statutory regime, by allowing ***530*** scope for dealings between miners and officers of the executive government in relation to the relaxation of the requirements of the legislation. One can be confident that such a state of affairs was not intended by the Act.

[66] A consideration of the language of the Act, to which one may now turn, does not reveal any intention to depart from the settled approach to the construction of such a legislative regime, save to the limited extent expressly indicated by [s] 75(6)(b) ...

The language of the Act

Sections 74, 74A and 75

[67] The clear meaning of s 74(1)(ca)(ii), as a matter of ordinary parlance, was that the documentation relied upon must have been lodged at the same time as the application was lodged, as each of the courts below held. The text of s 74(1)(ca) did not admit of any ambiguity or doubt on this point. The tenor of s 74(1)(ca)(ii) was both precise and prescriptive, conveying an intention not to countenance any degree of non-compliance with the requirement.

[68] The prefatory words of ss 74A(1), 75(2a), 75(4a) and 75(8) distinguish such applications from those where a choice was made to proceed by way of lodging a mining proposal under s 74(1)(ca)(i). It is not open to read those provisions as if they provided 'if the application for the mining lease is accompanied *or followed* by the s 74(1)(ca)(ii) documentation'. In contrast, the specific provision for late lodgement of a mining proposal in s 74(1AA) served to reinforce the requirement of contemporaneous lodgement in that it deemed a proposal lodged within the prescribed time after the application to have been a proposal that accompanied the application. This contrast confirms the ordinary meaning and prescriptive effect of the language of s 74(1)(ca).

...

[70] In addition, an applicant for a mining lease who chose to proceed by way of mineralisation report under s 74(1)(ca)(ii) engaged the powers ***531*** and duties of each of the Director, Geological Survey and the warden in the process leading to the grant by the Minister. Once an application was to be pursued in that way, the Director, Geological Survey became empowered and obliged to prepare a report under s 74A(1) based on the mineralisation report that accompanied the application, and no other. The Court of Appeal erred in holding that, while it was an essential preliminary condition that the mineralisation report be lodged at 'some time', the report did not have to accompany the application.

[71] In departing from the terms of the Act in this way, the Court of Appeal failed to take into account the circumstance that, as the express words of sub-ss (1) and (7) of s 74A made clear, the Director, Geological Survey was obliged to provide a s 74A report based on a mineralisation report that accompanied the relevant application, not some other mineralisation report provided at some unspecified other time. The mineralisation report that the Director, Geological Survey was required to consider in producing his or her report pursuant to s 74A was expressly defined in s 74A(7) to mean *the* mineralisation report that accompanied the application. No power was conferred on the Director, Geological Survey to extend time or to act upon some other document. The Director, Geological Survey was not authorised to receive or act upon a mineralisation report in any way other than that prescribed. Section 74A(7) had to be allowed to work according to its express terms and ordinary meaning.

[72] ... Under s 74A(1), the power and duty of the Director, Geological Survey to prepare a report arose only '*[i]f* an application for a mining lease *is accompanied* by the documentation referred to in section 74(1)(ca)(ii)'. Similarly, the warden's power to hear an application was expressly conditioned by the opening words of s 75(4), '[s]ubject to subsection (4a)'. Sub-section (4a) was engaged only '*[i]f* the application for the mining lease *is accompanied* by the documentation referred to in section 74(1)(ca)(ii)'. As a matter of ordinary parlance, those words referred not to something that has not been done, but rather, to something that has been done. In so doing, they reinforced the express requirement of contemporaneous lodgement contained in sub-ss (1), (3) and of s 74A ...

[73] The phrase '[i]f the application for the mining lease is accompanied by the documentation referred to in section 74(1)(ca)(ii)' was ***532*** substantially repeated in each of sub-ss (2a), (4a) and (8) of s 75. These were the three provisions that grounded the decision-making authority of the mining registrar, the warden, and the Minister respectively. These provisions left no room for the possibility that the documentation referred to in s 74(1)(ca)(ii) might be relied upon other than as an accompaniment to the application for a mining lease; on the contrary, each reinforced the essentiality of the requirement in s 74(1)(ca)(ii) itself.

[Section] 75(6) ...

[74] The express provision made by [s] 75(6) in relation to the consequences of noncompliance with the requirements of the Act preliminary to the exercise of the Minister's powers under s 71 is itself an indication that matters of non-compliance with the Act outside the scope of [s] 75(6) were fatal to the validity of a grant so affected.

[75] Section 75(6)(b) allowed the Minister to grant or refuse a mining lease notwithstanding an applicant's non-compliance in all respects with the provisions of the Act. It did not manifest an intention that any and all non-compliance with the provisions of the Act regarding applications for mining leases could be disregarded when the Minister determined whether to grant a lease. In particular, it did not purport to allow the Minister to make a grant where the warden had failed to comply with the Act, as, for example, by proceeding to a hearing under s 75(4) contrary to the requirements of s 75(4a).

...

The objects of the regime

534 [82] The conclusion of the Court of Appeal that 'there is no justification in principle or purpose for concluding that contemporaneous lodgment is a condition precedent to the mining registrar or the warden making a recommendation' was focused upon the 'delays, cost and other prejudice' already experienced by the second and fourth respondents. Quite apart from the consideration that these delays and costs resulted from those respondents' own non-compliance with the Act, this focus overlooked the consideration that nonobservance of the requirements of the regime governing the grant of mining leases was apt to disadvantage both the public interest and individuals in ways that the Act did not intend.

[83] In accordance with *Project Blue Sky* [(1998) 194 CLR 355, 390–391 [93]], the necessary inquiry is:

> as to whether the statutory purpose of the duty, when considered within the particular statutory scheme of which it forms part, would or would not be advanced by holding an exercise of decision-making power affected by breach of the duty to be invalid.

[84] Compliance with the regime established by ss 74, 74A and 75 was apt to improve administrative efficiency and to avoid backlogs by reducing the number of defective applications for mining leases that mining registrars, wardens, Directors, Geological Survey, and officers of the Department administering the Act have to manage and follow up. The Court of Appeal failed to appreciate that reduction of the problems of management of applications for mining tenements, an object of the prescriptive regime constituted by ss 74, 74A and 75 of the Act acknowledged by the Court of Appeal, would be furthered by the Act denying validity to acts done in disregard of the statute.

535 [85] Compliance with the requirement that a mineralisation report accompany an application was apt to reduce the administrative burden upon the Department. Officers of the Department should not have been troubled by the uncertainty and expense of attending to an application that was not accompanied by the documentation necessary to allow it to proceed.

[86] The Act's insistence upon a mineralisation report as an accompaniment to the application also served the purpose of ensuring that owners and occupiers of subject land were not troubled unnecessarily or prematurely by half-baked proposals. The Court of Appeal did not advert to the consideration that owners and occupiers of land affected by an application might be disadvantaged by an administration of the Act which proceeded in disregard of its requirements.

[87] The Act, in requiring any objection to be lodged by an owner or occupier of land affected by an application for a mining lease within a prescribed time from the service of the application, ensured that an objection would be informed by reference to the information concerning mineralisation which accompanied the application for the mining lease ...

[88] The provision of the informed views of those who objected to an application was apt to improve the quality of decision-making by those ***536*** charged with the administration of the Act. An objection lodged before the mineralisation report was made available would necessarily be framed without the benefit of that information. A failure to comply with the requirements of s 74(1)(ca)(ii) could thus compromise the rights of objectors. Non-compliance with statutory provisions designed to ensure that a right of objection to proposed action is exercised effectively has been regarded as invalidating the decision-making process.

[89] In addition, the relaxed view of the effect of non-compliance with the Act favoured by the Court of Appeal was apt to enure to the disadvantage of miners in competition for access to the State's resources. Compliance with the regime

established by ss 74, 74A and 75 was necessary to prevent 'land-banking', whereby holders of existing prospecting, retention or exploration licences that were soon to expire, who had not yet encountered a specific geological foundation for lodgement of a mineralisation report, might be minded cynically to use the mechanism of applying for a mining lease to extend their time for exploration.

[90] In introducing ss 74(1)(ca)(ii) and 74A into the Act by passage of the Mining Amendment Bill 2004 (WA), the Explanatory Memorandum for the Bill stated that the changes were to 'ensure a mining lease is *only applied for* when accompanied by a notice of intent to commence productive mining operations or a statement that significant mineralisation exists' (emphasis added). Similarly, the Minister for State Development referred in his second reading speech to the significant problem that exploration title holders were using the mechanism of a mining lease application as a way to seek 'further exploration rights rather than a title for productive mining'. The Minister explained that the Bill would address this problem by 'limit[ing] new applications for mining leases to those cases where significant mineralisation has been discovered or mining proposals are lodged with the application'.

Conclusion

[91] For these reasons, the appeal to this Court should be allowed and the relief sought by Forrest granted ...

[Citations omitted]

Improper delegation

O'Reilly v Commissioners of the State Bank of Victoria (1983) 153 CLR 1

Income Tax Assessment Act 1936 (Cth)

[As at relevant date]

264 Commissioner may require information and evidence

The Commissioner may by notice in writing require any person, whether a taxpayer or not, including any officer employed in or in connexion with any department of a Government or by any public authority—

(a) to furnish him with such information as he may require; and

(b) to attend and give evidence before him or before any officer authorized by him in that behalf concerning his or any other person's income or assessment, and may require him to produce all books, documents and other papers whatever in his custody or under his control thereto.

Taxation Administration Act 1953 (Cth)

[As at relevant date]

> **8 Delegation by Commissioner**
>
> (1) The Commissioner of Taxation may, in relation to a matter or class of matters, or in relation to a State or part of the Commonwealth, by writing under his hand, delegate to a Deputy Commissioner of Taxation or other person all or any of his powers or functions under this Act or an Act which is an Act with respect to taxation (except this power of delegation).

Facts

Pursuant to s 8 of the *Taxation Administration Act 1953* (Cth), the Commissioner of Taxation delegated to the Deputy Commissioner (Eric Unger) his power to issue notices under s 264 of the *Income Tax Assessment Act 1936* (Cth). In turn, the Deputy Commissioner gave the Chief Investigation Officer of the Australian Taxation Office ('ATO') written authority to 'Authorise issue of notices other than notices requiring the giving of information or evidence on oath' and 'Imprint facsimile of [Mr Unger's] signature upon such notices'.

The Chief Investigation Officer of the ATO, together with two other ATO officers, decided to issue a notice to a taxpayer, David Lawson, requiring him to give evidence and produce documents. The notice was in the following terms:

> TAKE NOTICE that in the exercise of the powers and functions conferred upon me as Deputy Commissioner of Taxation by delegation from the Commissioner of Taxation under the provisions of the Taxation Administration Act 1953, I, ERIC JOHN UNGER, do by this notice REQUIRE YOU ... TO ATTEND at ... and give evidence before Edward Henry Cornell (an officer of the Australian Taxation Office, who is authorised in that behalf) concerning your income and assessments., and in connection therewith I DO FURTHER HEREBY REQUIRE YOU TO PRODUCE at the same place and time the following books, documents and papers.

The Chief Investigation Officer affixed the facsimile signature of the Deputy Commissioner to the notice. The Deputy Commissioner had no knowledge of the notice. A similar notice was issued to Lawson's solicitor, John Perry.

The issue in the case was whether the issue of the notices constituted a valid exercise of the power under s 264. Did that power have to be exercised personally by the Commissioner (or his delegate the Deputy Commissioner)? Or was it permissible for another official to exercise the power on behalf of the Commissioner or Deputy Commissioner?

Wilson J

> ***30*** It seems to me that a clear distinction is to be drawn between the delegation of a power and the exercise of that power through servants or agents ... In *Carltona Ltd v Commissioners of Works* [[1943] 2 All ER 560, 563] Lord Greene MR described, in words which have become well-known, the necessity in modern government for the shared performance of duties short of delegation. He said:

> It cannot be supposed that this regulation meant that, in each case, the minister in person should direct his mind to the matter. The duties imposed upon ministers and the powers given to ministers are normally exercised under the authority of the ministers by responsible officials of the department. Public business could not be carried on if that were not the case. ***31*** Constitutionally, the decision of such an official is, of course, the decision of the minister. The minister is responsible.

[Editors' note: Wilson J then set out a quote to similar effect by Denning LJ in *Metropolitan Borough and Town Clerk of Lewisham v Roberts* [1949] 2 KB 608, 621.]

The defendants ... would dismiss the English authorities to which I have referred as dealing with the relationship of Ministers of the Crown to their departments. It is true that the emphasis in the cases is primarily expressed in that way. Yet I find the logic of the principle equally persuasive in its application to the head of any large government department, and, a fortiori, to a Deputy Commissioner of Taxation responsible within a State for the implementation of the Commonwealth's laws with respect to taxation. No permanent head of a department in the Public Service is expected to discharge personally all the duties which are performed in his name and for which he is accountable to the responsible Minister. I share the view expressed by Sachs J in *Commissioners of Customs and Excise v Cure & Deeley Ltd* [[1962] 1 QB 340, 371]:

> The commissioners are in a position parallel to that of the Ministers referred to in the judgment of Lord Greene in the *Carltona Case,* in that their functions are so multifarious that they could never personally attend to them all, and the powers given to them are normally exercised under their authority by responsible officials of the department.

However, the defendants further argue that the existence of the power to delegate (s 8, *Taxation Administration Act*) makes it unnecessary to resort to the *Carltona* principle, with the result that a formal delegation to Mr Holland was necessary to empower him to issue the notices. I note that in [*Re Reference under Ombudsman Act, s 11* (1979) 2 ALD 86, 94] the advisory opinion of the Administrative Appeals Tribunal on the reference under the *Ombudsman Act* to which I have referred, Brennan J said, when discussing the possibility that a person may be both a delegate ***32*** of a power and a servant exercising the like power on behalf of another:

> Is a dual character consistent with the statutory scheme for reviewing determinations under s 14 of the *Social Services Act?* I think not. The practical administrative necessity which warrants an authority's exercising his power by the acts of another disappears when the authority is empowered to delegate all of his powers and functions to that other.

That observation is, of course, to be understood in the context of the examination which his Honour was making of the *Social Services Act 1947* (Cth), as amended. In any event, the statement which I have cited can afford no analogy to the present case, because here the Deputy Commissioner, himself a delegate, has no power to delegate his power to Mr Holland. The question is whether the existence of the power of delegation requires that the Commissioner or his delegate must direct his mind personally to the exercise of every power or function vested in him. Stated in that way, in my opinion, the question admits only of one answer. The practical administrative necessity to allow a Deputy Commissioner to exercise the powers delegated to him by the actions of officers authorized by him is evident. The opposing argument would oblige the Commissioner himself to delegate his powers, not only to the Deputy Commissioners, but to a host of departmental officers throughout Australia, rendering each of them a Commissioner in his own right. It would be wholly destructive of any semblance of administrative order and efficiency.

...

Each of the notices which are under challenge is expressed to be an exercise by the Deputy Commissioner of the power under s 264 which was duly delegated to him. Each notice bears his signature. In my opinion each notice is what it purports to be. In resolving to ***33*** issue the notice, Mr Holland was acting for the Deputy Commissioner, in exercise of an authority duly vested in him. His action was the action of the Deputy Commissioner, notwithstanding that the latter had no personal knowledge of it.

[Citations omitted]

Mandatory and prohibited considerations

Minister for Aboriginal Affairs v Peko-Wallsend Ltd (1986) 162 CLR 24

This case was introduced in Chapter 3 in relation to statutory implications. In the extract below, Mason J (at 45) derives from the subject-matter, scope and purpose of the statute conferring the power 'an implication that the decision is to be made on the basis of the most current material available to the decision-maker'.

Aboriginal Land Rights (Northern Territory) Act 1976 (Cth)

[As at relevant date]

11 Recommendations for grants of Crown land, other than that described in schedule 1

(1) Where—

(a) the Commissioner ... recommends, to the Minister in a report made to him under paragraph 50(1)(a) that an area of Crown land should be granted to a Land Trust for the benefit of Aboriginals entitled land, whether or not the traditional entitlement is qualified as to place, time, circumstance, purpose or permission; and

(b) the Minister is satisfied—

(i) that the land, or a part of the land, should be granted to a single Land Trust to be held for the benefit of Aboriginals who are the relevant Aboriginals in relation to that land or that part of that land; ...

the Minister shall

(c) establish—

(i) in a case where he is satisfied that the land, or a part of the land, should be granted to a single Land Trust – a single Land Trust under section 4 to hold that land, or that part of that land, for the benefit of Aboriginals who are the relevant Aboriginals in relation to the land, or the part of the land, proposed to be held by that Land Trust; ...

(d) ... and

(e) ... recommend to the Governor-General that a grant of an estate in fee simple in that land be made to that Land Trust.

50 Functions of Commissioner

(1) The functions of the Commissioner are—

(a) on an application being made to the Commissioner by or on behalf of Aboriginals claiming to have a traditional land claim to an area of land, being unalienated Crown land or alienated Crown land in which all estates and interests not held by the Crown are held by, or on behalf of, Aboriginals—

(i) to ascertain whether those Aboriginals or any other Aboriginals are the traditional Aboriginal owners of the land; and

(ii) to report his findings to the Minister and to the Minister for the Northern Territory, and, where he finds that there are Aboriginals who are the traditional Aboriginal owners of the land, to make recommendations to the Minister for the granting of the land or any part of the land in accordance with sections 11 and 12;

...

(2) In making a report in connexion with a traditional land claim the Commissioner shall have regard to the strength or otherwise of the traditional attachment by the claimants to the land claimed, and shall comment on each of the following matters:-

(a) the number of Aboriginals with traditional attachments to the land claimed who would be advantaged, and the nature and extent of the advantage that would accrue to those Aboriginals, if the claim were acceded to either in whole or in part;

(b) the detriment to persons or communities including other Aboriginal groups that might result if the claim were acceded to either in whole or in part;

(c) the effect which acceding to the claim either in whole or in part would have on the existing or proposed patterns of land usage in the region; and

(d) where the claim relates to alienated Crown Land the cost of acquiring the interests of persons (other than the Crown) in the land concerned.

Facts

Since 1967, Peko-Wallsend Ltd and several other mining companies had held exploration licences for land in the Alligator Rivers region of the Northern Territory. They had found a large uranium deposit ('Ranger 68') that they wished to exploit. Ranger 68 was located in an area of land known as the 'Barote Block'.

In 1978, the Northern Land Council made a claim, under the *Aboriginal Land Rights (Northern Territory) Act 1976* (Cth), on behalf of groups of Aboriginal people with a traditional connection to the land, over land in the Alligator Rivers region. The Aboriginal Land Commissioner investigated the claim, including the potential detriment to the mining companies. The director of Peko-Wallsend, John Elliston, was vague in his evidence about the location of Ranger 68, telling the Commissioner that Ranger 68 was 'in the centre' of the Barote Block. In fact, Ranger 68 was in the extreme eastern corner of the Barote Block.

The Commissioner prepared a report for the Minister under s 50 recommending that a land grant be made over an area of land, including 10 per cent of the Barote Block. This included the entire Ranger 68 deposit. The report commented on the detriment the exploration companies would suffer if a land grant were made. However, the comments on detriment reflected the Commissioner's lack of knowledge of the precise location of Ranger 68.

Following the publication of the Commissioner's report, the mining companies wrote to the Minister for Aboriginal Affairs, Senator Baume, explaining that Ranger 68 was wholly within the area of the recommended land grant, and that the detriment they would suffer was greater than that indicated in the Commissioner's report. The Minister decided to recommend a land grant over the recommended area, except certain areas, including the Barote Block, in respect of which he deferred his decision.

After the change of government in the 1983 election, a new Minister for Aboriginal Affairs was appointed. The new Minister read the Commissioner's report, but was unaware of the subsequent correspondence between the mining companies and Senator Baume. He then decided to recommend that a land grant be made over the remaining areas, including the relevant part of the Barote Block.

The mining companies commenced judicial review proceedings in the Federal Court under the *Administrative Decisions (Judicial Review) Act 1977* (Cth), on the ground that the new Minister had failed to consider relevant matters: namely, the representations they had made following the publication of the Commissioner's report.

The judge at first instance dismissed the proceedings, but the Full Court reversed that decision. The Minister appealed to the High Court. The High Court dismissed the appeal.

Mason J

> ***39*** The failure of a decision-maker to take into account a relevant consideration in the making of an administrative decision is one instance of an abuse of discretion entitling a party with sufficient standing to seek judicial review of ultra vires administrative action. That ground now appears in s 5(2)(b) of the *AD(JR) Act* which, in this regard, is substantially declaratory of the common law. Together with the related ground of taking into account irrelevant considerations, it has been discussed in a number of decided cases, which have established the following propositions:

(a) The ground of failure to take into account a relevant consideration can only be made out if a decision-maker fails to take into account a consideration which he is *bound* to take into account in making that decision.

(b) What factors a decision-maker is bound to consider in making the decision is determined by construction of the statute conferring the discretion. If the statute expressly states the considerations to be taken into account, it will often be necessary for the court to decide whether those enumerated factors are exhaustive or merely inclusive. If the relevant factors – and in this context I use this expression to refer to the factors which the decision-maker is bound to consider – are not expressly stated, they must be determined by ***40*** implication from the subject-matter, scope and purpose of the Act. In the context of judicial review on the ground of taking into account irrelevant considerations, this Court has held that, where a statute confers a discretion which in its terms is unconfined, the factors that may be taken into account in the exercise of the discretion are similarly unconfined, except in so far as there may be found in the subject-matter, scope and purpose of the statute some implied limitation on the factors to which the decision-maker may legitimately have regard. By analogy, where the ground of review is that a relevant consideration has not been taken into account and the discretion is unconfined by the terms of the statute, the court will not find that the decision-maker is bound to take a particular matter into account unless an implication that he is bound to do so is to be found in the subject-matter, scope and purpose of the Act.

(c) Not every consideration that a decision-maker is bound to take into account but fails to take into account will justify the court setting aside the impugned decision and ordering that the discretion be re-exercised according to law. A factor might be so insignificant that the failure to take it into account could not have materially affected the decision. A similar principle has been enunciated in cases where regard has been had to irrelevant considerations in the making of an administrative decision.

(d) The limited role of a court reviewing the exercise of an administrative discretion must constantly be borne in mind. It is not the function of the court to substitute its own decision for that of the administrator by exercising a discretion which the legislature has vested in the administrator. Its role is to set limits on the exercise of ***41*** that discretion, and a decision made within those boundaries cannot be impugned. It follows that, in the absence of any statutory indication of the weight to be given to various considerations, it is generally for the decision-maker and not the court to determine the appropriate weight to be given to the matters which are required to be taken into account in exercising the statutory power. I say 'generally' because both principle and authority indicate that in some circumstances a court may set aside an administrative decision which has failed to give adequate weight to a relevant factor of great importance, or has given excessive weight to a relevant factor of no great importance. The preferred ground on which this is done, however, is not the failure to take into account relevant considerations or the taking into account of irrelevant considerations, but that the decision is 'manifestly unreasonable'...

42 **(e)** The principles stated above apply to an administrative decision made by a Minister of the Crown. However, in conformity with the principle expressed in (b) above, namely that relevant considerations may be gleaned from the subject-matter, scope and purpose of the Act, where the decision is made by a Minister of the Crown, due allowance may have to be made for the taking into account of broader policy considerations which may be relevant to the exercise of a ministerial discretion.

In the present case, the respondents submit that the Minister, in failing to consider the submissions which they had made to his predecessors, neglected to take into account a consideration which he was bound to take into account in making his decision. It is convenient to divide this central issue into two separate, but related, questions. The first is whether the Minister is bound to take into account the comments on detriment which the Commissioner is required by s 50(3)(b) of the Act to include in his report to the Minister. The second is whether he is also bound, as opposed to ***43*** merely entitled, to take into account submissions made to him which correct, update or elucidate the Commissioner's comments on detriment.

...

44 The Act does not expressly state that the Minister is bound to take into account the Commissioner's comments on the matters in pars. (a) to (d) of s 50(3) in exercising his power under s 11(1)(b) to decide whether or not he is satisfied that a land grant should be made. But a consideration of the subject-matter, scope and purpose of the Act indicates that such a finding is necessarily implied by the statute. The factor that leads irresistibly to this conclusion is the specific requirement in s 50(3) that the Commissioner comment in his report on each of the four matters enumerated in the sub-section, including of course detriment. That provision recognizes that the granting of land to a Land Trust may adversely affect the interests of many people, in some cases in a very substantial way. The legislature was clearly concerned that the Minister should not overlook crucial considerations which might counterbalance or outweigh the fairness and justice of granting the land when making his decision under s 11(1)(b). Accordingly, it provided the means whereby such factors would be analyzed and drawn to his attention for the purpose of having them taken into account. That purpose would not be achieved if the Minister was merely entitled, but not bound, to consider these factors ...

The second question, which lies at the heart of this appeal, is whether the Minister is also bound to take into account submissions made to him which correct, update or elucidate the Commissioner's comments on detriment. Once it is accepted that the subject-matter, scope and purpose of the Act indicate that the detriment that may be occasioned by a proposed land grant is a factor vital to the exercise of the Minister's discretion, it is but a short and logical step to conclude that a consideration of that factor must be based on the most recent and accurate information that the Minister has at hand. ***45*** Considerable time may elapse between completion of the Commissioner's report and the date at which the Minister makes his decision; in the present case it was well over one and a half years. In that time there may be such a change of circumstances that the Commissioner's comments may no longer prove to be an accurate guide, there may be uncertainties or ambiguities in his comments that deserve clarification, or, as in the present case, even though there may have been no change of circumstances, interested parties may have become aware that the Commissioner's report omitted material matters on the subject of detriment. It would be a strange result indeed to hold that the Minister is entitled to ignore material of which he has actual or constructive knowledge and which may have a direct bearing on the justice of making the land grant, and to proceed instead on the basis of material that may be incomplete, inaccurate or misleading. In one sense this conclusion may be seen as an application of the general principle that an administrative decision maker is required to make his decision on the basis of material available to him at the time the decision is made. But that principle is itself a reflection of the fact that there may be found in the subject-matter, scope and purpose of nearly every statute conferring power to make an administrative decision an implication that the decision is to be made on the basis of the most current material available to the decision-maker.

This conclusion is all the more compelling when the decision in question is one which may adversely affect a party's interests or legitimate expectations by exposing him to new hazard or new jeopardy. The granting of land to a Land Trust for the benefit of Aboriginals is a decision of this nature because an Aboriginal Land Council established under the Act has power to refuse to grant a mining interest over Aboriginal land (s 40), or to grant it on such terms and conditions as to payment or otherwise as are provided for by agreement: s 43. When the Act specifically provides for the Commissioner to comment on the manner in which persons may be adversely affected by the making of a land grant, and provides the means whereby those comments are brought to the Minister's attention, there may readily be found in the subject-matter, scope and purpose of the Act an implication that the Minister is bound to take resultant detriment into account when making his decision. There is no sound reason for confining that obligation to a consideration of the comments in the report; matters put to the Minister by interested parties correcting, updating or elucidating the Commissioner's comments can be of no less relevance.

...

46 For these reasons, and the further reason that it cannot be said that the omitted factor was so insignificant that the failure to take it into account could not have materially affected the decision, I conclude that the Minister was bound to consider the submissions made by the respondents to his predecessors in office.

[Citations omitted]

Tickner v Chapman (1995) 57 FCR 451

Aboriginal and Torres Strait Islander Heritage Protection Act 1984 (Cth)

[As at relevant date]

10 Other declarations in relation to areas

(1) Where the Minister:

(a) receives an application made orally or in writing by or on behalf of an Aboriginal or a group of Aboriginals seeking the preservation or protection of a specified area from injury or desecration;

(b) is satisfied:

(i) that the area is a significant Aboriginal area; and

(ii) that it is under threat of injury or desecration;

(c) has received a report under subsection (4) in relation to the area from a person nominated by him and has considered the report and any representations attached to the report; and

(d) has considered such other matters as he thinks relevant;

he may make a declaration in relation to the area.

(2) Subject to this Part, a declaration under subsection (1) has effect for such period as is specified in the declaration.

(3) Before a person submits a report to the Minister for the purposes of paragraph (1)(c), he shall:

(a) publish, in the Gazette, and in a local newspaper, if any, circulating in any region concerned, a notice:

(i) stating the purpose of the application made under subsection (1) and the matters required to be dealt with in the report;

(ii) inviting interested persons to furnish representations in connection with the report by a specified date, being not less than 14 days after the date of publication of the notice in the Gazette; and

(iii) specifying an address to which such representations may be furnished; and

(b) give due consideration to any representations so furnished and, when submitting the report, attach them to the report.

(4) For the purposes of paragraph (1)(c), a report in relation to an area shall deal with the following matters:

(a) the particular significance of the area to Aboriginals;

(b) the nature and extent of the threat of injury to, or desecration of, the area;

(c) the extent of the area that should be protected;

(d) the prohibitions and restrictions to be made with respect to the area;

(e) the effects the making of a declaration may have on the proprietary or pecuniary interests of persons other than the Aboriginal or Aboriginals referred to in paragraph (1)(a);

(f) the duration of any declaration;

(g) the extent to which the area is or may be protected by or under a law of a State or Territory, and the effectiveness of any remedies available under any such law;

(h) such other matters (if any) as are prescribed.

Facts

This case was part of the long-running dispute over the construction of a bridge linking Hindmarsh Island to Goolwa in South Australia. The Commonwealth Minister for Aboriginal and Torres Strait Islander Affairs commissioned Professor Cheryl Saunders to produce a report under s 10 of the *Aboriginal and Torres Strait Islander Heritage Protection Act 1984* (Cth). As a result of the public consultation process required by the Act, Professor Saunders received over 400 submissions, which were summarised in her report to the Minister. In addition, the Minister was given all the submissions. The report also included two annexures (one provided by Ngarrindjeri women and one by an anthropologist) containing secret, sacred knowledge (that came to be known as 'secret women's business') of the Ngarrindjeri women, with a note that the annexures were only to be read by a woman.

The Minister read part of the report but did not read all the submissions. He relied on a staff member, Suzanne Kee, who read some (but not all) of the submissions and told the Minister that the report accurately summarised the submissions. Further, the Minister did not read the annexure containing the secret women's business but relied on Ms Kee's summary of that material. The Minister made a declaration, under s 10, effectively prohibiting any development on the site.

The Chapmans challenged the declaration under the *Administrative Decisions (Judicial Review) Act 1977* (Cth). At first instance, a judge of the Federal Court (O'Loughlin J) quashed the declaration. The Minister appealed to the Full Court. The appeal was dismissed.

One of the grounds of review was that the submissions, and the secret women's business, were relevant considerations that the Minister had failed to consider. The Full Court held this ground was established.

Black CJ

462 The Minister must personally consider the report and any representations attached to it. This is because the powers and functions of the Minister under s 10 ... are specifically excluded from the power of delegation conferred by s 31(1) ...

The meaning of 'consider' used as a transitive verb referring to the consideration of some thing is given in the *Oxford English Dictionary* (2nd ed) as 'to contemplate mentally, fix the mind upon; to think over, meditate or reflect on, bestow attentive thought upon, give heed to, take note of'. Consideration of a document such as a representation or a submission (there is little, if any, difference between the two for these purposes) involves an active intellectual process directed at that representation or submission.

It is not surprising that the Minister should be required personally to participate in this way in a process that may lead to a declaration under s 10. The powers given to the Minister under the Act for the purposes of protecting Aboriginal heritage are capable of affecting very seriously the interests of third parties, and for this reason the Parliament has provided for decision-making at the highest level. It is this feature of the scheme of the Act – the explicit requirement that the Minister consider the representations – that removes the process under s 10 from the general rule that a Minister is not expected to do everything personally. ...

The requirement of substantial and non-delegable personal ministerial involvement is consistent with the evident intention of s 10 ... that interested persons will have an effective opportunity to provide information and to express opinion concerning important issues involved in the consideration of an application under s 10(1) and that the decision-maker, the Minister, shall make an informed decision on the questions in issue, having considered the representations of interested persons.

It must also be remembered that the obligation to consider, imposed separately upon both the reporter and the Minister, is an obligation to consider each representation. The degree of effort that the consideration of a particular ***463*** representation may involve will of course vary according to its length, its content and its degree of relevance.

...

464 [T]he process that counsel on behalf of the Minister sought to put forward as the Minister's 'consideration' of the representations was, in my view, flawed. As I have said, the consideration of a representation involves an active intellectual process directed at that representation and again the point must be made that s 10 is explicit in its requirement that not only must the reporter give consideration to the representations but the Minister must do so as well. A report, written after due consideration of the representations by the reporter, might or might not, 'reflect' them. In either event, the section makes it clear that the Minister must personally consider the representations and it is the representations that must be contemplated, not another document which is thought by someone else to 'adequately to reflect' the representations.

This does not mean that the Minister is denied the assistance of a staff member in the process of considering the representations. A staff member might, for example, sort the representations into categories. He or she might put together all the representations that are in common form so that they can be considered together. In some cases, a summary of technical supporting material, such as legal and financial documents, might be provided and it would certainly be in order, in my view, for a competent staff member to assist the Minister by making sure that supporting technical documents were what they purported to be. I would not rule out the possibility of some representations being quite capable of effective summary, yet there would be other cases where nothing short of personal reading of a representation would constitute proper consideration of it.

Examples of the sort of representation that would need to be read personally may be found amongst the 400 or so representations forwarded with, and notionally attached to, Professor Saunders' report. Some of these make important points by the use of photographs and the form of some representations conveys meaning in other ways. Such representations need to be seen to be 'considered'.

Whilst, then, a Minister may certainly have assistance for the purpose of ***465*** considering representations, they must be truly considered and the process adopted in the present case, relying as it did upon Ms Kee's opinion about the adequate 'reflection' of the representations, was insufficient. I therefore conclude that the trial judge was correct in holding that the obligation imposed by s 10(1)(c) of the Act to consider the representations had not been fulfilled.

[Editors' note: Black CJ then considered the way the Minister had dealt with the two annexures containing secret women's business.]

...

In the present case there can, in my view, be no doubt that the obligation imposed upon the Minister by the Act to consider any representations attached to a report submitted to him for the purposes of s 10(1)(c) is not subject to any implied exception to the effect that the Minister need not consider them if, according to Aboriginal tradition, the matters contained in them are only to be disclosed to a person of the opposite sex. The Act proceeds upon the clear basis that the actual decision-maker, the Minister, must consider the report and the representations attached to it.

...

466 In these circumstances, the remaining question is, again, whether the Minister considered the part of the representations comprising the confidential appendices to [the anthropologist's] report.

The Minister did not look at the confidential appendices himself but Ms Kee did read them and she assured the Minister that there was nothing in the confidential appendices that did not support what was said in Professor Saunders' report. For the reasons given earlier concerning the issue of consideration generally, I conclude that what occurred did not amount to the required consideration of these representations.

Burchett J

[Editors' note: Burchett J considered another way the Minister might have dealt with the secret women's business.]

470 The argument about the effect of the Minister's failure to consider the confidential portion of the representations concerning 'women's business' proceeded on the assumption that the practical alternatives were limited to his taking the course which he in fact took, or his making himself aware of the secret information. It seems to me that the Minister had available to him a third course. If he thought the Aboriginal women's claim to confidentiality required a departure from the normal way of dealing with the matter, it did not follow that the ordinary rights of other citizens, protected by the express provisions of the Act, had to be jettisoned. He could have asked the Prime Minister to appoint a female Minister or member of the Executive Council to act for the time being on his behalf during the consideration of the report and recommendations.

[Citations omitted]

Murphyores Inc Pty Ltd v Commonwealth (1976) 136 CLR 1

Customs (Prohibited Exports) Regulations 1958 (Cth)

[As at relevant date]

9 Prohibition of export of minerals, & c

...

(3) The exportation from Australia of goods to which this regulation applies is prohibited unless an approval in writing to the exportation of the goods issued by the Minister of State for Minerals and Energy or by an authorized person is produced to the Collector.

...

Facts

The goods to which reg 9(3) applied included minerals. Murphyores Inc Pty Ltd held mining leases over parts of Fraser Island and wanted to extract, and export, mineral sands. They sought the approval of the Minister for Minerals and Energy to export the mineral sands. While the Minister for Minerals and Energy was considering the application, the Minister for the Environment directed an inquiry into the environmental impact of mining on Fraser Island under the *Environment Protection (Impact of Proposals) Act 1974* (Cth). The Minister for Minerals and Energy informed Murphyores that he would not grant approval to export the mineral sands until the inquiry had been completed, and he had considered the report of the inquiry.

Murphyores commenced proceedings in the High Court under s 75(v) of the *Constitution,* seeking a declaration that the direction to hold an inquiry was beyond power and an injunction preventing the inquiry from proceeding.

One of Murphyores's arguments was that environmental impact was an irrelevant consideration in the exercise of the power under reg 9(3). This argument was rejected.

Stephen J

12 [H]as the maker of the decision duly exercised his decision-making power or, on the contrary, is his decision vitiated by the nature of the considerations, extraneous to the power conferred, to which he has had regard in arriving at that decision? This question must depend for its answer primarily upon the legislation which confers the power. Where the extent of the power is delineated, perhaps by specific enumeration of matters to be considered, perhaps as a result of implications which may be drawn from the subject matter dealt with, the courts will relieve against excesses of power affecting the rights of a subject. It will be seldom, if ever, that the extent of the power cannot be seen to exclude from consideration by a decision-maker all corrupt or entirely personal and whimsical considerations, considerations which are unconnected with proper governmental administration; his decision will not be a bona fide one since these considerations will, on their face, not be such as the legislation permits him to have regard to. In other instances the task for the court will be to discern what restraints, if any, the legislation places upon considerations to which he may have had regard.

13 In the present case the *Customs (Prohibited Exports) Regulations* confer wide powers upon a variety of decision-makers. Regulation 4 prohibits the export of an assortment of goods specified in the Second Schedule to the regulations, ranging from 'ships' to 'the skeletons ... of Australian or Tasmanian Aboriginals' and it is the Minister of Customs who is given power to relax the prohibition by granting his consent in writing. No express limitation of that power is stated and, in the absence of lack of bona fides in the sense mentioned above, the heterogeneous nature of the goods is in itself enough to dispose of any suggestion that a court should seek to construct limits to the considerations to which the Minister may have regard. The Minister's reasons for permitting the export of dolphins, of anthropological specimens derived from Australian Aborigines, of barrage balloons, of cocoa beans, of fortified wine less than six months old, of foreign coins bearing a date earlier than 1901 or of the diaries of Australian explorers (to take but a few instances) must be as various as the goods themselves.

...

Regulations 5A, 6, 6A, 6B, 7 and 8 impose a variety of other prohibitions, in each case coupled with a relieving power vested in various Ministers or their departmental officers. Some identify what may not be exported by reference to the country of destination ...; others by reference to a combination of goods and destination, no anhydrous ammonia may be exported to any 'place in Africa'; others again by reference simply to types of goods, as in the case of sugar, aircraft and various biological substances ...

What emerges from this examination is that no general criteria can be inferred which will serve to limit the considerations to ***14*** which the various Ministers and their officers may have regard in exercise of their power to grant approvals for the export of goods so long as no absence of bona fides in the sense already referred to manifests itself. The very nature of the power to relieve against a prohibition imposed upon the export of classes of goods itself suggests that it may be exercisable having regard to a wide spectrum of considerations. The character of some of the classes of goods export of which is prohibited is clearly inconsistent with any concept that considerations confined to matters of trade and commerce alone may enter into a decision to relax the prohibition. It is enough to refer to the various categories of historical and anthropological interest, some of which I have already mentioned, and to the weapons of war, all dealt with under reg 4, and also to the goods associated with nuclear reactor construction and atomic energy capacity dealt with under reg 11. The unrestricted export of goods may produce a wide variety of effects, both within and without Australia. It may stimulate local production, create local shortages, endanger local species of flora or fauna and otherwise affect conditions within the exporting country. It may also produce a variety of effects upon the foreign country to which exports are sent, whether by way of increasing its warlike potential or affecting for good or ill the physical or economic welfare of its people and, perhaps, the attitude of its government towards that of Australia. Again the relations with third party countries and their governments may be involved, as may be the observance of obligations arising under treaties or international conventions on a variety of topics, some quite unconnected with trade and commerce. When such a breadth of considerations is involved only something amounting to lack of bona fides could justify curial intervention in decisions made in the exercise of the power to relax export prohibitions.

It follows from all that I have said that in my view the Minister for Minerals and Energy is free to have regard to the environmental effect of such sand mining operations as the plaintiffs may conduct on Fraser Island in deciding whether or not to allow the export of the plaintiffs' concentrates.

[Citations omitted]

CHAPTER

14

GROUNDS ARISING FROM THE GENERAL LAW

Introduction 404

Improper purpose 404

R v Toohey; Ex parte Northern Land Council (1981) 151 CLR 170 404

Shop Distributive and Allied Employees Association v Minister for Industrial Affairs (SA) (1995) 183 CLR 552 407

Fettering discretion 411

Green v Daniels (1977) 13 ALR 1 411

Bread Manufacturers of New South Wales v Evans (1981) 180 CLR 404 415

Unreasonableness 417

Minister for Immigration and Citizenship v Li (2013) 249 CLR 332 417

Minister for Immigration and Border Protection v SZVFW (2018) 264 CLR 541 421

Irrationality and illogicality 427

Minister for Immigration and Citizenship v SZMDS (2010) 240 CLR 611 427

CRL18 v Minister for Immigration, Citizenship, Migrant Services and Multicultural Affairs (2020) 171 ALD 50 432

No evidence 437

Australian Broadcasting Tribunal v Bond (1990) 170 CLR 321 437

Minister for Immigration, Citizenship, Migrant Services and Multicultural Affairs v Viane (2021) 96 ALJR 13 439

Introduction

This chapter complements Chapter 14 of *Government Accountability: Australian Administrative Law*, third edition. The grounds of review in this chapter arise as a matter of general presumption or implication, unless excluded by statute. The extracts relate to the grounds of improper purpose, acting under dictation and inflexible application of policy (both of which are instances of fettering discretion), unreasonableness, irrationality/illogicality, and no evidence. As in Chapter 13, the cases have been chosen not only because they contain important statements of law, but also because their facts provide useful examples of how the legal principles apply to specific fact situations.

Several of these cases illustrate the interplay between different grounds of review. Three cases have been included under the heading 'Fettering Discretion': two on the topic of acting under dictation and one raising the issue of inflexible application of policy (or, arguably, application of a policy that was inconsistent with the statute). Reading these cases side-by-side reveals the common threads of reasoning that appear in these two grounds. *Minister for Immigration and Citizenship v SZMDS* (2010) 240 CLR 611 tells us about the relationship between the grounds of irrationality/illogicality and unreasonableness.

Improper purpose

R v Toohey; Ex parte Northern Land Council (1981) 151 CLR 170

This case has a complex procedural history and is important for its consideration of several administrative law issues, including the amenability of delegated legislation and the decisions of high-level office holders to judicial review (see extract in Chapter 10 at pp 282–4). The extract in this chapter deals with the issue of improper purpose.

Aboriginal Land Rights (Northern Territory) Act 1976 (Cth)

[As at relevant date]

[Editors' note: Sections 11 and 50 of the Act are set out in Chapter 13 (at pp 390–1) in the extract of *Minister for Aboriginal Affairs v Peko-Wallsend Ltd* (1986) 162 CLR 24.]

3 Interpretation

(1) In this Act, unless the contrary intention appears –

...

town has the same meaning as in the law of the Northern Territory relating to the planning and developing of towns and the use of land in or near towns, and includes any area that, by virtue of regulations in force under that law, is to be treated as a town.

...

unalienated Crown land means Crown land in which no person (other than the Crown) has an estate or interest, but does not include land in a town.

...

Planning Act 1979 (NT)

[As at relevant date]

4 Interpretation

...

town means-

(a) a town within the meaning of the *Crown Lands Act*;

(b) a municipality; or

(c) land specified by the regulations to be an area which is to be treated as a town;

...

165 Regulations

(1) The Administrator may make regulations, not inconsistent with this Act, prescribing all matters required or permitted by this Act to be prescribed, or necessary or convenient to be prescribed for carrying out or giving effect to this Act ...

...

Facts

The Cox Peninsula in the Northern Territory (or, to use its Larrakia name, Kenbi) covers an area of approximately 800 square kilometres. At its closest point to Darwin, it is only six kilometres west of the city, but, being a peninsula, it is separated from Darwin by the sea; the journey from Darwin to Cox Peninsula by road is about 80 kilometres.

On 20 March 1979, the Northern Land Council, on behalf of Aboriginal people claiming to be the traditional owners of the Cox Peninsula, made a claim (the 'Kenbi Land Claim') under the *Aboriginal Land Rights (Northern Territory) Act 1976* (Cth) ('*Land Rights Act*').

On 31 July 1979, the Administrator of the Northern Territory made a regulation under s 165 of the *Planning Act 1979* (NT) that, among other things, extended the town boundaries of Darwin. Previously, the town of Darwin had covered an area of 142 square kilometres. Under the new regulation (Regulation 5), the town of Darwin increased to a size of 4350 square kilometres, including the Cox Peninsula.

The Aboriginal Land Commissioner (Toohey J) held a hearing to determine the effect of Regulation 5. The Northern Land Council submitted that Regulation 5 had been made for an improper purpose. Toohey J held that it was not open to him to inquire into the motives for making the regulation. On this basis, he found that the Cox Peninsula was now part of a 'town' and, therefore, was no longer 'unalienated Crown land' and could not be the subject of a claim under the *Land Rights Act*.

The Northern Land Council commenced proceedings in the High Court, seeking a writ of certiorari to quash the Commissioner's decision, and mandamus to compel him to determine the Kenbi Land Claim.

For present purposes, the key issue was whether the Administrator's decision could be challenged on the ground that it was made for an improper purpose.

The High Court issued a writ of mandamus, directing the Aboriginal Land Commissioner to deal with the land rights claim in accordance with the law, thereby requiring the Commissioner to inquire into whether the Administrator's decision under the *Planning Act* had been made for an improper purpose.

Gibbs CJ

186 Under a statutory provision such as the present, the nature and extent of the power 'must be inferred from a construction of the Act read as a whole': *Padfield v Minister of Agriculture, Fisheries and Food* [[1968] AC 997, 1033]. The principle, which is clearly settled, at least in the case of authorities subordinate to the Crown, is that a statutory power may be exercised only for the purposes for which it is conferred. As Latham CJ said in *Brownells Ltd v Ironmongers' Wages Board* [(1950) 81 CLR 108, 120]:

> No inquiry may be made into the motives of the Legislature in enacting a law, but where a statute confers powers upon an officer or a statutory body and either by express provision or by reason of the general character of the statute it appears that the powers were intended to be exercised only for a particular purpose, then the exercise of the powers not for such purpose but for some ulterior object will be invalid. ...

187 In the present case, it is not open to doubt that the powers conferred by s 165 of the *Planning Act*, read in conjunction with the definition of 'town' in s 4(1), are to be exercised only for planning purposes, using that expression widely to include such matters as subdivision and development. It is incontestable that the power is not intended by the Act to be conferred for the purpose of defeating the traditional land claims of Aboriginals. If it was used for that purpose the exercise of the power was invalid, unless the Administrator enjoys some privilege that enables him to transcend and disregard the limitations which the statute on its proper construction imposes. It would be surprising in principle if this were so. It seems fundamental to the rule of law that the Crown has no more power than any subordinate official to enlarge by its own act the scope of a power that has been conferred on it by the Parliament.

...

193 In the present case, the appellant was in my opinion entitled to challenge the Planning Regulations ... on the ground that they were made for a purpose which was not a planning, or a town planning, purpose. The challenge might be made either on the ground that the regulations were invalid on their face, or on the ground that evidence would show that they were in fact designed to defeat the traditional land claims of Aboriginals. It was necessary for the Commissioner to decide on the validity of the Planning Regulations to enable himself to determine whether the application was made in respect of land to which s 50(1)(a) of the *Land Rights Act* applied. If the regulations were invalid, there was no justification for him to fail to continue to exercise his function under s 50(1)(a). For the reasons given the Commissioner has not exercised his functions in accordance with law and the case is a proper one for mandamus.

Shop Distributive and Allied Employees Association v Minister for Industrial Affairs (SA) (1995) 183 CLR 552

Shop Trading Hours Act 1977 (SA)

[As at relevant date]

4 Interpretation

(1) In this Act, unless the contrary intention appears –

...

exempt shop means –

(a) a shop (not being a hairdresser's shop) –

(i) the floor area of which does not exceed 200 square metres;

...

(b) ... a shop the business of which is the retail sale of all or any of the goods set out in any one of the following subparagraphs:

(i) antiques (other than coins or stamps);

(ii) live fish, fish food, aquariums, accessories for aquariums;

(iii) paintings, reproductions, drawings, etchings, pottery, sculptures, artifacts, wood carving, leatherware, weavings, hand-made goods of glass, iron, copper or silver;

(iv) newspapers, books, periodicals, greeting cards, posters, wrapping paper, stationery;

...

(x) food –

- for consumption on the shop premises; or
- prepared on the shop premises for consumption off those premises;

(c) a hairdresser's shop ...

(d) ... a shop –

(i) the business of which is the sale of foodstuffs;

(ii) which has a floor area –

(A) that does not exceed 200 square metres;

or

(B) that does not exceed 400 square metres and in which not more than three persons are physically present at any one time for the purpose of carrying on, or assisting in carrying on, the business of the shop;

and

(iii) which does not adjoin, and is not adjacent to, a building, with a floor area exceeding one-half the floor area of the shop, that is used as a storeroom for the purposes of the shop;

(e) a shop in relation to which a certificate of exemption, issued by the Minister, is in force; ...

but does not include any shop the business of which is solely or predominantly the retail sale of –

(g) meat;

(h) motor vehicles or boats;

or

(i) motor spirit or lubricants: ...

5 Certificate of exemption

(1) The Minister may issue a certificate of exemption to a shopkeeper in relation to a shop specified in the certificate.

...

13 Closing times for shops

(1) Subject to this section, the closing time for a shop situated within the Central Shopping District, or any other shopping district, or part of a shopping district, to which this subsection applies by virtue of a proclamation under subsection (6), is –

(a) 6.00 p.m. on every weekday other than a Friday;

(b) 9.00 p.m. on a Friday;

and

(c) 5.00 p.m. on a Saturday.

...

(6) Subject to subsection (7), the Governor may, by proclamation, order that the closing times specified in subsection (1) or such other closing times as are specified in the proclamation apply, as from a time specified in the proclamation, in any shopping district or part of a shopping district specified in the proclamation and those closing times will apply accordingly –

(a) until the date (if any) specified in the proclamation as the date at which the proclamation is to cease to have effect; or

(b) until the publication in the *Gazette* of a proclamation revoking that proclamation,

whichever occurs first.

(7) A proclamation under subsection (6) cannot be made unless the Minister –

(a) is satisfied that a majority of interested persons desire that the proposed proclamation be made; and

(b) gives a certificate to that effect.

(8) In subsection (7) –

interested persons means –

(a) persons resident in the relevant shopping district, or part of a shopping district;

and

(b) shopkeepers and shop assistants who work in shops within that shopping district or part of a shopping district.

(9) The Governor may, by proclamation, authorize the opening of shops during hours, specified in the proclamation, when it would otherwise be unlawful to open those shops.

(10) A proclamation under subsection (9) –

(a) may relate to shops generally or to a specified shop or to specified classes of shops;

(b) may apply generally throughout the State or in specified shopping districts or in a specified part of a shopping district or in other parts of the State;

(c) cannot operate in respect of a period greater than one month; and

(d) may be revoked by subsequent proclamation.

(11) Notwithstanding any other provision of this Act, it is lawful for a shop to be open in accordance with a proclamation under subsection (9).

...

14 Shops to be closed at closing time

...

(3) Except as otherwise provided in this Act, a shopkeeper must keep the shop closed and fastened against the admission of the public for the whole of each Sunday, each other public holiday and during such other period that the shop is required by this Act to be closed.

...

(6) A person who fails to comply with subsection ... (3) ... is guilty of an offence.

Penalty: $10 000.

...

(11) In any proceedings for an offence against this section, it is a defence for the defendant to prove that at the time of the alleged offence ... the shop, in relation to which it is alleged the offence was committed, was an exempt shop.

Facts

In the early 1990s, Sunday trading was a controversial topic in South Australia, with the Government in favour of deregulating shopping hours and some groups opposing this move. On 9 August 1994, the Minister issued a press release announcing that Sunday trading was to be permitted in Adelaide city centre from 11 am to 5 pm. The press release stated that retailers who were not already exempt would 'be able to apply for and obtain Section 5 Certificates of Exemption to permit the limited extended Sunday ... retail trading announced in this statement.'

The Shop Distributive and Allied Employees Association ('SDA') was the union representing retail workers. SDA applied for a declaration that certificates of exemption under s 5 issued for the purpose of establishing general Sunday trading in Adelaide city centre would be invalid. SDA argued that such certificates would be issued for an improper purpose.

Brennan, Dawson, Toohey, Gaudron and McHugh JJ

559 In an Act dealing with shop trading hours, the use of the word 'exempt' without qualification indicates in our view an intention that an exempt shop should stand outside the regime with respect to shop trading hours which the Act lays down. The use of that word certainly ***560*** does not suggest that the power to issue a certificate of exemption was intended to be a power to lay down an alternative regime in relation to trading hours. True it is that a certificate of exemption may be subject to specified restrictions and conditions, but a partial exemption, that is, an exemption confined to particular hours on a particular day of the week, can hardly be regarded as a complete exemption subject to a restriction or a condition. The type of restriction or condition contemplated by s 5 may be seen from the restrictions or conditions imposed by the certificates in this case. Moreover, in the definition of 'exempt shop' in s 4(1), all of the categories of exempt shops, apart from that in question, are defined, not by reference to trading hours, but by reference to such considerations as floor are and the nature of the goods or services offered for sale. It would be incongruous if the category of exempt shops constituted by 'a shop in relation to which a certificate of exemption, issued by the Minister, is in force' could be afforded a partial exemption defined by reference to trading hours. Furthermore, specific provision is made by s 13a for the Minister to grant a permit to certain types of hardware shop to trade on Sundays and other public holidays. Similar provision is made in s 17 for the Minister to grant licences permitting the sale of motor spirits and lubricants on Sundays and other public holidays. Those provisions would be unnecessary were s 5 to be construed as the Minister seeks to construe it.

But the strongest indication that the power given to the Minister to issue certificates of exemption does not extend to their use for the purposes of laying down shop trading hours in a shopping district is to be found in s 13. That section provides a means for the alteration by executive act of opening and closing times. Not only does it so provide, but where hours of trading are to be extended, interested persons are to be consulted unless the extension is confined to a period of one month. Understandably, having regard to the Act's concern for employees, where trading hours are to be reduced, the section does not impose any restriction. If it were possible to issue certificates of exemption prescribing shop trading hours which were different from those required by the Act, those protections which s 13 affords to interested persons might be bypassed and this can scarcely have been the intention of the legislature.

In our view, the power vested in the Minister by s 5 of the Act is a power to issue a certificate of exemption which exempts a shop from the operation of the Act in the same manner as other exempt shops. The power does not extend to relieving a shopkeeper from the observance of the required trading hours only on a particular day of the week and then only within certain hours on that day. Such an exemption (if it can be called an exemption at all) is only partial. A partial exemption is something which the Act does not envisage. In any event, the power should not be construed as allowing the Minister to effect an alteration of shop trading hours within a shopping district. The means of effecting such an alteration are contained in s 13 of the ***561*** Act and, having regard to the protections afforded by that section, s 5 cannot properly be regarded as intended to provide an alternative means.

It should be added that even if s 5 did in some way vest in the Minister a discretion to prescribe shop trading hours by the issue of certificates of exemption, it would be a wrongful exercise of that discretion to issue certificates in pursuance of a scheme to vary or displace the shop trading hours prescribed by the Act in a shopping district. It would be wrong to do so because the shop trading hours prescribed by the Act are the very thing from which there may be an exemption. But there is no exemption when different shop trading hours are prescribed by a certificate of exemption; what purports to be an exemption in fact becomes a prescription itself. In other words, the discretion vested in the Minister by s 5 is for the purpose of exempting a shop from the observance of the trading hours laid down by Parliament or by proclamation. Any discretion vested in the Minister by s 5 must be exercised for the purpose for which the discretion is conferred. The power conferred by s 5 may not be exercised for the purpose of laying down the trading hours to be observed generally in a shopping district.

For the foregoing reasons, it is our view that the certificates of exemption which the Minister has purported to issue pursuant to s 5 are beyond power. The parties are agreed that, in the event of the Court reaching that conclusion, it should declare that the certificates of exemption issued by the Minister pursuant to s 5 of the Act for the purpose of establishing general Sunday trading in the Central Shopping District in accordance with the ministerial statement of 9 August 1994 are invalid. We would make that declaration.

[Citations omitted]

Fettering discretion

Green v Daniels (1977) 13 ALR 1

Social Services Act 1947 (Cth)

[As at relevant date]

107 Unemployment benefits

... Subject to this Part, a person who—

(a) has attained the age of sixteen years but, being a male, has not attained the age of sixty-five years or, being a female, has not attained the age of sixty years;

(b) is residing in Australia on the date on which he lodges his claim for a benefit and—

(i) has been continuously so resident for a period of not less than twelve months immediately preceding that date; or

(ii) satisfies the Director-General that he is likely to remain permanently in Australia; and

(c) satisfies the Director-General that he—

(i) is unemployed and that his unemployment is not due to his being a direct participant in a strike;

(ii) is capable of undertaking, and is willing to undertake, work which, in the opinion of the Director-General, is suitable to be undertaken by that person; and

(iii) has taken reasonable steps to obtain such work,

shall be qualified to receive an unemployment benefit.

Facts

The Department of Social Security developed an 'Unemployment and Sickness Benefit Manual' containing guidelines for departmental officers to use when considering applications for social security benefits. One of these guidelines addressed concerns that students were applying for unemployment benefits at the end of the school year with no genuine intention to look for work; instead, they intended to claim benefits over the summer holidays and then return to study. The Manual provided:

> As a general rule ... people who leave school and register for employment within 28 days prior to the end of the school year, or at any time during the long vacation, will not be in a position, until the end of the school vacation, to satisfy the conditions of eligibility for unemployment benefit which require the claimant to be unemployed and to have taken reasonable steps to obtain work.
>
> ...
>
> A student who intends to enter the workforce and not resume his studies will, as a general rule, be eligible for unemployment benefit from the date of commencement of the following school year or from the seventh day after the date of lodgment of the claim, whichever is the later.

Karen Green completed her fourth form of school (the equivalent of Year 10) at the age of 16, on 26 November 1976. She decided to leave school and seek employment. In December 1976, she applied for unemployment benefits, but social security officers told her she would not receive benefits until the start of the new school year on 22 February 1977. Ms Green continued to look for work without success, and did not return to school. She began receiving unemployment benefits after 22 February 1977.

Ms Green applied to the High Court under s 75(v) of the *Constitution* for a declaration she had been entitled to unemployment benefits between 27 November 1976 and 22 February 1977. Her application was heard by a single judge of the High Court. Stephen J held that the manner in which the policy had been applied was unlawful.

Stephen J

> ***7*** Whatever hint of flexibility and of room for consideration of exceptional cases may be thought to be conveyed by the Manual's use of the phrase 'as a general rule', ...

the application of the general rule to the plaintiff contained no suggestion of anything other than an inflexible rule, a rule which prevented her from being considered for unemployment benefit at any time prior to 22 February 1977. It is said on behalf of the defendants that the plaintiff has herself to blame for this, since she failed to tell the Department … at any time prior to 22 February 1977 what she had done on her own behalf by way of efforts to find employment.

To this, the plaintiff replies that she was not only not asked for such information, but was expressly told that it should only be supplied … at the end of the school holidays. But more than that, there was, in any event, nothing very exceptional about the plaintiff's position of which she had to tell. I must, I think, infer that very many other school leavers would have been in precisely her position; that is, having decided to leave school, they would have taken some steps on their own account to seek employment, but would have met with no success.

8 Accordingly, this is not, I think, a case of a person in an exceptional situation being denied the opportunity of having her particular circumstances considered on their particular merits, but rather one in which the plaintiff, together no doubt, with very many others, has been dealt with in accordance with a general administrative rule intended for just such an ordinary case as hers.

The question is, then, whether this general rule is no more than a permissible instruction by the Director-General to those to whom he has delegated his powers under s 107(c) as to how they are to determine whether they are satisfied of the matters there referred to; or whether on the contrary it reveals an attempted substitution of inconsistent departmental criteria for those which the Parliament has enacted as appropriate to qualify an applicant for unemployment benefit.

…

9 [T]he function of the Director-General under s 107 is to be distinguished from that of [decision-makers] which, in their exercise of discretionary powers … may give effect to some general policy that they see as desirable so long as in doing so they do not preclude themselves from considering on its merits the exceptional case. The Director-General is not concerned, in his administration of s 107, with the carrying out of any policy. No general discretion is conferred upon him; instead specific criteria are laid down by the Act and all that is left for him to do is to decide whether or not he attains a state of satisfaction that the facts exist to which each of these criteria refer. He must, no doubt, for the benefit of his delegates and in the interests of good and consistent administration, provide guidelines indicating what he regards as justifying such a state of satisfaction. But if, in the course of doing this, he issues instructions as to what will give rise to the requisite state of satisfaction on the part of his delegates and these are inconsistent with a proper observance of the statutory criteria he acts unlawfully; should his delegates then observe those instructions, their conclusions concerning an applicant's compliance with the criteria will be vitiated.

This is what has happened in the present case. The criteria in s 107(c)(i) and (iii), those of being 'unemployed' and of having 'taken reasonable steps to obtain such work', have had superimposed upon them a requirement which prevents them from being satisfied by any school leaver during the school holidays, a period of about three months, and which, in effect, renders them inoperative during that period.

The position may be tested by examining the matters arising for consideration under each of those two statutory criteria and the effect, in each case, of the Director-General's requirement. I take first sub-par (i) of s 107(c). The state of being 'unemployed' I regard as satisfied as soon as a student leaves school, with the intention of not returning but, instead, of entering the workforce, and begins to seek employment. The only element in that set of circumstances which is not readily ascertainable by the Director-General is the school leaver's intention. That intention he has chosen to ascertain by waiting until the outcome reveals itself at the end of the school holidays. To do so no doubt ensures that the Director-General's state of satisfaction of mind will accord with the truth of the matter in the case of those applicants, surely only a small proportion, who seek to deceive him when they say that they do not intend to return to school; as to them his refusal to be satisfied until the end of the holidays will ensure that he is not deceived. But he has only attained this result at the cost of being wrong in the case of all those other applicants who have truthfully told him that they have ended their school days but whose statement he has refused to accept until proved correct at the end of the school holidays. In the case of all these, unemployment benefits will have been denied them during the school holidays and this because the Director-General will erroneously have failed to be satisfied as to their true position ... ***10*** Any method which produced erroneous results of this magnitude is clearly unacceptable as a means open to the Director-General in satisfying himself as to the subject matter of s 107(c)(i).

This must be the more so when other, conventional means of learning of applicants' intentions are not only open to him, but are in fact used by him; the 'Record of Applications made for Employment' issued to school leavers itself contains a form of declaration to be made by applicants that 'I will not be undertaking full time education or training in 1977'; in the present case, the plaintiff made such a declaration. Such declarations the Director-General presumably disregards. In addition to such declarations, he could have regard also to the nature of the efforts by the school leaver to seek employment ...

The second criterion, that in sub-par (iii) relating to the taking of steps to seek work, no doubt presents considerable scope for the giving of instructions by the Director-General to his delegates as to what is involved in 'reasonable steps'; it does not, however, in my view, entitle him to impose a quite arbitrary time of almost three months before this criterion is to be regarded as having been complied with. It is arbitrary [because] it depends not at all upon matters relevant to the application – upon factors such as the range of available employment opportunities consistent with the applicant's qualifications, skills and general capacity, the current state of the employment market and the locality in which employment is being sought. ...

11 [T]he quite understandable desire to prevent what is seen as an abuse of the Act by dishonest school leavers cannot be made the occasion for disregarding the statutory criteria of eligibility in favour of a requirement which finds no place in the legislation and the effect of which is to deny, for almost three months, to the great body of honest school leavers an opportunity to qualify for unemployment benefits.

[Editors' note: Stephen J made the following orders.]

> ***15*** Declare that upon receipt of the plaintiff's claim for unemployment benefits ..., the Director-General should have considered all the circumstances of the plaintiff's claim, making such investigations as he determined, and in the light thereof should have decided whether the plaintiff answered the descriptions contained in pars (a) and (b) of s 107 of the *Social Services Act 1947* and whether she had also satisfied him as to the several matters referred to in par (c) thereof and should by that means have determined whether the plaintiff was qualified to receive an unemployment benefit.
>
> Declare further that in his consideration of the plaintiff's claim, the Director-General might have had regard to the fact that it was made during the period of school holidays and at a time after the plaintiff had left school at the end of the year but should not treat that fact as of itself decisive in determining whether the plaintiff had satisfied him of any one of the several matters referred to in par (c) of s 107.

[Citations omitted]

Bread Manufacturers of New South Wales v Evans (1981) 180 CLR 404

Prices Regulation Act 1948 (NSW)

[As at relevant date]

20 Determination of maximum prices, rates, etc.

(1) The Commission may, with respect to any declared goods, from time to time, by order published in the Gazette—

(a) fix and declare the maximum price at which any such goods may be sold generally or in any part of the State or in any proclaimed area; or

...

(1A) Notwithstanding subsection (1), the Commission shall, before causing an order referred to in subsection (1) to be published in the Gazette, serve a copy of the proposed order on the Minister and shall not cause the proposed order to be so published—

(a) unless the Minister has informed the Commission that he does not propose to give it a direction under paragraph (b); or

(b) if the Minister, in the public interest, has directed the Commission not to publish the proposed order.

Facts

The Prices Commission made an order (Order No 798) fixing the maximum price of bread in New South Wales. There was evidence suggesting the Commission had met with the Minister and discussed the order before reaching a final decision. The Bread Manufacturers Association, a trade association representing the manufacturers of bread and bread products, challenged the order. Among other grounds of review, they argued the Commission acted under the dictation of the Minister.

At first instance, a judge of the Supreme Court of New South Wales quashed the order, but the Court of Appeal reversed that decision. The Bread Manufacturers Association appealed to the High Court.

The relevant issue for present purposes was whether discussing a proposed order with the Minister could amount to the Minister improperly dictating to the Commission. The High Court rejected this argument.

Gibbs CJ

> ***418*** The attack on Prices Regulation Order No 798 commences with the proposition that a statutory authority must not, in the purported exercise of its discretion, act under the dictation of some other person. This proposition is plainly correct. The Commission is the body entrusted with power to fix the price, and its decision must be its own. If it acted under pressure exerted by the Minister, or simply gave automatic effect to a decision of the Minister, the decision would not then really be that of the Commission but would be that of the Minister. It does not follow that it was impermissible for the Commission to consider the views of the Minister in coming to its decision. For the Commission to take ministerial policy into account in making a decision of its own is a different thing from automatically following ministerial policy. In [*R v Anderson; Ex parte Ipec-Air Pty Ltd* (1965) 113 CLR 177, 193, 201–2] the whole Court accepted that when a discretion is vested in the head of a government department, the policy of the government is not necessarily an extraneous matter which he must not consider. Although the members of the Commission are not all public servants and the Commission is an independent body, the Commission is required to give effect to views of public policy, with which the Minister also has a legitimate concern ... Further, the Minister is given important powers in connexion with the making of price- fixing orders, by s 20(1A) ...
>
> ***419*** [T]he effect of s 20(1A) is that the Minister has complete power to prevent the Commission from fixing prices in any case. It would be a futility for the Commission to make an order which it knew that the Minister would veto, and it would therefore not be wrong for the Commission, in considering what price it should fix, to take into account the Minister's views, provided that in the end the decision reached by the Commission was its own. If the Commission can consider the Minister's views, it can treat them as decisive. There is obviously a fine line between a case in which the Commission automatically obeys a ministerial pronouncement, and that in which it decides for itself to grant the largest increase in price that the Minister will not veto. The fact that the Minister has a statutory power of veto makes the case an exceptional one.
>
> In the present case the evidence does not in my opinion support a finding that the Commission acted under the dictation of the Minister, or that the Minister exercised undue influence on the Commission ...

[Citations omitted]

Unreasonableness

Minister for Immigration and Citizenship v Li (2013) 249 CLR 332

Part of French CJ's judgment in this case is extracted in Chapter 3, as an example of the interpretation of a statutory discretion.

Migration Act 1958 (Cth)

[As at relevant date]

PART 5—REVIEW OF DECISIONS

353 Tribunal's way of operating

(1) The Tribunal shall, in carrying out its functions under this Act, pursue the objective of providing a mechanism of review that is fair, just, economical, informal and quick.

(2) The Tribunal, in reviewing a decision:

(a) is not bound by technicalities, legal forms or rules of evidence; and

(b) shall act according to substantial justice and the merits of the case.

DIVISION 5—CONDUCT OF REVIEW

357A Exhaustive statement of natural justice hearing rule

(1) This Division is taken to be an exhaustive statement of the requirements of the natural justice hearing rule in relation to the matters it deals with.

...

(3) In applying this Division, the Tribunal must act in a way that is fair and just.

360 Tribunal must invite applicant to appear

(1) The Tribunal must invite the applicant to appear before the Tribunal to give evidence and present arguments relating to the issues arising in relation to the decision under review.

...

363 Powers of the Tribunal etc.

(1) For the purpose of the review of a decision, the [Migration Review] Tribunal may:

...

(b) adjourn the review from time to time;

...

Migration Regulations 1994 (Cth)

[As at relevant date]

880.22 Criteria to be satisfied at time of decision

...

> A relevant assessing authority has assessed the skills of the applicant as suitable for his or her nominated skilled occupation, and no evidence has become available that the information given or used as part of the assessment of the applicant's skills is false or misleading in a material particular.

Facts

Xiujuan Li was residing in Australia and training as a cook. On 10 February 2007, she applied for a Skilled-Independent Overseas Student (Residence) ('Class DD') visa. Under reg 880.22 of the *Migration Regulations 1994* (Cth), one of the conditions for the grant of this visa was that a 'relevant assessing authority' had given a favourable assessment of the applicant's skills in their chosen occupation. Ms Li supported with her application with a favourable skills assessment from an assessing authority, Trades Recognition Australia.

On 13 January 2009, the Minister's delegate refused to grant the visa, because the skills assessment had been based on false information provided by Ms Li's migration agent. Ms Li promptly engaged a new migration agent.

On 30 January 2009, Ms Li applied to the Migration Review Tribunal for a review of the delegate's decision. On 4 November 2009, she applied to Trades Recognition Australia for a fresh skills assessment. On 18 December 2009, before the new skills assessment had been completed, the Tribunal held a hearing in Ms Li's matter. The forthcoming skills assessment was discussed. Two days after the hearing, the Tribunal wrote to Ms Li's migration agent inviting further comment on some aspects of the application.

On 18 January 2010, the migration agent informed the Tribunal that Ms Li's second skills assessment had been unsuccessful, but that there had been two 'fundamental errors in the assessment process, and Ms Li had applied to Trades Recognition Australia for review of the assessment. He requested that the Tribunal refrain from making its decision until the skills assessment was finalised.

On 25 January 2010, without waiting for Trades Recognition Australia to complete the skills assessment, the Tribunal decided to affirm the delegate's decision refusing the visa. Its reasons included the following passage:

> The Tribunal considers that the applicant has been provided with enough opportunities to present her case and is not prepared to delay any further and in any event, considers that clause 880.230 necessarily covers each and every relevant assessing authority's assessment.

Ms Li commenced judicial review proceedings under s 476 of the *Migration Act 1958* (Cth), which confers on the Federal Magistrates Court jurisdiction equivalent to that conferred on the High Court under s 75(v) of the *Constitution.* Both the Federal Magistrates Court and, on appeal, the Full Court of the Federal Court held that the refusal to adjourn proceedings until the skills assessment had been finalised was unreasonable. The Minister appealed to the High Court. The High Court dismissed the appeal, holding that the Tribunal's decision had been unreasonable.

Hayne, Kiefel and Bell JJ

> ***362*** [63] Because s 363(1)(b) contains a statutory discretionary power, the standard to be applied to the exercise of that power is not derived only from s 357A(3), but also

from a presumption of the law. The legislature is taken to intend that a discretionary power, statutorily conferred, will be exercised reasonably.

[64] A standard of reasonableness in the exercise of a discretionary power given by statute had been required by the law long before the first statement of '*Wednesbury* unreasonableness' in *Associated* ***363*** *Provincial Picture Houses Ltd v Wednesbury Corporation* [[1948] 1 KB 223] ... In *Re Refugee Review Tribunal; Ex parte Aala* [(2000) 204 CLR 82, 100-101 [40]], Gaudron and Gummow JJ said that the requirement of reasonableness represents the development of legal thought which began before federation and accommodates s 75(v) to that development.

[65] In *Sharp v Wakefield,* it was said that when something is to be done within the discretion of an authority, it is to be done according to the rules of reason and justice. That is what is meant by 'according to law'. It is to be legal and regular, not arbitrary, vague and fanciful. The discretion must be 'exercised within the limit, to which an honest man competent to the discharge of his office ought to confine himself' [[1891] AC 173, 179]. ... [T]he legal conception of discretion dates from at least the sixteenth century. ...

[66] This approach does not deny that there is an area within which a decision-maker has a genuinely free discretion. That area resides within the bounds of legal reasonableness. The courts are conscious of not exceeding their supervisory role by undertaking a review of the merits of an exercise of discretionary power. Properly applied, a standard of legal reasonableness does not involve substituting a court's view as to how a discretion should be exercised for that of a decision-maker. Accepting that the standard of reasonableness is not applied in this way does not, however, explain how it is to be applied and how it is to be tested.

[67] ... [W]here discretions are ill-defined (as commonly they are) it is necessary to ***364*** look to the scope and purpose of the statute conferring the discretionary power and its real object. The ordinary approach to statutory construction, reiterated in *Project Blue Sky Inc v Australian Broadcasting Authority* [(1998) 194 CLR 355], requires nothing less. The legal standard of reasonableness must be the standard indicated by the true construction of the statute. It is necessary to construe the statute because the question to which the standard of reasonableness is addressed is whether the statutory power has been abused.

[68] Lord Greene MR's oft-quoted formulation of unreasonableness in *Wednesbury* has been criticised for 'circularity and vagueness', as have subsequent attempts to clarify it. However, as has been noted, *Wednesbury* is not the starting point for the standard of reasonableness, nor should it be considered the end point. The legal standard of unreasonableness should not be considered as limited to what is in effect an irrational, if not bizarre, decision – which is to say one that is so unreasonable that no reasonable person could have arrived at it – nor should Lord Greene MR be taken to have limited unreasonableness in this way in his judgment in *Wednesbury.* This aspect of his Lordship's judgment may more sensibly be taken to recognise that an inference of unreasonableness may in some cases be objectively drawn even where a particular error in reasoning cannot be identified. ...

365 [72] The more specific errors in decision-making, to which the courts often refer, may also be seen as encompassed by unreasonableness. This may be consistent with the observations of Lord Greene MR, that some decisions may be considered unreasonable in more than one sense and that 'all these things run into one another' [*Associated*

Provincial Picture Houses Ltd v Wednesbury Corporation [1948] 1 KB 223, 229] ... ***366*** Whether a decision-maker be regarded, by reference to the scope and purpose of the statute, as having committed a particular error in reasoning, given disproportionate weight to some factor or reasoned illogically or irrationally, the final conclusion will in each case be that the decision-maker has been unreasonable in a legal sense.

...

367 [76] As to the inferences that may be drawn by an appellate court [on an appeal from the exercise of a judicial discretion], it was said in *House v The King* [(1936) 55 CLR 499, 505] that an appellate court may infer that in some way there has been a failure properly to exercise the discretion 'if upon the facts [the result] is unreasonable or plainly unjust'. The same reasoning might apply to the review of the exercise of a statutory discretion, where unreasonableness is an inference drawn from the facts and from the matters falling for consideration in the exercise of the statutory power. Even where some reasons have been provided, as is the case here, it may nevertheless not be possible for a court to comprehend how the decision was arrived at. Unreasonableness is a conclusion which may be applied to a decision which lacks an evident and intelligible justification.

The Tribunal's exercise of discretion

[77] The starting point is that the Tribunal, for the purposes of reviewing the delegate's decision, exercises all the powers and discretions of the Minister. Further, and as the Minister concedes, in making a decision neither the delegate nor the Tribunal is confined to the material which was initially provided to support satisfaction of the relevant visa criteria. Those criteria are expressed to be satisfied at the time of the decision [*Migration Regulations 1994,* sch 2, subdiv 880.22]. If a further skills assessment is completed by TRA before the Tribunal makes its decision, the Tribunal may have regard to it. ...

[79] ... The discussion of the forthcoming second skills assessment during the hearing on 18 December 2009, and the subsequent request for an adjournment of the Tribunal's review while TRA reviewed the second skills assessment, must have conveyed to the Tribunal that Ms Li did not consider that she had presented her case. In ***368*** deciding whether to adjourn, that was what the Tribunal had to consider in the context of the statutory purpose of s 360, but it does not appear that it did so.

[80] The decision to refuse the adjournment request was explained by the Tribunal on the bases that (a) Ms Li had been provided with enough opportunities to present her case; and (b) the Tribunal was not prepared to delay the matter any further. The reference to delay was not further explained by the Tribunal. The only significant delay would appear to be attributable to the Tribunal, which took some nine months to contact Ms Li after the lodgment of her application. In any event, what pressing need for a conclusion of the review was the Tribunal adverting to, a need which would have to be weighed against the object of s 360? ... It may be accepted that the Tribunal is to act with some efficiency, as is stated in s 353(1) of the *Migration Act,* but such a consideration would again have to be weighed against the countervailing consideration of the purpose of s 360 and Div 5.

...

[82] It cannot be suggested that the Tribunal is under an obligation to afford every opportunity to an applicant for review to present his or her best possible case and to improve upon the evidence. Of course it may decide, in an appropriate case, that 'enough is enough', but it is not apparent how that conclusion was reached in the present case, having regard to the facts and to the statutory purpose to which the discretion to adjourn is directed.

[83] The purpose of s 360(1) has already been referred to. It is to provide an applicant for review the opportunity to present evidence and arguments 'relating to the issues arising in relation to the decision under review'. The question which remained in issue when the Tribunal made its decision was the satisfaction of a visa criterion by a complying skills assessment. Although the Tribunal could not be expected to assume that the second skills assessment, when reviewed, would favour Ms Li, it did not suggest that there was no prospect of the second skills assessment being obtained, or that the outcome could ***369*** not be known, in the near future. In these circumstances it is not apparent why the Tribunal decided, abruptly, to conclude the review.

...

[85] The Tribunal's error might be identified as giving too much weight to the fact that Ms Li had had some opportunity to present evidence and argument and insufficient weight to her need to present further evidence. It would not appear that the Tribunal had regard to the purposes for which the statutory discretion in s 363(1)(b) is provided in arriving at its decision. It is not possible to say which of these errors was made, but the result itself bespeaks error. In the circumstances of this case, it could not have been decided that the review should be brought to an end if all relevant and no irrelevant considerations were taken into account and regard was had to the scope and purpose of the statute. Because error must be inferred, it follows that the Tribunal did not discharge its function (of deciding whether to adjourn the review) according to law. The Tribunal did not conduct the review in the manner required by the *Migration Act* and consequently acted beyond its jurisdiction.

[Citations omitted]

Minister for Immigration and Border Protection v SZVFW (2018) 264 CLR 541

Migration Act 1958 (Cth)

[As at relevant date]

PART 7—REVIEW OF PROTECTION VISA DECISIONS

415 Powers of Refugee Review Tribunal

(1) The Tribunal may, for the purposes of the review of an RRT-reviewable decision, exercise all the powers and discretions that are conferred by this Act on the person who made the decision.

(2) The Tribunal may:

(a) affirm the decision; or

(b) vary the decision; or

(c) if the decision relates to a prescribed matter—remit the matter for reconsideration ...; or

(d) set the decision aside and substitute a new decision.

...

420 Refugee Review Tribunal's way of operating

(1) The Tribunal, in carrying out its functions under this Act, is to pursue the objective of providing a mechanism of review that is fair, just, economical, informal and quick.

(2) The Tribunal, in reviewing a decision:

(a) is not bound by technicalities, legal forms or rules of evidence; and

(b) must act according to substantial justice and the merits of the case.

DIVISION 4—CONDUCT OF REVIEW

422B Exhaustive statement of natural justice hearing rule

(1) This Division is taken to be an exhaustive statement of the requirements of the natural justice hearing rule in relation to the matters it deals with.

...

425 Tribunal must invite applicant to appear

(1) The Tribunal must invite the applicant to appear before the Tribunal to give evidence and present arguments relating to the issues arising in relation to the decision under review.

...

425A Notice of invitation to appear

(1) If the applicant is invited to appear before the Tribunal, the Tribunal must give the applicant notice of the day on which, and the time and place at which, the applicant is scheduled to appear.

(2) The notice must be given to the applicant:

(a) ... by one of the methods specified in section 441A; ...

(4) The notice must contain a statement of the effect of section 426A.

426A Failure of applicant to appear before Tribunal

(1) If the applicant:

(a) is invited under section 425 to appear before the Tribunal; and

(b) does not appear before the Tribunal on the day on which, or at the time and place at which, the applicant is scheduled to appear;

the Tribunal may make a decision on the review without taking any further action to allow or enable the applicant to appear before it.

(2) This section does not prevent the Tribunal from rescheduling the applicant's appearance before it, or from delaying its decision on the review in order to enable the applicant's appearance before it as rescheduled.

441A Methods by which Tribunal gives documents to a person other than the Secretary

Coverage of section

(1) For the purposes of provisions of this Part or the regulations that:

(a) require or permit the Tribunal to give a document to a person (the ***recipient***); and

(b) state that the Tribunal must do so by one of the methods specified in this section;

the methods are as follows.

...

Dispatch by prepaid post or by other prepaid means

(4) Another method consists of a member, the Registrar or an officer of the Tribunal, dating the document, and then dispatching it:

(a) within 3 working days (in the place of dispatch) of the date of the document; and

(b) by prepaid post or by other prepaid means; and

(c) to:

(i) the last address for service provided to the Tribunal by the recipient in connection with the review; or

(ii) the last residential or business address provided to the Tribunal by the recipient in connection with the review; ...

441C When a person other than the Secretary is taken to have received a document from the Tribunal

(1) This section applies if the Tribunal gives a document to a person other than the Secretary by one of the methods specified in section 441A (including in a case covered by section 441AA).

...

Dispatch by prepaid post or by other prepaid means

(4) If the Tribunal gives a document to a person by the method in subsection 441A(4) (which involves dispatching the document by prepaid post or by other prepaid means), the person is taken to have received the document:

(a) if the document was dispatched from a place in Australia to an address in Australia—7 working days (in the place of that address) after the date of the document; or

(b) in any other case—21 days after the date of the document.

...

Facts

SZVFW and his wife were residents of China. They applied for protection visas, claiming to fear persecution as a result of their opposition to government authorities following the compulsory acquisition of their land. A department official wrote to SZVFW and his wife, scheduling an interview to assess their claim. Later, another official contacted SZVFW by telephone to reschedule that interview. Despite this, SZVFW and his wife did not attend the interview. A delegate of the Minister refused to grant protection visas.

SZVFW and his wife applied to the Refugee Review Tribunal ('RRT') for review of the decision. The application specified an address in Roselands as the address to which correspondence could be sent, and also included a mobile number and email address. On 12 May 2014, the RRT sent a letter to the Roselands address, acknowledging receipt of the application and inviting SZVFW and his wife to provide material or written arguments. On 15 August 2014, the RRT sent another letter ('the Invitation Letter') to the Roselands address, informing the applicants that their hearing was scheduled for 10 September 2014. This letter included a warning that, if the applicants did not attend the hearing, 'the Tribunal may make a decision without taking any further action to allow or enable you to appear before it'. SZVFW and his wife did not respond to either letter. They did not provide any material or arguments, did not contact the RRT, and did not appear at the hearing of 10 September 2014.

The RRT exercised its discretion to make a decision without making further attempts to hear from the applicants. The RRT affirmed the visa refusal.

SZVFW and his wife sought judicial review in the Federal Circuit Court. The Federal Circuit Court held that the RRT decision was unreasonable because the RRT did not make further attempts to contact the applicants, and did not satisfy itself that they had received notification of the hearing date. The Full Court of the Federal Court dismissed an appeal. The Minister appealed to the High Court.

The High Court allowed the appeal, holding that there had been no unreasonableness in the RRT's decision. The extracts from the judgment of Nettle and Gordon JJ illustrate the importance of statutory context when applying this ground of review.

Nettle and Gordon JJ

> ***572*** [78] The task of the court, where it has been alleged that a decision is legally unreasonable, is to ask whether the exercise of power by the decision-maker was beyond power because it was legally unreasonable.
>
> [79] That task requires the court to assess the quality of the administrative decision by reference to the statutory source of the power exercised in making the decision and, thus, assess whether the decision was lawful, having regard to the scope, purpose and objects of the statutory source of the power.
>
> [80] Parliament is taken to intend that a statutory power will be exercised reasonably by a decision-maker. The question with which the legal standard of reasonableness is concerned is whether, in relation to the particular decision in issue, the statutory power, properly construed, has been *abused* by the decision-maker or, put in different terms, the ***573*** decision is beyond power. That question is critical to an understanding of the task for a court on review.

[81] How that abuse of statutory power manifests itself is not closed or limited by particular categories of conduct, process or outcome. The abuse of statutory power is not limited to a decision affected by specific errors which bring about an improper exercise of power because, for example, the decision-maker took into account an irrelevant consideration or failed to take into account a relevant consideration; or exercised the power in bad faith, or for a purpose other than a purpose for which it was conferred; or exercised the power in such a way that the result of the exercise of power is uncertain.

[82] Nor is the abuse of statutory power limited to a decision which may be described as 'manifestly unreasonable', or to what might be described as an irrational, if not bizarre, decision that is so unreasonable that no reasonable person could have arrived at it. A conclusion of legal unreasonableness may be outcome focused – where, for instance, there is no 'evident and intelligible justification' for the decision. As Gageler J explained in *Minister for Immigration and Citizenship v Li*, '[r]eview by a court of the reasonableness of a decision made by another repository of power "is concerned mostly with the existence of justification, transparency and intelligibility within the decision-making process" but also with "whether the decision falls within a range of possible, acceptable outcomes which are defensible in respect of the facts and law"'.

[83] Indeed, grievous error may result if a court on review had to identify a particular error to found its conclusion of unreasonableness. If the court approached the assessment in this way, at least one important part of the lens for assessing legal unreasonableness would be removed: namely, error identified by observing that the *result* is so unreasonable that it could not have been reached if proper reasoning had been applied in the exercise of the statutory power in the particular circumstances. In that situation, the court is not undertaking merits ***574*** review of an exercise of a discretionary power by a decision-maker. Rather, the court is asking whether the decision-maker's purported exercise of power was beyond power because it was legally unreasonable.

[84] Moreover, legal unreasonableness is invariably fact dependent and requires a careful evaluation of the evidence. That is, assessment of whether a decision was beyond power because it was legally unreasonable depends on the application of the relevant principles to the *particular* factual circumstances of the case, rather than by way of an analysis of factual similarities or differences between individual cases. Where reasons are provided, they will be a focal point for that assessment. It would be a rare case to find that the exercise of a discretionary power was unreasonable where the reasons demonstrated a justification for that exercise of power.

...

575 [88] The standard of reasonableness is derived from the applicable statute but also from the general law.

[89] First, there is a legal presumption that a discretionary power, statutorily conferred, must be exercised reasonably in the legal sense of that word. That is, when something is to be done within the discretion of the decision-maker, it is to be done according to the rule of reason and justice; it is to be done according to law.

[90] Second, in this appeal, the applicable statutory power was to be found in s 426A of the Act ... There was no express list of factors which the Tribunal was required to take into account in making its decision on the review without taking any further action to allow or enable an applicant to appear before it. However, the power was not without limitation. The scope and purpose of the Act provided limits on the exercise of the Tribunal's power under s 426A.

...

[Editors' note: Their Honours summarised the effect of ss 425 and 425A].

576 [94] Third, the Tribunal's statutory task, as revealed by a consideration of the Act as a whole and, in particular, the provisions of Pt 7 ... is to arrive at the correct or preferable decision in the case before it, according to the material before it.

[95] Fourth, the range of powers, discretions and obligations granted to the Tribunal by Pt 7 of the Act, and the way in which the statute ***577*** conditions them, contains an exhaustive statement of the rules of natural justice in relation to the 'matters' that Part deals with.

[96] Fifth, Parliament has conferred on the Tribunal the necessary flexibility to ensure that the Tribunal can fully perform its statutory task. Indeed, the discretion in s 426A itself provides flexibility so that the Tribunal's statutory task can be performed. Put in different terms, the legislative scheme of the Act concerning review of decisions in Pt 7 is not one that *requires* the exercise of power, or the performance of obligations, where conferred on the Tribunal, on a once only basis. The nature of the subject matter of the review and the manner of the exercise of the review may, on occasion, mean than the power may be exercised and the function or duty must be performed from time to time, as occasion requires, in order to arrive at the correct or preferable decision in the case before the Tribunal according to the material before it. But, of course, the exercise of the discretion in s 426A does not *require* the Tribunal to postpone or refrain from making a decision on a review every time an applicant suggests they wish to provide further information, cannot meet a deadline, or fails to appear.

[97] The discretion in s 426A recognises that the exercise of the discretion in a given case will be affected by the subject matter of the particular review, the course the review has taken, the Tribunal's approach throughout the review and the other surrounding circumstances. That is, there is an area within which the decision-maker has a genuinely free discretion which resides within the bounds of legal reasonableness.

...

[Editors' note: Their Honours noted that the effect of ss 441A and 441C was to deem the Invitation Letter to have been received by SZVFW.]

581 [119] The significance of compliance with s 441A(4) was that the deeming effect of s 441C(4) was engaged and ss 425 and 425A were satisfied. The Tribunal was then permitted to engage s 426A and make a decision on the review without taking any further action to allow an applicant to appear before it. And that is what the Tribunal did in this case.

[120] The primary judge's analysis paid no regard to the fact that s 441C had been satisfied, the place of that presumption in the statutory scheme, or the fact that there was no attempt to rebut that statutory presumption. Granted, as the primary judge put it, s 425 of the Act imposed an obligation on the Tribunal to give SZVFW and his wife a 'meaningful opportunity' to appear and present evidence and arguments in support of the Review Application. But the Tribunal did not deny them that opportunity.

[121] Moreover, the primary judge paid no regard to the lack of interaction of SZVFW and his wife with the delegate of the Minister when they did not attend to be interviewed by the delegate, where there could be no suggestion that they had not received a written invitation to attend that interview and even after being contacted by telephone. That is, there was no suggestion that the failure of SZVFW and his wife to attend the hearing before the Tribunal was unexpected or remarkable.

...

[123] The exercise of the statutory decision-making power by the Tribunal was not beyond power. Having regard to the statutory source of the power exercised in making the decision, the subject matter of the particular review, the course the review had taken, the Tribunal's approach throughout the review, the situation and conduct of SZVFW and his wife throughout the review and the other surrounding circumstances, the exercise of the power was not unreasonable.

[Citations omitted]

Irrationality and illogicality

Minister for Immigration and Citizenship v SZMDS (2010) 240 CLR 611

Migration Act 1958 (Cth)

[As at relevant date]

36 Protection visas

(1) There is a class of visas to be known as protection visas.

(2) A criterion for a protection visa is that the applicant for the visa is:

(a) a non-citizen in Australia to whom the Minister is satisfied Australia has protection obligations under the Refugees Convention as amended by the Refugees Protocol;

...

65 Decision to grant or refuse to grant visa

(1) After considering a valid application for a visa, the Minister:

(a) if satisfied that:

...

(ii) the ... criteria for it prescribed by this Act or the regulations have been satisfied;... is to grant the visa; or

(b) if not so satisfied, is to refuse to grant the visa.

430 Refugee Review Tribunal to record its decisions etc.

(1) Where the Tribunal makes its decision on a review, the Tribunal must prepare a written statement that:

(a) sets out the decision of the Tribunal on the review; and

(b) sets out the reasons for the decision; and

(c) sets out the findings on any material questions of fact; and

(d) refers to the evidence or any other material on which the findings of fact were based.

...

Convention Relating to the Status of Refugees

Opened for signature 28 July 1951, 189 UNTS 137 (entered into force 22 April 1954), as amended by *Protocol Relating to the Status of Refugees*, opened for signature 31 January 1967, 606 UNTS 267 (entered into force 4 October 1967), art 1.

Article 1 Definition of the term 'refugee'

A. For the purposes of the present Convention, the term 'refugee' shall apply to any person who:

...

(2) ... owing to well-founded fear of being persecuted for reasons of race, religion, nationality, membership of a particular social group or political opinion, is outside the country of his nationality and is unable or, owing to such fear, is unwilling to avail himself of the protection of that country; or who, not having a nationality and being outside the country of his former habitual residence as a result of such events, is unable or, owing to such fear, is unwilling to return to it.

Facts

SZMDS was a citizen of Pakistan. He married in 1991, and had four children in Pakistan. According to SZMDS, he developed an attraction to other men between 2005 and 2007, when he was living and working in the United Arab Emirates ('UAE'). By the end of 2006, he was cohabiting with another man, Mr R. Also late in 2006, SZMDS spent two months in the United Kingdom before returning to the UAE. At some point, SZMDS and Mr R commenced a sexual relationship with a third man, Mr H. In March 2007, SZMDS confronted Mr H, claiming Mr H was a drug addict and was having unprotected sex with other people. Mr H responded violently, bashing SZMDS. Mr R and SZMDS went into hiding. In May 2007, SZMDS returned to Pakistan before leaving, in June 2007, for the UAE and then travelling to Australia.

In 2007, he arrived in Australia on a temporary visa, and subsequently applied for a protection visa on the ground that he feared persecution in Pakistan if his homosexuality became publicly known. A delegate of the Minister, and, on review, the RRT, rejected SZMDS's application. The RRT's reasons explained that it did not accept SZMDS was homosexual.

SZMDS applied for judicial review of the RRT's decision in the Federal Magistrates Court under judicial review proceedings under s 476 of the *Migration Act 1958* (Cth), which confers on the Federal Magistrates Court jurisdiction equivalent to that conferred on the High Court under s 75(v) of the *Constitution.* He was unsuccessful, and appealed to the Federal Court. In the Federal Court, Moore J allowed the appeal on the ground (which had not been raised before the Magistrate) that the RRT's reasoning was irrational or illogical. The Minister appealed to the High Court. The High Court dismissed the appeal.

The issues for the High Court were whether irrationality or illogicality in the reasoning process could amount to jurisdictional error; and, if so, whether the RRT's reasoning in this instance had been irrational or illogical.

Crennan and Bell JJ

> [129] It can be acknowledged that the contemporary invocation of 'illogicality' or 'irrationality' as a basis for judicial review may well have first emerged in Australia, as intimated by Gleeson CJ in [*Re Minister for Immigration and Multicultural Affairs; Ex parte Applicant S20/2002* (2013) 77 ALJR 1165],[1] as a reaction to the ouster of the review ground of '*Wednesbury* unreasonableness' in immigration law. Equally it may be that the development of 'irrationality' as a basis for judicial review in England grew out of dissatisfaction with the inherent circularity of the *Wednesbury* test and the implicit suggestion in *Wednesbury* that there were degrees or grades of unreasonableness. Be that as it may, accepting that an allegation of 'illogicality' or 'irrationality' must mean something other than emphatic disagreement ... and also accepting that a demonstration of bona fides will not save an illogical or irrational decision or finding on a jurisdictional fact ... how do 'illogicality' and 'irrationality' fit with the clearly related body of law concerned with error, particularly jurisdictional error, in respect of reasoning which is 'clearly unjust', 'arbitrary', 'capricious' or '*Wednesbury* unreasonable'?
>
> [130] In the context of the Tribunal's decision here, 'illogicality' or 'irrationality' sufficient to give rise to jurisdictional error must mean ***648*** the decision to which the Tribunal came, in relation to the state of satisfaction required under s 65, is one at which no rational or logical decision maker could arrive on the same evidence. In other words, accepting, for the sake of argument, that an allegation of illogicality or irrationality provides some distinct basis for seeking judicial review of a decision as to a jurisdictional fact, it is nevertheless an allegation of the same order as a complaint that a decision is 'clearly unjust' or 'arbitrary or 'capricious' or 'unreasonable' in the sense that the state of satisfaction mandated by the statute imports a requirement that the opinion as to the state of satisfaction must be one that could be formed by a reasonable person. The same applies in the case of an opinion that a mandated state of satisfaction has not been reached. Not every lapse in logic will give rise to jurisdictional error. A court should be slow, although not unwilling, to interfere in an appropriate case.

1 At 1170 [20]. At the time of the decision, s 476(2)(b) of the *Migration Act 1958*, as it then stood, ousted review on the ground 'that the decision involved an exercise of a power that is so unreasonable that no reasonable person could have so exercised the power'.

[131] What was involved here was an issue of jurisdictional fact upon which different minds might reach different conclusions. The complaint of illogicality or irrationality was said to lie in the process of reasoning. But, the test for illogicality or irrationality must be to ask whether logical or rational or reasonable minds might adopt different reasoning or might differ in any decision or finding to be made on evidence upon which the decision is based. If probative evidence can give rise to different processes of reasoning and if logical or rational or reasonable minds might differ in respect of the conclusions to be drawn from that evidence, a decision cannot be said by a reviewing court to be illogical or irrational or unreasonable, simply because one conclusion has been preferred to another possible conclusion.

Was the Tribunal's fact finding 'illogical' or 'irrational'?

[132] Because illogicality or irrationality may constitute a basis for judicial review in the context of jurisdictional fact finding as explained above, it becomes necessary to decide whether the Tribunal's conclusion about the state of satisfaction required by s 65 and its findings on the way to that conclusion revealed illogicality or irrationality amounting to jurisdictional error. It is clear ... that the Federal Court emphatically disagreed with the Tribunal's finding that [SZMDS's] return to Pakistan and failure to seek asylum in the United Kingdom was conduct which was inconsistent with the claimed fear of persecution arising as a result of homosexuality. It also seems clear that the Federal Court, acting on the same material or evidence on which the decision was based, would have been satisfied that [SZMDS] feared persecution as alleged.

[133] However, the correct approach is to ask whether it was open to the Tribunal to engage in the process of reasoning in which it did engage and to make the findings it did make on the material before it. There was evidence that [SZMDS] was married with four children and that he regularly visited Pakistan to see his family after the time at which he said he commenced, as he put it, 'the practice of ***649*** homosexuality' in the UAE. In particular, he visited his family for three weeks before coming to Australia. During the time when he said he engaged in the 'practice of homosexuality' in the UAE, and when he visited the United Kingdom, the evidence was that under both civil law and Shari'a in the UAE homosexual activity was criminalised. [SZMDS] also gave comprehensive evidence of homosexual activity in the UAE which was uncorroborated. The Tribunal saw [SZMDS] give evidence and sought answers and explanations from him. Such was the evidentiary context in which the Tribunal determined that [SZMDS'] conduct, first in returning to Pakistan and secondly in failing to seek asylum in the United Kingdom, was conduct which was inconsistent with his claimed fears of persecution as a result of homosexuality.

[134] The process of reasoning followed by the Tribunal, which needs to be considered in the light of all of the evidence set out above, was as follows: the Tribunal appeared to accept that homosexuals as a social group in Pakistan were the subject

of persecution. It also appeared to assume that a person with a genuine fear of persecution as a homosexual in Pakistan would not go back to Pakistan and that a person with such a fear would seek asylum at the first available opportunity. The Tribunal then examined [SZMDS'] conduct in the United Kingdom in 2006 and in returning to Pakistan for three weeks in 2007. The Tribunal asked whether that conduct was consistent with a fear of persecution based on the practice of homosexuality said to have occurred in the UAE. The Tribunal then concluded that the conduct was not consistent with the claims of homosexual conduct said to form the basis for the fear of persecution. The Tribunal essentially found that it was improbable that [SZMDS] feared persecution because of homosexuality as claimed. It is that conclusion which the Federal Court found illogical and irrational; it would have come to a different conclusion which appears to be largely based on the view that no-one in Pakistan would necessarily discover that [SZMDS] had, as claimed, engaged in the practice of homosexuality. The Federal Court differed from the Tribunal in finding that [SZMDS'] fear of persecution as a result of homosexuality was plausible whereas the Tribunal had found it improbable.

[135] On the probative evidence before the Tribunal, a logical or rational decision maker could have come to the same conclusion as the Tribunal. Whilst there may be varieties of illogicality and irrationality, a decision will not be illogical or irrational if there is room for a logical or rational person to reach the same decision on the material before the decision maker. A decision might be said to be illogical or irrational if only one conclusion is open on the evidence, and the decision maker ***650*** does not come to that conclusion, or if the decision to which the decision maker came was simply not open on the evidence or if there is no logical connection between the evidence and the inferences or conclusions drawn. None of these applied here. It could not be said that the reasons under consideration were unintelligible or that there was an absence of logical connection between the evidence as a whole and the reasons for the decision. Nor could it be said that there was no probative material which contradicted [SZMDS'] claims. There was. The Tribunal did not believe [SZMDS'] claim that he had engaged in the 'practice of homosexuality' in the UAE and accordingly it was not satisfied that he feared persecution if he returned to Pakistan.

[136] There is no sense in which the decision that [SZMDS] did not fear persecution, or the findings upon which that decision was based, could be said to be 'clearly unjust', 'arbitrary', 'capricious', 'not bona fide' or '*Wednesbury* unreasonable'. Whilst these analogous categories were not relied on, they serve to confirm the want of jurisdictional error by reference to the closely related complaints of illogicality and irrationality. Neither the decision that the Tribunal was not satisfied that [SZMDS] feared persecution nor the findings on the way to that conclusion were 'irrational' or 'illogical' in the sense explained in these reasons. The Tribunal's decision did not show any jurisdictional error.

[Citations omitted]

CRL18 v Minister for Immigration, Citizenship, Migrant Services and Multicultural Affairs (2020) 171 ALD 50

Migration Act 1958 (Cth)

[As at relevant date]

5H Meaning of *refugee*

(1) For the purposes of the application of this Act ... to a particular person in Australia, the person is a ***refugee*** if the person:

(a) ... is outside the country of his or her nationality and, owing to a well-founded fear of persecution, is unable or unwilling to avail himself or herself of the protection of that country; ...

36 Protection visas – criteria provided for by this Act

...

(2) A criterion for a protection visa is that the applicant for the visa is:

(a) a non-citizen in Australia in respect of whom the Minister is satisfied Australia has protection obligations because the person is a refugee; ...

Facts

CRL18 and his brother M were Sunni Muslims and citizens of Lebanon. Both applied for Safe Haven Enterprise Visas ('SHEV') on the ground that they were refugees. They claimed that Hezbollah (a Shia militant group) had repeatedly attacked them and other family members. In particular, CRL18 claimed that Hezbollah had attacked the family's shop, stealing goods, assaulting everyone present, and wounding CRL18's brother A and their father. Australian immigration authorities interviewed CRL 18 and M about these claims on several occasions.

CRL18's visa application was refused by a delegate of the Minister and this refusal was affirmed by the Immigration Assessment Authority ('the Authority'). The Authority identified seven inconsistencies in the accounts CRL18 had given across his three interviews, and between the evidence of CRL18 and M. Because of these inconsistencies, the Authority found that CRL18 was not a credible witness and, therefore, did not accept his claims about the Hezbollah attacks.

CRL18 commenced judicial review proceedings in the Federal Circuit Court, arguing that four factual findings on which the Authority based its conclusion on credibility were irrational or illogical. The Federal Circuit Court did not accept this argument. CRL18 appealed to the Federal Court. Stewart J found that there *was* illogicality or irrationality in relation to each factual finding. The decision was quashed and remitted to the Authority.

As a decision of a single judge of the Federal Court, this case has limited authority as a precedent. It is included in this book as an example of the contemporary approach to the illogicality or irrationality ground of review. In the interests of brevity, we have included the discussion of only two of the four factual findings that were held to be illogical or irrational.

Stewart J

52 [12] The four factual premises adopted by the Authority which the appellant challenged before the Circuit Court as having resulted in error were:

(1) The 'Timing Premise', referring to the Authority's reasoning ... concerning an internal inconsistency in the appellant's evidence as to when the attack on his shop occurred;

(2) The 'Subsequent Attacks Premise', referring to the Authority's reasoning ... concerning an inconsistency between the evidence of M that agents clashed with A a further five times after the shop attack, with the evidence of the appellant who when questioned 'gave a relatively vague response [and] said he had experienced many problems ...';

(3) The 'Tripoli Family Premise', referring to the Authority's finding ... that the appellant had said in the interview that he did not have any family around Tripoli; and

(4) The 'Targeting of the Father Premise', referring to the Authority's reasoning ... that M's claim that the attackers were 'mainly trying to attack the sons because they are younger compared to his father' was 'vague and unconvincing and inconsistent' with the claim that the father was assaulted during the attack on the shop.

...

53 [17] The four premises ... are all related to findings of 'inconsistencies' in the evidence given by the appellant and M when assessed together and individually which gave rise to credibility concerns. The grounds of appeal and the particularisation of the grounds are targeted towards a finding of illogicality being made in regard to the factual findings made by the Authority, rather than the adverse credibility finding itself or the overall finding that the appellant did not face a real chance of persecution or a real risk of significant harm if removed to Lebanon. It is important, however, to keep in mind that the overarching question is whether the decision was affected by jurisdictional error.

[18] The fact that credibility is a matter for the Authority to determine as a question of fact does not mean that challenges to credibility are not amenable to judicial review on jurisdictional error grounds. It does indicate, however, that considerable caution must be exercised before concluding that errors in an adverse credibility assessment result in the decision being affected by jurisdictional error, in order to avoid judicial review transgressing into the impermissible area of merits review.

...

Timing premise

[21] The Authority ... found that the appellant's evidence was 'internally inconsistent' about when the attack on his shop occurred. The Authority further found ... that the appellant 'claimed, in his application for protection, that he opened the shop in 2012 and during his arrival interview he claimed the attack on the shop occurred in March/April 2013 but during this SHEV interview he claimed the attack occurred several months after they opened the shop which would have been in 2012'.

[22] The basis of this finding was information that the appellant had filled out as part of the SHEV application process and answers given during his SHEV interview. In a part of the SHEV application form which asked the appellant to list his employment history, he had written that he had opened his charcoal shop in '09/12' (ie September 2012).

54 [23] The portion of the SHEV interview which is said to have contradicted this previous statement was as follows:

OFF: How long had you been running the shop before this happened, had you had it a few months, or was it open a couple of years? How long had it been open?
[APP]: Just a few months, like –
OFF: Just a few months.
[APP]: Yeah.

[24] The appellant submits that this is an illogical or irrational conclusion. There was no contradiction between the appellant's claim that the shop was opened in September 2012 and his claim that the shop was attacked 'several' or 'a few' months later in March/April 2013.

[25] The appellant also draws attention to the context in which the answer was provided in the SHEV interview. The question to the appellant posed two alternatives, 'a few months' and 'a couple of years'. It was not an open question. The appellant's answer, 'Just a few months', was the most accurate of the two alternatives he was given.

[26] The Minister submits that the primary judge was correct in finding that it was open to the Authority to have found that the appellant's evidence in the interview placed the attack as having occurred in 2012, and not in March/April 2013 as stated in the protection visa application. A decision will not be illogical or irrational if there is room for a logical or rational person to reach the same decision on the material before the decision-maker.

[27] In [*Minister for Immigration and Citizenship v SZRKT* (2013) 212 FCR 99], Robertson J (at [143]) warned against situations where the Court is impermissibly invited on an appeal in judicial review proceedings to involve itself in choosing between contestable facts. Illogicality is taken to refer to 'extreme illogicality or irrationality, measured against the standard that it is not enough for the question of fact to be one on which reasonable minds may come to different conclusions and against the framework of the inquiry being as to whether or not there has been jurisdictional error on the part of the Tribunal'.

[28] I do not find that the Timing Premise on its own reaches the level of extreme illogicality or irrationality required. A reasonable decision-maker in the position of the Authority could reason, however tenuously, from the statement that the attack happened 'a few months' after the store opened in September 2012 to a finding that the appellant's evidence from the SHEV interview was that the attack occurred in 2012. It is not irrational to say, as the Authority and primary judge did, that 'a few months' is less than six months. However, consideration must be given to how that finding was used by the Authority in its reasoning.

[29] This issue is dealt with in [*AQV15 v Minister for Immigration and Border Protection* (2018) 266 FCR 83]. Especially relevant here is [28]:

> ... even where it is reasonably open to find that a person has given inconsistent evidence, the decision-maker needs to assess the significance of that inconsistency and the weight to be given to it. This requires consideration of, for example, the

> significance of the inconsistency having regard to the person's case as a whole and whether the inconsistency is on a matter which is central to the person's case or is at its periphery ***55*** and involves an objectively minor matter of fact. It also requires the decision-maker to remain conscious of the particular challenges facing asylum seekers in giving accounts of why they fear persecution, including that they may have to give multiple accounts, using interpreters, and that they may reasonably expect an interview or a review process will provide an opportunity for them to elaborate on, or explain, the narratives they have previously given. Consideration should also be given to whether there is an acceptable explanation for the person having given inconsistent evidence such that the fact of the inconsistency should attract little, if any, weight. How all these matters are weighed and evaluated in a particular case is a matter for the decision-maker, but a failure by the decision-maker to appreciate the particular nature of the task, or to perform it reasonably and fairly, may be the subject of judicial review.

[30] Taking into account the information which was before the Authority, the inconsistency which was said to arise regarding the date of the attack on the shop was of such a minor nature that it could not rationally form the basis, even with other material, to affect the assessment of the appellant's credibility.

[31] In making this finding I take into account these relevant factors.

[32] Firstly ..., the question posited by the Departmental officer provided two examples of periods of time, one measured in months and the other in years. The appellant chose the one that was most accurate without qualifying it or giving his own third alternative. The relevance of this factor in an interview where the appellant was unrepresented and which required an interpreter, many years after the events which are described, cannot be understated.

[33] Further, the appellant's statement that it had been 'Just a few months, like –' with the interjection by the Departmental Officer of 'Just a few months' further limited the possible range of answers that could be expected to be provided by him.

[34] It was entirely natural for the appellant in these circumstances to reply 'a few months' rather than specifying six months later, several months later or many months later. It is not part of the visa application process to criticise an applicant's choice of words with a lexicographer's zeal for precision in the use of a phrase which even native English speakers struggle with, ie just how many months is 'a few' months or 'some' months? These circumstances are an acceptable explanation for the appellant having given what the Authority characterised as inconsistent evidence. They do not form a basis to reasonably, fairly or rationally reject the appellant's version as false.

[35] On the above bases, it was irrational of the Authority to take the finding of inconsistency as one of the bases for rejecting the appellant's claims. Further, what the Authority did in assessing the Timing Premise was to set out the variation in the appellant's accounts, and then set out its conclusion about his credibility on the basis of the inconsistency, without explaining why it came to that conclusion. That is an inadequate basis to reject the appellant's account.

...

***58* Tripoli family premise**

[52] In … the Authority's reasons, another inconsistency between the evidence of the appellant and M was said to be whether the brothers had family around Tripoli:

> [M] claimed that, after the attack [on the shop], his family moved to an area between Tripoli and Akkar to stay with family, however, the applicant claimed they did not have any family around Tripoli when asked by the delegate.

[53] In the SHEV interview the appellant gave the following answers:

OFF: Do you have family near Tripoli?
APP: Do I have family in?
OFF: Or around Tripoli?
APP: In Tripoli? No, no. No, no.

[54] In his SHEV interview, M stated that he had family 'around Tripoli':

OFF: Yeah. So, after this incident happened, what happened? Did your family leave the area? Did they go back to Akkar?
[M]: No, we left an area before Akkar to – with relatives, stay with relatives.
OFF: Okay, in Beirut.
[M]: No, in close – close Tripoli.
OFF: After Tripoli?
[M]: After Tripoli.
OFF: Okay, all right, and so the Sunni area –
[M]: Before Akkar.
OFF: Okay, okay. So you have family around Tripoli?
[M]: Yeah, yeah.

…

[57] The Minister submits that in the context of the interview it was reasonable for the Authority to interpret the appellant's answer 'In Tripoli? No, no. No, no' as being a negative response to the question asked '[Do you have family] around Tripoli?' Whilst a different decision-maker might have interpreted the exchange during the interview in a different way this does not rise to the required level of illogicality.

…

[59] Beirut is located approximately halfway along the coast of Lebanon from north to south. Tripoli is also located on the coastline, approximately 80kms to the north of Beirut. Akkar District is the northern-most district of Lebanon, ***59*** sharing its northern and north-eastern borders with Syria. The Akkar District begins approximately 25kms to the north-east of Tripoli.

[60] As was submitted by the appellant, there is a difficulty of objectively defining whether a location between Akkar and Tripoli is 'around' Tripoli or not. Although the distance between the places is only 25kms, there are a multitude of different locations in the area between Tripoli and the boundary of the Akkar District which may or may not be considered to be 'around' Tripoli depending on one's perspective.

[61] Setting this difficulty aside, it is clear from the answer provided by the appellant, 'In Tripoli? No, no. No, no.' that he was saying that he had no family in Tripoli.

That is quite a different thing to saying he had no family around Tripoli – having family somewhere between Tripoli and Akkar, as identified by M, is different to having family in Tripoli. Therefore, for the appellant to say that he has no family 'in Tripoli' is no contradiction to M saying that they have family 'after Tripoli', 'before Akkar' and 'around Tripoli'. M also did not say that they had family in Tripoli. To find the two accounts inconsistent is illogical and irrational.

[62] Once again, this is an inadequate basis to reject the appellant's account, particularly if one also takes into account that the interviews were conducted through interpreters. There is no logical, rational or probative basis to reject the appellant's account on the basis of the Tripoli Family Premise.

[Citations omitted]

No evidence

Australian Broadcasting Tribunal v Bond (1990) 170 CLR 321

Facts

The facts, and relevant sections of the *Broadcasting Act 1942* (Cth) are set out in the extract of this case in Chapter 9. While the High Court did not conclude that any of the arguments based on the 'no evidence' ground of review were made out, Mason CJ's explanation of the relationship between the common law ground of 'no evidence' and the *AD(JR) Act* has been influential.

Mason CJ

355 The question whether there is any evidence of a particular fact is a question of law. Likewise, the question whether a particular inference can be drawn from facts found or agreed is a question of law. This is because, before the inference is drawn, there is the preliminary question whether the evidence reasonably admits of different conclusions. So, in the context of judicial review, it has been accepted that the making of findings and the drawing of inferences ***356*** in the absence of evidence is an error of law.

But it is said that '[t]here is no error of law simply in making a wrong finding of fact': *Waterford v The Commonwealth* [(1987) 163 CLR 54, 77], per Brennan J ...

[A]t common law, according to the Australian authorities, want of logic is not synonymous with error of law. So long as there is *some* basis for an inference - in other words, the particular inference is reasonably open - even if that inference appears to have been drawn as a result of illogical reasoning, there is no place for judicial review because no error of law has taken place.

...

357 The foregoing brief summary of the authorities relating to review for error of law is by no means decisive of the interpretation of the grounds of review in the AD(JR) Act. It does, however, provide part of the context by reference to which one must determine the scope of the relevant grounds of review contained in that Act.

Moreover, the content of the 'error of law' ground of review in s 5(1)(f) is necessarily influenced by the scope and purpose of the AD(JR) Act as an element in the statutory scheme of review constituted by that Act and the [*Administrative Appeals Tribunal Act 1975* (Cth)]. Two elements of that scheme are significant for present purposes. The first is that the [*Administrative Appeals Tribunal Act 1975* (Cth)] alone provides for review on the merits; the second is that the two Acts draw a sharp distinction between errors of fact and errors of law. These two elements provide strong support for the view that, in general, the concept of 'error of law' in s 5(1)(f) is intended to reflect the content of that expression as it was understood at common law in this country before 1977. Of course, unlike the antecedent common law, s 5(1)(f) does not require that the error of law appear on the face of the record.

The ground of review in s 5(1)(h), 'that there was no evidence or other material to justify the making of the decision', must be read with s 5(3) ...

The effect of s 5(3) is to limit severely the area of operation of the ground of review in s 5(1)(h). If we put to one side the situation to which [s 5(3)](b) is directed (proof of the nonexistence of a fact ***358*** critical to the making of the decision), the opening part of par. (a) restricts the 'no evidence' ground to decisions in respect of which the decision-maker was required by law to reach that decision only if a particular matter was established. In such a case the ground of review is that there was 'no evidence or other material ... from which he could reasonably be satisfied that the matter was established'.

As the respondents do not seek to bring this case within s 5(3)(a) or (b), the ground of review in s 5(1)(h) has no direct application here. But the presence of s 5(3) tells against an expansive interpretation of s 5(1)(f). Indeed, it might be argued from the presence of s 5(1) and (3) that they constitute a definitive and exhaustive statement of the 'no evidence' ground of review for the purpose of s 5, thereby excluding such a ground from the concept of 'error of law' in s 5(1)(f). However, such a result would verge upon the extreme and would pay scant attention to the traditional common law principle that an absence of evidence to sustain a finding or inference of fact gives rise to an error of law. The better view, one which seeks to harmonize the two grounds of review, is to treat 'error of law' in s 5(1)(f) as embracing the 'no evidence' ground as it was accepted and applied in Australia before the enactment of the AD(JR) Act and to treat the 'no evidence' ground in s 5(1)(h), as elucidated in s 5(3), as expanding that ground of review in the applications for which pars and (b) of s 5(3) make provision. Within the area of operation of par (a) it is enough to show an absence of evidence or material from which the decision-maker could reasonably be satisfied that the particular matter was established, that being a lesser burden than that of showing an absence of evidence (or material) to support the decision ...

[Citations omitted]

Minister for Immigration, Citizenship, Migrant Services and Multicultural Affairs v Viane (2021) 96 ALJR 13

Migration Act 1958 (Cth)

[As at relevant date]

501 Refusal or cancellation of visa on character grounds

...

(3A) The Minister must cancel a visa that has been granted to a person if:

(a) Minister is satisfied that the person does not pass the character test because of the operation of:

(i) paragraph (6)(a) (substantial criminal record) ...; and

(b) the person is serving a sentence of imprisonment, on a full-time basis in a custodial institution, for an offence against a law of the Commonwealth, a State or a Territory.

...

(6) For the purposes of this section, a person does not pass the ***character test*** if:

(a) the person has a substantial criminal record (as defined by subsection (7));

...

(7) For the purposes of the character test, a person has a ***substantial criminal record*** if:

...

(c) the person has been sentenced to a term of imprisonment of 12 months or more; ...

501CA Cancellation of visa – revocation of decision under subsection 501(3A) (person serving sentence of imprisonment)

(1) This section applies if the Minister makes a decision (the ***original decision***) under subsection 501(3A) (person serving sentence of imprisonment) to cancel a visa that has been granted to a person.

(2) For the purposes of this section, ***relevant information*** is information ... that the Minister considers:

(a) would be the reason, or a part of the reason, for making the original decision; and

(b) is specifically about the person or another person and is not just about a class of persons of which the person ... is a member.

(3) As soon as practicable after making the original decision, the Minister must:

(a) give the person, in the way that the Minister considers appropriate in the circumstances:

(i) a written notice that sets out the original decision; and

(ii) particulars of the relevant information; and

(b) invite the person to make representations to the Minister, within the period and in the manner ascertained in accordance with the regulations, about revocation of the original decision.

(4) The Minister may revoke the original decision if:

(a) the person makes representations in accordance with the invitation; and

(b) the Minister is satisfied:

(i) that the person passes the character test (as defined by section 501); or

(ii) that there is another reason why the original decision should be revoked.

Facts

Alex Viane was born in American Samoa and raised in the Independent State of Samoa (known as Samoa) before moving to Australia at the age of 14. Despite living in Australia and having an Australian-born daughter, Mr Viane never acquired Australian citizenship. Mr Viane was convicted of several offences, including a serious assault against his partner. These convictions meant that Mr Viane did not pass the 'character test' in s 501 of the *Migration Act 1958* (Cth), and that a delegate of the Minister was required to cancel Mr Viane's visa under s 501(3A).

In accordance with s 501CA(3)(b), the Minister invited Mr Viane to make representations about revocation of the cancellation. Mr Viane did not submit that he passed the character test; instead he argued there was 'another reason', within the meaning of s 501CA(4)(b)(ii), to cancel the visa revocation. In his representations, Mr Viane argued that, if he were deported, he, his partner, and his young daughter would have to live in American Samoa (or, possibly, Samoa). He argued that they would experience hardship because of their lack of social ties, job prospects, and the lack of available welfare. In particular, he argued that his daughter's lack of familiarity with the local language would be an impediment to her 'schooling and advancement in life'.

In general, the Minister accepted Mr Viane's submissions about the effect that cancelling the visa would have on Mr Viane's daughter. However, the Minister added two qualifications. First:[2]

> I find that the whole family, may, at least initially, experience problems relating to employment, income, housing and lack of family or social support and this would negatively impact on [Mr Viane's daughter]. English, however, is widely spoken in American Samoa and Samoa and healthcare, education and some welfare support are available in either location.

Second, while the Minister accepted that the services in American Samoa and Samoa may be of a lower standard, and/or more expensive, than those in Australia, the Minister said that Mr Viane and his family would have 'equal access to welfare, healthcare and educational services as do American Samoans and Samoans in a similar position'.[3]

There was no evidence or other objective material to support the Minister's finding that English was widely spoken in American Samoa and Samoa; or the finding that Mr Viane and his family would have equal access to services.

2 Quoted in *Minister for Immigration, Citizenship, Migrant Services and Multicultural Affairs v Viane* (2021) 96 ALJR 13, 16 [3].

3 Ibid 16 [5].

The Minister decided not to revoke the cancellation. He found that Mr Viane's family would be 'significantly impacted', and that it was in the best interests of Mr Viane's daughter to revoke the visa cancellation. Nonetheless, these considerations were outweighed by the risk of harm to the Australian community if Mr Viane were not deported.

In judicial review proceedings, Mr Viane argued that there was no evidence to support the Minister's findings about the prevalence of English, and the likelihood that Mr Viane's family would have access to services equal to that of other people, in American Samoa or Samoa.

A judge of the Federal Court rejected the judicial review application. The Full Court of the Federal Court allowed an appeal. The Full Court held that s 401CA(4) required the Minister state of satisfaction to 'be formed on the basis of factual findings that are open to be made on the evidentiary materials'.[4] A majority of the Full Court held that the impugned findings of fact were not supported by the Minister's personal knowledge or other material. Therefore, the Full Court allowed the decision and quashed the refusal to revoke the visa cancellation.

The High Court allowed an appeal by the Minister.

Keane, Gordon, Edelman, Steward and Gleeson JJ

***17* Fact finding for the purposes of s 501CA**

[12] The legal capacity conferred on the Minister by s 501CA of the Act to revoke a decision to cancel a visa is premised upon the prior exercise of the power of cancellation conferred by s 501(3A). Importantly, once the conditions of s 501(3A) are fulfilled, the power of cancellation is mandatory; the Minister must cancel the visa. In contrast, the power of revocation is broad. Upon receiving representations about revocation in accordance with s 501CA(4), the Minister must determine whether to be satisfied that the person passes the character test ... or whether there is 'another reason why the original decision should be revoked'.

[13] The relevant statutory scheme mandated by s 501CA of the Act comprises: the giving of relevant information to a person whose visa has been cancelled; inviting that person to make representations about why that cancellation decision should be revoked; the receipt of representations by the Minister made in accordance with that invitation; and, thereafter, the formation of a state of satisfaction, or not, by the Minister that the cancellation decision should be revoked. That scheme necessarily requires the Minister to consider and understand the representations received. What is 'another reason' is a matter for the Minister. Under this scheme, Parliament has not, in any way, mandated or prescribed the reasons which might ***18*** justify revocation, or not, of a cancellation decision in a given case. It follows that there may be few mandatorily relevant matters that the Minister must consider in applying s 501CA(4)(b)(ii). Thus, the Minister is not obliged to take account of any non-refoulement obligations, as expressed in the Act or otherwise, when determining whether there is another reason to revoke a cancellation decision where the materials 'do not include, or the

4 *Viane v Minister for Immigration, Citizenship, Migrant Services and Multicultural Affairs* (2020) 278 FCR 386, 400 [47] (Kerr and Charlesworth JJ).

circumstances do not suggest, a non-refoulement claim'. The power must otherwise be exercised reasonably and in good faith.

[14] No part of the statutory power conferred by s 501CA of the Act obliges the Minister to make actual findings of fact as an adjudication of all material claims made by an applicant. Based upon the representations made by an applicant, the cancellation decision and the 'relevant information' given to the applicant pursuant to s 501CA(3)(a), the Minister must, when the Minister is not satisfied that an applicant passes the character test, then determine relevantly whether to be satisfied that there is 'another reason' why the cancellation decision should be revoked. Deciding whether or not to be satisfied that 'another reason' exists might be the product of necessary fact finding, or the product of making predictions about the future, or it might be about assessments or characterisation of an applicant's past offending.

[15] If the representations made lack any substances altogether, then this of itself might justify a decision not to be satisfied that 'another reason' exists to revoke the cancellation decision, without any need to make any findings of fact about the various claims made. Moreover, some of the topics that might be traversed might not lend themselves to be addressed by way of evidence. They may involve matters of judgment, especially when weighing factors for and against revocation. The breadth of the power conferred by s 501CA of the Act renders it impossible, nor is it desirable, to formulate absolute rules about how the Minister might or might not be satisfied about a reason for revocation.

...

[17] If the Minister exercises the power conferred by s 501CA(4) and in giving reasons makes a finding of fact, the Minister must do so based on some evidence or other supporting material, rather than no evidence or no material, unless the finding is made in accordance with the Minister's personal or specialised knowledge or by reference to that which is commonly known. By 'no evidence' this has traditionally meant 'not a skerrick of evidence'.

[18] There is otherwise nothing in the statutory ***19*** language of s 501CA(4) of the Act that prohibits the Minister from using personal or specialised knowledge, or commonly accepted knowledge, for the purpose of considering the representations made by an applicant, and in determining whether the Minister is satisfied that there is 'another reason' for revocation. Indeed, there are simply no limitations on the sources of information that may be considered by the Minister in determining whether to reach the state of satisfaction prescribed by s 501CA(4)(b)(ii). Nor is there any express requirement that the Minister disclose whether a material finding was made from personal knowledge. In the circumstances of the present case, where no evidence or other material has been identified in support of the Minister's findings about the speaking of English and the availability of services in American Samoa and Samoa, it can be assumed that the findings proceeded from the Minister's personal or specialised knowledge or were matters commonly known.

[19] In exercising the power conferred by s 501CA(4) of the Act, the Minister is free to adopt the accumulated knowledge of the Department of Immigration, Citizenship,

Migrant Services and Multicultural Affairs ('the Department'). Indeed, it is now well established that the Minister may adopt as the Minister's own written reasons a draft prepared by a departmental officer, provided that such reasons actually reflect the reasons why the Minister had reached her or his decision.

[20] There is no necessary dividing line, for the purposes of s 501CA of the Act, between the use of personal or specialised knowledge, or the use of that which is commonly known, as against the need for some evidence or other material to support a finding which the Minister may make. Where the Minister wishes to make a finding in support of a conclusion that she or he is not satisfied that there is 'another reason' for revocation, and the Minister has personal or specialised knowledge which supports that finding, the Minister may use that knowledge. The Minister may also supplement or support such a finding with evidence or other material. Where the finding is not within such personal or specialised knowledge, and is not a matter commonly known, it will need to supported by some evidence or other material. It cannot be asserted without any basis at all. Different considerations might arise if the finding in question was material to the process of reasoning and was incorrect. But that has not been suggested here.

[21] It would, one would hope, be a rare case where a fact is asserted in support of a reasoned outcome under s 501CA of the Act which has no basis for its existence. However, there have been exceptions in extreme and rare cases where the Minister has made particular or personal findings about an applicant, which could not have been the subject of any pre-existing personal or specialised knowledge (or common knowledge), and were not otherwise supported in any way. Examples of this have included findings made in the absence of any evidence or supporting material about the danger an applicant might pose in the future to the Australian community, and about the type of hardship an applicant might personally suffer if deported.

[22] It finally remains to be observed, and emphasised, that an applicant's prospects of persuading the Minister to revoke a cancellation decision will doubtless be all the greater if the applicant adduces evidence, or other supporting material, to make good the claims that she or he makes. The production of such evidence or other material in the applicant's representations would engage the need for the Minister to consider such evidence and, if necessary, to answer it with further or different evidence, or other material, if the claims are to be rejected.

...

20 [25] [In the Full Court of the Federal Court], Besanko J found that both matters were within the Minister's personal knowledge. His Honour also found that the respondent had made no relevant claim about the extent to which English is spoken in American Samoa and Samoa, and that this impugned finding had not, in any event, been shown to be 'wrong'. ...

[26] With respect, Besanko J was correct. In the circumstances of this case, the obvious inference is that the two impugned findings were the product of the Minister's personal or specialised knowledge. Senior counsel for the respondent expressly disavowed any suggestion that the Minister had merely made things up.

[27] ... Given the store of knowledge the minister will have built up over many years, from dealing with individuals from so many countries and territories, the source of such specific observations about conditions in American Samoa and Samoa could only have been from the Minister's experience. In that respect, to reiterate, it had not been shown that either observation was incorrect.

[28] It follows that the majority's observation [in the Full Court of the Federal Court] that the Minister's satisfaction or non-satisfaction for the purposes of s 501CA(4) of the Act must be formed on the basis of factual findings that are open to be made on the evidentiary materials is not, with great respect, entirely correct. First, and as already mentioned, the Minister is not prohibited from using the accumulated knowledge of the Department. Secondly, representations may be received which are no more than bare assertions about a course of future events. The Minister may simply not be persuaded that such assertions can constitute 'another reason' for revocation. Such a conclusion does not require the Minister to make any factual findings. ...

[29] It also follows that the Minister did not err in law when making the two impugned findings. ...

[Citations omitted]

CHAPTER

15

CONSEQUENCES OF UNLAWFUL ACTION

Introduction 446

Consequences of breaching a statutory provision 446

Project Blue Sky Inc v Australian Broadcasting Authority (1998) 194 CLR 355 446

Cavo Pty Ltd v Minister for the Environment and Sustainable Development (2016) 313 FLR 241 449

Consequences of jurisdictional error 454

Minister for Immigration and Multicultural Affairs v Bhardwaj (2002) 209 CLR 597 454

Remedies 456

Ainsworth v Criminal Justice Commission (1992) 175 CLR 564 456

Wingfoot Australia Partners Pty Ltd v Kocak (2013) 252 CLR 480 457

Plaintiff M61/2010E v Commonwealth (2010) 243 CLR 319 461

Corporation of the City of Enfield v Development Assessment Commission (2000) 199 CLR 135 463

Statutory remedies 467

Administrative Decisions (Judicial Review) Act 1977 (Cth) 467

Chapman v Tickner (1995) 55 FCR 316 468

Introduction

This chapter complements Chapter 15 of *Government Accountability: Australian Administrative Law*, third edition. If an applicant is entitled to judicial review and successfully argues one or more grounds, what is the outcome? When judicial review is successful, the government action or decision that has been challenged will have been found to be unlawful. The sources in this chapter consider the consequences that flow from that finding, and the remedies that may be available.

Consequences of breaching a statutory provision

Project Blue Sky Inc v Australian Broadcasting Authority (1998) 194 CLR 355

Broadcasting Services Act 1992 (Cth)

[As at relevant date]

158 Primary functions of the [Australian Broadcasting Authority]

The primary functions of the ABA are:

...

(h) to assist broadcasting service providers to develop codes of practice;

(i) that, as far as possible, are in accordance with community standards; and

(j) to monitor compliance with those codes of practice; and

(k) to develop program standards relating to broadcasting in Australia; and

(j) to monitor compliance with those standards;

...

160 General obligations of the ABA

The ABA is to perform its functions in a manner consistent with:

(a) the objects of this Act and the regulatory policy described in; and

(b) any general policies of the Government notified by the Minister under section 161; and

(c) any directions given by the Minister in accordance with this Act; and

(d) Australia's obligations under any convention to which Australia is a party or any agreement between Australia and a foreign country.

Facts

The Australian Broadcasting Authority ('ABA') made a program standard requiring television stations to broadcast a minimum amount of Australian content. Project Blue Sky, a company that aimed to promote the growth of the New Zealand film and television industry, argued that this standard was inconsistent with a free trade agreement between Australia and New Zealand, under which each country agreed to grant the other traders access to local markets equal to that afforded to local traders. The High Court held that clause 9 of the Australian Content Standard was inconsistent with the trade agreement and in breach of the Act.

Extracts of this case appear in Chapter 9 in relation to statutory construction. The extracts below focus again on statutory construction to determine whether parliament intends that a failure to comply with a statutory provision should lead to the invalidity of an administrative decision. In this case, the High Court held that while s 160 imposed a legal duty on the ABA, and acts done in contravention of s 160(d) are unlawful, it was not a purpose of the legislation that a decision made in breach of that condition would be invalidated.

McHugh, Gummow, Kirby and Hayne JJ

> ***388*** [91] An act done in breach of a condition regulating the exercise of a ***389*** statutory power is not necessarily invalid and of no effect. Whether it is depends upon whether there can be discerned a legislative purpose to invalidate any act that fails to comply with the condition. The existence of the purpose is ascertained by reference to the language of the statute, its subject matter and objects, and the consequences for the parties of holding void every act done in breach of the condition. Unfortunately, a finding of purpose or no purpose in this context often reflects a contestable judgment. The cases show various factors that have proved decisive in various contexts, but they do no more than provide guidance in analogous circumstances. There is no decisive rule that can be applied; there is not even a ranking of relevant factors or categories to give guidance on the issue.
>
> [92] Traditionally, the courts have distinguished between acts done in breach of an essential preliminary to the exercise of a statutory power or authority and acts done in breach of a procedural condition for the exercise of a statutory power or authority. Cases falling within the first category are regarded as going to the jurisdiction of the person or body exercising the power or authority. Compliance with the condition is regarded as mandatory, and failure to comply with the condition will result in the invalidity of an act done in breach of the condition. Cases falling within the second category are traditionally classified as directory rather than mandatory. ***390***
>
> [93] In our opinion, the Court of Appeal of New South Wales was correct in *Tasker v Fullwood* [[1978] 1 NSWLR 20, 23–4] in criticising the continued use of the 'elusive distinction between directory and mandatory requirements' and the division of directory acts into those which have substantially complied with a statutory command and those which have not. They are classifications that have outlived their usefulness because they deflect attention from the real issue which is whether an act done in breach of the legislative provision is invalid. The classification of a statutory provision as mandatory or directory records a result which has been reached on other grounds. The classification is the end of the inquiry, not the beginning. That being so, a court, determining the validity of an act done in breach of a statutory provision, may easily focus on the wrong factors if it asks itself whether compliance with the provision is mandatory or directory and, if directory, whether there has been substantial compliance with the provision. A better test for determining the issue of validity is to ask whether it was a purpose of the legislation that an act done in breach of the provision should be invalid. This has been the preferred approach of courts in this country in recent years, particularly in New South Wales. In determining the question of purpose, regard must ***391*** be had to 'the language of the relevant provision and the scope and object of the whole statute' [*Tasker v Fullwood* [1978] 1 NSWLR 20, 24].

An act done in breach of s 160 is not invalid

[94] Section 160 proceeds on the hypothesis that the ABA has power to perform certain functions and directs that it 'is to perform' those functions 'in a manner consistent with' the four matters set out in the section. In the present case, for example, s 158(j) ... authorised the making of a standard relating to the Australian content of television programs ... The fact that s 160 regulates the exercise of functions already conferred on the ABA rather than imposes essential preliminaries to the exercise of its functions strongly indicates that it was not a purpose of the Act that a breach of s 160 was intended to invalidate any act done in breach of that section.

[95] That indication is reinforced by the nature of the obligations imposed by s 160. Not every obligation imposed by the section has a rule-like quality which can be easily identified and applied. Thus, s 160 requires the functions of the ABA to be performed in a manner consistent with: the objects of the Act and the regulatory policy described in s 4; any general policies of the Government notified by the Minister under s 161; any directions given by the Minister in accordance with the Act. In particular situations, it is almost certain that there will be room for widely differing opinions as to whether or not a particular function has been carried out in accordance with these policies or general directions. When a legislative provision directs that a power or function be carried out in accordance with matters of policy, ordinarily the better conclusion is that the direction goes to the administration of a power or function rather than to its validity.

[96] Furthermore, while the obligations of Australia under some international conventions and agreements are relatively clear, many ***392*** international conventions and agreements are expressed in indeterminate language as the result of compromises made between the contracting State parties. Often their provisions are more aptly described as goals to be achieved rather than rules to be obeyed. The problems that might arise if the performance of any function of the ABA carried out in breach of Australia's international obligations was invalid are compounded by Australia being a party to about 900 treaties.

[97] Courts have always accepted that it is unlikely that it was a purpose of the legislation that an act done in breach of a statutory provision should be invalid if public inconvenience would be a result of the invalidity of the act. Having regard to the obligations imposed on the ABA by s 160, the likelihood of that body breaching its obligations under s 160 is far from fanciful, and, if acts done in breach of s 160 are invalid, it is likely to result in much inconvenience to those members of the public who have acted in reliance on the conduct of the ABA.

[98] Among the functions of the ABA, for example, are the allocation and renewal of licences (s 158(c)) and the design and administration of price-based systems for the allocation of commercial television and radio broadcasting licences (s 158(e)). It is hardly to be supposed that it was a purpose of the legislature that the validity of a licence allocated by the ABA should depend on whether or not a court ultimately ruled that the allocation of the licence was consistent with a general direction, policy or treaty obligation falling within the terms of s 160. This is particularly so,

given that the 'general policies of the Government notified by the Minister under section 161' unlike the 'directions given by the Minister in accordance with this Act' [see s 162(2) ...] are not required to be publicly recorded and that even those with experience in public international law sometimes find it difficult to ascertain the extent of Australia's obligations under agreements with other countries. In many cases, licensees would have great difficulty in ascertaining whether the ABA was acting consistently with the obligations imposed by s 160. Expense, inconvenience and loss of investor confidence must be regarded as real possibilities if acts done in breach of s 160 are invalid.

[99] Because that is so, the best interpretation of s 160 is that, while it ***393*** imposes a legal duty on the ABA, an act done in breach of its provisions is not invalid.

[100] In a case like the present, however, the difference between holding an act done in breach of s 160 is invalid and holding it is valid is likely to be of significance only in respect of actions already carried out by, or done in reliance on the conduct of, the ABA. Although an act done in contravention of s 160 is not invalid, it is a breach of the Act and therefore unlawful. Failure to comply with a directory provision 'may in particular cases be punishable'. That being so, a person with sufficient interest is entitled to sue for a declaration that the ABA has acted in breach of the Act and, in an appropriate case, obtain an injunction restraining that body from taking any further action based on its unlawful action.

[Citations omitted]

Cavo Pty Ltd v Minister for the Environment and Sustainable Development (2016) 313 FLR 241

Planning and Development Act 2007 (ACT)

[As at relevant date]

27 Authority to keep public register

(1) The planning and land authority must keep a register (the *public register).*

(2) The planning and land authority may keep the public register in any form the authority considers appropriate.

29 Inspection etc. of public register and associated documents

(1) The planning and land authority must ensure that, during business hours, the public register and associated documents are available for public inspection.

(2) The planning and land authority must allow people inspecting the public register and associated documents to make copies of, or take extracts from, the register and associated documents.

30 Meaning of associated document—pt 3.6

(1) For this part, each of the following is an ***associated document*** for a development application (other than an application that has been withdrawn):

(a) information required under section 139(2)(c), (d) or (f)(i) to accompany an application;

(b) an assessment required under section 139(2)(e) to accompany the application;

(c) a completed [environmental impact statement] required under section 139(2)(f)(ii) to accompany the application;

(d) a survey certificate required under section 139(2)(i) to accompany the application;

(e) if the planning and land authority has asked for further information under section 141—information provided in accordance with the request;

(f) if the planning and land authority corrects the application under section 143— the notice of the correction (see s 143(2));

(g) if the applicant has asked the authority to amend the development application under section 144—any document provided by the applicant to support the request;

(h) an agreement by an entity to the development proposed in the application (see s 148(2)(b));

(i) if the application is referred to an entity under division 7.3.3—the advice of the entity in relation to the development application (see s 149(2));

(j) if 1 or more representations have been made under section 156 about the application—each representation (other than a representation that has been withdrawn);

(k) if the Minister decides the application—the statement by the Minister in relation to the application presented to the Legislative Assembly under section 161(2);

(l) the notice of the decision on the application given under division 7.3.8;

(m) if the applicant for the development application applies under section 191 for reconsideration of a decision to refuse to approve the development—any information included in the application;

(n) if the planning and land authority reconsiders a decision to refuse to approve the development—the notice of the decision on reconsideration under section 195;

(o) a plan, drawing or specification of a proposed building, structure or earthworks if the plan, drawing or specification –

(i) is part of the application (whether as originally made or as amended); or

(ii) is approved as part of the approval of the application under section 162; or

(iii) is required to be prepared by the applicant under a condition of an approval before the development, or a stated part of it, starts;

(p) if an inquiry panel inquires about an [environmental impact statement] for the development proposal to which the application relates—the report the panel gives the Minister under section 230 on the results of the inquiry.

...

Facts

This case was heard by the Court of Appeal of the Australian Capital Territory after remittal from related proceedings in the High Court that determined standing: *Argos Pty Ltd v Corbell* (2014) 254 CLR 394 – see Chapter 10.

The Minister granted development approval for a shopping centre, including a supermarket, in the Canberra suburb of Giralang. Operators of supermarkets in nearby suburbs challenged the approval under s 5 of the *Administrative Decisions (Judicial Review) Act 1989* (ACT). Of the grounds originally argued before the primary judge, the grounds considered by the Court of Appeal were: that the Minister failed to take into account relevant considerations or, the decision was unreasonable; the Minister had breached the rules of natural justice; and the decision involved an error of law. The extracts below concern the Court of Appeal's consideration of *Project Blue Sky* and invalidity arising from non-compliance with statutory procedures.

The development application was required to include documents addressing relevant criteria, including criterion C33 that concerned significant adverse economic impact on other local centres. In this case, the development application stated that C33 had been complied with and referred readers to an economic impact assessment report ('the 2011 Duane report').

Under s 29(1) of the *Planning and Development Act 2007* (ACT), the ACT Planning and Land Authority was required to make certain documents available for public inspection. The 2011 Duane report was before the Minister when the development decision was made and should have been made public, but was not. The Court of Appeal held that failure to make the documents available in accordance with s 29(1) in this case did not invalidate the Minister's decision to approve the development.

Penfold J, Cowdroy and Nield AJJ

***Project Blue Sky* invalidity**

266 [123] At the hearing, both parties relied on *Project Blue Sky Inc v Australian Broadcasting Authority* (1998) 194 CLR 355 (*Project Blue Sky*) in addressing the impact of the failure to publish the 2011 Duane report on the decision of the Minister. In *Project Blue Sky* at [41], Brennan CJ said:

> [41] The purpose of construing the text of a statute is to ascertain therefrom the intention of the enacting Parliament. When the validity of a purported exercise of a statutory power is in question, the intention of the Parliament determines the scope of a power as well as the consequences of non-compliance with a provision prescribing what must be done or what must occur before a power may be exercised. If the purported exercise of the power is outside the ambit of the power or if the power has been purportedly exercised without compliance with a condition on which the power depends, the purported exercise is invalid. If there has been non-compliance with a provision which

does not affect the ambit or existence of the power, the purported exercise of the power is valid. To say that a purported exercise of a power is valid is to say that it has the legal effect which the Parliament intended an exercise of the power to have.

[Editors' note: The Court then quoted McHugh, Gummow, Kirby and Hayne JJ in *Project Blue Sky* at [91], [93]; these passages are above at p 447.]

267 [126] Thus, the matters that are relevant in the current enquiry are:

(a) the language of the statute;

(b) its subject matter and objects; and

(c) the consequences for the parties of holding void every act done in breach of the requirement found in s 29 of the Planning Act or, more relevantly for present purposes, every act done following a breach of that requirement (given that there is no specific provision making compliance with s 29 a pre-condition to considering or deciding on a development application).

...

268 [131] ... In determining whether there was a legislative purpose to the effect that non-compliance with s 29, of the kind identified in this case, would render the Minister's decision invalid, we have had regard to submissions from the parties that are summarised as set out below. As will appear, at certain points we have not been able to separate the invalidity arguments from the procedural fairness arguments without losing the full flavour of the relevant submission.

[132] The appellants pointed to the following matters:

(a) that the maintenance of the retail hierarchy in the ACT (although not intended to provide any guaranteed protection for other local centres) was an intent of the legislation that was paramount (or at least relevant) to the decision-making process, and that the failure to exhibit 'the single document that addresses that issue means axiomatically that procedural fairness is not accorded';

(b) that the failure to publish the 2011 Duane report deprived the appellants of the capacity to make proper submissions in response to the case put forward by the applicant;

(c) that in the absence of evidence of any hardship to the applicant (AMC Projects) or inconvenience to the public, 'the enforcement of due process is paramount', and that any hardship to the applicant for development approval is clearly outweighed by the public interest in complying with due process;

(d) ***269*** that, in determining whether a failure to comply with the relevant provisions of the Planning Act affected the validity of a development approval given under that Act, it was necessary to consider the reasons for the requirement to make aspects of the development application publicly available (being in this case, not directly to inform interested members of the public, but to ensure that interested members of the public were able to bring to the decision-maker's attention any relevant information in response to the development application, with a view to ensuring that the decision-maker was properly informed when the fate of the development application was determined – in summary, the intent of the legislation was said to be properly informed decision-making on development applications).

[134] The respondents said:

(a) that the wide range of documents potentially covered by s 30 (and the difficulty in determining whether some documents are included in the scope of s 30, described in submissions as 'the lack of a rule-like quality' [*Project Blue Sky* at [95]] in the definition of 'associated document') tells against a finding that any breach of s 29 should automatically produce invalidity;

(b) so does the fact that some of the documents covered by s 30 are created after a DA is approved – clearly a failure to publish these could not render the prior decision invalid;

(c) that the appellants are treating C33 as a 'guarantee against competition', but that in the instant case, C33 did not require any particular outcome to be achieved by a development application, only that the development application *had regard to* economic impacts on other commercially viable local centres; as such, C33 had 'a relatively minor role in the planning regime', and its relative unimportance tells against a finding that a failure of public disclosure in relation to C33 is intended to lead to invalidity ...

(d) ***270*** that finding invalidity in this case would produce serious public inconvenience (due to the delay in providing a new shopping centre in Giralang that would result);

(e) that it is accepted that public participation in the planning process is important – as shown by the requirement for publication of development applications and associated documents, and the obligation under s 120 of the *Planning Act* for the decision-maker to take account of public representations – but this doesn't mean that every failure to comply, or even every failure that can be shown to have affected public participation, renders the final decision invalid.

[135] ... [T]he ACT legislation does not identify the publication, or the expiry of a publication period, as a prerequisite to a decision whether to give or refuse approval. Instead, the ACT legislation requires that decision to be made within a specified period after the development application is made: that is, the NSW *EPA Act* [in another cited case] focuses on delaying a decision until after the consultation period, whereas the ACT legislation is aimed at ensuring that decisions are made quickly.

272 [151] The appellants' submissions focus on the desirability of strict compliance with the legislative scheme. This is a noble aspiration, but the decision in *Project Blue Sky* makes it clear that not every legislative scheme must be strictly complied with in every respect before it can have any valid operation. It is necessary to assess the real significance of particular kinds of non-compliance, and to take a principled but also practical approach to determining when non-compliance invalidates a decision and when it does not.

[152] We are satisfied that it was not a legislative purpose of the *Planning Act* that non-compliance of the kind that occurred in this case would invalidate the Minister's decision; we have reached that conclusion having regard in particular to:

(a) the scope for uncertainty about the identification of associated documents in relation to a development application;

(b) the non-specific nature of the requirement set out in C33, the uncertainty about the proper form of an adequate response to that criterion in a development application, and the vagueness of the decision-maker's obligations in relation to it; and

(c) the nature and circumstances of the particular non-compliance in this case, in that although the 2011 Duane report was not published with the DA, the existence of further relevant material was identified in the published material ... ;

273 (d) the fact that the Minister's decision was made with knowledge of both the 2011 Duane report and other material challenging aspects of that report ... ;

(e) the fact that, given the publication of the DA and most of the supporting material, the appellants could have made their own submissions about the economic viability of relevant local centres: between the contents of the DA and the appellants' own (presumably deeper) knowledge of the operations of their own businesses, theappellants had access to material on which to base substantive submissions to the Minister even without seeing the 2011 Duane report or its conclusions.

[153] We are accordingly satisfied that it is not a purpose of the *Planning Act* that a failure in the nature of the Minister's failure to make the 2011 Duane report available for public inspection should invalidate the Minister's decision on the relevant development application.

[Citations omitted]

Consequences of jurisdictional error

Minister for Immigration and Multicultural Affairs v Bhardwaj (2002) 209 CLR 597

Facts

This case involved a review by the Immigration Review Tribunal of a decision to cancel Rajiv Bhardwaj's student visa. Late in the afternoon of the day before the hearing was due to take place, the Tribunal received a letter from Mr Bhardwaj's immigration agent explaining that Mr Bhardwaj was too ill to attend the hearing and requesting an adjournment. The Tribunal member who had responsibility for deciding the matter was not advised about the letter and as a result the Tribunal considered the matter in Mr Bhardwaj's absence and decided against him. The Tribunal then learned of the existence of the letter and convened another hearing that Mr Bhardwaj was able to attend. This time, the Tribunal decided in his favour. The Minister for Immigration sought judicial review on the grounds that, having made the first decision against Mr Bhardwaj, the Tribunal's power was spent and it had no power to make the second decision. The majority in the High Court held that the first decision had been affected by jurisdictional error because Mr Bhardwaj had not been accorded procedural fairness. This was a purported decision taken beyond power and the High Court majority held that it had no legal effect. That meant that the Tribunal had the power to make the further decision on the same matter.

Gaudron and Gummow JJ

613 [46] In our view, it is neither necessary nor helpful to describe erroneous administrative decisions as 'void', 'voidable', 'invalid', 'vitiated' or, even, as 'nullities'. To categorise decisions in that way tends to ignore the fact that the real issue is whether the rights and liabilities of the individual to whom the decision relates are as specified in that decision. And, perhaps more importantly, it overlooks the fact that an administrative decision has only such force and effect as is given to it by the law pursuant to which it was made. Further, the use of the term 'appeal' and the proposition that an administrative decision must have sufficient vitality to provide the subject matter of such a curial proceeding should not obscure the fundamental proposition that such an 'appeal' or other proceeding for judicial review is an exercise of original jurisdiction by the court concerned. ...

Decisions involving jurisdictional error: the general law

614 [51] There is, in our view, no reason in principle why the general law should treat administrative decisions involving jurisdictional error as binding or having legal effect unless and until set aside. A decision that involves jurisdictional error is a decision that lacks legal ***615*** foundation and is properly regarded, in law, as no decision at all. Further, there is a certain illogicality in the notion that, although a decision involves jurisdictional error, the law requires that, until the decision is set aside, the rights of the individual to whom the decision relates are or, perhaps, are deemed to be other than as recognised by the law that will be applied if and when the decision is challenged. A fortiori in a case in which the decision in question exceeds constitutional power or infringes a constitutional prohibition ... ***616***

[53] ... [A] decision involving jurisdictional error has no legal foundation and is properly to be regarded, in law, as no decision at all. Once that is accepted, it follows that, if the duty of the decision-maker is to make a decision with respect to a person's rights but, because of jurisdictional error, he or she proceeds to make what is, in law, no decision at all, then, in law, the duty to make a decision remains unperformed. Thus, not only is there no legal impediment under the general law to a decision-maker making such a decision but, as a matter of strict legal principle, he or she is required to do so.

[Citations omitted]

Remedies

Ainsworth v Criminal Justice Commission (1992) 175 CLR 564

Facts

A report made to the Queensland Parliament by the Criminal Justice Commission on the proposed introduction of poker machines in Queensland was critical of the conduct of the Ainsworth group of companies and recommended that those companies not be allowed to participate in the gaming machine industry. This had a potential practical effect on the business reputation of those companies and so gave them a right to be heard before the report was delivered.

The Ainsworth companies commenced judicial review proceedings, seeking certiorari (to quash the report) and mandamus (requiring the Commission to disclose the evidence it had against the companies, and allow them to put forward a case in response).

The High Court held that the Commission had breached the rules of procedural fairness in making its report. The Court further held that certiorari was not available, but granted a declaration.

Mason CJ, Dawson, Toohey and Gaudron JJ

> ***580*** The precise relief sought by way of certiorari is that 'the ... proceedings of the Criminal Justice Commission [be removed] for the purpose of quashing all findings of the ... Commission in the Report on Gaming Machine Concerns and Regulations which relate to the [appellants] or the "Ainsworth group", as that term is used in the ... Report'.
>
> The function of certiorari is to quash the legal effect or the legal consequences of the decision or order under review. The report made and delivered by the Commission has, of itself, no legal effect and carries no legal consequences, whether direct or indirect. It is different when a report or recommendation operates as a precondition or as a bar to a course of action, or as a step in a process capable of altering rights, interests or liabilities. A report or a recommendation of that kind may be quashed, that is to say its legal effect may be nullified by certiorari. But the Commission's report is not in that category. The report may bear ***581*** upon the appellants' prospects of obtaining licences under the *Gaming Machine Act 1991* (Qld). However, ... the report does not 'legally affect ... rights', for it may be that the appellants will be granted such licence or licences under the *Gaming Machine Act 1991* as they request 'even ... in direct opposition to any recommendations [made] in it' by the Commission. There being no legal effect or consequence attaching to the report, certiorari does not lie to correct the failure of the Commission to comply with its duty to proceed in a way that was fair to the appellants.
>
> It does not follow that, because mandamus and certiorari are inapplicable, the appellants must leave this Court without remedy. The law with respect to procedural fairness has developed in spite of the technical aspects of the prerogative

writs. Moreover, had the appellants had advance notice of the Commission's intention to report adversely, its failure to observe the requirements of procedural fairness would have entitled them to relief by way of prohibition preventing it from reporting adversely without first giving them an opportunity to answer the matters put against them and to put submissions as to findings or recommendations that might be made. Instead, the report has been made and delivered in accordance with ... the Act. And, although it had no legal effect or consequence, it had the practical effect of blackening the appellants' reputations. Prima facie, at least, these matters suggest that the appellants are entitled to declaratory relief. It is now accepted that superior courts have inherent power to grant declaratory relief. It is a discretionary power which '[i]t is neither possible nor desirable to fetter ... by laying down rules as to ***582*** the manner of its exercise.' However, it is confined by the considerations which mark out the boundaries of judicial power. Hence, declaratory relief must be directed to the determination of legal controversies and not to answering abstract or hypothetical questions. The person seeking relief must have 'a real interest' and relief will not be granted if the question 'is purely hypothetical', if relief is 'claimed in relation to circumstances that [have] not occurred and might never happen' or if 'the Court's declaration will produce no foreseeable consequences for the parties'.

The present case involves no mere hypothetical question. At all stages there has been a controversy as to the Commission's duty of fairness. A report has been made and delivered under ... the Act. That report has already had practical consequences for the appellants' reputations. For all that is known, those consequences may extend well into the future. It is appropriate that a declaration be made in terms indicating that the appellants were denied natural justice. That may redress some of the harm done.

The appeal should be allowed. The order of the Full Court of the Supreme Court of Queensland should be set aside and, in lieu thereof, it should be declared that, in reporting adversely to the appellants in its *Report on Gaming Machine Concerns and Regulations,* the Commission failed to observe the requirements of procedural fairness.

Wingfoot Australia Partners Pty Ltd v Kocak (2013) 252 CLR 480

Accident Compensation Act 1985 (Vic)

[As at relevant time]

68 Opinions

(1) A Medical Panel must form its opinion on a medical question referred to it within 60 days after the reference is made or such longer period as is agreed by the Conciliation Officer, the County Court, the Authority or self-insurer.

> (2) The Medical Panel to whom a medical question is so referred must give a certificate as to its opinion and a written statement of reasons for that opinion.
>
> ...
>
> (4) For the purposes of determining any question or matter, the opinion of a Medical Panel on a medical question referred to the Medical Panel is to be adopted and applied by any court, body or person and must be accepted as final and conclusive by any court, body or person irrespective of who referred the medical question to the Medical Panel or when the medical question was referred.

Facts

A medical panel was required under s 68(2) of the *Accident Compensation Act 1985* (Vic) to give a certificate as to its opinion on a medical question. The case involved an application for compensation for a neck injury suffered by Eyup Kocak at work. Mr Kocak's application for compensation under the statute was dismissed based upon the medical panel's report and he sought to have the report quashed by the Supreme Court of Victoria to avoid it being used in a separate common law compensation claim. The grounds argued by Mr Kocak to have the medical opinion quashed included that the medical panel had failed to give adequate reasons.

Mr Kocak's application for an order, in the nature of certiorari, quashing the opinion of the Medical Panel was dismissed by the primary judge. However, on appeal, the Court of Appeal held that the reasons given by the panel were inadequate and quashed the opinion of the Medical Panel. That decision was reversed by the High Court on appeal.

The following extracts discuss the grant of certiorari for jurisdictional error and error of law on the face of the record. Mr Kocak failed in his attempt to get the report quashed by certiorari, but nevertheless benefitted from the decision that the report would have no legal consequences for his common law compensation claim.

French CJ, Crennan, Bell, Gageler and Keane JJ

> **Availability and utility of certiorari**
>
> ***491*** [24] The jurisdiction of the Supreme Court to make an order in the nature of certiorari is an aspect of its jurisdiction as 'the superior Court of ***492*** Victoria'. The exercise of that jurisdiction is regulated by rules of the Supreme Court which require that it be exercised only by way of judgment or order.
>
> [25] The function of an order in the nature of certiorari is to remove the legal consequences or purported legal consequences of an exercise or purported exercise of power. Thus, an order in the nature of certiorari is available only in respect of an exercise or purported exercise of power which has, at the date of order, an 'apparent legal effect'. An order in the nature of certiorari is not available in respect of an exercise or purported exercise of power the legal effect or purported legal effect of which is moot or spent. An order in the nature of certiorari in those circumstances would be not simply inutile; it would be unavailable.
>
> [26] Jurisdictional error constitutes one basis on which the Supreme Court can make an order in the nature of certiorari to remove the purported legal

consequences of a purported exercise of power under a State statute. That basis for the Supreme Court making an order in the nature of certiorari is entrenched by the *Commonwealth Constitution.* Error of law on the face of the record constitutes a separate and distinct basis on which the Supreme Court can make an order in the nature of certiorari to remove the legal consequences or purported legal consequences of an exercise or purported exercise of power under a State statute. That basis for the Supreme Court making an order in the nature of certiorari is not entrenched by the *Commonwealth Constitution;* its application can be excluded by statute. Where it is not excluded, however, it applies independently of jurisdictional error. That is to say, where error of law on the face of the record is not excluded by statute as a basis for making an order in the nature of certiorari, and where an error of law on the face of the record is found, an order in the nature of certiorari can be made so as to remove the legal consequences or purported legal consequences of an exercise or purported exercise of power irrespective of whether the error of law also constitutes a breach of a condition of the valid exercise of that power.

[27] Recognition of the availability of certiorari for error of law on the face of the record, independently of jurisdictional error, goes much of the way towards meeting the Employer's challenge to the conclusion ***493*** of the Court of Appeal that certiorari is available to quash an opinion of a Medical Panel where the Medical Panel has given reasons for that opinion which are inadequate to comply with its duty under ... the Act. Not only is error of law on the face of the record as a basis for making an order in the nature of certiorari quashing an opinion of the Medical Panel not excluded by statute, but the 'record' of the opinion by reference to which such an error of law can be discerned has been expanded by statute to include whatever reasons the Medical Panel in fact gives for that opinion.

[28] Within the meaning of the *Administrative Law Act 1978* (Vic), a Medical Panel is a 'tribunal' and the opinion of a Medical Panel on a medical question referred to it is a 'decision'. Section 10 of that Act provides:

> Any statement by a tribunal or inferior court whether made orally or in writing ... of its reasons for a decision shall be taken to form part of the decision and accordingly to be incorporated in the record.

The effect of s 10 is to make whatever reasons a Medical Panel in fact gives for its opinion on a medical question referred to it part of that opinion and part of the record of that opinion. An error of law manifest on the face of such reasons as a Medical Panel in fact gives for its opinion on a medical question referred to it is therefore an error of law on the face of the record of that opinion. A Medical Panel which in fact gives reasons that are inadequate to meet the standard required of a written statement of reasons under s 68(2) the Act fails to comply with the legal duty imposed on it by s 68(2) and thereby makes an error of law. Inadequacy of reasons will therefore inevitably be an error of law on the face of the record of the opinion of a Medical Panel, and certiorari will therefore be available to remove the legal consequences of an opinion for which non-compliant reasons have been given.

[29] Whether non-compliance by the Medical Panel with its duty to give a written statement of reasons also constitutes a breach of a condition of the valid performance of the duty imposed on it by s 68(1) and (2) of the Act to form, and to give a certificate as to, its opinion on a question referred to it is not to the point. That issue would only be determinative in an application to the Supreme Court for an order in the nature of certiorari to remove the purported legal consequences of a medical opinion on the basis of jurisdictional error. In an ***494*** application for an order in the nature of certiorari to remove the legal consequences or purported legal consequences of a medical opinion on the basis of error of law on the face of the record, the issue simply does not arise.

[30] The Court of Appeal was therefore correct to conclude that an order in the nature of certiorari is available to remove the legal consequences or purported legal consequences of an opinion in respect of which reasons given by a Medical Panel are inadequate to meet the standard required of a written statement of reasons under s 68(2) the Act.

[31] Because an order in the nature of certiorari to quash an opinion is limited to removing the legal consequences or purported legal consequences of an exercise or purported exercise of power, however, the Court of Appeal was also correct to ask a threshold question. That threshold question was whether the opinion of the Medical Panel, sought to be quashed by certiorari in the application made to the Supreme Court by the Worker, had any continuing legal consequences, given that the opinion was on medical questions arising in the statutory compensation application, which by then had been dismissed.

[32] The Court of Appeal's affirmative answer to that threshold question was based on a conclusion that the opinion of the Medical Panel had two legal consequences for the continuing serious injury application. One was that the County Court would be compelled by s 68(4) of the Act to adopt and apply the opinion in the determination of the serious injury application.

...

[Editors' note: The other was that an issue estoppel arose.]

496 [36] The correct construction of s 68(4) of the Act, ... is to read the word 'any' in the introductory expression '[f]or the purposes of determining any question or matter' as referring to 'a question or matter' not '*all* questions and matters'. In respect of a particular opinion of a Medical Panel on a medical question referred to it, formed under s 68(1) and certified under s 68(2), the question or matter to which s 68(4) refers is the question or matter in which the medical question arose and in respect of which the medical question was referred to the Medical Panel.

[37] What s 68(4) of the Act on that construction requires is that an opinion of a Medical Panel on a medical question referred to it must thereafter be adopted and applied for the purposes of determining *the* question or matter, arising under or for the purposes of the Act, in which the medical question arose and in respect of which the medical question was referred to the Medical Panel. What s 68(4) does not require is that the opinion must thereafter be adopted and applied for the purposes of determining some *other* question or matter.

[38] The operation of s 68(4) of the Act in the present case was therefore to require the opinion given by the Medical Panel on the medical questions referred to it in the statutory compensation application to be adopted and applied by all courts and persons in the determination of the question or matter the subject of the statutory compensation application. That question or matter comprised the controversy between the parties to the statutory compensation application about the Worker's entitlement to the statutory compensation he claimed under Pt IV of the Act, and was brought to a conclusion when the statutory compensation application was dismissed. Section 68(4) did not have, and does not have, the further effect of requiring the opinion given on the medical questions referred in the statutory compensation application to be adopted and applied if and to the extent that the same medical question may arise in the determination of the question or ***497*** matter the subject of the serious injury application. That quite distinct question or matter, which remains unresolved, comprises the controversy between the parties to that application as to whether the Worker should have leave to bring common law proceedings

...

[40] The answer to the threshold question properly asked by the Court of Appeal is that the opinion of the Medical Panel sought to be quashed by an order in the nature of certiorari had no continuing legal consequences. The only legal effect of the opinion was that given to it by s 68(4) of the Act. That legal effect was spent when the question or matter, in respect of which the medical question was referred to the Medical Panel, was brought to a conclusion by the order dismissing the statutory compensation application. The Employer's foreshadowed reliance on the opinion having legal effect in the serious injury application would be of no avail.

[41] The order in the nature of certiorari made by the Court of Appeal was not available to quash the opinion of the Medical Panel because that opinion had no continuing legal consequence which could be removed by that order. Despite the irony of this being relied on by the Worker as respondent and eschewed by the Employer as appellant, that is a sufficient reason to allow the appeal.

[Citations omitted]

[Editors' note: Their Honours went on to consider adequacy of reasons which was an independent reason for allowing the appeal.]

Plaintiff M61/2010E v Commonwealth (2010) 243 CLR 319

Facts

The case concerned two Sri Lankan asylum seekers (M61/2010E and M69/2010) who arrived on Christmas Island by boat. Each challenged assessments made by government officers and private contractors about their refugee status on the grounds of error of law and breaches of procedural fairness. The High Court held that s 46A of the *Migration Act 1958* (Cth), which conferred a power on the Minister but imposed no duty to exercise that power or to consider exercising it, was constitutionally valid.

The High Court held that there had been an error of law and a breach of procedural fairness in the process conducted by an independent reviewer who made a recommendation to the Minister about Australia's protection obligations. However, mandamus was not available to compel the exercise of the power by the Minister and there was no utility in granting certiorari. A declaration was made.

French CJ, Gummow, Hayne, Heydon, Crennan, Kiefel and Bell JJ

***358* What relief may be granted?**

[99] Because ... the Minister does not have a duty to consider whether to exercise the power given by the section, mandamus will not issue to compel the Minister to consider or reconsider exercising either power. That the Minister decided to consider exercising the powers and, for that purpose, directed the making of Refugee Status Assessments and Independent Merits Reviews does not entail that, if the process of inquiry miscarried, the Minister can be compelled again to consider exercising the power.

[100] As was explained in *Re Minister for Immigration and Multicultural and Indigenous Affairs; Ex parte Applicants S134/2002* [(2003) 211 CLR 441, 461 [48]], the unavailability of mandamus entails that there is no utility in granting certiorari to quash the recommendation which the reviewer made in each of these matters. It is thus not necessary to consider whether certiorari to quash the recommendations would lie. More particularly, it is not necessary to examine whether, as was submitted on behalf of the Commonwealth and the Minister, certiorari will not go to quash a decision or recommendation prior to the final exercise of a discretion that directly affects legal rights unless that decision or recommendation ***359*** *must* be taken into account by the ultimate decision-maker. (In considering the exercise of power ... the Minister might, but need not, take account of the recommendations made by those who had conducted an assessment or review of an assessment of an offshore entry person's claim that Australia owes that person protection obligations.) Nor is it necessary to examine whether, or how, the proposition advanced on behalf of the Commonwealth and the Minister, expressed as it is in absolute terms, might permit or require modification to accommodate cases such as the present, where the right that is affected by conducting the impugned process of decision making is a right to liberty. The claims to certiorari and mandamus must be refused.

[101] Although the plaintiffs' claims for certiorari and mandamus should be rejected, a declaration should be made in each case that the processes undertaken to arrive at the reviewer's recommendation were flawed in the respects that have been identified. In many cases, the conclusion that certiorari and mandamus do not lie would require the further conclusion that no declaration of right should be made. Why should a declaration be made in these matters?

[102] The power to grant declaratory relief is a power which '[i]t is neither possible nor desirable to fetter ... by laying down rules as to the manner of its exercise'. As pointed out in *Ainsworth v Criminal Justice Commission* [(1992) 175 CLR 564, 582], it is a form of relief that is confined by considerations which mark out the boundaries of judicial power.

[103] In the circumstances of this litigation it cannot be said that a declaratory order by the Court will produce no foreseeable consequences for the parties. Declaratory relief is directed here to determining a legal controversy; it is not directed to answering some abstract or hypothetical question. Each plaintiff has a 'real interest' in raising the questions to which the declaration would go. In these cases, the procedures which are said to be infirm were conducted for the purpose of informing the Minister of matters directly bearing upon the exercise of power to avoid breach by Australia of its international obligations. The statutory powers to the exercise of which the inquiries were directed are placed in the statutory and historical context earlier described. That context demonstrates the importance attached to the performance of the relevant international obligations by both the legislative and executive branches of the Government of the Commonwealth. Moreover, there is a considerable public interest in the ***390*** observance of the requirements of procedural fairness in the exercise of the relevant powers.

[104] Accordingly, each plaintiff should have a declaration moulded in terms similar to the declaration made by this Court in *Ainsworth.*

Orders

[105] In each matter there should be a declaration that, in recommending to the Minister that the plaintiff was not a person to whom Australia has protection obligations, the third-named defendant made an error of law, in that he (or in the matter of Plaintiff M69, she) did not treat the provisions of the *Migration Act 1958* (Cth) and the decisions of Australian courts as binding, and further, failed to observe the requirements of procedural fairness.

[Citations omitted]

Corporation of the City of Enfield v Development Assessment Commission (2000) 199 CLR 135

South Australia Supreme Court Rules 1987 (SA)

[As at relevant date]

JUDICIAL REVIEW

98.01 Orders of mandamus, prohibition, certiorari and quo warranto to be sought by action for judicial review

(1) An order in the nature of mandamus, prohibition, certiorari or quo warranto shall be sought by way of judicial review by summons in accordance with the provisions of this Rule.

Prerogative writs not to be issued but orders to be made in the nature of such writs

(2) The prerogative writs of mandamus, prohibition and certiorari shall no longer be issued by the Court and informations in the nature of quo warranto are hereby

abolished, but in any case in which relief could have been granted by means of any of the said writs or of the said information, the Court shall have jurisdiction to make an order in the nature, and to have the effect, of the remedy or of the remedies which would have been available if this Rule were not in force.

Declarations and injunction may be sought and granted on summons for judicial review

(3) Declarations or injunctions may be sought in a summons for judicial review, and on such a summons the Court may grant the declaration or injunction claimed in lieu of, or in addition to, any order in the nature of, or having the effect of, a prerogative writ at common law if it considers that having regard to:

(a) the nature of the matter in respect of which relief may be granted by way of an order having the effect of an order for mandamus, prohibition, certiorari or quo warranto;

(b) the nature of the persons and bodies against whom relief may be granted by way of such an order; and

(c) all the circumstances of the case; it would be just and convenient for the declaration or injunction to be granted on a summons for judicial review.

Judicial review does not exclude other jurisdictions

(4) The existence of a remedy by way of judicial review does not exclude any jurisdiction of the Court to grant relief which could be invoked if this Rule had not been included.

Facts

Collex Waste Management Services Pty Ltd ('Collex') operated a waste treatment plant on its land at Kilburn in South Australia. Collex applied for provisional development plan consent (a form of development approval) to alter and expand the waste treatment plant. The local council, the City of Enfield, commenced judicial review proceedings in the Supreme Court of South Australia seeking a declaration that the provisional development plan consent was void. The facts of the case are set out in Chapter 13 along with extracts concerning the concept of jurisdictional fact. The following extracts consider the availability and nature of equitable remedies in public law. In a return to the theme of this book, Gaudron J also discusses the concept of accountability.

Although the High Court allowed an appeal from the Full Court of the Supreme Court of South Australia, it did not finally determine whether to grant the declaration sought by the City of Enfield. Instead, it remitted the matter to the Full Court. In the following extracts, the High Court considers the differences between equitable remedies in public law and the prerogative remedies.

Gleeson CJ, Gummow, Kirby and Hayne JJ

143 [16] Rule [98.01] of the *Supreme Court Rules 1987* (SA) (the Rules) ... provides that an order in the nature of mandamus, prohibition, certiorari or quo warranto shall be sought by way of judicial review by summons in accordance with the provisions of that rule. Declarations and injunctions may be sought in such a summons and equitable relief of this nature may be granted if the court considers that it would be just and convenient to do so, having regard, among other things, to all the circumstances of the case (r 98.01(3)). The existence of a remedy by way of judicial review does not exclude the jurisdiction of the Supreme Court to grant other relief (r 98.01(4)).

[17] Significant questions of public law, including those respecting ultra vires activities of public officers and authorities, are determined in ***144*** litigation which does not answer the description of judicial review of administrative action by the medium of the prerogative writs or statutory regimes such as that provided by the *Administrative Decisions (Judicial Review) Act 1977* (Cth).

144 [18] ... The jurisdiction of the Supreme Court which Enfield invoked was its jurisdiction as a court of equity to grant equitable relief to restrain apprehended breaches of the law and to declare rights and obligations in respect thereto.

[19] ... In *Bateman's Bay Local Aboriginal Land Council* v *Aboriginal Community Benefit Fund Pty Ltd* [(1998) 194 CLR 247], Gaudron, Gummow and Kirby JJ referred to the part played by the declaration and the injunction in the shaping of modern administrative law and continued:

> In this field, equity has proceeded on the footing of the inadequacy (in particular the technicalities hedging the prerogative remedies) of the legal remedies otherwise available to vindicate the public interest in the maintenance of due administration.

...

145 [21] The substance of the matter is that Enfield asserts apprehended breach by Collex of the statutory provisions which forbid the proposed development without the approval of the relevant authority (the Commission) together with the concurrence of Enfield. Enfield seeks a declaration as to the invalidity of the approval upon which Collex relies as establishing the legality of its development ... In his oral submissions in this Court counsel for Collex did not dissent from this understanding of the nature of the proceedings. However, he rightly pointed out that Enfield itself had tended to confuse matters in its notice of appeal by categorising the Full Court as having dealt with the litigation as an application for 'judicial review'.

[22] There will be differences between, on the one hand, the availability in public law of equitable remedies, and judicial review by mandamus, prohibition and certiorari on the other. At least under s 75(v) of the Constitution, rules as to standing may be more generous for ***146*** prohibition and certiorari. However, an applicant with standing still may fail to obtain an order absolute for reasons which would not have precluded the availability of a declaration. This was the case in *Ainsworth v Criminal Justice Commission* [(1992) 175 CLR 564] ... However, where the question is whether the decision-maker has erred as to the jurisdictional facts, as in this case, that question has to be answered by the court in which it is litigated upon the evidence before that court. In this respect, where the issue requires determination of whether jurisdictional facts existed, the task of the court to determine that question is essentially the same whether the relief sought be equitable or, for example, prohibition.

[23] In the present case, no question arises as to the sufficiency of the interest of Enfield in the absence of the Attorney-General's fiat. Section 85(1) of the Act provides:

> Any person may apply to the [Environment] Court for an order to remedy or restrain a breach of this Act ... (whether or not any right of that person has been or may be infringed by or as a consequence of that breach).

That section does not purport to displace or limit the jurisdiction of the Supreme Court, nor does it do so by implication. However, in administrative law, as elsewhere, the grant of injunctive and declaratory relief is attended by discretionary considerations. As Menzies J put it in *Cooney* [(1963) 114 CLR 582, 605], '[t]he wide discretion of the Court is an adequate safeguard against abuse of a salutary procedure'.

...

Gaudron J

156 [54] The potential for executive and administrative decisions to affect adversely the rights, interests and legitimate expectations of the individual is now well recognised. So, too, is the inadequacy of the prerogative writs as general remedies to compel the executive government and administrative bodies to operate within the limits of their powers. The introduction of comprehensive statutory ***157*** schemes such as that embodied in the *Administrative Decisions (Judicial Review) Act 1977* (Cth) owes much to the recognition of these two basic factors.

[55] The other factor that informs comprehensive statutory schemes for the review of executive and administrative decisions is what is sometimes referred to as 'accountability'. In this context, 'accountability' can be taken to refer to the need for the executive government and administrative bodies to comply with the law and, in particular, to observe relevant limitations on the exercise of their powers.

[56] Those exercising executive and administrative powers are as much subject to the law as those who are or may be affected by the exercise of those powers. It follows that, within the limits of their jurisdiction and consistent with their obligation to act judicially, the courts should provide whatever remedies are available and appropriate to ensure that those possessed of executive and administrative powers exercise them only in accordance with the laws which govern their exercise. The rule of law requires no less.

[57] As already indicated, the prerogative writs are not wholly effective as general public law remedies. Nor, perhaps, are equitable remedies which, in the absence of legislative provision to the contrary, are available only at the suit of a person with a direct or special interest in the subject matter in question. However, equitable remedies have long had a role to play in public law. And, because of the limitations and technicalities which beset the prerogative writs, that role is a continuing and important one.

[58] Equitable remedies are available in the field of public law precisely because of the inadequacies of the prerogative writs. Thus, ... ***158*** it is not incongruous that equitable relief should be available although prerogative relief is not. What is incongruous is the notion that equitable remedies should be subject to the same or similar limitations which beset the prerogative writs. In the field of public law, equitable remedies are subject to the same considerations, including discretionary considerations, as apply in any other field. There is no need for the importation of other limitations.

[Citations omitted]

Statutory remedies

Administrative Decisions (Judicial Review) Act 1977 (Cth)

[As at 1 December 2022]

16 Powers of the Federal Court and the Federal Circuit and Family Court of Australia (Division 2) in respect of applications for order of review

(1) On an application for an order of review in respect of a decision, the Federal Court or the Federal Circuit and Family Court of Australia (Division 2) may, in its discretion, make all or any of the following orders:

(a) an order quashing or setting aside the decision, or a part of the decision, with effect from the date of the order or from such earlier or later date as the court specifies;

(b) an order referring the matter to which the decision relates to the person who made the decision for further consideration, subject to such directions as the court thinks fit;

(c) an order declaring the rights of the parties in respect of any matter to which the decision relates;

(d) an order directing any of the parties to do, or to refrain from doing, any act or thing the doing, or the refraining from the doing, of which the court considers necessary to do justice between the parties.

(2) On an application for an order of review in respect of conduct that has been, is being, or is proposed to be, engaged in for the purpose of the making of a decision, the Federal Court or the Federal Circuit and Family Court of Australia (Division 2) may, in its discretion, make either or both of the following orders:

(a) an order declaring the rights of the parties in respect of any matter to which the conduct relates;

(b) an order directing any of the parties to do, or to refrain from doing, any act or thing the doing, or the refraining from the doing, of which the court considers necessary to do justice between the parties.

(3) On an application for an order of review in respect of a failure to make a decision, or in respect of a failure to make a decision within the period within which the decision was required to be made, the Federal Court or the Federal Circuit and Family Court of Australia (Division 2) may, in its discretion, make all or any of the following orders:

(a) an order directing the making of the decision;

(b) an order declaring the rights of the parties in relation to the making of the decision;

(c) an order directing any of the parties to do, or to refrain from doing, any act or thing the doing, or the refraining from the doing, of which the court considers necessary to do justice between the parties

(4) The Federal Court or the Federal Circuit and Family Court of Australia (Division 2) may at any time, of its own motion or on the application of any party, revoke, vary, or suspend the operation of, any order made by it under this section.

Chapman v Tickner (1995) 55 FCR 316

Facts

This case was part of the long-running dispute over the construction of a bridge linking Hindmarsh Island to Goolwa in South Australia that was opposed by a group of Ngarrindjeri women. Mr and Mrs Chapman and their son were the developers who sought to build the bridge. The Commonwealth Minister for Aboriginal and Torres Strait Islander Affairs commissioned Professor Cheryl Saunders to produce a report under s 10 of the *Aboriginal and Torres Strait Islander Heritage Protection Act 1984* (Cth). Professor Saunders published a notice in the Commonwealth *Government Gazette* and the *Adelaide Advertiser*. One of the grounds of review was that the notice did not satisfy the requirements of s 10 because it did not specify the precise area the subject of the application, nor the injury or desecration threatening the area.

As a result of the public consultation process required by the Act, Professor Saunders received over 400 submissions, which were summarised in her report to the Minister. In addition, the Minister was given all the submissions. The report also included two annexures (one provided by Ngarrindjeri women and one by an anthropologist) containing secret, sacred knowledge (that came to be known as 'secret women's business') of the Ngarrindjeri women, with a note that the annexures were only to be read by a woman. The Minister read part of the report but did not read all the submissions. Further, the Minister did not read the annexure containing the secret women's business but relied on a summary of that material prepared by an advisor to the Minister, Suzanne Kee. One of the submissions was provided by Mr Barton who commenced separate judicial review proceedings that were joined with the Chapmans'.

The Minister made a declaration, under s 10, effectively prohibiting any development on the site. The Chapmans challenged the declaration under the *Administrative Decisions (Judicial Review) Act 1977* (Cth). At first instance, O'Loughlin J in the Federal Court quashed the declaration. The Minister appealed to the Full Court and the appeal was dismissed (*Tickner* v *Chapman* (1995) 57 FCR 451). Extracts from the appeal decision concerning grounds of review are in Chapter 14.

The following extract is from the first instance decision of O'Loughlin J, granting relief under s 16(1)(a) of the *Administrative Decisions (Judicial Review) Act 1977* (Cth).

O'Loughlin J

372 In my opinion, the conclusions that I have reached require the intervention of the Court.

The Minister did not 'consider', in any sense at all, Mr Barton's representation to Professor Saunders. If that omission had been the only error, it would have been appropriate for the Court to refrain from interfering because, despite their obvious importance to him, the subjects in Mr Barton's representations were covered adequately in other representations, the most notable of which was the detailed representation of the Chapmans.

The Minister did not 'consider', in any sense at all, the detail of the women's business; his reporter did not set out that detail in her report because she had given her undertaking to treat the matter as confidential and the Minister denied himself the right to read the contents of the secret envelopes which, presumably, would have given him the opportunity to consider that most important representation. It may be true that the Minister did not make his decision on the contents of the secret envelopes (he could not have relied on the ***373*** contents as he had not read them). But he did make his decision as a result of women's business, the subject matter that was discussed in the secret envelopes. The detail of the Minister's reasons for his decision, as set out in the amended s 13 statement has already been set out; it shows quite clearly, the importance that was attached to the women's business. ... Despite the gravity of this error, if it were the only cause for concern, the matter could have been sent back to the Minister so that he might reconsider the matter in accordance with these reasons: but there is more.

I am of the opinion that the published notice in the *Gazette* and local press was fatally flawed. For the reasons that I have already addressed in some detail, it failed sufficiently to identify the area that was to be the subject of the report and it failed totally to apprise the interested members of the public of the information to which they were entitled. As events transpired, an aspect of particular significance of the bridge area to Aboriginals was the secret women's business. The public were entitled to know that significance and to know the nature and extent of the perceived threat. ... The notice did not address either of these issues for the reason that Professor Saunders did not know of their existence at the time of the publication of the notice. She was, therefore, left with a choice; she could have continued her reporting functions, ignoring the subject of women's business, or she could have advertised afresh with the new advertisement containing the required information. She was not entitled to proceed as she did, nor was the Minister entitled to make his declaration. The inadequacy of the notice meant that the Minister lacked jurisdiction to make the s 10 declaration.

The nature of this error is so fundamental that it cannot be rectified by further consideration by either the Minister or the reporter. This is a case where the Court must use its powers under s 16(1)(a) of the *ADJR Act* to quash each decision ab initio.

...

374 In the Chapmans' application, No SG 57 of 1994 -

The Court orders that:

1. The decision of Cheryl Anne Saunders dated 8 July 1994 be quashed with effect as from that date.
2. The decision of the Minister for Aboriginal and Torres Strait Islander Affairs dated 9 July 1994 be quashed with effect as from that date.

As the decision of Professor Saunders was not challenged by Messrs Barton and Knott there will only be an order in their action, No SG 78 of 1994, quashing the aforementioned decision of the Minister.

INDEX

Aboriginal and Torres Strait Islander Commission, 111–12
Aboriginal heritage, 36
Aboriginal land rights
  disallowance of, 70–6
accountability
  administrative law values and, 7–11
  modern challenges to, 12–16
  parliament
    response to challenges to, 95
  reasons for, 3–7
administrative action
  distinguishing acts of legislative and administrative character, 62–7
  unlawful action. *See* unlawful action
Administrative Appeals Tribunal, 178
  creation of, 206
  framework, 206–26
  merits review function, 225
  reasons for decisions, 172–3
administrative decisions
  reasons for, 165–74
    Administrative Appeals Tribunal, 172–3
    Administrative Review Council, 168–71
    judicial review, 173–4
    no general obligation to provide, 165
    Ombudsman, 172
administrative law
  statutory interpretation and, 47–53
  values, 7–11
administrative powers and discretions
  automated decision-making, 43–7
  discretionary power, 43
  statutory power, 41–2
Administrative Review Council
  The Contracting Out of Government Services, 34–5
  effect of internal review on decision-making, 180
  Federal Judicial Review in Australia, 320–2
  reasons for decisions and, 168–71
administrative review tribunals
  amalgamation of, 212
    effects, 213
  tribunal design issues, 197–206
    independent appointments, 197–8
    procedure, 199–200
archival resources
  meaning of property and, 131
asylum seekers
  breach of personal information security, 137, 141–2
  Malaysia Arrangement, 373–4
  Nauru Regional Processing Centre, 25–6
  offshore processing
    contract management of, 102
  public interest criterion and, 79
Auditors-General, 96–106
Australian Broadcasting Tribunal, 254
Australian Competition Tribunal, 52
Australian Conservation Foundation, 288–9
Australian Public Service
  Values and Code of Conduct, 22
Australian Secret Intelligence Service, 6
Australian Security Intelligence Organisation, 5, 79
AWB International Ltd, 30

change of sex, 365
Commonwealth Administrative Review Committee. *See* Kerr Committee
confidential information, 134–7
  government information and, 135
Council of Australasian Tribunals, 197
Crown
  Crown immunity, 35–9
  executive and
    terminology and constitutional framework, 20–2
cultural relics
  custodians of, 291

delegated legislation
  judicial review of, 76–85
  legislative regulation and parliamentary review of, 70–6
  problems with reliance on, 58

reasonableness and proportionality in relation to, 82
types of, 68–70
deportation of criminals, 200, 215
dual citizenship
politicians and, 21
Duane report, 451

executive entities, 22–4

freedom of information, 148–65
Osland case, 160–5, 231, 232
summary of exemptions, 156–7

Hindmarsh Island bridge, 397, 468

information security
personal information, 137–43
International Treaties Obligations Assessments, 141
invasion of privacy
listening devices and, 48

judicial review
grounds arising from the general law
fettering discretion, 411–16
irrationality and illogicality, 427–37
no evidence, 437–44
unreasonableness, 416–27
grounds arising from the statute conferring a power
improper delegation, 387–90
jurisdictional facts, 367–78
mandatory and prohibited considerations, 390–402
misconceiving the scope of a power, 364–7
procedural error, 378–87
grounds of review, 317–18
statutory grounds, 318–22
jurisdictional error and error of law on the face of the record, 258–77
distinction between, 278–80
legitimate scope of, 230–1
limits on judicial review
justiciability, 282–8
no-invalidity clauses, 308–11
privative clauses, 297–308
restricting access to information before the courts, 311–15
standing to commence judicial review proceedings, 288–97
of delegated legislation, 76–85
Ombudsman reporting function and, 117
origins of common law and constitutional judicial review, 246–9
prerogative writs, 246
reasons for judicial review of administrative decisions, 173–4
review of legality, 235–7
scope of, 236
sources of judicial review jurisdiction, 241–5
State Supreme Courts, 242–5
statutory construction, 238–41
statutory judicial review, 249–58
statutory review on a question of law, 231–5

Kakadu National Park
World Heritage Listing, 285
Kenbi Land Claim, 405–6
Kerr Committee, 41
Report, 179, 197, 206
terms of reference, 178

legal professional privilege, 160
legislative power
executive exercise of, 58–61

merits review
Administrative Appeals Tribunal, 225
de novo merits review, 186, 187, 219
examples of merits review decisions, 187–95
internal review, 180–7
statute providing avenues of review, 183
reasons for, 178–80
Migration Agents Registration Authority, 219

National Competition Council, 52
National School Chaplaincy Program, 90–1
no-invalidity clauses, 308–11
non-refoulement, 141
non-statutory powers, 53–6

Office of the Australian Information Commissioner, 137, 141, 156
Ombudsmen, 106–19
  amenability of reporting function to judicial review, 117

Palace Letters, 131
parliament
  as public investigatory body, 90–6
parliamentary scrutiny, 58
personal information
  security of, 137–43
prerogative of mercy, 53
prerogative power
  Cabinet and, 54
privative clauses, 297–308
procedural fairness
  bias rule, 352–62
    apprehended bias, 357, 360
    deemed bias, 352
  breach of, 277
  hearing rule, 349–52
  statutory exclusion, 336–49
  threshold test, 324–36
public interest
  nature of discretion and, 52
public interest disclosure, 143–8
public investigatory bodies
  Auditors-General, 96–106
  investigation and scrutiny through parliament, 90–6
  Ombudsmen, 106–19
  Royal commissions, 119–25
public servants
  duties of, 127–34
public sphere
  private bodies in, 24–35

Ranger 68 uranium deposit, 392
Refugee Review Tribunal, 246, 261
remedies, 455–66
  statutory remedies, 466–9
Royal Commission into the Home Insulation Program, 119–25
Royal commissions, 119–25
rule of law, 3–4
  limits on executive power and, 6–7
  relationship to executive, courts and legislation, 5–6

separation of powers
  individual liberty and, 4
Sheraton Hotel incident, 6
statutory interpretation
  administrative law and, 47–53
statutory powers, 47–53
  discretion and its limits and, 50
subjective opinion clauses, 370
Sunday trading
  South Australia, 409–10

unlawful action
  consequences of
    consequences of breaching a statutory duty, 446–54
    consequences of jurisdictional error, 454–5
    remedies, 455–66
    statutory remedies, 466–9

whistleblowers, 143